D1213792

Emotion

Emotions suffuse our lives: a symphony of feeling – usually whispering and murmuring in pianissimo but occasionally screaming and shouting in fortissimo crescendo – filling every waking moment and even invading our dreams. We can always be conscious of how happy, sad, annoyed, or anxious we feel, and also of the feelings we have relative to other persons: pride, envy, guilt, jealousy, trust, respect, or resentment. Developments in brain imaging and in capturing nuances of nonverbal display now enable the objective study of emotion and how biologically based primary emotions relate to higher-level social, cognitive, and moral emotions. This book presents an integrated developmental-interactionist theory of emotion, viewing subjective feelings as voices of the genes: an affective symphony composed of dissociable albeit interactive neurochemical modules. These primordial voices do not control, but rather cajole our behavior with built-in flexibility enabling the mindful application of learning, reason, and language.

ROSS BUCK is Professor of Communication Sciences and Psychology at the University of Connecticut.

STUDIES IN EMOTION AND SOCIAL INTERACTION
Second Series

Series Editors

Keith Oatley
University of Toronto

Antony S. R. Manstead
Cardiff University

Titles published in the Second Series:

The Psychology of Facial Expression, edited by James A. Russell and José Miguel Fernández-Dols

Emotions, the Social Bond, and Human Reality: Part/Whole Analysis, by Thomas J. Scheff

Intersubjective Communication and Emotion in Early Ontogeny, edited by Stein Bråten

The Social Context of Nonverbal Behavior, edited by Pierre Philippot, Robert S. Feldman, and Erik J. Coats

Communicating Emotion: Social, Moral, and Cultural Processes, by Sally Planalp

Emotions across Languages and Cultures: Diversity and Universals, by Anna Wierzbicka

Feeling and Thinking: The Role of Affect in Social Cognition, edited by Joseph P. Forgas

Metaphor and Emotion: Language, Culture, and Body in Human Feeling, by Zoltán Kövecses

Gender and Emotion: Social Psychological Perspectives, edited by Agneta H. Fischer

Causes and Consequences of Feelings, by Leonard Berkowitz

Emotions and Beliefs: How Feelings Influence Thoughts, edited by Nico H. Frijda, Antony S. R. Manstead, and Sacha Bem

Identity and Emotion: Development through Self-Organization, edited by Harke A. Bosma and E. Saskia Kunnen

Speaking from the Heart: Gender and the Social Meaning of Emotion, by Stephanie A. Shields

Emotion

A Biosocial Synthesis

Ross Buck
University of Connecticut

CAMBRIDGE
UNIVERSITY PRESS

CAMBRIDGE
UNIVERSITY PRESS

University Printing House, Cambridge CB2 8BS, United Kingdom

Cambridge University Press is part of the University of Cambridge.

It furthers the University's mission by disseminating knowledge in the pursuit of education, learning and research at the highest international levels of excellence.

www.cambridge.org
Information on this title: www.cambridge.org/9780521813167

© Cambridge University Press 2014

First published 2014

Printed in the United Kingdom by Clays, St Ives plc

A catalogue record for this publication is available from the British Library

Library of Congress Cataloguing in Publication data
Buck, Ross.
Emotion : a biosocial synthesis / Ross Buck.
pages   cm. – (Studies in emotion and social interaction, second series)
ISBN 978-0-521-81316-7 (Hardback)
1. Emotions–Social aspects. I. Title.
BF531.B783 2014
152.4–dc23   2014008996

ISBN 978-0-521-81316-7 Hardback

To Nora, Maya, Will, Hannah, and all the children

People learn to hate, and if they can learn to hate, they can be taught to love, for love comes more naturally to the human heart than its opposite.

Nelson Mandela, *Long Walk to Freedom*

We live in a world where we have to hide to make love, while violence is practiced in broad daylight.

John Lennon

Contents

Figures

Tables

Foreword

One of the defining pursuits of humanity is arguably to find answers to the *big questions*, such as where do we come from, where are we going, and who are we? Understanding humanity, in turn, cannot be achieved without a grasp of the concepts we currently refer to as *cognition*, *motivation*, and *emotion*. While thinkers in all cultures have tackled these for more than two thousand years, I join a significant number of fellow contemporary researchers in tracing the beginnings of scientific emotion research to the nineteenth century. Today's emotion science is standing on the shoulders of giants like Charles Darwin and William James. With the power of their interdisciplinary interests and their intellectual ideas they forged both the foundations and the prototypes of modern emotion theories. When reflecting on these achievements – and I recommend going back to read some of these texts in the original – I cannot help but marvel regarding one fact: someone like Darwin, or James for that matter, could be aware of basically *all* relevant research of the day. With respect to the output, all relevant research could fit in a decent library.

How times have changed! Today, knowledge is produced at a rate that prevents many a scientist from even retrieving, let alone reading all relevant material that is published, and this does not include the digestion of pertinent studies and publications. Today, we are further away from such a holistic analysis, and even more so from the capacity to synthesize the necessary bigger picture of emotion research. Yet, given the flood of research, we need an integrative view more than ever. Emotion science is a particularly tough cookie to swallow. An understanding of emotions does not just *benefit* from an interdisciplinary approach, emotion science *requires* a multidisciplinary approach! Affective processes cannot be understood at one level alone – they demand the multilevel approach that, for example Cacioppo and Berntson (1992), propagate. In "pop psychology," and the science columns of major national news outlets, there is presently much talk of how neuroscience provides *the* answers, *all* answers, to psychological questions. And while it should be clear to even the most critical reader that neuroscience has advanced our understanding of many psychological concepts, including emotions, it is completely false to believe that the new tools will do the trick on their own. Permitting myself an analogy, modern DNA analyses have revolutionized forensics – but they do not solve cases. In my mind, it is the same with the fine tools we now have for looking at the activity of the living brain. For me, personally, all the bits and pieces we have accumulated in the last century regarding emotions, whether they are at the level of cells, of organs, of the organism, of psychological processes, of interactions in networks of different sizes, or of descriptions of cultural values and practices – all these pieces are like an enormous puzzle that requires to be put together, using creativity, critical analysis, and the capacity to really transcend a view that is solely based on one of these individual levels, viewing the others only as auxiliaries. I am still baffled by how some people, and not only lay-people, are surprised when a newly published study demonstrates a psychological process to be accompanied by specific brain activity. Where did they think this would happen? And yet, just because there is a specific central nervous activation, I would not be able to tell whether this pattern is learned or hard-wired. If it is learned, whether it can be derived from mere observation of a few cases, or whether it takes a lifetime of learning to make the connections. It is here that other disciplines must work with neuroscience. Personally, I find it important to underscore how much of emotion psychology in 2014 is still focused on the individual alone. Emotions, and already Darwin pointed that out, have very important intrapersonal *and* interpersonal functions. In fact, in some cases, it makes much more sense to think of emotional processes in terms of larger units than the individual. But, this is perhaps easier to say for a biologist than for a modern, or post-modern, psychologist. The pervasiveness of social processes in all of emotion is still not yet something that is in the minds of many.

Emotion research is notorious for a multitude of definitions and approaches. Cornelius (1996) likens the stories emotion theorists weave to the ancient tale of the blind men who try to describe an elephant; their descriptions differ wildly because each of them can grasp, literally, only a part of the animal and not the elephant in its entirety; in fact, this analogy is echoed in the preface later in the present book. This is the challenge at stake in the here and now. And it is here that attempts are needed to put all of these pieces together. We need attempts at perceiving *The Big Picture* and converting it to a coherent narrative. And it is here where this book comes in that you are holding in your hands whether in the good old-fashioned print format or on a digital device. Ross Buck's *Emotion: A Biosocial Synthesis* draws that Big Emotion Picture with bold strokes. I am not surprised at the scope and the power of synthesis that Ross wields in this text – however, I sit in awe as it is revealed page by page. Ross Buck's writing had a significant influence on my thinking at an early stage in my career. While attending grad school at Dartmouth College, in the late 1980s, two of his books left a particularly strong impression on me – *Human Emotion and Motivation* (1976) and – even more so – *The Communication of Emotion* (1984). I remember very well the first time I witnessed Ross in action, asking very thoughtful questions at the 1994 meeting of the International Society for Research on Emotion (ISRE), for which I have the honor of presiding at the moment. Since then we have met many times and I continue to enjoy his views on emotion research, as he continues to integrate biological and social aspects of emotion theories.

This book, using a systems approach, convincingly ties together all the levels I mentioned before – and it particularly bridges that still wide-open divide between neuroscience and the social layers – which might be due to the fact that unlike many of our colleagues in the "emotion business," Ross is located in a Communication as well as a Psychology Department. The result is inspiring. This is the type of big synthesis of which we see perhaps less than a handful per decade. I am glad to benefit once again from his deep and broad insights. And I know that this book will inspire many students and scholars of the emotions. It provides not only a very useful conceptual framework, but also a guideline, a kind of road-map for the future trajectory of emotion research. Surely, as new research, particularly in social neuroscience, provides new insights on specific processes or structures in the years to come, details of the story will change, but just as in Magda Arnold's opus magnum *Emotion and Personality*, it is the functional analysis that will likely stand the test of time for quite a while.

To be clear – this is no product of a "consensual analysis" like Kleinginna and Kleinginna's attempt at defining emotions (1981b). This is a highly personal view, with a specific framework, idiosyncratic terminology, and strong choices – Ross Buck's power of vision is the strength of this book. Yet, it does not require the reader to believe every bit, or to buy into each element. Doubtlessly, this book will stimulate exchanges, discussions, as well as controversies, while pushing emotion research to the next frontier.

Arvid Kappas
Bremen, December 2013

Preface

"There will never be an integrative theory of emotion."
Niedenthal and Brauer (2012, p. 275)

Emotion is attracting burgeoning interest in the social, behavioral, and life sciences, but although the empirical evidence demonstrating its importance is overwhelming, important conceptual and definitional difficulties remain. In the issue of the journal *Emotion Review* current at this writing there was an extensive section on the definition of emotion, with one paper asserting that it is a concept "in crisis" and seriously questioning whether the concept of emotion "can be expected to operate as part of a truly scientific lexicon" (Dixon, 2012, p. 338). Emotion is widely considered to be momentary, fleeting, ephemeral, and resistant to study; while cognition is somehow stable, enduring, and well suited to empirical investigation. Also, the *Annual Review of Psychology* summary of the emotion field current at this writing began by questioning whether scientists can or should study emotion, and concluded that an integrative theory of emotion is impossible because the very definition of the term "emotion" is useful only in the context of a given research program (Niedenthal and Brauer, 2012). This recalls the famous parable from India about ten blind men arrayed around an elephant, each trying to describe the nature of the beast from his restricted experience of feeling a trunk, a leg, a tail; and arguing heatedly.

In this book I aim to present a general synthesis of the biological and social aspects of emotion. I regard emotion as an ever-present phenomenon central to all living things, evolving from the first stirrings of life nearly four billion years ago. I submit that only by understanding emotion can we understand *motivation* and *cognition*: each of these is involved with the others so closely that we cannot fully comprehend one without understanding how it relates to the others. Also, only by understanding emotion can we appreciate the fundamental similarities between human beings and other animals, as well as the fundamental difference: the human capacity for language. And, only by understanding emotion can we appreciate how fundamentally we differ from even the most impressive of computing machines. Computers are, in the final analysis, merely tools.

A major conceptual aim of this book is to describe how biological emotions are *natural kinds* discoverable by science, and how they relate to higher-level social, cognitive, and moral emotions. *Biological emotions* are seen to constitute natural kinds at two levels. First, they are based upon primary motivational-emotional systems (*primes*) associated with *readouts* of specifiable neurochemical systems in the brain. Second, biological emotions are natural kinds in that they are organized by their functions in the *ecology*: e.g. the physical and social environment in which the individual lives. It is at the ecological level that emotions can be organized and defined in terms of specifiable and observable displays, such as facial expressions, vocalizations, body movements, and postures; as well as intimate touches, scents, and odors. These displays are responded to automatically by preattunements to those displays in receivers, this process often involving mirror neuron systems. These display–preattunement associations take the phenomenon of emotion out of the head of the individual, as it were, into the social and communicative environment.

Chapter 1 introduces a general biosocial approach that views emotions in terms of emergent systems involving an interaction between biological potential and social experience over the course of development: a *developmental-interactionist* theory. Emotions emerge naturally and effortlessly from underlying biological potential as self-organizing dynamical systems over the course of development. This view might be termed "emotiocentric" in contrast to other approaches in the behavioral and social sciences. The chapter considers how experienced emotion, or *affect*, relates to other aspects of experience; as well as other aspects of emotional responding: expressive displays and physiological responses. The chapter also considers the process of *emotional education*: the complex ways that we learn to label and understand our subjective affective feelings and hopefully attain *emotional competence*.

The next three chapters consider basic *biological emotions* that are directly related to specifiable neurochemical systems in the brain: the active ingredients to the emotion cocktail, as it were. These include widely recognized dimensions of emotion – arousal and valence – as well as discrete emotions: the *primary affects* of happiness sadness, fear, anger, and disgust. They also include less widely acknowledged *reptilian emotions* (sex and power) and *prosocial emotions* (attachment, love, nurturance, bonding, separation anxiety).

Later chapters in the book consider "higher-level" social, cognitive, and moral emotions, and how these are grounded in the biological emotions but emerge to respond to universal ecological contingencies. I regard biological emotions as contributing the physiological bases for higher-level emotions. This book takes an *ecological-systems* view of higher-level emotions; they obtain their primordial experiential "fire" from biological emotions associated with attachment, expectancy, and a hypothesized emotion of moral approbation termed *gust*. Thus "fired" biologically, higher-level emotions respond as emergent dynamical systems to ecologically universal social and situational challenges occurring naturally during development.

Acknowledgments

It is a pleasure to acknowledge the support from others that made this book possible. Many thanks to Keith Oatley for his careful and useful editorial work. Collaborative work in recent years has led to publications with Michael Beatty, Rebecca Chory-Assad, Jack Dovidio, Jeff Fisher, Mark Hamilton, Rob Henning, Tim Levine, Adam Pearson, and Tessa West. In particular, collaborative work with R. Thomas Boone on emotional expressivity in social dilemma games; Reuben Baron on perceptual theory; Arjun Chaudhuri on emotion and persuasion; Whitney A. Davis and Mohammed Kahn on emotion in risk communication; Benson Ginsburg on the theory of communicative genes; Yumi Iwamitsu on emotion expression in cancer; David A. Kenny on dyad-level data analysis; Kent Kiehl on fMRI analysis of responses to spontaneous facial displays; Elliott D. Ross on brain mechanisms of emotion; and C. Arthur Van Lear on communication theory has contributed immeasurably to this book.

I am indebted to many students, including Erika Anderson, Emil Coman, Mats Georgson, Christian Rauh, Ipshita Ray, Nanciann Norelli Smith, and Georgios Triantis. In particular, a number of my doctoral students have contributed ideas and research particularly relevant to a number of aspects of the developmental-interactionist analysis offered here. These include work with Arjun Chaudhuri on emotion and persuasion; Michelle Pulaski Behling on music and emotion; Caroline Easton and Jacquie Cartwright-Mills on emotional communication in schizophrenia patients; Cheryl Goldman on emotional communication in behaviorally disordered children; and Megan Sheehan on emotional communication and personality. I particularly wish to acknowledge in this regard the work of Mike Miller, Christopher Kowal, Stacie Renfro Powers, Stephen Stifano, Rebecca Ferrer, Makoto Nakamura, Emil Coman, Ed Vieira, Maxim Polonsky, and Christian Rauh. Also, I am indebted to students in my graduate seminars on Nonverbal Communication, Motivation and Emotion, and Emotion and Persuasion who have read and commented on parts of this book as it has developed over the years; to Hillary Siddons, who did yeoman work assisting with the preparation of the references; and to Mike Miller, who was enormously helpful in obtaining permissions. Needless to say, none of my colleagues is responsible for any failings of this book, but they have contributed greatly to its strengths.

The cover figure is based on the idea of a mandala combining a brain, globe, and Greek masks. It was brilliantly realized by Donna Drasch, an artist from Ashford, Connecticut, USA; and was the logo for the Newsletter of the International Society for Research on Emotions (ISRE) when I was editor and is still used occasionally by ISRE. I am very grateful to the artist and to ISRE for permission to use it for a cover illustration, as it captures the essence of the view of emotion as a biosocial synthesis. I am also very grateful to Arvid Kappas, current president of ISRE, for writing the Foreword. With his broad and deep understanding of emotion, Arvid's views are greatly valued.

Finally, I am deeply indebted to my family for their support and encouragement: my children Ross William Buck, Maria Lenore Buck, Nancy Jenney Buck, and Theodore Reed Buck; my daughters-in-law Meghan Gaffney Buck and Jennifer Saraceno Buck; and grandchildren Eleanor Violet and William Christopher Buck (Bill and Meghan's children) and Maya Rose and Hannah Judith Buck (Ted and Jenn's daughters). This book is dedicated to my grandchildren. And of course this work would have been impossible without the help and support of my wife, Marianne Jenney Buck: the love and joy of my life.

PART I

A biosocial view of emotion

CHAPTER 1

A developmental-interactionist theory of emotion

As you read the words on these pages, information pours into your brain. You can experience the feel of the constant tug of gravity pulling you into your chair, the pages in your hand, and the clothes and shoes on your body. You can be aware of the lights and noises in your surroundings. Your sensory receptors constantly pick up information physically present in the light, air, and surfaces of the terrestrial environment, and this is automatically correlated with proprioceptive cues about the position of your eyes, ears, and parts of the body. Together, this amalgam of information tells you where you are located relative to your surroundings. However, as you try to concentrate on reading, you do not typically pay attention to these things. If your surroundings are comfortable, it is relatively easy to concentrate. But, if your chair is too hard, or your shoes are too tight, or if it is too dark or noisy in the room, it is difficult to shut this annoying information out. You experience the offending stimulation with a sense of frustration, and are distracted from your task.

Not all of the potentially distracting stimulation comes from your external surroundings. You may be hungry, or thirsty, or too warm or cold, or you may experience sexual urges, or a headache. Also, you may be in a bad mood, or you may feel slightly euphoric and just not "feel like reading." Any of these may interfere with your task, but the source of the distraction is not in the external surroundings, but rather is within your body. Information associated with these feelings and desires is always with you, pouring into your brain just like the information from the external surroundings. Interoceptors monitoring the nutrients, fluids, and tissues of the body inform us of bodily needs; generating a cocktail of *desires*. Also, interoceptive systems generate a cocktail of specific *feelings*: the subjective aspects of emotion. You can always "call up" the experience of these feelings and desires. You can call up the experience of how hungry, or thirsty, or warm/cold, or sexy you feel at the moment; and also how happy, sad, afraid, angry, and disgusted you are; just as you can call up the experience of the feel of your shoes on your feet. You can also call up feelings such as love or hate, but only if you think of a particular individual with whom you have a personal relationship. Normally, all these feelings are at low levels, whispering, but like the feel of your shoes on your feet *they are always "there."*

You may experience other feelings that do not distract from your reading, but actually nourish and sustain your attention. You may experience excitement in discovery, in seeing the world from another viewpoint, in understanding something about yourself and your relationships with others. Curiosity is one of the fundamental emotions underlying the development and maintenance of the cognitive system: as Albert Einstein put it, "our longing for understanding is eternal."

The essences of emotion

Can we approach these subjective feelings and desires, simultaneously distinct and ineffable as they are, from the viewpoint of objective science? Emotion is at the same time compelling and intimate, and mysterious and enigmatic. Virtually everyone will agree on the direct phenomenal reality of emotion: the subjective reality of our feelings and desires seems self-evident. However, when pressed it becomes difficult to define exactly what emotion is, how we distinguish one emotion from another, or how we even know that an emotion is occurring. For scientists, this difficulty of definition and measurement constitutes a significant challenge. Can one define and measure emotional phenomena in an objective way that is open to public verification, the hallmark of science?

For most of the twentieth century, the answer to this question on the part of most social and behavioral scientists, and many philosophers, was an unequivocal "no!" Emotions have been seen to be ineffable and unobservable, because subjective experience – considered by most to be an essential aspect of emotion – cannot be objectively observed. The originator of behaviorism, J. B. Watson, argued that science must confine its attention to publicly observable events, such as objective stimuli and responses, and that emotions simply do not qualify (1919). Many behaviorists acknowledged that subjectively experienced "private events" may exist, but argued that they cannot be studied by objective scientific methods and are therefore beyond the reach and ken of science; although B. F. Skinner in his 1953 book *Science and Human Behavior* presciently acknowledged that future technology might make private events objectively observable.

Others have gone farther, questioning the very existence of emotion. To the language philosopher Gilbert Ryle (1949), emotion is a "ghost in a machine": a category mistake involving a misuse of language.

The philosopher Ludwig Wittgenstein (1965) noted that often different things named by the same term are often truly different one from the other, and related only by what he termed "family resemblances." Tracing the history of the word "emotion," Dixon (2012) concluded that the word does not name "either a natural kind or any kind of innate or 'folk' psychological concept" (p. 343). An *Annual Review of Psychology* summary of the emotion field current at this writing began by questioning whether scientists can or should study emotion, and concluded that an integrative theory of emotion is impossible because the very definition of the term "emotion" is useful only in the context of a given research program (Niedenthal and Brauer, 2012). So, are different sorts of phenomena named "emotion" actually distinct and only related indirectly, with no fundamental essence?

I suggest that all of the words that refer to feelings and desires can be understood in terms of two related and complementary but distinct "essences" of emotion: at one level of analysis there are neurochemical systems and at another level, ecological demands and functions (Buck, 2010a). At the biological level, neurochemical systems contribute to subjective emotional experiences much like the ingredients to a cocktail or musical instruments to a symphony. At the ecological level, emotions are identified with displays, including facial expressions, body postures, spatiotemporal cues, touches, and pheromone releases. In addition, there are interrelated systems of higher-level social, cognitive, and moral emotions reflecting interactions between biological potential and universal ecological contingencies. Importantly, all of these emotions have publicly observable aspects that can be scientifically investigated – operationalized and objectively measured – including aspects that have heretofore been unobservable.

The biological essence: neurochemical systems

Primes. The subjective aspects of biological emotions – feelings and desires – are associated with specific neurochemical systems. As is described in detail in Chapter 2, neurochemical systems are defined by neurotransmitters and agonists or antagonists that respectively facilitate or impede such transmission. These systems constitute *primary motivational/emotional systems* or *primes* (Buck, 1985): distinct and dissociable but interrelated *modules* that are analogous to ingredients making up the subjectively experienced affective cocktail; or individual instruments contributing to the symphony of feeling.

Specific primes can be identified with specific neurochemical systems that can be located within the brain. They include systems in the brainstem involving arousal and behavioral activation/inhibition;

systems in the hypothalamus involving biological drives such as hunger and thirst; systems in subcortical brain structures involving raw sex and aggression; and systems in paleocortical brain structures involving a variety of individualist and prosocial emotions. The functioning of the primes is increasingly open to observation by advanced biological and physiological techniques, from the investigation of the functioning of specific genetic systems to double-blind studies of the behavioral effects of important neurochemicals to the online functioning of brain systems by advanced electrophysiological and scanning technology.

Voices of the genes. The molecules underlying the primes can be directly linked with specific genetic systems. Peptide neurotransmitters are direct genetic products constructed by DNA in the nuclei of their parent neurons. They are physically transported down the axon of the cell to the synapse, where they are released to carry on the message of the genes. On one hand, these peptide molecules are among the most ancient components of living systems, appearing in virtually unmodified form in microbes (bacteria, slime molds, yeast) and highly developed animals including human beings. On the other hand these molecules are closely related to the subjective experience of emotion, or affect, in human beings, interacting and participating in a cocktail or symphony of feelings whose precise recipe or score is discoverable, and affective neuroscience is hot on the trail to discover recipes for these cocktails or the scores for these symphonies. The feelings and desires so engendered carry the influence of the genes to the behaving organism. Usually whispering and murmuring in pianissimo, sometimes speaking out forcefully, and occasionally screaming and shouting in crescendo, affects function as *voices of the genes* that, acting together, can produce the equivalent to a *symphony of the genes* (Buck and Ginsburg, 1997a).

The ecological essence: display, behavior, and communication

Neurochemical systems evolved in the context of ecological requirements: that is, necessities born from functioning in the terrestrial environment of objects and events, and the social environment of other organisms. This terrestrial/social ecology can require, for example, approach, avoidance, escape, aggregation, separation, exploration, investigation, competition, cooperation, sex, play, and nurturance. These functional requirements took the phenomenon of emotion outside the organism and brain into the communicative social environment. Emotions are displayed as well as felt, and these displays are "picked up" by partners in communicative exchanges that may involve a number of specific primes.

The primes as individual modules are gathered together into "packages" due to their similar ecological implications regarding display, behavior, and communication. For example, the following feeling states can be considered to reflect modular primes based upon specific neurochemical systems: *stress* associated with corticotropin releasing hormone (CRH); *panic* with cholecystokinin (CCK); and *anxiety* with diazepam binding inhibitor (DBI). These are ecologically "packaged together" in that they all relate to similar escape/avoidance behavior patterns and specific displays (e.g. well-described facial expressions, gestures, postures, vocalizations) associated with the emotion that we term *fear*. In this view, fear per se is not associated with any single brain system: rather the feeling of fear represents a cocktail or symphony of neurochemicals whose precise recipe is variable, and, in principle, measurable; and fearful displays and behaviors can reflect any of a number of interacting primes (Buck, 2010a).

An example of a variety of primes underlying a complex emotional state was presented in the February 2011 "Valentine's Day" issue of *Scientific American* summarizing studies of brain systems underlying love (Fischetti, 2011). Neurochemicals at high levels included dopamine (DA) reflecting feelings of pleasure and activation; oxytocin (OXY) reflecting attachment and trust; vasopressin (AVP) reflecting attraction and sexual arousal;, and cortisol (CORT) reflecting stress and alertness. Sadness, fear, anxiety, and pain sensitivity were all low. Interestingly, serotonin (5-HT) was at a low level, reflecting tendencies toward insecurity, jealousy, aggression, and obsessive thinking associated with love. One can imagine how different specific examples of love may be reflected in different levels of these constituent neurochemicals interacting to yield a variable symphony of feelings and desires that nevertheless are all associated with "love" at the ecological level. At the ecological level, love is celebrated in story and song, particularly in "silly love songs" which, despite their ubiquity, are typically overlooked and ignored as inconsequential (Buck, 2010b). As we shall see in Chapter 5, such songs are extraordinarily diverse, ranging from "Some Enchanted Evening"[1] to "If you Want to Keep your Beer Ice Cold (Set it Next to my Ex-Wife's Heart)"[2]: thus the metaphorical symphony of felt love is embodied, as it were, in a plethora of actual songs. These reflect the wide variety of feelings and desires that can be associated with love; and our fascination with these songs reflects our fascination with these feelings and desires.

[1] From the 1949 Rodgers and Hammerstein musical *South Pacific*.
[2] © 1989 by Doug Vaughn and Pete Samson.

The ecological reality of emotion with respect to display, behavior, and communication is just as "real" as are biological neurochemical systems, and just as open to objective observation and investigation. As there has been a revolution in our ability to record, examine, manipulate, and image phenomena at the biological level, there has been a simultaneous and complementary revolution in our ability to image, measure, and time the fleeting nuance of display and expression occurring during social interaction. This involves, for example, using inexpensive low-light video technology and high-speed computer analysis. This revolution in observation has rendered the ephemeral permanent, allowing us objectively to record and examine the "body language" of nonverbal communication in human beings and other animals as never before.

Developmental-interactionist theory

Emotion, then, is based in biological potential inherent in the primes. However, this potential must be realized and actualized in social communication and interaction over the course of development. This interaction between biological potential and social experience is at the heart of the biosocial synthesis and is described by *developmental-interactionist theory*.

Defining motivation and emotion

Motivation and emotion. I begin by defining the fundamental terms, motivation and emotion. Kleinginna and Kleinginna (1981a; 1981b) surveyed definitions of motivation and emotion in the scientific literature, and suggested consensual definitions for each. *Motivation* has been traditionally defined in terms of the control of behavior: that is, the *activation and direction of behavior toward a goal* (Young, 1961). Such control may be manifested at many levels, from simple reflexes such as the knee-jerk reaction, to "instincts" or fixed action patterns including migratory behavior patterns, to drives such as hunger, thirst, and sex, to complex higher-level motives involving power, attachment, exploration, and achievement. *Emotion* has also traditionally been associated with goal-directed behavior, but in contrast with motivation, emotion typically involves *affects*: subjectively experienced feelings and desires. These may involve dimensions of quiescence-arousal and reward-punishment; the specific primary affects such as happiness, sadness, fear, and anger; and also higher-level affects such as pride, guilt, jealousy, trust, and resentment. Kleinginna and Kleinginna noted that emotion is also typically associated with *expressive behaviors*, including facial expressions, postures, patterns of spacing and eye contact, etc., and *peripheral physiological responses*, including changes in heart rate, sweating, blood pressure, and muscle tension.

Developmental-interactionist theory is consistent with these traditional definitions, but goes beyond them in suggesting that motivation and emotion are functionally linked. Motivation is defined as *potential for the activation and direction of behavior that is inherent in a system of behavior control*; while emotion is defined as the *realization or "readout" of motivational potential when activated by challenging stimuli*. So, motivation is the potential for behavior, and emotion is the readout of motivational potential. In this view, motivation and emotion are seen as two sides of the same coin: aspects of a *motivational-emotional system* (see Buck 1985, p. 9, 1988a, p. 5).

The relationship of emotion and motivation is analogous to that of matter and energy in physics. Energy is a potential that is not seen in itself, but rather is manifested in matter: in heat, light, and force. The potential energy in an explosive is manifested in heat, light, and force when it explodes, and the potential energy in a coiled spring is manifested in force when the spring is released. The energy per se is never seen. Similarly, motivation is conceptualized as potential that is not shown in itself, but rather is manifested in emotion: in physiological arousal, expressive displays, and affective experience.

Levels of motivational-emotional systems. Like motivation, motivational-emotional systems are manifest at many levels. For example, in a simple *spinal reflex* like the knee-jerk reaction, the motivational potential exists in the arrangement of sensory and motor neurons between the knee and spinal cord. The motivational potential is released with the stimulus: the neurologist's tap on the knee. In *fixed action patterns* such as those underlying migratory behavior, the potential exists in a system that activates complex sequences of behavior in response to a specific challenging stimulus (*releaser*) that may involve the day/night cycle, the magnetic fields of the Earth, and other environmental changes. In eating behavior, the motivational potential (the "hunger drive") exists in a complex system of energy regulation and metabolism that is functioning constantly – we always have specific needs for food that vary – and that can respond to environmental stimuli including the presence, sight, and smell of attractive food. Thus, motivational potential is activated by challenging stimuli – a tap on the knee, the day/night cycle, attractive food – in appropriate circumstances. This view of motivation in itself is not extraordinary: what is different is linking the activation of motivational potential with emotion. Reflexes, fixed action patterns, and drives are not traditionally associated with "emotion," but this linkage is an important aspect of developmental interactionist theory.

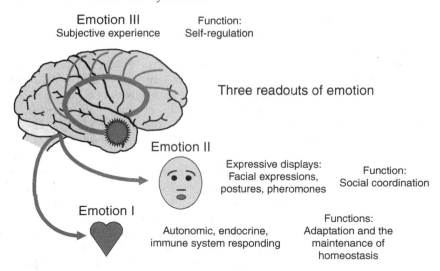

Figure 1.1 Three readouts of emotion. See text for details.

Three readouts of emotion

Emotion includes three aspects identified by Kleinginna and Kleinginna (1981a, 1981b): subjective experience, expressive displays, and physiological arousal. I characterize these three aspects of emotional responding as *readouts* (Buck, 1985, 1994a), and they are illustrated in Figure 1.1. There are ways to measure objectively and directly both physiological arousal and expressive behavior, but the aspect of emotion that in many ways seems most essential – the subjective experience of feelings and desires, or affects – has long seemed impossible to measure directly.

Affect: the subjective readout. In recent years, there has been a revolution in the ability to observe biological processes closely associated with feelings and desires, leading to the potential for what Jaak Panksepp termed an *affective neuroscience* that relates subjectively experienced feelings and desires directly to the activities of specific neurochemical systems (Panksepp, 1991, 1998). Brain scanning and electrophysiological techniques give access to events occurring within the functioning brain. Not only human beings, but also other mammals show evidence of the subjective experience of affects, in that they can demonstrate in their behavior that they have awareness of the states of neurochemical systems that are associated with affects. Moreover, viewing emotional displays of other persons can activate the areas of the brain associated with the experience of those emotions in the viewer: these *mirror neuron* (MN) systems suggest the possibility that even empathy may be observable.

I define *affect* as *the direct subjectively experienced knowledge of feelings and desires.* Human beings (and presumably many other animals) experience feelings and desires directly and immediately: the phenomenological subjective reality of affect is self-evident. Importantly, feelings like fear, anger, and happiness can *guide* the organism without actually *controlling* its behavior. A jealous man may be furious, and know that he is furious, but he is able to control his behavior so as not to make a suicidal attack on a large and menacing rival. In effect, the affects *cajole rather than control* – the organism is *persuaded* to fight, flee, or make love with a level of insistence that varies with the strength of the affect, but the locus of control remains with the individual (Buck and Ginsburg, 1997b).

In addition, *affects are always present.* There is a constant readout of feelings and desires available to us at all times. We can always turn our attention to how hungry, or thirsty, or warm we are; and also how happy, sad, or angry. We tend spontaneously to *notice* this affective information only when it is strong or sudden, but like the feel of our shoes on our feet, *it is always with us.* Relatively strong affects associated with specific eliciting stimuli are typically termed "emotions" as compared with *moods,* which are longer lasting and not so closely associated with specific elicitors (Ekman and Davidson, 1994). There is persuasive evidence that subjectively experienced affects are *not* epiphenomena or based upon visceral-autonomic or facial-somatic feedback: they are independent phenomena involving internal perceptual systems – *interoceptive* systems evolved in response to challenges reflecting the organism's "need to know" – serving their own vital functions based ultimately upon central neurochemical systems (see Buck, 1980, 1990, 1993a).

Display: the expressive readout. At the same time that subjectively experienced affects have become the subject of objective analysis, inexpensive videotape technology using unobtrusive cameras with low-light capability has made accessible brief and fleeting nuances of spontaneous facial expression and gesture that can be revealing even when the responder is trying to conceal her "true feelings."

Consider an example. Your friend is giving a party, but has a splitting headache. She strives to cover up her feelings of pain by smiling and acting happy, but you note a fleeting expression of pain that appears and fades suddenly. If the hostess were someone you did not know well, you might dismiss the short-lived and almost ephemeral change in expression. However, since she is familiar to you, you know that such an expression is uncharacteristic, and when given an opportunity to speak to her alone you ask if anything is wrong. Your friend confesses that she really feels terrible but doesn't want to spoil the fun at the party, and you comfort her as best you can. This simple exchange illustrates how people follow *display rules* to try to control the expression of their "true feelings" to fit social conventions, and how personal relationships can help one to see through these controls. At the same time, it is likely that your ability to see your friend's "true feelings" is not rebuffed by her but actually welcomed, and helps to foster accurate emotional communication that further supports and cements your relationship, enhancing its intimacy; as well as serving functions of bioregulation, contributing to the well-established stress-buffering effects of social relationships (see Buck, 1993c).

Arousal: the peripheral physiological readout. The third readout of emotion – arousal – involves peripheral physiological responses which can be assessed by such measures as heart rate, blood pressure, sweat gland activity, hormone levels, and T-cell activities of the immune system. In normal social interaction, these responses are not readily accessible, either to the responder or to others. Thus while we may occasionally be aware of our heart pounding, and others may sometimes notice that we are blushing, normally neither we nor others notice these sorts of responses and we certainly do not have detailed knowledge of, say, our blood pressure levels or T-cell counts.

Thus, the manifestations of motivational potential take three forms, or readouts. Arousal is the manifestation of motivational potential to serve functions of adaptation and homeostasis via the autonomic, endocrine, and immune systems and is termed *Emotion I* in Figure 1.1. The display (*Emotion II*) serves functions of social coordination via expressive behaviors (pheromones, touches, gestures, facial expressions, and the like). Subjectively experienced affects (*Emotion III*) serve functions of self-regulation (subjective *qualia* signaling needs, feelings, and desires).

Learning about affects: emotional education

Accessibility and emotion. The subjective, expressive, and arousal readouts are all reflections of the same emotional state, and early in life they are closely correlated to one another. Expression and feeling, for example, are typically shown together in young children (Izard, 1978). However, the three readouts are differentially *accessible* to the responder and to other persons. Subjectively experienced affect is accessible only to the responder; the expressive display is accessible more to the other than to the responder; and peripheral physiological arousal is normally not accessible to either without special physiological measuring equipment. Because of this difference in accessibility, these responses are shaped differently in the process of social learning,

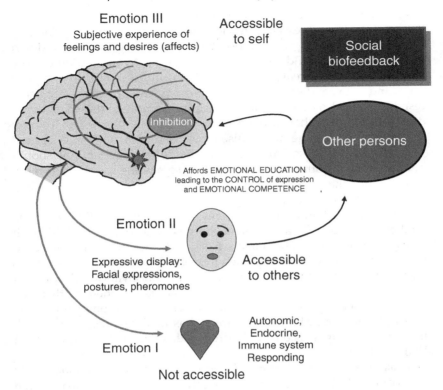

Figure 1.2 Emotional expression, emotional communication, and social biofeedback. See text for details.

and they become related to one another in increasingly complex ways over the course of development.

Affects are accessible directly only to the responder: the parent does not have direct access to the child's affect or the child to the parent's affect. Therefore, affects must undergo a different sort of social learning – be shaped differently by experience – than are openly accessible events. Because directly experienced affects are not accessible to others, we must learn *about* affects indirectly, through emotional communication (Buck, 1983). That is, the social learning process by which emotions are educated is different from other sorts of social learning, and accurate emotional communication between parent and child is essential (see Figure 1.2).

Emotional education. Consider a young boy Tommy playing with blocks: his carefully built structure falls down and he becomes enraged. He screams and throws his blocks around the room. His mother nearby has no access to the child's subjective experience of rage but she is all too aware of his expressive behaviors. She might say firmly: "Tommy, you've been playing with those blocks too long; they fell down so you're frustrated and angry. That's too bad, but you shouldn't throw your blocks; you'll break something. Go to your room, play with your train, and relax, and come back when you're ready to behave." Such a response provides rich information helping Tommy to understand and deal with the rage that rose within him when the blocks fell. Tommy learns that the feeling was caused by frustration, that it is termed "anger" in the English language, and that when it occurs one should not throw things but rather relax and do something different. Tommy learns about the affect – *emotional education* – and what to do when it occurs – *emotional competence.*

On the other hand, and especially perhaps with a little girl, the mother might say "Gina, you are a bad girl!" and strike the child. Such a response does not label Gina's feeling of rage or guide her about what caused it or what to do when it occurs. Indeed, if angry reactions were consistently punished in this way, Gina conceivably may not learn to label angry reactions at all, instead associating them with being "bad" and being punished and rejected. This may be one reason why harsh physical punishment by parents has long been associated with high levels of aggression in children and adolescents (Bandura and Walters, 1959).

Social biofeedback and modeling. Children learn about their subjectively experienced feelings and desires largely through the feedback from others responding to their expressive behaviors. This fact was pointed out by B. F. Skinner in his operational analysis of psychological terms (1945), but its implications have perhaps not been fully grasped. I have termed this *social biofeedback* because the behavior of the other provides the child with feedback which, like biofeedback, is about a bodily process that is otherwise inaccessible to the child (Buck, 1988a). But then, consider an older Tommy at puberty, when erotic feelings and desires come on line with the sexual hormones. In Western culture, Tommy is unlikely to express such feelings and desires to parents, teachers, or other adults who might provide social biofeedback. Instead, he may rely upon another way that human beings learn from others: watching their behaviors. Children *imitate* and *model* the emotional behaviors of others, and that perhaps is another reason why children with punitive parents tend to be aggressive: by aggressing against the weak they are, in effect, modeling their parents. However, in Western culture sex-related behaviors are rarely exhibited openly. Instead, young adolescents are strongly drawn to media depictions, particularly of affects (like sex and aggression) that are difficult to deal with interpersonally. Media are often criticized for their sexual and aggressive content, but such content is clearly popular: perhaps reflecting a need in American culture to deal more openly and frankly with sexual and aggressive feelings.

Learning about affects means being able to label and linguistically understand them and to respond appropriately and effectively when they occur. This requires the same kind of learning and information processing that is required for learning about events in the external environment. Indeed, there is an intrinsic interest and curiosity about the experience of affects just as there is about understanding other aspects of experience: a natural fascination with both "positive" and "negative" affects (Buck, 1988b; Buck and Powers, 2011; Stifano, 2011).

Emotional competence. The outcome of emotional education is a greater or lesser degree of *emotional competence*: children learn, or fail to learn, how to express their feelings and desires appropriately and what to do when these affects occur. Successful emotional education leads to emotional competence: the ability to follow cultural display rules to label, understand, control, and appropriately express feelings and desires. Contrariwise, deficits in emotional education lead to a kind of emotional helplessness that may contribute significantly to psychopathology (Buck et al., 1995, 1998).

Relating emotion and cognition

Defining cognition

Cognition. I define motivation and emotion as linked in motivational-emotional systems. In this view, one cannot exist without the other: they are aspects of the same phenomenon, two sides of the same coin. Similarly, I submit that one cannot coherently conceptualize or define cognition without considering motivation and emotion. Each is involved in both of the others: motivation intrinsically involves emotion and cognition, cognition involves motivation and emotion, and emotion involves motivation and cognition.

I define *cognition* generally as *knowledge of events*, and this can include knowledge of events in the physical environment, the social environment, and the internal bodily environment. In this view, affective feelings and desires constitute a kind of knowledge – a kind of cognition – involving events in the bodily environment. The "raw" experience of events is spontaneously restructured over the course of development into more differentiated knowledge structures based upon experience in the physical and social environment. That is, knowledge about emotion emerges naturally from experiences in which one (a) displays emotion and receives social biofeedback, (b) observes displays in inter-action partners with their descriptions of feelings and desires, and (c) observes a model (live or via media) displaying an emotion and receiving feedback. For example, Piaget (1971) noted how, based on experiences with physical events, a child's knowledge structures become progressively differentiated: initially based on direct sensory-motor experiences, later being influenced by concrete logical rules, and finally being structured by formal logical principles. In this process, two sorts of cognition can be distinguished: *syncretic cognition* is raw, holistic, direct, immediate, and self-evident acquaintance; *analytic cognition* is sequential, linear, propositional, and can involve rational information processing (see Epstein et al., 1996; Tucker, 1981).

Knowledge by acquaintance versus knowledge by description. The analytic–syncretic cognition distinction is related to, but not identical with, a distinction between *knowledge by acquaintance* (KA) versus *knowledge by description* (KD). KA is always syncretic: direct, immediate, and holistic. KA was described by Bertrand Russell as the "presenta-tional immediacy of experience" that is completely self-evident (1912, p. 73). Analytic cognition in contrast always involves KD, or knowledge *about* knowledge, which is not self-evident but can be false. In analytic cognition information is processed sequentially in a linear fashion, so that discrete pieces of information are related to one another. Syncretic cognition may also be known by description, as when one element is known spatially relative to another (see Buck, 1990).

KA constitutes the raw data of perception, based upon ancient per-ceptual systems evolved to detect information in the form of stimulus energy physically present in the environment: in light, vibration, and volatile chemical substances (Gibson, 1966, 1979). James J. Gibson's theory of ecological realism provides a coherent and detailed account of the evolution of knowledge from the earliest organisms to human perception. Gibson (1979) termed raw perception *awareness*: "To perceive is to be aware of the surfaces of the environment and of oneself in it" (p. 255). According to Gibson, species evolved to be sensitive to those aspects of the environment which afford possibilities or opportunities for behavior: *affordances*. There are three sorts of "raw" awareness. First, there is awareness of affordances in the terrestrial environment, such as "sitability" and "walkability." Second, there is awareness of *social affordances* provided by other animals. As Gibson (1979) put it, "other animals afford, above all, a rich and complex set of interactions, sexual, predatory, nurturing, fighting, playing, co-operating, and communicat-ing" (p. 128); and he noted that other animals "can only give off information about themselves insofar as they are tangible, audible, odorous, tasteable, or visual" (p. 135). This information is provided in great part by Emotion II displays, that are social affordances (McArthur and Baron, 1983). Third, Gibson recognized awareness via interoceptors of vague sensations of internal origin – feelings and emotions – the "pangs and pressures of the internal environment" (1966, p. 31). These may be conceptualized as bodily affordances, and in my view affects – awareness of the Emotion III readout – constitute awareness of bodily affordances.

In contrast with raw awareness or KA, KD is constructed from the restructuring or processing of raw perceptual data into an internal representation of reality. Thus we have direct perceptual acquaintance with events in the terrestrial environment, social environment, and internal bodily environment; and knowledge *about* these events based upon information processing and inference. The distinction between KA and KD has long been made in epistemology: it was made by St. Augustine in *De Magistro* (Marsh, 1956), and it is reflected in many languages, as in the French *connaître* versus *savoir* and the German *kennen* versus *weissen* (James, 1890). The relevance to emotion theory of the distinction between KA and KD has been widely recognized (see Epstein et al., 1996; Laird, 1996; Strack, 1996).

I suggest that KA and KD are based in different systems that interact over the course of development. This interaction is illustrated in Figure 1.3, which shows the relative influence of KA (or emotion) and KD (or reason) across situations involving knowledge. KA is always present, and in the figure its level is assumed to be constant across situations. KD may vary from not being present at all (pure raw experience, left extreme of figure) to having much more influence than KA (e.g. listening to a lecture or contemplating an equation). However, even when dominated by KD, KA is always present (right side of figure).

Special-purpose versus general-purpose processing systems

The perceptual systems that provide KA are innate: that is, they are phylogenetic adaptations reflecting the operation of genetic systems selected over the course of evolution. These are *special-purpose processing systems* (Buck, 1985). In the case of perceptual systems, the function is to provide access to information physically present in the terrestrial environment: e.g. in the light, in vibration, and in volatile chemicals. In the case of the primary motivational-emotional systems or primes defined previously, the function is to respond to events that have constituted specific sorts of challenges to individual and species survival over the course of evolution. The responses to such challenges include arousal, approach-avoidance, aggression, sex, and other behaviors supportive of the survival of the individual and the species. In contrast, KD is

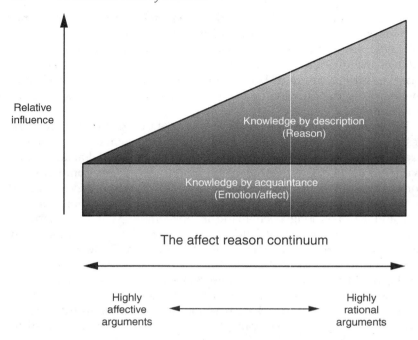

Figure 1.3 The relationship between knowledge by acquaint-ance and knowledge by description. At the extreme left, the influence of "raw" knowledge by acquaintance is total, and the relative influence of knowledge by description increases toward the right until it dominates, but the influence of knowledge by acquaintance never falls to zero. See text for details.

a function of *general-purpose processing systems* which are structured over the course of individual development: that is, by the individual's experience during ontogeny. They reflect the capacity of the species for learning via classical conditioning, instrumental learning, higher-order cognitive processing, and, in human beings, language. Figure 1.3 can also represent the interaction between special- and general-purpose processing systems.

Biologically based primes are special-purpose processing systems arranged in a hierarchy, in which the interaction with general-purpose processing systems becomes more important as one goes up the hier-archy, as illustrated as one goes from left to right on Figure 1.3 (Buck, 1985). The simplest sorts of primes are reflexes like the knee-jerk reaction: here the response is wholly "hard-wired" and innate, with virtually no flexibility. At the next point on the hierarchy are instincts or fixed action patterns, such as those that motivate the homing and migration of birds and fish. These can involve complex patterns of behavior, which are quite inflexible when examined closely: one cannot teach salmon to change their migratory behavior. The next level of the primes does, however, involve flexibility. Drives involve bodily needs that are signaled to the organism by subjectively experienced affects: feelings and desires (Buck, 1993a). The organism is signaled that it is hungry, or thirsty, or cold, or in pain by specific bodily messages. These serve to activate and direct behavior so that the organism has the capacity to explore its surroundings in search of the relevant resources. If the organism is successful in finding food, water, or other resources that satisfy its needs, *satiation* occurs and the behavior leading to the reward is *reinforced*. Stimuli associated with reward become *positive incentives* that can serve as cues in the future when similar needs arise, so that the organism is "steered" efficiently to the goal. Contrariwise, punishment produces *negative incentives* that are avoided.

The drives involve specific bodily needs and consummatory behaviors that function to satisfy those needs. The next level of the hierarchy does not involve specific needs or consummatory behaviors. This is the level of the *primary affects* of Tomkins (1962–92), Ekman and Friesen (1969a), and Izard (1971, 1977): happiness, sadness, fear, anger, and disgust. These signal the bodily state but do not directly influence behavior. The individual knows that he or she is happy, or angry; and may or may not know why; but unlike some I do not believe that any specific behavior tendencies are activated. Indeed, affects function to facilitate flexibility and *choice* among alternative behaviors: the individual has a *choice about what to do*, and if for example anger is felt toward a large person or a small person the behavior will be different.

As one proceeds up the hierarchy from reflexes, to instincts, to drives, to affects, the interaction between special-purpose and general-purpose processing systems has increasingly favored the latter. Arguably, the resulting dimension presented in Figure 1.3 more accurately reflects the relationship between innate factors and learning than does the more usual categorical distinction between emotion and cognition. Also, other phenomena may be meaningfully placed on this dimension. For example, the dimension mirrors the phylogenetic scale, with simple creatures' behavior being mostly a matter of reflexes (ants and bees, for example); and creatures with significant analytic-cognitive capacities being at the other extreme. The progressive evolution of learning and cognitive abilities that confer increased behavioral plasticity has been termed *anagenesis* (Gottlieb, 1984). Also, the developmental scale may be represented, with the more hard-wired infant at the left and the adult at the right. Similarly, this dimension represents the evolution of the nervous system, with functions served by more "primitive" structures to the left and to the right increasingly complex functions based upon brainstem, midbrain, hypothalamic, reptilian, paleocortical, and neocortical processing.

The notion of an interaction between special-purpose and general-purpose processing systems that takes place in developmental context is basic to developmental-interactionist theory. Figure 1.3 illustrates this fundamental interaction; in Chapter 5 a similar figure is used to represent the interaction between syncretic and analytic cognition and spontaneous and symbolic communication, and in Chapter 6 it is applied to a typology of cognition.

The epistemology of affect

Definition. Emotion II involves preattunements affording a direct KA of others' displays – social affordances in the Gibsonian sense – serving functions of social coordination (Buck and Ginsburg, 1997b). Preattunements may well be based upon mirror neuron systems. Emotion III is a direct KA of one's own feelings and desires: interoceptive knowledge of bodily processes serving functions of self-regulation. "Bodily processes" in this context do not necessarily refer to autonomic responses or expressive behaviors: rather Emotion III involves systems of internal perception or interoception that have evolved to inform the organism of specific events in the bodily milieu. The experiential aspects or *qualia* associated with these interoceptive perceptual systems are feelings and desires, or affects. The events of which they inform include the organism's needs for food (hunger), for water (thirst), for warmth or cold, for sex, etc.: these are drives involving specific bodily needs. We are also informed of more general need states involving the primary affects of happiness, sadness, fear, anger, etc.

More specifically, I define *affect* formally as *the direct knowledge by acquaintance of feelings and desires, based upon readouts of specifiable neurochemical systems evolved by natural selection as phylogenetic adaptations functioning to inform the organism of bodily events important in self-regulation* (Buck, 1985, 1993a, 1994). Affects are special-purpose, gene-based, neurochemical readouts which function to confer behavioral flexibility and choice. Human beings experience affects immediately and directly: the phenomenological subjective reality of affect is self-evident.

In addition, as noted previously, *affects are always present*: a constant readout of feelings and desires is available to the organism at all times, like the feel of your shoes on your feet. Information concerning these bodily events is always with us: we can always turn our attention to "pick up" how hungry, or thirsty, or warm we are; and also how happy, sad, or angry. We tend spontaneously to *notice* this information only when it is strong or sudden, but like the feel of our shoes on our feet, it is always with us. Relatively strong affects associated with specific elicitors are termed in ordinary language "emotions" as compared with "moods" which are longer-lasting and not so associated with specific elicitors (see Ekman and Davidson, 1994).

As we have seen, the aspect of affects that makes them problematic for objective science is that they are essentially subjective private events. B. F. Skinner (1953) described the realm of "the world within one's skin" in terms of private events which "may be distinguished by (their) limited accessibility but not, so far as we know, by any special structure or nature" (p. 257). He emphasized that what is different and unique about such events is their "degree of accessibility to the community" (p. 262), which makes it difficult to establish a reliable vocabulary to describe such events. Indeed, this makes affects singular from a social learning point of view, so that the process of achieving emotional education and competence differs significantly from other sorts of social learning, requiring expressive display on the part of the child and social biofeedback on the part of the interaction partners.

Affective curiosity. Knowing affects by description – that is, being able to respond appropriately and linguistically to label and understand them – requires that same kind of learning and information processing that is required for learning about events in the external environment. Indeed, there is an intrinsic interest and curiosity about the experience of affects just as there is about understanding other aspects of experience. As we shall see, this may explain the natural fascination with both "positive" and "negative" affects that is reflected in humans' attraction to emotionally arousing media: literature, drama, music, and film. Thus MTV has its roots in DNA (Buck and Powers, 2011).

Measuring affects. Based upon the assumptions that affects are always present and that their subjective reality is self-evident, measuring affect by self-report is a relatively straightforward proposition. People *know* how they feel, simply and directly: one need only ask the right questions. A useful approach is to use Differential Emotion Scales (Izard, 1977): five- or seven-point scales that vary from "Not at all" to "Very much." Based upon brain research that we will be examining in this book, Buck (1999) posited six major varieties of affect: *Positive Selfish* (confident, secure, satisfied); *Negative Selfish* (insulted, angry, hostile); *Positive Prosocial* (loving, caring, intimate); *Negative Prosocial* (ashamed, embarrassed, guilty); *Reptilian Sex* (erotic, sexually aroused, sexy); and *Reptilian Power* (powerful, vigorous, energetic).

Levels of cognitive processing

The distinctions between KA and KD, and special-purpose and general-purpose control systems, are related to evidence of multiple levels of cognition associated with different processing and memory systems in the brain. Many have acknowledged that there must be distinct sorts of cognition – basic sensory processing that all agree is necessary for emotion, and higher-order cognitive processing (Averill, 1994; Bargh and Ferguson, 2000; Ekman, 1994; Frijda, 1994; Leventhal and Scherer, 1997).

Levels of appraisal. Appraisal theories emphasize that what makes an event emotional as opposed to non-emotional is its personal relevance as appraised by the individual. *Appraisal* is the "process whereby the personal relevance of an emotional event is apprehended" (Parkinson, 1997, p. 63). The theory of appraisal in emotion was introduced by Magda Arnold (1960). To Arnold, appraisal is instinctive and immediate: "even before we can identify something we may like or dislike it . . . There seems to be an appraisal of the sensation itself, before the object is identified and appraised" (1960, Vol. 2, p. 36). Appraisal is based upon a *multilevel estimative system* that "serves the evaluation of incoming sensation" (1960, Vol. 2, p. 34).

The "low road" and "high road" to cognition. Arnold's conceptualization of appraisal accords well with the work of Joseph LeDoux (1996), who studied appraisal using advanced techniques that allowed him to follow the course of neurochemical pathways in the brain. This research demonstrated that there is direct sensory input to the amygdala and that this input is necessary for the learning of conditioned fear responses. In the auditory system, the "classic" auditory pathway proceeds from the cochlea of the ear to the brainstem, thence to the medial geniculate body (MGB) near the thalamus, and from there to the part of the neocortex specialized for auditory sensation. LeDoux and colleagues identified another, parallel, pathway in the auditory system that proceeds from the MGB to the amygdala (LeDoux et al., 1984), and similar direct amygdala pathways exist in the visual system as well (LeDoux et al., 1989). Thus the amygdala has its own subcortical sensory inputs. These constitute evolutionarily primitive "early warning systems" that trigger fast emotional responses to threatening stimuli essential in the quick "assignment of affective significance to sensory events" (LeDoux, 1996, p. 110). LeDoux termed this the *low road* to cognition. Amygdala inputs are several synapses shorter than those of the classical sensory systems and therefore offer "a temporal processing advantage at the expense of perceptual completeness" (p. 112). Microseconds after this initial sensory input is received, more completely processed input enters the amygdala from the neocortex

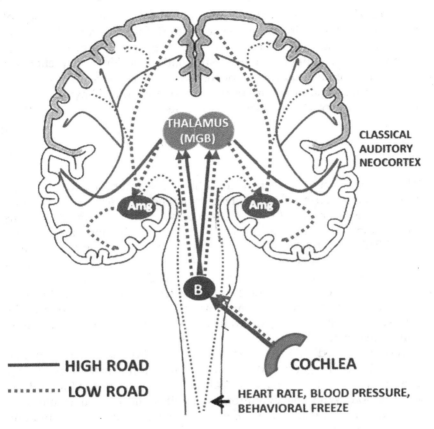

Figure 1.4 The low and high roads to cognition. The "classical" auditory pathway proceeds from the cochlea of the ear to the brainstem, then to the medial geniculate body (MGB) near the thalamus, and on to the part of the neocortex specialized for auditory sensation (solid arrows). A parallel auditory pathway proceeds to the MGB and thence directly to the amygdalae, thus affording the amygdala its own sensory inputs (dotted arrows). Incomplete but highly involving information passes quickly to the amygdalae, which initiate the fight-or-flight pattern of response. Information is also relayed to the neocortex to be processed more completely and initiating coping behavior, eventually moderating the amygdala response. Amg = Amygdala. B = Brainstem nuclei.

and other centers associated with higher-order cognition, so that we are able to "know" what caused the emotional reaction and initiate appropriate coping behavior (see Figure 1.4). The latter is the *high road* to cognition.

LeDoux's research speaks to the fundamental theoretical issue of the nature of the brain's initial response to emotional events. It appears that "low road" emotional responding precedes and can guide "high road" cognition. Indeed, stimulation, lesions, and chemical manipulations (e.g. by drugs) of the central nervous system can lead to apparently complete emotional experience and behavior with no higher-level cognitive appraisal of the state.

Conclusions

The necessary and sufficient conditions for emotion consist of the *readout, in response to a challenging stimulus, of potential built-in to a system of behavior control*. This states necessary and sufficient conditions for defining, not only "emotion," but also "motivation" and "cognition." The primitive terms of the definition – including "challenge," "built-in," and "behavior control" – imply the naturally evolved organism–environment interaction described by Gibson (1966). All organisms have evolved perceptual systems that can be informed by (or can become aware of) certain sorts of events – affordances – in the terrestrial environment. Affordances *inform the organism*: thus they constitute *information*.

Gibson argued that the organism, the environment, and information define each other: without an organism (on a lifeless planet, for example) there is a physical reality but no environment and no information. With the evolution of a self-replicating molecule such as DNA, an organism, environment, and information are simultaneously created; and with the commencement of natural selection, prototypical motivation, emotion, and cognition as well. Information implies cognition and motivational-emotional systems sort out the relative importance of information – they evolve to prioritize, to respond to the extent to which events are challenging. Thus prototypical motivational-emotional systems emerged with the natural selection of the organisms based upon adaptation to environmental events.

It might be noted that, in this definition, "motivational-emotional systems" and "emotional readouts" occur in even the simplest of creatures, but cannot occur in even the most sophisticated of computers. Computers can be very efficient at processing information but *they are never actually "informed."* They respond only to what they are told; they lack independent knowledge or awareness of affordances in the environment and the capacity independently to adapt that is demonstrated by the most elementary of life forms.

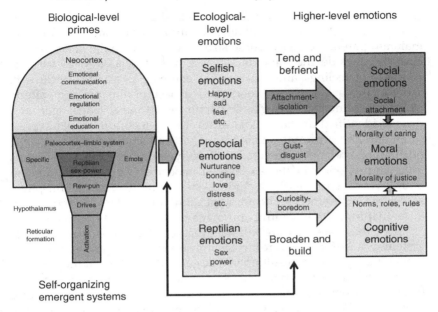

Figure 1.5 General model of biological and higher-level emotions. See text for details. REW-PUN = Reward-Punishment, EMOTS = Emotions.

A biosocial synthesis of emotion

The primes

A summary of the motivational-emotional systems to be considered in this book appears in Figure 1.5. On the left side of the figure is the anatomical hierarchy of the brain. Basic activation systems are associated with the reticular formation of the brainstem; specific drives including hunger, thirst, and sex with the hypothalamus; behavioral activation and inhibition (reward-punishment) systems course from the brainstem through the hypothalamus into frontal regions of the brain. None of these systems have executive functions, however: we shall see that three levels of executive functions are associated generally with MacLean's (1993) differentiation of levels of the triune brain. The most basic associated with sex and power are represented in subcortical structures and the amygdala, termed *reptilian systems* because they mediate social and sexual behavior seen in the basic lifestyles of reptiles (e.g. territoriality). Next are specific emotions associated with paleocortical (3–5 layered) structures labeled *paleomammalian* because they are largely absent in reptiles but functional in early mammals, and support the cardinal behavioral triad of mammals of nursing/maternal care, play, and audiovocal communication to maintain parental contact. These structures comprise the *limbic system*, and also include the amygdala. These are associated with variable cocktails of feelings and desires that combine in various recipes to provide the subjectively experienced aspect of the primary affects including elements of the classic happiness, sadness, fear, anger, and disgust identified at the ecological level by pancultural facial expressions; and also prosocial emotions involving attachment, bonding, love, nurturance, and separation anxiety. Finally, there are executive systems involving emotion in the six-layered neocortex, or new mammalian brain. These particularly include systems in the right hemisphere associated with emotional communication, and systems in the frontal lobes that function to control and manage emotional responding.

All of these systems are intimately associated with neurochemical systems whose functions are increasingly open to study and even experimental manipulation, resulting in a large and complex but increasingly coherent literature that is the subject of much of this book. In addition to traditional studies of brain lesioning and stimulation that span over a century, studies on animal behavior now include paradigms where the very genes that control the functioning of specific neurochemical systems can be manipulated and altered experimentally. These animal studies are complemented by studies of the effects of drugs and brain damage in human beings, where the sites of action or damage can be precisely specified and related to symptoms. The result is that we can now tell an increasingly coherent story about the nature of emotion and its place in human nature that is extraordinarily complex and detailed, but based squarely upon observation and experimental fact. At the same time, this story is relevant to understanding how emotions function in ordinary human beings in their daily lives and social relationships.

As noted previously, in my view the neurochemical systems in this hierarchy constitute primary motivational-emotional systems or primes. Although they are highly interactive, each prime has its own identity, which in principle and increasingly in practice can be distinguished and assessed experimentally. Each prime is like an ingredient in the cocktail of feeling and desire, or a musical instrument contributing to a symphony. Each prime is a *module of emotion*, as it were; and as previously discussed each prime is an irreducible biological reality underlying the concept of emotion. But, we do not typically express or label emotions based upon the primes. Emotion has another level of reality, an ecological reality based upon the evolved functions of emotions in the social and physical environment. The ecological reality is not irreducible because it is composed of primes. For example, we saw that at least three specific neurochemical systems constitute modules of what we call at the ecological level *fear*. One is anxiety, associated with DBI and the amygdala; another is stress, associated with the CRH and cortisol; another is panic, associated with CCK (Buck, 2010a). Experienced fear is analogous to a cocktail composed of a mixture of these basic ingredients, or a symphony in which they contribute like individual musical instruments. The precise recipe of the cocktail or score of the symphony may differ from situation to situation, but they are in principle observable and discoverable. Similar analyses can be made involving happiness, sadness, anger, and disgust; as well as a variety of prosocial emotions including love.

The role of communication

The ecological reality of emotion crucially involves communication, so it is not surprising that the primary affects are distinguished by distinct pancultural facial expressions. From a functional, ecological, and communicative point of view, it does not matter much whether danger results in panic, anxiety, or stress: the important thing is that one must freeze or flee, and communicate the danger to others. Less is known about the displays associated with prosocial emotions. They do not seem to involve specific facial expressions, perhaps because they operate at close personal distances where facial expression is not so useful a communicative signal (Hall, 1966). Other displays, perhaps involving pheromone exchanges, touch, eye contact, and soft musical vocalizations, are more useful at intimate distances.

There is evidence that, while survival emotions such as happiness, sadness, fear, anger, and disgust are displayed by facial expressions, intimate emotions such as love and sympathy are displayed through touch, and social dominance emotions such as pride, guilt, embarrassment, and shame are displayed by body posture (App et al., 2011).[3] For example, Aviezer et al. (2012) found that body cues, not facial expressions, discriminate between peak positive and negative emotions. There is evidence that communication by touch, like facial expression, has universal elements (Clynes, 1977, 1980, 1988; Miller, 2012). For example, Manfred Clynes argued that basic and universal expressive time forms, or *sentic forms*, are associated with specific emotions and can be expressed in touch, sound, and gesture. He studied these with a *sentograph* which assessed expressive form by recording dynamic finger pressure. Miller (2012) replicated and extended Clynes'

---

[3] This evidence emphasizes the point that the function of the display is communication rather than feedback.

work by demonstrating accurate communication of emotion via touch, using time series and Fourier analysis to describe universal sentic patterns associated with anger, disgust, love, sadness, joy, and sexual arousal that are distinct from one another. He also constructed a neural network that could be "trained" to recognize universal sentic forms using artificial intelligence. The machine's performance was comparable to that of human judges, and could guess all emotions except disgust.

The interaction during development

Thus, the mechanism of the interaction between physiological potential and ecological reality involves emotional communication: by facial expression, body posture, touch, and vocalization. This interaction occurs during the process of individual development, and the typical events experienced during infancy, childhood, and adolescence represent a coupling of emotional potential and social/communicative experience. The research of Harry F. Harlow (1971) on the development of rhesus monkeys showed how an initial *parental affectional system* is introduced through physical touch: contact comfort with a soft skin-like surface. This produces basic feelings of trust and attachment, which were the necessary conditions for a *peer affectional system* in which the youngster began to explore both the physical environment and the social environment through rough-and-tumble play. These experiences form the basis for rhesus monkey emotional communication: displays of threat, submission and appeasement, courting, and warning appear in play; to later be transformed after puberty into the signals that underlie rhesus social organization in the *sexual affectional system* (Buck, 2010b).

Higher-level emotions: an ecological-systems view

In this interaction between biological affects and the ecological realities of terrestrial and social experience with development, motivational-emotional systems form the basis for the emergence of three great *systems* of higher-level emotions: thus this conception is termed an *ecological-systems view* of higher-level emotion. The first motivational-emotional system is *attachment-detachment*, with its roots in the parental affectional system. With normal development, creatures are highly motivated to attach to others. A second is *curiosity-boredom*, which depends upon initial attachment, with the mother being the initial "safe base" from which the infant begins to explore the environment (Bowlby, 1969–80), and continues as the youngster acquires increasing motor and exploratory skills. A third system whose importance has only recently become apparent is *gust-disgust*: the biological basis of moral emotion. Disgust is well known and widely studied as a basis of morality, but I suggest that a similarly strong and powerful emotion of moral approbation – gust – is the "positive" counterpart of disgust.

Motives for attachment are the basis for *social emotions*, which as we shall see are hypothesized to exist *in a system* as four twins: *pride/ arrogance*, *guilt/shame*, *envy/jealousy*, and *pity/scorn*. *Embarrassment* plays a role in development, as do *regret* and *remorse*; the latter functioning to turn shame to guilt. Unlike many accounts, I suggest that the social emotions are pancultural, appearing in all human cultures and historical periods regardless of linguistic labels, in many animals as well as human beings, emerging naturally and effortlessly from the basic ecological contingencies of social interaction. The development of social emotions has been associated with tendencies to *tend and befriend* (Taylor et al., 2000).

Similarly, curiosity motives are the basis for exploratory behaviors and a wide variety of systematically related *cognitive emotions* ranging from *awe* to *ennui*. Among other things, cognitive emotions underlie the learning of social rules and expectations for conduct: the basis of social *norms* and *roles*. Cognitive emotions are also hypothesized to be pancultural, appearing in all human cultures and historical periods regardless of linguistic labels, in many animals as well as human beings, emerging naturally and effortlessly from the basic contingencies of interaction with the terrestrial ecology. The development of cognitive emotions has been associated with tendencies to *broaden and build* (Fredrickson, 2001).

Both social emotions based in attachment and cognitive emotions based in curiosity feed into *moral emotions*. There are two bases for morality, a *morality of justice* based upon knowledge and acceptance of the rules and a *morality of caring* based upon attachment. Moral emotions are also hypothesized as noted to be energized by gust, the emotion of moral approbation, and disgust, the emotion of moral indignation. Like social and cognitive emotions, systems of moral emotions are hypothesized to be pancultural, appearing in all human cultures and historical periods regardless of linguistic labels, in many animals as well as human beings, emerging naturally and effortlessly from the basic ecological contingencies of social interaction in terrestrial context.

Competence and success in social and cognitive emotions are held to be highly rewarding, but a lack of such competence is held to be associated with depression. A lack of social competence is hypothesized to be particularly related to Type B major depression (associated with depletion of serotonin [5-HT]) and a lack of cognitive competence is particularly associated with Type A major depression (associated with norepinephrine depletion). Again, this is hypothesized to be pancultural, appearing in all human cultures and historical periods regardless of linguistic labels, in many animals as well as human beings, emerging naturally and effortlessly from the basic ecological contingencies involving a lack of competence in social or terrestrial arenas.

In the Preface, I discussed the parable about blind men arrayed around an elephant trying to explain the nature of the beast. In a sense, the approaches summarized briefly in this chapter represent the experiences of the blind men, each accurate and valid in its own right but incomplete; representing restricted points of view. Figure 1.5 aims to present an overall, general view of the elephant, that hopefully can begin to reconcile these different points of view, and also to demonstrate that an understanding of emotion is at the very center of understanding human nature. With new means to observe and objectively measure events in the depths of the brain, and the fleeting nuances of body language, the nature of the beast is slowly coming into focus.

PART II

Biological emotions: a readout view

CHAPTER 2

Neurochemical systems: evolution and function

The discussion in Chapter 1 suggested that there is an irreducible essence at the biological level associated with all things labeled emotion. This chapter seeks to specify the nature of that essence. Biological emotions involve specific *neurochemical systems*, and neurochemical systems underlie both a constant subjective readout of subjectively experienced feelings and desires, or affects (Emotion III), and a constant readout of expressive displays (Emotion II). Neither the subjective readout nor the readout in display is necessarily conscious, in fact they normally operate below the radar of consciousness. Nevertheless, they exert pervasive influences on behavior.

The explication of the nature of neurochemical systems in this chapter does not reflect their importance per se, but rather is due to the proposition that these neurochemical systems form the irreducible, objectively observable, and manipulable basis of subjective affective *qualia*, which at the psychological level are experienced as feelings and desires. As noted, subjective experience is the most controversial and problematic aspect of emotion from a scientific point of view because it seemingly cannot be objectively studied. Objective measures and manipulations of neurochemical systems (e.g. through drugs and other means including the direct alteration of genes) are reliably and consistently linked to emotional displays and behaviors in animals and matching changes in subjective affect reported by human beings (Buck, 1993a; Panksepp, 1998).

There is persuasive and converging empirical evidence that certain specific neurochemicals are associated with specific subjective affective tonalities or *qualia* (Buck, 1993a). A given emotion defined at the ecological level – love, fear, anger, happiness – can be associated with a variable cocktail or symphony of specific feelings and desires, which can in principle be manipulated and measured via manipulations and measurements of the relevant neurochemical systems. Although of course not all neurochemical systems are associated with biological emotions, it is arguably the case that all biological emotions are associated with neurochemical systems. These systems are in principle specifiable and their activities observable and manipulable. Of course, any given neurochemical may have different effects in different individuals, because genetic or environmental/developmental influences, or interactions with other systems, can produce individual variation in the effect of any given neurochemical.

Neurochemical systems: neurotransmission and neuromodulation

Neurochemical systems

In an expansion of Hebb's (1949) classic notion of "cell assemblies," neurochemical systems are defined as functionally arranged sets of neurons – individual nerve cells – that communicate with other cells, that is, that both send to and receive information from other cells. It is possible in principle, and increasingly in practice, to define biological emotions objectively in terms of activities of specifiable neurochemical systems. Biological emotions in turn underlie higher-level social, cognitive, and moral emotions: biological emotions constitute affective potential that emerges in ecological context over the course of development. So, neurochemical systems constitute an irreducible essence of *all* emotions.

Investigations of the brain and emotion often emphasize the localization of emotion within specific brain structures. Although this can be useful, as we shall see in the next chapter, it is also the case that emotions can be associated with neurochemical systems that cross brain structures. Thus, emotional phenomena may be biologically based in observable and manipulable brain systems, and yet not associated with any specific brain structure.

The nerve cell is a structural unit of neurochemical systems (see Figure 2.1). A typical nerve cell or *neuron* communicates by sending and receiving chemical influences vis-à-vis other cells using specific *neurotransmitters*: molecules that carry influences across small spaces between cells termed *synapses*. The *cell body* of the neuron contains the genes and most of the metabolic machinery of the cell. The neuron receives influences at *dendrites*, which may activate the cell sufficiently for a *nerve impulse* to be generated. The nerve impulse in a typical neuron is an electrochemical signal that is propagated down the *axon*. The nerve impulse sets up chemical processes at *end buttons*, structures at the terminus of the axon, which in turn lead to the discharge of neurotransmitter molecules into the synaptic space. There, the neurotransmitters influence *receptor sites* in the membranes of the next cell in line, which may be dendrites of another neuron or *effector cells* such as muscle cells. The sending cell is the *presynaptic* cell, and the receiving cell, *postsynaptic* (see Figure 2.1).

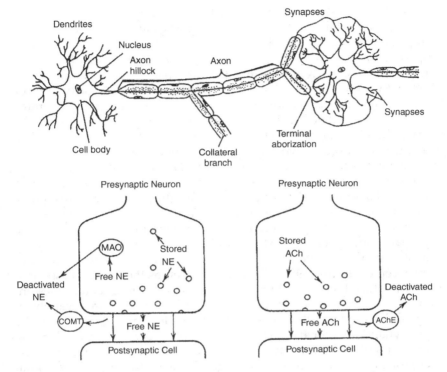

Figure 2.1 Neurochemical systems. Simplified diagram of a neuron (above), an adrenergic synapse (left below), and a cholinergic synapse (right below). In the adrenergic synapse, norepinephrine (NE) is broken down by monoamine oxidase (MAO) within the neuron and by catechol-O-methyl transferase (COMT) in the synaptic space. In the cholinergic synapse, acetylcholine (ACh) is broken down by acetylcholinesterase (AChE) in the synaptic space. See text for details.

Neurotransmission. Synaptic transmission has many variations, but general themes can be discerned. First, neurotransmitters are synthesized within the cell from precursor compounds, generally influenced by specific enzymes. The neurotransmitters are stored in vesicles in the end button. Second, the neurotransmitters are released through the presynaptic membrane into the synaptic space, typically in response to the arrival of a nerve impulse traveling down the axon. Third, the transmitter substance crosses the synaptic space and binds to receptor sites in the membrane of the postsynaptic cell. The molecular structure of the transmitter fits into the receptor site much like a key in a lock, and in doing so it activates the receptor site, allowing a flow of ions to pass through the membrane, temporarily depolarizing the postsynaptic membrane, and making it easier for the postsynaptic cell to fire a nerve impulse. Fourth, the transmitter substance is cleared from the synaptic space, either by an enzyme that degrades or breaks down the neurotransmitter, or by reuptake into the presynaptic cell, or both (Pinel, 1993). Synaptic transmission is illustrated in Figure 2.1 for two major kinds of neurotransmission: *cholinergic transmission* involving the transmitter acetylcholine (ACh), and *aminergic transmission* involving the catecholamines *dopamine* (DA) and *norepinephrine* (NE), and the indole amine *serotonin* (or 5-hydroxytriptamine, abbreviated 5-HT).

Neuromodulation: the second messenger. Neuromodulation is a more complex process in which the substance crossing the synaptic space is termed a *neuromodulator*: it does not affect the postsynaptic membrane directly, but rather acts through a *second messenger*, molecular structures within the postsynaptic cell. Briefly, the neuromodulator acts as the primary messenger, but instead of altering the postsynaptic cell membrane directly it activates a protein structure – a G-protein – coupled to the receptor (Beatty, 1995). The G-protein acts as the second messenger. It can initiate biochemical processes that serve as intracellular messengers, potentially affecting the membrane and the cell in a variety of ways. For example, the membrane may be depolarized, activating the postsynaptic cell; or the membrane may be hyperpolarized, inhibiting the cell and making it more difficult to initiate a nerve impulse. The G-protein may also potentially trigger the synthesis of proteins within the postsynaptic cell, altering the internal metabolism and even modulating gene expression of the postsynaptic cell; affecting the production of enzymes important in neurotransmission, and sprouting new synaptic connections (DeWeid and Gispen, 1977). Such effects could underlie learning and memory processes. These effects are often mediated by cyclic adenosine monophosphate (cAMP), a ubiquitous substance that has widespread effects on bodily functions (Matthews, 1998). The changes induced by the second messenger can cause long-term or permanent alterations in the cell's functioning, so that the cell, in effect, remembers the influence. The actions of neuromodulators are generally slower and longer lasting than those of simple neurotransmitters; acting on a scale from minutes to hours and persisting for weeks, months, or longer (Purves et al., 1997).

Receptor sites. A given type of neurotransmitter molecule can have different effects depending upon the receptor site to which it binds. As noted, the transmitter molecule fits into the receptor site like a key in a lock, and because transmitter molecules are complex three-dimensional structures, it is possible for the same molecule to fit into different types of receptor sites that may be distributed differently within the brain's anatomy, and may underlie different kinds of effects that have implications for drug sensitivity and side effects. For example, there are at least four kinds of DA receptor sites, abbreviated D1, D2, D3, and D4. Serotonin (5-HT) acts on at least twelve different receptor types. This allows a single type of molecule to be responsible for complex patterns of effects, which may be quite different and even apparently inconsistent with one another.

Genetic biosynthesis of peptides

There are two main categories of neurotransmission that will be discussed later, small-molecule neurotransmission and large-molecule neurotransmission involving the peptides. Peptides are particularly closely associated with subjective experiences of feelings and desires, as we shall see. Peptides are synthesized as relatively large precursor molecules that are direct products of genes. In a peptide-secreting neuron, the genetic transcription takes place in the cell body. The transcription process results in a *pre-propeptide*, which is processed in the endoplasmic reticulum of the cell, where a section of amino acids termed the signal sequence is removed. The remaining substance is a *propeptide*, that passes through the Golgi apparatus of the cell and is packaged into vesicles. Further processing of the propeptides by enzymes into active peptides occurs as the vesicles are physically transported in a process termed fast axonal transport down microtubule tracks in the axon from the cell body to the end button. Finally, the active peptide transmitters are released into the synaptic space, where they diffuse often affecting a number of nearby receptor locations. For example, pre-proopiomelanocortin is a pre-propeptide, and proopiomelanocortin (POMC) is the corresponding propeptide that, in company with specific enzymes, produces the active peptides ACTH, MSH, and beta-endorphin (Purves et al., 1997).

Many of the peptides involved in emotion have effects both in the central nervous system, acting like neurotransmitters and neuromodulators, and in the periphery of the body, acting like hormones. The functions of peptide hormones from endocrine glands that act via the bloodstream have long been recognized. It was once thought that peptide hormones are produced only in the specialized glands: ACTH from the pituitary, insulin from the pancreas, and so on. Now, peptides have been found throughout the body: in the brain, the placenta, the vas deferens, and cells of the immune system. Indeed, it has been suggested that virtually *any* bodily cell can produce virtually *any* peptide in small amounts (Niall, 1982). Moreover, the central effects of the peptides upon the brain are often related to their peripheral effects. Cholecystokinin

(CCK) acts peripherally in digestion and centrally in the regulation of appetite; oxytocin (OXY) is involved peripherally in childbirth and the production of milk and centrally in nurturance and attachment; and corticotropin releasing factor (CRH) is involved peripherally in the production of ACTH and other stress hormones and centrally in facilitating avoidance behavior (Panksepp, 1993).

Mechanisms of drug action: agonists and antagonists

The neurotransmission process can be influenced in a variety of ways by drugs or other manipulations. First, the synthesis of the transmitter from precursors can be facilitated or inhibited. Second, the actions of enzymes that break down neurotransmitters can be facilitated or inhibited. Third, the reuptake of transmitters into the presynaptic cell can be facilitated or inhibited. Finally, a drug can act as a transmitter *agonist*, itself activating the receptor on the postsynaptic cell and mimicking the effect of the transmitter; or the drug can act as a transmitter *antagonist*, binding to the postsynaptic receptor site without activating it and thereby preventing its activation by the transmitter.

The evolution of neurochemical systems

The fundamental chemical units of neural transmission evolved long before the appearance, within the phylum Chordata, of the vertebrate brain and spinal cord. The earliest traces of the latter appear in fossils of creatures from the Cambrian period, beginning 570 million years ago (Walker, 1987). In contrast, the classical transmitter molecules evolved at least 1000 million years ago, and they are found in virtually all phyla. These transmitters evolved the ability to activate a range of ion channels in membranes; resulting in excitation, inhibition, or other influences; acting via receptor sites. Homologies between invertebrate and vertebrate receptors suggest that the basic receptor subunits evolved at least 800 million years ago (Walker et al., 1996).

The evolutionary antiquity of the neurochemicals

There are two striking aspects of neurochemical systems in relation to biological emotions. One is the great evolutionary age of the molecules functioning in these systems, which evolved long before the appearance of the vertebrate brain and spinal cord. These molecules are more than ancient, they are primordial. The vertebrate brain/spinal cord arrangement evolved during the Cambrian era, in company with all of the other phyla of multi-celled animals presently on the Earth, including sponges, arthropods, mollusks, brachiopods, echinoderms, and chordates (Dixon et al., 2001). Indeed, the first known member of *chordata*, the phylum that includes human beings and all other animals with backbones, is the segmented wormlike swimmer *Pikaia*, found among the Cambrian-era fossils in the Burgess shale (Margules and Sagan, 1995).

In contrast with the relatively recent evolution of the brain/spinal cord, there is evidence that many of the molecules that now function as neurotransmitters evolved much earlier. For example, peptide neurohormones appear not only in the nervous systems of mammals including human beings, but also in insects, segmented worms, plants, and single-celled yeast and bacteria (Pert, 1985; Loumaye et al., 1982). Single-celled protozoa have peptides similar to adrenal-cortico-tropic hormone (ACTH) related in human beings to stress; the endogenous opiate beta-endorphin related to pain; cholecystokinin (CCK) related to digestion and satiety; gonadotropin-releasing hormone (GnRH) related to erotic feelings and sex; and insulin related to metabolism (LeRoith et al., 1980, 1982; Miller et al., 1983). This implies that these peptides must have existed in the common ancestors of, on one hand, mammals including human beings, and on the other hand, single-celled bacteria and yeast. Such ancestors must have lived well over one billion years ago, long before the evolution of the brain. Also, if the peptides evolved so early in the unicellular stage of life, the genes specifying these peptide molecules and their receptors must have existed and been conserved virtually unchanged throughout invertebrate and vertebrate evolution (Niall, 1982). Indeed, we share about 40 percent of our genes with simple single-celled creatures: such genes must be involved in constructing the peptides and their receptors, underlying the most fundamental sorts of intracellular and intercellular communication.

Neurochemicals, protoawareness, and affects

The second striking aspect of the neurochemical systems is that they are closely related to the most mysterious and ineffable aspect of emotion: subjective emotional experience, or *affect* (Pert, 1997). Evidence for this comes from the effects of drugs that alter the functioning of these neurochemical systems. In human beings drugs can induce strong feelings: intense euphoria, panic, increased or decreased fear and anxiety, sexual feelings, calm or angry feelings, all largely in the absence of rational or cognitive explanations for such emotional states. These effects in humans are directly comparable to similar kinds of effects in animals. Indeed, our rapidly increasing knowledge in this

Table 2.1 Major types of psychoactive drugs

Neurotransmitter system	Classification	Common examples
Acetylcholine (ACh)	ACh agonists	Nerve gases soman and sarin; nicotine
	ACh antagonists	Acetylcholine esterase; atropine; scopolamine
Dopamine (DA)	DA reuptake inhibitors	Cocaine, amphetamine
	DA releasers	Amphetamine
	DA agonists	L-DOPA
	DA antagonists	Haloperidol, many antipsychotics
Norepinephrine (NE)	NE reuptake inhibitors	Tricyclic antidepressants (TCAs)
	NE releasers	Ephedrine
Serotonin (5-HT)	5-HT agonists	LSD, psilocybin, mescaline
	5-HT reuptake inhibitors	SSRIs including fluoxetine (Prozac) TCAs including imipramine
	5-HT releasers	MDMA (ecstasy)
	5-HT receptor antagonists	Atypical antipsychotics
Endogenous opiates (endorphins)	Agonists	Morphine, heroin, codeine, oxycodone
	Antagonists	Naloxone, naltrexone
gamma-Aminobutyric acid (GABA)	GABA receptor agonists	Ethanol, barbiturates, benzodiazepines, diazepam (Valium), chlordiazepoxide (Librium)
N-Methyl-D-aspartic acid (NMDA)	NMDA receptor antagonists	Ethanol, PCP, ketamine, nitrous oxide
Cannabinoid receptor	Agonists	THC, cannabidiol, cannabinol

area involves complex but converging and largely consistent evidence from many sources, as we shall see.

The effects of some major drugs, including drugs of abuse, are summarized in Table 2.1 and are discussed later in the context of particular neurotransmitter systems. In examining these drug effects, a close correspondence becomes apparent between, on one hand, concrete and observable neurochemical systems, and on the other, private and ineffable emotional experience. This is one way that the essence of emotion can be objectively operationalized and measured by public observation. As Candace Pert put it in her book *Molecules of Emotion*:

> We ... knew how the mind drugs heroin, opium, PCP, lithium, and valium entered the network and worked on the receptors, and how the endogenous, or "in-house," substance, endorphin, communicated over a wide range. If we were to characterize exactly what these chemicals were doing, we would have to say they affect the emotional state of the person who takes them, making him or her happy, sad, anxious, or relaxed ... And when we focus on emotions, it suddenly becomes very interesting that the parts of the brain where peptides and receptors are richest are also the parts of the brain that have been implicated in the expression of emotion. (Pert, 1997, p. 178)

It is noteworthy that subjectively experienced affects are related to neurochemicals with the most ancient origins. For example, the peptides insulin and CCK enable the simplest single-celled creatures to regulate their eating behavior relative to their bodily needs for food. The raw "protoawareness" possessed by these creatures of their need for food is apparent in their behavior, in that they eat only when they need to. Certainly this does not involve the conscious experience of hunger as it may be experienced by more complex creatures. However, this elementary protoawareness may well lay the biological and epistemological groundwork, as it were, for the conscious subjective experience of affect. These neurochemicals provide a way for organisms to have access to, and eventually to evolve to become consciously aware of, their own basic needs via feelings and desires.

Affects as voices of the genes

So, the ancient peptides associated with feelings and desires are direct products of specific genes. The peptidergic neurochemical systems provide a way for these genes to communicate, constituting *interoceptive perceptual systems* informing the organism of bodily states critical in self-regulation. In effect, as suggested in Chapter 1, affects function as *voices of the genes*. Genes produce peptides which in turn are associated with the subjective experience of feelings and desires. Through the affects the genes do not *control* the organism, rather they *cajole*: wheedle, entice, coax, and persuade. This allows the organism a range of *choice* in how to respond. For example, feelings of hunger and thirst register long before the organism has a physical need for food or water, but they signal that these needs must eventually be attended to with an insistence that varies with the strength of the feeling or desire. It is the same with fighting, fleeing, making love, celebrating, mourning. Affects are always with us – we can always turn our focal conscious attention to our affective feelings and desires just as we can to the feel of our shoes – but we generally do so only if they are at relatively high levels. They are always with us, but usually the voices of the genes whisper in pianissimo. But, there are times when they scream and shout in crescendo.

This arrangement allows, indeed necessitates, flexibility of response. In contrast with relatively simpler control mechanisms such as reflexes and instincts or fixed action patterns, drives and biological affects do not control the response of the organism. They set the agenda, specify the priority, and dictate the significance, but leave the actual resolution to the organism. Thus, the most inflexibly determined aspect of human nature is *flexibility*. So, paradoxically, *free will is biologically determined*.

Neurochemical systems: structure and function

There are many kinds of transmitter substances: we will consider major ones including *acetylcholine* (ACh), *dopamine* (DA), *norepinephrine* (NE), *gamma-aminobutyric acid* (GABA), and *serotonin* (5-HT); as well as peptides such as the *enkephalins*. For each neurotransmitter, there are chemical *agonists* that can facilitate its functions as well as *antagonists* that inhibit its actions (Pert, 1997). The responsiveness of a neurochemical system is influenced by many factors, including the number and excitability of nerve cells in the system, the availability of neurotransmitters with their agonists and antagonists, and receptor sites of a specifiable number, anatomical location, and degree of sensitivity.

Small-molecule neurotransmitter systems

Systems of neurotransmission can be divided into small-molecule neurotransmitter systems, and neuropeptides, which involve relatively large transmitter molecules (Purves et al., 1997).

Cholinergic transmission. The fact that neurotransmission involved chemicals was first demonstrated in 1921 by the Austrian physiologist Otto Loewi, and the transmitter involved, ACh, was isolated in 1933. There are two major sorts of ACh receptors, termed nicotinic and muscarinic based upon their sensitivity to the toxic plant alkaloids nicotine (derived from the tobacco plant) and muscarine (derived from a poisonous red mushroom). The nicotinic receptor is relatively uncomplicated: ACh is synthesized in the nerve cell from precursors choline and acetyl coenzyme A in a process requiring the enzyme choline acetyltransferase (CAT). The assembled ACh is stored in sacs in the end button of the presynaptic cell adjacent to the synapse. When an impulse arrives down the axon, the ACh is released into the synaptic space where it temporarily alters, or depolarizes, the membrane of the postsynaptic cell by binding to ACh-sensitive receptor sites (Eccles, 1965). In effect, ACh molecules act to open a physical gate in the postsynaptic membrane, allowing a flow of sodium and potassium ions through protein channels that thereby depolarize the cell. The ACh is rapidly broken down by a powerful enzyme in the synaptic space, *acetylcholine esterase* (AChE), which allows the postsynaptic membrane to quickly repolarize (Purves et al., 1997). AChE breaks ACh down into acetate and choline, the latter of which is recycled into the presynaptic cell in a reuptake process (see Figure 2.1).

ACh is a peripheral neurotransmitter in the autonomic nervous system and at the neuromuscular junction, acting via nicotinic receptors to cause the skeletal muscles to contract. It is also present in the central nervous system, although its role there is not so well understood (Purves et al., 1997). Over 99 percent of the cholinergic receptors in the central nervous system are muscarinic, which involve second messengers and produce more complex and varied effects compared with the simpler nicotinic receptors (Beatty, 1995). The ACh acts as the primary messenger, but instead of altering the postsynaptic cell membrane directly it activates a G-protein coupled to the receptor, which in turn acts as the second messenger, initiating a variety of effects.

The simpler nicotinic ACh receptor is the target organ of several natural poisons, which act to shut down the receptor site, causing paralysis because skeletal muscles can no longer be activated by motor neurons. The venom of snakes such as the cobra, sea snake, and banded krait paralyze prey using this method, as does the plant toxin *curare* used by native South Americans as an arrowhead poison. Also, drugs acting on the nicotinic ACh receptor are used and abused as social drugs. These include tobacco and the active ingredient of betel nuts, which are chewed in many parts of the world (Purves et al., 1997). Both of these substances are highly addictive, where *addiction* is defined by the high involvement in and compulsive use of a drug, and a high tendency to relapse after use of the drug is discontinued (Jaffe, 1985). Nicotine is currently the most commonly used addictive drug in the world. Tobacco smoking was brought to Europe from the Americas, and indeed nicotine was named for the French ambassador to Portugal in 1550, Jean Nicot, who ironically was an early advocate of the medicinal qualities of tobacco smoking. Of course, tobacco smoke is now known to be highly toxic, both to the user and to others in the environment, as well as being highly addictive. Peripherally, nicotine acts as a muscle relaxant, while centrally it produces arousing and alerting effects, both via the release of dopamine and norepinephrine and via central cholinergic systems (Beatty, 1995).

Cholinergic transmission is also targeted by the organophosphates, examples of which include insecticides and also poison gases: mustard gas first used in World War I, and the nerve gases Sarin and Soman. Sarin was the compound used by Japanese terrorists on the Tokyo subway in 1995 and by Iraq's leader Saddam Hussein against Kurdish villagers in Iraq. These compounds inhibit AChE, causing ACh to build up in the synaptic space, resulting in muscular convulsions, eventual paralysis, and a slow and painful death (Purves et al., 1997). Sarin is countered by atropine (belladonna), which itself is a toxin (derived from deadly nightshade) that blocks the muscarinic ACh receptor. Soldiers in contemporary armies are equipped with atropine with which to inject themselves if under nerve gas attack.

Aminergic transmission. Aminergic transmission involves the biogenic amines, which exist in two major classes. One involves a set of related compounds termed *catecholamines,* which includes dopamine (DA), norepinephrine (NE), and epinephrine (Epi). They are directly related to one another in that all are derived from a common precursor, tyrosine. Tyrosine is converted by an enzyme within the cell to *L-dopa,* which is in turn converted by an enzyme to DA, which is then converted to NE, which is then converted to Epi. The second class of biogenic amines includes the indole amine serotonin (5-HT) and histamine. Serotonin is produced from the amino acid *tryptophan.* Much production of the amines is centered in brainstem nuclei: the *substantia nigra* in the case of DA, the *locus coeruleus* in the case of NE, and the *raphe nuclei* in the case of serotonin.

Amines neurotransmission is illustrated in Figure 2.1. Amine neurotransmitters are constructed within the end button of the presynaptic cell and exist both stored in sacs and in a free state. They are deactivated within the cell by the enzyme monoamine oxidase (MAO). After they are released into the synaptic space they are inactivated by catechol-O-methyl-transferase (COMT).

The mechanisms of amine synthesis and functioning of the synapse provide a number of ways to intervene in aminergic functioning. These are of particular interest because at the psychological level, they are involved in emotional processes related to a general elation–depression continuum of behavior. The amines can be manipulated directly by injection or restriction of critical dietary elements such as tyrosine, from which DA and NE are produced. Drugs that reduce DA and NE activity, such as reserpine, induce sedation, feelings of fatigue, and, in some persons, depression. A wide variety of drugs has been developed to facilitate aminergic transmission and thereby act as antidepressants, and these are among the most widely prescribed drugs worldwide. One class of antidepressants includes MAO inhibitors (MAOIs) such as *iproniazid*, which act by reducing the concentration of amine-destroying enzymes within the cell, thereby increasing levels of DA, NE, and serotonin. A second approach is taken by tricyclic antidepressants such as *imipramine*, which inhibit the reuptake of the amines and thereby increase their levels in the synaptic space by a different mechanism. A more discriminating approach is taken by *Selective Serotonin Reuptake Inhibitors* (SSRIs), which work by selectively inhibiting the reuptake of serotonin in the synaptic space. The well-known antidepressants *fluoxetine* (Prozac), *sertraline* (Zoloft), and *paroxetine* (Paxil) are SSRIs, and generally have fewer side effects than the older antidepressants (Purves et al., 1997). The efficacy and tolerability of the NE reuptake inhibitor *reboxetine* has been evaluated (e.g. Rampello et al., 2005), but Selective NE Reuptake Inhibitors (SNRIs) are not yet in widespread use.

At the psychological level, aminergic neurotransmission is linked with the social drugs cocaine and amphetamine (*dexedrine*), which have a long history of use and abuse (Wise and Bozarth, 1987). Both are DA agonists: both cocaine and amphetamine block the reuptake of DA, and amphetamine increases its release as well. Both have antidepressant effects, elevating mood, increasing energy and alertness, and suppressing appetite: "The mind is filled with energy and a sense of purpose and power" (Panksepp, 1981, p. 360). With high doses, the effects of the two drugs are similar: experienced cocaine users cannot distinguish between pharmacologically equivalent injections of cocaine and dexedrine (Fischman, 1984). Injections produce a pleasurable and sexual rush that is distinct from that produced by opiate injections. This euphoria is accompanied by a sense of enhanced physical and mental capacity, the loss of the subjective sense of a need for food or sleep, and reports of delayed and intensified orgasm in both women and men. With continued use, progressively larger doses are required to achieve the same level of euphoria, and schizophrenia-like symptoms may appear, including paranoia and hallucinations (Beatty, 1995; Pinel, 1993).

Serotonin. Serotonin (5-HT) is an indole amine neurotransmitter involved in a wide variety of psychophysiological functions. There are at least fourteen different serotonin receptors divided into seven main families. Alterations in these receptors occur in a variety of psychological disturbances, including personality disorders, anxiety, depression, eating disorders, schizophrenia, and drug-induced psychotic states (Roth, 1994).

Animals given lesions that interfere with serotonin function show symptoms of impulsive aggression (Siever and Trestman, 1993), and reviews of studies in humans have also identified links between low levels of serotonin function and impulsiveness, hostility, and domestic violence, particularly in men (Asberg, 1994; Brown et al., 1994; Coccaro, 1992; George et al., 2001; Tuinier et al., 1995). Symptoms of these conditions include failures to delay gratification or to suppress punished behavior, and New et al. (2002) suggested that low serotonin is associated with low activity in orbitofrontal cortex (OFC) brain areas associated with planning and long-term behavior regulation (see Chapters 3 and 7).

A review by Carver and Miller (2006) confirmed the links between low serotonin and impulsive hostility, and reviewed studies in which serotonin levels were experimentally elevated in normal samples by SSRIs or administration of tryptophan, a precursor of serotonin. Elevated serotonin led to decreases in aggressiveness and increases in cooperation, and there were also increases in confident dominance or what Carver and Miller termed "social potency" (2006, p. 7). Persons with elevated serotonin during everyday interactions reported more dominant behaviors (Moskowitz et al., 2001), and were more cooperative and affiliative in a game situation, while at the same time being rated as less submissive and showing more dominant eye-contact behavior (Tse and Bond, 2002a, 2002b).

Monoamine oxidase (MAO). As noted, monoamine oxidase is an enzyme that breaks down the amines DA, NE, and also serotonin. The variant MAO-A removes serotonin and NE, while MAO-B degrades DA (Bortolato and Shih, 2011). Lower levels of MAO translate into higher levels of the amines, and natural MAO concentrations can be assayed in humans from blood platelets (Murphy, 1973). These concentrations show wide individual variations, which at the psychological level have been related to behaviors in both animals and human beings which appear relevant to a general introversion–extroversion dimension of personality which we examine in Chapter 3. For example, relatively high MAO levels have been associated with passivity, inactivity, and a lack of social responsiveness in rhesus monkeys; while low levels are associated with high activity, play behavior, and social contact (Redmond and Murphy, 1975; Redmond et al., 1979). In humans, low MAO persons describe themselves as more social and report greater interest in social contacts (Coursey et al., 1979).

Variations in the MAO genotype are associated with a number of pathological conditions in humans, including antisocial personality disorder (Bortolato and Shih, 2011; Reti et al., 2011), and there is evidence that this genetic potential interacts with environmental influences involving early sexual and physical abuse. A high activity MAO-A genotype appears to serve to protect against experiences of early maltreatment in males, in that they are relatively less likely later to develop antisocial problems (Craig, 2005), while a thirty-year longitudinal study showed that males with the low-activity MAO-A variant who were exposed to abuse in childhood were significantly more likely to report later hostility, conduct problems, and offending (Furgusson et al., 2011). These observations of a gene × environment interaction may explain some of the variability in developmental outcomes associated with sexual and physical maltreatment. In general, MAO levels are negatively related to sensation seeking and impulsiveness, and positively related to inhibition (Castrogiovanni et al., 1990–91; Zuckerman, 1993; Zuckerman et al., 1980), and high and low levels of MAO have been linked respectively with inhibitory and disinhibitory psychopathology (Bongioanni, 1991; Sher et al., 1994).

GABAergic transmission. An additional type of small-molecule neurotransmission particularly relevant to emotion involves gamma-aminobutyric acid (GABA). GABA is an inhibitory transmitter that inhibits the ability of the postsynaptic cell to depolarize and fire. As many as one-third of brain synapses use GABA as the neurotransmitter (Purves et al., 1997).

GABA is synthesized from the precursor *glutamate* via the enzymes glutamic acid decarboxylase and pyridoxal phosphate, derived from vitamin B6. Dietary deficiencies of vitamin B6 have led to diminished GABA synthesis and resulted in seizures caused by the lack of inhibition. Most GABA is removed by active reuptake into the presynaptic cell. Drugs that are agonists or that otherwise increase GABA effectiveness, such as *barbiturates* (e.g. *phenobarbital*), have been used as anti-seizure medications and as sedatives (Purves et al., 1997). Also, the *benzodiazepines* (BZD) appear to work by increasing the ability of GABA to bind to its receptor, effectively slowing nerve activity. BZDs include the widely prescribed anti-anxiety drugs *chlordiazepoxide* (Librium) and *diazepam* (Valium). The binding sites for BZD are particularly dense in the amygdala, a brain structure known to play a major role in fearful and angry emotions (Pinel, 1993). As discussed later, the actions of the anti-anxiety drugs are antagonistic to those of the peptide transmitter *diazepam-binding-inhibitor* (DBI), also known as the "anxiety peptide" (Marx, 1985).

The peptide neurohormones

Definitions. As noted, neuropeptides involve relatively large transmitter molecules (Purves et al., 1997). There are sixteen amino acids that can be linked by the carboxyl group of one amino acid and the amino group of another, and thereby strung together like beads on a string. Amino acid chains are the building blocks of the peptides, and of protein. *Peptides* are defined as relatively short chains of two or more amino acids (Pert, 1997). The order in which the amino acids are joined determines the shape of the molecule and, thereby, the physiological activity of the peptide. Like the other neurotransmitters, peptides fit into receptor sites like a key in a lock, and the amino acid sequence determines the shape of the key. A change in only one amino acid can cause a dramatic change in the effects of a peptide.

Relatively long chains of approximately 100 or more amino acids are termed *polypeptides*, and polypeptide chains of more than 200 amino acids are *proteins*. Short chains of peptides often function like neurotransmitters, with relatively fast but transient effects: these are termed *neuropeptides*. The neuropeptides far outnumber the small-molecule neurotransmitters. Generally, longer peptide chains function like *hormones*, with relatively slow but long-lasting effects, often caused by distribution through the circulation in the bloodstream. Indeed, many of the neuropeptides were originally identified as hormones. The discovery of the neuropeptides blurred the traditional distinctions between neurotransmitters and hormones, leading to the combined term *peptide neurohormones*, which includes both sorts of function.

Another reason that the transmitter–hormone distinction was blurred is that short and long peptides often have structural similarities because they share amino acid sequences: they thereby presumably have similar shapes, can fit into similar receptor sites, and may have similar effects. An example is the polypeptide *beta lipotropin*, consisting of 91 amino acid sequences. Bolles and Fanselow (1982) noted that the first 41 of these sequences characterize *adrenocorticotropin hormone* (ACTH), which appears in single-celled creatures and plays an important role in the stress response in human beings. Sequences 42 to 60 consist of *melanocyte-stimulating hormone* (MSH), a pituitary hormone that darkens the skin in response to ultraviolet light (sun tanning) by stimulating melanin dispersion in pigment-containing cells. Sequences 61 to 91 comprise the molecule *beta endorphin*, a natural hormone found in the pituitary gland. The term endorphin comes from a contraction of endogenous morphine, and beta endorphin is a powerful analgesic (pain-killer). A fragment of beta endorphin – sequences 61 to 65 – constitute the molecule methionine enkephalin (*met-enkephalin*). Leucine enkephalin (*leu-enkephalin*) is similar, differing by one amino acid (Purves et al., 1997). Enkephalins are found in the brain, and have less powerful but faster-acting analgesic effects: they may function like neurotransmitters in contrast to the hormone-like beta endorphin.

In recent years advances in techniques for studying and manipulating genetic systems have helped to identify specific roles of neuropeptides in influencing and controlling behavior. Specifically, *knock-out* experiments work by breeding an animal in which the specific gene encoding a given peptide is eliminated; and *knock-in* experiments do the reverse, breeding an animal with a gene grafted on from another species. Such experiments can also be employed to study the small-molecule transmitters, by targeting genes that synthesize enzymes critical to the transmitter's functioning. The technology for such studies has been developed for mice (known as "transgenic mice") since the late 1980s and is now in wide use. Studies have tested the effects on socio-emotional behaviors of knockout strains involving the peptides AVP (Caldwell et al., 2010) and OXY (Macbeth et al., 2010), as well as serotonin (Lewejohann et al., 2010) and NE (Haenisch et al., 2009).

Genetic mechanisms for peptide biosynthesis are similar in vertebrates and non-vertebrates. As noted previously, the functioning of the peptides as messengers is evolutionarily ancient and primordial. In fact, the peptides are far older than the small-molecule neurotransmitters. The hydra is a member of the most ancient animal group with a nervous system, the *Cnidarians* (including corals, jellyfish, and sea anemones), and has a nerve net containing peptides, but not acetylcholine, serotonin, or catecholamines (Kandell et al., 2000), indicating that the nerve system of the common ancestor of the hydra and other animals functioned using only peptide messengers.

Peptides and subjectively experienced affects. With the peptides, there are tantalizing links between the functioning of ancient genes on one hand, and subjectively experienced feelings and desires, or affective *qualia*, on the other. Pert (1985, 1997) noted that the peptides are distributed in mood-regulating areas of the brain. She suggested that each peptide may bias information processing in a unique way when occupying a given receptor site, such that each peptide's "tone" might produce a typical mood state. Similarly, Panksepp (2003) has suggested that affective feelings emerge from specific subcortical circuits rich in neuropeptides.

The following sections examine peptides that show evidence of having important affective properties: beginning with the endorphins or endogenous opiates.

The opiates

The endogenous opiates. Opium, extracted from the opium poppy, has long been used and abused for its euphoria-producing effects and analgesic (pain-killing) properties. The Greeks discovered the euphoric effects of the wild poppy by 380 BC, and the active ingredient of opium is *morphine,* named for Morpheus, the Greek god of dreams (Pinel,

1993). Over 2,300 years later, Pert and Snyder (1973) discovered that certain areas of the brain are sensitive to opiates, including opium, morphine, and heroin, and also to the opiate antagonists *naloxone* or naltrexone. These brain areas are particularly associated with pain mechanisms (Panksepp, 1991). Opiate-like substances were identified in the vas deferens of the mouse, and later in the brain, by Hughes and colleagues (Hughes et al., 1975). Since then, over twenty opioid peptides have been identified in three classes: *endorphins, enkephalins,* and *dynorphins.* Each of these is associated with a distinct gene or pre-propeptide precursor: e.g. pre-POMC; pre-proenkephalin (proENK); and pre-prodynorphin (proDYN), respectively (Purves et al., 1997). Thus, unlike the small-molecule transmitters that are constructed from chemical precursors via enzymes, the opioids like other peptides are *constructed directly by specific genes.*

The opiates and pain. Substance P is a peptide neurotransmitter in the spinal cord that conveys pain information. The more substance P is released in these sensory nerves, the greater the transmission, and subjective perception, of pain. Endorphins apparently act to regulate the sensation of pain by modulating the release of substance P (Iversen, 1979). The release of substance P can be inhibited by opioid peptides, resulting in the analgesic (pain-killing) effects of the opiates. The resulting system of pain modulation is similar in many ways to the Gate Theory of pain regulation proposed by Melzack and Wall (1965) long before the role of the opiates was understood (Purves et al., 1997). Melzack and Wall proposed that signals from the brain can activate gating circuits in the spinal cord to block incoming pain messages, thus accounting for the ability of cognitive and emotional factors to block pain perception.

The opiates function by in effect "closing the gate" to pain in con-junction with other neurochemical systems. Disruption of serotonin, or destruction of certain serotonergic raphe nuclei in the brainstem, can disrupt the analgesic effects of the opiates (Basbaum et al., 1976). The mechanism of opiate analgesia generally accepted today was outlined by Fields and Basbaum (1984; Basbaum and Fields, 1978). The first step is the stimulation of opiate-sensitive neurons in the *periaqueductal gray* (PAG) in the midbrain, the gray matter surrounding the cerebral aque-duct. These neurons can be stimulated by opiate drugs, by electrical stimulation, or by influences from higher brain centers presumably including cognitive and emotional influences (Panksepp, 1998). The PAG cells project downward to serotonergic cells in the raphe nuclei in the medulla (particularly the nucleus raphe magnus), which in turn project down to cells in the dorsal horn of the spinal cord. The seroto-nergic raphe neurons synapse on endorphin-containing neurons that, when activated, inhibit the release of substance P, and therefore close the gate, reducing the pain message (Beatty, 1995).

The analgesic effects of the opiates can be blocked by the opiate antagonist *naloxone*, which competes with the opiates for the specific receptor sites, thereby blocking the effects of the opiates. Research using naloxone has produced evidence that the analgesic properties of both the placebo effect and acupuncture are based upon endorphin mechanisms (Purves et al., 1997). The *placebo effect* is defined as a curative response to a pharmacologically inert substance, and it is well established that pharmacologically inert substances such as saline solutions will significantly reduce pain. Early studies showed that naloxone can reverse the analgesic effects of placebo following the extraction of wisdom teeth (Levine et al., 1978): that is, when naloxone was used rather than an inert substance, the placebo effect disappeared and pain intensity was not reduced. There is also evidence that acupuncture analgesia can similarly be antagonized by naloxone (Mayer et al., 1977). These findings were supported by evidence suggesting that placebos and acupuncture normally have real pain-reducing effects due to their ability to activate the opiates (ter Riet et al., 1998). In a study involving real-life stress, Janssen and Arntz (2001) studied pain sensitivity in novice parachute jumpers, showing that, consistent with the opioid-mediated analgesia interpretation, a placebo led to lower reports of pain sensitivity compared to naloxone. They also found a large increase in plasma B-endorphin immediately after the jump, which correlated with reports of anxiety and loss of control during the jump. On the other hand, there have been reports of placebo effects that were insensitive to naloxone (Amanzio and Benedetti, 1999), so non-opioid mechanisms may be involved as well.

Opiate addiction. Panksepp (1991) suggested that the role of the opiates in regulating pain is related to their role in social dependence and addiction. As noted, addiction is defined behaviorally in terms of the compulsive involvement in and use of a drug, and a high tendency to relapse after discontinuing use (Jaffe, 1985). Other definitions of addiction emphasize the physical dependence to a drug, as indicated by the emergence of *tolerance* during use and *withdrawal* after discontinuing use of a drug (Beatty, 1995). Tolerance refers to the decreased sensitivity to a drug caused by repeated use, so that a given dose has progressively less psychological and/or physiological effect and therefore progressively larger doses must be taken to achieve a given effect. This may be because the taking of a drug may shut down the endogenous sources of the corresponding neurotransmitter, decrease the sensitivity of receptor sites, or both. The withdrawal syndrome, involving disturbances associated with the discontinuation of drug use, may be associated with the same phenomenon: normal functioning of the transmitter system is disrupted due to drug use.

Like the effects of cocaine and amphetamine, the euphoric and addictive effects of the opiates may be related to their effects on DA reward systems: indeed most addictive substances, including nicotine and benzene (alcohol), affect the DA system in some way (see Wise and Bozarth, 1987). However, there are differences between DA-mediated reward (wanting) and opiate-mediated reward (liking) that are functionally important, as discussed in the next chapter.

Other neuropeptides

Diazepam-binding inhibitor (DBI): the anxiety peptide. DBI is a chain of 87 amino acids first isolated in the rat brain in 1983 based upon its ability to displace diazepam (the anti-anxiety drug Valium) from its receptor sites on the GABA receptor and also from receptor sites on the outer membrane of mitochondria (Costa and Guidotti, 1991). It has since been identified in the human brain, and also in the fruit fly *Drosophila melanogaster*, used in much genetics research by virtue of its rapid rate of reproduction (Kolmer et al., 1994). The genes encoding DBI in the rat and human were sequenced and compared (Kroll et al., 1996). Named the *anxiety peptide* (Marx, 1985), DBI has been associated with depression, anxiety disorders, and panic attacks in humans (Guarneri et al., 1990), as well as aggressive behaviors in rodents (Alho et al., 1985; Kavaliers and Hirst, 1986). DBI is found in highest concentrations in the hypothalamus, amygdala, cerebellum, and discrete parts of the thalamus, hippocampus, and neocortex: we shall see that these include areas of the brain particularly associated with fearful and aggressive reactions. Peripherally, DBI is found in the adrenal gland, testes, liver, and kidney.

It appears that DBI has biological actions in addition to the regulation of diazepam binding sites (Costa and Guidotti, 1991; Owens et al., 1989). Indeed, the DBI molecule is identical to a molecule called acyl-CoA-binding protein (ACBP) previously studied for its effects upon lipid metabolism (Yanase et al., 2002). Importantly for its relationship with emotional functions, DBI appears to modulate the production of steroids, both in the brain and in the adrenal glands (Ferrarese et al., 1993).

Steroids are lipid compounds that are diffusible and membrane permeable, so unlike transmitters, steroid hormones are capable of entering and affecting cells without operating on specific receptor sites. Instead, they are often produced in large quantities by specialized organs – the endocrine glands – and spread throughout the body via the bloodstream. The steroid hormones include the *gonadal hormones* (the female *estrogens* and *progesterone* produced by the ovaries; the male *androgens* such as *testosterone* produced by the testes). They also include the *corticoid hormones* produced by the adrenal cortex, such as *cortisol* (CORT), which are often termed stress hormones. These steroids are also produced in the brain, in much smaller quantities, by a type of glial cell. Glial cells or neuroglia are supportive cells within the central nervous system, some of which have been discovered to have important functions. DBI is present in astroglia and Bergmann glia, which are steroidergic: that is, they produce steroids in the brain (*neurosteroids*). The neurosteroids in turn regulate GABA receptor functions (Costa and Guidotti, 1991).

Another indication that DBI is related to stress is that DBI levels have been found to be significantly correlated with levels of corticotropin releasing hormone (CRH) in the cerebrospinal fluid, suggesting that by blocking GABA, DBI may have a role in releasing CRH in the human brain (Roy, 1991; Roy et al., 1989). We shall see that, during stress, CRH releases ACTH from the pituitary, which in turn releases corticoid stress hormones from the adrenal cortex (Ferrarese et al., 1993). This evidence suggests that DBI may be intimately involved in the activation and regulation of the hypothalamus-pituitary-adrenal (H-P-A) stress response. Indeed, recent evidence suggests that psychological stress induced by conditioned emotional stimuli, but not physical stress, increases DBI gene expression in the mouse brain (Katsura et al., 2002).

Cholecystokinin (CCK) and panic. CCK, a peptide involved in appetite regulation, has been identified in unicellular organisms (Loumaye et al., 1982). There is converging evidence that CCK causes subjective feelings of fear and panic (Bowers et al., 2012). In rats, CCK systems have been found to mediate freezing behavior (Farook et al., 2001; Tsutsumi et al., 2001) and acoustic startle responses (Josselyn et al., 1995; Fendt et al., 1995; Frankland et al., 1996). Interestingly, a CCK antagonist has been found to reduce state anxiety in mice (measured by the animal's preference for a dark rather than a light environment), but not trait anxiety (measured by a free exploratory test: Belzung et al., 1994). Also in mice, novel predator and non-predator odors were found to increase CCK gene expression (Hebb et al., 2002).

In humans, injections of CCK induce feelings of anxiety and fear without external cause (Abelson and Nesse, 1990; Bradwejn, 1993; de Montigny, 1989; Harro et al., 1993). Patients subject to panic attacks recognize the feelings associated with CCK to be like those associated with their attacks (Bradwejn et al., 1991). A study of healthy volunteers showed that the effects of a CCK agonist on subjectively experienced anxiety, apprehension, and fear were substantially decreased by a CCK antagonist (Bradwejn et al., 1994, 1995). Koszycki et al. (1993) found that healthy volunteers with preexisting high anxiety reported more panicky thoughts and fears of somatic symptoms, but they were not more susceptible to experiencing a panic attack to CCK than medium or low anxiety volunteers, and the authors concluded that cognitive factors were not critical determinants of CCK-induced panic attacks. Also, studies using positron emission tomography (PET) scanning and magnetic resonance imagery (MRI) showed that CCK increases blood flow in limbic areas associated with fear (Benkelfat et al., 1995; Javanmard et al., 1999; Reiman et al., 1989).

There are indications that CCK responsiveness is related to personality in humans (Kennedy et al., 1999). Volunteers completed self-administered anxiety scales, including the State-Trait Anxiety Inventory (STAI) and Beck Depression Inventory (BDI). They were then injected with a CCK agonist or a placebo, and the latency, number, intensity, and duration of panic-like symptoms were recorded. Results indicated that the STAI and BDI predicted the CCK-induced symptoms, the fear response to panic symptoms, and the post-injection anxiety (Jerabek et al., 1998).

Another study suggests that a traditional Chinese medicine, Gotu Kola, may be a CCK antagonist, with anxiety-reducing effects because of binding on CCK receptor sites. Although Gotu Kola did not significantly affect self-rated mood, it did attenuate the acoustic startle response in humans (Bradwejn et al., 2000). Other evidence suggests that CCK release may be antagonized by endogenous *cannabinoid* activation (Chhatwal et al., 2009; Javanmard et al., 1999), possibly contributing to the calming effects of tetrahydrocannibinol (THC: e.g. cannabis and marijuana). In a review, Bowers et al. (2012) concluded that endocannabinoids have a specific role in the extinction of aversive learning.

Oxytocin (OXY) and nurturance. OXY was the first peptide to be synthesized outside the body, in 1953 by Victor de Vigneaud. This was a major milestone in peptide research, for it allowed the manufacture of large quantities of these substances, both for research and in the production of drugs. OXY is released from the pituitary to bind with receptors in the uterus during childbirth, where it causes uterine contractions. A synthetic analog of OXY, Piocin, is used to induce and speed labor. OXY also is involved in uterine contractions of the female sexual orgasm, and in the control of lactation (Pert, 1997). These peripheral functions of OXY are specific to mammals, which are characterized by placental birth and feeding of the young after birth by mother's milk (Gore, 2003). Such behavior requires relatively strong social bonds and tendencies to bond and nurture that are not required in non-mammals, and we shall see in Chapter 4 that there is plentiful evidence that OXY – sometimes called the cuddle hormone – is involved in nurturance and social bonding as well.

In the central nervous system, OXY is strongly associated with maternal behavior (Insel, 1992; Panksepp, 1992; Pederson et al., 1990). In many species, OXY and maternal behaviors are regulated by sex steroids and stimuli associated with offspring (Bale and Dorsa, 1995; Pederson, 1997). Also, OXY is related to sexual behaviors. Both male and female orgasm are associated with increased OXY release (Richard et al., 1991). In rats, OXY enhances sexual receptivity in the female, and OXY antagonists decrease receptivity (Arletti and Augusta Bertolini, 1992; Caldwell 1992). Central administration of OXY increases sexual behavior in both males and females (Richard et al., 1991), reduces infanticide in animals (McCarthy, 1990), and decreases separation distress (Panksepp, 1992).

There are dramatic differences in the region of the brain associated with OXY depending upon whether a species is monogamous – mated for life – as opposed to non-monogamous. This research, particularly studies relating to a small rodent, the monogamous prairie vole, is considered in Chapter 4 (Donaldson and Young, 2008; Young, 2002). We shall also see that OXY is associated with trust and social bonding in human beings. In a review, Panksepp (1993) concluded that OXY is a prime candidate for mediating feelings of acceptance and social bonding (p. 93). Relevant to this, in a double-blind study in which OXY was administered in nasal spray, Rockliff et al. (2011) reported that participants given OXY reported increases in the ability to image compassionate emotions. However, the effects of OXY were influenced by individual differences: less positive responses to OXY were found in participants high in self-criticism and low in self-reassurance, social safeness, and attachment security.

In another double-blind experiment using intranasal administration of OXY, Cardoso et al. (2012) found significant anxiety reduction with OXY only among women high in emotion-focused coping. Healthy participants were tested in a live social rejection paradigm in which they were engaged in a ten-minute conversation with two other persons (actually confederates) who gradually began to ignore, and then exclude completely, the participant. As we shall see in later chapters, such procedures are effective in making people feel isolated and ostracized. OXY was found to reduce the anxiety engendered by ostracism only in women who were high in emotion-focused coping, a style of coping generally associated with poor interpersonal function-ing. That is, women who reported that they tended to respond to stress with emotion and therefore were vulnerable to such interpersonal stress showed reduced anxiety with OXY. Men were generally less responsive to the ostracism manipulation.

One of the remarkable facts about OXY is that it does not exist as an active neuropeptide in non-mammals. Along with argenine vasopressin (AVP), OXY is derived from an evolutionary divergence of an ancestral hormone, *vasotocin*, which has been identified in unicellular organisms (Loumaye et al., 1982) and facilitates socio-sexual responses in reptiles and birds (Donaldson and Young, 2008; Moore, 1987). The central functions of OXY and AVP are similar in some respects, particularly with regard to parental behaviors, and quite different in others (Carter et al., 2009). The fact that they share the same ancestral hormone raises questions about how the behaviors that they regulate differ in mammals from similar behaviors in reptiles, birds, and other non-mammals. Specifically, there is evidence that OXY and AVP are relevant to the differentiation of female- and male-typical patterns of sexual and aggressive-protective behaviors in mammals.

Argenine Vasopressin (AVP). Formerly known as antidiuretic hormone, the peripheral effects of AVP include inhibiting water excretion in the kidney and raising blood pressure. Peripherally, AVP is associated with defense behaviors, including sympathetic nervous system responding (Carter and de Vries, 1999). In the central nervous system, although AVP does not affect separation distress or female sexual behavior, male socio-sexual behaviors are promoted, including pair-bonding in monogamous prairie voles (Windslow et al., 1993) and aggressive behaviors (Koolhaas et al., 1990). More specifically, AVP induces selective intraspecies aggression, perhaps acting via the central amygdala (Gingrich et al., 1997). Conversely, AVP antagonists reduce male intraspecies aggression in hamsters (Potegal and Ferris, 1989) and rats (Ferris et al., 2008). In humans, administration of AVP with nasal spray in men has been found to increase aggressive tendencies (Cocaro et al., 1998), stimulate antagonistic facial displays in response to the faces of unfamiliar men (Thompson et al., 2006), and impair the recognition of facial displays of negative emotions (Uzefovsky et al., 2012). This evidence is consistent with Panksepp's (1993) suggestion that AVP may be a specific carrier for male dominance and persistence urges mediating heightened tendencies for males to exhibit aggression; and that the underlying subjective emotional correlate is one of increased irritability and anger (pp. 93–94).

AVP is associated with testosterone levels: androgens are involved in AVP synthesis, and castration in rats reduces AVP neural systems in the brain by approximately one half (de Vries et al., 1985, 1994). In monogamous prairie vole males, it is AVP rather than OXY that facilitates partner preferences: pair-bond formation and other behaviors associated with monogamy are facilitated by AVP agonists and pre-vented by AVP antagonists (Carter et al., 2008). Also, Pitkow et al. (2001) demonstrated that transferring the gene for the AVP receptor into the brain of male prairie voles increased the density of AVP binding, increased affiliative and anxiety behavior, and facilitated pair-bonding. We examine the social and emotional lives of voles further in Chapter 4.

Gonadotropin-releasing hormone (GnRH). Gonadal function is regulated by the brain through the hypothalamus, which controls the secretion of luteinizing hormone (LH) and follicle stimulating hormone (FSH) from the anterior pituitary gland. These LH and FSH releases are regulated by an interaction of sex steroids (female estrogen and progesterone; the male androgen testosterone) and the peptide *gonadotropin-releasing hormone* (GnRH). Puberty is initiated when GnRH secretion is stimu-lated via the peptide *kisspeptin* (KP), and GnRH is thereafter secreted from the hypothalamus into the portal system that supplies blood to the anterior pituitary. It enhances the release of both LH and FSH in mammals, and is active in birds, reptiles, and fish as well (Schally et al., 1978). Indeed, GnRH is among the peptides that show evidence of great evolutionary age. A peptide mating pheromone of the single-celled yeast *Saccharomyces cerevisiae* is similar to GnRH (Loumaye et al., 1982). Loumaye and colleagues (1982) noted that it is intriguing that a pheromone responsible for mating and zygote formation in a unicel-lular organism serves a key role in mammalian reproduction.

The peripheral effects of GnRH include stimulating the production of estrogen and progesterone in the female and androgens in the male, therefore promoting spermatogenesis in males and preparing the female body for ovulation. Centrally, GnRH increases sexual procliv-ities: indeed, Panksepp (1993) suggested that GnRH may well prove to be a prime mover in human subjective sexual feelings, or *libido* (p. 94). In hamsters, chemosensory and other sensory inputs trigger GnRH release in the brain, which then facilitates mating behavior (Meredith and Fernandes-Fewell, 1994). Meredith and Fewell (2001) studied the effects of electrical stimulation of the *vomeronasal organ*, which responds to chemosensory stimulation. They mapped the acti-vation of the brain using *Fos*, a marker of neuronal activation. The stimulation of the vomeronasal organ activated neurons of chemosen-sory pathways also activated by mating and sexual chemical stimuli, and Fos was also activated in GnRH neurons in the medial preoptic region of the brain. They suggested that these GnRH neurons mediate chemosensory influences on sexual behavior.

GnRH has rewarding effects as demonstrated by their abilities to establish conditioned place preferences in male rats. In this test, rats are exposed to a two-compartment chamber, and their preference for the two compartments is assessed. They are then exposed to a drug (i.e. GnRH) while in one compartment and a saline placebo in the other. Twenty-four hours later, their preference is assessed again. This has proved to be a sensitive self-report measure, as it were, of the rewarding or punishing effects of a drug: to the extent that the drug is rewarding, the animal will show a preference for the compartment that was associated with the drug. The rewarding effects of GnRH are, however, absent in gonadectomized animals (de Beun et al., 1991). This suggests that the GnRH is rewarding because of its effects on the gonadal steroids.

Corticotropin releasing hormone (CRH). CRH is released from the periventricular hypothalamus and causes the release of ACTH from the pituitary, which in turn releases a variety of stress hormones: steroids including cortisol from the adrenal cortex. Previously, we discussed the relationship between CRH and DBI in this regard. Centrally CRH is associated with a coordinated central stress response that has a major impact on the elaboration of both fear/anxiety and separation distress in the brain (Panksepp, 1993, p. 92). CRH has been implicated in mediating the negative affects associated with withdrawal from drugs of abuse, including alcohol, cocaine, opiates, and cannabis (Rodriguez de Fonesca et al., 1997). Stress experienced early in life can cause permanent increases in CRH activity and chronic disregulation of the hypothalamic-pituitary-adrenal axis (H-P-A axis) response to stress (Kolber et al., 2010).

Panksepp (1993) has suggested that CRH is associated with a particular kind of chronic stress-induced depression or *burnout* in human beings. Normally, CRH turns itself off, in a negative feedback loop via increased NE: CRH excites NE activity, but NE in turn inhibits CRH activity. Long-term CRH activity due to chronic stress can lead to NE over-activation and the eventual depletion of brain NE that is difficult to reverse because with the low levels of NE, there is no longer any way to turn off the CRH (Risch, 1991). In this way, chronic stress can promote semi-permanent brain changes that at the psychological level may be experienced as despair (Panksepp, 1993, p. 92; Kolber et al., 2010).

Conclusions: emotion
and the arousal/arousability of neurochemical systems

This chapter has summarized evidence that subjectively experienced affects at the psychological level are associated with specifiable neurochemical systems, and that the functioning of such neurochemical systems thus constitutes an irreducible essence associated with emotion. This review has demonstrated the multiplicity and complexity of neurochemical systems associated with subjectively experienced affects – feelings and desires – but at the same time it is clear that converging evidence concerning how these systems function, from traditional animal research, from new techniques involving the manipulation of genes, and from evidence relating to drug effects in humans, is consistent, coherent, and expanding. To summarize, Table 2.2 organizes the neurochemical systems we have considered, the nature of the subjective affects with which they have been associated, and commonly used and abused drugs that are agonists or antagonists of these systems.

The consideration of the neurochemical bases of biological emotions furnishes a conceptual springboard from which other important aspects of emotion can be considered. Figure 2.2 summarizes some hypothesized relationships between the functioning of neurochemical systems and the subjective experience of feelings and desires, moods and emotions. As considered previously, in my view the neurochemical systems associated with biological emotions constitute readouts: voices of the genes evolved to notify the organism of critical information. Such information includes specific need states of the organism – needs for food, water, sex, warmth, or coolness – associated with primary drives of hunger, thirst, sex, etc. It also includes information about states of arousal, approach and avoidance, agonistic competition, and prosocial cooperation, which are fundamental functions of emotion (Buck, 1999). All of these readouts are active all of the time: we *always have access* to the awareness of a certain level of hunger, thirst, sexiness, warmth/ coolness; and also a variable symphony of biological affects associated with arousal, approach and avoidance, agonistic tendencies, and cooperative tendencies. They are available for inspection in the brain, just as the feel of our shoes on our feet or the hardness of our chair are always available for inspection. The nature of this awareness is in the form of direct, immediate, and self-evident knowledge by acquaintance (KA), discussed in the previous chapter. However, we attend to this information only if it changes suddenly or is at a sufficiently high level. This information is directly related to the state of arousal of the specifiable neurochemical systems underlying the affects.

More specifically, I suggest that with a lack of effective stimulation, neurochemical systems are normally at a low level, like a pilot light, and are normally accessed only if attention is explicitly drawn to them, as on the left side of Figure 2.2. Here, the voices of the genes are whispering, as it were. If the system is weakly stimulated by, say, changes in the day/night cycle or an attractive scent of perfume in the air (S1),

Table 2.2 Common drugs, neurochemical systems, and associated affects

Drug	Neurochemical systems	Associated subjective experiences
Cocaine, amphetamine	Dopamine (DA) Norepinephrine (NE)	Wanting/pleasure; energy vs. sadness/ depression
LSD, psilocybin, mescaline, MDMA (ecstasy)	Serotonin (5-HT)	Hallucinogen, euphoriant, paranoid horror (bad trip)
Selective serotonin reuptake inhibitors (SSRIs) including fluoxetine (Prozac)	Serotonin (5-HT)	Confident dominance vs. depression (social?)
Morphine, heroin, codeine, oxycodone	Endorphins	Liking/elation, analgesia vs. pain sensitivity
Oxytocin (OXY)	Oxytocin (OXY)	In-group attachment, pair-bonding, trust vs. fear, suspicion, narcissism
Vasopressin (AVP)	Vasopressin (AVP)	Attraction, sexual arousal, protectiveness
Ethanol (alcohol), benzodiazepines including Librium and Valium	Diazepam binding inhibitor (DBI)	Anti-anxiety
Barbiturates	GABA	Depressant
Nicotine	Acetylcholine (ACh)	Stimulant
Caffeine	Adenosine antagonist	Stimulant, focus
Tetrahydrocannabinol (THC), cannabis, marijuana, hashish	Cannabinoid	Relaxation, sensory alterations
Cholecystokinin (CCK)	CCK	Panic
Corticotropin releasing hormone (CRH)	Pituitary– adrenal axis	Stress vs. relaxation
Gonadotropin-releasing hormone (GnRH)	Pituitary– gonadal axis	Erotic feelings

the individual may experience what most theorists consider to be a *"mood"*: it is relatively long lasting, and the precipitating stimulus is often not readily apparent. Here, in effect, the genes murmur and purr. If the system is more effectively stimulated – say by a sudden loud noise,

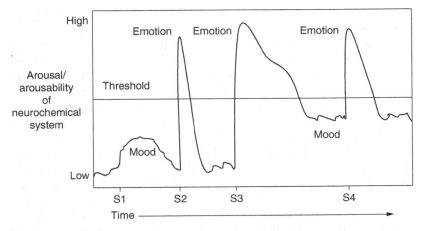

Figure 2.2 Neurochemical arousal and subjective experience. Hypothesized relationships between the arousal and arousability of neurochemical systems and subjectively experienced mood and emotion. See text for explanation.

the sight of an attractive and receptive sexual partner, the aggressive display of a rival (S2) – the system is activated and appropriate readouts are organized, including arousal reactions (Emotion I), displays (Emotion II), and subjective experiences (Emotion III) that suddenly dominate consciousness. Here, the genes suddenly shout. In my view, this constitutes the arousal of what most theorists consider to be an "emotion": it is readily experienced and is easily associated with the precipitating stimulus.

If the stimulus is quickly withdrawn, the system soon returns to its normal level (S2). If, however, the neurochemical system has been strongly stimulated, for example by a traumatic event such as the 9/11 attacks on the United States, the system may not return to its original state (S3). New neurochemical connections may have been created, additional neurotransmitters may have been synthesized, receptor sites may have multiplied, and inhibitory neurochemical systems may have been suppressed, so that the arousal and arousability of the strongly stimulated neurochemical system may be increased. As a result of increased tonic arousal, the neurochemical system may now function at a level close to the threshold of consciousness, so that it is relatively easily noticed even with a minor stimulus (strong mood). Also, if the *arousability* of the neurochemical system – the ease with which it is aroused – is increased, the emotion may be easier to elicit in the future, and it may dissipate more slowly (S4).

Each of the neurochemical systems we have considered in this chapter can be considered to be a semi-independent system or module potentially responding as illustrated in Figure 2.2, each one contributing to the symphony of experienced affect. Extending the analogy, individual synapses can be considered to be individual musical instruments, and neurochemical modules as analogous to collectivities of instruments, e.g. clarinets, trumpets, snare drums, violins. Moreover, different collectivities may be interrelated: for example, orchestral woodwinds include clarinets, piccolos, bassoons, oboes, etc; brasses include trumpets, trombones, and French horns. These may generally play together, but not always. For example, we saw that the functioning of neurochemical systems involving CRH and DBI often occur together. Also, some sections such as percussion may be involved throughout virtually all performances, while other sections typically observe periods of silence. Analogously, neurochemical systems involving functions of arousal, reward and punishment, agonistic competition, and prosocial cooperation may be considered analogous to sections of musical instruments, some of which, like arousal and reward/punishment, are involved in virtually all emotions. In both the symphony of music and feeling, there may be synchrony or asynchrony and harmony or disharmony affecting the whole performance: little is known about the factors that organize and direct the symphony of feelings and desires, although that too is potentially discoverable. In the next chapter, we see that the physical arrangement of these systems in brain anatomy reflects the structure of their functioning.

This consideration of biological emotions as based upon neurochemical systems allows a fresh approach to such fundamental issues as the nature of attachment, love, pleasure, and desire; the origins of despair; the emotional bases of competition and cooperation; and the relationships between emotions and physical health. The notion of subjectively experienced affect as reflecting a symphony of arousal and arousability in a variety of neurochemical systems affords an objective basis for measuring, manipulating, and understanding this most problematic aspect of emotion. In the next chapter, I examine the physical structure of the brain as a hierarchy of these neurochemical systems that may reveal something of the basic structure of experienced emotion.

At the same time, the functioning of the neurochemical systems both illustrates and reflects a basic theme running through all emotional phenomena: *dynamic regulation through communication*. It is apparent that neurochemical systems function through communication: a sender cell conveys information to a receiving cell through chemical transmitter substances, so that all biological emotions involve communication processes. A basic function of these communication processes is bodily regulation, adapting the organism to environmental changes and maintaining homeostasis (the Emotion I readout). In addition, neurochemical systems also are involved in communication between organisms, in which information is expressed by displays in sending organisms, and is picked up through preattunements to those displays by receiving organisms (Buck and Van Lear, 2002). The basic function of these communication processes is social regulation, adapting a collectivity of organisms to environmental changes and maintaining social organization (the Emotion II readout). Again, all of these communication processes – the display mechanisms, the messages involved, the receiving processes – can be defined objectively in terms of observable phenomena that are increasingly open to measurement. Finally, neurochemical systems are involved in interoceptive communication processes in which a symphony of information is registered in the subjective awareness of desires and feelings (the Emotion III readout). The basic function of this involves self-regulation and behavioral flexibility – a.k.a. free will – via the usually whispering in pianissimo, sometimes shouting in crescendo, but always present and insistent, voices of the most basic units underlying evolution and behavior: the genes.

CHAPTER 3

Structure of neurochemical systems of emotion

The central nervous system as a hierarchy of neurochemical systems

The central nervous system comprises a hierarchy of anatomical structures that vary from relatively simpler and phylogenetically older systems deep in the brain, to more complex and phylogenetically newer systems closer to the outer surface of the brain and associated with higher-order brain functions. Arousal and reward-punishment systems associated with arousal and valence dimensions of emotion are deep in the brainstem and the midbrain, coursing through the hypothalamus into the forebrain. These, however, are not executive systems, but rather they function according to specific decision rules: they allow us to ignore a great variety of sensory stimuli (the feel of our shoes) but to orient to strong and unexpected stimuli. Also, we are drawn toward stimuli associated with experiences of reward and shrink from stimuli associated with punishment, based upon principles of classical and instrumental conditioning. The simplest executive systems are subcortical structures associated with aggression and sex, but activation of these systems does not appear to be associated with subjectively experienced affects. The latter are associated instead with the limbic system, comprising paleocortical (3–5 layered) structures in contrast with the six-layered neocortex that covers most of the human brain. In this chapter, I review classic literature on the functioning of the brain in biological emotions, based largely upon studies of animals, which established general principles that have largely been confirmed and expanded upon by more recent studies in humans.

The central nervous system (CNS) includes the brain and spinal cord; while the peripheral nervous system (PNS) includes the sensory and motor nerves entering and exiting the CNS. Often the location of structures within the nervous system is indicated by anatomical terminology. *Dorsal* refers to the top of the brain and *ventral* to the bottom, while *anterior* is toward the front of the brain and *posterior* is toward the back. *Medial* is toward the middle, and *lateral* is toward either side.

In upright animals such as monkeys, apes, and human beings, the head and the brain are at right angles to the body, and to maintain consistency with other animals, below the head the directional terms are changed so that "dorsal" refers to the back and "ventral" the front of the body.

The CNS can be divided into sensory, association, and motor elements. Generally, sensory systems are located in posterior regions of the brain, motor systems in anterior regions, and association areas are in between. Sensory systems convey information from the sensory organs to the brain and motor systems convey information from the brain to effector organs such as muscles and glands. These systems are often composed of nerve fiber tracts specialized for fast transmission of nerve impulses: this fast transmission is facilitated by a fatty *myelin sheath* covering the fibers that gives them a white appearance. Therefore, the sensory and motor fibers are known as the *white matter* of the brain. These are often named for the brain structures that they connect: for example, the thalamocortical pathway connects the thalamus and the cortex.

Association areas of the brain are areas in which information processing occurs: input from the sensory systems is organized and structured, and response tendencies are initiated. These areas are composed largely of nerve cell bodies and connections which have a gray appearance, so they constitute the *gray matter* of the brain. A cluster of cell bodies and connections in the CNS is termed a *nucleus*. In the periphery of the body, fiber tracts are termed *nerves* and a cluster of connections is a *ganglion*.

Emotion I: peripheral physiological arousal

Somatic motor systems

Peripheral systems involved in emotion include the *somatic motor system* that innervates the skeletal muscles, the *autonomic nervous system* that innervates the smooth muscles of the heart and viscera, the *endocrine system* of ductless glands that operates via chemical hormones released into the bloodstream, and the *immune system*. The somatic motor system can be further subdivided into the *pyramidal motor system* that functions in voluntary movement, and the *extrapyramidal motor system* that functions in nonvoluntary movement including facial expression.

The pyramidal motor system. The physical structure of these systems reveals much about how they function. In the pyramidal motor system, there is typically a one-to-one relationship between a point in the *motor neocortex* of the brain and a body muscle. Single motor neurons originate in the brain and go directly to a muscle without synapses through pyramid-shaped structures in the brainstem: hence the name "pyramidal system." Because of the one-to-one relationship between areas of the brain and areas of the body, a pictorial representation of the body can be visualized based upon its representation in the brain, resulting in a figure termed a *motor homunculus*. Areas of the body that are associated with more precise motor control are associated with a larger area of the motor neocortex, so that the muscles of the hands, fingers, lips, tongue, pharynx, and larynx appear large on the homunculus reflecting their greater representation in the brain's motor cortex. In contrast, areas such as the chest and back appear constricted because of their relatively sparse motor innervations.

The motor neocortex and pyramidal system are responsible for voluntary movement, and lesions in this system typically result in paralysis. Because the pyramidal motor fibers cross from the left to the right side of the body in the midbrain, the paralysis is typically on the side of the opposite to the site of the lesion in the brain. For example, damage to the left side of the brain will generally produce right hemiplegia: paralysis in the right side of the body. This principle applies to the complex movements of lips, tongue, pharynx, and larynx that are responsible for spoken language in human beings: control of the muscles underlying speech is accomplished by *Broca's area* in the left hemisphere of the brain just anterior to the left motor cortex associated with control of the lips, tongue, pharynx, and larynx. The control of language expression is almost always sited in the left hemisphere of the human brain, even for left-handed persons whose handedness implies a relatively greater degree of right-hemisphere control than for right-handers.

The extrapyramidal motor system. Whereas the pyramidal motor system subserves voluntary movement, the extrapyramidal motor system is responsible for the nonvoluntary coordination of movement, including spontaneous facial expression. Its physical organization contrasts with that of the pyramidal motor system in ways that reflect how the systems function differently. The extrapyramidal system is controlled via the *supplemental motor cortex* at the top of the head, and it is diffuse, with a point in the supplemental motor cortex not associated with specific bodily muscles in any simple way.

The functions of the extrapyramidal system are perhaps best revealed in the well-known medical condition where it is disrupted: *Parkinson's disease*. The functioning of the extrapyramidal motor system is dependent upon the neurotransmitter DA, and Parkinson's disease is caused by the death of DA-generating cells in the substantia nigra. Major symptoms include motor rigidity, difficulty with walking, and a mask-like dearth of facial expression. The extrapyramidal system, therefore, functions to maintain free and flexible motor movement including expressive body movements and facial expression.

Fight-or-flight versus relaxation

The autonomic nervous system. The *autonomic nervous system* (ANS) and also the *endocrine system* serve basic functions of bodily adaptation to change and the maintenance of homeostasis via the regulation of such automatic functions as respiration, digestion, and temperature regulation. It also responds to emergency and stressful situations. The ANS is controlled via the hypothalamus and innervates the smooth muscles of the viscera, blood vessels, heart, and lungs. There are two branches of the ANS: the sympathetic nervous system (SNS) and the parasympathetic nervous system (PNS). The PNS is controlled by the anterior hypothalamus and the SNS by the posterior hypothalamus. The functions of the SNS and PNS are generally opposed, with the SNS functioning to use up the body's resources in response to emergency and threat: the *fight-or-flight* response. The PNS functions to shore up bodily resources, and its effects have collectively been termed the *relaxation response* (Benson, 1975).

The endocrine system. Another "backup" to the SNS fight-or-flight response, which is also potentially responsible for stress-induced mischief to physical health, involves the endocrine system acting via the hypothalamus-pituitary-adrenal axis (HPA). The pituitary gland is physically connected to the floor of the hypothalamus, and arousal of the HPA axis is initiated by the release of CRH from the periventricular hypothalamus into the pituitary, where it stimulates the release of ACTH into the bloodstream. ACTH acts on the cortex of the adrenal glands to release a variety of stress-related steroid hormones into the bloodstream collectively termed *corticoids*, including *cortisol* (CORT). Effects of the corticoids include reducing swelling and inflammation, and decreasing the immune system response.

The immune system. The structures of the immune system include the *thymus gland, bone marrow, spleen,* and *lymph nodes.* Cells of the immune system are collectively termed white blood cells and include natural killer cells, macrophage ("big-eater") cells, *T cells* from the thymus, and *B cells* from the bone marrow. These cells are congregated in the spleen and lymph nodes which function to "filter" the blood and lymphatic fluid, respectively. That is, they respond to the presence of foreign substances or *antigens*, such as viruses, by initiating an immune system response.

The effective activation and functioning of the immune system requires the identification of cells that belong to the body, using a *major histocompatibility complex* (MHC) protein that is present on the membrane of all body cells. MHC proteins are slightly different for every individual, and therefore can function to identify cells belonging in the body as distinguished from foreign antigens. Cells with the correct MHC protein are identified as "self" and are not attacked; cells without the critical MHC protein are attacked by the immune system as antigens.

When antigens are found, they are engulfed and broken down by macrophages and B cells, which display a fragment of the antigen on their membrane. These activate T cells and give them the information needed to recognize the antigen.

T cells play a variety of roles in the immune response. *Inducer* T cells cause the division of these into millions of clones, all having the critical information. *Helper* T cells induce the differentiation of B cells into millions of clones, which produce specific chemical antibodies that target and attack the specific antigens that have not yet entered body cells to infect them. *Killer* T cells search out body cells which express both the MHC protein and antigen fragment, which signal that they are infected, and kill these cells, hopefully ending the infection. When the infection is ended, the immune system response is brought to an end by *Suppressor* T cells. A few *Memory* T cells and B cells remain, which retain the information about the particular antigen fragment, so that if reinfected a local immune system response can quickly be initiated and the antigen eliminated. At this point, the organism is said to be "immunized" against that particular antigen. Artificial immunization is typically performed by injecting an inactive or killed fragment of a virus, thus initiating an immune system response which will set up Memory B and T cells sensitive to it (Buck, 1988a).

The immune system exists in a state of delicate balance. If its response is too weak it may not detect an abnormal cell as "foreign" and may not attack it: such is typically the case in cancer. On the other hand, if the immune system response is too strong it may attack healthy body cells, a condition known as autoimmune disease. Examples of autoimmune diseases include forms of lupus, arthritis, psoriasis, colitis, and Type 1 diabetes.

The stress syndrome

Hans J. Selye was the first to use the word *"stress"* in a biological context to identify a situation where the demands of the environment challenge or exceed an organism's ability to adapt. In 1935, studying the responses to hormone injections in rats, Selye noted a similar responses to injections of any irritant: the adrenal glands became enlarged, the thymus and lymph nodes shrank, and the stomach became ulcerated. He deduced that the common feature was that they were reactions to a general irritant. He then put animals in other stressful situations and found the same pattern of response, which he termed the *stress syndrome*. Further testing identified three typical stages in the adaptation of the organism to stress, which Selye (1956) termed the *general adaptation syndrome*.

Alarm reaction. The first stage is the *alarm reaction*, where in the initial *shock* to the stress, bodily resistance to stress drops. It is characterized by SNS arousal, release of Epi from the adrenal medulla, release of ACTH and the corticoids including CORT, and immune system suppression. If the shock is too severe, death may result immediately, but if it is not that severe but continues, a second, *countershock* phase is organized. The characteristic signs of stress appear – adrenal enlargement, shrinking of thymus and lymph nodes, and ulceration – but the overall resistance to stress increases above the initial level. Selye suggests that local adaptive responses are organized to maintain life.

Stage of resistance. As the local defenses against stress are organized, Selye suggested that the overall stress response becomes unnecessary. In the *stage of resistance*, local adaptation to stress is at optimum, and the symptoms of the stress syndrome disappear.

Stage of exhaustion. However, if the stress continues too long or if other stresses are piled on, the ability of the organism to resist stress ends. The HPA system is again activated, CORT rises, immunosuppression occurs, and the stress symptoms return (see Figure 3.1). Selye suggested that at this stage the appearance of the pituitary and adrenal hormones may in itself be stressful to the weakened organism, and he described the disorders resulting from the body's attempts to deal with stress as "diseases of adaptation."

Peripheral arousal and subjective emotional experience

A classic theory of emotion advanced by William James (1884/1968) suggested that the experience of emotion is the feeling of peripheral bodily changes occurring when we respond to an emotional stimulus. Thus when we see a dangerous bear, visceral (heart pounding) and somatic (running) responses occur. As James put it, "our feeling of these same changes as they occur *is* the emotion . . .Without the bodily states following the perception, the latter would be purely cognitive in form, pale, colorless, destitute of emotional warmth" (1884/1968, p. 19; italics in the original).

Spinal cord injuries would block such bodily feedback to the brain, so James' theory predicts that emotional experience would be diminished

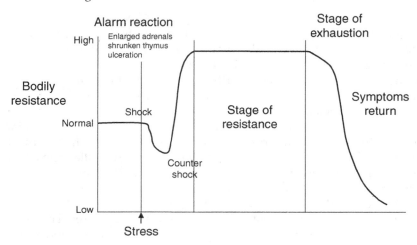

Figure 3.1 Selye's General Adaptation Syndrome. The first stage of the stress syndrome is the *alarm reaction*, where bodily resistance to stress drops in the initial *shock* to the stress, followed by a *countershock* phase. Characteristic symptoms appear: adrenal enlargement, shrinking thymus and lymph nodes, and ulceration. Bodily defenses are organized in the *stage of resistance*, and these symptoms disappear. But, if the stress continues too long, the symptoms return in the *stage of exhaustion*, which can lead to death.

by spinal cord injury. Hohmann (1966) reported just such an effect: men with spinal cord injuries asked to compare their emotional experiences before and after their injury did report decreased emotional experience, and the decrease was greater if the spinal lesion was higher, and the loss of visceral/somatic sensation therefore greater. In a related observation, Delgado (1969) reported that a patient whose sympathetic nervous system was severed on one side of the body "found that his previous and customary sensation of shivering while listening to a stirring passage of music occurred in only one side and he could not be thrilled in the sympathectomized half of his body" (pp. 134–35).

Taken together, these observations suggest that peripheral factors contribute to some kinds of emotional experience. However, two subsequent studies failed to confirm Hohmann's results: neither Chwalisz et al. (1988) nor Lowe and Carroll (1985) found evidence of lessened emotional experience in spinal cord injured patients. The authors of both studies suggested that Hohmann's result may have reflected depression stemming from the long hospitalization and lack of effective rehabilitation that typically characterized the treatment of spinal cord injuries in the 1950s, when Hohmann's data were collected. The reduction in reported affective experience may have been "the result of a discouraging outlook rather than a disrupted nervous system" (Lowe and Carroll, 1985, p. 136).

James himself recognized the relevance to his theory of having emotional feelings when bodily sensation is blocked. At the end of his 1884 paper, he cited an 1882 case of total anesthesia published by a Professor Strümpell reporting that the patient expressed shame at soiling his bed and grief because he could no longer taste a favorite dish. Upon questioning by James, Strümpell reported that the patient also expressed and appeared to experience fear and anger. James acknowledged that if "the patient recognized explicitly the same mood or feeling known under those names in his former normal state, my theory would of course fall. It is, however, to me incredible that the patient should have an identical feeling, for the dropping out of the organic sounding-board would necessarily diminish its volume in some way" (1884/1968, p. 205). Some have attempted to maintain a neo-Jamesian view in the face of the spinal cord injury evidence by suggesting that once emotions have been experienced via bodily feedback, this experience is somehow maintained centrally even after such feedback is unavailable (Damasio, 1994). For example, Lindquist et al. (2012b) asserted that "a functioning peripheral nervous system is not necessary for a person to experience a core affective state ... as long as they have some prior experiences to provide them with a central nervous system representation of bodily states" (p. 124). However, there is no evidence that prior experiences could fill such a role. Altogether, there is what Rolls (1999) characterized as "rather over-whelming evidence against an important role for bodily responses in producing emotions or emotional feelings" (p. 72), and the evidence from the direct effects that psychoactive drugs can have on subjective experience in human beings argues persuasively that, although periph-eral bodily feedback may well contribute to some kinds of subjective emotional experience, it is neither necessary nor sufficient for such experience (see Buck, 1980).

The physiologist W. B. Cannon (1927) reviewed clinical and experi-mental evidence relating to the James–Lange theory, and outlined strong objections. In particular, he argued that visceral sensation from ANS responding is far too slow, diffuse, and insensitive to account for the speed and range of emotion experienced by human beings. He argued instead that the ANS functions to prepare the body for emergency action – the fight-or-flight response – and has little if any role in emotional experience. Cannon and Bard suggested that emo-tional stimuli are processed by phylogenetically older parts of the brain, and that these systems simultaneously inform the newer parts of the brain – the *neocortex* – in the form of emotional experience, and the body in the form of the fight-or-flight response. Thus in their view, central nervous system mechanisms are responsible for emotional experience (Bard, 1928; Cannon, 1932).

Conclusions

Selye's general adaptation syndrome summarized the typical course of the peripheral physiological responses to extreme and continuing stress: Emotion I responses. It is noteworthy that these responses are not normally accessible in detail to the individual responder or to others: the responses associated with the ANS, endocrine, and immune systems are normally not detectable without special equipment. We may occasionally be able to detect our heart pounding, or flushing in the cheeks, but we do not normally have access to our blood pressure or immune system activation. Because of this, these Emotion I responses are under the influence of dramatically different influences during the course of social and emotional development compared with Emotion II responses, to which we now turn. These latter responses are accessible to others. Indeed, they have arguably evolved with the function of being accessible to others, to display externally the state of certain internal motivational-emotional states to support social organization.

Emotion II: display and communication

Display

There is plentiful evidence of the genetic basis for both sending and receiving mechanisms that is the foundation of the discipline of sociobiology (Wilson, 1975). The social behavior of many insects is controlled by such systems that function with few degrees of freedom. In classic studies of cricket calls, Bentley and Hoy (1974) demonstrated a genetic basis for both sending and receiving mechanisms such that they constitute a fail-safe system for effective communication within species and genotype. Males generate species-specific calls that attract conspecific females, and hybrid males generate calls with different temporal patterns and harmonic content that attract appropriate females. In a review of such communication systems in a variety of species including frogs, toads, and vampire bats, Moon-Fanelli noted that "the genetics of communication delineate boundaries for sociality and speciation" (2011, p. 870).

Brainstem mechanisms of display. In mammals, some of the basic elements of emotional displays, including audiovocal, facial, and postural/gestural displays, appear to be "hard-wired" in the brainstem although their activation is organized by higher structures. Among the earliest relevant observations were those made in the classic experiments of Bard (1928), who systematically studied the brain systems necessary for the defensive "sham rage" response in cats by progressively removing higher brain structures.[1] He demonstrated that the organized response of hissing, spitting, clawing, heart rate and blood pressure increases, and erection of the hair required that the posterior hypothalamus be intact. If it were lesioned, isolated elements of the sham rage response could still occur, but were not organized. These conclusions were supplemented by the contemporary work of W. R. Hess (1928; Hess and Brugger, 1943), who showed that electrical stimulation of the hypothalamus could produce a well-coordinated and directed attack response.

Displays in coydogs. The nature of the genetic bases of displays and how they can be altered by environmental experience has been illuminated in studies of coyote–beagle hybrids, or coydogs (Moon-Fanelli, 2011). Although they are closely related genetically, dogs, wolves, and coyotes differ in many aspects of their behavior. Coyotes produce a distinctive defensive gape-threat display that differs from that of dogs and wolves: the mouth is open and gaping, the head is lowered with arched back, and there is a distinct hiss vocalization. In contrast, dogs and wolves produce a snarl-threat, characterized by a closed mouth with lips retracted to reveal the canine and incisor teeth accompanied by a low rumbling growl, and the back is not arched. Dogs have not been observed to display the gape-threat, while coyotes can produce either display depending on the social context.

In a longitudinal study of sixty-one coydogs carried out over eighteen years, Moon-Fanelli (2011) reported that the expression of the gape-threat was influenced by developmental, experiential, genetic, and hormonal factors. Many of the coydogs appeared to have the genetic potential for both types of display. Some animals displayed a "pre-gape" pattern of partial expression of the coyote display such as a "hissy-growl." Fifteen never expressed the coyote gape-threat and thirty-one were early-gapers who emitted the gape-threat prior to puberty. Once the coyote gape-threat fully appeared, it tended to be maintained and expressed in subsequent defensive encounters. The appearance of the gape-threat did not appear to be greatly influenced

---

[1] It was termed "sham" rage because it was assumed that the decorticate animal did not subjectively experience an emotional response.

by learning or modeling: early-gapers were as young as two weeks of age, before the eyes and ears were completely functional, and the appearance of the gape-threat was not related to conditions of being housed with gapers or non-gapers.

There were three varieties of late-gapers. Five coydogs spontaneously switched to the snarl-threat during or shortly after puberty, suggesting that hormonal factors may have influenced the changeover. Eight more switched following social stress, involving being housed with more dominant animals. The changeover in the socially stressed animals was accompanied by a precipitous rise in levels of endogenous CORT. Subsequently, two of three non-gapers switched to the gape-threat following priming with exogenous CORT. Moon-Fanelli (2011) deduced that the expression of genetically encoded potential over the course of development depended upon environmental events that influence internal mechanisms that in turn control that expression.

Facial expressions. Observations of newborn human infants support the notion of brainstem mechanisms of genetically encoded facial displays. J. E. Steiner (1979) observed the facial reactions of newborns to tastes, showing that a sweet taste produced lip licking, sucking, and "smiling," a sour taste lip pursing, nose wrinkling, and blinking, and a bitter taste mouth opening, spitting, and retching. Similar responses were seen in full-term and premature infants, and even anencephalic infants. Anencephaly is a tragic and hopeless condition in which the infant is born literally without a brain above the level of the brainstem. Steiner concluded that facial expressions are organized in the brainstem, and that influences from higher centers normally shape and refine the basic expressions. In line with Darwin's (1998/1872) theory of emotional expression, he suggested that facial displays serve communicative functions in the infant–caretaker relationship. We shall see that such communication is critical to the formation and development of social bonds, secure socio-emotional attachment, and well-organized and functional social and moral emotions.

In studies of the brain systems involved in reactions to negative and positive tastes, Berridge (2009) demonstrated cross-species homologies in expressive facial responses. Species including rats, monkeys, apes, and human beings show common microcomponents such as gaping, tongue protrusion, head shaking, spitting, and low mouth corners; and the speed and duration of these components is closely correlated with the body weight of the species in question. These homologies of expression offer a window into cross-species comparisons of brain systems underlying positive and negative taste experiences, using observation of the expressive facial display as the measure.

Facial expressions of primary affects. Charles Darwin (1998/1872) proposed that expressive displays have evolved in many species, including facial expressions in human beings. This notion was disputed by those who argue that facial expressions are learned and culturally patterned, a contention that seemed to be supported by early studies (e.g. Landis, 1924, 1929). Silvan Tomkins (1962–92, 1982) suggested that eight primary affects – happiness, sadness, fear, anger, surprise, disgust/contempt, interest, and shame – are associated with characteristic and universal facial displays in human beings (Tomkins and McCarter, 1964). Paul Ekman and Carroll Izard each carried out a series of studies involving the judgment of such posed photographs, and both found support for Darwin's proposal and developed conceptualizations of emotion based upon Tomkins' general theory.

Ekman and his colleagues (1972) used photographs representing six of Tomkins' primary affects: happiness, sadness, fear, anger, surprise, and disgust/contempt. Ekman et al. (1969) used these photographs in a study which, perhaps more than any other, brought the study of facial expression and emotion to the attention of a wide audience of scholars. They studied judgments of these photographs by members of the Fore tribe, an isolated and preliterate tribe in the New Guinea highlands. They told the judges a brief story ("his child died and he felt sad"), showed them a set of three photographs, and asked them to choose the face appropriate to the story. Results indicated that a larger percentage than chance chose the expected photograph, although the face showing fear was not distinguished from surprised faces. Furthermore, Ekman and his colleagues asked nine of the Fore to show how their own face would look if they were the person described in the story, and videotaped the resulting expressions. American college students were able to discriminate between Fore's expressions of happiness, sadness, anger, and disgust, but not surprise and fear.

Although these and other data convinced most that facial expressions have an innate basis, it was also clear that facial expressions are influenced by learned rules about what displays are appropriate under what circumstances, or display rules. Recall the example in Chapter 1 of the hostess with the headache giving the party: she attempted to display happiness because that was what is expected. Ekman and Friesen (1975) noted that a person might *qualify* the display of a felt emotion by adding an additional expression as a "comment." Thus, a smile may be added to the display of negative affect (sadness, fear, anger) to indicate "I can take it," or "I won't go too far." Also, one can *modulate* the intensity of one's expression, showing more or less than one actually feels; and *falsify* one's expression in several ways: *neutralizing* and

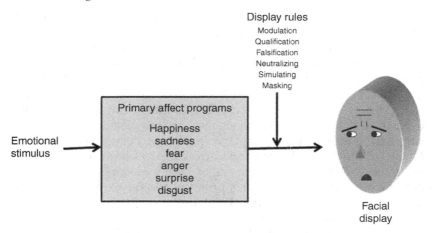

Figure 3.2 The neurocultural model of facial expression. Facial expressions reflect influences from universal primary affect displays and culturally influenced emotional stimuli and display rules.

showing no affect, *simulating* an unfelt emotion, or *masking* what one actually feels by showing a different, unfelt display.

Ekman and Friesen (1969a, 1975) developed a *neurocultural* model of facial expression that described how innate factors and sociocultural learning interact in producing the facial display (see Figure 3.2). An affective stimulus is responded to by a combination of innate primary affect mechanisms, which initiate a tendency to produce the associated facial display. The display, however, is influenced by learned display rules, so that the resulting display is an amalgam of innate and learned influences, including the sorts of experiences studied in coydogs by Moon-Fanelli (2011).

Higher brain mechanisms involved in display. The general pattern of displays represented in the brainstem organized and controlled by higher brain centers has been observed in studies of expressive vocalizations in monkeys. Many monkey species show an extensive repertoire of calls that signal warning, threat, submitting, greeting, and courting; and these displays can be precisely specified by the sound spectrograph, which records the frequency of the vocalization across time. In a series of brain stimulation and lesioning studies, Jurgens (1979), Ploog (1981, 1988), and colleagues found evidence of a hierarchy of mechanisms responsible for the control of these vocalizations. At the lowest level of the hierarchy are the facial nuclei in the hindbrain, through which pass all of the nerve fibers controlling facial movement. If this area is stimulated electrically, the result is a disorganized noise that does not resemble a natural display. The second level is in the *limbic midbrain area* (LMA), specifically the central gray and laterally adjacent tegmentum between the inferior colliculus and brachium conjunctivum. If this area is stimulated, the animal produces a vocalization that can be virtually identical to a natural display: e.g. a typical cackle, growl, trill, chirp, shriek, caw, or groan (Ploog, 1988). However, the animal does not *act* emotionally in other respects. This may be the brain area preserved in the anencephalic infants studied by Steiner (1979). The third hierarchical level involves limbic system structures that project directly to the LMA. If these structures are stimulated, vocalizations virtually identical to natural displays can occur, but the animal also *acts* as if it is feeling emotion, showing a range of behavioral and physiological responses that vary with the limbic structure being stimulated as we shall see. Based upon the readout model presented in Chapter 1, I suggest that input from primary motivational-emotional systems (primes) in the limbic system trigger appropriate vocalization and facial expression patterns in the LMA which are expressed via the hindbrain.

There are two additional brain systems involved in the control of vocalization. One is at or near the cingulate gyrus: in human beings the supplemental motor cortex that controls the extrapyramidal motor system and therefore non-voluntary facial movement. Electrical stimulation here can produce vocalizations virtually identical to natural displays but, as when the LMA is stimulated, the animal does not act emotionally. Jurgens and Ploog suggested that this area allows the animal to voluntarily initiate the expression of a display pre-formed, as it were, in the LMA. They termed this *voluntary expression initiation*. A call virtually identical to a natural call is produced, but the limbic system structures associated with other aspects of emotional response are bypassed so that the call can be produced "cold," as it were. Presumably this is accomplished via extrapyramidal motor input to the LMA (Buck, 1984).

The fourth brain area is associated with vocalization only in human beings. It is the area of the primary motor cortex that innervates via the pyramidal motor system the mouth, tongue, pharynx, and larynx; and is just posterior to the classic Broca's area speech center, almost always in the left hemisphere. Stimulation of this area produces a meaningless noise, similar to the stimulation of the facial nuclei in the hindbrain. Jurgens and Ploog suggested that here the organization of the vocalization is formed voluntarily by the individual via Broca's area, and termed it *voluntary expression formation*. This is accomplished by direct pyramidal system motor input to the muscles of the mouth, tongue, larynx, and pharynx via the hindbrain facial nuclei (Buck, 1984; see Figure 3.3).

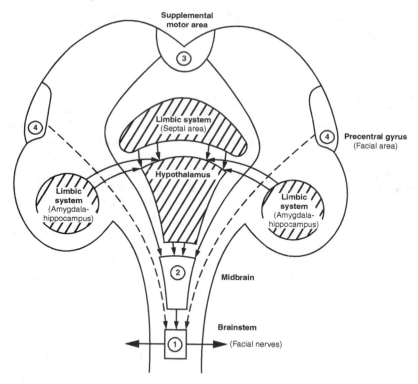

Figure 3.3 A hierarchical model of emotional display and control. See text for details.

Automatic and voluntary factors in display

Two streams of communication. The activities of the brain systems studied by Jurgens and Ploog result in three sorts of communication. First, there is the direct display of the state of primary motivational-emotional systems from limbic structures to the LMA. This display is biologically based, unlearned, and nonvoluntary; and its elements are externally accessible aspects or *signs* of the internal state. Because the sign requires presence of the state, the display cannot by definition be false, so it is *nonpropositional*. This is the Emotion II readout illustrated in Figure 1.1, and it results in *spontaneous communication*. Second, there is the voluntary formation or *encoding* of a linguistic message in the brain of a human sender via Broca's area. Information is encoded into *symbols*, which are defined as having an arbitrary relationship with a referent, such as the word "tree" in English. The system of symbols and rules of grammar is learned and culturally patterned, and this process is

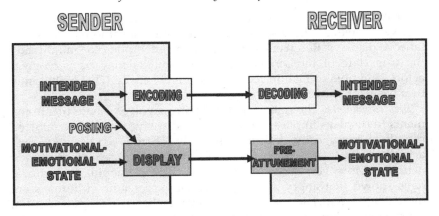

Figure 3.4 Symbolic, spontaneous, and pseudospontaneous (posing) communication. See text for details.

voluntary at some level although it is not necessarily conscious. Because the relationship of symbols and referents is arbitrary, the statement may be false: I may say "the tree is blue" when it is in fact green. Therefore, these statements are *propositions* capable of logical analysis such as tests for truth or falsity, and the result is *symbolic communication* (see Buck, 1984; Buck and Van Lear, 2002).

This analysis implies that the brain is involved at all times in two simultaneous "streams" of communication: symbolic and spontaneous (see Figure 3.4). These require different sorts of response on the part of receivers of these messages. With symbolic communication, the receiver must *decode* the symbols. This requires that the sender and speaker both have learnt the same particular vocabulary and grammar: that they "speak the same language." In the case of spontaneous communication, this is not necessary. There are natural sensitivities or *preattunements* to displays that presumably involve mirror neuron systems. Preattunements must co-evolve with displays so that the spontaneous communication can occur. Therefore, such "nonverbal communication" can occur across cultures to an extent (see Buck, 1984; Buck and Van Lear, 2002).

Voluntary expression initiation. However, displays may not function only as signs reading out the state of inner motivational-emotional systems. They can also be manipulated by the sender via voluntary expression initiation, where displays virtually identical to natural displays are voluntarily produced. Buck and Van Lear (2002) termed this *pseudospontaneous communication*, because from the point of view of the sender it is voluntary and perhaps intended to manipulate the receiver for tactical or strategic purposes. From the point of view of the receiver, however, the displays are virtually identical to natural spontaneous displays. Receivers may respond by attempting to "mind-read" the true state of the sender, but some senders may be very good actors, and able to take in receivers relatively easily. This ability may be a basis for *charisma*.

Preattunements. The notion that receiving involves innate preattunements to displays implies that emotional displays must be recognized rapidly, automatically, and unconsciously. There is evidence for such a biologically based, direct receiving process in research on mirror neurons. Moreover, studies using classical conditioning procedures have shown that angry and fearful facial expressions in humans are more readily associated with aversive events than are happy or neutral expressions (Ohman and Dimberg, 1978). Also, an angry face is picked out of a group of happy faces more quickly than a happy face is picked out of a group of angry faces, presumably because of evolutionary advantages such recognition affords (Hansen and Hansen, 1988). Studies have shown that different facial stimuli evoke specific neural activity in the human amygdala (Morris et al., 1998; Whalen, 1998), that amygdala damage in humans impairs the recognition of specific facial expressions (Adophs et al., 1994), and that subconscious presentations of happy and angry facial expressions elicit corresponding unconscious responses in the facial muscles (Dimberg et al., 2000) and amygdalae (Whalen et al., 1998) of observers.

Direct evidence for emotional preattunements in human beings was demonstrated in a study of two patients with unilateral destruction of the visual cortex, and subsequent *cortical blindness* in one half of the visual field so that visual stimuli cannot be consciously perceived on one side (Tamietto et al., 2009). Pictures of facial and bodily displays of emotion were presented to both the blind and sighted visual fields of these patients, while their facial expressions were recorded via electromyography and arousal by pupil dilation. Results indicated that facial reactions were faster and arousal reactions were greater when the stimuli were presented to the blind visual field, so they were not consciously perceived. The pictures of facial and bodily display produced similar reactions, indicating that the patients "resonated to their affective meaning." The authors concluded that these affective reactions were "mediated by visual pathways of old evolutionary origin, bypassing cortical vision," while still providing for emotional communication (Tamietto et al., 2009, p. 17661). In effect, this convincingly demonstrated in humans a fast "low road" to visual affective perception in human beings analogous to that demonstrated by LeDoux (1994) for auditory perception in rats.

Spontaneous emotion communication accuracy. The studies of emotional communication via facial expression carried out by Tomkins, Izard, and Ekman primarily used photographs of posed facial expressions as opposed to spontaneous displays. Robert E. Miller and colleagues developed a *cooperative conditioning* procedure to measure spontaneous emotional communication in rhesus monkeys. Two monkeys were taught to press a bar when a light came on, and then were paired so that a "sender" could see the light and a "receiver" in another room could press the bar. The receiver, however, was provided with a video feed showing the sender's face. If the sender made a facial expression when the light was turned on, and if the receiver could perceive and correctly interpret that expression, the receiver could press the bar, solving the problem. Miller found that normal monkeys could solve this problem with relative ease, thus demonstrating communication via spontaneous facial expression (Miller et al., 1967).

Miller's procedure was adapted to the study of spontaneous emotional communication in human beings by showing human "senders" emotionally loaded pictures and recording ratings of their emotional reactions to each picture. Unknown to them, their facial/gestural reactions were filmed with an unobtrusive camera. Judges viewing their expressions attempted to guess the type of slide presented and their emotional reactions. Results demonstrated significant sending accuracy with wide individual differences. Women were better senders than men, and sending accuracy was positively related to self-report measures of extroversion and self-esteem. Interestingly, good senders showed fewer skin conductance deflections to the slides (Buck et al., 1972, 1974). Subsequent studies with preschool children as senders showed similar evidence of internalizing and externalizing response modes with both skin conductance measures and teacher's ratings, although there was less evidence of a gender difference (Buck, 1975, 1977).

From the viewpoint of the model of emotional development and emotional education presented in Chapter 1, accurate sending must be a critical element in socio-emotional development. If a child does not clearly express her emotions in ways understandable to interaction partners, the partners cannot give the child effective and accurate social biofeedback (see Figure 1.2). This would lead to deficits in the child's ability to accurately recognize, label, and understand her own feelings and desires; in effect to deficits in emotional education, as discussed in Chapter 1. This would lead in turn to a deficient vocabulary of emotion, termed *alexithymia* (no words for mood). If the child shows too little expression the partner would be unable to know the true feelings of the child and could not provide social biofeedback. The result would be *hypoexpressive alexithymia*. On the other hand, if there is too much,

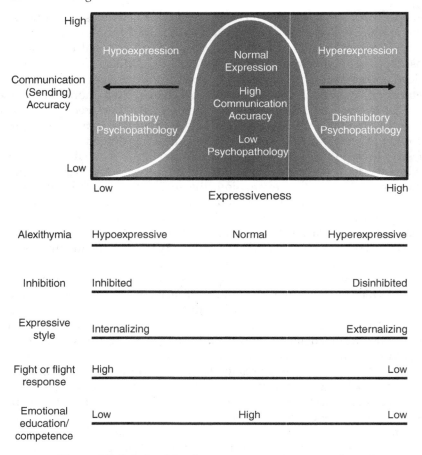

Figure 3.5 Relationships between expressiveness and sending accuracy. Either extremely low or high expressiveness leads to deficits in emotional communication, and thence emotional education and emotional competence, leading to *inhibitory psychopathology* or *disinhibitory psychopathology*, respectively. See text for details.

uncoordinated expression as has been observed in behaviorally disordered children (Goldman, 1994) and schizophrenia patients (Easton, 1994), the partner again could not judge the child's true feelings and the result would be *hyperexpressive alexithymia* (Buck and Powers, 2013). The best level of expressiveness from the viewpoint of emotional education would be a moderate level where the child's "true feelings" are apparent to the partner. Figure 3.5 illustrates the resulting curvilinear relationship between emotional communication accuracy and emotional expressiveness. As it illustrates, either extremely low or high expressiveness would be expected to lead to deficits in emotional education and emotional competence, leading to *inhibitory psychopathology* or *disinhibitory psychopathology*, respectively.

Emotional sonar, IFF, and emotional intelligence. The accurate display of one's emotions enables others to respond with social biofeedback and affords emotional education and the achievement of emotional competence, but it does far more. One's expressions actually *influence the expressiveness of the interaction partner*, such that the partner's expressiveness is enhanced or reduced. Watch the expressiveness of grocery clerks as they interact with a number of customers. Although a few may be unfailingly sociable or dour, most will match the expressiveness of the customer, brightening or darkening in response to the customer.

Thus, a good sender tends to encourage expressivity in interaction partners, while a poor sender (either hypoexpressive or hyperexpressive) tends to discourage such expressivity. As a result, we carry through our lives a "bubble of expressivity" wherever we go, encouraging or discouraging the expressiveness of our interaction partners. This can have significant consequences, in that we actually create our own enriched or deprived emotional environment. Boone and Buck (2003) compared this process to "emotional sonar," where we send emotional displays into the interpersonal environment much as a ship sends sound signals or "pings" into the aquatic environment in search of a submarine. Our displays are reflected in the displays of partners. Our display can also be a challenge analogous to the military "identification of friend or foe" (IFF), where we attempt to determine whether the partner is trustworthy. Such testing appears to happen naturally and unconsciously, as when people seem able to detect cooperators or defectors in social game situations from brief interactions unrelated to the game, as we shall examine in Chapter 6.

The effects of expressivity on trustworthiness were investigated in a sales context by Kowal (2012). Participants were professional real-estate salespersons from a variety of offices in the northeast United States. Sending accuracy was assessed by the slide-viewing technique (SVT). Good senders were found to have better sales records in the office, suggesting that they were regarded as more trustworthy by their clients. Interestingly, men were overall better senders than women in this study, a reversal of the usual finding: perhaps the role of a real-estate salesperson obliges men to be relatively outgoing and extroverted, and women to be more reserved and "businesslike."

Accurate emotional expression, then, enhances interpersonal emotion skills underlying such concepts as intuition, empathy, and rapport.

It is certainly a, and could be *the*, critical skill underlying what has widely been labeled "emotional intelligence" (Boone and Buck, 2003; Buck and Powers, 2013).

Conclusions

Spontaneous, symbolic, and pseudospontaneous communication takes emotion out of the brain of the individual sender, and puts it into social context. Indeed, developmental-interactionist theory posits that emotional communication is at the core of social organization and that it has important implications for the emotional functioning of the individual (Buck and Powers, 2013). The displays organized in the LMA of the brainstem play a critical role in translating emotion from the individual brain to the social and cultural environment.

Emotion III: subjective experience of affective feelings and desires 1 – arousal and reward-punishment mechanisms

Systems of arousal

The brainstem. The neurochemical systems at the base of the anatomical hierarchy – the hindbrain and midbrain – make up the *brainstem*. The brainstem houses sensory and motor tracts connecting the brain with the spinal cord, nuclei of cranial nerves that leave the CNS at this level, and a network of nuclei at the core termed the *reticular formation* (Steriade, 1996). These nuclei include the *locus coeruleus* and the *raphe nuclei*, which as noted in Chapter 2 are involved in the production of the neurotransmitters norepinephrine (NE) and serotonin (5-HT).

Arousal. The reticular formation is a network ("reticulum") of gray matter and small nuclei in the core of the brainstem extending from the spinal cord through the midbrain to the reticular nucleus of the thalamus. From there, diffuse thalamocortical pathways connect with the rest of the brain. The reticular formation has been associated with arousal, attention, and sleep. Its role in arousal and attention was suggested by Bremer (1935), who demonstrated that separation of the reticular formation from the rest of the brain, even when sensory input to the cortex was left intact (*cerveau isole*), resulted in coma. In such coma, sensory areas of the brain could continue to show responses to external stimuli, but the organism could not be aroused. Moruzzi and Magoun (1949) found that electrical stimulation of the reticular formation produces alerting and EEG arousal, and Lindsley (1951, 1957) suggested that the Ascending Reticular Activating System (ARAS) is the physiological basis for general arousal.

Habituation. The anatomical position of the reticular formation in relation to incoming sensory systems suggests how it can fill the crucial function of the *habituation* or filtering of incoming stimuli. As noted in Chapter 1, many stimuli are available to the brain but are not important, such as the feel of one's shoes. We can easily turn our attention to such stimuli, but attention normally soon "naturally" returns to other, more pressing, matters. But, how can the brain "know" whether stimuli are important or not important without first identifying those stimuli? The reticular formation accomplishes this by, in effect, using a simple decision rule to arouse the brain and initiate attention. Stimuli like the feel of one's clothes, or the sound of traffic in the background, or the hum of a furnace tend to be relatively weak and repetitive. Sensory systems ascending into the brain send fibers into the reticular formation, so that the reticular formation is in a good position to respond to the relative strength and novelty of a stimulus. If a stimulus is strong and/or novel, an alerting response may be initiated; if not, the brain as a whole is not aroused. Therefore, the reticular formation can respond to whether a stimulus is important without "knowing" what the stimulus is.

Emotion. The reticular formation extends upward into the thalamus, and the thalamic reticular nucleus (TRN) plays a key role in the control of attention, shifting attention to relevant stimuli and away from distracters. The TRN receives "bottom-up" projections from sensory and motor systems, and also "top-down" projections from prefrontal cortices that play key roles in emotion, cognition, and memory: the dorsolateral prefrontal cortex (DLPFC), the posterior orbitofrontal cortex (pOFC), and associated mediodorsal thalamic nuclei (MD). It is thought that the DLPFC and pOFC control attention via these projections (Barbas and Zikopoulos, 2007). In addition, the amygdala has also been found to project to the TRN in primates in a pathway only recently discovered, which uses specialized synaptic terminals which are larger and more efficient that those from the pOFC and MD (Zikopoulous and Barbas, 2012). The amygdala is a key structure processing emotion, and Zikopoulous and Barbas suggest that this pathway provides a powerful mechanism for rapidly shifting attention to emotional stimuli important to survival. In conjunction with the input from the frontal cortices, this allows a purposeful assessment and contemplation of events with emotional import.

The hypothalamus

The hypothalamus is a collection of nuclei about the size of the end of the thumb, located in the base of the brain below the thalamus.

It gathers and integrates information relevant to bodily functioning from the central nervous system and peripheral bodily sources and influences that functioning through the autonomic and endocrine systems. The hypothalamus is well situated to send and receive chemical information from bodily fluids: it has the richest supply of blood vessels of any nervous system structure; it borders the third ventricle, a cavity in the brain filled with cerebrospinal fluid; and within the hypothalamus, the blood–brain barrier that normally prevents chemicals in the bloodstream from crossing into the brain is weaker. The hypothalamus directly controls the sympathetic nervous system via the posterior nucleus, the parasympathetic nervous system via the anterior hypothalamus, and the endocrine system via the pituitary gland. Classic studies have established that lesion and stimulation of specific hypothalamic nuclei have dramatic effects upon behaviors associated with primary drives such as hunger, thirst, and sex; and also with aggressive/defensive/submissive behaviors, and social attachment.

Aggressive/defensive/submissive behaviors. The hypothalamus participates in the integration and expression of at least two distinct kinds of aggressive behavior: defensive attack and submission, and offensive attack and dominance. We noted previously that the posterior hypothalamus is required for the organization of the defensive "sham rage" response in cats (Bard, 1928). In the same year that Bard published his work, Hess (1928) demonstrated that electrical stimulation of the perifornical region near the ventromedial hypothalamus produced defensive attack. Similar effects were found with stimulation of the midbrain central gray, and MacLean (1969) suggested that rage reactions are channeled from the perifornical region of the hypothalamus to the central gray.

Adams (1979) suggested that defensive attack evolved to defend the individual against attack by predators, but was modified in social species to reduce disruptive and dangerous within-group fighting. The modification took the form of a "submission system" so that when confronted with an attack from a dominant and familiar group member or consociate as opposed to a predator, an animal would assume a submissive posture which would inhibit the attack. He suggested that both defensive attack and submission are activated by the perifornical hypothalamus-central gray mechanism, but the defensive attack is inhibited by the information that the antagonist is a familiar and dominant consociate. Defense and submission have several specific elements in common: a defensive posture and vocalization, freezing, and fleeing. Submission has in addition a submissive posture and vocalization, while defensive attack lacks these but includes striking and lunge-and-bite attack.

Another kind of aggressive behavior – confident offensive attack – is associated with the lateral hypothalamus. Animals stimulated in this area do not express rage, but rather quietly stalk and make predatory attacks on smaller animals. For example, Roberts and Kleiss (1964) found that cats which did not initially attack rats would learn a maze to stalk and kill a rat when stimulated in the lateral hypothalamus. They would leave food to take up the hunt, suggesting that they were not motivated by hunger, but rather a drive to hunt and kill.

Social attachment. The notion that social behaviors are based upon basic brain mechanisms was once controversial but now arguably the evidence is in, and it is overwhelming. Adams' (1979) theory that the hypothalamus contains mechanisms that turn defensive attack into submission has been joined by theories that basic neural mechanisms underlie social attachment (Panksepp, 1991).

One of the qualities that distinguishes the typical lifestyle, or ethogram, of mammals (and also birds) from that of reptiles is the helplessness of the infant and consequent requirement on the part of adults to provide protection and nurturance. One consequence is that the young of many species produce distress vocalizations when separated from consociates: this is true of puppies, kittens, guinea piglets, and of monkey, ape, and human infants (see Scott, 1974). Jaak Panksepp and colleagues have suggested that distress vocalizations elicit caregiving and maternal behavior from adults. They found that areas of the brain that when stimulated elicit distress vocalizations are rich in the brain's endogenous opiates. These include limbic structures (particularly the cingulate gyrus and septal area) extending down through the hypothalamus into the midbrain central gray. Panksepp (e.g. 1982) argued that these areas constitute the physiological substrate for social cohesion. Very low, nonanalgesic doses of morphine reduce distress vocalizations in several species "seemingly substituting for mother in a dose-dependent fashion" (Panksepp, 1981, p. 299). In contrast, the opiate antagonist naloxone increases distress vocalizations, and Panksepp suggested that this may "indicate the specificity of endogenous brain opiate systems in organizing social behavior" (1981, p. 300).

The relationship of the endogenous opiates to social cohesion suggests that opiate addiction may be related to brain mechanisms of social attachment, and the intriguing possibility that strong social attachments are analogous in some respects to opium addiction: that humans are, as the song says, "addicted to love" (Panksepp, 1986). Panksepp suggested that the euphoria associated with being in love derives from high levels of endorphins, that the tolerance that comes with morphine dependence is analogous to the decrease in the experienced attractiveness of a lover over time, and that the "pain" associated with separation from the loved one and bereavement may be literally due to a hypersensitivity to pain due to lowered levels of the endorphins. This link between attachment and the endorphins may also explain the protective stress-buffering effects of social relationships, whereas separation and bereavement often increase susceptibility to stress and disease (Buck, 1993c).

Subjective experience and the hypothalamus. The hypothalamus is intimately involved in a wide range of motivational and emotional phenomena, but the motivational-emotional states mediated by the hypothalamus are incomplete in a crucial respect: the subjective experiences associated with such states are largely missing. Humans stimulated in the hypothalamus have pronounced autonomic nervous system changes, but do not report unusual sensations, alterations in consciousness, or emotional feelings (White, 1940). Sem-Jacobson (1968) found few changes in mood or consciousness in a report of hypothalamic stimulation at 2,651 electrode sites in eighty-two patients. In addition, diseases of the hypothalamus in human beings can produce a variety of sexual abnormalities and eating disorders, and also psychic disturbances such as expressions of rage and compulsive attacks of laughing and crying (Bauer, 1954). However, the nature of the subjective experiences associated with these conditions is not clear, and Reynolds (1971) suggested that the laughter associated with hypothalamic lesions is entirely compulsive and not associated with the subjective experience of humor. In contrast, patients with lesions in the limbic system that produce laughter also make the patient *feel* funny, similar to a person that continually laughs at his own bad jokes.

Systems of reward and punishment

The midbrain region of the brainstem contains several important emotion-relevant areas that were discussed in Chapter 2. The midbrain lies between the cerebellum and the forebrain (Pinel, 1993). The dorsal surface of the midbrain is the *tectum*, which means "roof." In mammals, there are two sets of bumps on the tectum termed the *colliculi* (meaning "little hills"): the anterior pair (superior colliculi) have visual functions and the posterior pair (inferior colliculi) have auditory functions. The region below, or ventral to, the tectum is termed the *tegmentum*. In addition to sensory and motor pathways, and part of the reticular formation, the tegmentum contains the red nucleus and *substantia nigra*. The latter contains neurons that produce and release DA, which travels to the *striatum* via the nigrostriatal pathway. Also, DA pathways from the ventral midbrain have reciprocal connections with the *basal ganglia* and limbic forebrain. In particular, DA neurons in the ventral midbrain that project to the *nucleus accumbens* (NAcc) mediate reward effects. The tegmentum also contains the *periaquaductal gray* or PAG, gray matter surrounding the cerebral aqueduct, a duct in the center of the brainstem containing cerebrospinal fluid. As discussed in Chapter 2, the PAG responds to opiates, and in company with serotonergic fibers in the raphe nuclei, it is involved in the regulation of pain (Purves et al., 1997).

Emotional valence 1: approach-avoidance. The limbic midbrain area or LMA of the midbrain involved in display is also associated with general approach and avoidance. These systems cross hierarchical levels from the midbrain through the hypothalamus into the forebrain, and involve reward and punishment effects associated respectively with the *behavioral activation system* (BAS) and *behavioral inhibition system* (BIS: Gray, 1982a, 1982b). The BAS corresponds to the classic "reward system" discovered by James Olds (1956, 1958) when he was studying the reticular formation. He noticed that a rat with an off-target stimulating electrode would repeatedly return to the place where the stimulus was applied. By giving rats a bar to self-stimulate in this area, Olds and Milner (1954) demonstrated that rats would press the bar untiringly over long periods of time, and would solve complex mazes and cross electrified grids to get to the bar. In particular, food-deprived rats with electrodes in the *medial forebrain bundle* (MFB) would continue to self-stimulate even ignoring the presence of food. Olds (1956) suggested that the MFB and also the septal area constitute "pleasure centers" in which stimulation elicits feelings of pure and presumably vivid hedonic pleasure: ecstasy, perhaps.

At about the same time that Olds discovered evidence of pleasure centers, Delgado et al. (1954) found brain regions where stimulation was punishing: animals would avoid behavior associated with stimulation in those areas. Olds and Olds (1963) found stimulation of the *periventricular system* (PVS) to be punishing. The PVS runs medial to and parallel with the MFB, and Stein (1964) suggested that reward effects are mediated by the MFB and punishing effects by the PVS: the BAS and BIS, respectively.

The functioning of the reward and punishment systems illustrates how fundamentally "hard-wired" special-purpose processing systems can become "programmed" by experience in the environment: indeed, they are *hard-wired to be programmable*. Consider a mouse sleeping under a tree, which awakens hungry. It becomes active and begins to explore the environment. As it explores, it comes into mortal danger – it encounters a cat – and it quickly escapes. After reaching safety, it begins to explore again and eventually finds food. It eats and, satisfied, returns to the tree and falls asleep. The next time it awakens hungry and begins to explore the environment, it tends to avoid the area associated with the cat and goes more directly to the food. Eventually, with additional similar experience it goes directly and quickly to the food. In effect, it has learned to avoid the cat and approach the food. Experiences in the environment *steer* behavior toward reward and away from punishment. This process is termed goal-directed or *instrumental learning*, in which the dangers of the external environment come to be avoided and its fruits come to be approached.

The cat is an *unconditioned stimulus* to fear to the mouse: a natural sign of danger and fear that activates the BIS. Stimuli in the environment around the cat become associated with fear and danger: they become *negative incentives* that activate the BIS because of their association with the cat. When the BIS is activated, the mouse responds with anxiety and avoidance behavior: it avoids not only the cat, but everything associated with the cat, with the strength of the avoidance tendencies correlated with degree of association. Conversely, food serves as an unconditioned stimulus to reward that activates the BAS. Stimuli in the environment around the food become *positive incentives* that activate the BAS because of their association with the food. When the BAS is activated, the mouse responds with approach behavior. Thus acting together, the BAS and BIS steer the mouse away from stimuli associated with punishment and toward stimuli associated with reward.

The reward and punishment systems act via the BAS and BIS in several ways: they activate behavior in times of challenge, steer it in the right direction, and terminate it when the goal is reached and satiation is achieved (Stein, 1978). The activating function is particularly associated with DA, the steering with NE, and the satiation with the endorphins. That is, the DA system acts to modulate cognitive flexibility (Cohen et al., 2002), the NE system acts to direct attention to salient sensory stimuli (Oades, 1985), and the endorphin system provides pleasurable satiation (Esch and Stefano, 2004). These systems also inhibit behavior associated with punishment. Whereas the BIS punishment system accounts for passive avoidance, it does not account for active fight-or-flight responses: those are associated with the amygdala, as we shall see (MacLean, 1993; Gray, 1982a, 1982b).

In his *Reinforcement Sensitivity Theory*, Gray suggested that the BAS, BIS, and fight-or-flight systems interact in emotional situations. In particular, Gray suggested that sensitivity to rewards is associated with high relative BAS activity, and there is in fact evidence in human subjects that psychometric measures of reward sensitivity are related to activation of reward-sensitive areas of the brain (Beaver et al., 2006; Hahn et al., 2009). Thus, the BAS reflects sensitivity to rewards in the environment and involves activation of appetitive DA systems. The BAS initiates both approach behavior relative to positive incentive stimuli, and active avoidance behavior relative to negative incentive stimuli. Thus, the DA systems promote "a generalized ability for response initiation" to both positive and negative incentives (Panksepp, 1986, p. 90).

In contrast, the BIS reflects sensitivity to punishment: it modulates BAS-driven behavior through activation of the amygdala and the septo-hippocampal-frontal system (SHF system: see later). The BIS responds to conditioned or innate aversive stimuli with anxiety and passive avoidance behavior. Gray (1982a, 1982b) suggested that the BIS continually compares actual with expected stimuli. While expected and actual match, the BIS remains in a "checking mode" and the control of behavior resides elsewhere. If the match does not occur, or if a stimulus associated with punishment (negative incentive) is encountered, the BIS takes on a "control mode": any behavior being executed is inhibited and identified as "faulty" so that it will be performed with more caution in the future. Also, the organism scans the environment to identify stimuli associated with punishment, failure, or nonreward. Gray suggested that NE and serotonin are both involved in increasing the range of environmental stimuli that "need checking," with NE particularly responding to "important" stimuli and serotonin to "aversive" stimuli. In effect, NE systems increase sensitivity to relevant positive or negative stimuli, serving as a central amplifying system increasing the signal-to-noise ratio in sensory systems, increasing the sensitivity to central, relevant cues and reducing sensitivity to peripheral cues (Easterbrook, 1959). High levels of response inhibition are associated with anxiety, and excessively high levels with phobias and obsessive-compulsive neuroses. Gray suggested further that introverts have high levels of BIS activity relative to extroverts, so those introverts are more prone to anxiety and inhibition and more susceptible to punishment.

Emotional valence 2: wanting versus liking. Doubts have long been expressed that the motivation underlying self-stimulation necessarily involves hedonic pleasure. On one hand, the motivation must be extremely strong and compelling because animals will go through so much and work so hard to obtain the stimulation. On the other hand, there are puzzling differences between rewarding brain stimulation and rewards that satisfy real biological needs, such as food and drink. Deutsch (1972) noted that if brain stimulation is withheld for a time, animals will seem to lose interest in it. He suggested that the brain stimulation itself produces the drive for brain stimulation, with each stimulation having the double function of rewarding the previous response and creating the drive for the next response. If too much time elapses between reinforcements, the drive decays and the animal appears to lose interest. Panksepp (1998) noted that the behavior of the rat engrossed in self-stimulation in the MFB does not generally appear to be enjoying the experience. Rather, its behavior seems frantic and compulsive. Given the opportunity for self-stimulation in the septal area, in contrast, the animal does not press the bar frantic-ally. It stimulates and then pauses to stretch and groom itself, as if enjoying the effect of the stimulation. If motivation is defined as the number of bar presses in a given time, the MFB does produce greater numbers, but the evidence suggests that the animal's experience, while "rewarding" in a behavioral sense, might not be so pleasant in a hedonic sense.

Berridge (2007, 2009) suggested that there are in fact two sorts of positive valence involved in brain stimulation, which he termed *wanting* versus *liking*. Wanting involves positive incentive motivation that can produce approach behavior, while liking involves hedonic pleasure. Wanting and liking are mediated by partially dissociable neural substrates that make up the integrated reward system. Whereas wanting reactions are associated with the MFB reward system, liking is associated with a limited number of "hedonic hotspots," particularly in the nucleus accumbens (NAcc), *ventral pallidum*, and brainstem *parabrachial nucleus* (see Figure 3.6). Berridge and Kringelbach (2008) referred to the hedonic hotspots as "pleasure generators" (p. 464). Whereas the MFB is associated with DA as a principal neurotransmit-ter, the hedonic hotspots are rich in opioid and also endocannabinoid receptors. Anatomically the hotspots are highly localized, a cubic millimeter in size in the rodent brain that translates into approximately a cubic centimeter in the human brain. A hotspot in the posterior ventral pallidum appears to be strongly necessary for pleasure, in that damage to it actually replaces liking reactions with "disliking" reac-tions (e.g. tongue protrusions associated with sweet tastes are replaced by gaping responses normally associated with bitter tastes: Berridge and Kringelbach, 2008).

Both wanting and liking may be conscious or non-conscious. The notion of "unconscious affect" seems at first glance something of a contradiction in terms, but Berridge and Winkielman (2003) argued that effects of affective stimuli on behavior can be dissociated from subjective experience. They demonstrated subliminal presentation of happy and angry faces could influence choice behavior without influencing ratings of subjective experience. They defined unconscious affect as "a reaction caused by valenced stimuli that has valenced behavioral consequences, but which nevertheless is not subjectively felt, even upon introspection" (Winkielman and Berridge, 2003, p. 666).

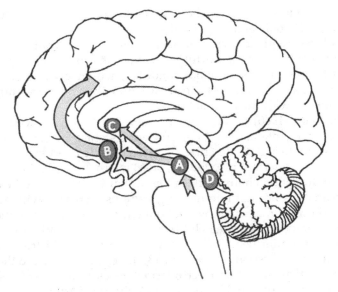

Figure 3.6 Areas of the brain associated with reward. These include the dopaminergic MFB associated with wanting and opiate "affective hotspots" associated with liking. An additional affective hotspot in the ventral pallidum is not visible in this midline view of the human brain. Arrows = Medial forebrain bundle (MFB); A = Ventral tegmental area (VTA); B = Nucleus accumbens (NAcc); C = Septal area; D = Parabrachial nucleus.

Arousal and reward-punishment systems and temperament

Externalizing and internalizing. Acting together, the arousal and reward-punishment systems are involved in determining general patterns of personality and temperament. For example, there is evidence that reactivity in the reward and punishment systems is associated with peripheral physiological responses (Buck, 1979). There has long been evidence that persons who are overt in their emotional responding are less reactive on certain autonomic nervous system measures such as electrodermal responses. Electrodermal responses measure changes in the conductivity of the palmar and plantar surfaces of the hands and feet to the passage of a slight electric current, termed *skin conductance* (SC) responses. They have been described as among the most sensitive physiological indicators of psychological events. In a review of this literature in 1920, Prideaux concluded that electrodermal responses are associated with emotional suppression: "the greater the visible signs of emotion ... the less the response on the galvanometer" (1920,

p. 66). Studying adolescent boys in emotionally charged situations, Landis (1932) confessed surprise that those who showed overt expression had less frequent electrodermal responses: "one would expect that the frightened, angry, or tearful individual, that is all those giving all outward signs of an emotional condition, would give very frequent (electrodermal responses). Instead, we find that they are much less frequent than with the normal" (p. 285).

H. E. Jones (1960) found similar results in studies of electrodermal responding in infants, children, and adolescents; and suggested the term "externalizing" to describe a pattern of little overt expression but frequent electrodermal responding, and "internalizing" to describe the opposite. In young children Jones found that infants showed externalizing patterns, and that internalizing patterns increased with age, and he hypothesized that this was due to increasing inhibition of the overt display of emotion: "in older children, the increase in inhibition . . . may not imply a diminished emotionality but merely a shift from outer to inner patterns of response" (1960, p. 13). Jones then turned to the study of extreme high and low electrodermal reactors among adolescents who were part of the University of California Adolescent Growth Study. He found the high reactors, who showed the internalizing pattern, to be quiet, reserved, controlled, calm, poised, good natured, cooperative, and responsible. The extreme low reactors in contrast were characterized as uninhibited, talkative, animated, impulsive, assertive, and bossy. Jones suggested that the low reactors were manifesting an infantile and maladaptive mode of response.

Jones' conclusions contrast with those of a study of externalizing/internalizing patterns by Jack Block (1957), who studied high and low electrodermal reactors among medical school applicants. In this study, low reactors were judged in more positive terms, being: "independent, aggressively direct, and relatively non-conforming" (p. 13). High reactors were judged to be more "maladjusted": being withdrawn and worrying individuals who "turn their anxieties toward inner routes of expression" (p. 13). These differing conclusions may reflect the difference in the samples: perhaps reserved and cooperative behavior judged to be appropriate in an adolescent is seen to reflect undue caution and submission in a medical school applicant. Similarly, behavior judged to be impulsive and bossy in an adolescent may be seen as appropriate and "aggressively direct" in a medical school applicant (Buck, 1979).

Extroversion/introversion. The functioning of reward and punishment systems and the internalizing/externalizing phenomenon are also relevant to constructs of inhibition/disinhibition studied in research on personality and temperament. These include concepts of approach and withdrawal identified in the New York Longitudinal Study of Temperament (e.g. Thomas et al., 1970), concepts of behavioral inhibition and disinhibition studied in the long-term longitudinal research of Jerome Kagan and colleagues (e.g. Kagan et al., 1984), and personality constructs of extroversion and introversion (Rothbart, 2012).

The constructs of extroversion and introversion have roots in the work of C. G. Jung (1977) and Ivan Pavlov's distinction between strong and weak nervous systems (1927). The latter was based upon observations of individual differences in the responsiveness of different dogs in Pavlov's famous experiments on classical conditioning: dogs with strong nervous systems are said to be relatively resistant to external stimulation, and are therefore difficult to condition, while dogs with weak nervous systems are more reactive and therefore susceptible to classical conditioning. H. J. Eysenck (1967) developed a three-factor personality theory encompassing concepts of extroversion and introversion (linked to strong and weak nervous systems, respectively), and neuroticism linked to anxiety. He related extroversion/introversion to differences in the arousability of the reticular formation. J. A. Gray (1971, 1977) reformulated Eysenck's theory based upon notions of BAS and BIS systems which interact with the reticular formation responding to the arousal qualities and novelty of stimuli; and the fight-or-flight system, associated with the amygdala. Gray suggested that extroversion/introversion is associated with the relative arousability of the BAS and BIS, with extroversion associated with being relatively easy to reward, and introversion with being relatively easy to punish (see Rolls, 1999). Consistent with the notions of emotional sonar and IFF, extroversion is also the personality trait most easily identified by others (John and Robins, 1993).

Longitudinal studies by Kagan and colleagues (Kagan, 2007; Kagan et al., 2007) identified continuities and discontinuities in expressiveness from childhood to adulthood which shed light on the extent to which extroversion and introversion are genetically based. One method involved categorizing children as inhibited or uninhibited early in life (4–24 months) and then testing them in later childhood, adolescence, and adulthood. For example, Schwartz et al. (2003) found that young adults (mean age = 21.8 years) classified as inhibited at age 2 showed greater amygdala fMRI arousal responses to novel faces than did adults classified as disinhibited, and also greater responses to novel than to familiar faces. This suggested that extroversion and introversion are associated with different brain responses to novelty that are preserved from infancy to early adulthood, constituting a genetically based predisposition or *diathesis* for inhibited or disinhibited behavior.

Conclusions

This section has demonstrated that the interplay of reward and punishment systems is involved in essential aspects of behavior, including the determination of critical aspects of personality and temperament. In terms of the developmental-interactionist model presented in Chapter 1, it provides particularly clear examples of how specific neurochemical systems function as interacting modules underlying emotion in all of its aspects: physiological responding, display, and subjective experience. Thus the tendency to be easily rewarded is reflected physiologically in less evidence of certain fight-or-flight responses, in enhanced expressive displays leading to attributions of an extroverted personality and temperament, and in tendencies toward positive affect. The latter can be subdivided into dissociable modules: activity in the MFB related to wanting and activity in the hedonic hotspots related to liking.

This discussion has amplified the previous discussion of spontaneous and symbolic communication in taking emotion out of the exclusive realm of the individual level of analysis into the dyadic, social level. The accuracy with which a person displays her feelings and desires enables the dyadic partner to respond with social biofeedback, but beyond this, accurately sent emotional signals invite and even demand responses, and this is a major determinant of the richness of the affective environment that we, in effect, carry with us through our lives. Emotions exist not only in the head of the individual, but in the collective social realm as well, as will become increasingly clear as we consider social and moral emotions.

Normal emotional development requires accurate emotional communication, so the individual child must *learn how to label and use* the complement of biological emotions conferred at birth. In this process, arousal and reward-punishment systems are important, but there is much more to the biological basis of emotion. Executive systems associated with more complex and more recently evolved brain structures set the agenda for a complex array of specific feelings and desires, some of these functioning to preserve the individual and others to preserve the species.

Emotion III: subjective experience of affective feelings and desires 2 – selfish competition versus prosocial cooperation

Brain systems of subjective emotional experience

Papez and the limbic system. We saw that Cannon (1932) argued that emotional experience is associated with central nervous system rather than peripheral mechanisms. He suggested that emotional stimuli are first processed by phylogenetically older parts of the brain, and that these systems inform the neocortex in the form of emotional experience and the body in the form of the adaptive/homeostatic responses. Cannon incorrectly identified the old systems with the thalamus. In 1937, the anatomist James Papez suggested a different anatomical basis for emotion in the brain. He noted that the neocortex tends to be reciprocally connected to the thalamus, but that older paleocortical tissues tend to be reciprocally connected with the hypothalamus, which directly controls both the ANS and endocrine systems.[2] Papez reasoned that these paleocortical tissues constitute the cortical representation of emotion. Previously, these tissues had been called the rhinencephalon or "smell brain," because much of their sensory input came from the olfactory apparatus.

Paul D. MacLean (1952) introduced the most widely used contemporary term describing these structures: the *limbic system*. The name derives from the Latin word for "border," and was originally used by French neurologist Paul Broca to describe the way the paleocortical structures surround the brainstem (see Figure 3.7). The limbic system includes the paleocortical tissues of the brain plus the amygdala (Grossmann, 1967). Papez argued that the hypothalamus and limbic system together represent the anatomical basis of emotion, with the hypothalamus responsible for initiating peripheral emotional *arousal* and the limbic system responsible for emotional *experience*. Thus, his theory is closely related to Cannon's conceptualization, with the limbic system taking the place of the thalamus.

MacLean's Triune Theory. MacLean contributed one of the major conceptualizations of how the limbic system functions in emotion and relates to the rest of the brain (MacLean, 1958, 1973, 1990, 1993). Based upon experimental studies of animals and clinical evidence particularly from cases of psychomotor epilepsy, he suggested that the brains of human beings and other advanced mammals reflect three major evolutionary developments, "retaining the anatomy and neurochemistry that relate to the behavior of reptiles, early mammals, and late mammals" (1993, p. 67).

MacLean (2001) noted that all three classes of terrestrial vertebrates – reptiles, birds, and mammals – show a behavioral profile or *ethogram*

---

[2] Cortical tissues consist of *gray matter*: networks of interconnected cells where information processing takes place; as opposed to *white matter*, consisting of pathways going from one place to another. The term *cortex* comes from the Latin for "layered": cortical parts of the brain have a layered structure. The phylogenetically newest *neocortex* has six distinct layers. *Paleocortex* or "old cortex" tissue is also layered but simpler in structure, having 3–5 layers. *Subcortical* tissue is defined as gray matter which is not layered. Subcortical tissues are generally oldest in phylogenetic origin, and are located deep in the brain. Virtually all of the visible outer layers of the human brain consist of neocortex.

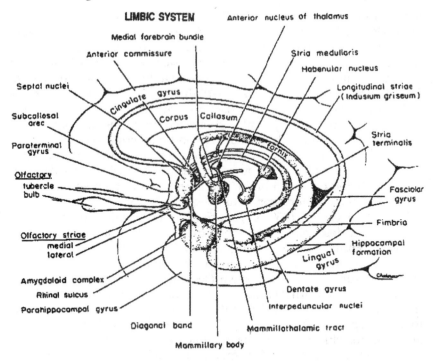

LIMBIC SYSTEM

Figure 3.7 The major limbic system pathways. Note the direct input from the olfactory apparatus, the amygdala and stria terminalis, the hippocampus and fornix terminating in the mammillary body, and the cingulate gyrus. The insula is not shown in this view.

with more than twenty-five like kinds of behavior in common, and he suggested that the "basic animality" that orchestrates the daily *master routine* typical of the species are subserved by the *reptilian brain* (Murphy et al., 1981). The reptilian brain consists of subcortical structures of the basal ganglia, including the caudate, globus pallidus, and putamen (collectively termed the *striatum* because of their striped appearance due to interweaving gray and white matter), the nucleus accumbens (NAcc), olfactory tubercle, and satellite aggregations of gray matter (see Figure 3.8). The master routine serves functions of both species survival (procreation) and individual survival (self-preservation): the creature "does what it has to do" to survive (MacLean, 1993, p. 74). MacLean suggested that the master routine is performed virtually automatically, without felt emotion, unless the performance is thwarted or frustrated.

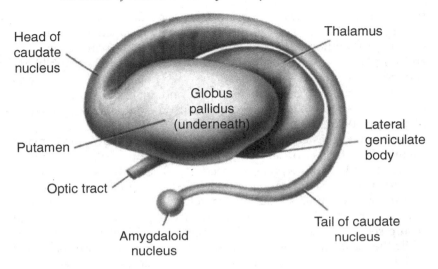

Figure 3.8 Human basal ganglia.

In reptiles such as lizards, the daily master routine is carried out within a domain that includes a home site within a variably sized *territory*, which is itself within a larger *home range*. The territory generally provides food, water, and zones for excreta, and is defended against intrusion; the home range also provides resources but is not defended. Reptilian social behavior is organized by basic displays communicating threat, submission, and courtship. Damage to the reptilian brain in animals eliminates or fragments these displays. The displays of lizards involve, fundamentally, sex and aggression: they include signature (self-assertive), challenge (territorial), appeasement (submissive), and courtship displays. Reptiles are generally born self-sufficient, and in most such species there is no strong requirement for parental behavior or long-term bonds between individuals. The organization of social and sexual behavior in reptiles is facilitated by the neuropeptide *vasotocin*, which controls courting, sexual vocalizations, and birthing (MacDonald and MacDonald, 2010). Vasotocin is also involved in the regulation of social behavior in fish, amphibians, and birds (Moore, 1987; Panksepp, 1993).

The reptilian brain and its associated master routine and displays are also seen in mammals, but with significant additions associated with the evolution of the limbic system, which MacLean (1993) considered the "common denominator in the brains of all mammals" (p. 74). Mammals by definition *must* engage in parental behaviors, including "three cardinal forms of behavior that characterize the evolutionary transition from reptiles to mammals" (MacLean, 1993, p. 74). This "family-related triad" consists of (a) nursing in conjunction with maternal care, (b) audiovocal communication to maintain parental contact, and (c) play. It is noteworthy that the vasotocin of fish, amphibians, and reptiles diverged and evolved into two neuropeptides – *oxytocin* (OXY) which is important in lactation and maternal behavior, and *vasopressin* (AVP) which is associated with male dominance behavior (Panksepp, 1993, 1998).

MacLean suggested that the limbic system includes three major circuits. The first two, labeled 1 and 2 in Figure 3.9, are centered in the amygdala and *septum*, respectively. These can be identified in modern fish: thus they apparently existed in the common ancestors of fish and mammals and are therefore phylogenetically ancient. The *amygdala division* plays a basic role in motives and emotions that ensure self-preservation, including angry/fearful/defensive behavior; while the *septal division* is associated with emotions that are concerned with the preservation of the species, including sociability and sexuality. These circuits have strong connections with the brainstem and the olfactory apparatus, which reflects the importance of the sense of smell in their functioning. It is noteworthy that, although the olfactory apparatus has decreased in relative size over the course of evolution, the size of the septal area increased during primate evolution and reaches its greatest size in human beings (Andy and Stephen, 1968). Also, the septal area both produces and has receptors for OXY and AVP. We shall see that it plays a major role in human prosocial behavior including moral emotions.

The third circuit, the *thalamocingulate division* in Figure 3.9, includes the tract connecting the mammillary bodies in the hypothalamus with the anterior thalamus (AT) and the fibers going on to the cingulate gyrus. This is a phylogenetically newer structure: it is virtually absent in reptiles, and it is not connected with the olfactory apparatus. MacLean suggested that the elaboration of this system during evolution reflects the shift in emphasis from the olfactory to the visual regulation of behavior. The thalamocingulate division is particularly associated with the emotions associated with the preservation of the species involved in the family-related triad: maternal behavior, audiovocal communication, and play.

It is noteworthy that OXY, AVP, and other neurochemicals functioning in limbic system brain structures are associated with emotional displays and reports of subjective affective experiences in human beings. As Panksepp (2002) put it, the "apparently homologous neurochemical codes for many emotional and motivational processes in all mammals [allow] us to go from studies of animal emotional behaviors

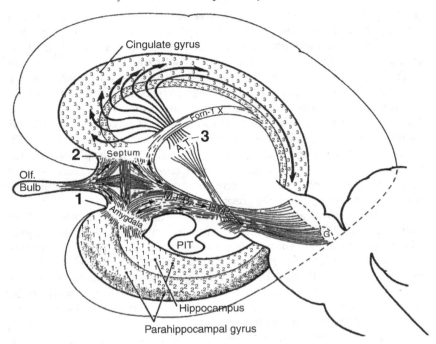

Figure 3.9 MacLean's three subdivisions of the limbic system. MacLean (1993) suggested that the limbic system includes three major circuits. The first two, labeled 1 and 2, include the *amygdala division* which plays a basic role in motives and emotions that ensure self-preservation; and the *septal division* associated with emotions concerned with species preservation. These circuits have strong connections with the brainstem and the olfactory apparatus. The third circuit, the *thalamocingulate division*, includes the tract connecting the mammillary bodies in the hypothalamus with the anterior thalamus (AT) and the fibers going on to the cingulate gyrus; and is associated with the family-related triad of maternal behavior, audiovocal communication, and play. AT = Anterior thalamic nuclei; G = Dorsal and ventral tegmental nuclei of Gudden; HYP = Hypothalamus; MFB = Medial forebrain bundle; PIT = Pituitary gland; OLF = Olfactory bulb.

to human affective experiences" (p. xxv). Moreover, in addition to animal studies, MacLean's triune brain analysis was also informed by clinical observations of reports of subjective emotional experiences in patients with psychomotor epilepsy, a condition characterized by an aura followed by automatic behaviors for which the patient has no memory. As MacLean (2001) noted, "words used in describing the aura add up to a thesaurus of feelings" (p. 84), and these self-reported subjective reports are considered to constitute clinical evidence of an epileptic focus in or near limbic brain structures.

Triune theory has been criticized as oversimplified and outdated by many neuroscientists, as it has been seen to be based on interpretations of brain organization and evolution that are now recognized as faulty (Reiner, 1990; Campbell, 1992). These criticisms have been countered as misrepresenting and oversimplifying MacLean's ideas (Cory, 2002; MacLean, 2001; Panksepp, 2002). Certainly, any implication that brain evolution involves a simple linear hierarchy where fish become amphibians become reptiles become mammals is incorrect. Reptiles did not stop evolving after the reptilian lifestyle was established, and indeed all creatures alive today are evolutionary success stories in their own right that have adapted to specific environmental challenges. Many species of non-mammals demonstrate audiovocal communication, and complex cognitive processing has evolved independently in many species (Patton, 2008). Also, dinosaurs and birds evolved a lifestyle with mechanisms of nurturance quite different from those in mammals, a point that was clearly acknowledged by MacLean (Cory, 2002). Nevertheless, while it is perhaps not useful from the point of view of the technical understanding of brain evolution, triune theory remains compelling as a broad and general organizing theme or heuristic because it relates three levels of brain structure to three distinct stages of evolutionary adaptation (Ploog, 1992), specifically to mammalian evolution which added affectional and other-interested behavior to the primarily self-interested behavior of ancestral vertebrates (Cory, 2002), and because the triune theory explicitly considers the brain bases of the subjective affective aspect of emotion (Panksepp, 2002).

In this regard, Panksepp (2002) and Cory (2002) defended the usefulness of MacLean's conceptualizations (Cory and Gardner, 2002). Panksepp suggested that MacLean's view has been marginalized by some behavioral neuroscientists because "MacLean gives provisional solutions to a problem most behavioral neuroscientists would rather not address" (2002, p. xx), specifically the problem of subjective affective experience. Panksepp also acknowledged that although MacLean's organizational framework for understanding emotions is preliminary and the need for corrections and elaborations is inevitable, "MacLean's insight has proven fundamentally correct" (p. xxiv). Panksepp's position that "raw affective experiences are critically linked to the neurodynamics of sub-neocortical limbic networks" (p. 38) is consistent with the position that affects are emergent phenomena arising from the interactions of specific neurochemical systems: ancestral voices of the genes cajoling, but not controlling, our behavior through our subjectively experienced feelings and desires.

Neurochemical emotion systems:
meta-analyses of human neuroimaging studies

A meta-analysis of human neuroimaging studies is relevant to a contemporary evaluation of MacLean's ideas. Kober et al. (2008) performed a meta-analysis of 162 human neuroimaging studies of emotion, using multivariate statistical techniques to identify consistent patterns of co-activation across studies (Buck, 2012). The data for most of these studies were measures of brain metabolic activity via functional magnetic resonance imaging (fMRI) in situations involving emotion compared with similar situations where no emotion was involved. Differences were assumed to be due to brain metabolic activity associated with the emotional content. This inductive or data-driven technique identified six coherent *functional groups* of co-occurring emotion-related brain activity (Lindquist et al., 2012b). These are summarized in Figure 3.10, redrawn from data presented in Kober et al. (2008).

The Core Limbic group. The first, *Core Limbic* group consists of subcortical and paleocortical structures identified in much animal work on emotion, including the amygdala, hippocampus, and thalamus extending down into the PAG; areas of the ventral striatum and globus pallidus; and lateral hypothalamus. The Core Limbic group includes structures included in the reward-punishment systems we have considered plus structures identified by MacLean with the reptilian brain. The Core Limbic group connects strongly to the next two, both of which include paleocortical structures identified in MacLean's theory with the limbic system.

The Lateral Paralimbic group. The *Lateral Paralimbic* group includes the insula, areas of the ventral striatum and dorsal putamen, hippocampus, orbitofrontal cortex (OFC), and temporal pole and cortex. Kober et al. (2008) suggest that the Lateral Paralimbic group is involved in motivation, with the OFC and ventral striatum particularly contributing to the valuation of stimuli, especially rewards. The insular regions are associated with interoception, being the cortical representation of the viscera and other bodily responses. Insula regions have been associated with both experiencing disgust and recognizing it in others (see Calder et al., 2007; Wicker et al., 2003). The hippocampus was associated with the amygdalar division of the limbic system in MacLean's (1993) conceptualization (see Figure 3.9).

The Medial PFC group. The *Medial PFC* group includes the dorsomedial prefrontal cortex (DMPFC) and anterior cingulate cortex (ACC).

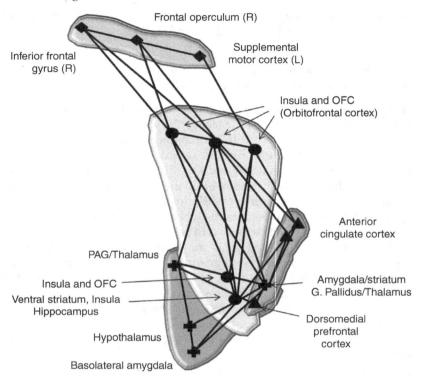

Frontal operculum (R)

Inferior frontal
gyrus (R)

Supplemental
motor cortex (L)

Insula and OFC
(Orbitofrontal cortex)

Anterior
cingulate cortex

PAG/Thalamus

Insula and OFC

Ventral striatum, Insula
Hippocampus

Amygdala/striatum
G. Pallidus/Thalamus

Dorsomedial
prefrontal
cortex

Hypothalamus

Basolateral amygdala

◆ Cognitive-motor group
▲ Medial PFC group
● Lateral paralimbic group
✚ Core limbic group

Figure 3.10 Emotion systems emerging from analyses of
human neuroimaging studies. Consistent with classic
descriptions of the brain systems underlying emotion, the
Core Limbic group includes subcortical and paleocortical
structures involving reward-punishment systems plus reptilian structures: the amygdala, hippocampus, and thalamus extending down into the PAG; areas of the ventral
striatum and globus pallidus; and lateral hypothalamus.
The *Lateral Paralimbic group* includes the insula, areas of
the ventral striatum and dorsal putamen, hippocampus,
orbitofrontal cortex (OFC), and temporal pole and cortex.
The *Medial PFC group* includes the dorsomedial prefrontal
cortex (DMPFC) and anterior cingulate cortex (ACC). This
Figure 3.10 (*cont.*) differentiation of the Lateral Paralimbic
and Medial PFC groups is consistent with MacLean's (1993)
differentiation of individualistic/selfish amygdala and

prosocial/cooperative septal and thalamocingulate circuits within the limbic system (see Figures 3.8 and 3.9). The *Cognitive/Motor group* consists of the right frontal operculum (neocortex covering the insula) and inferior frontal gyrus; and the left pre-supplemental motor cortex.

The ACC has been associated with conflict resolution and empathy, the response to pain including the release of endorphins in response to placebo, and to serotonin-based Type B depression (Behrendt, 2011). The DMPFC has been associated with voluntary emotion regulation, and Lindquist et al. (2012b) suggested that it plays a role in emotion conceptualization. One study has related DMPFC activation to the degree of poignant autobiographical memory experienced during the playing of an excerpt of popular music, suggesting that it is involved with the association of music and emotionally salient memories (Janata, 2009).

Lindquist et al.'s (2012b) differentiation of the Lateral Paralimbic and Medial PFC groups is consistent with MacLean's (1993) differentiation of individualistic/selfish amygdala and prosocial/cooperative septal and thalamocingulate circuits within the limbic system (Buck, 2012; Lindquist et al., 2012a; see Figures 3.9 and 3.10). The Lateral Paralimbic group seems clearly concerned with self-preservation. The ACC in the Medial PFC group was included in MacLean's prosocial thalamo-cingulate circuit based upon stimulation studies, and it indeed is involved in empathy (Decety and Jackson, 2004; Jackson et al., 2006) and audiovocal communication including maternal behavior and distress calls (Behrendt, 2011). This region is also involved in pain regulation, which is relevant to Panksepp's (1991) hypothesis linking social bonding and attachment to pain regulation via the endorphins discussed previously.

The Cognitive/Motor group. The Lateral Paralimbic group in turn is closely connected with the *Cognitive/Motor* group, consisting of the right frontal operculum (neocortex covering the insula) and left pre-supplemental motor cortex; and the inferior frontal gyrus. Kober et al. (2008) suggest that these areas are involved in cognitive control and the voluntary regulation of emotional responses. This seems consistent with evidence summarized earlier that the supplemental motor cortex is involved in the voluntary control and initiation of emotional displays in monkeys (Jurgens, 1979; Ploog, 1981), or pseudospontaneous communication (Buck and Van Lear, 2002).

Medial Posterior and Occipital/Visual Association groups. The *Medial Posterior* group includes the primary visual cortex and posterior cingulate cortex. It is closely connected with the *Occipital/Visual Association* group, which includes cortical regions in the occipital cortex, right occipital/temporal cortex, and cerebellum. Kober et al. (2008) suggest that these two groups are likely to play roles in the visual processing of emotional stimuli (75 percent of the studies included in the meta-analysis used visual stimuli) and are likely not specific to emotion.

The picture emerging from the Kober et al. (2008) analysis is generally consistent with classic descriptions of the brain systems underlying emotion that developed with Broca, Papez, MacLean, and Panksepp, in that it shows a richly interconnected central core of subcortical and paleocortical structures, which in turn interconnect widely with other brain regions including sensory and motor regions (Buck, 2012). Thus the meta-analysis demonstrates the applicability to human behavior of major themes coming out of animal research. Like all meta-analyses, it is only as complete as the studies that have in fact been conducted and that are included in the analysis. Thus 75 percent of the Kober et al. studies used visual stimuli, and that fact may have magnified the apparent importance of the Medial Posterior and Occipital/Visual Association groups. Different stimulus modes may produce different groupings of networks of co-occurring activity. On the other hand, this problem applies more to the peripheral networks: the central networks replicate many aspects of previous research including the differentiation by MacLean into a reptilian circuit and two limbic circuits.

More specifically, the extensively interconnected Core-Limbic, Lateral Limbic, and Medial PFC groups seem analogous to the reptilian, selfish-limbic, and prosocial-limbic divisions suggested by MacLean largely on the basis of studies of nonhuman primates. This is a remarkable convergence of evidence derived as it is from studies using significantly dissimilar participants and methodologies. The implication is that MacLean's triune theory may well merit Panksepp's (2002) description as "not mere speculation but a superb theoretical structure, with abundant predictions, built upon a solid functional body of data from an extensive study of the functional systems of our brethren species" (p. x).

A meta-analysis of discrete emotion categories. Kober et al. (2008; Lindquist et al., 2012b) noted that the patterns they discovered do not correspond to discrete emotion categories such as happiness, sadness, fear, anger, or disgust. They suggested instead that these categories "result from the interplay of more basic psychological processes" and that the nature of these processes is "a matter for scientific discovery" (2008, p. 1000). The Kober et al. position is actually compatible with the notion that discrete emotion categories are meaningful at the ecological but not necessarily the biological level, and at the biological level the meaningful units are specific neurochemical modules or primary motivational-emotional systems (primes) that are widely distributed in the brain. It is noteworthy that the definition of the primes is consistent with the notion of "basic psychological processes" as described by Kober et al. (2008) and Linquist et al. (2012b; see Buck, 1985; 2012). These combine in various ways to form the symphony of experienced affect.

Another approach to the meta-analysis of human neuroimaging studies, which was explicitly designed to evaluate whether discrete emotion categories are associated with dissociable patterns of activation in the brain, was reported by Vytall and Hamann (2010). The structure found by Kober et al. (2008) was data-driven and did not consider emotion labels. In contrast, Vytall and Hamann included only studies that analyzed at least one of the discrete emotions of happiness, sadness, fear, anger, or disgust in healthy participants. Their results were consistent with basic emotion theory. First, each emotion was characterized by consistent neural correlates across studies. Second, the activation patterns associated with each emotion were discrete, that is, discriminable from the other emotions in pairwise contrasts. Third, the activation patterns overlapped with results obtained using other approaches, providing "converging evidence that discrete basic emotions have consistent and discriminable neural correlates" (Vytall and Hamann, 2010, p. 2864).

Evaluation. The results of Kober et al. (2008) and Vytall and Hamann (2010) are arguably complementary. Neither supports the notion that discrete emotion categories are represented in specific anatomical locations in the brain: this position is oversimplified and maintained by no one. The discriminable clusters of neural systems associated with discrete emotion terms by Vytall and Hamann were distributed across the brain. As we learn more about the specific neurochemicals associated with these clusters, more may be learned about the biological bases of the subjective experiences associated with the basic emotions. From the point of view of subjective experience of emotion being analogous to a cocktail or symphony of feelings, the Vytall and Hamann approach might be compared to combining many recipes to find what is common in the recipe of a given cocktail: of a Mojito, Bloody Mary, Margarita, etc.; or Bach, Beethoven, Stravinsky symphonies. While arguably capturing the "essence" of these cocktails or symphonies, this misses the variability that can be built into intoxicating mixed drinks, symphonies, and subjectively experienced feelings and desires associated with basic emotions. Also, it might be commented that

Vytall and Hamann included only those basic emotions associated with universally recognized facial expressions. These are selfish-competitive emotions displayed at a distance and do not include emotions displayed primarily by body posture, such as dominant and submissive emotions; nor do they include prosocial/cooperative emotions displayed by intimate touch, physical distance, contact comfort, pheromones, and the like.

The remainder of this section is organized into the analysis of selfish-competitive versus prosocial-cooperative biological emotions at two levels: the reptilian-subcortical which is largely unconscious and the mammalian-paleocortical which involves subjectively experienced affects.

Reptilian emotions: sex and violence

The reptilian brain. MacLean (1993) traced the reptilian ethogram to the evolution of the amniote egg, which made it possible for the first time for animals to adapt to an entirely terrestrial existence. Taking the lizard as representative, this basic behavioral profile included its "master daily routine" and its communicative displays: self-assertive signature displays, territorial displays, submissive displays, and courting displays. A male lizard will establish a territory and defend it against intrusion by other males, but will display courting signals to attract females. When joined by a female, a nest will be constructed and eggs laid and fertilized. At this point the parents leave the territory and the young, when they emerge from their egg, are on their own. Inspection of the displays suggests that a kind of "raw" sex and violence characterizes the social organization of the reptiles and serves individual and species survival in birds and mammals as well, including human beings.

Lesions to the basal ganglia in lizards and monkeys cause selective disruption of communicative displays. Moreover, symptoms in diseases in human beings which affect the corpus striatum, such as Huntington's disease and Sydenham's chorea, include deficits in planning and organizing daily activities, and ritualistic obsessive-compulsive behaviors. MacLean noted that in human beings compulsive acts are "notably unaccompanied by emotional feelings" and that the performance of the daily routine "occurs almost automatically, as though propelled by propensities without associated emotion unless the intended acts are thwarted or meet with frustration" (1993, p. 73). Many of MacLean's reptilian brain structures are included in the Core-Limbic grouping of Kober et al. (2008).

Reptilian aggression: an illustration. Reptilian aggression differs from paleomammalian anger in terms of its compulsive and apparently uncontrollable quality. The well-known case of Charles Whitman offers an anecdotal illustration. This University of Texas graduate student wrote a letter on the night of July 31, 1966 which stated in part:

> I don't understand what it is that compels me to type this letter ...
> I have been a victim of many unusual and irrational thoughts. These
> thoughts constantly recur, and it requires a tremendous mental effort
> to concentrate on useful and progressive tasks ... After my death
> I wish that an autopsy would be performed on me to see if there is
> any visible physical disorder ... It was after much thought that
> I decided to kill my wife, Kathy, tonight after I pick her up from
> work ... I love her dearly, and she has been as fine a wife to me
> as any man could ever hope to have. I cannot rationally pinpoint
> any specific reason for doing this ... I intend to kill her as painlessly
> as possible. (Cited in Johnson, 1972, p. 78)

That night, Whitman killed his wife and mother, and the next morning he purchased two pistols, three rifles, a shotgun, and about 600 rounds of ammunition. He then climbed a commanding tower on the University of Texas campus and began to fire on those below. He killed fourteen more and wounded thirty-two before he was killed by police. An autopsy revealed a highly malignant, slow-growing tumor in the right hemisphere basal ganglia near the amygdala.

It is noteworthy that there was no evidence of rage, anger, or strong emotion of any kind in the description of Whitman's actions. Rather, his actions were methodical, calm, and appropriate enough that he was able after killing his wife and mother to purchase a small arsenal on credit. The letter suggests that Whitman was in the grip of a compulsion that *accomplished irresistible control of his violent intentions and goals without influencing the higher-level rational control of his moment-to-moment actions and verbal statements.* That compulsion led to ruthless and merciless violence that was not accompanied by rage or anger, or indeed by any strongly experienced emotional feeling.

Compulsive sex and violence. There are other examples of compulsive violent and also sexual behavior that do not seem to be accompanied by felt affect. Psychomotor or temporal lobe epilepsy (TLE) is a brain seizure condition which does not result in convulsions, but rather an aura followed by a loss of consciousness where apparently purposeful behavior may continue. In TLE, the patient may experience a variety of emotional feelings, including those that "come into play in the struggle for survival ... hunger, thirst, nausea, suffocation, choking ... which may be conjoined with a variety of intense emotional feelings such as terror, fear, anger, sadness, foreboding, strangeness, and paranoid feelings" (MacLean, 1973, pp. 14–15). TLE seizures typically last a few seconds or minutes but may last hours or days. A patient may look at a clock and realize that hours had passed and have no memory of events that transpired. One man, driving a trailer truck, blacked out in Los Angeles and did not wake up until he was near Reno, Nevada (Mark and Ervin, 1970). The medial temporal lobe including the amygdala is particularly susceptible to TLE attacks.

A small minority of TLE seizures have been associated· with bizarre antisocial behavior. Mark and Ervin (1970) described several examples, one of which involved a young woman, Julia, who suffered psychomotor seizures and had woken up several times in unfamiliar surroundings, so she carried a knife for self-protection. One night at age 18 she was at a movie with her parents, when she recognized the familiar aura signaling an attack coming. She went to the ladies' lounge, and automatically took out the knife from her purse. Inside the lounge another woman inadvertently brushed against Julia's arm. Julia struck viciously with the knife, penetrating the other woman's heart. The ensuing scream alerted Julia's father, a physician, who fortunately was able to save her life. Later, Julia drove a pair of scissors into the lung of a nurse, and had assaulted twelve people by age 21.

Julia was referred for a depth electrode protocol which can be an effective treatment for intractable TLE that does not respond to drug treatments (Keysers and Gazzola, 2010). Electrodes were placed in a number of likely regions, and recordings revealed seizure activity in the amygdala. These regions were then remotely stimulated on two occasions. On one, Julia was peacefully strumming on a guitar, and when the amygdala was stimulated she violently smashed the guitar; on the other, she scowled and hurled herself against the wall in apparent rage. Selective lesioning of these epileptogenic regions using a higher current applied through the same electrodes ended the attacks.

Another example from Mark and Ervin (1970) was a girl aged 14 named Jennie, who had murdered two younger siblings because she could not stand their crying. A thorough medical and psychiatric examination found no abnormality, but depth electrode studies identified seizure activity in the amygdala and hippocampus region. A recording of a baby crying produced seizure activity and angry and anxious expressive displays. It is significant that this seizure activity was not apparent from electrodes placed on the scalp, and indeed a depth electrode placed 1 mm away failed to pick up the seizure. Mark and Ervin (1970) suggested four behavioral symptoms as markers for hidden brain disease: (1) violent physical assault such as spousal beating, (2) pathological intoxication where the drinking of small amounts of alcohol triggers violence, (3) many traffic violations and accidents, and (4) impulsive sexual behavior.

Anneliese Pontius (2002) suggested the label Limbic Psychotic Trigger Reaction (LPTR) for a condition which unlike TLE does not involve a loss of consciousness, but involves limbic seizures triggering apparently motiveless homicides. These episodes typically are atavistically regressive acts that are unplanned, unpremeditated, brief-lasting, out-of-character, and performed with flat affect by a lone individual, typically against a stranger who happens to provide a "trigger stimulus," a memory of a past mild-to-moderate stress. She described twenty-one bizarre cases that fit no other known diagnosis. In one example, a man who had been the only one of five brothers who did not fulfill his father's wish of becoming an officer in the armed services fatally stabbed a female stranger while she was talking about her husband and son being officers in the armed forces. In another, a man whose wife spoke approvingly of a restaurant owner shot and killed the owner and shot at other persons after seeing his wife's car near the restaurant. The violent acts were recalled fully and with remorse, with the individual often voluntarily reporting their crimes, taking full responsibility, not blaming others, and sometimes undertaking serious suicidal acts.

Pontius differentiated LPTR from bizarre acts that have been committed by schizophrenic men, including two dismemberment murders in which the perpetrators tried to create an ancient-god-like male/female combination of their victims; and three firesetters who sought to unite extreme opposites by fire. She noted that these behaviors reflect the acting-out of basic themes shared by ancient myths and rituals worldwide. The uneducated men who committed these acts were unaware of these myths, suggesting that these patterns may reveal "built-in constraints of subjective experience" (2002, p. 183) that are universal, resembling Jungian archetypes (Jung, 1977). In contrast, the acts associated with LPTR do not resemble archetypical themes: rather they resemble primitive animal-like patterns of predatory or defensive killing and destruction. Nevertheless, Pontius (2002) noted that the archetypical patterns found in some schizophrenics and the animalistic patterns found in LPTR both imply a "hard-wired organic basis for species-specific patterns of experience and behavior even in humans" (p. 183), and these patterns critically involve limbic brain structures.

Whatever the specific brain systems underlying violent behavior, there is evidence for an additional common risk factor across many sorts of murder – involving strangers, friends, or family members; carefully planned or apparently random actions; done for profit or apparently motiveless; involving mass murders or individual killings; with male or female perpetrators – and that factor is early abuse and neglect. Neurologist Jonathan Pincus reported on his examination of some 150 murderers, and found that, despite differences between the crimes, there were common factors of early abuse that generated a combination of disordered attachment and violent impulses; plus neurological and psychiatric brain diseases that impaired the ability to inhibit and control such impulses (Pincus, 2001). The normal course of brain development can be distorted by abuse, neglect, and emotional deprivation. This is not a question of the relative influence of innate versus environmental factors, for the innate factors emerge and must be nurtured over the process of development, particularly early development, if they are to be successfully realized. The genetic endowment of the individual – the *encoded genotype* – can be twisted by a lack of normal expressed affection and presence of brutal mistreatment, and like the coyote–beagle hybrids described by Moon-Fanelli (2011), the expression of the genes – the *effective genotype* – is altered and in this case deformed by environmental experience. As Pincus put it: "There is a window, the first two years of life, during which an infant must receive a parental 'love bath,' or be at risk, permanently, of suffering the effects of this early deprivation" (2001, p. 125). We shall examine other examples of the importance of early care and contact in essentially "nurturing the genome" in Chapter 4.

Limbic system emotions: selfish and prosocial

The limbic system conception of emotion has three aspects: anatomical, evolutionary, and functional. First, the limbic system is classically defined as comprised of paleocortical structures (old cortex or allocortex, comprising stratified brain tissue with three to five definable layers) plus the amygdala (Grossman, 1967). Paleocortical structures include the hippocampus, septal area, insula, parahippocampal gyrus, and cingulate gyrus (see Figure 3.7). Second, as we have seen, these structures were related to the broader evolutionary context as paleomammalian in MacLean's (1993) triune theory. These brain structures define a higher hierarchical level of organization compared with the subcortical structures associated with the reptilian brain. Third, these structures are related functionally to emotion, and particularly to Emotion III subjective affective experience in at least three ways: (1) as considered in Chapter 2, drugs associated with agonistic or antagonistic effects on the neurochemical systems associated with these structures produce reports of subjectively experienced affects; (2) subjective affects are often experienced in epileptic aura stemming from abnormal seizure activity in these structures; and (3) electrical stimulation of these structures produces reports of subjective affective experiences. The latter is illustrated by the following example.

Limbic system and affect: an anecdotal illustration. Some of the most persuasive evidence that the limbic system is associated with subjectively experienced affect comes from observations in human beings of the effects of electrical stimulation. The behavior of persons stimulated in limbic systems structures such as the amygdala can be quite different from compulsive aggression. Here there is evidence of subjective affect without the behavioral compulsion: although the *feelings* are uncontrolled, they are not acted upon. Individuals seem to maintain considerable control of their *goal-directed behavior*.

This is illustrated in an interview conducted by King (1961, pp. 484–85), during which the amygdala of a woman with epilepsy was stimulated. The woman sat with the interviewer, and the amygdala was stimulated via telemetry. The interviewer questioned the subject about how she feels.

SUBJECT: "I just feel like everything is all wrong. Like I can't be a part of anything. Like I didn't belong and everything is a dream or something."

INTERVIEWER: "Did you feel this way before the operation?" (*He is referring to the implanting of electrodes.*)

SUBJECT: "Yeah I felt the same way. I didn't want anything and I didn't belong anymore." (*The subject's voice tone was extremely flat and lacking in emphasis. Her facial expression was blank and unchanging.*)

The region of the amygdala was then stimulated by a 5 ma. current.

INTERVIEWER: "How do you feel now?"

SUBJECT: (*Voice much higher in tone*) "I feel like I want to get up from this chair! Please don't let me do it!" (*There is a change to strong voice inflection and marked alteration in facial expression to express pleading.*) "Don't do this to me. I don't want to be mean!"

INTERVIEWER: "Feel like you want to hit me?"

SUBJECT: "Yeah, I just want to hit something." (*Appears and sounds aroused and angry*) "I want to get something and just tear it up. Take it so I won't" (*She hands her scarf to interviewer; he hands her a stack of paper, and without further verbal exchange she tears it to shreds.*) "I don't like to feel like this!"

The level of stimulating current was then reduced to 4 ma.

SUBJECT: (*Immediately changing to wide smile*) "I know it's silly, what I'm doing."

INTERVIEWER: "Now feel better?"

SUBJECT: "A little bit."

INTERVIEWER: "Can you tell me any more about how you were feeling a moment ago?"

SUBJECT: "I wanted to get up from this chair and run. I wanted to hit something; tear up something – anything. Not you, just anything. I had no control of myself."

The level of stimulating current was then increased to 5 ma. again.

SUBJECT: (*Voice loud and pleading*) "Don't let me hit you!"

INTERVIEWER: "How do you feel now?"

SUBJECT: "I think I feel a little better like this. I get it out of my system. I don't have those other thoughts (*her pre-existing mental symptoms*) when I'm like this . . .Take my blood pressure. Make them cut this thing off, its killing me! Take my blood pressure, I say!" (*Strong voice inflection and facial appearance of anger*) "Quit holding me! I'm getting up! You'd better get someone else if you want to hold me! I'm going to hit you!" (*Raises arm as if to strike*).

The stimulating current was then reduced to 4 ma.

SUBJECT: (*Wide smile and laugh*) "Why does it make me do this? I couldn't help it. I didn't have any control. I wanted to slap your face. I don't like to be done like that." (*Voice relaxed, tone apologetic*)

When stimulated, the woman's voice rose and she displayed and apparently experienced strong anger, but she maintained considerable control of her behavior. This pattern of strong and *uncontrollable affective experience*, combined with some ability to *control and choose how one responds* to this experience, contrasts with the lack of affect but compulsive and uncontrollable behavior exemplified by Charles Whitman and the cases of LPTR, and exemplifies the cajoling of behavior by voices of the ancient genes. This is the hallmark of the hierarchical level of primes associated with subjectively experienced affects, and it is essential to the *controlled* expression and communication of emotion that is arguably critical to complex social life (Buck and Powers, 2013).

Selfish affects and the amygdala circuit. Interest in the amygdala can be traced to the *Klüver–Bucy syndrome*, which results when the amygdala is removed bilaterally (Klüver and Bucy, 1937, 1938, 1939). Animals which have undergone this procedure generally demonstrate a striking lack of evidence of anger, fear, and disgust. Defensive aggressive responses disappear; flight responses vanish even to stimuli such as snakes and fire which are innately feared in monkeys; the affected animal mouths even such distasteful and painful stimuli as dirt, feces, rocks, and burning matches. Amygdalectomized human beings show analogous patterns of response (Terzian and Dalle Ore, 1955; Buck, 1988a). Stimulation of the amygdala produces effects generally opposite to those of lesions, producing rage-like attack and fear-like defensive behaviors in a variety of species including human beings such as in the illustration given previously (King, 1961). We saw that LeDoux and colleagues demonstrated direct sensory input to the amygdala to be necessary for the "low road" to cognition and the learning of conditioned fear responses. LeDoux (1993) concluded that the amygdala is essential in the "assignment of affective significance to sensory events" (p. 110).

Prosocial affects and the septal and cingulate circuits. Stimulation and lesioning of the septal and cingulate areas produce responses that are strikingly different from manipulations of the amygdala. Septal stimulation in human beings has been associated with positive affect, often with a sexual tinge. Heath (1964) reported the results of a study of septal stimulation in fifty-four patients with depth electrodes. Stimulation was typically delivered during interviews without the patient's knowledge, similar to King's (1961) illustration of amygdala stimulation. Septal stimulation often produced positive changes in the interview, with expressions of depression and despair changing to optimism and reports of pleasant experiences, and patients were typically at a loss to explain their sudden change in thinking. For example, one patient, on the verge of tears,

> described his father's near-fatal illness and condemned himself as somehow responsible, but when the septal region was stimulated, he immediately terminated this conversation and within 15 seconds exhibited a broad grin as he discussed plans to date and seduce a girlfriend. When asked why he had changed the conversation so abruptly, he replied that the plans concerning the girl suddenly came to him. (Heath, 1964, p. 225)

MacLean suggested that the septal area is concerned with "primal sexual functions and behavior conducive to procreation" (1993, p. 77). He reported that following septal stimulation a patient reported "I have a glowing feeling. I feel good" (1973, p. 16).

Gray (1982a, 1982b) suggested that the medial septal area is involved in inhibition by driving theta-rhythm brain waves from the hippocampus, which in turn influences the BIS under overall executive control of the frontal cortex. He termed this the septal-hippocampal-frontal (SHF) system. Septal lesions produce temporary viciousness and disinhibitory effects (Grossman, 1967). Gorenstein and Newman (1980) suggested that these symptoms in animals are similar to what they termed "disinhibitory psychopathology" in humans, including an insensitivity to punishment (feared stimuli become effective only when they are immediately at hand) and poor impulse control in the face of rewards (leading to an inability to delay gratification). They suggested that this condition applies to many disorders including psychopathy, hysteria, impulsivity, and hyperactivity. I examine these issues further in Chapter 7, in discussing moral emotions.

As noted, MacLean (1993) suggested that the thalamocingulate circuit functions in a "family-related triad that distinguishes the transition from reptiles to mammals" (p. 77): nursing and maternal care, audio-vocal communication, and play (see Figure 3.9). Panksepp (1991) suggested that the pain mechanism was elaborated to support social bonding. We saw in Chapter 2 that pain is modulated by the opiates, and also discussed the role of the opiates in addiction. Panksepp's suggestion implies that human beings are, in a very real sense, "addicted to love." It is noteworthy that the ACC is activated by painful stimuli via the medial thalamus (Zhuo, 2008), it has a high concentration of opiate receptors, and it is associated with pain-related vocalizations including distress vocalizations and separation cries (Behrendt, 2011). In Chapter 7, we shall see that in human subjects, social rejection and humiliation manipulated by exclusion have been associated with ACC activation, paralleling results from studies of physical pain (Eisenberger et al., 2003). Moreover, cingulate lesions have been found to interfere with maternal behavior (Slotnick, 1967; Stamm, 1955), and play (Murphy et al., 1981).

Play is a fundamental process – a vehicle for the development of complex social abilities – that occurs even in the absence of the neocortex (MacDonald, 1993; Panksepp, 1996). Birds and mammals including dolphins, monkeys, and humans adjust vocalizations in response to group influences, with both aggression and affiliation being important in the process. Play is central to the establishment of early peer relationships that are critical for later socio-emotional functioning (Harlow, 1971), and play deprivation produces significant social deficits that may be secondary to deficits in emotional communication and emotional education (Harlow and Mears, 1983; Miller et al., 1967).

Selfishness/prosociality and political orientation. The amygdala is particularly important in the selfish emotions and the ACC in the prosocial emotions, and it is interesting in view of this that there is evidence that the relative sizes of these regions have been related to political orientation. Kanai et al. (2011) found a correlation between larger size of the amygdala in young adults with a right-wing political orientation, versus a larger size of the ACC in those with a left-wing political orientation. This is consistent with other evidence that conservatives are often motivated by threat, fear, and anger, and "bleeding heart" liberals by empathy and sympathy. We return to this evidence in Chapter 7. It should be noted this does not suggest that brain size necessarily determines political orientation. Indeed the causal relationship may be the opposite: it is conceivable that those who regularly think and feel a certain way will foster the development of brain structures whose functioning reflects those priorities.

The neocortex

The *neocortex* (new cortex) consists of brain tissue with six definable layers. The neocortex covers most of the outside of the brain, so that in the human brain, virtually the only tissues visible from the outside are neocortical, with the structurally simpler paleocortical tissues buried within. The neocortex is organized into folds, with ridges termed gyri (singular *gyrus*) separated by furrows termed fissures or sulci (singular *sulcus*). The posterior parts of the neocortex (occipital, and parietal lobes) are separated from anterior parts (frontal lobes) by the central sulcus, a large furrow. The temporal lobes are to either side, separated from the rest of the brain on each side by the lateral or Sylvian fissure. Different areas of the neocortex have been identified based on their microstructure as numbered *Brodmann areas* (BAs, see Figure 3.11).

Posterior parts of the brain are generally associated with sensory functions. In the temporal lobe the *primary auditory cortex* on the superior temporal gyrus receives input via subcortical nuclei from the cochlea of the ear. In the occipital lobe at the back of the brain, the *primary visual cortex* receives input from the retina, also relayed via subcortical nuclei. The *primary olfactory cortex* mediating the sense of smell is in the *uncus* of the *piriform* region of the temporal lobes; and the *primary gustatory cortex* mediating the sense of taste is in the insular cortex. The *primary somatosensory cortex* is on the postcentral gyrus in the anterior parietal lobes, just posterior to the central sulcus. Specific areas of the body are associated with specific areas of the somatic sensory cortex, so that a sensation in the arm is associated with brain activity in a different place than the leg, for example. More sensitive areas of the body are associated with larger brain areas on the post-central gyrus, so that it is possible to produce a *sensory homunculus* with body areas proportional to their associated brain areas, as we saw in the discussion of the pyramidal motor system. Surrounding the sensory regions are *association areas* which organize raw sensory information to produce meaningful perceptual experiences.

In contrast, the frontal lobes that comprise the anterior parts of the brain are generally associated with motor functions, including the executive regulation of planning and action. The pre-central gyrus

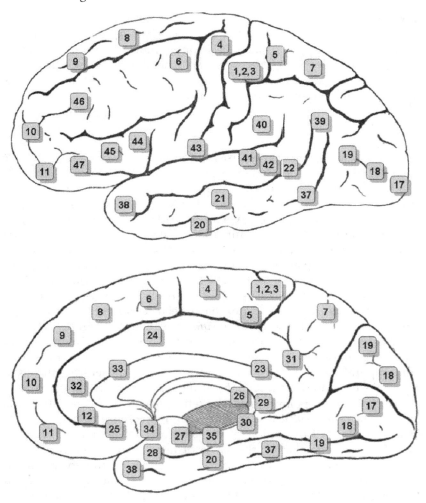

Figure 3.11 Brodmann areas. Brodmann areas (BAs) are regions of the cerebral cortex defined based on the structure and organization of cells. Wernicke's area is associated with the posterior part of BA 22; Broca's area is associated with BA 44 and 45.

anterior to the central sulcus is the primary motor cortex. As noted in the discussion of the pyramidal motor system, areas of the pre-central gyrus are devoted to more precise motor functions.

Classical language areas. Two areas of the left neocortex have been associated with language in most persons (over 90 percent). Part of BA

22 in the left posterior cortex near the primary sensory cortex for audition comprises the association area of the classic auditory cortex and has been termed *Wernicke's area*. As first described by Carl Wernicke (1874, 1875/1995), damage to this area can cause deficits in comprehending speech and language, although the person can still speak and write. One patient with this condition was asked by a neurologist to explain the proverb, "It's always darkest before the dawn." The patient answered, "Don't mix ions with ions." The neurologists asked, "What are ions?" and the patient answered by spelling "I. . .n. . .I.a.o.n. . ." The neurologist asked, "Is that some kind of metal?" and the patient answered, "Sure!" The patient could speak clearly and there appeared to be a kind of internal organization of what he saying, but it was "word salad" that did not make sense and did not relate to the proverb. This pattern of reduced comprehension while retaining the ability to speak is termed *Wernicke's aphasia* or *receptive aphasia*. Often such patients do not comprehend the degree to which they have lost the ability to communicate.

It is quite different when damage occurs in the BA 44/45 in the left frontal cortex, anterior to the part of the motor neocortex that controls the mouth, tongue, pharynx, and larynx. This is termed *Broca's area*, and its anatomical location suggests that it is involved in voluntary expression formation. The pattern of results of damage to this area was first described by Paul Broca (1861), and typically includes problems with expressing speech and language, although the person can still comprehend. One patient with this condition was asked by a neurologist to point to an object on the wall that measures the passage of time, and he immediately pointed to a wall clock. Upon being asked to name the clock, the patient could not and was obviously frustrated by his inability to do so. This pattern combining the inability to speak and write while retaining comprehension is termed *Broca's aphasia* or *expressive aphasia*.

Agnosia. *Agnosia* is a disorder of recognition where the ability to identify familiar objects, persons, sounds, smells, etc. is lost without any dysfunction in the specific sense involved: elementary perception is intact but "stripped of meaning" (Bauer, 1984, p. 457). Also as noted, each of the primary sensory areas of the brain has a linked association area nearby. Agnosias often occur when sensory and association areas are disconnected. A sensory stimulus is perceived normally but the individual cannot recognize it: that is, past associations with the stimulus are lost and they cannot usually be regained. As suggested in Chapter 1, knowledge by acquaintance (KA) of the stimulus is intact but knowledge by description (KD) is lost. Such disorders are termed *disconnection syndromes* (Geschwind, 1979).

The primary visual cortex and visual association area are in the occipital lobe at the back (posterior) of the brain. When these are disconnected, a version of agnosia termed *prosopagnosia* may result, in which the individual cannot recognize the faces of familiar persons (the self, the spouse, famous persons) even though the face is perceived normally. The sudden and frightening onset of prosopagnosia in a patient who suffered a stroke while talking to his speech therapist was described by Lhermitte et al. (1972, p. 339):

> He suddenly realized that he could no longer "recognize" the young woman in front of him. He exclaimed . . . "But Miss, what is happening to me? I can no longer recognize you!". . . (He) could still see the young woman and . . . knew that he was speaking to her and that she must be his speech therapist. . . When she spoke, however, he recognized her and remembered their previous associations from her voice.

The primary auditory cortex is in the temporal lobe just below the lateral fissure, next to the auditory association area that on the left side in human beings has been identified as Wernicke's area. Receptive or Wernicke's aphasia, in which the comprehension of language is disrupted, may be a kind of auditory agnosia caused by the disconnection of the auditory association area from the primary auditory cortex.

Mirror neurons. We noted in Chapter 1 that certain mirror neurons fire when an individual is performing an action or experiencing an emotion, and also fire when that individual observes someone else performing that action or expressing that emotion; and I suggested that they reflect preattunements to emotion displays. Mirror neurons were discovered by Di Pellegrino and colleagues (1992) after it was noticed that neurons in the ventral premotor cortex of monkeys which fire during hand movement also fired when the monkey observed a researcher reaching for food. As Gallese et al. (2004) put it, "although we do not overtly reproduce the observed action, part of our motor system becomes active 'as if' we were executing that very same action that we are observing" (p. 397). Kohler et al. (2002) found that mirror neurons were activated by the sounds as well as the sight of activities. Gazzola et al. (2007) found that when an industrial robot was observed to "pick up" an object, mirror neurons associated with picking up an object were activated even though the kinematics of "picking up" were different in robot and human. Gazzola et al. suggested that the mirror neurons appear to be responding to the perceived goals and intentions of the action: "The goal alone, without matching kinematics, is sufficient to activate our mirror neuron system" (2007, p. 1682).

The evidence suggests that mirror neurons allow us to detect the intentions of others – even robots – directly and immediately via visual and auditory information. There is also evidence that mirror neurons afford the detection of the emotions of others via their displays, and investigators have suggested that mirror neurons are involved in empathy (Decety and Jackson, 2004; Preston and de Waal, 2002; Gallese, 2001; Keysers, 2011). For example, Wicker et al. (2003) exposed participants to disgusting odors, then films of the facial expressions of others smelling the disgusting or a pleasant odor. Viewing the disgusted facial expressions activated a region of the anterior insula also activated when actually smelling the disgusting odors. Similarly, participants' neural responses when they experienced pain personally were comparable to when they observed a loved one present in the same room experiencing the pain (Singer, 2006; Singer et al., 2004).

In monkeys, mirror neurons have been observed in inferior frontal and inferior parietal regions: specifically the ventral premotor cortex (VPMC) and inferior parietal lobule (IPL: Keysers and Gazzola, 2010). Gallese et al. (1996) proposed that the VPMC region in the monkey brain is homologous with Broca's area. The reality of mirror neurons in the human brain has been questioned by some because single-unit recording is ordinarily not possible for ethical reasons, so research in human beings using fMRI, for example, has typically been described in terms of mirror neuron *systems* rather than mirror neurons per se. However, Mukamel et al. (2010) studied twenty-one patients undergoing depth electrode study for epilepsy. These patients had electrodes placed in likely epileptogenic areas for clinical reasons. The patients were shown movies of smiles, frowns, precision finger grips, and hand grips; and were asked to perform these actions by presenting the words "smile," "frown," "finger," and "hand." Mukamel et al. found neurons in human beings that acted exactly like classic mirror neurons studied in animals, discharging during both the observation and execution of one specific action but not another. Mirror neurons were identified in the supplemental motor cortex, entorhinal cortex, hippocampus, and parahippocampal gyrus. Mukamel et al. (2010) also found "anti-mirror" neurons in the supplemental motor cortex that increased when a given action was performed but *decreased* when the same action was observed. Keysers and Gazzola (2010) noted that anti-mirror neurons could disambiguate actions of self from the actions of others and selectively block automatic motor imitation. They also pointed out that fMRI recordings would be blind to the difference between mirror and anti-mirror neurons, because the fMRI is sensitive to changes in metabolism and both excitation and inhibition consume energy.

The discovery of mirror neurons is arguably among the most important recent developments in neuroscience because of its implications for communication. As Gallese et al. (2004) put it, "social cognition is not only thinking about the contents of someone else's mind … Our brains, and those of other primates, appear to have developed a basic functional mechanism, a mirror mechanism, which gives us an experiential insight into other minds" (p. 401). This experiential insight arguably results from the action of mirror neuron-based preattunements to displays, that is, from spontaneous communication (Buck and Powers, 2011; Powers et al., 2007). We experience the intentions and feelings of others immediately, directly, and intuitively: in Gibsonian terms a direct perception or "pickup" of meaning via socio-emotional affordances (Gibson, 1966, 1979). This notion is controversial, because the idea that the perception of the intentions and emotions of others – "knowledge of other minds" – may be coded at the level of individual neurons flies in the face of much Western philosophy. As Churchland and Winkielman (2012) put it, "a neuron, though computationally complex, is just a neuron. It is not an intelligent homunculus" (p. 142). However, perhaps what is in operation is not just a neuron, but an evolved *communicative system* involving genetically based displays in the sender and genetically based preattunements in the receiver. Mirror neurons may be readouts of communicative genes (Buck, 2011; Buck and Ginsburg, 1991).

Frontal lobe functions. It has long been known that damage to the frontal lobes, or *prefrontal cortex* (PFC), can produce serious deficits in decision-making, emotional processing, and social skills. This may be attributable to an overall insensitivity to future consequences, an inability to generate normal emotional responses to events, or both. Part of the PFC, the *orbitofrontal cortex* (OFC) is involved in the processing of incentive or reward value. The OFC is in the front of the brain immediately above the eyes (Brodmann areas [BA] 10, 11, and 47), and receives strong inputs from the amygdala. Damage to the OFC in humans, particularly in childhood, can lead to diminished inhibition and severe antisocial and reckless behavior or "rash impulsiveness" (Andersson et al., 1999).

Bechara and Damasio's *Somatic Marker Hypothesis* (2005) stated that the positive or negative incentive values associated with appraisal and decision-making are stored as *somatic markers* in the ventromedial prefrontal cortex (VMPFC), which includes the OFC. Activation of these markers produces bodily feelings that contribute to decision-making. Also as noted in the discussion of the James–Lange theory, Rolls (1999) countered that the involvement of peripheral somatic processes is unnecessary, and that brain activity in the OFC and amygdala, and brain structures connected with them, is related to felt emotion directly.

Decision-making involves choosing an optimal course of action when multiple alternatives are available. Usually, such choices involve *risk,* defined as uncertainty about outcomes whose probability is known (Loewenstein et al., 2008). Traditional economic theories suggest that human beings are rational actors motivated to maximize the expected utility of outcomes. However, there is much evidence that the traditional model of humans as *homo economicus* is incomplete. For example, the *risk as feelings hypothesis* suggests that when there is tension between rational evaluations and feelings, behavior tends to be determined by the feelings anticipated as outcome at the point of the decision (Loewenstein et al., 2001). I consider the role of the frontal lobes in decision-making and risk, including differences between purely logical decisions and decisions with emotional and moral significance, in later chapters.

Lieberman (2007) summarized evidence relating to frontal lobe mechanisms emphasizing the core distinction between controlled and automatic cognitive processing. The automatic reflexive or "X" *system* involves the basal ganglia and amygdala, the dorsal ACC, the lateral temporal cortex (LTC), and the VMPFC. It is characterized as phylogenetically older, spontaneous, fast, and involving parallel (e.g. holistic) processing. The controlled reflective or "C" *system* involves the lateral prefrontal cortex (LPFC), medial prefrontal cortex (MPFC), dorsomedial prefrontal cortex (DMPFC), ventrolateral prefrontal cortex (VLPFC), medial temporal lobe (MTL), lateral parietal cortex (LPC), medial parietal cortex (MPC), and rostral ACC (see Figure 3.12). It is characterized as phylogenetically newer, intentional, slow, and involving serial (e.g. linear) processing.

Lieberman (2007) made another core distinction between "*internally focused*" and "*externally focused*" cognitive processing. Internally focused means cognitive processes that focus on one's own *or another person's* "mental interior" (thoughts, feelings, intentions, experiences). Externally focused means cognitive processes that focus on physical features and actions that are experienced as part of the material world. Lieberman stated that this distinction is data-driven, in that it has emerged from empirical findings across many domains of social-cognitive neuroscience. This distinction is similar to that made in Chapter 1 between core themes in motivational-emotional development: to "tend and befriend" (Taylor et al., 2000) and "broaden and build" (Frederickson, 2001), in that the former critically involves dealing with one's own and others' feelings and the latter involves dealing with objective events in the material world. Certainly it makes sense that cognitive processes focusing on one's own or another's mental interior may be motivated by emotions associated with attachment and bonding; and that cognitive processes focusing on physical features and actions in the material world may be motivated by emotions associated with curiosity and

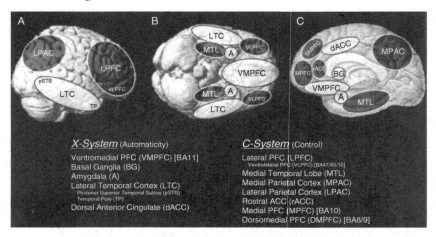

Figure 3.12 Brain systems involving automatic versus controlled processing. Hypothesized neural correlates of the
C-System supporting reflective social cognition (analogous
to controlled processing and analytic cognition), and the
X-System supporting reflexive social cognition (analogous
to automatic processing or syncretic cognition) displayed on
a canonical brain rendering from (A) lateral, (B) ventral, and
(C) medial views. The basal ganglia (BG) and amydgala (A)
are subcortical structures displayed here on the cortical
surface for ease of presentation.

exploration. In Lieberman's analysis, internally focused versus externally focused cognitive processing can be either automatic or controlled.

Lieberman expressed the hope that these two core distinctions will
help researchers to "carve social processes at their joints" (2007, p. 279).
However, an additional distinction critical to social and cognitive
neuroscience was not considered in his paper: the phenomenon of
cerebral lateralization.

The cerebral hemispheres

The left and right hemispheres of the brain are different in many
respects – in embryological origin, in microstructure, and in gross
anatomy – and these differences have functional implications. Lateralization of function appears in vertebrates including fish, reptiles, birds,
and mammals (Denenberg, 1981, 1984). Species with eyes placed laterally tend to scan for predators with the left eye, indicating right
hemisphere (RH) involvement; while communicative vocalizations
tend to be processed in the left hemisphere (LH: Des Roches et al.,

2008). Aggressive behavior is right-lateralized in the brain of the lizard *Anolis* (Deckel, 1995). In rats, right-hemisphere damage decreases mouse-killing tendencies (Denenberg and Yutzey, 1985) and emotionality (Denenberg, 1981, 1984).

The human brain is more lateralized than most other vertebrate brains because the corpus callosum, which connects the left and right neocortex, increased greatly in size during evolution, while the size of the anterior commissure, which connects left and right paleocortical and subcortical regions, did not. For this reason, many paleocortical and subcortical regions of the human brain are more directly connected with the ipsilateral neocortex than they are with corresponding paleocortical and subcortical regions on the other side (Ross, 1992). Most obviously, the LH is associated with language in the vast majority of human beings. The functions of the RH are less well understood, but there is evidence that RH responding is particularly involved in emotional communication (Geshwind, 1979).

Tucker (1981) suggested that syncretic and analytic styles of cognition noted in Chapter 1 are associated with the RH and LH, respectively. The RH can holistically integrate and synthesize analog information from a variety of sources into a sort of nonverbal conceptualization in which sensory, affective, and reasoning elements are fused into a global construct that Tucker termed syncretic cognition. Syncretic ideation is suited to picking up the affective meaning of complexes of nonverbal information provided by facial expression and gesture, body movement and posture, and vocal prosody and tone. In contrast, the LH is characterized by linear, serial, and sequential cognitive operations that can logically and rationally differentiate and articulate concepts. Language provides a prime example of the operation of analytic cognition. The global, holistic, and nonverbal knowledge of the RH is compatible with emotional cognition; while the verbal, linear, and sequential knowledge of the LH is compatible with rational cognition. These concepts have some elements in common with Lieberman's (2007) distinction between automatic or X cognition versus controlled or C cognition, but it is unclear how cerebral lateralization relates to this distinction. Some kinds of syncretic cognition, such as spatial reasoning, are controlled.

The split-brain. The cognitive capacities of the two hemispheres can be compared in cases where the corpus callosum is sectioned, essentially disconnecting RH and LH cognitive processing. This has been done in human patients to combat epilepsy in which activity in one hemisphere initiates an epileptic seizure by passing abnormal brain activity from one hemisphere to the other. This typically causes few serious side effects because sensory systems usually present the two hemispheres with the same information, but special tests can reveal striking effects demonstrating that the two hemispheres become essentially two brains with dissociable information and dissociable cognitive processes to deal with it. For example, a patient might be asked to view a brief exposure of a picture showing the half-face of a young woman in the left visual field (going to the RH) and an old man in the right visual field (going to the LH). The patient will typically report seeing the old man, and will confidently report seeing a full rather than a half-face. However, if asked to point with the left hand (controlled by the RH) to the picture being viewed, the patient will point to the picture of the young girl.

Sperry et al. (1979) placed a contact lens over the eye of split-brain patients that could be manipulated to selectively send visual information to the RH or LH permitting free scanning and prolonged examination on the part of the patient. Patients were shown neutral pictures interspersed with emotionally loaded material including pictures of the patient, family, friends, belongings, and famous figures. Patients evaluated the items with a "thumbs up" or "thumbs down," and pointed to pictures they recognized, liked, or disliked. When presented to the LH, the emotional stimuli produced prompt recognition and evaluation; but when presented to the RH they produced striking emotional responses which the patient could not verbally explain. In one example, a photograph of the patient was unexpectedly presented. The patient examined it for a few seconds, and then exclaimed "Oh, no! . . . Where did you g... What *are* they? . . . (laugh) . . . Oh God!" (Sperry et al., 1979, p. 158). When the examiner asked what was in the picture, the patient responded emphatically and loudly: "'Something nice whatever it was . . . Something I wouldn't mind having probably.' This was followed by another loud laugh" (p. 158). Sperry and his colleagues noted that the emotional responses from the RH were "more intense and less restrained" than those from the LH (p. 156), and suggested that the emotional reaction to the picture crossed to the LH through the brainstem while the patient remained unaware of the exact nature of the material that caused the RH emotional response.

Cerebral lateralization and selfish vs. prosocial emotion. There are two major theories of brain lateralization with respect to emotion. The *right hemisphere hypothesis* states that the RH is specialized for all emotional processing (Borod et al., 1998), while the *valence hypothesis* holds that the RH is specialized for negative and the LH for positive emotion (Bogen, 1985; Davidson and Fox, 1982). A variant of the valence hypothesis suggests that the LH is specialized for approach emotions and the RH for avoidance emotions (Davidson and Irwin, 1999).

Examination of the literature reveals that the right hemisphere hypothesis appears to be correct for emotional *communication*, both expression and recognition aspects (Borod and Koff, 1990; Borod et al., 1986; Ross, 1981, 1992; Strauss, 1986). There is extensive evidence that systems in the anterior and posterior RH are involved in the display and recognition of emotion, respectively. Buck and Van Lear (2002) suggested that these play roles in spontaneous communication that are analogous to roles that Broca's and Wernicke's areas in the LH play in the expression and comprehension of intentional symbolic communication, notably language. Differences between spontaneous and symbolic communication were discussed earlier in this chapter (see Figures 3.4 and 3.5).

The valence hypothesis, that the RH is specialized for negative/ withdrawal and the LH for positive/approach emotions, may be relevant to the question of the brain loci of emotional *experience* as opposed to communication. Despite evidence favoring the valence hypothesis, there are data that are difficult to reconcile. For example, the experience of disgust is associated with the left insula (Calder, 2003; Calder et al., 2000; Straube et al., 2010). This may be compatible with the approach-avoidance version of the valence hypothesis because, like anger, disgust albeit hedonically negative has been described as an approach emotion, and indeed a prosocial emotion, as a common response to disgust is to invite others to experience the disgusting object for themselves (Rozin et al., 1993). The function of such behavior may be to communicate to the community about what is disgusting. On the other hand, there is evidence that orgasm is based in RH mechanisms (Janszky et al., 2002; Holstege et al., 2003), and that the arousability to erotic films in the ovulatory phase of the menstrual cycle compared with other phases is primarily right-sided (Zhu et al., 2010). This latter evidence seems difficult for either the valence or approach-avoidance theory accounts.

Ross et al. (1994) suggested an alternative to the valence hypothesis that may address some of its problems. This was based upon a study of patients undergoing the *Wada test*, where a brain hemisphere is temporarily deactivated by sodium amobarbitol in preparation for brain surgery for intractable epilepsy. This is done to make sure the language areas of the brain will be spared during the operation. In the test, the person lies awake with both arms extended up counting backward from 1,000 aloud, and sodium amobarbitol is introduced into the right or left carotid artery under local anesthetic. When the LH is deactivated, the right arm becomes paralyzed and drops, and the person normally becomes temporarily aphasic, unable to speak. When the RH is inactivated, the left arm drops but the patient can still speak.

Before the operation, patients were asked to describe an event they had experienced that gave rise to strong emotion. During the Wada test while the RH was deactivated, they were asked about the same event. After the operation, they again described the event. The RH inactivation did not change the factual content of the life event, but eight of the ten patients showed evidence of minimizing or denying a primary emotion such as fear or anger. In a few cases, the RH inactivation seemed to produce a change in emotion. A man who described himself as "angry and frustrated" at the inability of physicians to diagnose his condition described himself as "sorry for people that they had so much trouble finding out what was wrong" when the RH was inactivated. A woman who said that she was "mad and angry" at being teased for her epilepsy as a child, when the RH was inactivated stated that she was "embarrassed" at the abuse. Later, when RH functioning was restored, the patients denied being sorry or embarrassed, and insisted that they had been angry.

Ross et al. (1994) suggested that the RH inactivation produced changes consistent with a change from selfish to prosocial emotion (Buck, 2002a). This was consistent with an observation by Buck and Duffy (1980) in LH and RH damaged patients in responding to emotionally loaded slides, who found that most patient groups accentuated positive displays and attenuated negative displays, as would be expected from display rules. However, LH-damaged patients did not attenuate their reaction to negative slides: indeed one elderly veteran cried at a picture of a starving child. This suggested the possibility that the RH might be associated with the spontaneous expression of emotion, while the LH is associated with display rules – learned expectations about how and when emotions should be expressed – involved in what we have termed pseudospontaneous communication (Buck and Van Lear, 2002). The veteran may have been expressing true feelings that most of us have learned to hide while viewing such pictures.

The Ross et al. (1994) results suggested an extension of this: that the RH is associated with individualistic/selfish emotions, both negative and positive (e.g. the right-lateralization of orgasm), while the LH is associated with prosocial/cooperative emotions, including the voluntary modulation of RH-mediated basic emotions via display rules. Indeed, social/cooperative emotions may often appear to be positively valenced because display rules often (but not always) encourage the expression of cheerful and positive albeit perfidious displays that are at variance with the "true feelings" of the responder. For example, Davidson and Fox (1982) found that social smiling is associated with LH activation in human infants, and interpreted this as consistent with the association of the LH with positively valenced emotions. However, another explanation is that infants' social smiles reflect prosocial attachment emotions as opposed to "selfish" pleasure. Indeed, stimuli used to elicit positive emotion may often elicit prosocial emotions as well (e.g. pictures of cute children, a baby gorilla). Unfortunately, stimuli used in these studies sometimes are not sufficiently described to judge whether positive slides are actually prosocial in nature (e.g., Balconi et al., 2009).

Several studies are relevant to the lateralization of selfish/individualistic versus social/cooperative emotions. Prodan et al. (2001) showed that upper facial displays, which are more likely to reflect basic emotions, are processed in the RH; while lower face displays which more likely reflect the moderating effects of display rules, are processed in the LH. Shamay-Tsoory et al. (2008) found support for the selfish/prosocial hypothesis in two studies. In the first, they tested the ability of left versus right PFC lesioned patients to recognize photographs of six basic emotions (happy, sad, afraid, angry, surprised, disgusted) and seven complex-social emotions (interested, worried, confident, fantasizing, preoccupied, friendly, suspicious). Shamay-Tsoory et al. found that left PFC-damaged patients were significantly more impaired in recognizing complex-social emotions; and right PFC-damaged patients were slightly albeit not significantly more impaired in recognizing basic emotions. In the second study they showed pictures of eyes posing basic versus complex-social emotions in left or right visual field presentations to normal persons. They found the RH to be significantly better at recognizing basic than complex-social emotions, and the LH to be slightly more accurate in recognizing complex-social than basic emotions. Shamay-Tsoory et al. (2008) concluded that there is a RH advantage in recognizing basic emotions and a LH advantage in recognizing complex-social emotions.

Another study relevant to the lateralization of selfish versus prosocial emotions was conducted by Gur and colleagues (Gur et al., 1995), who studied resting metabolism in brain areas associated with emotion. Participants lay for 90 minutes in a quiet room with instructions to remain "quiet and relaxed without either exerting mental effort or falling asleep" (Gur et al., 1995, p. 528). Results indicated that, for both women and men, metabolic activity was highest in the basal ganglia and the groups showed similar metabolism in non-limbic frontal, parietal, and occipital regions. However, men showed higher relative metabolism in temporal-limbic regions: the raw absolute metabolic rates were higher in men than women in the temporal region, including the temporal pole, amygdala, hippocampus, and OFC. In contrast, women had higher relative metabolism in the cingulate gyrus. This pattern suggests that men had more relative activity in brain areas associated with selfish emotions and women in brain areas associated with prosocial emotions. It might be noted that such patterns of brain activity could be a result of sex role-related social learning. Another aspect of the Gur et al. (1995) study was that it examined the right versus left lateralization of brain activity in different brain regions. Importantly, activity in the "prosocial" cingulate gyrus was left lateralized, but right lateralized in most "selfish" temporal regions of the limbic system and basal ganglia.

In conclusion, the evidence regarding the nature of the differences between the LH and RH in emotion is suggestive and attention should be paid to the selfish versus prosocial nature of stimuli as well as their valence and approach-avoidance implications. Studies of the lateralization of the amygdala and PFC may shed further light on this issue.

Lateralization of the amygdala. There is evidence that the left and right amygdalae are asymmetrical, both structurally (Szabo et al., 2001) and functionally (Baas et al., 2004). We saw that LeDoux and colleagues showed the amygdalae to be necessary in the conditioned fear response. Subsequent research suggested that the right amygdala may make a greater contribution than the left in fear. Coleman-Mesches and McGaugh found that the temporary inactivation of the right, but not the left, amygdala by microinjection of drugs disrupted the retention of passive avoidance responding in rats (1995a, 1995b, 1995c). Consistent with the notion that the right amygdala is involved in the memory for aversive experience, inactivation of the right but not left amygdala attenuated the response to a reduction in reward (Coleman-Mesches et al., 1996). Also, lesions to the right amygdala have been associated with larger reductions in fear than lesions to the left amygdala (Baker and Kim, 2004). In humans, right but not left temporal lobectomies led to lessened ability to recall unpleasant emotional events (Buchanan et al., 2006). Also, Smith et al. (2008) described a case of post-traumatic stress disorder (PTSD) in a patient with no left amygdala, and suggested that because PTSD persisted in the absence of the left amygdala, the right amygdala normally plays a greater role in its symptoms: fear conditioning, modulating arousal and vigilance, and maintaining memory for emotional context.

In a meta-analysis, Baas et al. (2004) found that the left amygdala is more often activated than the right in studies of emotional processing, and it is activated by positive as well as negative emotion. Hardee et al. (2008) demonstrated that the left more than the right amygdala discriminated between increases in eye white area that signaled fear versus a similar increase in white eye area associated with a lateral shift in gaze direction. This is consistent with a suggestion by Markowitsch (1998) that the left amygdala has a relatively greater affinity to respond to emotional information with detailed feature extraction and language, while the right amygdala responds to pictorial or image-related emotional information in a relatively fast, shallow, or gross response.

While the right amygdala appears to respond to fear, there are suggestions that the left amygdala may be involved with the left OFC and *fusiform face area* (FFA) in the functioning of a "social brain network" (Kleinhans et al., 2008). The FFA is an area on the fusiform gyrus on the ventral surface of the temporal lobe and is specialized for face recognition (BA 37). There is evidence that the functioning of this system is compromised in Asperger Syndrome (AS). A core feature of AS is impaired social and emotional cognition: it is distinguished from autistic spectrum disorder (ASD) in that there are no clinically significant delays in language, cognitive development, curiosity, or adaptive behavior other than in social interaction. Fine et al. (2001) reported a case study of a patient with early left amygdala damage who was diagnosed with AS in adulthood. This person showed no indication of executive function impairment, but had severe impairment in the ability to represent mental states (*Theory of Mind*, or *ToM*). This suggests both a dissociation between ToM and executive functioning, and that the left amygdala may play a role in the development of circuitry mediating ToM. Ashwin et al. (2007) found that AS participants showed less activation to fearful faces in the left amygdala and OFC compared to controls. Kleinhans et al. (2008) found that connectivity between the FFA and left amygdala was greater in controls than ASD participants; and that among the latter connectivity was negatively correlated with a measure of ASD clinical severity: that is, the less the conductivity, the more severe the clinical symptoms. Another study showed a positive correlation between FFA cortical thickness and left amygdala volume in normal controls, but a significantly different negative correlation in ASD participants (Dziobek et al., 2010). In a normal sample, Suda et al. (2011) reported a negative correlation between a measure of ASD characteristics and blood flow in the left superior temporal sulcus.

While AS and ASD have been associated with evidence of lessened activity in the left amygdala region and its connections, there is evidence of left amygdala *hyper*activation in response to emotional faces in *Borderline Personality Disorder* (BPD: Donegan et al., 2003; Koenigsberg et al., 2009). The contrast between the symptoms of AS versus BPD on one hand, and left amygdala hypoactivation and hyperactivation on the other, may therefore be relevant to understanding the unique functions of the left amygdala.

Both AS/ASD and BPD are associated with disrupted interpersonal relations, but for different reasons. AS is associated with something of an obliviousness to other persons. Major symptoms include the impairment of social interaction and communication, including deficits in the use of nonverbal behaviors (e.g. eye-to-eye gaze, facial expression) to regulate social interaction. There is a typical lack of empathy (awareness of others or their needs), a lack of social or emotional reciprocity, and a preference for solitary activities (American Psychiatric Association, 1994). Based upon the evidence summarized previously, these symptoms could be related to left amygdala hypoactivation.

In contrast, major symptoms of BPD involve intense emotional *over-involvement* with other persons. The symptoms include impulsivity and emotional instability which can involve episodes of intense dysphoria, irritability, anxiety, and inappropriate anger that is difficult to control (American Psychiatric Association, 1994). The instability may be related to a heightened sensitivity to social cues (Koenigsberg et al., 2009), in which the individual may make frantic efforts to avoid real or imagined separation, rejection, or abandonment. This can lead to intense, unstable interpersonal relationships that alternate between extremes of idealization and devaluation. In contrast with AS, BPD has been associated with evidence of *increased* empathy (Wagner and Linehan, 1999; Lynch et al., 2006); particularly affective empathy involving sharing emotional feelings (Harari et al., 2010). This pattern may result from a kind of social and emotional hypervigilance, which based upon the Donegan et al. (2003) and Koenigsberg et al. (2009) findings, could be related to left amygdala hyperactivation.

Lateralization of the prefrontal cortex. These issues are relevant to neocortical systems closely connected with the right and left amygdala: the right- and left-sided PFC and their subregions. We noted the importance of the PFC in decision-making: particularly the VMPFC and OFC subregions, and that there is evidence that, like the amygdala, the functions of the PFC are lateralized. The amygdala is closely connected with the OFC, and persons with AS showed relatively less activation to fearful faces in both the left amygdala and left OFC (Ashwin et al., 2007). Shamay-Tsoory et al. (2008) noted that, while emotion recognition has been associated with the right PFC, recognition tasks involving ToM skills are associated with the left PFC. They suggested that the right PFC plays a role in mediating basic emotions and the left PFC has a unique role in complex social emotions involving ToM.

Sex differences in selfish versus prosocial emotion. So, the left amygdala/PFC may function along a social-emotional obliviousness to hypervigilance dimension, with normal social behavior and emotional communication involving a moderate level of functioning. It is noteworthy in this regard that AS is more common among men, and BPD among women, and indeed normal women and men are sometimes said to vary along something of a vigilance-to-obliviousness dimension when it comes to emotional communication and sociality. A popular book compared the relationship strategies and communication patterns of men to Mars and those of women to Venus (Gray, 1993). Extending the metaphor, could the right amygdala/PFC be functionally analogous to Mars and the left to Venus?

There indeed is evidence of sex differences in amygdala and PFC lateralization. In women, activity in the left, but not right amygdala predicted subsequent memory for emotional stimuli; while right amygdala activity predicted emotional memory in men (Cahill et al., 2004); and Cahill (2005) suggested that, in processing emotional experiences, women generally use the left and men the right amygdala, which among other things helps women remember details and men the holistic central ideas of events. Moreover, Killgore et al. (2001) hypothesized that cerebral functions are redistributed from the amygdala to the PFC from childhood to adolescence, reflecting greater self-control over emotional behavior. They reported that women showed an age-related increase in PFC relative to amygdala activation in the left hemisphere in response to fearful faces, whereas men did not show a significant age-related change. Killgore and Yurgelun-Todd (2001) found both sexes to have greater left amygdala activation in response to fearful faces, while happy faces produced greater right than left amygdala activation in men but not women.

Conclusions: lateralization of selfish vs. prosocial emotion. In conclusion, there appears to be evidence from a variety of sources that a selfish–prosocial hypothesis is a viable alternative to the valence and approach-avoidance hypotheses of cerebral lateralization. Neither the valence hypothesis nor the approach-avoidance analysis seems compatible with the right-lateralization of orgasm, the evidence that AS and BPD relate respectively to left (but not right) amygdala hypo- and hyperactivation, or the observed sex differences. The selfish–prosocial hypothesis is compatible with these observations, and allows them to be placed in a wider context of the neurochemical basis of socio-emotional functioning including basic sex differences that are relevant to evolutionary theory with women being more nurturing, empathic, and verbal in accord with their greater caregiving role; and men being protective providers.

A problem with the selfish–prosocial hypothesis is that it is difficult to specify ahead of time just what is selfish and what is prosocial. Disgust and anger appear to be left-lateralized, and there is reason to believe that although considered to be hedonically negative they actually function as approach emotions with prosocial functions. The left-lateralization of anger was a basis of the replacement of the valence hypothesis with approach-avoidance (Davidson and Irwin, 1999); and Rozin has described how when something disgusting is encountered, the tendency is to share it with members of the community, perhaps so that a social consensus on what is disgusting can emerge (1999; Rozin and Fallon, 1987). Some types of aggression, such as predatory attack, seem clearly selfish; while others such as territorial aggression may have prosocial functions (Moyer, 1968). Ultimately, the foundation of the definition of how selfish and prosocial factors differ may be biological rather than logical: demonstrating the laterality of a function may be an instructive clue to its selfishness or prosociality.

Emotional communication and the right hemisphere

By far the most obvious and important function relating to brain laterality is communication, and particularly language, including reading and writing. Left hemisphere (LH) damage normally leads to deficits in not only speech and language, but also in analogic and "nonverbal" modes of intentional communication such as gesture, pantomime, sign-language, and finger spelling (Buck and Van Lear, 2002; Duffy et al., 1975; Duffy and Duffy, 1981). In contrast, speech and language are usually preserved in patients with RH damage, but they often lose emotional qualities of voice – *vocal prosody* – and speak in a monotone, a condition termed *aprosodia* (Ross 1981, 1992). Brain damage to the anterior RH, including the RH analogs of Broca's area, BAs 44 and 45, has been associated with *expressive aprosodia*: the inability to express emotion in the voice. For example, when asked to repeat a standard sentence such as "I am going to the other movie" as if they were happy, sad, angry, etc., such patients reply with a monotone that does not differentiate the emotions. Damage to the posterior RH including Wernicke's analog BA 22 is associated with an inability to comprehend emotion in the voice, or *receptive aprosodia*. Such patients typically cannot differentiate between recordings of standard sentences spoken in happiness, sadness, anger, etc. Thus, while damage to Broca's and Wernicke's areas in the LH are associated respectively with expressive and receptive aphasia; damage to analogous areas in the RH are associated respectively with expressive and receptive aprosodia (Ross, 1992; see Borod, 2000).

Nonverbal sending accuracy. Most formal studies of nonverbal communication in aphasia patients have studied only the deliberate and intentional use of gesture and pantomime as opposed to spontaneous nonverbal behavior. However, Buck and Duffy (1980) used the slide-viewing technique (SVT) in brain-damaged patients which assesses abilities at spontaneous communication as we have defined it. As discussed previously, the SVT employed slides to evoke emotional expressions (see Buck, 1979, Buck and Powers, 2013). In its application to brain-damaged patients, patients were shown a series of color slides with different emotional content – familiar people, scenic, unpleasant, and unusual slides – while their facial/gestural responses to the slides were recorded by an unobtrusive camera. Later, receivers viewed the recorded expressions and guessed what kind of slide the patient viewed on that trial. The resulting accuracy scores indicated the ability of receivers to correctly guess the slides viewed, or the "sending accuracy" of the patients. Results indicated that receivers could determine the category of slide viewed by the aphasia patients as well as they could from the expressions of non-brain-damaged comparison patients. Furthermore, RH damaged patients showed significantly lower sending accuracy scores relative to LH damaged patients and comparison patients, and in fact, RH damaged patients did not differ significantly in sending accuracy from patients with Parkinson's disease, a disorder long associated with a "mask-like" dearth of facial expression.

Communication via sign language and pantomime are "nonverbal" in two senses: the vocal apparatus is not involved, and such channels potentially make use of spatial and analogical abilities that may be RH-based and therefore spared with LH damage. Therefore, the abilities of LH damaged persons at communication by sign-language and pantomime are of interest. Duffy and Buck (1979) investigated relationships between pantomimic communication abilities and spontaneous sending accuracy in LH damaged patients. Pantomime expression was assessed by the examiner showing the patient a picture, and asking the patient to pantomime using the object (e.g. a drinking glass). Pantomime recognition was assessed by the examiner pantomiming an action (e.g. drinking from a glass) and the patient being asked to point to an appropriate picture (e.g. a glass, a lock, a hammer). Pantomime expression and recognition were strongly related to measures of verbal ability: patients who could use pantomime could typically use speech and language as well. A meta-analysis of studies of pantomimic and verbal abilities demonstrated a general pattern of positive relationships between pantomimic and verbal abilities, suggesting that these tasks are similar in that both involve symbolic communication (Buck and Van Lear, 2002). On the other hand, spontaneous sending accuracy scores of the LH damaged patients were unrelated to verbal or pantomimic ability, supporting the view that these scores reflect spontaneous communication which is dissociable from symbolic communication. These results were supported by Borod et al. (1985), who found deficits in rated facial expression and emotional intonation in patients with anterior RHD (Borod and Koff, 1990). The highly positive correlations demonstrated between verbal ability and pantomime expression and recognition show that the fact that both are symbolic overrides the fact that pantomime is spatial, analogical, and "nonverbal." The negligible correlations between spontaneous sending accuracy on one hand, and verbal ability and pantomime on the other, illustrate the essential independence of spontaneous emotional communication as opposed to verbal and analogic-pantomimic symbolic communication. Moreover, the results demonstrate that spontaneous sending accuracy is associated with the RH, and symbolic verbal and pantomimic abilities are associated with the LH (recall Figure 3.4).

The evidence suggests that there are essentially two simultaneous and independent *streams of communication*: intentional symbolic communication associated with the LH and emotional spontaneous communication associated with the RH. Additional evidence for this has come from studies using fMRI to measure LH and RH brain activity. More RH activation has been observed while viewing human-like interactions simulated by animated geometric shapes (Schultz et al., 2003) and cartoons (Mar et al., 2007), as well as live actors (Pelphrey et al., 2003, 2004).

Nonverbal receiving ability. Many studies implicate the RH in emotion recognition. In normal persons, the left ear better recognizes emotion expression in speech in dichotic listening tasks (e.g. *how* the statement is expressed as opposed to what is expressed: Safer and Leventhal, 1977). Similarly, RH damaged patients have difficulty recognizing and discriminating emotional faces and pictures (see reviews in Gainotti, 2000; Heilman et al., 2000). Also, there is a left visual field superiority for the processing of faces (indicating RH involvement), particularly faces expressing emotion (Ley and Bryden, 1979; Suberi and McKeever, 1977).

The latter result has been supported by studies of chimeric stimuli in which the sides of the face differ (with, for example, the left side male and the right side female). Using computer graphic techniques, Burt and Perrett (1997) produced realistic chimeric faces in which the right and left sides differed in age, attractiveness, gender, emotional expression, and lip-reading. Stimuli were constructed by computer averaging or morphing of photographs of faces: for example the "male aging" blend combined twenty-one male faces average age 22 years with eighteen male faces average age 51 years (Burt and Perrett, 1995). Results indicated that judgments of age, attractiveness, gender, and expression were influenced more by the left side of the face (judge's viewpoint), indicating greater RH involvement. In contrast, the right side of the face, indicating LH involvement, was more influential in judgments of lip-reading. Burt and Perrett concluded:

the left hemisphere seems to predominate during processing of facial information about speech (lip-reading), and the RH seems to predominate during processing of other facial dimensions (age, gender, expression, and attractiveness). Both of these findings are concordant with the neuropsychological studies of brain damaged subjects. (1997, p. 15)

The results of these studies have been confirmed in studies using fMRI measures. Lawrence et al. (2006) showed participants items from the Profile of Nonverbal Sensitivity (PONS: Rosenthal et al., 1979), an instrument designed to assess nonverbal sensitivity which used brief video clips of a model enacting emotionally loaded scenarios. Participants viewing clips while fMRI measures were taken were asked to make nonemotional judgments (indicating whether the face was visible or only the body: e.g. FACE vs. BODY) and emotion judgments (choosing a word indicating the emotional state portrayed: e.g. ANGRY vs. HAPPY). Results indicated that the emotion judgment task elicited more RH activation overall; with bilateral activation of BA 44/Broca's area and greater right-sided activation in the dorsolateral prefrontal cortex (DLPFC: BA 46) extending to the insula, inferior frontal gyrus, and pre-central gyrus; in the superior frontal gyrus extending to the cingulate gyrus; and in the fusiform gyrus extending to the inferior temporal gyrus, parahippocampal gyrus, superior temporal gyrus, and middle temporal gyrus. Lawrence et al. (2006) noted that the bilateral BA 44/Broca's area activation is of particular interest because of suggestions that it contains mirror neuron systems (Lieberman, 2007; Molnar-Szakas et al., 2005).

Semrud-Clikeman et al. (2011) studied the processing of dynamic representations of socio-emotional interaction. Participants in the fMRI viewed actors portraying vignettes of positive (happy) or negative (angry) scenarios: e.g. a child with friends opening a desired birthday present versus a teen being teased by peers. Significantly greater RH than LH activation to both positive and negative scenes were found in the amygdala-hippocampus, fusiform gyrus, inferior frontal gyrus, medial temporal gyrus, and superior temporal gyrus. In addition, significantly greater RH than LH activation to positive scenes was found in the anterior cingulate gyrus (ACC). The authors concluded that the results were consistent with their expectation that the RH is more involved in socio-emotional processing.

In another study investigating patterns of activation in these RH regions when viewing dynamic emotional stimuli, Powers (2009; Powers et al., 2007) presented judges in the fMRI with films taken of senders' expressions to familiar, unpleasant, unusual, and neutral slides. Results indicated that viewing senders responding to all of

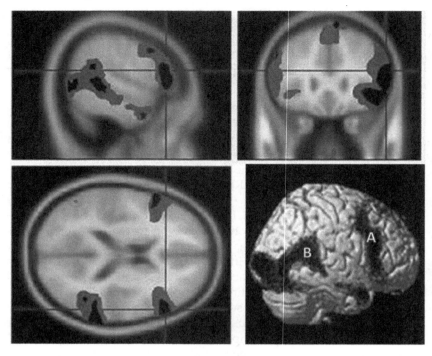

Figure 3.13 Patterns of brain activation when viewing spontaneous emotional displays. Judges in the fMRI viewed films
taken of spontaneous facial/gestural expressions to emotionally loaded slides. Results showed activation in areas associated with response to emotionally salient stimuli, much of
it right-sided. Expressions to familiar and unpleasant
slides activated RH analogs of Broca's (BAs 44 and 45) and
Wernicke's (BA 22) areas. A = Broca's, B = Wernicke's.
Crosshairs identify BA 45.

the emotional slide categories activated areas associated with attention
and arousal to emotionally salient stimuli, and much of the activation
was right-sided. Importantly, the expressions of senders viewing
familiar and unpleasant slides activated areas of the RH analogs of
both Broca's (BAs 44 and 45) and Wernicke's (BA 22) areas (Powers
2009; see Figure 3.13). As noted, these areas have been associated with
mirror neuron activity, and with Lawrence et al. (2006) this suggests
that dynamic representations of dynamic spontaneous emotional
expression activate mirror neuron system activity. The pattern shown
in Figure 3.13, plus converging evidence from other studies, suggests
that the RH analogs of Broca's and Wernicke's areas are associated

with a stream of spontaneous emotional communication existing alongside the stream of symbolic propositional communication associated with the LH.

Summary

Taken together, a convergence of evidence from a variety of perspectives supports a distinction between symbolic communication based in the LH and spontaneous communication based in the RH. Communication proceeds in two simultaneous streams: one intentional, propositional, learned, and culturally patterned; the other nonintentional, nonpropositional, innate, and pancultural. Species have evolved, however, such that the spontaneous stream can be hijacked, as it were, by intention, allowing the sender to control or suppress the display and thus manipulate the receiver through convincing display rules and deception that effectively activate preattunements in the partner via mirror neuron systems (Buck and Powers, 2013). Display of one's "true feelings" can be increased or decreased, and unfelt emotions simulated. The control and suppression of the display are central to *emotion regulation*, which is how we try to influence the emotions we have, when we have them, and how we experience and express them (Gross and Levenson, 1997).

Summary and conclusions

Low and high roads to appraisal

Subcortical systems filter our experience with reality based upon innate releasers and conditioned emotional responses to environmental events. Stimuli are first picked up by subcortical systems and, if challenging, the low road to cognition is engaged and they are attended to and *only then seen*. At that point, the high road appraisal process occurs and coping processes engaged. Specific subcortical systems respond quickly to specific sorts of challenge, mirror neurons pick up displays of affect and intention in others directly, and amplified and directed voices of the genes cajole our response via direct readouts of feelings and desires.

This process is illustrated in Figure 3.14. It begins with a challenging stimulus (e.g. a stimulus with motivational/emotional implications) that may either be internal or external to the organism. Internal stimuli might include low blood sugar associated with fasting, bodily changes associated with lengthening of the time of darkness as winter approaches, and increased levels of sex hormones at the onset of puberty. External

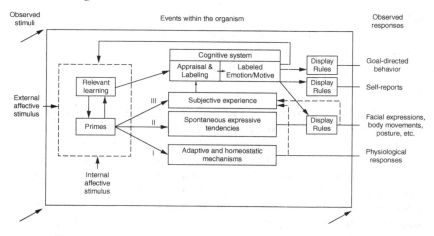

Figure 3.14 A developmental-interactionist model of the appraisal process. See text for details.

stimuli might be the sight of an enemy or a lover, an order from an authority figure, or the presence of a novel stimulus to a child. These impinge on what amounts to a pre-attentive subcortical/paleocortical *filter* that represents the unique characteristics and learning experiences of that individual (dotted lines). This filter includes two elements. The first involves the primes: the unique pattern of neurochemical systems inherited by the individual (*encoded genome*) plus any changes in arousal/arousability in the functioning of those systems due to experience vis-à-vis those stimuli during development (*effective genome*). These systems also include mirror neurons "picking up" directly the feelings and intentions of others. The second element in the filter involves the unique learning experiences of the individual relevant to those stimuli, including classically conditioned associations as well as direct or vicarious learning experiences.

The filter determines the impact of those particular stimuli for that particular individual in that particular situation. Thus, the impact of emotional stimuli is determined by (1) the state of arousal/arousability of the neurochemical systems comprising the primes in question, and (2) the individual's relevant learning experiences associated with those stimuli over the course of development. This implies that the stimuli impinge upon neurochemical systems underlying motivation and emotion directly and without the mediation of analytic cognition – the LeDoux (1996) low road to cognition – and that we respond emotionally before we can appraise a stimulus (Tamietto et al., 2009; Zajonc, 1980, 1984).

On the emotional level, the stimuli activate adaptive and homeostatic responses (Emotion I); and tendencies to spontaneously display

(Emotion II) and to directly subjectively experience (Emotion III) the emotional state. Subjective experience may also include feedback from display and physiological responding (dashed lines), although evidence suggests that such feedback is neither necessary nor sufficient for emotional experience. The impact of the stimuli in "raw" awareness thus has two aspects: the syncretic KA of the stimuli themselves and the syncretic KA of the emotional response to the stimuli (Emotion III). This is the first stage of Arnold's (1960) estimative system, and results in the "low road" primary appraisal of the stimuli on the basis of past experience, present situation, and the subjective emotional responses or *qualia* associated with the stimuli. This initial *primary appraisal* gives the individual a basis for labeling and coping with the stimuli: higher-level information processing systems organize *secondary appraisal* – the knowledge by description (KD) of the stimuli and their subjective emotional impact – resulting in a consciously label-able motivational/emotional response. The individual then has a basis for *coping* with the stimulus. Coping includes the initiation of appropriate goal-directed behaviors (Lazarus, 1966), and also involves feeding back to become a stimulus in its own right. For example, the stimulus to a sudden fright may be quickly recognized as innocuous, dampening the emotional response; or it may be recognized as highly dangerous, greatly increasing the emotional response.

The Emotion II display and Emotion I response are observable in the form respectively of pheromones, facial expressions, body movements, etc.; and autonomic, endocrine, immune system, etc., responses. One aspect of these responses involves modulation by display rules: learned rules about appropriate emotional displays and self-reports. Thus, self-reported emotional experience and emotional displays may therefore not reflect one's "true feelings." Physiological responses, in contrast, do not directly reflect the influence of display rules because they are typically not accessible during social learning. Children can be rebuked by adults for hitting, or crying, or even saying that they are angry or afraid; but not for having skin conductance responses. This is one reason physiological responses are sometimes considered useful in "lie detection."

The person's overt coping response may of course act to alter the original emotional stimulus, a process not illustrated in Figure 3.14. If an angry person attacks, the enemy may flee or stand her ground, and the consequences may alter the functioning of the filter and appraisal process on subsequent occasions.

The aspects of this process that are observable in ordinary life include external stimuli and the observed goal-directed behaviors, self-reports, and displays. These typically comprise the information used by others to provide social biofeedback to the responder. Observers are not typically aware of internal stimuli, such as might be caused by abnormal brain activity associated with some pathological state, changes in sex hormones, or hormonal variations associated with seasonal changes in the day/night cycle. Behaviors associated with these may seem puzzling to observers. Similarly, with the possible and typically rare exception of observing such reactions as blushing, sweating, and pupil dilation reactions, observers are not typically aware of autonomic, endocrine, and immune system responses. All of these processes occur largely within the organism and are not accessible to observers.

The influence of the primes on appraisal constitutes the interactive aspect of developmental-interactionist theory: the subjective experience of an initial emotional response serves as a critical source of information to appraisal, and the products of the appraisal process can become effective stimuli in their own right. The developmental aspect of the theory is represented by the fact that the interaction process takes place in the context of the developmental history of the individual (diagonal arrows on Figure 3.14). As we shall see in the next chapter, encoded genetic potential is actualized, implemented, and regulated in the context of experiences in which the primes are repeatedly aroused and responded to in interactive social context.

Disconnecting the filter

The first stage in appraisal is the pre-attentive subcortical/paleocortical filter involving the primes and the unique learning experiences of the individual. The functioning of this filter can be illustrated by manipulations in which different aspects of the process are damaged, resulting in *disconnection syndromes*: disorders caused by interruptions of transmission along neurochemical pathways (Geschwind, 1979). Three such disconnection syndromes have been discussed in this chapter, and are illustrated in Figure 3.15.

The first such syndrome involves the sectioning of the reticular formation from the rest of the brain, leaving sensory input intact (*cerveau isole*). This prevents the nonspecific arousal of the cortex, resulting in coma (A in Figure 3.15). The second disconnection syndrome involves bilateral lesioning of the amygdala, resulting in the Klüver-Bucy syndrome in which emotional responses are diminished even to stimuli that normally reliably elicit fear, anger, and disgust behaviors (snakes, fire, feces). This has been termed *emotional agnosia* (B in Figure 3.15). The third disconnection syndrome results when the primary sensory and association areas of the brain are disconnected: elementary perception remains intact but is stripped of meaning, and

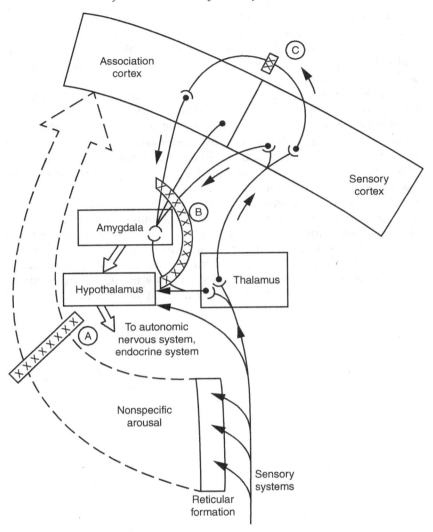

Figure 3.15 A model of initial sensory processing. Illustrating three *disconnection syndromes*. A shows the sectioning of the reticular formation from the rest of the brain, resulting in coma. B illustrates bilateral lesioning of the amygdala, resulting in the Klüver-Bucy syndrome and emotional agnosia. C shows disconnection between the primary sensory and association areas of the brain, resulting in agnosia.

the ability to recognize and identify familiar objects, persons, sounds, smells, etc. is lost (agnosia: C in Figure 3.15). As Figure 3.15 indicates, familiar stimuli may still be able to evoke peripheral autonomic and endocrine responses in agnosia, due to the preservation of subcortical and paleocortical systems.

This chapter examined several specific areas in which the analysis of biological emotions based upon specific neurochemical systems suggests new ways of distinguishing between emotions at a conceptual level. These included (1) two types of emotional valence, one based upon wanting (approach and avoidance) and the other based upon liking (pleasantness and unpleasantness); (2) reptilian emotion systems associated with the compulsive control of behavior; and (3) selfish versus prosocial emotion systems associated with felt affect and behavioral flexibility. Chapter 4 will go on to examine the biological bases of attachment, nurturance, and love. Thus far we have established how affects based upon a hierarchy of neurochemical systems function as primordial voices of the genes, cajoling our behavior and affording free will. A central theme of Chapter 4 is how the genes are nurtured via emotional communication: the *nurturing of the genome*.

Attachment: the evolution, development, and neurochemistry of sociality

The evolutionary biology of natural law: the state of nature and the social contract

The social contract

The question of whether human beings are essentially good or funda-mentally evil, cooperative or selfish, has had a long history in Western thought, with important social and political consequences. Perhaps because of the political implications, the debate has often been heated. This controversy arose in the seventeenth and eighteenth centuries in Europe. The theory of the divine right of kings was questioned, particularly in England, and philosophers sought a new theoretical basis for government authority and political legitimacy. This was found in the concept of a *social contract* established between individuals in a society (Russell, 1945, pp. 622–33). The reason for, and nature of, the social contract depended upon how the philosopher viewed the *state of nature* that existed prior to the establishment of the social contract. In *Leviathan* (1650), the British philosopher Thomas Hobbes (1588–1679) argued that all are motivated by the instinct of self-preservation to maintain their own freedom while dominating others. This resulted in a war of all against all that made life "nasty, brutish, and short." *Homo homini lupus*, he proclaimed: Man behaves as a wolf toward other men. Hobbes argued that the social contract was established out of fear as a peace treaty to end this universal war. The basic task of the state, he suggested, is to establish and maintain law and order. The state is most efficient at doing this when sovereignty is delegated to a central authority, preferably an absolute ruler.

In contrast to Hobbes' view, John Locke (1632–1704) held a more positive view of the state of nature as resembling a community of virtuous anarchists. People lived together peacefully without leaders according to reason and natural law. To Locke, natural law had a divine origin. This positive view of human nature was the basis of the rela-tively democratic and equalitarian political philosophy of Locke and

145

David Hume (1711–76), and it contributed to both the French and American revolutions. Bertrand Russell (1945) noted that this concept of human nature survives in modern liberalism, although it has lost its theological basis and thus its logical foundation.

Darwin's theory

Natural selection. This controversy arose again in the nineteenth century in the context of Darwin's theory of evolution. In *The Origin of Species* (1859) and *The Descent of Man* (1871), Charles Darwin (1809–82) argued that the force behind evolution is the "struggle for existence." Living things multiply faster than nature can provide for, so that at times of challenge, there will not be enough resources to go around. Those that survive will be those who are best adapted to their environment. It was in this sense that Darwin argued for the "survival of the fittest," by which he meant those who fit best with the species' particular environmental niche. This explains the evolution of the physical features of animals: the shell of the turtle, the hoof of the deer, the neck of the giraffe. At a time of challenge, such as a drought, a giraffe with a slightly longer neck will be able to eat more vegetation than a shorter-necked cousin, so the former will be more likely to survive and reproduce. Droughts, floods, and changes in climate bring about *selection pressures* that challenge the adaptive capacities of animals. It is important to note that this does not imply an active rivalry between individual animals: the animal with the better "fit" simply can take advantage of environmental resources more efficiently. This is *natural selection.* As Darwin put it: "It is not the strongest of the species that survives, nor the most intelligent, but the one most responsive to change."

The latter point was not, however, widely appreciated, and rightly or wrongly Darwin's ideas of the struggle for existence and survival of the fittest gave new credence to the Hobbesian view of human nature, with social and political consequences that Darwin himself regretted. Social philosophers including Darwin's half-cousin Francis Galton (1822–1911) misinterpreted the theory as implying an active intraspecies rivalry or competition: as Tennyson wrote "nature red in tooth and claw." A similar natural and inevitable competition was suggested in which only the fittest human beings are worthy of survival. This ideology of *Social Darwinism* was used as a scientific justification for a *laissez-faire* economic system and a rationalization for British imperialism and the exploitation of colonial and Native American populations (see Hofstadter, 1959). Social Darwinism was based on a fundamental misinterpretation and misunderstanding of Darwin's theory.

The evolution of behavioral and social structures. While it is relatively easy to appreciate the evolution of physical features of animals by natural selection, the evolution of behaviors and social structures is less obvious. For example, there is evidence that the cognitive emotion of curiosity is affected by evolution, in that species with an easy-to-obtain food supply and many natural enemies tend to be less curious than species with hard-to-obtain food and few enemies (Glickman and Schiff, 1967). Curiosity and exploratory behavior tendencies evolve only when they are adaptive, that is, only when selection pressures favor curious individuals. Similarly, infant monkeys would not survive long if they were not strongly attached to their mothers, and their mothers to them; so there are selection pressures favoring the survival of monkeys with strong tendencies for attachment and affection at birth.

These behavioral adaptations occur in individuals, so it is relatively easy to see how a strong attachment in an individual can select for the genes of that individual: the attached individual is more likely to survive, reproduce, and pass on its genes to the next generation. However, it is not so clear how social or group structures can evolve, because groups do not have genes. Mechanisms of *group selection* have been proposed, but as we shall see later in this chapter it is difficult to imagine group selection operating across evolutionary time-scales. Instead, I propose that social and group characteristics evolve via *communication*, that is by genetically based sending mechanisms (displays) and receiving mechanisms (preattunements to those displays). When these communicative signals are used in developmental context, particularly during the rough-and-tumble play of youngsters, social organization emerges naturally and directly as a self-organizing system (Buck, 2007).

Communication and the evolution of social organization

Emotion I involves bodily regulation and adaptation of the organism to environmental challenges and maintaining homeostasis. At the dawn of life, the chemical, energy, and temperature balances in the primordial seas were conducive to the functioning of the DNA molecule. As time went on, these balances began gradually to change, and the DNA molecules that survived were those that were protected from environmental change by a membrane made of protein that was constructed by the DNA. The temperature, energy, and chemical balances inside the membrane – inside the primordial cell – were more constant than those in the external environment, protecting the DNA. As time went on, the critical temperature, energy, and chemical balances were maintained inside the cell via the process of homeostasis. Indeed, through progressive adaptation, the temperature, energy, and chemical balances of the primordial seas lap quietly within our bodies even today (Asimov, 1957).

Emotion II involves information expressed by sending organisms via displays, and its pickup by receiving organisms through preattunements. The function of Emotion II is communication and social regulation, adapting a collectivity of organisms to environmental changes and maintaining social organization (Buck, 2007; Buck and Powers, 2013). Also, all of these communication processes – the display mechanisms, the messages involved, the receiving processes – can in principle be defined objectively in terms of observable phenomena that ultimately can be related directly to the most basic units underlying behavior: the genes and their primordial voices: quietly whispering, insistently instructing, and screaming in crescendo.

Spontaneous, symbolic, and pseudospontaneous communication

Brain mechanisms underlying spontaneous, symbolic, and pseudospontaneous displays were discussed in the last chapter (see Figure 3.3). In this section, these concepts are formally defined.

Spontaneous communication. Spontaneous communication is defined as having the following major qualities: (a) it is based upon a biologically shared signal system, (b) it is nonvoluntary, (c) the elements of the message are signs rather than symbols, and (d) it is nonpropositional. Displays are biologically based and are not symbolic because their relationship to their referents is not arbitrary. In the language of semiotics they are "signs" which bear natural relationships with their referents: like "dark clouds are a sign of rain," or "smoke is a sign of fire": the sign (the display) is an external manifestation of the referent (the emotional state). In contrast, a symbol is a signal which bears an arbitrary and socially learned relationship to its referent (Jenkins et al., 1975, p. 70). If signs are an external manifestation of emotional states, it does not make sense to inquire whether they are "true" or "false," for if the information did not exist, the sign would by definition be absent. Thus communication via signs is *nonpropositional* (Buck, 1984; Buck and Van Lear, 2002). The relationship of spontaneous communication and symbolic communication is summarized in Figure 4.1.

Symbolic communication. In contrast, symbolic communication is defined formally as (a) based upon a socially shared signal system which must be learned and shared by sender and receiver, (b) voluntary or intentional, (c) composed of arbitrary symbols, and (d) propositional, expressing statements which can be logically analyzed, e.g. can be false. The most

[handwritten margin note left: referants: thing that a word/phrase denotes or stands for]

[handwritten note bottom: non-propositional - concrete object, kind, or a property]

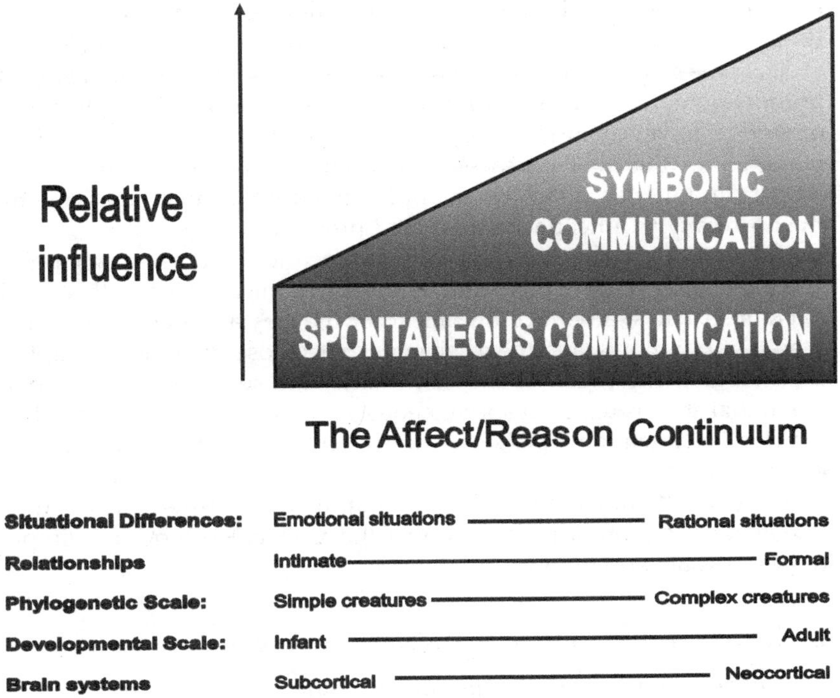

Figure 4.1 The relationship between spontaneous and symbolic communication. See text for details.

obvious example of symbolic communication is language, but there is a wide variety of "nonverbal" behaviors that involve symbols, including systems of sign-language, pantomime, and body movements and facial expressions associated with language, e.g. emblems, regulators, and illustrators (Ekman and Friesen, 1969a). Such "conversational" nonverbal expressions can involve well-established habits which, like many aspects of language, may be learned so well that they operate virtually automatically and outside conscious awareness.

Pseudospontaneous communication. By definition a spontaneous display cannot be "false," because it is dependent on the underlying biological state. However, expressions virtually identical to natural displays – also organized in the hindbrain – can be *used* propositionally, to follow social conventions or to deceive and/or manipulate the other. As discussed in Chapter 3, initiating a display in the absence of the corresponding internal biological state it is voluntary expression initiation (Jurgens, 1979; Ploog, 1981), or pseudospontaneous communication (Buck and Van Lear, 2002). To the receiver, this can be functionally equivalent to "valid" spontaneous displays. Pseudospontaneous communication is based upon a communication system shared biologically by sender and receiver, and the elements of pseudospontaneous communication are naturally occurring displays, or signs. However, in pseudospontaneous communication the sender manipulates the displays to send a specific message, or proposition, which can be false, as in the "I am having a good time" message by the hostess with a headache described previously.

The model of simultaneous and interacting streams of symbolic, spontaneous, and pseudospontaneous communication was illustrated in Figure 3.4. In symbolic communication, the message is encoded by the sender into symbols, and the receiver decodes those symbols to decipher the intended message. At the same time, the sender's motivational-emotional state is read out spontaneously and automatically in display, which given attention is picked up directly by the receiver via perceptual preattunements, presumably involving mirror neuron systems. The sender may attempt strategically to manipulate the display by pseudospontaneous communication, to control the receiver's response or simply to meet social expectations.

The relationship between spontaneous and symbolic communication

Communication in formal versus informal situations. The simultaneous streams of spontaneous and symbolic communication are, in principle, dissociable: one can vary independently of the other. Figure 4.1 is a modified version of Figure 1.3, which presented the relationship between syncretic knowledge by acquaintance (KA) and analytic knowledge by description (KD). In fact, spontaneous communication is associated with syncretic KA and symbolic communication with analytic KD. A given communication situation can be characterized as a particular mix of spontaneous and symbolic communication. For example, a large lecture falls at the right end of Figure 4.1, with symbolic communication relatively more important in conveying the overall message than spontaneous communication. On the other hand, a small seminar designed for more direct discussion and deliberation between participants allows more opportunity for spontaneous communication. It typically takes place in a small room with participants arrayed around a table facing one another as much as is possible. Thus, the seminar falls toward the left end of Figure 4.1.

In another sort of situation, symbolic communication becomes less relevant and spontaneous emotional display and communication may take over, and rational symbolic communication may virtually disappear at the far left end of Figure 4.1. An example might be a serious fire that interrupts the lecture or seminar. Suddenly the propositional content of the situation becomes irrelevant, and all attention is paid to avoiding and escaping from danger. Organized behavior may break down into panic in such situations, and it is useful therefore to prepare for such emergencies with such procedures as fire drills, life boat drills, and the ubiquitous safety lectures on air flights. Such procedures seek to forestall panic by providing a basis for at least a modicum of rational symbolic communication even in emergency situations.

Other dimensions of spontaneous versus symbolic communication. Other dimensions of communication situations can be related to Figures 1.3 and 4.1. There can be, for example, a dimension of interpersonal intimacy, from highly formal relationships between strangers on the right, where symbolic communication about the relative identities and roles of the interactants is negotiated. An example might be college roommates when they first meet: they might discuss where they are from, what their families are like, etc. As they get to know one another, the relative role of spontaneous emotional communication between them tends to increase. As people become even more intimate, symbolic communication becomes relatively less important, and long-together couples may actually not need to talk. And, on the left of Figures 1.3 and 4.1 are highly intimate encounters of lovemaking or fighting, where "irrational" impulses predominate. *[handwritten: phylogenetic-evolutionary history]*

Two other dimensions can fit as dimensions at the base of Figures 1.3 and 4.1: the phylogenetic scale and the developmental scale. As we shall see, there is communication between relatively simple creatures, including simple bacteria and virus, and it is entirely spontaneous. As species became more complex, more flexible systems of behavior control came online, and the influence of the programming of behavior by environmental experience became greater, and so the control of behavior gradually moved to the right along the dimension. However, the role of spontaneous communication did not disappear; rather it became less important relative to symbolic communication. We discuss in Chapter 5 how in human beings, the power of language gave great power to symbolic communication relative to communication in other animals. The role of spontaneous communication in human communication became less recognized, but it did not disappear. Similarly, the relative role of spontaneous communication over the lifespan is ordinarily greatest at birth, and declines as the relative role of symbolic communication increases with age and experience; and in human beings, language learning and development.

Still another dimension that can be related to Figures 1.3 and 4.1 involves the structure of the brain, as discussed in Chapter 3. The brain forms a hierarchy with the most basic reflexes and fixed action patterns or instincts associated with subcortical systems at the left side of the figures. Paleocortical systems are associated with subjectively experienced feelings and desires, which as noted function as voices of the genes affording more flexible action. Finally, at the right extreme of the figures, neocortical systems afford higher-level learning, cognitive processing, and in human beings, linguistic competence.

The evolution of sociality

As argued in Chapters 1 and 2, neurochemical systems constitute an irreducible essence of emotion. Specific neurochemical systems are associated with subjectively experienced feelings and desires: where there is a mood there is a molecule (Pert, 1985). Many of these molecules are associated not only with subjectively experienced moods, but also with the display and communicative functions of emotion, taking the phenomenon of emotion outside only the head of the individual, and into the social realm of conflict and cooperation.

The biological processes that regulate social organization and social bonds have received increased attention in recent years. Consideration of the neurochemical bases of emotion suggests that there are important biologically based prosocial emotional states that are often overlooked by contemporary emotion theory. These include "family-related" emotions involved in bonding, courting, play, and parental behaviors. These arguably meet the criteria for biologically based human emotions suggested by Ekman (1994): quick onset, automatic appraisal, common antecedents, presence in other primates, temporary duration, unbidden occurrence, distinctive physiology, and characteristic display.

We considered MacLean's (1973, 1993) view that some emotions are inherently selfish, directed toward the survival of the individual organism; while others are inherently social, directed at the survival of the species. The latter, prosocial affects arguably function to preserve the species via preserving the interactive, communicative *social relationship* (Buck, 2002a, 2011; Buck and Ginsburg, 1997b). As we saw in Chapter 2, these prosocial emotions are associated with a variety of specific neurochemical systems. In the remainder of this chapter, these prosocial emotions will be considered in detail, beginning with their evolutionary precursors involving primitive cooperative behaviors; and continuing with accounts of primate social structures and human social and emotional evolution; the specific neurochemical systems underlying attachment; and concluding with the issue of selfish gene theory.

Paleosociality

Individual single-celled organisms demonstrate what might be termed a "protoawareness" of self and environment, which can be aggregated into a collective protoawareness. Simple creatures – including single-celled cyanobacteria, slime molds, and sponges – demonstrate individual protoawareness of their internal state relative to the environment in various ways, such as regulating ingestive behavior: only eating prey when they need nourishment, for example. These creatures also demonstrate protoawareness on a collective level. *"Paleosociality"* refers to the social behavior and organization of microbes and other relatively simple organisms. In these creatures, fundamental principles of social organization can be discerned which, given the intrinsic conservatism of evolution, illuminate mechanisms and principles of social organization in more complex creatures including human beings. Certainly some of the chemical substances involved in fundamental communication processes between single-celled organisms have been conserved over enormous spans of time. For example, we noted in Chapter 2 the example of the GnRH molecule as being involved in the subjective experience of erotic feelings and also serving as a mating pheromone of the single-celled yeast *Saccharomyces cerevisiae.*

Stromatolites. The most ancient known organisms on Earth show evidence of paleosociality. Stromatolites are the fossilized colonies of cyanobacteria (aka blue-green algae) that appeared on Earth 3.5 billion years ago. Cyanobacteria are *prokaryotes,* the simplest of single-celled creatures lacking a cell nucleus surrounding their DNA. Contemporary examples are responsible for the pond scum that forms on stagnant water. Organized cyanobacteria once formed massive reefs, and through photosynthesis, using the energy of the sun and producing oxygen as a waste product, actually manufactured the oxygen atmosphere of the Earth (and ironically in the process poisoned themselves, as oxygen is highly toxic to them). Although they are almost extinct today, stromatolite colonies still live in the protective highly saline waters of Hamelin Pool in Shark Bay in Western Australia and along the coasts of Baja California (Olson, 1989). Through spontaneous communication, these ancient creatures self-organize and self-configure to create a working community that recovers collectively from damage.

Quorum sensing in bacteria. The signals or displays used by bacteria generally involve amino acids or peptides functioning as pheromones (Gallio et al., 2002). An example of such cellular communication is *quorum sensing* in bacteria. The term "quorum" refers to having a minimum number of individuals to perform a given action, as in a meeting that requires a certain number of participants in order to act. Quorum sensing

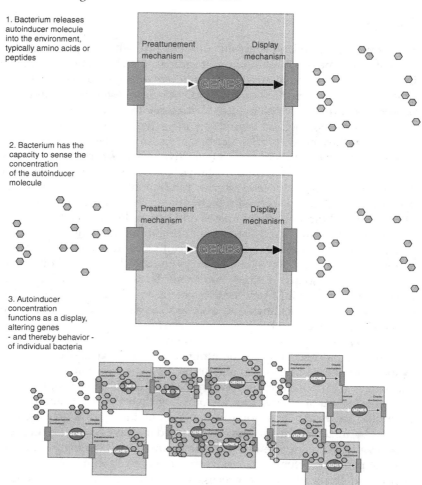

1. Bacterium releases autoinducer molecule into the environment, typically amino acids or peptides

2. Bacterium has the capacity to sense the concentration of the autoinducer molecule

3. Autoinducer concentration functions as a display, altering genes - and thereby behavior - of individual bacteria

Figure 4.2 Illustration of quorum sensing. See text for details.

in bacteria refers to the ability of bacteria to sense that their numbers in the area have reached a critical mass, and thereby to coordinate collective "social" behavior (Figure 4.2). One familiar example of quorum sensing involves the marine bioluminescent bacterium *Vibrio fischeri*, in which luminescence is induced by the accumulation of activator molecules in the environment reflecting a critical mass of individuals. This bacterium lives freely in a planktonic state, and also exists in symbiotic relationship with certain fish, squid, and insects (e.g. "lightning bugs") causing luminescence that functions as camouflage and to attract food and mates

(Ruby and McFall, 1999). The "display" molecule responsible for the activation of luminescence in *V. fischeri* was identified in 1981, and the genetic system analyzed in 1983 (Eberhard et al., 1981; Engebrecht et al., 1983).

Some bacterial infections involve quorum sensing such that when a quorum is attained, the regulation of bacterial genes is changed so that toxic "virulence factors" are produced. For example, in cystic fibrosis, when they reach a certain concentration, bacteria produce a *biofilm*: a tough shell that protects the bacteria from attack from the immune system of the victim and/or antibiotics. The bacteria then can reproduce, produce toxins, and damage tissues in relative safety (Riedel and Ebert, 2002). One function of quorum sensing is that the bacteria are quiescent – not activating a full immune system response – until their numbers are sufficient to overwhelm the victim. The mechanism of quorum sensing is of great interest because, if drug treatment can disrupt bacterial communication, the virulence of the bacteria can be greatly reduced. Moreover, since such a drug would target the mechanism of communication – in effect disrupting the dyad-level *communicative relationship between bacteria* rather than the bacteria as individuals – it would be less likely to leave drug-resistant individuals behind to reproduce and eventually create strains of drug-resistant bacteria (see Buck and Ginsburg, 1991).

The mechanism for quorum sensing in prokaryotic bacteria has been found to have a remarkable similarity with cellular communication in more complex organisms. In multi-celled organisms, the cells are not prokaryotes but rather are *eukaryotes* having a defined cell nucleus containing DNA, as well as organelles such as mitochondria, endoplasmic reticulum, and Golgi apparatus. Gallio and colleagues studied the genetic sequence of the Rhomboid gene associated with a mutation in the fruit fly *Drosophila* and found it in the ArrA gene which is involved in quorum sensing in the bacterium *Providencia stuartii*. Moreover, the Rhomboid and ArrA gene could swap roles, with ArrA functioning successfully in *Drosophila* and Rhomboid functioning successfully in *P. stuartii*. Gallio and colleagues noted that "peptide signaling in bacteria ... could be more widespread than anticipated, perhaps representing an ancient means of cell communication ... The use of peptides as signaling molecules is ... likely to be universal" and that similar mechanisms are "likely to be found in humans." They concluded that peptide mediated signaling is a "widely conserved mechanism for signal release ... not only the signal releasing mechanism seems conserved, but also the molecule that carries it out ... (suggesting that) ... these molecules share a common ancestry (2002, pp. 12212–13).

Slime molds. The life-cycle of the slime mold *Dictyostelium discoideum* illustrates in another relatively simple organism certain general concepts demonstrating implications of cell communication for larger issues of overall social organization. Slime molds are abundant: a spoonful of rich garden soil will contain millions of the creatures, and they are responsible for the slimy material found particularly on rotting wood. At one stage, *D. discoideum* are single-celled amoebae living independently of others. In this free-living stage the individual amoebae display negative chemotaxis: that is, they produce pheromones that repel other amoebae of the same species (Newell, 1995). The negative chemotaxis functions analogously to territorial/threat displays in more complex species: to disperse the amoebae and therefore afford an efficient utilization of the fruits of the environment; in the case of the *D. discoideum* its principal food is rotting organic material.

When available food is used up, the negative chemotaxis ends and a positive chemotaxis begins, attracting individuals to aggregation centers where the single-celled amoebae come together into a wormlike multi-celled form termed a grex, which may be made up of millions of individuals. In *D. discoideum* the pheromone upon which the positive chemotaxis is based is cyclic adenosine monophosphate (cAMP), a ubiquitous molecule which as noted in Chapter 2 is involved in the second messenger effects of many neurotransmitters. Cells at the front control the organized movement of the grex from the forest floor toward the light, in an inchworm-like journey that may take days. The mechanism of coordination is not well understood, but may involve axial gradients within the grex of pheromones such as cAMP that induce aggregation in the first place (Lackie, 1986). The control of the collective movement by the "head-end" is associated with a gradient of metabolism, with faster metabolism at the front. This may reflect an early stage of cephalization resulting eventually in the evolution of the brain at the front end.

The journey of the grex culminates in the differentiation of the cells into what is termed a *fruiting body*. Cells at the front end become a cellulose stalk, which becomes anchored to a secure footing, and a mass of cells from the rear then climb to the top of the stalk and form spores that become released into the environment. Given favorable conditions, the spores become individual amoebae and begin the life-cycle anew. In this process, the individual amoebae that form the stalk die, and therefore give up any possibility of passing on their genes, while the individuals that climb the stalk carry on the species. The giving up of potential to pass on one's own genes, while enhancing the genetic potential of other individuals, is the biological definition of *altruism* (Wilson, 1975). Thus, *D. discoideum* in its life-cycle demonstrates what might be termed proto-threat behavior in its negative chemotaxis, proto-attachment behavior in its positive chemotaxis, and proto-altruistic behavior in its stalk formation. The mechanism of the initial critical decision of an individual cell to altruistically die and join the stalk versus form a spore remains unclear: there may be a periodicity by which each cell is primed for stalk formation or spore formation at different times (Chattwood and Thompson, 2011). The differentiation process is regulated by cell communication: the decision of a given cell is communicated to other cells in the area via chemical signals.

D. discoideum is not alone in forming fruiting bodies. They are formed as well in single-celled prokaryotic bacteria, which as noted previously do not have the differentiated cell body and organelles that characterize the more advanced eukaryotic cells that characterize all complex multi-celled organisms. Thus, these simple bacteria too must be capable of communication and protosocial organization of remarkable complexity.

Sponges. Sponges have been identified as the simplest of animals, in that they appear to be the earliest creatures to show a core DNA sequence common to all animals (Harder, 2002). They have no nervous system and move only slowly, so they do not appear outwardly to be animals. However, they reproduce sexually, by the meeting of eggs and sperm, their cells are specialized and have the ability to communicate and share nutrients, and they carry out processes of growth and repair.

Sponges are multi-celled sea creatures characterized by many small pores, in which nutrient-rich water is pulled in, and a few large openings where the water is expelled. The sponge contains several kinds of specialized cells. One type pulls water into the pores of the sponge with hair-like filaments: these beat their filaments in synchrony which propels a stream of water past another type of cell that captures and ingests nutrients. However, one characteristic of sponges is particularly relevant to the study of cellular communication. It has long been known that if the cells of most sponges are dispersed (as in an electric blender), one at first simply has a container of cloudy water. However, with time, the individual cells making up most sponges reaggregate to re-form the characteristic organization of the multi-celled sponge (Buchsbaum, 1948). Moreover, if sponges of two species are blended together, they will reaggregate to form individuals of the two original species. To accomplish this, the cells must recognize one another and reassemble in such a way that the characteristic structure of the sponge is realized. Whether the individual cell types maintain their identity during dispersion, or revert to *stem cells* that can become any of the several cell types characterizing the sponge depending upon their spatial/communicative relationship with other cells, is not known.

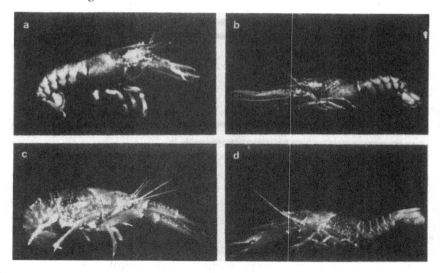

Figure 4.3 Lobster and crayfish dominance and submission postures induced by neurochemicals. Postures induced by injections of serotonin or octopamine. (A) Lobster (*Homarus americanus*, length 25 cm) injected with 5 mg serotonin or (B) 5 mg octopamine. (C) Crayfish (*Procambarus clarkii*, length 10 cm) injected with 1 mg serotonin or (D) 1 mg octopamine.

Lobsters and crayfish, dominance and serotonin. Threat and dominance versus submissive behaviors are among the most robust of paleosocial and social behaviors. They are demonstrated across phyla in high, prominent postures and active confrontative engagement with the environment; as opposed to low, less visible postures and retreat (Darwin, 1998; Wilson, 1975). The dominant–submissive relationship forms the ecological context for higher-level social and moral emotions, as we shall see.

We considered the negative chemotaxis in the slime mold, which can be regarded as a proto-threat behavior functioning to maintain territory. Another nonvertebrate species that demonstrates a notable analogy with the functioning of neurochemical systems involving dominance in higher vertebrates is the lobster *Homarus americanus*. Livingstone et al. (1980) demonstrated that injections of serotonin (5-HT) in freely moving lobsters produce a posture similar to the typical dominance posture. This involves a rigid flexion of the legs and abdomen so that the animal stands high with claws raised and open, and the tail tucked under (see Figure 4.3). On the other hand, octopamine (the phenol analogue of NE: Breen and Atwood, 1983) injections produce an opposite posture, similar to the typical subordinate posture:

a rigid hyperextension of the legs and abdomen so that the animal crouches low, with the claws stretched out in front (Livingstone et al., 1980; Weiger and Ma, 1993). The extremity and duration of these effects were dose-dependent. Similar results have been observed in crayfish (*Procambarus clarkii, Astacus fluviatilis*, and *A. astacus*: Livingstone et al., 1980). The triggering by serotonin or octopamine of particular motor programs in the central nervous system were responsible for producing these opposing postures (Kravitz, 1988; Ma and Weiger, 1993).

It is of interest that the effect of serotonin on dominance posturing may be dependent upon the social status of the individual. Cattaert et al. (2010) first placed two size-matched male adult crayfish (*P. clarkii*) together in an aquarium for ten days. Dominance between the two was determined based on observed dominance and submissive behavior: high postures, approaches and attacks vs. low postures, retreats and tail-flips. Only pairs in which the dominant partner won all of the fights during the last days of pairing were used for the study. It was found that serotonin showed evidence of producing motor changes associated with dominance posturing only in dominant animals, suggesting that the relevant neural networks are more reactive in dominant than subordinate animals, and indeed serotonin actually reinforced the divergence between dominant and subordinate individuals. Cattaert et al. (2010) noted other evidence that social dominance status influences escape reflexes in crayfish, and evidence of differences in the balance of serotonin receptors in dominant and submissive mammals as well.

This evidence is of particular interest because dominance and submission are not properties of an individual organism, but are defined in the context of specific social relationships. A given individual crayfish may become dominant when paired with one partner but submissive when paired with another. Indeed, it may be that dominance behaviors in an actor are created and maintained by the submissive behaviors of interaction partners. This implies that social experience in a dominant or submissive relationship can cause changes in the balance of serotonin receptors. This begs many questions: how much such social experience is required? How lasting are these changes in receptor balance? Clearly, the analysis of the social psychology of the crayfish has only begun!

Dominance in vertebrates. The relationship between serotonin levels and dominance exists in vertebrates as well, as we saw in Chapter 2. In vervet monkeys, the level of serotonin is twice as high in the blood of dominant as compared to subordinate males (McGuire et al., 1984), and similar findings have been observed in lizards (Summers and Greenberg, 1995), rats (Blanchard et al., 1994), and UCLA fraternity members. In the latter case, McGuire et al. (1984) found fraternity officers have higher serotonin levels than other members. Interestingly, there is evidence here too that the serotonin levels may be maintained by communicative displays. In vervet monkeys, the leader's high serotonin level falls if he is removed from the group: apparently it is maintained by the submissive behavior he elicits from submissive animals. Also, if the leader is removed and serotonin functioning is enhanced in one of the subordinate animals by giving the serotonin agonists tryptophan and the reuptake inhibitor fluoxetine (Prozac), the subordinate tends to acquire high dominance status in the group (Raleigh et al., 1991).

As noted in Chapter 2, both high and low serotonin levels have been associated with what might be termed "aggressive" tendencies. McGuire and colleagues found dominance to be associated with high levels of serotonin while other evidence links low serotonin levels with impulsive aggression, particularly in men (e.g. Asberg, 1994). Also, symptoms of impulsive aggression seen in antisocial personality disorders in humans are similar to behaviors shown by animals given lesions that interfere with serotonin function, including failures to delay gratification and to suppress punished behavior (Siever and Trestman, 1993). The crucial difference may be between *confident dominance* versus *frustrated hostility*. Contrary to conventional wisdom, the most powerful dominant "alpha" male is often not the strongest and most aggressive. In wolves the dominant male often is the most effective politician, who builds coalitions that cooperate in driving more aggressive males from the pack (Ginsburg, 1991). This is a case where consideration of the neurochemical systems underlying behavior can suggest distinctions between types of emotional processing that are not immediately apparent by the analysis of the behavior (e.g. aggressive tendencies) at the ecological/display level.

Conclusions: biological bases of paleosociality

We have considered communication mechanisms in creatures ranging from cyanobacteria to lobsters. Readers might object that none of these creatures is particularly noted for its complex *emotional* life. However, these examples demonstrate how communicative biological systems are involved in the organization and coordination of basic social behaviors in the simplest of living things. The governing principles and mechanisms illustrated by these relatively simple biological systems and social behaviors are arguably relevant to the understanding of social organization in more complex creatures, including human beings. Specifically, all of the communication mechanisms we have discussed in this section, involving cyanobacteria, bacteria like *V. vischeri*, slime molds, sponges, and lobsters, are examples of spontaneous communication as defined previously. All of the formal qualities of spontaneous communication are present in these examples of communication in the simplest creatures: thus in the quorum-sensing of single-celled bacteria, a bacterium's pheromonal display is not arbitrary. It is an externally accessible aspect of the bacterium's presence in the environment, a sign that has functional implications for collective action. Displays constitute signs of biological states in senders that activate preattunements in receivers, altering behaviors in ways that are adaptive, functioning to enhance the collective survival by the selection, not of the individual organism or the group, but rather the selection of the *communicative relationship* between individuals (Buck, 2011; Buck and Ginsburg, 1991).

Human social and emotional evolution

The governing principles and mechanisms of sociality demonstrated by simpler life forms are illustrated again in human evolution, and again, communication is at the core of sociality. New fossil evidence about human evolution, plus new techniques of measurement, including genetic analyses, have produced increasingly detailed scenarios of human social evolution. Such scenarios can take into account geological changes that created the environment in which human evolution occurred.

Origins in the rainforest. The primate line in evolution began before the extinction of the dinosaurs over 65 million years ago, with small, arboreal, nocturnal, insect-eating mammals. With the dinosaur extinction, the Cenozoic era began, with hot, wet, tropical rainforests and swamps covering much of the planet. For nearly 60 million years, the climate was relatively constant, without the spasms of glaciation that have occurred in the past 2 million years. Early primates adapted to this lush ecology, evolving efficient grasping hands, an omnivorous diet, binocular vision, and good brains, and they likely lived in social groups organized by audiovocal communication. New World monkeys, colorblind and with prehensile tails, diverged from Old World monkeys about 30 million years ago. Perhaps they migrated on rafts of vegetation from Africa to South America, which were relatively close at the time (700 km). Also around this time, the Earth began gradually to cool. About 25 million years ago, trichromatic color vision evolved in the Old World monkeys, which have tails, and early apes, which are tailless. About 12 million years ago, Earth's climate became drier and the forests shrank away toward the equator, where they remain today. With the rainforests went the forest-dwelling apes, whose numbers dwindled with the area of their habitat. Today only four species remain: the gibbon, orangutan, gorilla, and chimpanzee.

Adapting to the savannah: the garden of Ardi and Lucy. As rainforests were replaced by drier savannah, some monkey and ape species gradually adapted to the relatively difficult and dangerous life in the new environment. Unlike specialized herbivores, they could not digest the tough grasses of the savannah; and unlike specialized carnivores, they lacked speed, strength, and natural weapons. Moreover, their color vision, which served them well in the rainforest, held a significant disadvantage on the savannah: it was less efficient in the dark relative to the vision of powerful predators. However, they had the primates' efficient hands, binocular vision, good brain, probably an ability to make simple tools, and perhaps most important, social organization and communication.

Our closest genetic relative is the chimpanzee, but the chimpanzee remained in the forest while some monkeys adapted to the savannah. Among these were the ancestors of the baboon, which we might consider our closest ecological relative because they are primates which adapted to the savannah (Morris, 1967). Significantly, one of the major differences between chimpanzees and baboons involves the relationships between males and females. Although there is evidence that male wild chimpanzees do exchange meat for sex on a long-term basis (Gomes and Christophe, 2009), in general male and female chimpanzees rarely interact outside the relatively rare times when the female is in estrus. In contrast, male and female baboons often form long-term and even life-long "friendships" in which they stay physically close and move together. Morris suggested that baboons form *pair-bonds* to help enlist the support of the male in child-rearing, and a similar phenomenon may have occurred during human evolution.

Human beings and chimpanzees are both characterized by a larynx between the pharynx and lungs, indicating that this precursor to human speech was a feature of a common ancestor, known as the *chimpanzee last common ancestor* or CLCA (Lovejoy, 2009). The ancestors of human beings – termed *Hominins* – separated from those of the chimpanzees about 7 million years ago. In 1992 an archaeological team found the remains of *Ardipithecus ramidus*, including much of the skull, pelvis, lower arms, and feet. *Ardi*, as she became known, lived about 4.4 million years ago in what would become known as the Afar Triangle of Ethiopia. She stood about three feet tall and probably lived in woodland conditions, in that her feet were adapted to grasping and tree-climbing rather than walking for long distances. However, her pelvis, foot, and the angle of the foramen magnum indicate that she walked upright. Thus, the ability to maneuver in trees was preserved alongside the ability to walk upright.

The remains of some three dozen *Ardipithecus* individuals have been found, including *A. kadabba* who lived about 5.6 million years ago. *A. ramidus* had a small brain (300 to 350 cc), similar in size to modern chimpanzees. Importantly, *Ardipithecus* teeth resemble modern human teeth more than they do those of chimpanzees: specifically in the absence of large canine teeth in males (Lovejoy, 2009). The absence of these projecting canines is significant because they are used in aggressive male–male competition, and together with evidence that *A. ramidus* males are only slightly larger than females in body size, this suggests that *A. ramidus* was less aggressive than its chimpanzee-ancestor cousins, and that males may have contributed to parenting. We examine this further with the examination of the baboon lifestyle in a later section.

Ardipithecus lived over a long span of at least 1.2 million years, from relatively soon after the CLCA, to 4.4 million years ago. The next major hominid species was *Australopithecus*, who lived in savannah environments over an even longer span of time of nearly 3 million years: from over 4 to over 1 million years ago. The best-known representative is *Australopithecus afarensis*, who lived between 3.9 and 2.9 million years ago and left human-like footprints on volcanic ash in Laetoli, Kenya; providing strong evidence of bipedalism. A 40 percent complete skeleton of an individual *A. afarensis* was discovered in 1974 in Ethiopia's Afar Triangle and was named *Lucy*. She stood 3 feet 7 inches tall, and her pelvis and leg bones functioned similarly to those of modern humans. *Australopithecus* had a relatively small brain (380–450 cc). The relatively great size difference between males and females, plus their short legs, suggest that *A. afarensis* were relatively aggressive: the size difference between males and females is correlated with having shorter legs, and some have suggested that this was an adaptation for male-versus-male competition for females (Pennisi, 2006). Figure 4.4 illustrates the body proportions of Lucy compared to a modern chimpanzee and modern human being. The comparison of the pelvis and hip region are noteworthy: below the waist Lucy was more like a modern human being than a chimpanzee, yet her brain remained small.

Ice and the Stone Age. About 2.58 million years ago, the climate of the Earth changed; permanent ice sheets were established in Antarctica and perhaps Greenland, and cycles of ice ages began in which ice sheets covered great areas of the globe. An early ice advance, known in Europe as the *Gunz* glaciation and in North America as the *Nebraskan*, began about 1 million years ago and lasted 400,000 years. Lucy and her kind, after enduring for so long, disappeared. However, beginning about 2.3 to 2.4 million years ago, descendants of *Australopithecus* apparently sired

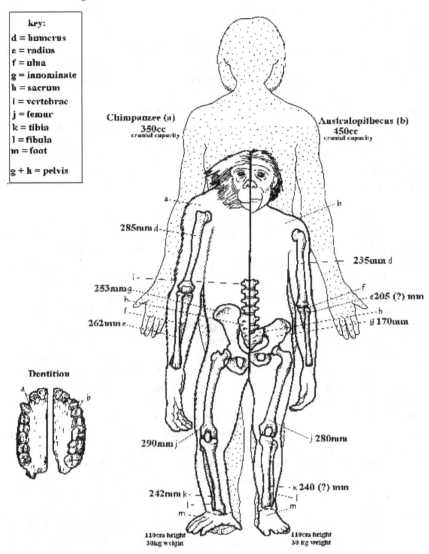

key:
d = humerus
e = radius
f = ulna
g = innominate
h = sacrum
i = vertebrae
j = femur
k = tibia
l = fibula
m = foot

g + h = pelvis

Chimpanzee (a)
350cc
cranial capacity

Australopithecus (b)
450cc
cranial capacity

a

b

285mm d

235mm d

i

f

253mm g

e205 (?) mm

h

f

h

262mm e

g 170mm

Dentition

290mm j

j 280mm

k 240 (?) mm

242mm k

i

l

m

m

110cm height
30kg weight

110cm height
30 kg weight

Figure 4.4 Comparison of Australopithecus (Lucy) and Chimpanzee bodies. See text for details.

a new species, the genus *Homo* that includes modern human beings. The most salient development in the new species was an increase in cranial capacity, from about 450 cc in *A. garhi* to 600 cc in *Homo habilis*. The emergence of *Homo* coincided roughly with the onset of the ice ages.

The advent of *Homo habilis* ("handyman") has been thought to match with the first evidence of stone tools: the *Mode One* pebble tools of the *Oldowan* industry which were used for chopping, scraping, and grinding (Napier, 1960). These are stone cores with flakes removed to create a sharpened edge. However, there is evidence from Ethiopia of earlier stone tool usage before 3.39 million years ago (McPherron et al., 2010), supporting the hypothesis of early tool-use by Australopithecines. *H. habilis* was short in stature, averaging 4 feet 3 inches tall, and had disproportionately long arms compared to modern humans; but had a less protruding face than Australopithecines, and remains of *H. habilis* are often accompanied by stone tools.

Homo habilis is thought to be the ancestor of *Homo ergaster* ("workman"), who appeared between 1.9 and 1.8 million years ago and introduced the first *Mode Two* or *Acheulean* stone tools. Acheulean tools include teardrop- or pear-shaped stone handaxes flaked over each side of the surface. As with the Oldowan, the flakes struck off the stone core were also used as scrapers and cutting instruments. These tools were used for a variety of tasks, including butchering, skinning, cutting, and digging.

H. ergaster stood over six feet tall and possessed larger brains (700–1100 cc) compared to *H habilis*. Their sexual dimorphism in size was smaller than that of *Australopithecus*, and it has been speculated that inter-male competition for females was reduced. It has also been suggested that *H. ergaster* was the first to control fire, had a breathing apparatus that could support speech, and had a social organization similar to human hunter-gatherer band-societies. Although it has been thought that the reduction in dimorphism and inter-male competition was associated with the advanced tool use and expansion of the brain, the fact that dimorphism was low in the much earlier *Ardipithecus ramidus* suggests that these elements are not necessarily causally related.

The next major *Homo* species to emerge was *Homo erectus*, associated with Acheulean tool technology (Pappu, 2001) and the control of fire (Goren-Inbar et al., 2004). *H. erectus* stood about 5 feet 10 inches and had a cranial capacity of 850 to 1100 cc, the latter figure overlapping with modern humans. This and evidence for the presence of Broca's area suggest the capacity for articulate language (Leakey and Lewin, 1992). Sexual dimorphism in size was slightly greater than that seen in modern humans, but much smaller than *Australopithecus*. It is theorized that *H. erectus* migrated from Africa around 2 million years ago, possibly during a wet phase in the Sahara, and dispersed throughout much of the world, including Europe and much of Asia.

Homo heidelbergensis ("Heidelberg Man") was probably a descendant of *H. ergaster* who migrated from Africa to Europe, and may be the direct ancestor of both *Homo neanderthalensis* ("Neanderthal man") in Europe and *Homo sapiens* in Africa (Rightmire, 1998). Evidence suggests that *H. heidelbergensis* lived between 600,000 and 400,000 years ago; used Acheulean stone tools; had a large cranial volume of 1100–1400 cc, overlapping the average 1350 cc of modern humans; and was tall, averaging 6 feet. *H. heidelbergensis* may have been the first species of the *Homo* genus to bury their dead. It is likely that they had a primitive form of language: the morphology of the ear suggests they had an auditory sensitivity similar to modern humans (Martínez et al., 2004). *Homo neanderthalensis* lived between about 300,000 and 24,000 years ago in Europe, and is associated with the *Mousterian* tool culture involving primarily flint handaxes and points (Haviland et al., 2009). They were shorter than *H. heidelbergensis*, with women averaging about 5 feet and men 5 feet 6 inches. Their cranial capacity matched or exceeded that of modern *H. sapiens*, with whom there may have been limited inbreeding.

Homo Sapiens and Toba. *Homo sapiens* probably originated between 200,000 and 150,000 years ago in Africa (Hetherington and Reid, 2010). They had a flat face with small brows and a protruding chin, and were tall and lanky. They were and are distinguished from all other animals by propositional language, which afforded systems of behavior control and organization that do not exist in other animals (Buck, 1988a). The matrilineal most recent common ancestor (M-MRCA), named *Mitochondrial Eve*, was a woman from whom all living humans today descend on their mother's side. She is estimated to have lived around 200,000 years ago in East Africa (Soares et al., 2009). The patrilineal most recent common ancestor (Y-MRCA), termed *Y-chromosomal Adam*, was a man from whom all living people are descended tracing back along paternal lines. He is estimated to have lived around 142,000 years ago (Cruciani et al., 2011).

There is evidence that there were multiple migrations by *Homo sapiens* groups from Africa between 125,000 and 60,000 years ago, and that these humans gradually replaced populations of *H. neanderthalensis* and *H. erectus* in Europe and Asia. There is also evidence of an eruption of a supervolcano between 69,000 and 77,000 years ago at Lake Toba in Sumatra, Indonesia. Some suggest that this eruption triggered a six- to ten-year volcanic winter and cooling that lasted 1,000 years, that devastated vegetation worldwide and may have contributed to the onset of the last ice age. There is evidence that humans and other species experienced a severe culling of the population, probably as a result of the Toba event, resulting in genetic bottlenecks that reduced human genetic variation (Gibbons, 1993). Estimates vary, but the human population could have plummeted to only 3,000 to 10,000 individuals. Archaeological evidence suggests that some archaic human groups survived the *H. sapiens* migrations and Toba event, including *H. erectus soloensis* on Java and the diminutive and small-brained "hobbit" *H. floresiensis* on the Indonesian island of Flores, but these species apparently did not leave genetic evidence of their survival.

Conclusions. Primates and early hominins evolved in rainforest conditions that gradually became drier, with woodland and savannah conditions replacing rainforest particularly in East Africa. Monkeys that adapted to the savannah conditions included the ancestors of present-day baboons: apes that adapted to the new conditions included *Ardipithecus ramidus* and *Australopithecus afarensis*: Ardi and Lucy, respectively. These species walked upright with a pelvis that resembles modern humans more than chimpanzees, and had efficient hands, but they retained small brains, not appreciably larger than those of chimpanzees. The increase in brain size did not occur until the appearance of ice ages, and also coincided with the first concrete evidence of propositional speech. Perhaps the basic motivational and emotional systems underlying human behavior, including attachment and family life, evolved during the long period of the Garden of Ardi and Lucy, and the evolution of human linguistic, intellectual, and complex cognitive capacities did not occur until the onset of severe selection pressures associated with the climate changes at the onset of ice ages. If this is correct, the motivational and emotional systems laid down during the long Garden period are of great interest, even more so as we realize that what evolved was an entirely new and different sort of sexuality.

The evolution of human sexuality

Sex in nonhuman primates. For many years nonhuman primates were assumed to be sexually insatiable, based on the observation of frequent and bizarre sexual behaviors in animals confined to Victorian-era zoos (Ardrey, 1966). Indeed, Sigmund Freud's observation of sexual behaviors among monkeys and apes in the London Zoo reportedly influenced his formulation that sexual drive or libido is basic to human nature (Morris, 1967). However, when the actual behavior of monkeys in the wild was observed, it became clear that the hypersexual behavior seen in zoos did not occur. Many monkey groups have sexual seasons with an almost complete lack of sexual behavior at other times of the year. *Estrus* is a period of heightened sexual interest and attractiveness in females that usually coincides with ovulation and the period of greatest fertility (Symons, 1980). It is signaled by displays of sexual readiness by the female including swelling, changes in coloration, and pheromones. These *sexual advertisements* excite arousal and courting behaviors in males. In most mammals, including most primates, sexual activity is restricted to the period. In a given female, estrus is suppressed when she is nursing, and she may nurse for months or years, so opportunities for sex can be few and far between.

Social bonds appear to play a role in regulating access to sexual opportunities in many nonhuman primate species. For example, the ability of a male to form coalitions with other males can affect his access to females. In baboons, Smuts (1987) described evidence of long-term "friendships," where a male and female tend to sit together, travel together, and groom one another. A male is more likely to come to the aid of a female and her offspring if she is a friend: indeed, of situations in which a male came to the aid of a female or her offspring, about 95 percent involved friends. Male–female friendships persist through phases of the reproductive cycle when the female is not sexually available, including the period of pregnancy and lactation that can last up to two years. Also, as baboons lack sexual exclusivity, friendships persist despite any apparent guarantee of paternity. Females commonly have two male friends, and males have up to eight female friends.

In contrast with baboons, the participation of male chimpanzees in the care of the young is relatively limited. Generally there is relatively little evidence of male–female bonding in chimpanzees, although Bonobos may exhibit a different pattern. In her long-term observation of chimpanzee groups, Jane Goodall (1986) reported that male–female relationships are restricted to short-term *consortships* where a male persuades/coerces a female, usually in estrus, to accompany him away from other community males. In general, the sex life of chimpanzees is communal, with males copulating if possible with any female who comes into estrus. The female tends to copulate with a number of males, although there are suggestions that females show preferences for males who are sexually mature, gentle, and who share food. The female chimpanzee typically shows little involvement in the sex act. There are no signs of orgasm when the male ejaculates and dismounts, and she reportedly "usually walks off as if nothing had happened" (Morris, 1967, p. 68). There is little evidence of a sense of paternity, and males generally play little part in caring for the young.

Chimpanzee social structure. Chimpanzee social structure differs from that of other nonhuman primates in several important respects (Ghiglieri, 1985). First, chimpanzees live in communities numbering fifty or more individuals within a *territory* from which strange male chimpanzees are excluded. Second, there is *female exogamy* in that females leave the natal group at sexual maturity and mate in another group; and *male philopatry*, in which males remain in their natal group forming a *patriarchy*. This ensures among other things that males within a community are genetically related to one another and have had much social experience with one another over the course of development. Third, the chimpanzees demonstrate a *fission-fusion* organization in that when food is sparse, the members of the community disperse with small foraging parties striking out on their own to find food. When food is plentiful, the community congregates to feed, mate, groom one another, and rest. This combination of territoriality, female exogamy, and a fission-fusion society is not found in any other nonhuman animals, but it is found in human beings: it is "typical of human societies in the hunting-and-gathering phase" (Ghiglieri, 1985, p. 102).

Another characteristic of chimpanzee and human hunting-and-gathering societies is the degree of cooperation manifested by males within the group, coupled with the degree of hostility manifested by them toward certain members – particularly males and infants – of other groups. The within-group cooperation extends to the sharing of scarce food and of mating opportunities. Often when a group comes across a fig tree bearing ripe fruit – a rare and precious event – males will vocalize with pant-hoots, apparently to alert other members of the community who subsequently arrive to share the bounty. Also, males do not usually attempt to exclude one another from relatively rare mating opportunities. A female chimpanzee normally is sexually receptive for only a few weeks every five years. A result of this sharing by males is a minimum of conflict within the community, with friendly interactions outnumbering antagonistic interactions by a factor of ten. Ghiglieri stated that "cooperation among genetically-related males in defense of the home range is one of the foundations of the community" (1985, p. 112).

Female chimpanzees, on the other hand, do not tend to be related genetically to other community members. Their reproductive success depends on the survival of her offspring, and the investment in the offspring is enormous. Each offspring requires nine months of gestation and at least four to five years of dependence, during which the mother is constantly with the youngster. Females begin to breed at age 15 and typically live 35 to 40 years, so each offspring represents about one-quarter of her adult lifespan.

A chimpanzee "war"? The general pattern of cooperation within the group can be combined with deadly hostility toward other communities. This was forcefully illustrated by the observation of a chimpanzee "war" by Goodall and colleagues that resulted in merciless killing. In 1970, some chimpanzees in the community originally studied by Goodall at the Gombe Stream Game Reserve in Kenya split and moved south along the shore of Lake Tanganyika. A stream valley became a territorial boundary across which male members of the original Kasakela group and the new Kahima group were observed to threaten each other without coming into physical contact: calling loudly, hurling rocks, drumming on trees, and dragging branches as they charged back and forth. The Kasakela group was observed to mount "patrols" near the boundary: traveling silently and cautiously, often stopping to listen. "Sometimes they climb tall trees and sit quietly for an hour or more, gazing into the 'unsafe' area of a neighboring community. They are very tense and at a sudden sound ... may grin and reach out to touch or embrace one another" (Goodall, 1986, p. 490).

Early in 1974, a single male of the southern Kahima group was caught by five members of the Kasakela group, who hit, kicked, and bit him for 20 minutes and left him to die. A month later, another Kahima male was similarly attacked, then an elderly male. An elderly female was next: attacked, pummeled, and beaten by four Kasakela males, she died five days later despite the vigil of her daughter, who brushed flies from her festering wounds. In 1977, the final two Kahima males were caught and killed. The Kasakela group had gradually exterminated the males of the southern group, with most attacks carried out by groups of Kasakela males deep in Kahima territory. Following that, the younger Kahima females joined the Kasakela group whose range now included the former Kahima territory.

Goodall (1986) concluded that the territorial conflict observed in the chimpanzees have most of the basic elements of human warfare at the preliterate hunter-and-gatherer stage. She considered carefully the question of whether there was an "intent to kill" in these attacks and concluded that there was. All observed attacks were gang attacks lasting 10–20 minutes, the victims after initial resistance crouched or lay passively during the onset while being held down, hit, bitten, kicked, and pulled in different directions. At the end, the victim was not only badly wounded but immobilized. The attacks showed patterns of behavior that were not seen during intra-community fighting but were seen during the killing of large prey: they twisted limbs, tore flesh, and drank the blood pouring from the victim's wounds. Eibl-Eibesfeldt (1979) used the term *pseudospeciation* to describe treating members of other groups as if they were members of a different species, and Goodall (1986) suggested that the wars of the Gombe chimpanzees may illustrate analogs of pseudospeciation in humans.

Sexuality in human beings. If there appear to be similarities between human beings and our chimpanzee cousins in the matter of warfare, we differ considerably in the matter of sex. Two of the cardinal differences in human sexuality from sex in other primates is invisible estrus and continuous sexual receptivity on the part of the female. There are no obvious signs or displays of estrus in human females, and Lovejoy (2009) suggested that this *ovulatory crypsis* was characteristic of *Ardipithecus ramidus* as well. He suggested that ovulatory crypsis was part of a major shift in reproductive strategy on the part of early hominids that transformed the social structure. This shift also involved the feminization of male canine teeth used in male–male conflict, more egalitarian sex roles as deduced by the reduced difference in the body size of females and males, and bipedal walking. Lovejoy argued that, together, these resulted in reduced intra-sexual antagonism, increased social attachment, and increased investment of the male in the care of the young. Females came to prefer nonaggressive males who were rewarded with sex and therefore reproductive success in exchange for valuable foods, which is technically termed *vested provisioning*. As noted previously, some have assumed that the reduction in sexual dimorphism and inter-male competition came about at the same time as the enlargement of the brain, the first speech, and Acheulean tools (e.g. between 1.9 and 1.8 million years ago with *H. ergaster*). The appearance of the former qualities 4.4 million years ago with small-brained *Ardipithecus ramidus* suggests that this shift in reproduction strategy occurred long before the expansion of the brain. Indeed, the basic motivational/emotional systems underlying human sexuality and family structure may have been in place for millions of years, through the times of Ardi and Lucy. The brain apparently did not expand until the challenges of the ice ages began.

With the loss of estrus displays, it is not the case that human females cease to advertise their sexual receptivity. Rather, many suggest that receptivity is advertised continuously (Symons, 1980; Morris, 1967). A number of physical features that distinguish human beings from other primates may have evolved to provide permanent sexual displays, including membranous lips; fleshy earlobes; protruding nose, breasts, and nipples; fleshy buttocks; odorous tufts of hair in the armpits and genitals; and the general hairlessness of the skin. Body shapes changed, with females becoming broader at the pelvis and males broader at the shoulders. As Desmond Morris noted in *The Naked Ape* (1967), many of these displays are accentuated by cosmetics and fashions, including earrings, perfumes, lipstick, makeup, and brassieres; as well as clothing and shoes that accentuate the shoulders of the male and hips of the female.

Along with this continued advertisement of sexual receptivity has evolved the female's capacity to be receptive sexually virtually continuously, even when menstruating, pregnant, and lactating. At the same time, the human female has evolved a greater capacity for orgasm and consequent involvement in the act of sexual intercourse (Masters and Johnson, 1966). Many have suggested that these changes function to support the pair-bond, make family life more rewarding, and enlist the male's help in caring for the offspring: as Morris put it, to "heighten the excitement of sexual activities and ... tighten the bond between the pair by intensifying copulatory rewards" (1967, p. 46). Others have countered that the basis of the human pair-bond is "not erotic but economic" (Lévi-Strauss, 1969, p. 38): that it typically involves more of an alliance of families or groups of people, and a reduction in sexual competition. Symons (1980) argued that "human sexuality may be adapted, not to promote marriage, but to promote reproductive success in a marital environment" (p. 175). This may be the case, but it seems unlikely that abstract notions of sexual rights, duties, and marriage would mean much to *Ardipithecus ramidus*.

Communication of ovulation. Although there are no obvious displays of estrus in human beings, there is evidence that the behaviors and preferences of both males and females can be unconsciously influenced by ovulatory status via accurate but inconspicuous displays. There is evidence that females in the fertile (estrus) phase of the menstrual cycle have more attractive body scent, facial appearance, body symmetry, and waist-to-hip ratio; as well as greater verbal creativity and fluency (Miller et al., 2007). In one well-known study, eighteen professional dancers working at gentlemen's clubs reported their menstrual periods, work shifts, and tip earnings for a period of 60 days; including about 5,300 lap dances. Normally cycling women (e.g. not using hormonal contraceptives) earned about US$185 per five-hour shift during menstruation, US$260 during the luteal phase, and US$335 during estrus. The study did not specify the cues that influenced tip earnings (Miller et al., 2007). Women using hormonal contraceptives ("the pill") did not show this effect, perhaps because the pill keeps the body in a state of hormonal pseudopregnancy (Gangestead et al., 2005).

Other studies have shown that the ovulatory cycle also alters social judgments in women, particularly with regard to mate preferences. In their *strategic pluralism model* of mating, Gangestead and Simpson (2000) proposed that women balance evidence of whether a male is a "good provider" and whether a male will contribute "good genes" to her potential offspring in making mating decisions (Simpson and Lapaglia, 2007). These considerations vary depending upon whether the relationship sought is short-term or long-term, and also with the stage of the ovulatory cycle. A number of studies have suggested that women prefer "macho" traits such a body symmetry, facial masculinity, self-assurance, and aggressiveness/arrogance; but only when they are evaluating men as short-term mates as opposed to long-term stable partners. Gangestead et al. (2004) sought to determine whether such judgments were affected by stage of the ovulatory cycle. Video clips were recorded of men being interviewed for a possible lunch date by an attractive woman. The men thought that she would choose either him or a "competitor." Following the interview they were filmed discussing with the competitor why the woman should choose him rather than the competitor. Observers rated "macho" qualities – the degree of social presence and intra-sexual competitiveness – of each of the men. Then, women viewed the clips and evaluated each man as a potential short-term mate (i.e. an "affair") or a long-term partner. Results indicated that women found the "macho" men more attractive, but only if the men were being evaluated as a short-term mate and only if the woman was at or near the peak fertility. The authors suggest that the results reflect an evolved mechanism for women to employ short-term mating to garner genetic benefits: the potential genetic benefits being greatest when fertility is highest (Simpson and Lapaglia, 2007).

In a second study, the same video clips were rated by a new group of women, who rated the men on a variety of qualities. Some were predicted to be associated with the selection of a long-term mate: faithfulness, warmth, intelligence, financial success, ability to be a good father. Other qualities were predicted to be associated with the selection of a short-term mate: influential, muscular, physically attractive, confrontative, and arrogant. As expected from the fertile-women-favor-good-genes hypothesis, women near ovulation preferred short-term qualities in short-term mates: they were also attracted to men rated as *less* faithful as short-term mates. Conversely, faithfulness, warmth, intelligence, financial success, and ability to be a good father predicted preferences for long-term mates regardless of stage of the cycle (Gangestead et al., 2007; Simpson and Lapaglia, 2007).

It is unlikely that the responses to stage of the ovulation cycle are conscious in either women or men. Miller et al. (2007) noted that in thousands of hours of interviews of dancers in their research on gentlemen's clubs, the dancers never reported noticing cycle effects on tip earnings, even though they had much opportunity to learn and were motivated to maximize their earnings. Displays and feeling states associated with the cycle are subtle but, apparently, powerful. Men's response to them and their effects on women's preferences are not governed by rational intention: they are responses to hushed but insistent voices of the genes.

Natural law

At the beginning of this chapter, I noted that the positive view of human nature of John Locke and David Hume, that human society is governed by reason and natural law, lost its logical foundation when the notion of natural law lost its theological foundation. Ironically, a Darwinian view of human nature emphasizing the evolved human capacity for attachment and bonding can perhaps supply this missing logical foundation. We saw above that Eibl-Eibesfeldt (1979) described treating members of other groups as if they were members of a different species as pseudospeciation, and suggested that it allows human beings to attack humans from other groups with a minimum of inhibition. He noted data from warfare in preliterate tribal cultures, including the tendency to refer to the enemy with dehumanizing names that is common to preliterate and modern warfare. Eibl-Eibesfeldt suggested that any functions that war may have had in human cultural evolution have become maladaptive, and that the only way to curb the "archaic intolerance" of humans is to reject pseudospeciation, to "realize that those different from us are nonetheless basically the same and that diversity constitutes the particular beauty of mankind" (Eibl-Eibesfeldt, 1979, p. 441). He suggested that the urge to bond constitutes a biologically based norm that is, among other things, the basis for the universality of the golden rule: "Thus the commandment 'Love thy neighbor as thyself' has a biological foundation" (Eibl-Eibesfeldt, 1979, p. 228). We shall see that there are in fact cross-cultural similarities in moral judgment that suggest a universal basis of moral reasoning. These are due to innate motives for bonding and attachment, plus universal features immanent in the ecology of social interaction, from which emerges Natural Law.

The development of sociality

The potential for sociality is genetically encoded in the human species, but to become effective that potential must be activated and implemented in social interaction. At the heart of this is emotional display and reception – emotional communication – in social interaction over the course of development.

Attachment theory

Theory development. The theoretical and empirical evidence for the existence of attachment motives stems largely from the work of psychiatrist and psychoanalyst John Bowlby (1907–91). Beginning in the 1930s, Bowlby was interested in the effects of maternal deprivation on personality development, and he combined insights from psychoanalytic theory, ethology, and control theory to develop attachment theory. After World War II, he hired James Robertson to observe children who had been separated from their parents and were hospitalized or institutionalized. Robertson had been trained in child observation at

Anna Freud's Hampstead residential nursery for homeless children during the war. His studies showed that when an infant is separated from its caregiver, the first response was typically to *protest*, including crying and active searching. This gave way to *despair*, involving passivity and sadness. If the caregiver continued to be absent, *detachment* may occur in which expressions of distress ceased and there was disregard and avoidance if the caregiver returned. Robertson made a film of the conditions of the children, and together with the work of Rene Spitz (1945), who also produced a film documenting the horrific effects of sensory and social deprivation on children, this helped to revolutionize the treatment of institutionalized children (Bretherton, 1992).

The World Health Organization (WHO) commissioned Bowlby to write a report on the conditions of homeless children in postwar Europe. The report, entitled *Maternal Care and Mental Health*, was published in 1951 and translated into fourteen languages (Bretherton, 1992). In it Bowlby pointed to the necessity for "the undifferentiated psyche to be exposed during certain critical periods to the influence of the psychic organizer – the mother" (1995 [1950], p. 53). His central conclusion was that "the infant and child should experience a warm, intimate, and continuous relationship with his mother (or permanent mother substitute) in which both find satisfaction and enjoyment" (1995 [1950], p. 13). He also emphasized the necessity for society to support the caregiver–child relationship: "If a community values its children it must cherish their parents" (1995 [1950], p. 84).

In the 1950s Bowlby began to introduce ethological concepts into his thinking about infant–mother attachment, rejecting claims by psychoanalytic and learning theorists that attachment is a by-product of the mother's satisfaction of the infant's needs. He distinguished attachment from dependency as being natural and healthy (Bretherton, 1992), and also incorporated evidence about the devastating effects of separation, drawing upon Robertson's data as well as evidence of the effects of maternal deprivation in Harry Harlow's studies of rhesus monkeys (Harlow, 1971). Bowlby's attachment theory was laid out in papers published in the late 1950s and early 1960s, and eventually published in three volumes: *Attachment* (1969), *Separation: Anxiety & Anger* (1973), and *Loss: Sadness & Depression* (1980). One center of his interest was always the intergenerational transmission of attachment patterns: that people who have themselves experienced secure attachment will tend to act in ways that transmit attachment security to their young (Bretherton, 1992). Unfortunately, it is also the case that neglect and abuse will tend to foster abuse and neglect of the next generation. In this Bowlby was one of the first to suggest that the effects of attachment or neglect could span generations: effects that are now understood to be *epigenetic influences*.

The strange situation. Mary Salter Ainsworth (1913–99), whose dissertation work emphasized the concept of security, joined Bowlby's research unit at the Tavistock Clinic in London in 1950 and assisted in the analysis of Robertson's data. Later, she studied mother–infant attachment behaviors in Uganda, seeing differences in the sensitivity of different mothers to the signals of their infants. She distinguished three attachment patterns: secure infants cried rarely and explored happily, insecure infants cried frequently and explored little, and nonattached infants did not behave differently to the mother. More sensitive mothers tended to have more secure infants. This contributed to a central concept of attachment theory: that infants develop secure attachments with adults who are sensitive and responsive to their signals.

To document types of attachment, Ainsworth developed the *strange situation* to observe attachment behaviors exhibited between caregivers and infants in a natural, albeit controlled, setting (Ainsworth and Bell, 1970). The procedure took place in a room with one-way glass allowing behavior to be observed. Infants aged between 12 and 18 months were observed during seven three-minute episodes: (1) Mother and infant alone. (2) Stranger joins mother and infant. (3) Mother leaves infant and stranger alone. (4) Mother returns and stranger leaves. (5) Mother leaves; infant left alone. (6) Stranger returns. (7) Mother returns and stranger leaves. Four categories of behaviors on the part of the infant were measured: separation anxiety when the mother left, willingness to explore, anxiety in the presence of the stranger, and reunion behavior when the mother returned. Ainsworth and Bell distinguished three types of attachment similar to those seen in Uganda. *Secure attachment* was demonstrated by 70 percent of the infants. They displayed distress when the mother left, avoided the stranger when alone but were friendly when the mother was present, and displayed happiness when the mother returned. Also, they used the mother as a safe base to explore the environment. *Insecure ambivalent attachment* was shown by 15 percent of the infants. They displayed intense distress when the mother left and showed fear and avoidance of the stranger. When the mother returned the infant approached but resisted contact and might push the mother away. These infants cried more and explored less than the other attachment types. *Insecure avoidant attachment* was shown by 15 percent of the infants. They showed no sign of distress when the mother left, did not fear the stranger, and did not show interest when the mother returned. Ainsworth and Bell (1970) suggested that the infant's behavior in the strange situation was determined by the behavior of the mother: secure attachment is associated with sensitive and responsive care; insecure ambivalent attachment is associated with inconsistent care; and insecure avoidant attachment is associated with unresponsive care.

Adult attachment. Bowlby's attachment theory and Ainsworth's empirical evidence for its validity had significant influence in the social and behavioral sciences, the full significance of which is still unfolding. Slightly different conceptualizations of attachment have emerged that are beyond the scope of this book, but one feature of particular interest is the notion of adult attachment. Most adults manifest a mixed attachment style, perhaps because in adulthood one has a variety of social relationships, some of which may be more secure than others. Shaver and Hazan (1993) translated Ainsworth's patterns of secure, ambivalent, and avoidant attachment to adult romantic relationships (Mikulincer and Shaver, 2003, 2005). *Secure* adults have positive views of themselves and their partners, trust the partner, and are comfortable with intimacy and independence. *Anxious-preoccupied* adults are less positive or trusting, and may show patterns of impulsiveness, high emotion, and worry about the relationship. *Fearful-avoidant* and *dismissive-avoidant* adults suppress their feelings and seek less intimacy; and dismissive adults additionally view themselves as self-sufficient and independent, not needing close relationships. We return to this analysis in Chapter 6, in the context of higher-order social emotions.

Attachment and communication

The potential for attachment and bonding in human beings requires emotional communication in the course of development to become actualized, and the specific requisites for this emotional communication are ordinarily supplied by evolved systems of social interaction activated naturally in the process of development across the lifespan: in infancy, childhood, adolescence, and adulthood. In particular, there is evidence that the neurochemical systems associated with some emotions are active at birth. This is particularly true of prosocial emotions associated with successful attachment implying the very early functioning of mirror neuron (MN) systems. Other emotions including fear, anger, and sexuality mature only when normally there has been adequate social experience and communication to allow them to be displayed and responded to effectively and competently. If this social experience and communication are not provided at the correct time, the result can be serious deficits in sociality.

Imitation. Converging evidence suggests the existence of functional MN systems in newborns (Lepage and Theoret, 2007). It has long been argued that newborns possess the capacity for imitation. Meltzoff and Moore (1977, 1983, 1997) exposed infants between 12 and 21 days of age to facial expressions and manual gestures, and demonstrated that observers viewing films of the infants could accurately judge the eliciting stimuli from the infants' responses: for example, viewing tongue protrusion tended to elicit tongue protrusion on the part of the infant. The investigators argued that infants were able to imitate these behaviors. Research on MN systems suggested a mechanism for this effect (Meltzoff and Decety, 2003); e.g. the matching mechanism underlying imitation is mediated by MN systems (Wohlschlager and Bekkering, 2002).

Mutual contingent responsiveness and primary intersubjectivity. There is other evidence of very early social responsiveness on the part of new-borns. Murray and Trevarthen (1986) demonstrated that 3- to 12-week-old infants interact naturally with their mothers via a video system. Mother and infant viewed a full-face, life-size image of the other on a video screen allowing "eye contact" to be maintained. When their interaction was played live and in real time, infant and mother demonstrated exquisite sensitivity to the timing and form of the communicative behaviors of the other: they "appeared to be communicating naturally" (Murray and Trevarthen, 1986, p. 17). The live video link allowed *mutual contingent responsiveness*: both mother and infant could respond "online" to the flow of the communicative behavior of the other. Trevarthen (1979) suggested that mutual contingent responsiveness naturally enabled *primary intersubjectivity* vis-à-vis infant and mother: that is, each was automatically attuned to the subjective state displayed by the other. With mutual contingent responsiveness, primary intersubjectivity may take place automatically, directly, naturally, and unconsciously, mediated by displays and MN preattunement systems. This pattern of smooth communicative flow changed dramatically, however, when either mother or infant unexpectedly viewed a playback of the other's behavior. Even though the behavior was physically identical to that played at another time, the playback made mutual contingent responsiveness impossible and disrupted the communication process: the infant looked away and expressed distress and the mother's characteristic pattern of baby talk changed (Trevarthen and Aitken, 2001).

Tronick (1978) demonstrated a similar phenomenon in the response of infants to a sudden unresponsiveness on the part of a social partner, termed a "still face." This occurs when an infant is happily interacting face-to-face with a responsive partner, when the partner suddenly stops all facial expression and looks past the infant. The infant's distress is immediate and wrenching. This phenomenon has proved highly replicable, and videos demonstrating the still-face effect are widely available on the Web. It is particularly interesting to note how painful it is to watch the infant's reaction to the still-face: our own strong empathic reaction to its distress reveals the existence of the strong prosocial emotions, usually hidden, that contribute mightily to social, emotional, and language development in the human species.

Distress calls. The presence of attachment needs in a species is demonstrated by *distress calls*. When attachment needs are not met, or when the newborn is in pain or in need, loud and insistent vocalizations result. The infant distress call at separation is one of the principal signs of the existence of a biologically based attachment mechanism in animal species, and it is typically associated with stress as assessed by cortisol (CORT) measures. Distress calls are communicative in that they tend to activate caring/nurturing inclinations in adults, who typically become intrinsically motivated to aid the infant, particularly those attached to the infant. The neurochemistry of distress calls is considered in the next section.

Babyfacedness and superdisplays. Another display that signals the helplessness of the infant and tends to activate nurturing responses is the characteristic "babyface" shape of the infant's head. The heads of infants tend to be large in proportion to the body, and are rounded with proportionately larger forehead and eyes, and smaller chin, with round and protruding cheeks. Lorenz (1966) suggested that these features are perceived to be "cute" and tend to draw out feelings of nurturance and caring. Eibl-Eibesfeldt (1970) noted that such features are exaggerated in dolls and cartoon characters such as Teddy bears, "Cabbage Patch" dolls, and cartoon characters from Mickey Mouse to Dora the Explorer. Although highly distorted from normal human appearance, these manipulations produce *superdisplays* that release super-normal caring responses and tendencies to pick them up and cuddle them. The influence of a babyface can carry on into adulthood. Berry and Zebrowitz-McArthur (1986) showed that adults with infantile head-shapes are perceived to be relatively honest, warm, kind, and naive: for example they elicit protective responses and in mock-jury trials babyfaced adults tend to receive lighter sentences for identical crimes than persons with mature faces (Alley, 1983). Unfortunately, infants who lack a characteristic infantile head-shape and babyface may be at risk for abuse. In particular, premature infants tend to have smaller and less rounded heads, and proportionally smaller eyes; and they are at more risk for abuse than siblings (Frodi et al., 1978).

As Eibl-Eibesfeldt (1970) noted, other aspects of body proportionality can be manipulated to produce superdisplays, and such manipulations are used in advertising as well. Extreme shoulder-to-waist ratios display masculinity, and are seen in cartoon characters such as Superman and Batman, as well as masculine fashions that include shoulder padding and epaulets. Large bosoms and extreme hip-to-waist ratios on the other hand display femininity, and are seen in Barbie dolls (actually derived from a pornographic doll), cartoon characters such as the Disney Princesses, and feminine fashions including breast enhancements and girdles. It is noteworthy that the Disney Princesses also display infantile head shapes, with small chins and large eyes and foreheads. Superman and other "good" superheroes, interestingly, often have infantile faces, perhaps to soften their super-masculine body proportions. Super villains and other evil characters, on the other hand, combine super-masculine bodies with facial configurations that display aggressive brutality and cruelty: the beady little eyes, small forehead, large mouth and jaw, and sharp teeth of the Big Bad Wolf.

Stages of emotional development

The infant is born with the motivational and emotional potential to form strong attachments, including capacities for imitation, mutual contingent responsiveness, and primary intersubjectivity. However, this potential must be realized in the context of social learning and communication. The newborn has the ability to display, and presumably experience, emotions of distress and love; but these do not function in a social vacuum. Emotional communication begins at or even before birth, and the socio-emotional milieu of the infant ordinarily nurtures its potential for attachment. Harry F. Harlow's (1971) classic studies of socio-emotional development in rhesus monkeys demonstrated that experiences of body contact, clinging, and nursing are *necessary and sufficient* factors in the establishment of reciprocal infant and mother-love. This establishes the essential emotional foundation of attachment and sociality, and results in a basic sense of security and trust that is critical to all later relationships.

Infancy: the parental affectional system. Harlow's (1971) classic studies of socio-emotional development in rhesus monkeys demonstrated that fundamental attachment is established early. The first three months or so of infant monkey existence is a time of contact comfort bliss, with almost unrestricted contact between mother and baby and virtually no punishment on the part of the mother. However, at about 4 months, punishment appears, peaks at about 5 months, and then declines. The increase is associated with a drop in infant–mother contact and, consistent with the developing motor skills of the youngster, increased contact with peers. With time, contact with the mother is largely replaced by contact with peers, the youngster makes fewer demands on the mother, and the punishment naturally declines. The necessary condition for this initial *parental affectional system* is contact comfort: contact with a soft skin-like surface. Harlow argued that this functions to establish a basic sense of trust in one's fellow monkey, even if the "mother" is an unresponsive terrycloth-covered surrogate. But the transition from a primary attachment to the mother (and father) to age-mates is not always easy. As Harlow wryly observed, Portnoy was not the only one to complain about the difficulties of breaking the apron strings with mom. But, this is necessary for normal socio-emotional development. Harlow noted that "maternal rejection during this period is truly one of many forms of mother love; a mother who loves her infant will emancipate him" (1971, p. 30).

Childhood: the peer affectional system. The feeling of trust established by contact comfort is a necessary condition for the *peer affectional system*. Young monkeys, having the common experience of contact, are at some point obliged by their own mothers' rejection to seek social contact elsewhere, and naturally with the ecology of the monkey social organization they tend to find similarly rejected peers with whom to interact. In these interactions, the basic communicative system underlying monkey social organization begins to emerge and become functional. Immature threat, submission, courting, and warning displays appear in the context of rough-and-tumble play, and are responded to by others, fostering the social biofeedback and emotional education processes. This affords the youngster practical experience in *using* the innate emotional display and communication system basic to rhesus monkey social organization.

The play of young animals is critical if they are to learn *how to use* the emotion communication typical to their species: to become emotionally educated and emotionally competent. Indeed, there is evidence that deprivation of play produces significant socio-emotional deficits that may be secondary to communicative deficits (Harlow and Mears, 1983; Miller et al., 1967). In the context of play, expressive and communicative displays and behaviors are not used as seriously as they are after puberty.

Adolescence: the sexual affectional system. With the maturation of sexuality, sexual and aggressive systems come online and the communicative displays are used with dangerous and even deadly seriousness. In this, the *sexual affectional system*, adult male and female roles and dominance orderings emerge from communicative interactions, forming the basis for rhesus monkey social organization.

Thus, each of the affectional stages sets up the necessary conditions for the next (see Figure 4.5). The basic sense of trust established in the parental affectional system is necessary to establish affectionate relations with peers, and the actualization of the display and communicative potential in the context of rough-and-tumble play is necessary to establish appropriate affectionate relationships with other adults of the same and opposite sex. Harlow argued that these interactive and

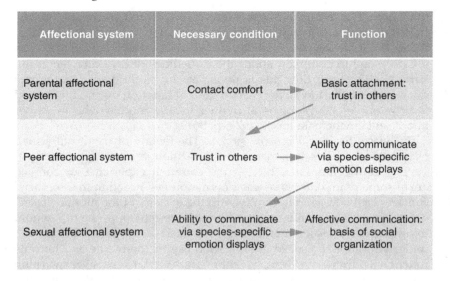

Affectional system	Necessary condition	Function
Parental affectional system	Contact comfort ━▶	Basic attachment: trust in others
Peer affectional system	Trust in others ━▶	Ability to communicate via species-specific emotion displays
Sexual affectional system	Ability to communicate via species-specific ━▶ emotion displays	Affective communication: basis of social organization

Figure 4.5 Stages of emotional development. See text for details.

communicative socio-emotional challenges correspond to those typical of infancy, childhood, and adolescence in human children. The result is an emergent system based first upon the basic sense of trust initially achieved by contact comfort. This illustrates the critical role of early attachment, and may help to explain why early abuse and neglect so often are common factors in disorders of attachment and in antisocial behavior.

Conclusions: emotional education and emotional competence

The stages of emotional development demonstrate a natural unfolding of the maturation of biological potential underlying subjective experiences of emotion (affective feelings and desires: Emotion III) and displays of emotion (facial expressions, postures, vocalizations: Emotion II) in social context in such a way as to afford emotional education and emotional competence. A full complement of emotions is not present at birth, but only those emotions functioning to keep the infant from harm (distress) and to establish and maintain social bonds (love and nurturance). These involve not only the private subjective experiences of the infant, but also displays that serve to communicate its needs; and these displays naturally initiate private subjective experiences and reciprocal displays in the caregiver that naturally synchronize with those in the infant during the parental affectional system. I discuss this natural synchrony and its biological correlates in the next section. For the present it is noteworthy that the infant's private experiences of distress and love, conveyed to the caregiver via infant displays, initiate displays on the part of the caregiver that function as social biofeedback and can naturally "explain" the infant's private subjective experiences, leading to emotional education: learning to understand and label these basic feelings and desires that underlie trust and security. A similar process occurs in the peer affectional system, in which the child comes to understand fearful and angry/aggressive feelings and desires in the context of play with peers; and with the sexual affectional system, in which the youngster comes to terms with the experience and display of newly matured sexual feelings and desires. Of course, events which interfere with this natural progression of communication and understanding have the capacity to erect significant roadblocks to emotional development and understanding. A consideration of the specific neurochemical systems underlying sociality and attachment allows us to understand the biological bases of this process in more detail, and these are suggestive of possibly effective interventions to enhance emotional education, competence, and sociality.

The neurochemistry of sociality

In this section, I explore how the human potential for attachment and bonding is based in specific neurochemical systems, including the opiates, oxytocin (OXY), and vasopressin (AVP) interacting with dopamine (DA).

The opiates and attachment

Separation and distress calls. One of the striking characteristics to emerge during the course of evolution as the behavioral flexibility of species increased, from fish, to amphibians, to reptiles, to birds, to mammals, is the increase in the helplessness of the infant at birth. The infant's initial helplessness is directly related to the complexity of the brain. As the brain became more complex, it was progressively less complete at birth, and it took time – in human beings decades – to fully mature. Infant helplessness is complemented by a progressively increased necessity for caregiving – attachment and nurturance – on the part of adults.

As noted, an objective sign of this increased need for caregiving is the evolution of distress vocalizations on the part of infants to separation from adults. Distress calls do not occur in most fish, amphibians, or reptiles. Most of these species are born relatively self-sufficient, without the need for parental care. Correspondingly, parental care is absent, so that distress calls might tend to be counterproductive. Indeed, in the absence of caregiving, such calls could be suicidal, particularly since many fish, amphibians, and reptiles eat their young. But nestling birds, chicks, mice, kittens, and puppies; and monkey, ape, and human infants show separation induced distress calls. Moreover, these calls appear to activate caregiving and maternal/parental behaviors in adults (Panksepp, 1981, 1982; Scott, 1974).

Panksepp studied the brain regions associated with distress calls, and found them to be rich in the opiates, or endorphins. He suggested that these data "indicate the specificity of endogenous brain opiate systems in organizing social behavior" (1981, p. 300), and that the brain endorphin systems constitute a physiological substrate for attachment and social cohesion (Panksepp et al., 1997). Moreover, Panksepp (1981, 1982) argued, based upon the neurotransmitter systems involved, that mechanisms of social attachment are related to, and may indeed have evolved from, mechanisms of pain modulation. As noted in Chapter 2, the neuropeptide carrying the pain signal – Substance P – is modulated by endorphins in the spinal cord. Panksepp suggested that attachment is associated with increased levels of endorphins, which in common with opium, morphine, and heroin, are associated with subjectively experienced relaxation and euphoria. Separation, on the other hand, is highly aversive, and is associated with *separation distress*, or what Panksepp (1981, 1982) termed *PANIC*. He suggested, "Separation has emerged from more basic pain systems during brain evolution" (1998, p. 267). The pain often described in bereavement ("like I lost a piece of myself") may be caused literally by hypersensitivity in pain systems associated with low opiate levels. Furthermore, Panksepp noted that opiate addiction might be related to brain mechanisms of social attachment: we literally may be, as the song says, "addicted to love." In addition, separation may be analogous to morphine withdrawal (see Panksepp, 1998, p. 255).

Pain and attachment. The brain systems underlying pain regulation and communication are closely related. As discussed previously, the modulation of pain is associated with limbic system structures projecting to opiate-sensitive neurons in the midbrain periaquaductal gray (PAG) or central gray. The PAG in turn is associated with two functions that at first glance do not "logically" seem related: emotion communication and pain regulation.

As noted, the PAG is the gray matter surrounding the cerebral aqueduct of the midbrain. It contains among other things nuclei associated with the modulation of pain perception, and it is highly sensitive to opiate drugs (Purves et al., 1997). The caudal PAG and laterally adjacent tegmentum is also part of the limbic midbrain area (LMA) that, as noted, is associated with display/call production functions in many species of vertebrates, including fish and mammals (Jurgens, 1979). This implies that, phylogenetically, call-production functions characterized this region of the brain in the common ancestor of fish and mammals, and thus dates at least from Devonian times (416 to 359 million years before present). As considered in Chapter 3, the midbrain region is also associated with basic facial displays in human beings (Steiner, 1979).

Moreover, the PAG is closely associated with emotion. Panksepp (1998) noted that the major neurochemical systems associated with discrete emotions project into the PAG, with rage/anger, fear, and separation distress projecting to dorsal portions and sex, nurturance, and play projecting to ventral portions. Such projections may generate a kind of primitive global value mapping, or "evaluation," that may have initially evolved from the modulation of pain. The fact that the same, quite "primitive," area of the brain is associated both with the modulation of pain and with social attachment is noteworthy. It implies that there may be some fundamental connection between the preservation of bodily tissues on one hand and that of the social fabric on the other. It also provides an example of a differentiation between selfish and prosocial emotions in a subcortical brain region.

The opiates and play. Panksepp and Burgdorf (1999) demonstrated that playful tickling arouses high frequency 50 kHz ultrasonic chirping in adolescent rats. Burgdorf and Panksepp (2001) found tickling to be rewarding to rats, as evidenced by approach behavior, conditioned place preferences, and elevated operant behavior. Rats actually showed preferences for being tickled by the relatively large (and one might imagine menacing) hand of an experimenter. Panksepp and Burgdorf (2000) suggested that this vocalization, which occurs during manual tickling, play, sex, and aggression, may express a "highly positive affective state" (p. 34), and that it may be "functionally or evolutionarily related to human laughter" (p. 26). Consistent with the opioid-dependence theory of attachment, this positive social affect appears to be modulated by the endogenous opiates (Panksepp, 1991, 1998).

All in all, there is considerable converging evidence supporting the role of the endogenous opiates in attachment, including distress calling, bonding, and play. However, the opiates are not the only neurochemicals associated with attachment: a different kind of attachment appears to be associated with OXY and AVP.

Oxytocin, vasopressin, and family-related emotions

As noted in Chapter 2, oxytocin (OXY) and vasopressin (AVP) diverged from the ancestral hormone vasotocin, which facilitates socio-sexual responses in reptiles and birds (Moore, 1987) and has been identified in unicellular organisms (Loumaye et al., 1982). The fact that OXY and AVP share the same ancestral hormone raises questions about how the behaviors that they regulate differ in mammals from non-mammals. Interestingly, there is evidence that OXY and AVP are relevant to the differentiation of female- and male-typical sexual and aggressive-dominant behaviors in mammals. Much of this evidence comes from the analysis of opposite-sex bonds and parental bonds in different species of voles.

Monogamy and the vole. The vole is a mouse-size rodent of the genus *Microtus*, some species of which are relatively monogamous, forming lasting female–male bonds. Prairie voles (*Microtus ochrogaster*) show monogamy as evidenced by a variety of behaviors. First, the prairie vole shows selective and lasting partner preferences (pair-bonds) that are activated by mating. A female prairie vole becomes sexually receptive when she is exposed to a chemical in the urine of a strange male (i.e. a male who is unrelated to her, so incest is avoided). After exposure, she will mate repeatedly with the male: in the process the two form a monogamous pair-bond, and soon become parents. The bonds are lasting: if the bonded partner dies, a surviving prairie vole will often live alone rather than take a new mate (Carter et al., 1997; Insel and Young, 2001). Bonded prairie voles live together, snuggling close to their mate over 50 percent of the time in side-by-side social postures, within a common nest and territory. After bonding either member of the pair will respond aggressively toward intruding voles, perhaps functioning to guard mate and territory. Both male and female prairie voles provide extensive care for the young pups, with the male helping to build the nest and spending almost as much time with the young as does the female. Also, if separated the pups become agitated and display ultrasonic distress calls and high stress response as evidenced by increases in CORT. Interestingly, compared with non-monogamous species, there is less sexual dimorphism of the brains of prairie voles: that is, relatively small differences in the brain between the sexes.

In contrast, closely related species – the meadow vole (*Microtus pennsylvanicus*) and montane vole (*Microtus montanus*) – are non-monogamous (Carter et al., 1997). They nest independently, breed promiscuously, the males play no parenting role, even the females abandon their pups soon after birth, and the pups do not appear to be distressed by abandonment. Generally, these animals show none of the signs of strong social bonding behaviors displayed by the prairie vole. Also, sex differences in brain systems are generally larger in promiscuous than in monogamous species (De Vries, 1996; De Vries and Villalba, 1997).

Roles of oxytocin and vasopressin. Studies have shown that OXY and AVP are both critical to the social bonding of the prairie vole. In the female prairie vole, OXY has been shown to be both necessary and sufficient for the development of pair-bonds (Insel, 1992; Williams et al., 1994). That is, an unbonded female exposed to a strange (i.e. unrelated) male and OXY agonists will become bonded without mating, while an OXY antagonist will block bonding despite mating. Similarly, AVP is necessary and sufficient for bonding in the male prairie vole: AVP stimulates the formation of a partner preference even without mating, and AVP antagonists will prevent the formation of partner preferences even after extensive mating (Insel and Young, 2001). In the natural setting, mating is associated with OXY release, which apparently functions to cement partner preferences in that the individuals prefer who they are with when OXY increase occurred (Carter, 1992).

The formation of the bond in prairie voles is related to other neurochemicals, particularly dopamine (DA). In fact, reward effects of OXY may often be mediated via DA release in brain reward areas (Leckman, 2011). Wang and colleagues (1999) found that, as with OXY, a nonspecific DA agonist and a D2 receptor agonist facilitated pair-bonding without mating in female prairie voles; and a nonspecific DA antagonist and a D2 receptor antagonist blocked pair-bonding. On the other hand, DA agonists and antagonists that work on the D1 receptor were not effective in either facilitating or blocking pair-bonding. The authors concluded that mating-induced pair-bonding requires activation of D2 receptors (Wang et al., 1999). Indeed, levels of DA increase during mating in the female in the "hedonic hotspot" NAcc associated with reward, as discussed in Chapter 3. Also, in rats, the effects of OXY on maternal licking/grooming of pups was found to be mediated by the effect of OXY on DA release in the reward system (Shahrokh et al., 2010).

Brain regions associated with OXY and AVP. One of the striking differences between monogamous prairie voles as opposed to non-monogamous voles is the amount of brain area devoted to OXY and AVP. Brain areas associated with OXY are much larger in the prairie vole compared to the more solitary and non-monogamous montane vole (Insel et al., 1997). This is particularly true in the NAcc and the prelimbic cortex. Similarly, the distribution of AVP receptors in the male brain is different, with the prairie vole having a relatively high density of AVP receptors in the ventral pallidum of the brain, which receives the major output of the NAcc (Young et al., 2001). Given that the prairie and montane voles are similar to one another in many respects, this difference in the distribution of brain neurochemicals is remarkable.

Studies have manipulated OXY and AVP genes to determine the neural substrates upon which they operate and their roles in social behavior. Young (2001, 2002) studied the OXY knock-out (OTKO) mouse, bred without the genes to produce OXY, and found profound changes in social behavior. As pups, OTKO mice appear to be less distressed by social isolation, as measured by fewer distress calls when isolated from their mothers. Also, they show no preference for their mothers compared to the strong preference shown by normal mice. As adults, OTKO mice demonstrate "social amnesia": whereas normal rats show a decline in the olfactory investigation of a stimulus rat after a few exposures, OTKO rats show no decline even after repeated exposures. This "social amnesia" is reversed by a single injection of OXY into the brain prior to, but not after, the initial exposure. Also, there is evidence that OTKO mice process social stimuli via different neural pathways than normal rats. Whereas normal rats show evidence of neural activity in the medial amygdala following a social encounter, OTKO rats do not, showing activation of other brain structures instead. Microinjections of OXY directly into the medial amygdala of OTKO mice restore social recognition (Young, 2001). Young (2001) pointed out a number of parallels between social deficits in OTKO mice and autism (ASD) in humans. As discussed in the last chapter, ASD is characterized by profound social impairments, including deficits in social engagement and abnormal brain processing of social stimuli, and there is suggestive evidence that autistic children have abnormally low concentrations of OXY in the blood.

A natural question arises from these studies: whether OXY, AVP, and other neurochemicals play an analogous role in human attachment and love. The role of OXY and AVP in human beings is a subject of great current interest. Both OXY and AVP are released into the bloodstream during sexual intercourse, and OXY in company with prolactin and other hormones are involved in the regulation of birthing and of milk production. Given the conservation of function that is generally found within mammals, as well as the suggestive parallels between human ASD and symptoms in the OTKO mouse, it seems reasonable to expect that OXY and AVP are involved in some way in the bonding process in humans (Young et al., 2011), and indeed there is increasing evidence that these peptide neurohormones play important roles in complex human social behavior.

The neurochemistry of sociality in human beings

Oxytocin and trust. Studies of the effects of the central nervous system effects of OXY in human beings have taken advantage of the fact that when administered in a nasal spray, neuropeptides cross the blood–brain barrier and affect the brain (Guastella and MacLeod, 2012). In one of the first studies to use this method, OXY or a placebo was administered by nasal spray in a double-blind study: that is, no one knew whether a given individual received OXY or the placebo until after the completion of the study (Kosfeld et al., 2005). Two persons played a *Trust Game* anonymously in roles of trustee or investor with real monetary stakes. The game was arranged as a social dilemma, in which if the investor trusts and the trustee shares, both benefit; but there is a risk that the trustee will abuse the investor's trust leaving the investor less well off. Results indicated that OXY significantly increased the investors' trust, with 45 percent in the OXY group showing the highest trust level while only 21 percent in the placebo group did so. In a similar study involving risk that did not involve interpersonal trust, the effect of OXY was not significant, suggesting that it influenced trust and not risk aversion per se. Other alternative interpretations of the results were considered and discarded, including possible OXY effects on mood, general prosociality, and general beliefs in the trustworthiness of others. Instead, the results were consistent with OXY fostering an increase in trust and a decreased aversion to betrayal, factors consistent with the effects of OXY in animals in increasing approach behavior by activating reward circuits (for example in the "hedonic hotspot" NAcc) and lowering social avoidance (Kosfeld et al., 2005).

Another study used a double-blind application of OXY to measure the effects of the breaching of trust on brain responding (Baumgartner et al., 2008). Participants played a Trust Game similar to that in the Kosfeld et al. (2005) study while in the fMRI machine. In a game associated with nonsocial risks, placebo and OXY groups did not differ. However, with social risks, those who received placebo and whose trust was violated showed a lessening of their trusting behavior, while those who received OXY continued to trust regardless of the violation. This maintenance of trust was associated with lower activation in brain systems mediating fear (the amygdala [bilaterally] and midbrain [left]) and adaptations to feedback (the dorsal striatum including the putamen/insula [left] and caudate [right]). It is also interesting to note that, prior to information about betrayal, those who had received placebo showed more activation in the dorsal anterior cingulate cortex (ACC), suggesting a greater disposition to monitor conflict between the inclination to trust and their suspicion of the partner. The authors suggested that OXY functioned to lower the perception of risks of betrayal: that they implicitly "know" that they can trust the partner. Moreover, these effects were automatic or unconscious. Importantly, participants were unaware of whether they had received OXY, and its influence was seen as automatic, intuitive, and unconscious (Baumgartner et al., 2008).

The findings of studies using OXY nasal spray are consistent with evidence from studies using other methodologies. Kosnik and Tranel (2011) compared participants with adult-onset focal brain damage to the amygdala to neurologically normal adults and adults damaged in other areas of the brain in a Trust Game with a simulated partner. Amygdala-damaged participants showed higher trusting behavior and did not decrease trust when betrayed. Also, testosterone was found to decrease trusting tendencies: women given sublingual (e.g. oral) administration of testosterone rated the faces of strangers as less trustworthy, with effects largest for those women who were initially more trusting (Bos et al., 2010).

These results suggest that OXY tendencies to increase trust moderate tendencies toward suspiciousness mediated by brain systems associated with anxiety and social vigilance. Johnson and Breedlove (2012) suggest that the activity of the amygdala in response to threat is associated with testosterone receptors that act on AVP neurons that activate fearful responses via brainstem systems. OXY may increase trust by exerting opposing effects.

Oxytocin and communication. There is, in fact, direct evidence that OXY interacts with the amygdala, although there are differences with different amygdala subregions. In a study on fMRI activation to a task involving the classification of emotional faces, OXY was found to attenuate the response to fearful faces but enhance the response to happy faces in lateral and dorsal regions of the anterior amygdala (Gamer et al., 2011). This suggested with other evidence that OXY enhances the processing of positive social stimuli. At the same time, Gamer et al. (2011) showed that OXY increased reflexive tendencies to attend to the eye region of others: OXY increased the gaze shifts toward the eye region regardless of the depicted emotion. This effect was associated with increased activation of the posterior amygdala and enhanced functional connectivity between it and the superior colliculus, a structure involved in the control of eye movements. This finding is significant because the eye region of the face is more likely than the lower face to display spontaneous "true feelings" as opposed to controlled and socialized expressions (Buck, 1984), and an implication may be that OXY functions to increase accurate emotional communication, whether it be "positive" or "negative." In fact, intranasal OXY has been demonstrated to substantially increase the ability to infer emotions expressed by the eyes (Domes et al., 2007b).

The studies using Trust Games could not be sensitive to the ability of OXY to increase accurate nonverbal communication because they are played anonymously, sometimes partnered with a computer-simulant rather than another human being. As Koscik and Tranel (2011) noted, behavior in the Trust Game is highly variable and greatly influenced by the actions of a partner, and the variability of the behavior of a given participant can be reduced if all have the same opponent. This is undoubtedly correct, but it is nonetheless an artificial situation and results can be misleading if they are applied uncritically to situations where interaction and communication occur. In fact, as we shall discuss later, it may be that nonverbal expressivity, which tends to enhance face-to-face emotional communication, can function as a marker of trustworthiness in interactive situations (Boone and Buck, 2003; Oda et al., 2009).

Oxytocin in interactional context

The effects of OXY have been examined in interactional context in an impressive series of studies by Ruth Feldman and colleagues (see Feldman, 2012a). Feldman suggested that there are three prototypes of attachment in human beings: *parental love* between parent and infant, *filial love* between friends, and *romantic love* between sexual partners: these correspond generally to the parental, peer, and sexual affectional systems noted previously. Feldman suggested that these prototypes share common brain mechanisms underpinned by OXY in the promotion of *biobehavioral synchrony*, which involves the temporal concordance of the biological and social behavior of interactants. Examples of such synchrony have long been reported in animals, from social insects (Wheeler, 1928) to flocks of birds and schools of fish. Interpersonal synchrony has been observed in human interaction as well (Condon, 1982; Condon and Ogston, 1966; Condon and Sander, 1974; Kendon, 1970), and it is a cardinal feature of mutual contingent responsiveness and primary intersubjectivity noted previously (Murray and Trevarthen, 1986). Feldman (2012a) argued that OXY plays a key role in the motivation to bond, particularly in interaction with the DA reward system including the "hedonic hotspot" NAcc; and she reports research involving the observation and micro-coding of human interaction behaviors such as touching, eye contact, emotion display, and soft vocalization; assessing the interactional coordination of these behaviors in parent–infant, filial, and sexual dyads; usually including measures of OXY and other relevant neurohormones and physiological responses.

Parental love. The parent–infant bond has been studied most extensively in this research, which has included longitudinal studies assessing the long-term effects of early parenting styles. In the first study of the role of OXY in maternal behavior in women, plasma OXY and cortisol (CORT) were assessed repeatedly from the first trimester of pregnancy to one month after birth. OXY levels were significantly higher in mothers compared with other women, in whom they tended to be stable, and OXY levels in the first trimester of pregnancy were associated with maternal bonding behaviors micro-coded during interaction with the infant, including gaze, the display of positive emotions, high frequency "motherese" vocalizations, and affectionate touch. The rise in OXY from the first to the third trimester was also associated with maternal bonding behaviors (Feldman et al., 2007). A second study differentiated mothers on the basis of their observed interaction behaviors with their infants: secure mothers coordinated their behavior with that of the infant, but intrusive mothers did not respond to infant signals. While viewing films of infant behaviors, secure mothers showed activity in the left NAcc, suggesting the involvement of reward-related neurochemical systems; while insecure mothers showed activity in the right amygdala, suggesting the involvement of anxiety and stress. Moreover, the brain activity of secure mothers was more organized, and correlations between OXY, NAcc activation, and amygdala activation were observed in the secure mothers only (Atzil et al., 2011).

Another study examined relationships between plasma OXY, synchronous parenting, and memories of parental care in a large sample including 272 mothers and fathers and their 4- to 6-month-old infants; and 80 non-parents. In addition, it examined variations in the OXTR gene, which codes for the oxytocin receptor; and the CD38 gene that is essential to the release of brain OXY. High-risk variations in these genes have been associated with increased risk for social dysfunctions including ASD. Parent–infant interactions were micro-coded for parental touch and gaze synchrony. Results revealed that OXTR and CD38 risk variations were associated with lower plasma OXY in all samples, showing that genetic and peripheral markers of OXY measures are interrelated. In addition, reduced plasma OXY and OXTR and CD38 risk factors were related to less parental touch; and high plasma OXY and low-risk CD38 variations predicted longer episodes of parent–infant gaze synchrony. Moreover, and relevant to Bowlby's concern about the intergenerational transfer of attachment styles, parents reporting memories of greater parental care showed higher plasma OXY, low-risk CD38 variations, and more infant touch. The authors concluded that the extended OXY system reflects core behaviors associated with parenting and social engagement in human beings (Feldman et al., 2012b).

Other studies reviewed by Feldman (2012a) involved OXY and the behavior of fathers. She noted that only 3–5 percent of mammalian species exhibit active paternal involvement in child care, but as we have seen, there is evidence that such paternal involvement may have been a factor in human evolution long before the expansion of the brain. Interestingly, maternal and paternal caregiving behaviors tend to differ, with mothers preferring *social-affective play* (face-to-face positioning, touching, licking, and grooming); and fathers preferring *object-oriented stimulatory play* (side-by-side positioning, stimulating the infant to encourage exploration, and providing rough-and-tumble contact. Feldman et al., 2007). As Feldman put it, "Mothers establish a sense of predictability and safety, while fathers prepare for novelty and excitement, and both components are needed for the formation of lasting attachments" (2012a, p. 6).

A number of studies investigated relationships between micro-coded parental behaviors, OXY, and other neurohormones. In a prospective longitudinal study, Gordon et al. (2010a) measured plasma OXY and salivary CORT in 160 first-time mothers and fathers with their infants in the first month and again at six months. Plasma OXY was at comparable levels in mothers and fathers, and higher than levels in non-attached women and men. OXY in mothers was associated with socio-affective play, and OXY in fathers with object-oriented play. Moreover, OXY in mothers and fathers demonstrated *physiological synchrony*, or associations between the OXY levels of cohabiting mothers and fathers, suggesting a process in which partners "shape each other's neuropeptide response through affiliative behavior and marital and coparental attachment" (Feldman, 2012a, p. 6).

In a study of 144 mothers and fathers interacting with 6-month-old infants, plasma OXY and AVP were at comparable levels in mothers and fathers, but OXY was associated with social-affective play and AVP with object-oriented stimulatory play. Also, the social and object play behaviors of the infant were differentially associated with the OXY and AVP measures in the parents, demonstrating that "attachment partners shape each other's physiology through joint interactive behavior in a social context" (Feldman, 2012a, p. 6). In a second study, 43 fathers were asked to engage in social-affective or object-oriented play, while plasma OXY and prolactin (PRL) were assessed. OXY was associated with the father's social-affective play and PRL with object-oriented play (Gordon et al., 2010b). A third study investigated triadic synchrony: points where parents and child share gaze and are in physical contact. These points were associated with high OXY and low CORT in both parents. In a fourth study, Feldman et al. (2011) found that plasma and salivary OXY were interrelated and associated with the number of positive communication sequences and the degree of interpersonal synchrony between parents and their 6-month-old children. All in all, these studies demonstrate convincingly the role of OXY in supporting parental affiliative behaviors.

Finally, a study manipulated OXY in fathers in a double-blind study that administered OXY or a placebo in nasal spray, and both fathers' and infants' behaviors were micro-coded during play. Salivary OXY was measured from both father and infant at baseline and in three 20-minute intervals. Fathers inhaling OXY showed longer durations of engagement with the infant and more frequent touch. Importantly, levels of OXY in the infant were dramatically raised when the father had inhaled OXY, despite the fact that OXY was not administered to the infant. Also, infants in the OXY condition had increased *respiratory sinus arrhythmia* (RSA), a measure of parasympathetic nervous system arousal associated with readiness for social contact (Porges, 1995); and they showed longer social gaze and toy engagement. Feldman concluded, "These findings are the first to demonstrate that OXY administrations to a parent can lead to alterations in the physiology and behavior of an infant in ways that induce greater readiness for social contact" (2012a, p. 7).

The fact that the father's OXY can shape the infant's physiology and behavior suggests a mechanism for the intergenerational transmission of attachment patterns that was a concern of Bowlby (Bretherton, 1992). Indeed, Feldman et al., (2010) found evidence of the intergenerational transmission of OXY responding. Salivary OXY was measured from mothers, fathers, and 6-month-old infants at baseline and following play, and behavioral synchrony was micro-coded. Parent and infant OXY levels were positively correlated with one another at baseline, as was the degree of OXY increase following play. Importantly, parent synchrony moderated the intergenerational effect: parent and infant OXY were associated only when parent and infant synchrony was high. Feldman concluded, "Behavioral coordination provides one channel through which parental OXY shapes the infant's emerging neuropeptide organization and its ensuing life-time effects on social affiliation" (2012a, p. 7).

Another study investigated the brain responses in fifteen married couples as they viewed films of their own child or another infant, and synchrony of the mother's and father's brain activity were assessed. Mothers showed greater activation than fathers in the amygdala and NAcc, and this was positively associated with maternal OXY. Fathers showed greater activation than mothers in emotion-regulatory areas, particularly the medial prefrontal cortex (MPFC), and this was positively correlated with AVP. Moreover, results revealed synchrony in the brain activations of mothers and fathers in areas implicated in empathy, ToM, and mirroring that support the intuitive understanding of infant displays: these included the MPFC, superior temporal sulcus (STS), inferior frontal gyrus (IFG), and insula (Atzil et al., 2013). Feldman noted, "These findings are the first to show that parents synchronize online brain activity in cortical networks that support intuitive understanding of the infant's communications and the planning of appropriate caregiving" (2012a, p. 7).

Filial love. In Harlow's (1971) account of socio-emotional development, the early interactions occurring during the parental affectional system set the stage for later interactions between peers by instilling a basic sense of trust in others. This process was studied in longitudinal follow-up studies of studies of parent–infant interaction reported by Feldman (2012a). In one, families seen in the prospective longitudinal study of Gordon et al. (2010a) at 1 and 6 months were seen again at age 3. Children were observed interacting with their mother, father, and best friend, and salivary OXY was collected before and after play. As expected, children who had received more synchronous interaction with their parents early in life were found to interact more easily with their best friends, showing greater reciprocity, empathy, concern for the other, emotional involvement, and affective attunement. Also, parents' early OXY and synchrony prospectively predicted child OXY at age 3.

A second study followed children's interactions with their parents at 5 months, 3 years, and 13 years of age. They were also observed at age 13 in interactions with a same-sex best friend in positive (planning a school activity) and negative (discussing a conflict in their relationship) interactions. Results indicated that reciprocity of the child with the parents was stable across the 13 years, and also that maternal and paternal reciprocity were interrelated at each age. Also, parental reciprocity in infancy predicted friendliness, cooperation, and ease of interaction with same-sex friends in childhood, and interaction skills in adolescence (Feldman and Bamburger, submitted).

Sexual love: pair-bonding in humans. Just as Harlow's peer affectional system (1971) makes way for the sexual affectional system at puberty, peer relationships are accompanied by sexually charged relationships in adolescence in human beings. Animal studies implicating the importance of OXY in pair-bond formation are echoed in studies in humans, who show culturally universal evidence of intense romantic love (Jankowiak and Fischer, 1992). Romantic love is associated with a complex of feelings and desires termed *limerance* (Tennov, 1979), which includes euphoria, energy, attention, obsessive thinking, emotional dependency, and a craving for emotional union with the beloved

(Hatfield and Sprecher, 1986). Studies suggest that the affective symphony associated with sexual pair-bonding has similarities with the affective symphony associated with parental and filial love, but significant differences as well, recalling discussions of the reward processes – wanting and liking – discussed in Chapter 3.

Brain imaging studies have compared the brain response to facial images of a partner in an intense early-stage romantic love relationship with the brain response to a picture of a highly familiar acquaintance (Aron et al., 2005). Results indicated the involvement of areas rich in DA, including the right ventral tegmental area (VTA) and medial caudate nucleus. Also, activation in the right caudate was correlated with self-report measures of romantic passion; activation in the left insula, putamen, and globus pallidus was associated with trait affect intensity; and activation in the left VTA was correlated with facial attractiveness of the person photographed. Acevedo et al. (2012) also found evidence of activation in the DA-rich reward centers such as the VTA and dorsal striatum in a study of long-term romantic lovers, suggesting that the reward value of a long-term partner may be sustained. They also found activation in neural systems associated with the opiates and serotonin, and suggested that intense romantic love may persist in long-term love relationships, but become calmer, losing obsessive aspects characteristic of early romantic relationships. Acevedo et al. (2012) noted that their results were consistent with several other studies implicating the right VTA in responding to romantic love and relational closeness. They also noted that long-term pair-bonds and maternal attachment both appear to activate "hedonic hot-spots" associated with the pleasure aspects of reward, discussed in Chapter 3 (Smith et al., 2009): "the 'wanting' motivation and reward associated with a long-term partner may be sustained, and can co-exist with 'liking' and pleasure, aspects of attachment bonding" (Acevedo et al., 2012, p. 13).

Feldman (2012a) noted the overlap in brain regions activated by long-term romantic attachments and parental bonding, and suggested that parental and romantic attachments share underlying mechanisms (Gordon et al., 2008; Feldman, 2012b). This was seen to be consistent with the results of a study by Schneiderman et al. (2012) involving 163 young adults, including 43 unattached singles and 120 new lovers (60 couples), shortly after the initiation of the romantic relationship of the latter. Six months later, 25 of the 36 couples who had stayed together were observed in dyadic interaction and interviewed about their relationships. Results indicated that plasma OXY was higher in new lovers than in unattached singles: in fact the OXY levels were higher in the new lovers than they typically were in new parents. These levels remained high in the six-month period between assessments and were stable within individuals. Also, the OXY levels were associated with the interactive synchrony of the couples, including social focus, affectionate touch, positive emotional displays, and synchronized dyadic states; as well as worries and preoccupations concerning the relationship.

Feldman (2012a) concluded that the three prototypes of human attachment – parental, filial, and sexual – are supported by common OXY-based neuroendocrine systems and expressed by similar dyadic behavior involving the online coordination of positive emotional displays, gaze, affectionate touch, and vocalization. From the point of view of the function of subjectively experienced feelings and desires that is at the heart of this book, it appears that the voices of the genes carrying messages to love and bond with our lovers, children, kin, and comrades are powerful indeed; contributing to a variable but persisting affective symphony that in many ways gives meaning to life and in many instances is stronger than any fear, even that of death. Also, although these influences are often below the radar of consciousness, their effects are objectively present for all who look carefully to see, in displays of interpersonal synchrony.

The dark side of oxytocin

There is evidence that OXY not only increases trust, empathic concern, and interactive synchrony, but also the categorization of others into in-group and out-group, and that the trust and concern may be reserved primarily for the members of the in-group (De Dreu, 2012). We saw in a previous section that OXY plays a role in social recognition and memory in rodents, and that it plays a role not only in maternal care but also in maternal aggression in defense of the young (Neumann, 2008). In one human study, participants were given OXY or placebo in nasal spray and then viewed pictures of faces. The next day, they were asked unexpectedly to perform a recognition task, and it was found that those who had seen the pictures with OXY rated the pictures they had seen as more familiar (Rimelle et al., 2009). In similar studies, Savaskan et al. (1989) showed that OXY increased the short- and long-term recognition of angry and neutral (but not happy) faces; and Gauastella et al. (2008) reported that OXY increased the ability of men to remember happy (but not angry or neutral) faces. Another study showed that OXY could increase negative as well as positive social emotions. In an economic choice game, OXY increased both reported gloating (*schadenfreude*, or pleasure at the distress of others) when one gained more than an opponent, and reported envy when the opponent was more successful (Shamay-Tsoory et al., 2009).

The results of the studies of parent–infant, peer, and romantic interaction reported by Feldman (2012a) are consistent with the developmental-interactionist view that emotional expression and communication link phenomena at the social/ecological level of analysis (e.g. play behaviors) and phenomena at the physiological level of analysis (e.g. neuropeptides). Emotional expression and communication simultaneously serve functions of self-regulation and social coordination (Buck, 1989b). We shall see in Chapter 7 that human tendencies for attachment are accompanied by tendencies to distinguish in-groups and out-groups, and that the social contract that regulates conflict and aggression within groups may actually include an implicit requirement for pseudospeciation: that is, to reject, attack, and even remorselessly destroy those who constitute a threat to the in-group. This indeed may be the answer to the question posed at the beginning of this chapter: whether human nature is essentially "good" and cooperative, or "bad," selfish, and competitive. Neurochemical systems associated with the OXY molecule support strong subjective affects supporting parental caring and joyful play, and well as deep friendship and romantic love, but at the same time they appear to foster *xenophobia*: the rejection and ostracism – even the destruction and annihilation (*"ethnic cleansing"*) – of those not deemed to be within the group. In the innocent and beautiful play of parent and child, friend and lover, lie the emotional roots of fascism.

Implications: the readout model of emotion

The research considered in this section expands the view of the process of emotional education and of emotional competence emerging naturally over the course of emotional development; and it adds detail regarding the specific neurochemical systems involved. In particular, this research provides a compelling and concrete illustration of the basic notion that emotions are "read out" constantly in arousal, display, and experience (Emotion I, II, and III). The OXY molecule and systems associated with it have effects upon Emotion I physiological responses such as CORT, Emotion II responses such as display behaviors, and Emotion III responses involving subjective experiences. At the same time, this research has demonstrated that the readouts of child and parent, peers, and lovers can be synchronous, indicating that the displays not only reveal the subjective lives of senders but simultaneously alter the subjective lives of receivers and their displays in response. The emotion readout is at once hidden in Emotion III private experiences,

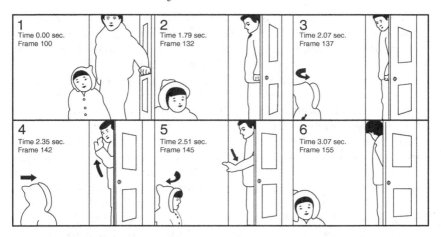

Figure 4.6 The affective microscope. Leave-taking sequence between father and preschool daughter, drawn from the film. See text for details.

and objectively observable in the stream of Emotion II expressive behavior, which if carefully recorded and observed can serve as an "affective microscope" revealing much about the interaction and the feelings and desires of those involved.

An example is illustrated in Figure 4.6 in a three-second sequence taken from a frame-by-frame analysis of leave-taking between a parent and child at a nursery school (Peery, 1978). A father brought his daughter to the school and waited at the door as she entered. After a few steps, the daughter stopped and turned back to her father, who waved. The girl then turned back to the schoolroom while the father left. Viewed at normal speed, this sequence appeared unremarkable, but when viewed in detail by frame-by-frame analysis it became clear that the father's "wave" took a particular form of first stopping the child similar to the action of a police officer stopping traffic, and then "pushing" her away and into the schoolroom. The first part of the father's gesture was associated with the daughter stopping her movement back toward the father (drawing 4). The father then brought down his hand and arm in a "pushing" motion, and on precisely the same frame as his action began, the daughter began turning her head away from her father and back into the schoolroom (drawing 5). Peery noted that when viewing the 0.16 seconds between frames 142 and 145, it "almost seems that the father has physically pushed the daughter away" despite the fact that there was no physical contact between them. "They look like puppets being manipulated by the same strings" (Peery, 1978, p. 60).

This simultaneous "dance" involving both intrapersonal and interpersonal synchrony is a constant albeit little noted aspect of human interaction. At every turn, we are expressing our reactions to the behaviors of others "online," and they are reacting to our behaviors. Paradoxically, although we are exquisitely sensitive to the cues of this dance we are at the same time largely oblivious to it. The synchronous dance is experienced by both parties as "flow," "presence," or "involvement" in the conversation and functions to punctuate and lubricate normal informal interaction (Buck and Powers, 2013). Often it only becomes noticeable on a conscious level when something goes wrong: something is out of place. Ray Birdwhistell (1950), in studying the nodding of psychotherapists in response to the stories of their patients, noted that most nods did not influence the stream of interaction unless they were unsynchronized with the beat of the patient's behavior. These "sore thumb nods" stood out from the flow of interaction like a sore thumb, indicating to the patient that the attention of his therapist had wandered. Lecturers are only too aware of cues in their audiences that indicate inattention: persons surreptitiously texting in the last row give clear evidence of their iniquity in their lack of synchrony with the class as a whole. And, the lecturer typically greets such inattention with annoyance and resentment. As we shall see, "higher-level" social and moral emotions emerge directly and naturally from these behaviors over the course of interaction.

Conclusions: emotion, communication, and social organization

The consideration of biological emotions as based upon neurochemical systems allows a fresh approach to such fundamental issues as the nature of attachment, love, pleasure, desire, and despair; the emotional bases of competition and cooperation; and a topic we have not considered in this chapter because of limitations of space: the relationships between emotion, stress buffering, and physical health (Buck, 1993c). Of fundamental importance in all of this is emotion communication. A major implication of the evidence discussed in this chapter – from evolution, from animal behavior and development, from the affective neuroscience of human interaction – is that spontaneous communication is a mechanism by which evolution can come to structure social organization (Buck, 2007).

Displays and preattunements must co-evolve, in that the evolution of one depends on the evolution of the other. In effect, evolution cannot select the display or the preattunement in isolation. In selecting the phenotype of communication, evolution instead selects the communicative relationship in the genotype, involving display and preattunement functioning together (Buck, 2011; Buck and Ginsburg, 1991, 1997b). The capacity of a species to communicate emotion and thereby to communicate about threat and submission, courting and mating, parenting and nurturance, separation and reunion, aggression and affiliation, social recognition, play, distress, and so on does much to determine the basic social organization of that species. Such emotion communication is inherently dyadic, and it must be learned and shaped in the context of dyadic interaction over the course of development in each generation; but at the same time it is related to concrete, potentially observable phenomena within both sender and receiver, such as the interpersonal synchrony of the micro-level social behaviors involving touch, gaze, vocalization, and emotion displays that have been demonstrated to be influenced by OXY and other specific neurochemicals. Such emotion communication reflects a universal interaction of ruthless selfishness and unconditional loving cooperation in a dynamic balance: a Yin and Yang of self-interest and altruism.

At the center of this communication process is one of the great motivational-emotional systems at the heart of human nature: attachment. In considering the neurochemical systems underlying attachment, and the developmental course of attachment in early life, we have seen evidence of continuity with attachment mechanisms in other animals, particularly primates. Initial parental affection sets the stage for affectionate relations between peers, which in turn set the stage for affectionate sexual relationships. However, in considering the evolution of attachment, there appears to be an important discontinuity involving the evolution of mechanisms such as invisible estrus, continuous sexual receptivity in females, the absence of projecting canines in males, more egalitarian sex roles suggested by smaller sex differences in body size, and the concomitant enhancement of sexual pleasure. All of these appear to function to involve the male in caring for the young. Significantly, we have seen that *Ardipithecus ramidus* showed evidence of these traits 5 million years ago, long before there is evidence of enlargement of the brain in the past 1–2 million years. If so, the quality that has most distinguished humanity from our fellow primate species may not be our ability to think so much as our ability to love.

PART III

Higher-level emotions:
an ecological-systems view

CHAPTER 5

Cognitive and linguistic emotions

From biological to higher-level emotions

One of the enduring puzzles in emotion theory has been understanding the relationship of biological emotions and higher-level emotions such as pride, resentment, pity, gratitude, and respect. As previously discussed, I regard biological emotions to be based in primary motivational-emotional systems or primes, which involve interactive but dissociable modules, each associated with specifiable neurochemical systems and, ultimately, with specifiable genes and genetic systems. Due to their similar functions, these modules are "packaged" ecologically by the forces of evolution into familiar emotions such as happiness, sadness, fear, anger, love, nurturance, and bonding.

Biological versus higher-level emotions: general principles

A central proposition in Silvan Tomkins' (1962–92) theory was that affect functions as a separate assembly, a *general motivational system*, working to amplify other aspects of behavior. I suggest that this is not the case for the primes: each of the primes has motivational force built into the system. Indeed, the activation of a prime is seen to be a readout of motivational potential, as illustrated in Figure 1.1. However, Tomkins' notion of a separate affect system is useful in conceptualizing the differences and similarities of biological and higher-level emotions.

An essential difference between biological and higher-level emotions is that the former can "stand alone" as it were: the complete Emotion I, II, and III package of arousal, display, and experience resides in the individual organism, although the proper functioning of this package requires social experience and communication as we have seen. In contrast, higher-level emotions involve biologically based affects, but these affects function as general motivational systems in Tomkins' sense, and the unique character of different higher-level emotions is determined externally, by events in terrestrial and social reality. For example, a child's general need for exploration can appear in the guise

205

of curiosity in a novel situation, surprise in an unexpected situation, and dread in a frightening or uncertain situation. Similarly, a child's need for social attachment can appear in the guise of pride when the child is successful, in resentment when another child succeeds unfairly, and pity when another child is punished unfairly.

An ecological view of higher-level emotions. Several principles differentiate biological from higher-level emotions. First, biological emotions are associated with specifiable neurochemical modules that can, at least in principle, be manipulated directly by drug or gene alterations within the body. Second, biological emotions are always "on," albeit normally at low levels and unnoticed. Third, biological emotions emerge developmentally in an internally programmed maturational sequence which is timed with their functions in the parental, peer, and sexual affectional systems.

In contrast, while they do involve general biologically based affects to provide their motivational force, higher-level emotions respond to specific ecological challenges in the terrestrial and social environments, and they therefore exist relative to external stimuli or other persons, including situations involving events in memory and imagination. Second, higher-level emotions are not always "on," rather they exist as potential until activated by those specific ecological challenges. Third, while higher-level emotions involve a general biologically based affective readiness, they require experience over the course of development with the specific ecological challenges to become appropriately, effectively, and competently experienced and expressed. Cognitive emotions require experience in terrestrial reality, social emotions require experience in social reality, moral emotions require experience in both.

Curiosity, attachment, and gust. At least two sorts of general affect-motivational systems can be distinguished: *curiosity* or *effectance motives* associated with cognitive emotions, and *attachment* associated with social emotions. As suggested in Figure 1.4, curiosity and effectance motives are associated with general tendencies to *broaden and build* (Fredrickson, 2001), and attachment motives are associated with general tendencies to *tend and befriend* (Taylor, 2000). In addition, *gust* may be a general affect-motivational system associated with moral emotions. Gust is hypothesized to be a basic motive firing moral approbation, the opposite of the widely recognized and studied disgust (Rozin et al., 1993).

The relationship of biological and higher-level emotions

The general model of the relationship of biological and higher-level emotions is presented in Figure 5.1. Biological affects based upon

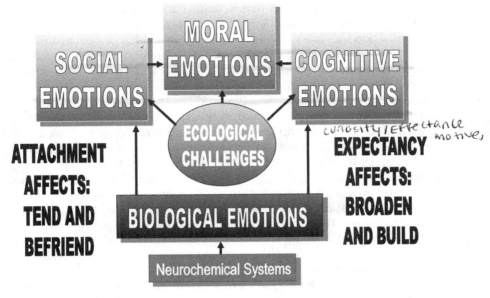

Figure 5.1 Relationships between biological and higher-level emotions. See text for details.

specifiable neurochemical systems are the source of general individual-istic *effectance affects* that underlie tendencies to broaden and build and that, when combined with ecological challenges in the form of combinations of situational contingencies, produce cognitive emotions. Specifiable neurochemical systems are also the source of prosocial *attachment affects* that underlie tendencies to tend and befriend that, when combined with ecological challenges in the form of combinations of interpersonal contingencies, produce social emotions. Moral emotions involve less well-understood affects of gust–disgust which are biologically based that combine with ecological challenges in the form of combinations of moral contingencies. There are two aspects of moral emotions: one is the understanding of rule systems engendered particularly by effectance affects, resulting in a *morality of justice*; and the other is caring that the rules are followed engendered particularly by attachment affects, resulting in a *morality of caring*.

Curiosity and effectance motives expose the child to events that evoke feelings of happiness and security, sadness and grief, fear and anxiety, anger and frustration, surprise and uncertainty, satisfaction and boredom: a vast array of cognitive emotions ranging from awe to ennui. Early on, the child must encounter a relatively safe environment of events and stimulation that is neither too sterile nor too rich, that affords the ability to assimilate new information and accommodate that information into one's cognitive system. Information that is assimilable but not completely accommodated constitutes a challenge, and the child is intrinsically motivated to approach and explore such stimuli until they are mastered.

Attachment motives expose the child to people and events that evoke prosocial emotions: love, warmth, intimacy, bonding, caring, nurturance; as well as the panic and despair associated with separation, isolation, and bereavement. In the case of attachment, we saw in Chapter 4 that normal social development and bonding requires the initial "turning on" of attachment motives via contact comfort; and later emancipation from parents with contact with peers in rough-and-tumble play. Early social deprivation, neglect, and abuse can lead to life-long disorders of attachment. Bowlby's (1988) work described how parents normally fulfill the dual roles of activating attachment motives and providing a safe base for exploration, with powerful potential influences on the child-rearing skills of their own children.

Least is known about gust, but I hypothesize it as a motive which exposes the child to do good and avoid doing evil. Morality has usually been approached in the negative sense of suppressing or controlling evil tendencies, including the "animal passions," rather than encouraging and celebrating the good. Thus, disgust is widely studied and acknowledged to be a moral emotion, but emotions of moral approbation remain poorly understood.

The functioning of these three motivational systems – curiosity, attachment, and a pervasive sense of right and wrong – is gloriously and sometimes disturbingly displayed in the play of the young: human and nonhuman alike. This is the great drama of the peer affectional system, where the affective seeds of adult behavior are sown and begin to take root. It is an interesting fact that in the great majority of children, aggressive behavior peaks between the ages of two-and-a-half and three-and-a-half. Children do not learn to be aggressive: they learn *not* to be aggressive (Tremblay, 2010). They learn through playful interaction to moderate their own hostile and selfish behaviors and begin spontaneously to follow the Golden Rule, to treat others as they themselves would wish to be treated. Of course, children are also known to tease and bully one another unmercifully, as well as to form gangs whose sense of propriety and morality may be very strong, but inconsistent with and hostile to that in the larger culture. In order effectively to mitigate the damage caused by these undesirable behaviors, we must better understand their affective roots.

Cognitive emotions: from awe to ennui

The readout model of cognitive emotions

As with biological emotions, cognitive emotions may be with us, whispering, even though we may not notice them; but unlike biological emotions and like social and moral emotions these exist with regard to external events: they always relate to something outside the organism. When we feel curious, interested, surprised, bored, or burned out, it is with respect to specific events or circumstances: we are interested *in* something; or surprised *at* something; stubborn, confused, or confident *about* something. It is only meaningful to inquire about cognitive emotions if some situational circumstances are specified or implied.

Curiosity/effectance: the biological bases of the cognitive emotions

Just as social emotions are based biologically in prosocial attachment systems, cognitive emotions are based biologically in individualistic reward and punishment systems coursing through the hypothalamus into the forebrain. As noted in Chapter 3, these have been termed the behavioral activation system (BAS) and behavioral inhibition system (BIS) respectively. They function together to enable an animal to adapt its behavior to the fruits and dangers of its environment so that it becomes through experience able to obtain the former and avoid the latter. Individual differences in these tendencies vary along the powerful personality dimension of introversion–extroversion, which expresses in part the general ease in being rewarded or punished (Gray, 1982a, 1982b). Panksepp (1982) suggested that this "expectancy system" provides the motivational component to a number of specific drives, and that it can also motivate more general exploratory behaviors, resulting in general motives to explore and to understand the unfamiliar.

Effectance motivation. In a seminal paper, Robert W. White (1959) pointed out that exploratory, stimulus-seeking behaviors have a common property: they have an effect on the environment. He cited a classic study of play by Gross (1901), who emphasized the child's "joy in being a cause" in altering and manipulating the environment. White proposed that "effective interaction with the environment" is intrinsically rewarding: that exploratory behaviors are directed, selective, and persistent, and motivated by an intrinsic need to deal with the environment which he termed *effectance motivation*. The result is that the child gains *competence* in dealing with the environment. To illustrate, White reviewed the work of Jean Piaget (e.g. 1971), that had relatively little impact on American psychology up to that time.

White's analysis implied that the process of coming to know the environment is not a "cold cognitive" process but rather is strongly charged affectively, with powerful feelings including expectancy, curiosity, boredom, interest, and surprise. Interest and surprise were among Tomkins' (1962–92) original primary affects, and surprise has been associated with pancultural facial expressions (Ekman and Friesen, 1975). Interest remained a fundamental emotion in Izard's (1977) analysis.

A number of *competence theories* have central concepts similar to White's competence: Rotter's (1966) *locus of control*, Heider's (1958) and de Charms' (1968) *personal causation*, Bandura's (1991) *self-efficacy*, and Deci and Ryan's (1991) *intrinsic motivation* are prominent examples. These have generally not considered in detail the affective concomitants of exploration: indeed, they often conceptualize emotions as negative influences disrupting smooth cognitive processing. For example, Deci and Ryan (1991) discussed "amotivation . . . (occurring when one is) ineffective . . . with respect to forces, such as affects or impulses, that are within" (p. 253). They regarded amotivated behavior as undesirable, and wrote of "amotivated hate" (p. 279). They did not, however, consider amotivated love. Both Bandura (1991) and Deci and Ryan (1991) acknowledged that there are human needs – social needs in particular – that fall outside the range of competence theories, but their theories at times seem to advocate an ideal of the independent, autonomous, competent self-actualizer (Deci and Ryan, 1991, pp. 276–77). This perhaps may reflect the view of a relatively "selfish" individualistic outlook that may not fully appreciate more communal values (see Buck, 1993d).

Broaden-and-build, and positive psychology. More recently, Barbara Fredrickson (2001) developed the concept of "broaden and build," which suggests that "positive" emotions such as joy, happiness, interest, and anticipation are different from "negative" emotions that tend to turn attention toward a specific challenging emotional stimulus. Positive emotions, in contrast, tend to broaden one's range of awareness, encouraging exploration and novel and creative thoughts and actions.

The broaden-and-build concept has been associated with a larger program of *positive psychology*, which has sought to concentrate on the positive promotion of mental and emotional health as opposed to the treatment of mental and emotional illness. Positive psychology has been defined as the study of processes that "contribute to the flourishing or optimal functioning of people, groups, and institutions" (Gable and Haidt, 2005, p. 104). These ideas have roots in the work of humanistic psychologists including Carl Rogers, Eric Fromm, and

Abraham Maslow, who originated the term in his book *Motivation and Personality* (Maslow, 1954). The viewpoint was powerfully encouraged in 1998 when Martin Seligman, known for his work on temperament, helplessness, and depression, chose positive psychology as the theme for his term as president of the American Psychological Association. In January 2000, Seligman and Mihaly Csikszentmihalyi edited a special issue of the *American Psychologist* devoted to positive psychology, which initiated what came to be known as the positive psychology movement (Gable and Haidt, 2005). To its credit, this movement has strongly encouraged empirical research on the concept, and it has indeed found considerable support. For example, optimism, humor, forgiveness, and curiosity have all been demonstrated to promote mental and emotional well-being (Gable and Haidt, 2005).

Although positive psychology has been successfully branded as new and unique, close examination reveals that in important respects it is not so different from earlier competence theories. Unlike the competence theories, positive psychology in general and the broaden-and-build concept in particular put positive emotion and affect at the core of exploration and discovery. But, like the competence theories, there is a prescriptive flavor to positive psychology and the broaden-and-build notion, as involving the promotion of "optimal" human functioning. Also like the competence theories, social and communicative aspects of human functioning tend to be overlooked in favor of the promotion of individualistic excellence. In this regard, Gable and Haidt (2005) noted that Seligman (2002) proposed "three pillars" of positive psychology – positive subjective experience, positive individual characteristics, and positive institutions and communities – and they acknowledged that the movement has produced much research in the first two areas but little in the third. Gable and Haidt also acknowledged the complexity of identifying what after all is "positive." Positivity can be defined as what is normally chosen, as what is seen as satisfying and pleasant, and as what is in accord with a system of values; and these three criteria of positivity may not agree. One may often buy gasoline, but that act is not necessarily seen as pleasant or consistent with one's values; sex outside a committed relationship may be seen as pleasant, but inconsistent with values and engaged in rarely if at all; jury duty may be consistent with one's values but seen as unpleasant and avoided if possible.

In a 2011 book billed as "a visionary new understanding of happiness and well-being," Seligman (2011) presented what one reviewer termed a "course correction" for positive psychology (Suttie, 2011). Acknowledging that positive psychology had been too focused on promoting momentary feelings of happiness, Seligman proposed a shift to increase

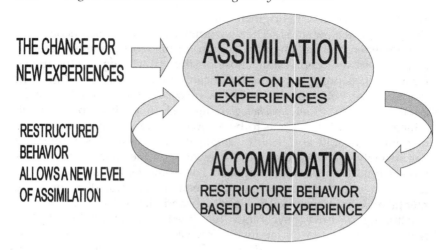

Figure 5.2 Exploration in children: cognitive growth cycles. See text for details.

personal well-being in a broader sense – termed "flourishing" – and to improve the community, not just the self. However, it is unclear what such a course correction will involve given the dependence upon a conceptualization of positive psychology based upon advancing personal happiness and well-being.

Cognitive development

Cognitive growth cycles. Effectance motives motivate exploration, and it is through experiences gained during exploration that the cognitive system develops. In Piaget's (1971) theory, cognitive development takes place in a process of *assimilation* and *accommodation*, where new information is assimilated into developing knowledge structures, which become enriched as they are accommodated to the information, allowing new, more complex information to become assimilable (see Figure 5.2). Assimilable bits of information are termed *aliments*: foods for cognitive growth. Piaget suggested that the individual intrinsically is motivated to explore the aliment: it elicits curiosity and interest. The *cognitive growth cycle*, to use Flavell's (1968) term, comes to an end when the information is completely accommodated. At this point *equilibration* occurs: the individual has nothing else to learn in the situation, and becomes bored with it, turning to a new situation to explore. In this example, we can see the operation of the cognitive emotions of interest and boredom in signaling to the individual the cognitive status of surrounding events: whether they be compelling and fascinating aliments or boring habituated redundancies.

White (1959) cited as an example an observation by the educator Maria Montessori, who watched a young girl engrossed in a puzzle. She picked up the girl, desk and all, and placed her on a table. The girl remained absorbed in the puzzle and it was some minutes before she looked up with a satisfied expression and realized she was on the table. Importantly, the girl never played with that puzzle again. After having mastered it, she went on to other pursuits. The puzzle ceased to be an aliment for cognitive growth.

Curiosity can be defined conceptually as the tendency to become interested, and operationally in terms of the range of stimuli that excite interest. This tendency can be encouraged by a safe and moderately complex environment in which many potentially assimilable experiences are made available. Tendencies to be curious can also be readily suppressed by sterile surroundings, and by a threatening or dangerous environment.

There is evidence that the range of stimuli that elicits exploratory behavior differs from species to species: some species are more curious than others. As noted, Glickman and Schiff (1967) observed that species that have a hard-to-obtain food supply and few natural enemies tend to be curious: for them, exploration is not particularly dangerous and is useful in finding food. On the other hand, species with an easily obtained food supply with more enemies tend to be more timid. Curiosity is more likely to kill a mouse than a cat.

Attachment and the cognitive emotions. We saw that there is evidence that individual differences in attachment as well as in extroversion–introversion may influence exploratory behaviors. Bowlby (1988) suggested that parents can serve as a secure base from which the child gains the capacity to explore the environment. Without such a base, a child's ability to discover that events can be rewarding could be severely restricted.

As summarized in Chapter 4, attachment styles include a *secure* style in which children are confident they are loved, an *anxious/ambivalent* style in which such confidence is lacking, and an *avoidant* style in which the child is relatively unconcerned about being loved. Mikulincer (1997) studied both curiosity and the integration of new information into cognitive structures. Securely attached and anxious/ambivalent persons described themselves as more curious and valued curiosity more than did persons with an avoidant attachment style. Also, secure persons were more open to new information in making social judgments and reported less preference for cognitive closure relative to both anxious/ambivalent and avoidant persons. Mikulincer suggested that a secure base of attachment in infancy encourages curiosity, exploration, and tolerance for ambiguity. Anxious/ambivalent persons have less trust in the world, and in addition may view exploration as competing with social activities used to shore up their confidence in being loved. In both anxious/ambivalent and avoidant persons, their insecurity and lack of optimism and sense of mastery may lead them to reject evidence that might cause confusion or uncertainty. This results in a high need for cognitive closure, intolerance of ambiguity, and a tendency to hold stable, stereotypical, and dogmatic beliefs.

Specific cognitive emotions

The general model of cognitive emotion is presented in Figure 5.1: expectancy affects combine with fundamental situational contingencies to produce cognitive emotions. Expectancy affects provide motivational force in the way suggested by Tomkins' (1962, 1963) theory, while the fundamental situational contingencies determine the nature of the cognitive emotion.

Ecologically fundamental situational contingencies. Ecologically fundamental situational contingencies are defined formally as *specific combinations of circumstances ecologically existent in the terrestrial environment with implications for well-being*. Situational contingencies vary along a number of dimensions which are naturally present in the terrestrial ecology: one is that they may be *actual or anticipated*; another is that they may be *positive, neutral, or negative*, and a third is that they may be *certain or uncertain*. Table 5.1 presents common words in English that are used to label feelings associated with these combinations of situational contingencies, which identify specific cognitive emotions. Thus, the anticipation of positive consequences is associated with feelings of hope, optimism, and confidence; anticipation of negative consequences is associated with feelings of fear, apprehension, and trepidation; anticipation of neutral consequences is associated with feelings of curiosity, interest, and attention. Actual positive consequences are associated with feelings of happiness, satisfaction, and contentment; actual negative consequences are associated with feelings of sadness, depression, and melancholy; actual neutral consequences are associated with feelings of boredom, tedium, and ennui. Anticipation of expected consequences is associated with feelings of certainty, confidence, and coolness; anticipation of unexpected consequences is associated with feelings of insecurity, uncertainty, and indecision. Actual expected consequences are associated with feelings of understanding, comprehension, and recognition; actual unexpected consequences are associated with feelings of surprise, astonishment, and amazement.

Table 5.1 Specific cognitive emotions: common words in English used to label feelings associated with combinations of situational contingencies

	Anticipated	Actual
Positive	hope	happiness
	optimism	satisfaction
	confidence	contentment
Negative	fear	sadness
	apprehension	depression
	trepidation	melancholy
Neutral	curiosity	boredom
	interest	tedium
	attention	ennui
Expected	certainty	understanding
	confidence	comprehension
	coolness	recognition
Unexpected	insecurity	surprise
	uncertainty	astonishment
	indecision	amazement

The reader may note that there is overlap between some labels of cognitive emotions and the primary affects of Tomkins, Ekman, and Izard, specifically happiness, sadness, surprise, and fear. These are emotions ecologically packaged together because they are associated with universal facial expressions that signal actual or anticipated positive, negative, and unexpected consequences. The visible display of such signals at a distance conveys information important for group organization and functioning, so it is not surprising that they can be seen to exist as both primary affects and higher-level cognitive emotions. The list of cognitive emotions is, of course, more extensive, linguistically capturing nuances of meaning that cannot be expressed by the face.

Language and higher-level emotions. In this analysis of higher-level emotions, including cognitive, social, and moral emotions, language is used to label and communicate about the feeling states involved. Some conceptualizations assume that higher-level emotions require complex cognitive processing including a consciousness of self and knowledge of cultural standards, and argue that the language used to label and communicate these emotions is critically culture-bound. For example, Tracy and Robins (2004a) stated, "self-conscious emotions cannot occur independently of elaborate self-processes" (p. 121). The notion that higher-level emotions involve a sense of self and knowledge of cultural standards has been interpreted as consistent with a relativistic view that higher-level emotions are cultural constructions: creations of the human mind (Lutz, 1988). Moreover, cultural differences in the emotion lexicon have been taken to be indicators of differences in emotional experience: as L. F. Barrett (2006) put it: "cultural variation in the experience of emotion . . . is intrinsically driven by cultural differences in emotion categories and concepts" (p. 39).

This issue will be explored in more detail in the chapters on social and moral emotions, where the implications for cultural differences are clear and the positions of advocates well developed, but some discussion on the role of language in understanding cognitive emotions is relevant here. Table 5.1 is not intended to be a listing of major cognitive emotions per se: rather it is a listing of words that are often applied in English to refer to feeling states elicited by the specific combinations of situational contingencies. The words are not relevant in themselves. The combinations of contingencies are universal, and labels can be applied to them in any culture, language, and historical period.

Three levels of knowledge

The need for understanding. The implicit goal of effectance motivation and its associated cognitive emotions is to reach an effective *understanding* of the world, which confers competence. Piaget's (1971) concept of equilibration and Flavell's (1968) cognitive growth cycles describe how this understanding is attained. The nature and complexity of understanding depends upon the general-purpose cognitive learning and memory capacities of the species in question, but in all sufficiently complex species a fundamental *need for understanding* underlies analytic-cognitive development and is expressed in exploratory behavior or the lack thereof (Buck, 1988a).

The ways in which understanding helps the individual organism to adapt are too obvious to belabor here, but it should be noted that human understanding is qualitatively different from the kind of knowledge developed from exploration and experience in other animals. Human understanding has a formal, linguistic character that takes it beyond the experience of a particular individual. In human beings understanding is organized and communicated via language. Therefore, understanding in human beings is uniquely structured by rules of logic, inference, induction, deduction, and coherence inherent in language.

Knowledge by acquaintance. To conceptualize the impact of language on the process of understanding, three levels of knowledge may be

distinguished. The first, as we saw in Chapter 1, is immediate perceptual knowledge: "raw" awareness, knowledge by acquaintance, or
KA. KA is based upon perceptual systems, which are special-purpose
processing systems shaped by phylogenetic adaptation responding to
the natural qualities of the terrestrial ecology: "the fundamentals of
the environment – the substances, the medium, the surfaces – are the
same for all animals . . . we were all, in fact, formed by them. We were
created by the world we live in" (Gibson, 1977, p. 130). The basic
substances of the terrestrial environment are solid (earth), liquid (water),
and gas (air); *surfaces* are the interfaces between any two of these three
states of matter. Gaseous and liquid *media* are illuminated, transmitting
electromagnetic radiation emitted by the sun, including what we call
the "visible spectrum" of light. These *afford vision* whereas solid substances do not. Also, gaseous and liquid media allow chemical diffusion from soluble or volatile sources, thereby they *afford olfaction*.
Gaseous, liquid, and also solid media transmit vibrations, pressure,
or sound waves, thereby they *afford audition*. The gaseous medium of
the air thus "contains *information* about things that reflect light, vibrate,
or are volatile" (Gibson, 1966, p. 17, italics in the original). Information
about the object or surface is physically present in the medium around
it. An object or surface in effect "broadcasts" its presence and properties
through the medium in a flux of potentially stimulating ambient light,
vibration, and diffusion that can be discovered, detected, or "picked
up" by perceptual systems which are phylogenetic adaptations evolved
by natural selection to be sensitive to this information.

Gibson's perceptual theory is applicable not only to the perception of
events in the terrestrial environment that afford behavior (affordances),
but also to social perception (*social affordances*: Buck, 1984; McArthur
and Baron, 1983) and to the perception of internal information via what
Gibson (1966, p. 31) termed *interoceptors*. Subjectively experienced affect
is an example of such internal perception.

Knowledge by description. KA provides the raw material of knowledge,
and in the simplest creatures this raw awareness is all there is to
knowledge. The second level involves knowledge *about* knowledge:
knowledge-by-description (KD). KD appeared with the evolution of
the simplest associative learning: classical conditioning. A certain
marine snail responds to being rotated by extending its foot: apparently
the rotation mimics ocean turbulence and the foot response functions
to help secure the snail. This is a simple unconditioned UCS–UCR reflex
response. If a light stimulus is paired with the rotation in a classical
conditioning procedure, the light soon comes to elicit the foot extension
by itself: that is, the light becomes a CS (Alkon, 1989). When the light
becomes a CS, there is an essential change in the way it is "known"

by the snail. Previously, the light may have been known only by acquaintance, but when it was associated with the rotation the snail learned something *about* the light: that it is associated with rotation. Through associative learning, the light becomes known by description in an elementary sense. The associative learning mechanism by which the light becomes a CS works automatically and is genetically determined: what is not genetically determined is that the CS is a light and not something else. Any stimulus can become a CS if it is associated with a UCS in the experience of an individual organism. This is the essence of a general-purpose processing system: it is literally hard-wired to be flexible. Its response is structured by the specific experience of the individual organism during development.

A more complex sort of KD is provided by instrumental learning of the sort discussed in Chapter 3: e.g. the mouse learning of the position of the dangerous cat and tempting food in the environment. The mouse learns something *about* the stimuli associated with the cat and the food, so that such stimuli become negative and positive incentives, respectively. More complex KD has evolved as more complex general-purpose processing systems involving learning, memory, and information processing have evolved with cognitive capacities associated with the neocortex.

The development of the analytic-cognitive system is motivated via biologically based systems evolved to enable the development of an understanding of reality (e.g. in effectance motivation and curiosity). In both human beings and other animals the content of the analytic-cognitive system is based upon the structure of reality as experienced by that individual. But in human beings an additional source for the organization of cognition is provided by language.

Linguistic knowledge: the ghost in the machine. The achievement of language introduces a system of behavior control that is fundamentally different from the sorts of systems that went before. Language freed us from our individual experience, allowing us to reason about events that have never been, and could never be, actually experienced, such as the number of angels that can stand on the head of a pin, or the nature of a black hole. In most cases the learning, knowledge, and understanding of creatures which lack linguistic competence die with the creature: language provides human beings the capacity to share complex experiences and understandings with those who have gone before. In this respect language actually resembles a "ghost in the machine": the phrase that Gilbert Ryle (1949) used to ridicule Descartes' dualism. Through language we can share the experiences and understanding of those long dead, as well as contemporary creatures of theatre, fiction, mass media, and the Internet. Ghosts, of a kind.

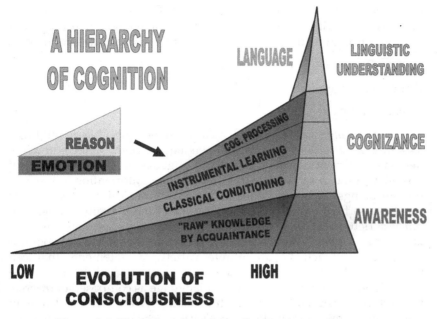

Figure 5.3 Hierarchy of cognition. See text for details.

Summary. The three levels of knowledge are represented in Figure 5.3, which is a modified version of Figure 1.3, which represented the interaction of syncretic KA and analytic KD; and Figure 4.1, which represented the interaction of spontaneous and symbolic communication. All of these involve interactions between special-purpose processing systems and general-purpose processing systems. Again the special-purpose processing systems of KA are along the base, influencing all behavior to some extent. The general-purpose processing systems are divided into those involving classical conditioning, instrumental learning, and higher-order cognitive processing. At the top is language, a general-purpose processing system unlike anything that went before. Language can take cognitive processing outside the limits of individual human existence and into human culture.

At the base of Figure 5.3, as in Figures 1.3 and 4.1, one can place the primes going from reflexes, to instincts, to drives, to affects, to effectance motivation; the phylogenetic scale going from simple creatures to human beings; the developmental scale from conception to adulthood; and the evolution of the brain. Furthermore, it can represent a scale of consciousness running from raw awareness to linguistically based sentience. It might be noted that – as ontogeny recapitulates phylogeny – the principles illustrated in Figure 5.3 are concretely demonstrated with every individual developmental course from conception, through fetal development, to birth and social development.

Language and emotion

Linguistic emotions

The magic of language. Language has its own biological bases, but has a structure and content that is independent of both biology and the personal experience of the individual. Language is one of a number of formal ways of organizing and categorizing information unique to human beings: others include mathematics, musical notation, dance notation, and computer programming. All of these involve systems of *symbols* (letters, words, numbers) that are related to one another according to *rules* (grammar, logic, mathematics, computer programming), and all achieve an infinite variety of statements that can be decoded by anyone who knows the symbols and the rules. For example, structural linguistics regard language as composed of discrete hierarchically arranged units, with a relatively few elemental human vocalizations or *phones* making up *phonemes* (the elements of language roughly corresponding to the letters of the alphabet). The phonemes are combined into *morphemes* (analogous to words) with arbitrarily assigned meanings, and the morphemes are combined to form *sentences*. The rules for combining phones to phonemes to morphemes to sentences constitute the *grammar* of the language. The "magic" of language is that a relatively few phones can be combined into a few dozen phonemes, which are combined into a few hundred thousand morphemes (constituting the vocabulary), which can be combined into an infinite variety of sentences that can be understood by anyone who knows the vocabulary and the rules of combination, e.g. the grammar.

The joy of language. The linguistic competence of human beings is unique, and the development, organization, and maintenance of linguistic control systems must require a kind of motivation that is absent in animals. Language is often viewed as a quintessentially "cold-cognitive" phenomena, but this misses the joy that human beings experience in the successful use of language and the grinding frustration when an idea just cannot be put into words (Buck, 1994b). Not only are humans *cognitively capable* of language, they *care* about language: about understanding phenomena in a linguistically consistent and coherent way, about communicating that understanding to others, about teaching children to do the same. Any writer is familiar with the "blank page" phenomenon: the entirely unpleasant affective response when one is confronted with a blank page on one's tablet or computer screen. Any writer or public speaker has also known-by-acquaintance the deep satisfaction that comes from having produced a well-turned phrase that stirs a positive response in the audience.

Chomsky (1972, 1980) argued that human children are innately equipped with a universal grammar that allows them to come to understand novel sentence constructions in all languages. Pinker (1994) termed this facility a "language instinct" characteristic of human beings, but he did not define "instinct" and in fact acknowledged the term to be "quaint" (p. 18). He noted that "spiders spin spider webs because they have spider brains" (p. 18), implying the analogy that humans have language because they have human brains. However, the term "instinct" by itself explains nothing about the motivational/emotional systems that underlie the learning, organization, and application of linguistic understanding. Certainly, beyond crude analogy what is "instinctive" about spiders spinning webs must be qualitatively different from what is "instinctive" about human language.

Presumably, biologically based reward-punishment/expectation systems are engaged to provide the affective readout of reward and frustration involved in the successful or unsuccessful use of language. Curiosity, interest, and exploratory motives are harnessed to support linguistic investigation, comprehension, and behavior as they are to support other sorts of exploration, producing affective phenomena that are unique to human beings: the pleasure occasioned by cognitive consistency and coherence, by understanding the causation of events, by understanding oneself.

The linguistic rewiring of the ancestral brain. Attempts to teach sign language to nonhuman primates have demonstrated that chimpanzees and gorillas can learn an impressive number of signs and perhaps can combine them in meaningful ways suggestive of grammar. However, there is no question that the gulf between human language competence and the sign language abilities of contemporary apes is enormous. As Pinker (1994) put it, "what impresses one most about chimpanzee signing is that, fundamentally, deep down, chimps just don't 'get it' . . . they never seem to *feel in their bones* what language is and how to use it" (p. 340, italics added). Indeed, one of the disappointments of the sign language studies of chimpanzees was that individuals who had been taught to sign failed to teach it to their offspring. The extraordinarily strong motives to teach language to the young – so apparent in all human cultures that it is taken for granted – appears to be absent in the apes.

Nevertheless, linguistic competence is associated with aspects of the human brain that are shared, to some extent, with monkeys and apes.

The extent of this sharing may reflect the extent to which the cognitive and affective precursors of linguistic competence had evolved in the common ancestors of humans and monkeys, and of humans and apes. For example, structures homologous to Broca's area and Wernicke's areas, and fibers connecting them, have been identified in the brains of monkeys (Deacon, 1988, 1989; Galaburda and Pandya, 1982). These regions do not control spontaneous monkey calls and gestures: the Wernicke's homologues are involved in the recognition of sound sequences and the discrimination of individual calls; the Broca's homologues are associated with the motor control of the mouth, tongue, and larynx. These regions receive extensive sensory inputs, including auditory inputs and tactile inputs from the mouth, tongue, and larynx. Pinker (1994) suggested that this primate brain circuit was likely characteristic of the common ancestor of humans, apes, and monkeys; and noted: "this arrangement would have given evolution some parts it could tinker with to produce the human language circuitry" (p. 350). For another example, the human brain typically shows anatomical asymmetry: the LH being longer and wider at the back, and the RH being wider at the front in most persons (Geschwind, 1979). This "linguistic twist" to brain anatomy is common to human beings and present-day apes, but not monkeys, so presumably it was characteristic of the common ancestor of humans and apes, but not that of humans and monkeys (see Balzeau et al., 2012).

Other features that distinguish the human brain involve connections between language areas and the limbic system. Ploog (1992) pointed out that there is an "increased limbic input into the human neocortex" that may represent "an increased differentiation of the limbic input being sent to the neocortex. And vice versa, through reciprocal connections . . . an increased ability to activate and control limbic structures through neocortical input" (p. 21). LeDoux (1986) noted that the inferior parietal lobule (IPL), a neocortical structure that receives both highly processed sensory input and input from limbic structures, is more developed in human beings than in other primates. On the right side, the IPL is involved in spatial processing; on the left it is part of the posterior language area bordering Wernicke's area. LeDoux (1982) suggested that the IPL plays a major role in the connection between emotion systems and language.

Such connections may be the basis of linguistic motivational/emotional systems unique to human beings: potentials inherent in linguistic control systems that provide the rewarding or punishing affective readout that accompanies the use and misuse of language. More specifically, there may be particular motives to maintain logical consistency in the structure of one's arguments; there may be motives to achieve an accurate comprehension of the causal structure of reality, and there may be motives to achieve an accurate linguistically organized understanding of oneself. These three sorts of motives – which should not exist in nonhuman animals – have been considered in cognitive consistency, attribution, and self theories, respectively.

● *Cognitive consistency theories.* Gestalt psychologists (Kurt Lewin, 1951; Fritz Heider, 1944) advanced the notion that a need to understand is a basic human motive. This theory suggested that psychological processes act to make psychological states as simple and orderly as possible. Cognitive consistency theories expressed this principle by the premise that there is a tendency for an individual's cognitions to be related to one another in a logical manner, so that, in effect, the human mind has a strong need for consistency. All of these theories involved *cognitive elements* and *relations* between elements.

In cognitive balance theories, advanced by Heider (1946) and Newcomb (1953) among others, the elements were expressed by nouns or noun phrases that are positively valued, negatively valued, or neutral; such as "friend," "enemy," "person." The relations may be positive, negative, or null. The resulting combination of elements and relations may be imbalanced (cognitively uncomfortable), balanced (comfortable), or irrelevant. If my friend likes my friend, or my friend dislikes my enemy, these cognitive elements are balanced: they make logical sense. However, if my friend dislikes my friend, or my friend likes my enemy, the elements are imbalanced and create an uncomfortable sense of inconsistency (see Figure 5.4).

Many examples of the application of balance theory can be found in advertising campaigns that seek to create positive images for their products – ranging from commercial products to political candidates – by associating them positively with positively valued elements and negatively with negatively valued elements. Products that are objectively similar to one another can be "differentiated" and "branded" by carefully associating them with such elements as health, beauty, youth, sociality, sexiness, and wealth. At the same time, associations of products with negative factors, such as risk, are minimized as much as is possible (Buck and Davis, 2010). The tobacco industry is faced with a particular problem in this regard because its products are uncomfortably linked with preventable death from cardiovascular disease and cancer. In the past, tobacco advertisers fought furiously against admitting the causal association of smoking with disease, and have successfully minimized it by presenting vivid images of young, sexy, rich, sociable, happy, healthy people who are smokers. These images are inconsistent with disease and death, and therefore tend to blur the link between smoking and disease, encouraging smokers to ignore or

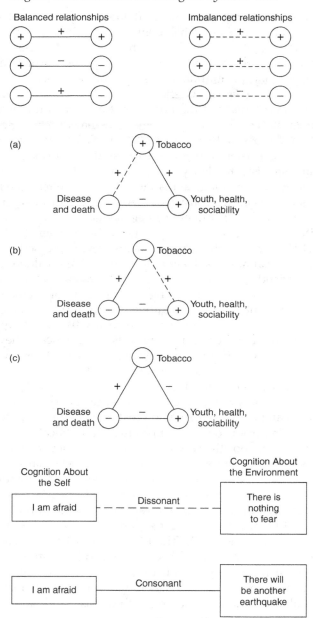

Figure 5.4 Cognitive consistency/balance; cognitive dissonance. See text for details.

mindlessly discount such information (Figure 5.4a). Anti-tobacco groups have often attempted to create negative images of smoking by emphasizing the link between smoking and disease while ignoring the positive images engendered by tobacco advertising (Figure 5.4b). A problem with this approach is that the positive images of youth and health are attractive in themselves, while negative images are easily resisted and ignored. An alternative is to attack instead the positive link between smoking and the positive qualities stressed by tobacco advertisers – portraying smokers as unattractive social outcasts, for example – while at the same time emphasizing the smoking–disease link with such techniques as presenting images of disease and death directly on tobacco packaging (Figure 5.4c). The latter sorts of images appear on tobacco packaging in much of the world, but at this writing the inclusion of such images is being fiercely contested by tobacco groups in the United States (Buck and Davis, 2010).

Leon Festinger (1957) advanced a different sort of consistency theory: cognitive dissonance theory. In it, the elements are expressed in sentences: one of which is about the self ("I am afraid"), the other about the environment ("there is danger"). The relations between elements are not explicitly stated but rather are implied in the elements. Festinger argued that a state of cognitive dissonance exists between two cognitive elements "if, considering these two alone, the obverse of one element would follow from the other" (1957, p. 13). Festinger suggested that, all else equal, cognitions about the self are more stable than cognitions about the environment. If one feels afraid, for example, a person will tend to look for elements in the environment to explain this fear: to find danger where it may not exist. This is important in that it suggests that our own feelings and actions may often mold our attitudes: for example, the hatred and fear of strangers might underlie prejudiced attitudes, rather than the reverse.

Cognitive dissonance theory is particularly relevant to the analysis of emotions, because the cognitive element about the self can be affective ("I am afraid," "I am happy"), and the theory therefore has the potential to deal with the relationship between emotion, behavior, and judgment. For example, it has been reported that Festinger got the essential idea behind dissonance theory by reading about the aftermath of a serious earthquake. The report stated that there were widespread rumors in the area about more and deadlier earthquakes to come, and Festinger wondered why the survivors of an earthquake were motivated to predict more earthquakes. He hypothesized that this phenomenon might be caused by the fear and panic experienced by many of the survivors. He reasoned that their knowledge of their own state of fear might be considered a cognitive element analogous to knowledge of

AFFeCt - describe experience/ feeling of emotion.
overt behaviors - Directly observable (vs. covert)
226   *Higher-level emotions: an ecological-systems view*

dissonance: The clash resulting from 2 unharmonious elements

an external object. However, the cognitive element "I am afraid" is inconsistent with the cognition that "there is nothing to fear." Because the fear could not be immediately suppressed, Festinger suggested that people changed their judgments about the external environment to become consistent with their inner state of fear: "there will be another earthquake" (see Figure 5.4, lower).

Cognitions about subjectively experienced affects are different from cognitions about overt behaviors: overt behaviors are said to have maximal effects upon dissonance when they are voluntary and public (Brehm and Cohen, 1962). Affective responses are not voluntarily chosen, and they may or may not be publicly displayed, so they are interesting from the point of view of dissonance theory. Because affective responses emerge naturally from the body, cognitions about one's spontaneous affective responses may be considered to be cognitions about the *body*, rather than cognitions about the "self." However, this possibility has not been systematically explored in the research inspired by dissonance theory.

2 *Attribution theory*. Fritz Heider was a founding figure in attribution theory as well as cognitive consistency theory, and attribution theory also has Gestalt origins. Like consistency theory, the central assumption is that human beings are motivated to acquire organized and valid information about the environment. Attribution theory emphasized the importance of correctly judging the causal relationship between events: we must know *why* an event has occurred to "attain a cognitive mastery of the causal structure of (the) environment" (Kelley, 1967, p. 193). Michotte (1963) demonstrated the dominance of causal attributions in his classic study in which subjects watched a film of two inanimate objects, a red disk A and a black disk B, moving on a screen. If A approaches and bumps B, and B immediately moves away from A, the observer has the impression that A *caused* the movement. If B moves with A, it is seen as being dragged along with A; if B's movement is delayed by ¼ to ½ second, the perception of causality disappears.

A particularly relevant aspect of attribution theory involves its treatment of *internal* and *external attribution*. Internal attribution occurs when causes are attributed to the actor: these are assumed to result from stable characteristics of the actor. The actor chose to perform such behaviors because of these characteristics, so the behaviors are the responsibility of the actor, and they can be expected to occur in the future. In contrast, external attribution occurs when the situational factors are seen to be the causes of behavior. Emotional behaviors do not easily fit either of these descriptions: they clearly result from the actor, but the actor does not *choose* to have them (Schneider et al., 1979). Rather, emotional behaviors are manifestations of *bodily* responding: of biological sources of behavior control.

Another aspect of attribution theory involves the notion of *mindlessness* (Langer et al., 1978). Langer and colleagues drew a distinction between "mindful" cognitive activity, in which the individual draws distinctions, analyzes and categorizes stimuli, and generally reasons about the stimulus; and "mindless" cognitive activity that relies upon distinctions already drawn. They suggested that the attribution process takes effort, and that mindful analysis is used only when it must be. Mindfulness is relevant to the question of the role of rational and emotional processes in attitude formation and change. Traditional theories of attitude change have tended to emphasize the mindful logical analysis of arguments: what Petty and Cacioppo (1986) termed the "central route" to persuasion. However, even a cursory acquaintance of television advertisements – messages designed at great cost to influence human behavior – reveals a marked lack of rational argument, and a great deal of emotional appeal. Are advertisers foolishly ignoring the rational analytic capacities of human beings? Or have they hit upon something fundamental about human nature?

● *Self theories.* As with other complex terms, the word "self" is often used in different ways in different contexts. In their classic volume, Hall and Lindzey (1970) used the term generally to refer to all qualities of the individual: feelings and desires, perceptions, judgments, attitudes, evaluations. In accordance with the distinction between KA, KD, and linguistic knowledge we can see that the self can be conceptualized as *self-by-acquaintance*, *self-by-description*, and *linguistic self*. Self-by-acquaintance is the immediate self-evident syncretic knowledge involving feelings, desires, percepts, and so forth; self-by-description is knowledge *about* such feelings, desires, and percepts. Self-by-acquaintance and self-by-description exist in nonhuman animals as well as human beings. The linguistic self in contrast is uniquely human: we not only know our feelings, desires, and percepts; and know *about* them; we also *organize* this knowledge linguistically, developing sometimes naive but often wise theories about our own nature and the nature of other persons.

This perspective has much in common with the self theory of Carl Rogers (1951), who distinguished between two systems of behavior regulation: the "organism" and the "self." The organism is known directly as part of the phenomenal field of experience; the self is a differentiated portion of that phenomenal field that is conscious. Consciousness to Rogers consisted of that which can be symbolized – in our terms that which can be known by description and organized and patterned by experience, and in human beings by language. Thus, Rogers defined the self as an "organized, fluid, but consistent conceptual pattern" (1951, p. 498). The view of the self as a linguistically organized, consistent, and coherent system is related to Kelly's (1955) theory that persons come to construe themselves and the world by recognizing repeated themes or rules, which serve like yardsticks in the measurement of persons, objects, and events, and facilitate predictions about the future.

The self in human beings may be conceptualized as involving a system of linguistically structured *rules about behavior* built up over the life of the individual. The system is governed by its own principles of internal organization, which in human beings are dominated by the principles of logic and reasoning mediated by language. Information from the three sources noted previously – the physical, social, *and bodily* environments – is integrated over time and linguistically structured into a system of rules about behavior. If there are significant changes in any of these, the rules constituting the self may no longer be valid. That is, if the physical environment changes due to moving to a different location, or the social environment changes due to marriage, birth, or bereavement, or the bodily environment changes owing to puberty, biological cycles, or physical illness, the basis of the self may change. Under such circumstances changes in the rules are required. Such changes can be difficult and painful, as we shall see in Chapter 7.

Emotional education and the construction of the self

Emotional education is learning *about* the bodily environment of feelings and desires, with the goal of emotional competence: the ability to deal with feelings and desires when they occur (see Figure 1.2). We saw in Chapter 4 that systems underlying subjectively experienced feelings and desires tend to mature in a temporal sequence appropriate to the typical social and communication environment of mammals. Love and distress are present at birth and typify the parental affectional system. Fear matures after basic social bonds have had time to be formed, presumably accompanied by appropriate social and communicative experiences. Anger appears during the peer affectional system as the capacity for social communication is established in the context of rough-and-tumble play. The maturation of potentially dangerous sexual motives and emotions does not occur until the ability to communicate fearful and angry feelings has normally been well established in the larger context of social bonding and attachment.

Emotions and the self. A natural outcome of emotional education is that feelings and desires become part and parcel of the "organized, fluid, but consistent conceptual pattern" that Rogers (1951, p. 498) defined as the self. The sorts of lessons that we learn about these feelings and desires form a critical but often overlooked aspect of the self-image. We may learn to accept our feelings and desires and find ways to express them appropriately in cultural context, so that we become emotionally competent. However, it may be that feelings and desires occur that we cannot accept because they are not consistent with our view of our self and/or our culture. Rather than regarding them as natural bodily/ biological phenomena which we did not choose to have, certain feelings and desires can be regarded as signs of weakness or even evil. The experience of such affects may be *suppressed* – not displayed – or *repressed*: not consciously acknowledged. In both cases there can be consequent deficits in emotional education and emotional competence. Feelings and desires regarding sex and aggression are perhaps particularly subject to such an interpretation and particularly likely to be suppressed or repressed.

Coping may be defined as the process of changing the rules that constitute the self, in order to adapt to changes in the physical, social, or *bodily* environments; and the addition of the bodily environment, including subjectively experienced feelings and desires, requires a reexamination of the traditional attribution theory point of view (Reardon and Buck, 1989). There are many potential sources of bodily information: what they have in common is that although they are inextricably *part of us*, we do not *choose* to have them. They come with the biological territory, as it were. In human beings, we noted that media are often critical in providing models for learning about, imitating, and controlling the expression of, for example, sexual and aggressive feelings, desires, and behaviors, in ways that are considered appropriate and valued within a community (Buck, 1988a). The onset of puberty in young people, accompanied as it is by novel feelings and desires that are difficult to share with others, ushers in a time of development where media use soars.

Sexual motives and emotions of a given individual may differ from the typical, as lesbian, gay, bisexual, and transgendered (LGBT) individuals are well aware. This can pose a challenge for emotional education, because useful and effective models may not be available in a given culture. There is of course a wide range in the flexibility of social structures in dealing with the natural variability of sexual feelings and desires. The power of media in presenting the feelings and desires of LGBT individuals as acceptable, or denying them and seeking to suppress them, is an issue of great contemporary import.

There are other sources of bodily information – inextricably bound to but not chosen by the individual – that are relevant to the issue of emotional education. Prominent among these are symptoms of serious illness.

Emotional education and serious illness. We have seen that the parent, peer, and sexual affectional systems can be viewed as developmental stages in which there are significant changes in the bodily information provided by feelings and desires, due to the physical maturation of the neurochemical systems underlying subjectively experienced affects. In effect, there are great changes in the whispering, murmuring, and occasionally screaming voices of the genes. Other major life changes may influence this bodily information less directly, such as moving away from home, marrying, having children, going through conflict and divorce, experiencing bereavement. Such changes have been demonstrated to cause stress which requires coping and adaptation, particularly when networks of social support and communication are disrupted (Buck, 1988a). Richard Lazarus (1966) distinguished two types of coping responses: *problem-focused* and *emotion focused*. Problem-focused coping involves targeting the causes of stress, aiming to reduce or eliminate the stressor; while emotion-focused coping involves attempting to reduce negative emotional responses associated with the stressor. However, the analysis of the body as a source of structured information implies a different sort of emotion-focused coping: learning to label, understand, and otherwise deal with the new patterns of feelings and desires associated with the altered circumstances. In cases where reducing or eliminating the stressor itself is not possible, this second sort of emotion-focused coping may be superior to simply attempting to reduce negative emotional responses, which may often involve the suppression of the display and not actually the experience of negative emotion. There is evidence that such suppression is itself stressful (Buck, 1993c).

Among the changes requiring coping, the process of coping with serious illness represents a unique category, where the changes requiring adaptation are themselves bodily changes: the symptoms of illness. Like the changes associated with the physical maturation of the emotion systems, these are inextricably linked with the individual responder, but are in no way intentionally chosen by the responder. As with changes associated with puberty, it may be difficult to communicate about such bodily changes, and often there are few models of social comparison and imitation. The particular needs of patients with serious illnesses to communicate about their experiences, and to learn to label and understand the new and unfamiliar feelings and desires engendered by their condition, are poorly recognized and understood (Iwamitsu and Buck, 2008; Iwamitsu et al., 2005a, 2005b; Reardon and Buck, 1989).

Emotions in relationships: silly love songs. The physical maturation of sexual systems occurring at puberty brings with it not only new feelings and desires, but feelings and desires that naturally involve other people – friends, lovers, sex partners, rivals, chums – all in the presence of authority figures with their own ideas about sexual feelings and desires and how they *should* be handled and expressed (if at all). The enormous complexity of learning how to handle these newly experienced feelings and desires in the context of unfamiliar social relationships is matched by the enormous complexity of a phenomenon largely taken for granted in the social and behavioral sciences: the ubiquity of silly love songs.

Paul McCartney reportedly wrote "Silly Love Songs" in 1976 in response to teasing by John Lennon and others for writing lightweight songs. But the huge popularity of such songs begs the question, why is it that people so like silly love songs? A possible explanation is that love songs allow us to explore strong prosocial feelings and desires in the context of personal and social relationships. Silly love songs can have the serious function of allowing us to explore feelings associated with attraction, affection, fulfilment, and love; as well as rebuff, rejection, betrayal, loss, and isolation.

We have an internal environment of biologically based feelings and desires that we did not choose, but we must explore, understand, and become competent in dealing with these feelings and desires in the context of a vast variety of social and personal relationships. So, just as we are motivated to explore and understand to achieve competence in the external physical environment, we are motivated to explore subjectively experienced feelings and desires to achieve emotional education. But the internal environment differs in that other persons do not have direct access to our feelings and desires, so that learning about these must be indirect, via social biofeedback. Such learning is intrinsically social as well as biological. Media come into the picture because there are many feelings and desires that cannot easily be explored in direct face-to-face interaction: these include socially dangerous sexual and aggressive feelings but also feelings of love, affection, and bonding, the direct expression of which can be socially inappropriate or embarrassing. Feelings associated with social loss – feelings of loneliness, separation, and isolation caused by rejection, absence, or bereavement – are also intrinsically difficult to share directly with others. These feelings and desires tend to be the subject of silly love songs, in the context of a vast variety of personal and social relationships ranging from "Some Enchanted Evening"[1] to "If you Want to Keep your Beer Ice Cold (Set it Next to my Ex-Wife's Heart),"[2] to say nothing of "Love Stinks!"[3]

---

[1] From the 1949 Rodgers and Hammerstein musical *South Pacific*.
[2] © 1989 by Doug Vaughn and Pete Samson.
[3] © 1980 by The J. Geils Band.

To assess whether specific emotions contribute to motives involved in the choice of specific media content, participants were asked to rate the emotions elicited by MTV music videos, and whether they liked the content (Buck, 1988b). A *specific emotional appeal* was defined as a positive correlation between the rating of the emotion and the rating of liking of the content. For example, if there was a positive correlation between ratings of happiness and liking, it suggested that people liked it if it made them happy, so the video therefore had a "happiness appeal." In a study conducted during the 1980s, seven music videos that appeared to have differing emotional appeals were presented to participants who rated the emotions elicited by the video and their liking (Buck, 1988b: see Table 5.2). Four videos, Lionel Ritchie's "All Night Long," Eric Martin's "Don't Stop," Linda Ronstadt's "What's New," and ZZ Top's "Sharp Dressed Man" had happiness appeals for both women and men, with ratings of happiness strongly correlating with ratings of liking (average $r = 0.59$). A video chosen for its aggressive content – Rolling Stones' "Under Cover of the Night" – showed a happiness appeal for men ($r = 0.63$) but not women; but it showed a power appeal for both women and men, in that liking was correlated with ratings of power (average $r = 0.54$). One video chosen for its anti-war content: "Fields of Fire" by Big Country, showed a child playing with toy soldiers inter-cut with scenes of combat. This video had a happiness appeal for women ($r = 0.52$), but for men liking was positively correlated with ratings of sadness, fear, and anger ($rs = 0.51, 0.44, 0.52$ respectively): men apparently liked "Fields of Fire" if viewing it made them feel sad, afraid, and angry.

On the other hand, ratings of two emotions were strongly correlated with liking for both genders across all seven videos: liking was positively correlated with interest (average $r = 0.62$) and negatively correlated with boredom (average $r = -0.56$). A second study, conducted during the 1990s with a new set of MTV videos, replicated these results (Pulaski, 1999): again, different videos showed different emotional appeals, but again liking was positively correlated with interest (average $r = 0.61$) and negatively correlated with boredom (average $r = -0.43$). Thus, different MTV videos had different emotional appeals: people liked some videos if the music made them sad, others if music made them happy, others if music made them feel powerful, etc. But, across all the videos in both studies, people liked them if the music made them interested and disliked them if the music made them bored.

This suggests that listening to silly love songs, and perhaps more broadly to music and entertainment in general, is a kind of exploratory behavior where one is exploring and coming to understand one's own feelings and desires. The more anger and sense of power elicited by

Table 5.2 Pearson product-moment correlations between rated emotion and rated liking for seven music videos

Rated emotion	Lionel Ritchie "All Night Long"		Eric Martin "Don't Stop"		Linda Ronstadt "What's New"		Rolling Stones "Under Cover of the Night"		ZZ Top "Sharp Dressed Man"		Police "Every Breath You Take"		Big Country "Fields of Fire"	
	M	F	M	F	M	F	M	F	M	F	M	F	M	F
Happy	89*	73*	52*	75*	52*	70*	63*	02	43*	70*	25	39*	-20	52*
Sad	-41*	-45*	-23	19	-17	-15	09	-10	-74*	-08	27	73*	51*	01
Afraid	-22	03	16	-11	-20	26	13	-19	-69*	-22	-20	04	44*	-04
Angry	-35	04	-12	-37*	-20	-19	-09	-42*	-59*	-03	-10	17	52*	-14
Surprised	14	28	40*	27*	02	31	30	03	09	29	-10	19	19	29
Disgusted	-37*	-01	-13	-16	-23	-19	-01	-36*	-69*	-21	-32	-17	32	-06
Sexually aroused	06	20	32	55*	11	52*	21	46*	29	50*	04	49*	-09	15
A sense of power	01	53*	41*	22	27	34	54*	54*	15	54*	28	24	-10	05
Interested	62*	77*	48*	69*	71*	61*	61*	63*	62*	80*	84*	67*	82*	45*
Bored	-76*	-64*	-46*	-37*	-76*	-68*	-54*	-46*	-69*	-61*	-72*	-78*	-58*	-37*

Source: From Buck (1988b).

*p <0.05. Subjects were 23 male and female college students.

an action-adventure movie, the more fear elicited by a horror show, the more tears elicited by a tearjerker, the more sexual arousal elicited by an erotic depiction, the better they are generally regarded. Of course, there are people who will not go near certain media content: some avoid horror films and others avoid tearjerkers. Perhaps these individuals do not need or want to explore certain feelings. But, from this point of view, a major factor in the pleasure of entertainment may be curiosity in the pursuit of emotional exploration and emotional education.

Emotional education and cinema: emotional communication in film. Another area of media studies where the investigation of emotion has been generally overlooked involves film theory. In a direct application of developmental-interactionist theory to the study of film communication, Stephen Stifano (2008, 2011) suggested that two streams of communication are involved in cinema: symbolic/rational and spontaneous/emotional. To investigate this, Stifano used professional-quality films in which he obtained ratings from the film creators (directors, actors, and editors) during the filming to relate to audience ratings of emotion, comprehension, and liking. This research measured spontaneous/emotional responding and communication by scales which asked how the responder felt while creating or watching the film. Symbolic/rational processing of the film was measured as the rational understanding of the content and meaning of the film (comprehension). Empathy was defined as the correlation between creator and audience ratings on the emotion scale. In an initial study using a haunting and surrealistic 6.5 minute film SMILO (2006), "correct" answers to comprehension and emotion measures were established by the answers of the co-director, chief cinematographer, and editor of the film. Stifano (2008) demonstrated that empathy was positively and significantly correlated with audience liking of the film ($r = 0.31$) while comprehension was not ($r = -0.05$). Group discussion of the film increased comprehension but decreased empathy scores, a result Stifano labeled the "film class effect" because of his observation that discussing the nuances and meaning of a film often increases understanding, but undermines one's enjoyment of the film engendered by sharing the emotions portrayed.

In subsequent studies, the empathy–liking relationship was replicated with advertisements and other short films (Stifano, 2010a, 2010b). Following these, Stifano produced and directed a full-length independent feature film, *Belief* (www.beliefmovie.com). Measures for film creators were assessed from all those involved in the production of the film: the director (Stifano), all principal actors, and members of the production crew. The creators responded to measures at the conclusion of each scene in which they were involved during the production of the film. The questionnaires assessed creators' emotional experiences, and their evaluations of the filming experience and the completed scene. For each scene, the average correlation between creators' emotion ratings defined the *emotional synchrony* of the scene. Creators were also asked about how much they felt and thought about while doing the scene. Creators also rated understanding of the scene, enjoyment of the scene, and quality of the scene. Their responses were related to each other and to appropriate responses of audience members viewing the completed film in theater-like settings. Results indicated that empathy with the director and overall emotional synchrony were positively correlated with evaluation of the scene. Interestingly, among actors, empathy was relatively more important in predicting evaluation than was understanding; while the reverse was true among crew members. Director-to-viewer empathy was again significantly correlated with audience liking ($r = 0.49$), which was significantly stronger than comprehension ($r = 0.24$). Actor–viewer empathy was significantly correlated with ratings of the actor's performance for the two main characters, but not for the supporting characters; and there was evidence that levels of empathy with some characters predicted levels of identification with others in interesting albeit complex ways, influenced by the gender of both the actors in question and the audience member. The results of the Stifano studies suggest that much can be learned about emotion and emotional education by studying such media.

Emotional aliments: can emotions be "negative"? The apparent attraction for experiencing negative events in theater has been termed the "paradox of tragedy" (Raphael, 1960). About 330 BCE, Aristotle in *Poetics* described tragedy as invoking emotions of pity and fear: "he who simply hears an account of them shall be filled with horror and pity at the incidents . . . The tragic pleasure is that of pity and fear" (1947, p. 641). The pleasure is based on imitation, exploration, and understanding of situations evoking such feelings. Aristotle wrote:

> The general origin of poetry was due to two causes, each of them part of human nature. Imitation is natural to man from childhood . . . and it is also natural for all to delight in works of imitation. The truth of the second point is shown by experience: though the objects themselves may be painful to see, we delight to view the most realistic representations of them in art . . . The explanation is to be found in a further fact: to be learning something is the greatest of pleasures not only to the philosopher but also to the rest of mankind. (1947 p. 627)

Thus, human beings are drawn to tragedy because of the pleasure of learning, even about pity and fear.

From this point of view, the whole notion of "negative" emotions is problematic. On one hand, there is considerable consensus that "people seek to maximize the experience of positive emotions and minimize the experience of negative emotions" (Ekman and Davidson, 1994, p. 412). Indeed, many subjectively experienced affects – sadness, fear, anger, disgust – normally *inform* us of negative things that we certainly do strive to escape and avoid, but why do people spend good money to expose themselves to materials that appear to effectively arouse these very affects? An excellent example is the motion picture *Titanic*, one of the highest grossing films of all time, which was re-released in 3D apparently to make the horror and grief more real, to "delight to view the most realistic representations" in Aristotle's terms.

An alternative hypothesis is that the experience of so-called negative affects is not necessarily unpleasant per se, but that in fact the safe experience of *any* affect can function as an aliment – food for cognitive growth – in the terms of Piaget's (1971) theory, encouraging assimilation and accommodation. The experience of affect can constitute new information which is assimilated into a developing knowledge structure of emotional understanding, enriching it and allowing new, more complex emotional information to become assimilable (see Figure 5.2). As Piaget suggested, the aliment naturally elicits curiosity and interest and intrinsically motivates exploration on the part of the individual: in this case it is emotional exploration. The result is that emotional understanding can become accommodated as an aspect of the self.

Emotional education as intervention: emotional inoculation

Dual-process theories of attitude change and persuasion. A distinction between mindful and mindless processing in responding to messages is a feature of dual-process theories of attitude change and persuasion. These suggest that reason and emotion involve different kinds of cognitive processing, or different sorts of knowledge of events. For example, Petty and Cacioppo's (1986) *elaboration likelihood model* (ELM) contrasted a rational *central route* to persuasion with a *peripheral route* in which emotion was seen to be important. The ELM considered the emotional processing of attitude objects to be important where the issue at hand has relatively "low involvement" or low personal relevance to the individual, and there is therefore little incentive to devote scarce cognitive resources to rationally and mindfully evaluating the arguments. Chaiken's (1980, 1987; Chaiken and Eagly, 1983) distinctions between systematic and heuristic processing paralleled this distinction in that central route and systematic processing demand and consume effortful and mindful analytic cognitive capacities. The theories differed in their conceptualizations of peripheral route versus heuristic processing, but in both cases such processing was regarded as less "mindful" and rational. In a different vein, Forgas' (1995) *affect infusion model* (AIM) predicted that the degree of affect infusion into judgments varies along a processing continuum, such that judgments requiring either heuristic or substantive processing are more likely to be infused by emotion than are direct-access or motivated judgments. All of these approaches imply that the persuasion process may be influenced or infused by emotion, but in all cases it is the judgment process that really counts, in a sense: persuasion per se is based upon a central rational or "cold-cognitive" analytic judgment process.

Decision-making and emotion. The effect of emotion on decision-making was long thought to be largely disruptive and contrary to rational thought, but it is now understood that emotions can also contribute positively to decision-making. It is important to consider the conditions under which emotions can facilitate or disrupt efficient decision-making. Unfortunately the conceptualization of emotion in the decision literature is generally oversimplified. For example, the experience of situations of risk described in the *risk as feelings hypothesis* is framed rather simply in terms of the anticipated experience of positive or negative evaluative feelings (Loewenstein et al., 2001).

The developmental-interactionist conceptualization of emotion in general and the notion of emotional education in particular have implications for the detailed design of interventions in situations involving risk. It is now generally acknowledged that emotions play a major role in decision-making in situations involving risk (Buck and Ferrer, 2012). Emotions can influence such decision-making in several ways. First, *anticipatory emotions* are responses to potential outcomes that are experienced at the time of the decision (Bagozzi et al., 1998). For example, one may actually *feel* erotic excitement when thinking about having sex; or *feel* worry, dread, and anxiety when thinking about being tested for a serious illness. There may well be mixed feelings, when erotic excitement may be mixed with worry about the possibility of sexually transmitted disease. Second, *anticipated emotions* refer to future emotions that are anticipated at the time of decision. Though not actually experienced at the time of the decision, they can contribute to rational decision-making, and can also contribute to the experience of anticipatory emotions (Loewenstein and Lerner, 2003; Loewenstein et al., 2001). For example, thinking about being diagnosed with a disease can conjure a rational realization that one's future could be accompanied by pain and loneliness. These anticipated emotions may then trigger actual experienced feelings of dread and separation anxiety. Third, *incidental emotions* unrelated to the decision may also be experienced at the time of the decision, and though not directly relevant may be influential nonetheless (e.g. Grunberg and Straub, 1992; Harlé and Sanfey, 2007;

Lerner and Keltner, 2000, 2001; Lerner et al., 2004). For example, one may feel generally happy or sad, and such moods may influence decision-making (e.g. Han et al., 2007; Loewenstein and Lerner, 2003; Loewenstein et al., 2001). A lively party atmosphere on spring break with alcohol, loud music, and dancing may conceivably make the anticipation of erotic excitement more likely – and the anticipation of worry, dread, and anxiety less likely – at the point of a critical decision. Also, inhibitions may possibly be lowered by such situations. Fourth, there are cases where *the feelings and desires in themselves present the risks*. We saw that in Festinger's (1957) cognitive dissonance theory, subjective feelings ("I am confident"), can alter judgments about the environment ("it is safe"), and such subjective feelings are generally expected to be more stable than judgments about the environment. If one feels specific emotions, one will tend to look for elements in the environment to explain them and overlook dissonant elements, so that one's feelings and desires may often mold one's attitudes. For example, people may be tempted to engage in risky behavior by sexual desires, or (false) perceptions of hunger, or feelings of power, or experiences of curiosity or wanting (Lerner and Keltner, 2000).

Perceptions and judgments regarding anticipated and anticipatory emotions may be shaped in a variety of ways. Personal experience may be a powerful source of influence, but many risky situations by their very nature are uncommon and unusual, so that they may well be novel to a given individual. Media models have their place, but expecting the provision of sober, accurate, and balanced accounts of the pros and cons of risky situations via media is problematic. Indeed, media often present significant risks in exciting, stimulating, and humorous contexts. In a meta-analysis of the relationships between media depictions of risky media and behavior, Fischer et al. (2011) found that risky media depictions encouraged risk-taking behaviors and risk-positive emotions and attitudes. This was particularly true for exposure to active (e.g. video games) than passive (music, film) media content. Moreover, sexual behavior is often presented by allusion and innuendo, and mention of safe sexual practices is rare. In 2005, out of the 68 percent of television shows that showed sexual content, only 15 percent discussed risk and responsibility (Common Sense Media, 2012). The treatment of spring break by MTV is a case in point.

I have likened the effects of subjectively experienced feelings and desires to the voices of the genes, which cajole and persuade. And when the voices of the genes begin to scream and shout, people may well be unprepared. In particular, the occurrence of novel and unexamined feelings may initiate an environmental search process as was demonstrated by Schachter and Singer (1962) with injections of epinephrine, which led to informal social comparison with an angry or euphoric confederate as a way to identify and understand the novel feeling (Festinger, 1950, 1954). Such social comparisons can put the individual at particular risk of labeling their own feelings based upon the displays of others, ignoring apparently obvious rules of conduct and safety concerns, and instead following the crowd in performing prohibited or risky behaviors.

The range of risks encountered by preteens and teens in twenty-first century American culture is impressive. They can expect their first experiences with teasing; bullies and gangs; tobacco, alcohol, and drugs; eating a diet they choose on their own; diving into swimming pools; texting while driving; having sex. Adults can also expect challenges of being tempted to overeat, drink and drive, smoke, use drugs, and have unprotected sex; as well as health changes including undergoing medical testing and diagnosis, and medical procedures and operations. In most cases, the emotional aspects of facing and overcoming these risks have not been explored, and there is precious little information disseminated that could prepare individuals to anticipate the feelings and desires experienced in these situations.

Emotional inoculation as intervention. The developmental-interactionist view of emotion and emotional education can be leveraged into a new approach to intervention in these and other risky situations. I hypothesize that if a person is *educated to anticipate the specific emotions they will likely experience* in a risky situation, they will be able to more accurately and rationally anticipate such feelings and desires when the situation arises and therefore better manage the risk. They would also be less at risk for labeling their feelings based upon informal social comparisons with the displays of other persons in the situation.

The key to the technique is to target *specific* emotions in *specific* situations. To do this, these emotions must be determined. Buck et al. (2004) assessed emotions involved in condom use. University students were asked to rate a range of emotions that "people feel" in sexual situations: e.g. discussing condom use with a potential partner; and having sex with or without a condom in a one-night-stand, with a friend, or with a long-term partner. Results indicated that a wide variety of emotions were rated to occur that varied greatly depending upon whether a condom was used and the nature of the relationship. Generally, positive emotions increased and negative emotions decreased as the relationship became more exclusive, but there were significant exceptions. For example, across relationships and for both women and men, erotic emotions were rated to be higher when condoms were *not* used; and condom use was rated to be associated with *more caring* but *less intimacy*. This suggests that there are "reptilian rewards" associated with condom non-use which might pose significant emotional barriers to safer sexual practices. Women and men reported different overall patterns in responses on anger and power to condom use. Men reported more anger and less power when condoms were used; women reported more anger and less power when condoms were not used (Buck et al., 2004).

Given that the patterns of specific emotions to be expected in specific risky situations can be established, the next step is to present this information to at-risk individuals in objective, non-threatening, and non-evaluative ways: e.g. "This is how people report feeling in situation X," or presenting videos showing people discussing their feelings. It may be counterproductive to tell people how they *should* or *should not* feel, but rather more useful to present factually those emotions typically experienced and leave the conclusions to the audience. Brief intervention "modules" presenting such information can be prepared for a wide variety of risky situations, targeted at teaching the at-risk individual to anticipate, label, understand, and deal effectively with feelings and desires in that specific situation of risk; e.g. educating emotions with the goal of instilling emotional competence in that particular situation. Potential uses include but are not limited to the following:

(a) *Moderating effects of risky human drives* involving safer sex, eating behavior, consumption of alcohol, tobacco, specific drugs, etc.
(b) *Moderating behavior in risky human activities* involving using firearms, diving, driving, texting, risk-taking, sports, etc.
(c) *Moderating reactions to risky human situations* involving being affected by the presence of street gangs; easy availability of drugs; violent crime; terrorism; joblessness; groupmind risks; natural disasters including aftermath of storms, floods, nuclear accidents, etc.; economic disasters; combat situations; new technology; ennui; etc.
(d) *Moderating effects of natural risks in human development* involving developmental stages of adolescence, young adulthood, midlife, aging, retirement, old age; marriage; having children; family conflict including parental neglect, divorce, abusive situations, etc.; serious illness; caring for family members; etc.

Ferrer (2007) studied the role of emotion in relation to information, motivation, and behavioral skills in explaining obesity-related behavior. Information, motivation, and behavioral skills are parts of the social-cognitive IMB model of health behavior intervention: participants are given information about a risky behavior, motivated to escape or avoid the risk, and given specific behavioral skills that will allow the risk to be escaped or avoided. Ferrer measured traditional IMB model variables of information, motivation, and behavioral skills in relationship to diet and exercise behavior on two occasions in an online questionnaire. She also assessed the possible role of feelings experienced while engaging in healthy and unhealthy behaviors, creating an extension to the IMB model including emotion: the IMB+E model. Ferrer demonstrated that the IMB+E model predicted more variance in intentions to comply with safer practices than the IMB model alone.

In a conceptual replication and extension of the diet and exercise study, Ferrer et al. (2011) studied the addition of an emotional education component to a brief intervention for sexual risk reduction. This study evaluated whether the addition of emotional education to a traditional IMB safer sex intervention increased efficacy, compared with both the traditional IMB and no intervention. The emotional education intervention involved using results from the Buck et al. (2004) study to design messages about what emotions are experienced in risky sexual situations. Participants received either the IMB+E intervention, the IMB intervention, or no intervention; and reported their condom use at three and six months following the intervention. At six months' post-intervention, individuals in the IMB+E intervention arm reported significantly increased condom use compared with both the IMB intervention and the no-intervention comparison group (see Figure 5.5). Although more research needs to be done, this constitutes suggestive evidence that the addition of an emotional education component can significantly enhance health interventions.

TEEMS: Targeted Emotional Education Modules. The Ferrer et al. (2011) results offer preliminary support for the notion that emotional education targeting specific emotions in specific risk situations, or Targeted Emotional Education Modules (TEEMs), have the potential to provide a wide range of brief and inexpensive but effective evidence-based interventions that enhance emotional competence and control and support healthy behavior. The TEEM approach is theoretically grounded and empirically based, yet practical, flexible, and applicable to many populations. More specifically, the TEEM approach recognizes the potency and potential danger of informal social comparison in shaping collective emotional responses when feelings and desires encountered in a situation are novel and strong. The evidence suggests that the displays of other persons can exert powerful influences on the labeling and understanding of one's own feelings and desires, potentially contributing to a *group mind* phenomenon (Le Bon, 1896; Gantt and Agazarian, 2011). Moreover, the TEEM approach allows for the understanding of complex and often apparently incompatible patterns of feelings, accepting them as normal given the situation so that they do not need to be suppressed but they do not need to be acted upon either. It allows individuals to linguistically represent and more clearly display and

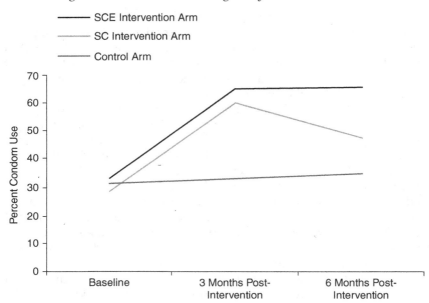

Figure 5.5 Effects of a social-cognitive intervention (SC) and an emotion education intervention (CSE) on reported condom use.

express these feelings in ways that are appropriate and adaptive. The overall effect is that the individual is better able to use subjectively experienced feelings and desires as informative signs rather than impulsive urges, and is therefore inoculated from the most problematic aspects of strong emotion.

There is in fact considerable evidence that putting one's feelings into words, or *affect labeling*, can attenuate dysfunctional emotional processing. James W. Pennebaker and his colleagues have demonstrated in numerous experimental studies that verbalizing emotional experience can reduce distress (Frattaroli, 2005; Pennebaker, 1997; Pennebaker and Chung, 2007). Neuroimaging research has found that affect labeling can reduce amygdala activity to emotional images, while increasing activity in the right ventrolateral prefrontal cortex (RVLPFC), which has been shown to down-regulate the amygdala (Lieberman et al., 2007). In a study on the effects of affect labeling in a study with a behavioral measure of fear, Kircanski et al. (2012) showed that affect labeling was better able to reduce skin conductance responses to spiders in spider-phobic persons than emotional reappraisal or distraction. Interestingly, affect labeling did not reduce self-reported fear, and in fact a greater use of fear and anxiety-related words during exposure to the spider was associated with a greater reduction in fear response. This perhaps counterintuitive finding was similar to that of Iwamitsu et al. (2005a, 2005b) who found that women who labeled their aggression and anxiety showed less distress during the course of cancer diagnosis.

Conceptually, the TEEM approach applies the theoretical principles of disclosure techniques such as those of Pennebaker *before the fact*, seeking to encourage affect labeling prior to exposure to a risky situation in which the affect actually occurs. The goal is perhaps analogous to that of Freud: to "make the unconscious conscious," but again, before the fact. The intent is to inoculate the participant by encouraging the mindful symbolic processing of the affect, therefore mitigating its effects on risky choices.

Linguistic control: an integrated view

There are two aspects to the analysis of linguistic competence and emotions: the emotions involved in the *development and use of linguistic systems*, and the linguistic *understanding of emotion itself*. The former aspect involves the motivational/emotional systems that underlie the learning, organization, and application of linguistic understanding: presumably, biologically based reward-punishment/expectation systems are engaged to provide the affective readout of reward and frustration involved in the successful or unsuccessful use of language. The second aspect is that, as well as understanding the physical and social environments, linguistic understanding includes understanding of the body, including the affects: emotional education about the internal "bodily environment" of feelings and desires (Buck, 1983).

We have seen that cognitive dissonance theory included cognitions about affects, which are in essence cognitions about the body; that attribution theories can involve attributions about the body, which are different in important respects from attribution about the "self"; and that the self involves rules about the body. The critical difference between the readout conceptualization and other analyses is that *affects are seen to afford knowledge about the body*: affects function as *voices of the genes* giving access to certain important bodily events. This bodily knowledge has self-regulatory functions that inform the individual of bodily based needs, feelings, and desires; and thereby allow the individual to learn to adapt flexibly and effectively to the external physical and social environment. Affects facilitate the ability of the individual to act in anticipation of homeostatic deficits; and to modulate, qualify, and falsify emotional responses in consideration of environmental circumstances.

Summary and discussion

A typology of knowledge/cognition was summarized in Figure 5.3. We have seen that the raw material of knowledge is KA, which following Gibson (1966) is termed *awareness*: thus we have an immediate acquaintance with the external physical environment (*terrestrial awareness*), of other organisms (*social awareness*), and of oneself (*self/bodily awareness*). The latter includes the affects: subjectively experienced feelings and desires. Knowledge by description might be termed *cognizance*: thus knowledge about the environment is *terrestrial cognizance*, knowledge about others is *social cognizance,* and knowledge about the self, including the affects and symptoms of disease (Reardon and Buck, 1989), is *self/ body cognizance.* Linguistic knowledge is termed *comprehension,* yielding *terrestrial comprehension, social comprehension,* and *self* and *bodily comprehension.* Because language is structured independently of biology, self-comprehension and bodily comprehension are distinguished at this level. Self-comprehension is the equivalent of Rogers' (1951) "organized, fluid, but consistent" system of rules that is structured by learning, cognition, and language over the life of the individual, including rules about affective experience and the expression of emotions.

Applying this analysis to cognitive consistency, attribution, and self theories suggests a basis for integrating and extending them. In all of these theories the motivational force is seen as being provided by linguistic motives – for understanding, causal explanation, coherence, consistency, order, a "good gestalt" – all involving language and linguistic emotions. An important proviso is that mild inconsistency may be tolerated and even be "cognitively invigorating" if it seems to be assimilable (Piaget, 1971). With this motivational basis in common, the three theories can be seen as differing according to the object of interest that they deal with and the specific sort of linguistic motive/emotion that they emphasize. With cognitive consistency theories, attitudes or attitude change are typically the objects of interest, and the motive is the need to maintain a "good gestalt." In attribution theory, the judgment of the causes of events is the object of interest, and the need for understanding and causal explanation is the motive emphasized. Self theories have the self as the object of interest, and they emphasize a variety of motives important in its development and maintenance.

All of these theories also have implications for understanding, not only the external environment and the self, but the body as well and the relationships between knowledge of the environment, self, and body. Introducing the body to these typically "cold-cognitive" theories gives them all a new source of richness and variety. Relationships between past emotional experience, social relationships, the sense of self, and one's own subjective affective responses can be explored using familiar theoretical orientations. For example, cognitive dissonance may involve dissonance between environment and body cognitions: "it is safe" versus "I feel afraid"; "everything is OK" versus "I feel depressed"; "the other is powerful" versus "I am angry." Attribution processes are relevant to how such dissonance might be resolved: thus such dissonance may motivate us to look toward the reasons for fear, depression, and anger beyond factors in the environment. Self theories are relevant as well: for example, dissonance might exist between self and body cognitions: "I am a courageous person" versus "I am afraid." Due to self-versus-affect dissonance, one might begin to define oneself as a fearful or depressed person, and one may begin to actually choose to enter situations appropriate to those feelings: to choose situations in which one is helpless, for example. This might be relevant to understanding why some people go from one abusive relationship to another: repeated abuse might lead a person to view themselves as one who somehow "deserves" abuse. Furthermore, dissonance, attribution, and self-theories may be used to help to understand the implications of attachment theory for social emotions.

The ultimate function of the interaction of syncretic and analytic cognitive processes is education: the capacity to learn *about* one's raw experience. This learning includes both education leading to competence in dealing with the physical and social environment, and emotional education leading to emotional competence: the ability to navigate successfully the internal bodily environment, and to label and express appropriately one's own feelings and desires. In human beings this emotional competence involves linguistic understanding.

CHAPTER 6

Social emotions

Emotional communication, involving displays and preattunements to those displays, takes emotion outside the individual into the social context, where they come under the influence of behavior-control systems structured at the group level. Simple creatures such as stromatolites and insect societies such as ant hills and bee hives exemplify complex group structures based upon special-purpose spontaneous communication systems. These systems lay the basic groundwork for the more complex social structures of reptiles and mammals including examples we have examined: voles, primates, and hominids including human beings. As general-purpose processing systems increased in relative importance and particularly with the evolution of linguistic competence, social structure became more flexible. But, actually, this flexibility is innate: in effect, flexibility is mandated by hard-wired special-purpose systems underlying knowledge and communication. In fact, *the most inflexibly determined attribute of human nature is flexibility.* Free will is biologically determined. At the same time, social organization takes on its own structure, in that it is governed by linguistically structured *rules* and *scripts* that are not biologically determined but vary widely across human societies.

This chapter and the next consider the nature of these rules and how we are so strongly motivated to follow them. The motivational-emotional bases of social influence are unexpectedly powerful, capable of controlling our behavior in ways that are independent of, and at times contrary to, the ways that would be chosen by the self acting independently. At the same time, these powerful motives are ordinarily below the radar of consciousness and taken for granted unless challenged. This chapter examines studies of conformity and obedience that demonstrate the power of social influence.

We saw in Chapter 4 that these motivational-emotional systems are rooted in attachment, and we see in this chapter how attachment needs combine with ecologically fundamental combinations of interpersonal contingencies involving meeting and failing to meet social expectations in self and comparison other, to form universal *primary social emotions.*

Primary social emotions emerge naturally and spontaneously from the combination of attachment needs and interpersonal contingencies experienced in social interaction. This is the central hypothesis of an original *ecological-systems* theory of higher-level social emotions: that a *system of social emotions* including pride/arrogence, guilt/shame, envy/jealousy, and pity/scorn is activated by attachment needs *functioning in the context of ecological challenges* involving social comparison of relative success and failure in meeting socio-emotional goals. Given that this system of social emotions is activated by ecological challenges, it is convenient to label it an ecological-systems theory of social emotions.

We begin by considering the powerful but typically hidden social motives that underlie social structure.

The nature of social structure

Social influence processes

Scripts: norms and roles. A great proportion of human behavior is determined, not by individual motives, emotions, goals, and intentions, but rather by complying with social influence and the expectations of ourselves and significant others. We do what we have learned is expected in a given situation. Behaviors follow *scripts*, which involve a succession of expected behaviors. Behaviors expected in a given situation across actors are termed the *norms* for that situation, while behavior expected of a given individual across situations is termed the *role* of that individual.

A classic study by Muzafer Sherif (1936, 1965) illustrated the natural emergence of norms in the course of social interaction. Sherif wanted participants to make judgments on an issue that had no objectively "correct" answer. He therefore used the *autokinetic effect*, which is the tendency to perceive movement in a single stationary light in an otherwise dark room. The apparent movement comes from natural eye movements. If asked, people experiencing this phenomenon can judge the extent of movement by speaking aloud. They typically begin with variable judgments, but then settle on a single "individual norm" of, say, nine inches for one person, six inches for another. If two people who have arrived at individual norms make audible judgments in each other's presence, Sherif found that they influence one another, arriving at a "group norm" that is usually a compromise between the individual judgments, say seven inches.

To test the power of this influence process, Sherif created three-person groups in which, unknown to the others, one person was instructed to give extreme judgments. That person was found to influence the other two, so that they, too, began to give extreme judgments. The first person then left the group and was replaced by a new, naive person. Even though the original person had left, the extreme judgments of the remaining two influenced the new person. Then another of the original persons left, and a new naive person was influenced, and so on. The extreme judgments of the original person lasted through many such "generations" of groups, despite the fact that the originator of the extreme judgments was long gone. This example illustrates how social influence processes with groups create shared expectations, or norms, that are not based upon the individuals making up the group, but rather on the past history of social influence communicated within the group. The two original naive persons were influenced by the extreme judgments of the first person and *conformed*: they did what they learned was expected in that situation. They continued to do so even when the original source of social influence had departed.

Conformity. Sherif used the autokinetic effect because there was no objectively correct answer. Solomon Asch (1952) in another classic study went to the opposite extreme to determine whether social influence could induce people to make an obviously incorrect judgment. Participants made simple judgments of the relative length of lines: on one large card were a long and short line labeled "A" and "B"; on another card was a line labeled "C" which was identical to either A or B. The correct answer was obvious. Asch had ten participants give their judgments verbally and in succession. The first nine were actually confederates of the experimenter, coached to answer in specific ways. On most trials the group gave the obviously correct answer, but on "social influence" trials the nine unanimously gave an incorrect judgment. Asch found that approximately one-third of the naive participants conformed to the group and gave the obviously wrong answer. Further research indicated that women were more conforming than men (Eagly, 1978, 1983), and that if only one participant disagreed from the majority (giving the real participant "social support"), conformity dropped to virtually zero (Asch, 1952).

Obedience

The Milgram experiments. The best-known – indeed notorious – studies demonstrating the power of social influence were studies of obedience to authority by one of Asch's students, Stanley Milgram (1963, 1974; Zimbardo, 2007). These studies were explicitly designed to address the justifications offered by Nazi officials for acts of genocide at the Nuremberg war criminal trials following World War II: that they were "following the orders" of their superiors. According to his friend Philip

Zimbardo, Milgram's interest came from "deep personal concerns about how readily the Nazis had obediently killed Jews during the Holocaust" (Zimbardo, 2007, p. 2).

In the initial study, middle-aged men were recruited, ostensibly for a study of the effects of punishment on learning. At the laboratory, two men were introduced and participated in a rigged draw in which one, actually a confederate of the experimenter, drew the role of "learner" and the naive participant drew the role of "teacher." The teacher was to read a list of paired words to the learner, who was to repeat the paired word when the teacher later read the stimulus word. If he made a mistake, the teacher was to punish the learner by pressing a switch to deliver an electric shock.

The learner was led into a separate room. As the teacher watched, he was strapped into a chair with shock electrodes attached that seemingly made it impossible for him to escape the shocks. Electrode paste was applied to, as the experimenter explained, "avoid blisters and burns." The learner stated that he had been recently diagnosed with a minor heart condition and asked whether the shocks could be dangerous. The experimenter replied: "No, although the shocks can be extremely painful, they cause no permanent tissue damage. Anything else? . . ."

The teacher then returned to the original room which contained a large shock apparatus equipped with thirty switches which supposedly delivered increasing intensities of shock. The switches were labeled with voltage readings increasing in 15 volt increments from 15 to 450 volts. Groups of four switches were labeled with increasingly disagreeable verbal descriptions: e.g. from "slight shock," to "strong shock, " to "extreme intensity shock," to "DANGER: severe shock." The last three switches were marked with three red Xs.

The teacher was told to give the learner a shock each time he made a mistake. The shock switch would then remain depressed so it was clear that intensity had been delivered, and the teacher was told to give the next most intense shock for each mistake. Once the experiment began, the learner made many mistakes and the teacher soon found himself giving strong shocks. At 75 volts, the learner began to moan and grunt when the shock was given. At 150 volts the learner declared that he did not want to take any more shocks and demanded that the experiment be discontinued: "I can't stand the pain, let me out of here!" As the shock intensities increased, the learner's pleas became more insistent – "You have no right to keep me here!" – and he stated that his heart was bothering him. At 180 volts he screamed that he could not stand the pain. At 300 volts, the learner stopped responding to the stimulus word: "I absolutely refuse to answer any more! You can't hold me here! My heart's bothering me!" At this point, the experimenter ordered the teacher to consider a non-response within a few seconds to be incorrect and to administer the appropriate punishment. At a higher voltage the learner's screams ceased and the shocks were met by silence. The teacher was told to continue up the shock scale anyway until he administered the highest shock on the scale, 450 volts, three times.

Most teachers objected and resisted giving further shocks, particularly after the learner demanded to be freed. The experimenter told him to continue in a series of four successive verbal prods: "Please continue," "The experiment requires that you continue," "It is absolutely essential that you continue," and "You have no other choice, you must go on." If the teacher still continued to resist after the four prods, the study was halted.

No shocks were actually delivered: the actual purpose of the experiment was to see how far the teacher would continue to apparently injure another person in obedience to the experimenter's commands. The results indicated that participants were much more obedient than expected. To illustrate this, Milgram asked forty psychiatric residents to predict the extent of obedience in the experiment. Their predictions are shown in Figure 6.1, along with the actual observed obedience. The residents – experts in human motivation – predicted that over half the teachers would stop by the 150 volt level when the learner first asked to be freed, that only 3.73 percent would go beyond the 300 volt level, and that less than 1 percent would go to the highest, 450 volt level. Actually in this experiment, 60 percent of the teachers complied fully with the experimenter's orders and went on to the 450 volt level. Milgram emphasized that even though most teachers complied, they clearly demonstrated great reluctance to injure the learner. They showed signs of extreme stress and tension, including trembling, sweating, stuttering, and groaning. Many had bizarre fits of nervous laughter, and several suffered uncontrollable seizures.

Replications and extensions. Milgram (1974) carried out nineteen different variations of the basic paradigm, testing the effects of various potentially important variables upon observed obedience. In one, he conducted a replication at a nondescript office in industrial Bridgeport, CT, to determine whether the prestige of Yale University explained the high level of compliance. Results revealed that although reduced (47.5 percent went to the end), the level of obedience was not significantly lower than at Yale. In other variations, Milgram varied the immediacy between the experimenter and learner. This did influence obedience significantly: if the experimenter gave his orders by telephone, only 21 percent of the teachers complied fully. Milgram also investigated the immediacy of teacher and learner, demonstrating less compliance as

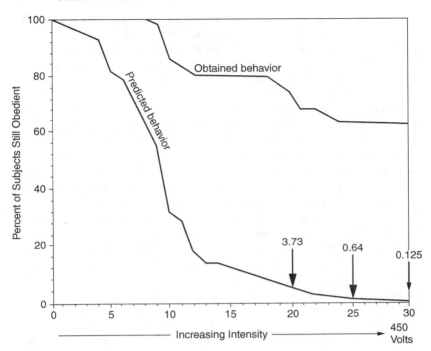

Figure 6.1 Predicted and obtained behavior of the teacher when the learner/victim responded to shocks by vocal objection.

the learner became more immediate. In one the learner was in the same room as the teacher, with his hand resting on the shock electrode plate. After the 150 volt shock, the learner refused to hold his hand on the plate, and the experimenter ordered the teacher to forcibly hold the learner's hand on the plate. Most complied, and 30 percent of the teachers complied to the last 450 volt shock. In another variation, the naive participant was a member of a "teaching team" assisting in other parts of the experiment while another person (a confederate) had the role of pulling the shock lever to punish the victim. In this condition, total compliance was over 90 percent. On the other hand, if "social support" was provided as Asch had done by including a confederate that resisted the orders, less than 10 percent finished the experiment. Thus, purely situational manipulations could produce variations in compliance from 10 percent to over 90 percent (Zimbardo, 2007).

Milgram's studies were criticized because, due to the stress experienced by the teachers, they do not meet current standards for the ethical treatment of participants in experiments. Nevertheless, his results have been replicated and extended. In an analysis of eight replications in the United States and nine in other nations conducted from 1963 to 1985, Blass (1991) found a mean obedience rate of 61 percent in the United States and 66 percent in other samples (Zimbardo, 2007).

Another study replicated the original Milgram study in an immersive virtual environment, where the victim-learner is a virtual human and it is clear to the teacher that no one is really in danger (Slater et al., 2006). In the Visible condition, the (female) learner-avatar was visible to the teacher, responded to the shocks with increasing signs of discomfort, protested that she had "never agreed to this" and asked to stop. At the penultimate shock she slumped forward and was unresponsive. In the Hidden condition, the learner-avatar was not visible, there were no protests, and answers were given through text. Results indicated that, even though the participants knew at the analytic-cognitive level that the situation was not real, they responded subjectively, behaviorally, and physiologically as if it were. They displayed stress, showed physiological arousal, and expressed concern for the learner. Several withdrew before the experiment ended, a rare event in simulator studies. The authors concluded that extreme social situations can be usefully simulated in virtual environments, allowing the empirical study of areas otherwise for ethical reasons not open to experimental study.

Obedience: an anecdotal example. The behavior of the naive participants in the obedience experiments is difficult to understand because it involves the activation of hidden motives and emotions that we normally ignore and take for granted but are actually quite powerful. Milgram illustrated the power of social influence in another, perhaps more easily appreciated way, by showing how difficult it is to violate common and apparently trivial social expectations by asking for someone's seat on the subway (Tavris, 1974).

In his classes at the City University of New York, Milgram often discussed violating social expectations with his students. On one occasion, he suggested that the students go up to a stranger on the New York City subway and courteously ask for their seat. This elicited much nervous laughter in the class, which Milgram recognized as a sign that an important but implicit social taboo was being violated. He persisted in asking for a volunteer, and eventually, a courageous student took on the assignment of making the request to twenty strangers on the subway. He found that about one-half of the passengers complied without question, but the student was unable to complete the assignment, explaining that it was one of the most difficult things he had ever done.

Curious to see why making such an apparently trivial request was such a difficult project, Milgram decided to repeat the assignment himself. He reported that, as he approached a seated passenger, he was overcome by a paralyzing inhibition. The words of the simple request seemed lodged in his throat. After several attempts, he finally went up to a stranger and choked, "Excuse me, sir, can I have your seat?" He reported that he was suddenly overcome by panic, but the stranger got right up and gave him the seat. Taking the seat, Milgram reported that he felt an overwhelming need to behave in a manner that would nonverbally *justify his request*: "My head sank, and I could feel my face blanching. I was not role-playing. I actually felt as if I were going to perish" (Tavris, 1974, p. 72). Significantly, he found that as soon as he left the car at the next stop, the tension disappeared.

Milgram suggested that this experience pointed up the enormous anxiety, ordinarily unnoticed, that prevents us from violating social expectations or norms. When the norm is breached, there is a powerful and unconscious need to justify that breach (by appearing sick or exhausted in this case). Milgram stressed that he was not acting, but rather his reaction was a "compelled playing out of the logic of social relations." Finally, this intense experience was created in, and limited to, the particular situation, thus illustrating the power of the immediate situation on feelings and behavior. He stated that this experience gave him a better appreciation of the feelings and behaviors of some participants in the obedience experiments: "I experienced the anxiety they felt as they considered repudiating the experimenter. That anxiety forms a powerful barrier that must be surmounted, whether one's action is consequential – disobeying an authority – or trivial – asking for a seat on the subway" (Tavris, 1974, p. 72).

Gender differences in obedient aggression. Gender differences in obedience are of interest because, although women are generally less aggressive than men in experiments (Brock and Buss, 1962; Buss and Brock, 1963), women tend to be more conforming in response to social influence. This raises the question, will obedient aggression be higher in men, reflecting the individual and cultural factors that make men more aggressive; or will it be greater in women, reflecting their greater tendencies to conform? There is evidence that women experience more conflict in the situation: when ordered to shock another same-sex person with intense shocks, mild shocks, or painless signals, women showed more skin conductance arousal both when given the instructions about shocking, and when actually administering the shocks (Buck, 1972).

Despite greater conflict about being aggressive, there is little evidence that women are less likely to show obedient aggression. Milgram conducted one study with female participants, and did not find a significant difference from males (reported in Sheridan and King, 1972). Larsen et al. (1972) described the Milgram situation to female and male college students, and asked them to predict what level of shock they themselves would give before breaking off. Women predicted that they would give fewer volts than did men (80 volts for women versus 147 volts for men). However, in an actual conformity study women from the same participant pool gave significantly more shocks than men (328 volts for women and 295 volts for men out of a possible maximum of 390 volts).

Another study compared the willingness of female and male participants to give increasingly severe shocks to an actual victim: a small cute puppy. Sheridan and King (1972) ordered participants to shock a puppy for making mistakes in an (actually insoluble) learning task. The puppy reacted to the shocks by initial foot flexion, then running and barking, and finally continuous yelping and howling. Many participants showed high levels of distress at this: some wept openly. Six of the thirteen males broke off before reaching the end of the shock scale, but none of the thirteen women broke off: all continued to the end of the scale.

The origins and development of conformity and obedience. This evidence that women show as much or more obedient aggression than men suggests that obedient aggression is more an act of conformity than an act of aggression. These studies demonstrate dramatically that persons may engage in aggressive behavior under social influence that is not associated with aggressive tendencies "within" them, and indeed is contrary to their individual wishes and values. Such behavior may be quite independent of any individual motives and goals beyond the motives to obey an authority figure and to do that which is expected. But then, the latter motives may be among the most powerful determinants of human behavior. Responsiveness to social influence and a tendency to conform may be a central fact of human nature: an innate response tendency that automatically emerges during development if supportive experiences are provided. This pervasive responsiveness to social influence is hidden and taken for granted until challenged, as it was in Milgram's study and other experimental paradigms including moral dilemmas that we consider in Chapter 7 (Fiske, 2010b).

The basic motive underlying responsiveness to social influence is attachment. We saw in Chapter 4 that the model of social development and attachment proposed by Bowlby suggested that the infant naturally orients toward and promotes contact with other persons. Natural responsiveness to social influence emerges in the parental affectional system, and is nourished and expanded in the peer and sexual affectional systems. Stayton et al. (1971) suggested that the attachment bond appears to "foster a willingness to comply with parental signals" (p. 1067). The first definite signs of obedience – compliance with maternal signals – emerges with locomotor exploration. Klinnert et al. (1983) noted that at this stage, infants begin to use *social referencing*: searching the faces of others for clues about how to respond. Thus, responsiveness to social influence is itself a basic aspect of human nature, and this fact helps to explain some apparent contradictions in human behavior. Human nature is not "good" or "evil," rather it is *flexible*. As noted previously, it could be emphasized again: arguably the most inflexibly determined attribute of human nature is flexibility itself. This responsiveness to immediate social and situational influences underlies much human cooperation and the achievement of constructive social enterprises. Ironically, it may also play a major role in the most dangerous and destructive of human crimes.

Attachment and social emotions

The general model of the relationship between biological and higher-level emotions was presented in Figure 5.1. In Chapter 5 we stated two general principles regarding this relationship: (1) that higher-level emotions respond to natural ecological challenges in the social and terrestrial environments, and they therefore exist relative to other persons, stimuli, and situations; and (2) that to become functional they require experience over the course of development with other persons, stimuli, and situations. Furthermore, like all emotions, higher-level emotions exist as potentials, hidden unless activated by challenge. Unlike biologically based emotions, the motivational force underlying higher-level emotions is seen to involve separate systems *à la* Tomkins' (1962; 1963) affect theory. In the case of social emotions, the motivational force or experiential "fire" underlying tendencies to "tend and befriend" is attachment, based in turn upon prosocial biological emotions including love, warmth, bonding, caring, and distress at separation and isolation.

To repeat, this chapter develops an ecological-systems theory of social emotions. In this view, attachment needs combine with experience with universal interpersonal contingencies in social interaction. From this combination, a system of primary social emotions emerges naturally and spontaneously as a self-organizing system. Social emotions are honed, as it were, in the crucible of social interaction. In this ecological-systems view, social emotions are not invented in the human mind but rather constitute "natural kinds" that are discovered in the course of social interaction and emerge naturally over the course of development.

Attachment: the biological bases of social emotions

Just as cognitive emotions are "fired" by effectance motives combining with ecological challenges in the form of combinations of fundamental situational contingencies, social emotions are motivated by attachment emotions combining with ecological challenges in the form of combinations of fundamental interpersonal contingencies. Social emotions exist with regard to other persons and events. When we feel proud, or ashamed, or jealous, it is with respect to other persons and specific situations. It is only meaningful to inquire about social emotions if other persons and situations are specified or implied.

We have examined a number of "positive" biologically based emotions, including emotions associated with different sorts of reward, satiation, erotic attraction, maternal/parental love, play, and bonding. We saw in Chapter 5 that positive individualistic/selfish emotions – involving curiosity, expectancy, reward, and satiation – underlie exploratory effectance motives that with experience lead to the emergence of cognitive emotions. Analogously, prosocial biological emotions underlie attachment motives – involving the needs to be loved and esteemed – that with social experience lead to the emergence of social emotions.

Prosocial/cooperative emotions involve attachment to others, and as considered in Chapter 4, the evolution of mammals was associated with the appearance of a number of attachment mechanisms that tend to moderate selfish tendencies. Attachment systems are inherent in basic territoriality, sexuality, and nurturance of the young; and they are strongest in species characterized by social recognition, social preference, negative responses to separation (including distress vocalization in the young), social repair of destructive conflicts, and play (see de Waal and Aureli, 1997; Mendoza and Mason, 1997; Panksepp et al., 1997). Brain regions associated with these behaviors are typically rich in OXY, AVP, and the endorphins (Carter et al., 1997; Panksepp, 1998; Panksepp et al., 1997). We saw that attachment-related neurochemical systems (e.g. OXY, AVP) have been demonstrated to strongly influence complex behaviors and feelings in human beings. Collectively, biologically based attachment mechanisms determine an individual's motivation to interact, communicate, and bond with others. In this way attachment constitutes the physiological basis of the social emotions: a powerful motivational force amounting to an "addiction to love."

Fundamental social motives

The motivation arising from attachment has two aspects: the need to be loved and the need to meet/exceed expectations (Buck, 1988a).

A person is strongly motivated to be loved; and a person is strongly motivated to conform, to do that which is expected and indeed to exceed expectations and attain the esteem of others. Experiences involving the satisfaction and frustration of such needs are essential to the affective side of social development. As we saw in Chapter 5, normal socio-emotional development requires the initial activation of attachment motives via contact comfort, and later experiences in playful contact with peers. Early social deprivation, neglect, and abuse can lead to life-long disorders involving insecure or avoidant attachment.

Before considering the ecological-systems approach to social emotions further, I examine another approach to higher-level social emotions which views them as necessarily involving a consciousness of self.

Self-conscious emotions

Social emotions in our definition include those that Michael Lewis (1993) termed *self-conscious emotions*: pride, hubris or arrogance, embarrassment, shame, and guilt. These are often considered to appear later in development than biologically based emotions and to require relatively elaborate cognitive processing involving a sense of self: that is, an evaluation of the self with respect to social standards, rules, or goals involving attribution processes (Barrett, 2005; Tangney, 1999; Weiner, 1986). In an extension of attribution theory (considered in Chapter 5), these authors argue that for these emotions to occur, one must appreciate that one's behavior is good or bad, for example, consistent with or contrary to rules. The self-conscious emotions flow from our explanations or attributions of the causes of good or bad behavior.

Attributions to self versus behavior

Pride, guilt, shame, and embarrassment. One of the major propositions involved in distinguishing different self-conscious emotions is that good or bad behavior can be attributed to the self as a whole, or to particular aspects of the self. *Global self-attributions* refer to the evaluation of the whole self (e.g. I am a good/bad person), while *specific self-attributions* refer to the evaluation of specific features or actions of the self (e.g. I did a good/bad thing). Helen Block Lewis (1971) suggested that guilt is focused upon specific negative actions (I did a bad thing), while shame involves a global negative evaluation of the self (I am a bad person: Tangney, 1995a; Tangney et al., 1996). M. Lewis (1993) agreed and extended this analysis to pride and hubris. Pride is focused on a specific self-attribution (I did a good thing), while hubris is focused on a global self-attribution (I am a good person). Hubris is similar to the perhaps more widely understood term "arrogance" (Tracy and Robins, 2004a). Specific self-attributions are thought to be generally *unstable*, in that your good behavior on one occasion may not be expected to be repeated. Global self-attributions on the other hand are *stable*: if you are a good person you will be expected to be consistently good across situations.

In a review of basic and higher-level emotions, Tracy and Robins (2004a, 2004b) suggested the following: self-conscious emotions (a) involve the activation of self-representations, (b) are judged to be relevant for one's identity, (c) are congruent or incongruent with one's identity, and (d) are attributed to internal causes (e.g. chosen by the responder and not caused by accident or outside pressures). Moreover, self-conscious emotions are interrelated: identity–goal congruence elicits positive self-conscious emotions (pride), while identity–goal incongruence elicits negative self-conscious emotions (shame, guilt, embarrassment). In the Tracy and Robins (2004a, 2006) model pride and guilt are similar in that both involve unstable specific attributions to one's behavior, while arrogance (hubristic pride) and shame are similar in that both involve stable global attributions to oneself (Campbell et al., 2004).

Other higher-level emotions. Self-conscious emotions theorists have tended to focus upon pride, guilt, shame, and embarrassment. However, other higher-level emotions can be related to this analysis, namely envy, jealousy, pity, and scorn. These can be viewed as referring to global or specific attributions concerning another person. For example, if another is successful in exceeding expectations, the corresponding tendency is that one tends to feel envy at the accomplishment, and when another receives love and esteem, the tendency is to be jealous (Guerrero et al., 2005; Parrott, 1991; Parrott and Smith, 1993; Vecchio, 2005). Although M. Lewis (1993) and Tracy and Robins (2004a, 2004b) did not include envy or jealousy in their analyses, the ideas that envy is specific to an accomplishment, and that in jealousy the other succeeds in obtaining a global positive evaluation arguably do fit. Similarly, if another person fails to meet expectations, she or he may be pitied. Pity is specific to a failed behavior, and the other is not rejected (Dijker, 2001; Dijker and Koomen, 2003). On the other hand, if the other loses love and esteem, he or she becomes an object of scorn (Anolli et al., 2002). Again, M. Lewis' (1993) analysis arguably fits: pity is specific to a failure on the part of the other, while the scorned other receives a global negative evaluation. Tracy and Robins' (2004a, 2004b) analysis also fits: pity and envy involve unstable specific attributions; and jealousy and scorn, stable global attributions.

There has been considerable research on the self-conscious emotions in humans, mostly from the point of view of cognitive-attribution theories of motivation and emotion (Frijda, 1986; Lazarus, 1991b; Scherer, 1993; Smith and Ellsworth, 1985; Weiner, 1986). These theories show considerable agreement and overlap with one another (Ekman and Davidson, 1994), and share a common assumption that emotions are based upon cognitive evaluations or appraisals of events relevant to one's well-being. This research has often used self-report methods based upon participants' evaluations of stories or their own remembered autobiographical experiences. For example, participants might be given stories involving success or failure due to luck or to personal effort, and asked to describe or rate the feelings experienced by the protagonists. Alternatively, they might be given a social emotion term such as "pride," and asked to describe a situation that would evoke that feeling, or to recall a situation in their own lives when that feeling was experienced.

Cognitive bases of self-conscious emotions

The concept of self-conscious emotions requires complex cognitive processing – even language. As noted, Tracy and Robins (2004a) argued that self-conscious emotions require elaborate self-processes involving a sense of self and knowledge of cultural standards; and L. F. Barrett (2006) suggested that emotional experience is driven by culture-specific emotion categories and concepts. However, recent studies have called both of these assumptions into question. K. C. Barrett (2005) studied guilt, embarrassment, and anxiety behaviors in 17-month-olds, and unexpectedly found no relationship between these behaviors and self-recognition: indeed, contrary to expectations, the relationship between embarrassment behaviors and self-recognition in boys was found to be negative. Also, Breugelmans and Poortinga (2006) found that even though the Raramuri Indians in Mexico have only one word for shame and guilt, they nevertheless differentiated between characteristics of shame and guilt in ways similar to populations that have two words. As Frijda put it, "experiences of what we would recognise as shame and what we would recognise as guilt differed as much as when separate labels are available" (2009, p. 1455).

Social emotions in nonhuman animals

The notion that social emotions necessarily involve elaborate self-representations vitiates against the notion that social emotions are involved in the social regulation of nonhuman animals. However, complex social bonds and alliances observed in animals arguably require social emotions (Buck, 2007; Buck and Powers, 2006; de Waal, 2008; Morris et al., 2008). Also, animals including laboratory rats have been demonstrated to engage in altruistic behavior where the only reward is helping another animal (Bartal et al., 2011). These phenomena require communication, and we saw in Chapter 3 that specific affective communication mechanisms supporting social organization have been observed in many species, including voles, wolves, and chimpanzees; and that learning how to use such communication mechanisms in interaction is critical to socio-emotional development.

An ecological-systems view of social emotions

Ecologically fundamental interpersonal contingencies

The notion from self-conscious emotion theories that higher-level social emotions are interrelated can be extended from pride, hubris, guilt, and shame to also include envy, jealousy, pity, and scorn. In fact, all of these emotions are interrelated, so that they fit the classic definition of a *system* as "a whole which functions as a whole by virtue of the interdependence of its parts" (Rapoport, 1986, p. xvii). On the other hand, a Gibsonian view suggests that cognition is not the basis of social emotions. Instead, attributions and appraisals are themselves structured by architectures inherent in the natural ecology of social interaction that emerge over the course of development: social emotions emerge spontaneously from active social comparison.

More specifically, *ecologically fundamental interpersonal contingencies* are antecedent to culturally variable attribution, appraisal, and labeling processes in social emotions; just as ecologically fundamental situational contingencies are antecedent to such analytic cognitive processes in cognitive emotions. Ecologically fundamental interpersonal contingencies are defined formally as *specific combinations of circumstances ecologically existent in the social interaction environment with implications for the comparative well-being of self and others.*

Fundamental social motives. Attachment has intrinsic motivational consequences that are fundamental to social life. The motivation arising from attachment has two aspects: the *need to be loved*, and the *need to follow/exceed the expectations of others* (Buck, 1988a). A person is strongly motivated to be esteemed and loved by others; and a person is motivated to conform, to do that which is expected and indeed to exceed expectations. Perceived challenges in the social environment involving social comparison can activate strong and persistent affective needs to be loved and esteemed. Persons (Ps) can themselves satisfy or fail to satisfy these affective needs; and they can compare themselves with another person, a *comparison other* (CO), who satisfy or fail to satisfy these needs for themselves.[1] A consequence of this view is that social emotions do not require complex cognitive processing – in fact they can exist in social animals as well as human beings – because given attachment motives they emerge naturally and effortlessly from the ecology of social interaction.

The distinction between two fundamental social motives is related to the distinction drawn previously between specific and global self-attribution. The motive to follow/exceed expectations focuses on specific expectations, while the motive to be loved involves a global self-attribution. However, in the ecological-systems view the level of cognitive processing required by the H. B. Lewis and M. Lewis analyses is not necessary. Given basic attachment, social emotions play out within the natural logic of interaction, and function also in social animals.

Affordances and social affordances. Gibson (1966) argued that organisms evolved to "pick up" naturally and effortlessly environmental information that affords behavior (*affordances*). This ecological determination has two aspects: phylogenetic and developmental. First, we have seen that critical architectures for biological emotions – neurochemical systems – emerged via natural selection as phylogenetic adaptations to the ecological realities of terrestrial environments (Buck, 1999). To paraphrase Gibson, what is in the head was determined by what the head has been in. Furthermore, critical architectures for higher-level social emotions are ecologically present over the course of development as social affordances naturally present in the course of social interaction and communication, so that social emotions are discovered effortlessly by the child and emerge naturally. Therefore, rather than being created by the brain or mind, social emotions emerge spontaneously as self-organizing systems from architectures objectively present over the course of development in the child's communicative interactions with others, including parents and other adults, peers, and also media models.

Displays as social affordances. Expressive displays function as social affordances in the Gibsonian sense (Buck, 1984; Buck and Ginsburg, 1997a; McArthur and Baron, 1983), and there are similarities in the

---

[1] The term "comparison other" (CO) is used here to indicate that the comparison in question is not necessarily with someone that one has a relationship with, either friendly or unfriendly. The term comes from World War II studies which showed that soldiers who compared themselves with soldiers in combat were satisfied, soldiers who compared themselves with soldiers stationed in the United States were not (Stouffer et al., 1949); and was used in social comparison theory (Festinger, 1954). CO is an abstract comparison other, not a concrete individual with whom the person (P) has a personal relationship (Polonsky and Buck, 2003).

expressive behaviors involved in emotion displays in humans and non-human animals. For example, pride and hubris/arrogance have been associated with expressive behaviors in human beings involving an erect and expanded upper body posture and upward head tilt (Tracy and Robins, 2004c), which is distinctly different from the downcast posture and head tilt associated with embarrassment and shame (Keltner, 1995, 1997; Keltner and Buswell, 1996, 1997; Keltner and Harker, 1998). These expressive displays are similar to displays of dominance and submission widely observed among nonhuman animals, including non-primates and even non-vertebrates as we have seen (e.g. lobsters; see Figure 4.3); and there is evidence in human beings consistent with the social affordance conceptualization that the perception of dominance and submission is direct and unmediated (Moors and de Houwer, 2005).

If social emotions are interrelated in a dynamic system, a display of *one* has *implications for all*: a display of pride implies arrogance and pity/scorn, and tends to stimulate envy/jealousy and guilt/shame in the comparison other, who tends to display submission. The evidence that the perception of dominance/submission is direct and unmediated therefore implies that *all* of the social emotions can be *directly perceived and communicated without cognitive mediation* in the course of interaction. I suggest that such communication occurs naturally, spontaneously, and constantly; although it is rarely noticed and consciously acknowledged (Buck, 1984). This results in the natural, effortless, and pan-cultural emergence of primary social emotions.

Primary social emotions

Definition. When success and failure at satisfying the two fundamental social motives on the part of a person and comparison other are combined, the result is an array of eight ecologically fundamental interpersonal contingencies that can be related to common English labels for social emotions, as well as labels in other languages. All else equal, a relatively successful person (P) is likely to experience a social emotion labeled in English *pride* and/or *arrogance* and to have *pity* and/or *scorn* for the less fortunate comparison others (COs). Proud persons are relatively unlikely to experience *guilt, shame, envy,* or *jealousy*. On the other hand, relatively unsuccessful COs comparing themselves with a successful P, are relatively likely to experience guilt and/or shame, and envy and/or jealousy toward P in comparison. These eight *primary social emotions* are summarized in Figure 6.2. The interdependence of social emotions stems from the natural architectures of ecologically fundamental interpersonal contingencies based upon social

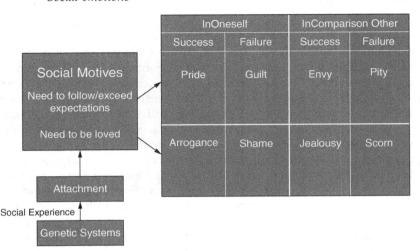

	InOneself		InComparison Other	
	Success	Failure	Success	Failure
Pride	Guilt	Envy	Pity
Arrogance	Shame	Jealousy	Scorn

Social Motives

Need to follow/exceed expectations

Need to be loved

Attachment

Social Experience

Genetic Systems

Figure 6.2 Hypothesized relationships between attachment, expectancy, social motives, and social emotions. Biologically based attachment systems produce directly needs to be loved/esteemed. Biologically based expectancy systems motivate exploration via curiosity, produce competence, with social exploration producing social competence and understanding of social expectations. The latter, combined with needs to be loved/esteemed, produces the need to meet/exceed expectations. The two social motives are combined with ecologically fundamental interpersonal contingencies involving success and failure in meeting these needs in the self and comparison other, yielding eight ecologically based social emotion categories that are labeled differently in different cultures and languages.

comparisons of relative gain and loss, or success and failure. Because these combinations of contingencies are naturally interrelated, primary social emotions themselves are interrelated so that one has implications for the others: this reflects the interdependence of system elements in Rapoport's (1986) definition.

Attachment provides the biological motivational basis of these primary social emotions: one cannot experience social emotions such as pride, guilt, shame, envy, etc. unless one *cares* about winning and maintaining the esteem and love of other persons. Social emotions are "fired" biologically by attachment, involving affects including needs for affection, bonding, and love; and also painful distress, panic, and anguish when these needs are threatened. Social emotions emerge from potential inherent in these biologically based attachment motives, realized via experiences in ecologically fundamental interpersonal contingencies over the course of development. Because of the universality of attachment needs on one hand, and ecologically fundamental interpersonal contingencies involving relative success and failure on the other, the emergence of primary social emotions is universal in human beings in all cultures and historical periods and dynamic interrelationships between social emotions should be consistent across cultures and historical periods, regardless of language differences in labeling them.

The dynamics of primary social emotions. The ecological-systems analysis implies that, because of the natural structure of fundamental interpersonal contingencies, each primary social emotion is related to others in specific respects. First, each primary social emotion associated with the need to meet/exceed expectations has a *twin* associated with the need to be loved: pride is the twin of arrogance, guilt is the twin of shame, envy is the twin of jealousy, and pity is the twin of scorn. There is considerable literature concerned with differentiating some twins from one another (particularly guilt versus shame and envy versus jealousy). However, attempts to differentiate them in terms of differences in appraisal have not been entirely successful, and no system of defining and differentiating these "twins" is generally accepted in the field (see Fontaine et al., 2006; Tangney et al., 1996).

Second, each primary social emotion associated with success has an *opposite* associated with failure. Pride is the opposite of guilt, arrogance is the opposite of shame, envy is the opposite of pity, and jealousy is the opposite of scorn.

Third, each primary social emotion has a *reciprocal*, such that if a person P feels X about him/herself, P would tend to feel its reciprocal toward a comparison other. Pride is the reciprocal of pity: that is, proud P would tend to pity the comparison other. Similarly, arrogance is the reciprocal of scorn, guilt is the reciprocal of envy, and shame is the reciprocal of jealousy.

Fourth, each primary social emotion has a *converse*, which is the opposite of the reciprocal. P would tend *not* to feel the converse about CO. For example, proud P would tend *not* to be envious of CO. Similarly, arrogance is the converse of jealousy, guilt is the converse of pity, and shame is the reciprocal of scorn.

From this analysis one can make specific hypotheses about the dynamics of primary social emotions. If one experiences a given primary social emotion, it is:

1. Likely that one would simultaneously experience its twin (positive correlation).
2. Unlikely that one would experience its opposite (negative correlation).

3. Likely that one would experience its reciprocal toward others (positive correlation).
4. Unlikely that one would experience its converse toward others (negative correlation).

Furthermore, this analysis implies that if P feels a given primary social emotion about him/herself, CO would tend to experience a pattern of *mirror* primary social emotions in comparison. First, it is unlikely that CO will experience the same mirror emotion as P, or its twin. That is, if P is successful in exceeding expectations and feels proud, CO would not tend to feel pride or arrogance.[2] Similarly, guilt and shame, envy and jealousy, and pity and scorn in P would tend to discourage similar emotions in O. Rather, O would tend to feel the *mirror-opposite* of P's emotion: that is, pride/arrogance in P would tend to encourage feelings of guilt/shame in CO toward P in comparison. On the other hand, P's guilt/shame would encourage pride/arrogance in CO. Moreover, P's envy/jealousy would encourage CO's pity/scorn; and likewise P's pity/scorn would encourage CO's envy/jealousy.

Based upon similar reasoning, O would tend *not* to feel the *mirror-reciprocal* of the emotion experienced by P. That is, pride/arrogance in P would tend to discourage pity/scorn in CO, P's guilt/shame would discourage CO's envy/jealousy. Likewise, pity/scorn in P would tend to discourage pride/arrogance in CO, P's envy/jealousy would discourage CO's guilt/shame. On the other hand, CO would be likely to feel the *mirror-converse* of the emotion experienced by P. That is, pride/arrogance in P would tend to encourage envy/jealousy in CO, and P's guilt/shame would encourage CO's pity/scorn. Likewise, envy/jealousy in P would tend to feed pride/arrogance in CO, and P's pity/scorn would encourage CO's guilt/shame.

One can therefore specify several additional hypotheses about the dynamics of primary social emotions. If P experiences a given primary social emotion, the comparison other is:

5. Unlikely to simultaneously experience that emotion or its twin (negative correlation).
6. Likely to experience its mirror-opposite (positive correlation).
7. Unlikely to experience its mirror-reciprocal (negative correlation).
8. Likely to experience its mirror-converse (positive correlation).

Thus, proud/arrogant P will tend to pity/scorn the envious/jealous other, who will feel guilty/ashamed (see Figure 6.3).

---

[2] Recall the assumption that there is no personal relationship between P and CO.

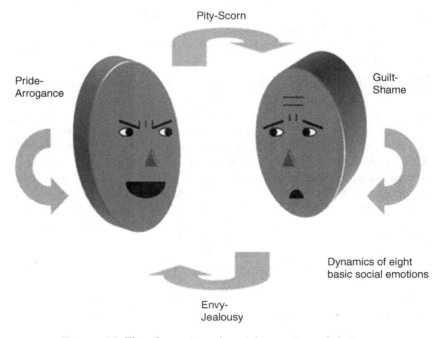

Pity-Scorn

Pride-
Arrogance

Guilt-
Shame

Dynamics of eight
basic social emotions

Envy-
Jealousy

Figure 6.3 The dynamics of social emotions defining a
dominant-subordinate relationship. See text for details.

Implications of the ecological-systems view of social emotions. One implication of the ecological-systems analysis is that there may be links
between esteem for others and esteem for the self: comparison with
persons who are relatively less successful than oneself at meeting/
exceeding expectations and being loved may tend to reinforce feelings
of pride and arrogance. Contrariwise, comparison with persons
who are relatively more successful than oneself may tend to reinforce
feelings of guilt and shame.

This analysis implies two hypotheses about the cultural generality or
"universality" of social emotions. First is the *hypothesis of universal
labeling*: there should be words describing the eight fundamental interpersonal contingency unions in all nations, cultures, languages, and
historical times. Second is the *hypothesis of universal dynamics*: these
words should be interrelated similarly in all nations, cultures, languages, and historical times.

Importantly, the ecological-systems analysis does not proceed one
emotion at a time: rather fundamental interpersonal contingencies
evoke simultaneously a *system* of social emotions, where the system

functions as a whole by virtue of the interdependence of its parts (Rapoport, 1986). The expressive display of one social emotion has implications for all of the others, such that *all of the social emotions are displayed simultaneously in dominance and submission behaviors*. Also, this implies that the measurement of one social emotion has implications for measuring all of the others, so that ratings of "pride," "guilt," "envy," and "pity," for example, do not constitute single-item measures of four emotions; rather they constitute a multi-item measure of a ecological system of primary social emotions.

Social emotions and dominance

The suggested pattern of dynamic interrelationships of the social emotions is illustrated in Figure 6.3. Note that the individual depicted in Figure 6.3 on the left seems happy and upbeat, and the other seems sad and downcast. This illustrates how the social emotions are experienced naturally in the *dominance relationship*. In general, dominant individuals are expected to feel the twin social emotions pride and arrogance vis-à-vis themselves and the reciprocal twin's pity and scorn to the subordinate comparison other. The subordinate other experiences the mirrors of these emotions: the twin's guilt and shame vis-à-vis the self and the reciprocal twin's envy and jealousy toward the dominant comparison other. From the evidence discussed earlier, one would expect that the communication of this dominance relationship within the dyad would tend to be associated with increased levels of serotonin (5-HT) at specific receptor sites in the dominant partner and corresponding decreases in serotonin in the subordinate partner. Such decreases might be expected to lead in turn to tendencies toward depression in the latter.

Envy and jealousy tend to encourage self-directed guilt and shame in the perceiver. This may help to explain the evidence that one may experience pleasure if the object of envy or jealousy suffers adversity (Ben-Ze'ev, 1992; Smith et al., 1996). Such pleasure in the suffering of others is termed *schadenfreude*, and it may be a typical response when a dominant comparison person is "brought to his knees."

The language of primary social emotions

The issue of the relationship of emotions and the language used to label them is complex and contentious. As noted, some have taken cultural differences in emotion lexicon to imply differences in emotional experience (E. F. Barrett, 2006), but empirical evidence calls this proposition into question (Breugelmans and Poortinga, 2006). In the ecological-systems approach, it is the combinations of contingencies represented in the fundamental interpersonal contingencies, not specific emotion labels, which are theoretically meaningful. In this view, *emotion terminology is largely irrelevant*: social emotion terms reflect fundamental interpersonal contingencies which exist in nature independently of emotion terms and are discovered rather than created by the human mind.

Accordingly, in the ecological-systems view, "guilt" and "shame" are *not emotions*; they are *words* that in English designate combinations of fundamental interpersonal contingencies that *are* ecologically universal attributes of interaction and social organization in human beings and other animals, and are universally the bases of social emotions (Buck, 2004). As relative success and failure and social comparison processes are universal experiences, dynamic relationships between social emotions should be consistent across cultures and historical periods, regardless of language differences in labeling. For example, in the ecological-systems view "shame" *is not an emotion. It is a word*. But, when someone who deeply desires to be loved perceives that she or he is in fact unloved and/or unlovable, *that* is a combination of fundamental interpersonal contingencies that *is* associated with emotion that can be expected to be related to other social emotions and to manifest distinct properties (unpleasant, heightened cortisol, lowered head, slumped posture . . .). It can exist in all normally socialized persons, in all cultures, in all historical periods, and in animals to the extent of their sociality. This emotion may be represented by many words in one culture and few in another, and this fact may be critically important for understanding those cultures, but the emotion also reflects ecologically fundamental events that can occur whenever social comparison of relative success or failure occurs in combination with strong attachment motives.

Thus, the intent is not to reify "pride," "guilt," etc. per se as universal social emotions; rather, the intent is to point out eight functional combinations of interpersonal contingencies that *are* ecologically fundamental and universal to social behavior, and therefore given social experience form the basis of a self-organizing system of primary social emotions. These combinations of contingencies may or may not correspond well in a given language with an appropriate label: this is an empirical issue (see Hupka et al., 1999). The proposed labels in English seem reasonably appropriate for most of these contingencies, but this is not really a problem from the point of view of the ecological-systems theory: the labels are regarded as more or less convenient and appropriate tools for communication, whose adequacy can be empirically investigated.

Attachment and social emotions

The assumption that social emotions are based upon attachment allows the use of attachment theory to understand and make predictions about who would experience which social emotion more strongly and under what circumstances. As discussed previously, attachment is the bio-logical basis of social emotions, and attachment has two fundamental motivational consequences: it stimulates a need to be loved, and a need to follow/exceed expectations (Buck, 1988a). Also, if emotion is defined as a readout of motivational potential, this implies that there are two aspects to social emotions: some social emotions represent a readout of needs to be loved, and others represent a readout of needs to follow/exceed expectations. Attachment theory has implications for under-standing how these two needs are related to different patterns of social emotions. For example, the need to be loved is present at birth, while the need to follow/exceed expectations requires cognitive development (e.g. ToM skills) and therefore emerges later in development.

Attachment styles in children

We saw in Chapter 4 that Bowlby described the infant's attachment with the caregiver, and that many naturalistic and laboratory studies supported Bowlby's theory (Bretherton, 1985). For example, studies using Ainsworth's Strange Situation, where the mother briefly leaves the child and then returns, established the distinction between secure, anxious/ambivalent, and avoidant attachment styles (Ainsworth et al., 1978). Secure attachments grow out of consistent expressions of love by the caregiver, giving the infant "confidence in the availability of attachment figures," with less tendency toward the "intense or chronic fear" experienced by those who lack such confidence (Bowlby, 1973, p. 235). Inconsistency on the part of the caregiver tends to produce an anxious/ambivalent attachment and signs of protest: the child tends to cry more and to explore the physical and social environment less than the securely attached child, and shows signs of anxiety and anger mixed with attachment behaviors. Consistent rejection of the infant can lead to the infant's learning to avoid the caregiver, producing detachment. Thus, the secure infant is confident in being loved, the anxious/avoidant infant is insecure that it is loved, and the avoidant infant may no longer need to be loved. Similarly, Robertson's studies showed a pattern of protest, giving way to despair, and finally detachment when an infant is separated from its caregiver over an extended period of time; an initially secure attachment took on the characteristics of anxious/ambivalent, and finally avoidant attachment.

Attachment style differentiates "twin" social emotions

All else equal, securely attached persons should be confident in being loved and therefore should be relatively less concerned about being not loved, so that their motives to be loved should not be particularly salient, and their greater concern would be with fulfilling expectations. Conversely, anxious/avoidant persons should be relatively more concerned about being loved. Therefore, I expect that, all else equal, securely attached persons should tend to experience pride, guilt, envy, and pity in situations in which anxious/ambivalent persons should experience the twins of these emotions: arrogance, shame, jealousy, and scorn. Avoidant persons, in contrast, should be relatively detached and not be expected to experience the social emotions as frequently or as deeply as other persons.

Thus, in the ecological-systems analysis, differences between pairs of twin social emotions lie not in the objective aspects of the eliciting situations, or even in the cognitive appraisals of those situations. Rather, the differences in the twins lie in whether the responder is most concerned about others' evaluation of his or her behavior, or of his or herself. This concern, I suggest, is based upon the individual's attachment security: identical circumstances can produce either twin. More specifically, securely attached persons generally have more confidence in being loved, compared to anxious/ambivalent persons. For that reason, I expect that secure persons are likely to experience pride in situations where anxious/ambivalent persons experience its twin, arrogance. Moreover, secure persons should feel guilt instead of shame and envy instead of jealousy, while anxious/ambivalent persons should be predisposed to feelings of shame and jealousy rather than guilt and envy. Finally, I expect anxious/ambivalent persons to be more susceptible to scorn than its twin, pity, compared with more secure persons.

Adult attachment

Attachment theory was based upon studies of children and their caregivers. Hazan and Shaver (1987, 1994) extended attachment theory to romantic relationships in adults, and a number of conceptualizations and measures of attachment in adults developed from this work. I will not attempt a comprehensive review of this research here, although there is evidence that attachment style impacts interpersonal communication patterns (e.g. Le Poire et al., 1999). One of the major differences between attachment in children versus adults is that adults tend to show mixed attachment styles: e.g. they seem to be secure in some relationships, anxious-ambivalent in others, and avoidant in still others. This may actually accurately reflect the state of interpersonal relationships in most normally socialized adults.

This has important implications for the ecological-systems model of social emotions. First, it suggests that it is useful to conceptualize adult attachment as a state as well as a trait. In addition to seeing a given individual as generally secure, anxious-ambivalent, or avoidant, it is useful to consider the individual as having a variety of attachment relationships, the security of which varies both across relationships and across time within relationships. Second, this implies in turn that the social emotions experienced vis-à-vis other persons vary across relationships and across time within relationships. For example, upon graduation, a college student might feel authentic pride when he considers his sainted grandmother who helped him through school; and virtually simultaneously he might feel arrogance when considering a high school rival. The student feels secure in the relationship with the grandmother, but anxious-ambivalent in the relationship with the rival. Mixed feelings are also possible. The student may feel pride vis-à-vis the grandmother about graduation, but simultaneously guilt or shame when thinking about the extra semester that it took to finish and the attendant cost to the grandmother.

The result is a flexible conceptualization that is based upon the emotions felt directly and immediately when contemplating a variety of complex social and personal relationships. Complex cognitive constructions such as self-consciousness or "working models" of attachment may exist, but they are not necessary for understanding the basic functioning of social emotions in human beings or other animals.

Research on primary social emotions

The most direct way to test the ecological-systems model would be to treat attachment style as an independent variable, and determine whether pride, guilt, envy, and pity are amplified under secure attachment conditions; and arrogance, shame, jealousy, and scorn enlarged with insecure attachment. However, this is an original conceptualization and such focused studies have not yet been done. Nevertheless, much research done from the point of view of self-conscious emotions is relevant to the ecological-systems model. This section examines relevant research organized by the hypothesized "twin" social emotions, including major attempts in the literature to define and distinguish the twin social emotions. It also examines their display and the developmental sequence in which they appear. In the process, I suggest specific hypotheses arising from the ecological-systems model. For example, the model predicts that pride, guilt, envy, and pity should appear later in development, after rules are learned and understood and the child can make basic causal attributions about the intentions of an actor including basic ToM skills. Their twins – arrogance, shame, jealousy, and scorn – should appear earlier because these cognitive capacities are not required for the ability to respond to needs to be loved. More specifically, social emotions involving needs to follow/exceed expectations should be preceded both phylogenetically and ontogenetically by social emotions involving the need to be loved: arrogance precedes pride; shame precedes guilt; jealousy precedes envy; and scorn precedes pity.

Pride/arrogance

Definitions. M. Lewis (1993) argued that pride involves pleasure focused upon a specific behavior, which affords the individual the ability to reproduce the positive state via similar behavior in the future. He used the term "hubris" for the case in which the individual succeeds in obtaining a global positive evaluation that includes the self as well as the behavior. Hubris is similar to the proposed twin of pride, which, following Tracy and Robins (2004a), I have termed "arrogance."

Display. Studies have described a typical nonverbal display associated with pride as involving the head tilted back with a small smile, and the torso expanded, arms akimbo or away from the body (Tracy and Matsumoto, 2008; Matsumoto and Hwang, 2012), and there is evidence that this display is recognized cross-culturally (Tracy and Robins, 2008). Hubristic pride or arrogance and authentic pride do not appear to differ in terms of their display, and this raised questions about whether they can be distinguished as distinct emotional states (Williams and DeSteno, 2010). Tracy and Prehn (2012) demonstrated that judgments of the same pride display could be manipulated into judgments of authentic pride or arrogance by altering contextual knowledge: that is, judgments of arrogance increased when the cause of the success was objectively attributed to ability rather than effort.

Developmental sequence. There is evidence that pride appears later in development than arrogance. According to Weiner's (1986) attribution theory, pride is the achievement of a positive outcome by personal effort. He suggested that there is a developmental sequence in the appreciation of emotions such as pride based upon children's abilities to consider causal attributions and situational outcomes together. Thus, Thompson (1987) presented participants with stories that varied in situation (achievement or moral), outcome (positive or negative), and causal attribution (personal effort, other's intervention, or luck), and asked participants to make inferences about the feelings of the protagonist. He found that younger children (second graders) tended to judge others as happy or sad based upon positive or negative outcomes, while older children and adults used causal attributions to infer pride. Similarly, Graham and Weiner (1991) used stories about protagonists who achieved success with the cause being either intended or external (eliciting or not eliciting pride), and protagonists in need of help, with the cause of the need manipulated to be uncontrollable (eliciting pity) or controllable (eliciting "anger" [scorn?]). They found developmental changes in attributions about pride but not pity or anger/scorn.

Relevant research. As noted, Tracy and Prehn (2012) demonstrated that judgments of hubristic pride or arrogance increased when the cause of the success of CO was objectively attributed to ability rather than effort. This was the case whether the successful COs themselves claimed success as due to effort or ability. The authors noted that this was surprising: they predicted that COs should have appeared arrogant when they falsely attributed their success to their ability when an objective observer judged that it was actually due to effort, as that would seem to imply over-claiming. However, that was not the case: the CO was judged to be arrogant when success was attributed to ability, regardless of whether CO claimed falsely that it was due to effort. A possible explanation based on the ecological-system model is that objective attribution to the CO's high ability made the participant feel less secure in comparison, and it was that insecurity on the part of the participant that led to judgments of arrogance as opposed to authentic pride. The ecological-systems view predicts that responders who are less secure, whatever the reason, would be more likely to judge a pride display as involving arrogance as opposed to authentic pride. Similarly, less secure responders are predicted to judge shame, jealousy, and scorn in situations where more secure responders judge guilt, envy, and pity.

Guilt/shame

Definitions. In the H. B. Lewis (1971) and M. Lewis (1993) analyses, guilt is focused like pride upon a specific behavioral transgression, which may motivate attempts to repair the failure. In contrast, shame involves a "painful" global negative evaluation of the self, leading to passivity, depression, and social withdrawal (Aron, 1997). Similarly, Lazarus (1994) related guilt to the core relational theme of "having transgressed a moral imperative" and shame to the core relational theme of "failing to live up to an ego-ideal" (p. 164). Frijda (1994) related guilt to "having unintentionally harmed someone within one's group," and shame to "risk of social rejection" (p. 156). Scheff (1988) suggested that nonconformity to social norms is punished by social rejection and shame. Welten et al. (2012) argued that all shame is related to a threat to the self.

The use of guilt as social control would tend to focus upon the rejection of the behavior and the expectation of repair, rather than the rejection of the individual. Some have suggested that most Western cultures tend to use guilt as social control, while Japanese culture for one tends to use shame (Benedict, 1946; Creighton, 1990; Davidson and Schaffner, 1977) but this is disputed and the reality may well be more complicated (de Rivera, 1989; Tatara, 1989).

There is a considerable literature on the distinction between guilt and shame. Smith and Ellsworth (1985) found the cognitive appraisals associated with guilt and shame to be "virtually indistinguishable from each other" (p. 833), and Tangney et al. (2011) noted that the types of events eliciting shame and guilt cannot be distinguished. Tangney (1992) asked participants to describe situations that induced guilt and shame. She found that descriptions of situations evoking guilt typically focused upon moral transgressions, often involving harm to others. Such situations could also evoke shame, and indeed, most situations involving a concern with one's effect upon others appeared to be capable of eliciting either guilt or shame. Shame could also be evoked by non-moral situations, such as one's failure in a performance. Significantly, shame was marked by a particular concern with others' evaluations. Stearns and Parrott (2012) found that transgressors who responded with either guilt or shame were rated more positively than those who did not. They could not, however, differentiate guilt from shame using manipulations focused on distinguishing a desire to apologize versus feelings of worthlessness: "our manipulation was successful but not emotion-specific: the terms 'guilt' and 'shame' do not solely evoke one emotion, but seem to evoke both emotions" (Stearns and Parrott (2012, p. 416). In a review, Tangney (1995b) concluded that judgments of guilt versus shame depend upon the individual's interpretation of the role of the self in the eliciting event, rather than the nature of the specific event per se. In guilt the focus is on the behavior, while in shame the focus is on the self. All in all, this literature suggests that guilt and shame are not distinguished by appraisals or by the eliciting situation. However, the hypothesis that shame and guilt can be distinguished according to the attachment concerns of the responder is consistent with this literature.

Display. Guilt and shame may differ in details of their display. To depict a shame display, Keltner and Buswell (1996) used photographs of faces showing head and gaze down. They compared this with an "embarrassment" display that also showed head and gaze down, but included as well a non-Duchenne smile, lip press, head movement to the left, and face touching. It is possible that these latter elements signal a less intense response that may signal repairable guilt. However, in general descriptions of guilt/shame displays suggest that they are opposite in most respects to displays of pride/arrogance. M. Lewis (1993) noted that the person experiencing shame shows behavior suggesting a wish to hide or disappear, such as hiding the face, averting the eyes, and shrinking the body. Studying spontaneous expressions following victory and defeat at the Olympic and Paralympic games, Tracy and Matsumoto (2008) described a slumping of the shoulders and narrowing of the chest following defeat in both sighted and blind athletes. Thus, as suggested previously, the display of pride/arrogance is similar to the ancient dominance display, while the display of guilt/shame is similar to submission and appeasement.

Developmental sequence. Consistent with the notion that guilt requires more cognitive processing than shame, there is evidence that guilt develops later. Izard (1978) described evidence of shame in 4- to 6-month-old infants, while signs of guilt were not detected until the beginning of the second year. Vaish et al. (2011) found that 5-year-olds but not 4-year olds responded appropriately to a film of a transgressor who either displayed or did not display guilt (looking down with furrowed brow). Graham et al. (1984) found developmental changes in the tendency of children aged 6 to 11 to link guilt with controllable negative events.

Relevant research. Tangney and Fischer (1995) distinguished individual tendencies to experience shame versus guilt as shame-proneness and guilt-proneness. Cohen et al. (2011) developed a scale intended to measure guilt- versus shame-proneness. Guilt-proneness was associated with more ethical decision-making, while shame-proneness was associated with negative self-evaluation. This is consistent with the ecological-systems view in that with guilt the responder is more secure in being loved and can therefore turn attention to repairing the breach in expectations. The anxious-ambivalent responder, in contrast, is concerned with being loved as reflected in the negative self-evaluation.

I suggest that attachment of the responder is critical to the distinction between shame and guilt: compared with more secure persons, anxious-ambivalent persons should be more susceptible to shame than guilt. This should be true of "state" attachment as well as "trait" attachment. Also, I suggest that given appropriate circumstances shame-proneness will be related to tendencies to feel and judge arrogance, jealousy, and scorn; while guilt-proneness will be related to tendencies to feel and judge pride, envy, and pity. Moreover, the ecological-systems view predicts that not only shame, but arrogance, jealousy, and scorn will be associated with a relatively negative self-evaluation on the part of the responder.

Envy/jealousy

Definitions. If a comparison other is successful in exceeding expectations and feels proud, the corresponding tendency is that one feels envy at their accomplishment; while if the comparison other receives love and esteem, the tendency is to be jealous. Traditionally, envy has been seen as a desire for something that someone else has, while jealousy is associated with the possibility of losing to a rival a relationship that one already has (Smith et al., 1988). Lazarus (1994) related envy to the core relational theme of "wanting what someone else has," and jealousy to the theme of "resenting a third party for loss or threat to another's affection or favor" (p. 164). Frijda (1994) related envy to "inequality of access to valued goods by social equals" and jealousy to "threats to exclusive sexual access" (p. 156). Ecological-systems theory views the similarities and differences between envy and jealousy somewhat differently: the difference is conceptualized in terms of whether the other's success is associated with a specific behavior or with a global assessment, in both cases generating an unfavorable comparative self-evaluation. Envy and jealousy were not explicitly considered in M. Lewis' (1993) analysis, but the notion that envy involves a CO's specific accomplishment while jealousy involves the other succeeding in obtaining a global positive evaluation of self does seem to fit.

A number of investigators have studied similarities and differences between envy and jealousy. Rodin and colleagues suggested that envy is a special case of jealousy – "social comparison jealousy" – that occurs "when we compare ourselves to others and find that we do not measure up" (Salovey and Rodin, 1984, p. 780; Bers and Rodin, 1984). Salovey and Rodin (1986) contrasted this with "romantic jealousy," which they suggested is stronger because it combines social comparison jealousy with other distressing features, including negative feelings about the self, lover, and rival. Defending the distinction between envy and jealousy, Parrott and Smith (1993) asked participants to read stories in which circumstances producing envy or jealousy were manipulated independently. For envy, the success of a rival and protagonist were manipulated in a domain self-relevant to the protagonist; for jealousy, the protagonist was depicted as seeing either one's lover or an unidentified person interacting romantically with a rival. They found that differing affective states were associated with the two kinds of stories:

envy stories elicited feelings of inferiority, longing, resentment, and disapproval of the emotion; while jealousy was associated with feelings of loss, distrust, anxiety, and anger.

Display. No specific displays have been associated with envy or jealousy: they are usually defined in terms of negative emotional responses in situations involving invidious comparisons with other persons. "Status symbols" might be considered to be displays that are used to show pride/arrogance and to incite their mirrors, envy/ jealousy, in others.

Developmental sequence. The emergence of envy seems to coincide with the development of ToM skills (Sawada, 2010). In contrast, several investigators have described the appearance of jealousy reactions during the first year of life based upon infant responses to a loss of parental attention to a social rival (Campos et al., 2010; Hart, 2010; Markova et al., 2010; Sawada, 2010). Mize and Jones (2012) first assessed the baseline EEG responding of 11- to 14-month-old infants. The mother then played with the infant for three minutes. Following this, the mother was given a lifelike doll or a book, and attended to that for three minutes while ignoring the infant. The mother then played again with the infant for three minutes. The infant's responses while being ignored were observed, with a jealousy profile including rated arousal, anxiety, aggression, gaze toward the mother, close proximity and touching the mother, and displays of negative affect including vocalizations. Results indicated that jealousy profile behaviors were higher in the social (doll) than non-social (book) rival condition. Also, jealousy profile responses related to maternal ratings of the infant's temperament, including activity, distress to limitations, and (negatively) smiling and laughing. Jealousy profile responses also predicted greater left frontal EEG activity, which is consistent with descriptions of left-sided activation being associated with approach behavior and/or prosocial responses (see Chapter 3).

Kolak and Volling (2011) used a similar procedure to assess jealousy in 4-year-olds with a younger (approximately 16-month-old) sibling. Parents (both mother and father) interacted with one child for three minutes, and then ignored that child and interacted with the sibling for three minutes. The toddlers tended to respond with distress when ignored (crying, whining, fussing), while the older children tended to respond with displays of sadness and anger. The relationship quality of the siblings was then observed two and a half years later. It was found that the jealousy reactions of the older siblings when interacting with the father predicted later sibling conflict. Negative sibling interactions tend to be stable from preschool through adolescence, particularly on the part of older siblings (Dunn et al., 1994), and Kolak and Volling

(2011) suggested that the relationship with the father has particular significance to the older sibling because of the mother's common preoccupation with the younger. Thus the older sibling may be particularly threatened when ignored in favor of the younger sibling by the father.

Relevant research. Fiske (2010a) presented positive, negative, or neutral daily events that happened to members of groups that tended to elicit caring (e.g. an elderly woman), scorn (a drug addict), or envy (a banker). Participants indicated whether the event would make them feel good or bad. The envied group received the least good ratings for their positive events and least bad ratings for their negative events. Also, facial electromyography records revealed that the zygomaticus major muscles involved in smiling activated more for the negative than the positive events only for the envied group, suggesting pleasure in another's misfortune, or *schadenfreude*. Fiske observed, "People can't help smiling a little when an investment banker 'steps in dog poo'" (2010a, p. 703).

Feelings of envy typically do not involve a judgment that the other's advantage is deserved. If the advantage is seen as deserved, *admiration* rather than envy might be the result. Feelings of envy may often be mixed with feelings of admiration, and vice versa. Admiration has been termed "pride-in-other" by Tesser and Collins (1988). They found that when the behavioral comparison is of low relevance to oneself, and the other is close rather than distant, pride in the other is enhanced. They suggested that this may reflect in part a "reflection process" in which one gains in self-evaluation due to the relationship with the other. This may counteract feelings of guilt that might otherwise occur as the reciprocal of envy. I consider admiration in the next chapter as a moral emotion.

Pity/scorn

Definitions. If COs fail to meet expectations, they tend to be pitied, and when COs lose love and esteem, they become objects of scorn. Again, the M. Lewis (1993) analysis fits: the pitied O fails at a specific behavior, and the scorned O receives a global negative evaluation. For pity, Lazarus (1994) used a related but perhaps more comprehensive term, "compassion," in which the core relational theme is "being moved by another's suffering and wanting to help" (p. 164). Scorn does not easily fit any of the core relational themes of Lazarus (1994): the closest perhaps is his "anger": "a demeaning offense against me and mine" (p. 164). A number of studies have investigated the conditions under which pity or anger toward another person is generated. I suggest that the particular kind of "social anger" evoked in these studies is actually scorn, the "twin" of pity, where it actually is the person who is rejected. For example, Weiner (1986) and his colleagues contrasted pity with social anger in a study that presented a protagonist in need of help. This was designed to arouse pity if the need was aroused for uncontrollable causes, but anger if the causes were controllable (Graham and Weiner, 1991). Similarly, Butler (1994) asked Israeli primary school teachers how they would feel about a student who was failing because of low ability or low effort. Teachers responded that they would feel pity for the low ability student but anger toward the low effort student. Similar results have been reported for American and Chinese participants (Stipek et al., 1989; Weiner, 1987) and in children (Graham and Weiner, 1986; Graham et al., 1984). This sort of social anger seems comparable to scorn: pity is specific to a failed behavior; while with scorn the person involved is angrily rejected.

The word "pity" originally described loving and tender feelings toward one who had experienced misfortune, as personified in Michelangelo's masterpiece, the *Pietà*; but more recently the term has been used condescendingly for people who are perceived as blameworthy (Gerdes, 2011). This appears to reflect a change in the evaluation of the person who suffered the misfortune, rather than the misfortune itself: e.g. a change from pity to its twin, scorn.

Display. No specific displays have been associated with pity or scorn, but displays of the related moral emotions sympathy and contempt have been suggested, as we shall see in the next chapter. Specifically, a facial display of sympathy blending attention and sadness has been suggested (Eisenberg et al., 1989; Haidt and Keltner, 1999), but that is disputed (Widen et al., 2011). Others have suggested that sympathy is best displayed by touch, as opposed to face or body expressions (App et al., 2011). Contempt was one of Tomkins' original eight primary affects associated with an asymmetrical facial expression, with the lip raised on one side of the face more than the other.

Developmental sequence. There is some evidence that anger/scorn develops earlier than pity. Weiner et al., (1982) showed that children as young as 5 could understand how a teacher's anger/scorn could be related to a lack of effort on the part of a child; but only children 9 years and older could understand how a teacher's pity could be related to a child's lack of ability. On the other hand, Graham et al. (1984) studied children aged 6 to 11 and did not find age-related changes in the tendency to link anger/scorn with controllable negative events, and pity with uncontrollable negative events.

Relevant research. A number of investigators have noted that anger and rage are often associated with the hypothesized mirror of scorn:

shame. Scheff and Retzinger (1991; Scheff, 1995) suggested that shame–anger sequences are at the core of destructive conflict and violence, stemming ultimately from threats to the social bond. Retzinger (1991, 1995) investigated covert shame–anger sequences in dysfunctional personal relationships, and Scheff (1997) reported that videotapes of interviews of combatants in Northern Ireland were full of shame–anger sequences. Similarly, in a review of Tangney and Fischer (1995), Aron (1997) noted a theme that "if the threat to the self is too overwhelming ... shame can quickly move into rage" (p. 590). The ecological-systems analysis agrees that shame is often associated with anger and rage, and that the basis of this association involves threats to the social bond, but offers a somewhat different conceptualization: that the particular sorts of anger and rage described in these studies involve scorn, and that scorn is linked to its mirror shame by the common low self-evaluation due to feeling unloved.

Scorn involves a kind of revulsion of the other that may be analogous to what has been termed "moral disgust" (Rozin et al., 1994). A sufficiently detested person becomes, in effect, a contaminant. Rozin and colleagues suggested that the emotion of disgust originated in revulsion at bad tasting food (Rozin and Fallon, 1987). As children become aware of the diffusion of physical substances and its lack of reversibility, they become sensitive to the possibility of contamination: unpleasant substances can then render otherwise edible food disgusting through physical contact (Rozin et al., 1985). Possibilities of associating unpleasant substances increase with the operation of laws of sympathetic magic: contagion (a permanent transfer of properties by brief contact) and similarity (an image having properties of an object). Thus, the laundered shirt of a disliked person, or acceptable food formed in the shape of a disgusting object, are rejected (Rozin et al., 1986). Also, scorn is associated with systems of social control that use shame: the offending individual is rejected by the group: scorned and perhaps shunned.

There is evidence that scorn can actually accomplish the ultimate in dehumanization: deactivating the brain's natural tendency to "mind-read," or consider the mind of the scorned person. Fiske (2010a, 2010b) noted that photographs of people normally produce activation in a "social-cognitive circuit" including the medial prefrontal cortex (MPFC) that is associated with casual mind-reading: e.g. in effect asking "What kind of person is this?" "What are they feeling?" I consider this circuit further in the next chapter. This response is essential for regarding the person in the photograph as an agent who has power to shape their environment, rather than an inanimate object. Fiske summarized research suggesting that pictures of members of scorned groups – e.g.

homeless persons, lazy poor people, drug addicts – elicited no MPFC system activation. They were apparently seen literally as objects. Distressingly, this was also the case for pictures of sexualized women being viewed by men who were high in hostile sexism. Cikara et al. (2010) showed that when men viewed pictures of women in bikinis, activity in regions in the MPFC (BA 10), dorsomedial PFC (DMPFC, BA 8), posterior cingulate cortex, and temporal poles were negatively correlated with scores in hostile sexuality. The results indicated that "more hostile attitudes predict less spontaneous activation of the network reliably associated with mentalizing" (Cikara et al., 2010, pp. 547–48). The women were, quite literally, perceived as objects.

Embarrassment and teasing

If an actor's failure to meet expectations is situational and associated with momentary clumsiness, and repair is not really necessary or possible, it is *embarrassment*. M. Lewis (1993) noted that embarrassment is linked with shame rather than guilt in some analyses (Izard, 1979; Tomkins, 1962–92), and himself distinguished two sorts of embarrassment: embarrassment as self-consciousness associated with public exposure, and embarrassment as mild shame. In the view of the ecological-systems model, embarrassment may result in a failure to meet expectations *or* a failure to be loved, so that embarrassment may be seen as a kind of mild guilt or mild shame.

Embarrassment and moral socialization. Embarrassment may be viewed as part of the process by which the child learns about social rules and expectations. Some suggest that embarrassment plays a unique role in socialization, involving the motivation to conform to social rules (Goffman, 1956; Scheff, 1988). The teasing of children, widely and perhaps rightly regarded as cruel and painful to the target, is perhaps a kind of scorn inducing shame in the other, and may be a powerful motivator to induce the target to conform and follow the rules (Keltner et al., 1998). Keltner and Buswell (1997) suggested that the response of the embarrassed individual functions to repair or remedy the social breach. In this regard, they cited Goffman's (1967) analysis of *facework*: the "social strategies that people rely on to honor, maintain, and when necessary, restore each other's desired public identities and the harmony of the 'expressive order'" (Keltner and Buswell, 1997, p. 262). They reviewed evidence that individuals who display embarrassment tend to receive sympathy, forgiveness, and liking from observers, thus restoring the breach, and suggested that embarrassment is "an emotional mechanism ... to maintain the stability of moral communities" (p. 250).

Embarrassment may be accompanied by specific displays similar in significant respects to shame/guilt displays (Keltner and Harken, 1998; M. Lewis, 1993; R. S. Miller, 1995a, 1996). Keltner and Buswell (1997) reviewed similarities between human embarrassment behaviors and nonhuman submission and appeasement displays, including gaze aversion, smiling, downward head movement, reduced physical size, self-touching or grooming, and submissive vocalizations. We noted that Keltner and Buswell (1996) used photographs of faces showing head and gaze down to signal shame, and that an "embarrassment" display also showed head and gaze down, but also included a non-Duchenne smile, lip press, head movement to the left, and face touching. Keltner and Buswell demonstrated that judges could distinguish these displays, but their embarrassment and shame displays both seemed to reflect submission and appeasement. Perhaps this difference between displays is indicative of whether a given episode has evoked shame-embarrassment focused upon the self, as opposed to guilt-embarrassment focused upon the act.

The focus on act or self may vary with the situation, which may influence attachment security in at least two ways. First, one's affective state can influence whether one feels secure in being loved (Mikulincer, 1998). Therefore, all else equal, guilt-embarrassment may be linked to generally positive affect and shame-embarrassment to generally negative affect. Second, understanding social rules, or *social competence*, can influence whether one is able to focus on the act as opposed to the self. All else equal, low social competence may be associated with shame-embarrassment, and high social competence with guilt-embarrassment.

Moral adaptation: shame, guilt, embarrassment, and social competence. More specifically, there may be a dynamic developmental relationship between shame, guilt, and embarrassment, in which shame-embarrassment is transformed into guilt-embarrassment as the responder becomes more secure and competent in understanding and meeting expectations. At an early stage of what might be termed *moral adaptation*, a child struggles both to learn what the rules are, and how to perform as expected. Failures at this stage reflect on the self, as the child is unable to attribute failure to specific actions. This is perhaps the stage in the social and moral development of children when teasing is common. The focus of teasing is the self rather than the behavior because, although both the teaser and the one being teased know that it is critically important to follow social rules, neither really understands what the rules are or how to follow them. Thus, teasing reflects ignorance and a lack of social competence on the part of both parties. At this stage, shame-embarrassment with its associated display would be common when lapses occur, as submission and appeasement displays may function to deflect teasing and restore dignity.

As the individual becomes more sophisticated and socially competent, the model suggests that individual differences in shame-embarrassment displays may become more evident. Securely attached individuals may tend to understand social lapses in a context in which being loved is assured, and will focus on repairing the behavior. A secure individual might experience considerable embarrassment, but manifest the shame-embarrassment display including a non-Duchenne smile, lip press, head movement to the left, and face touching as a guilt-embarrassment display. In contrast, an anxious-ambivalent person who is less certain of being loved might respond to the same social lapse with the same level of experienced embarrassment, but also display shame-embarrassment as a gesture of appeasement to restore dignity and maintain the regard of others. Avoidant individuals, on the other hand, might not be expected to experience embarrassment to the same extent as others.

This analysis predicts that shame-embarrassment displays will continue even in securely attached persons in response to momentary clumsiness or to unforeseeable and unexpected accidents. R. S. Miller (1996) gave a classic example of such a case: a woman whose slip came loose and dropped off while crossing a street in full view of waiting motorists. Social competence and security are low by definition in such cases, and a focus on action and its repair is not necessary or useful. At the other extreme, at high levels of social competence where the rules and procedures for following them are clearly understood by all, even anxious-ambivalent individuals are relatively secure and can come to focus on actions, with relatively few pure shame-embarrassment displays regardless of attachment. Accordingly, as social competence increases from low levels, an initial high level of shame-embarrassment should be replaced by increasing individual differences related to attachment, and finally by decreasing individual differences and replacement of shame-embarrassment by guilt-embarrassment. An implication of this view is that procedures that increase social competence – explicitly teaching what is expected of a person and how to achieve expectations – will aid in the process of transforming shame-embarrassment to guilt-embarrassment when lapses occur, and may lessen teasing.

Remorse and regret

Regret is focused upon specific behaviors that violate expectations, and occurs with guilt: the behavior rather than the individual is the focus of regret. In contrast, shame and scorn involve global negative evaluations where one loses the affection of others: one becomes unloved, and indeed unlovable and reviled. *Remorse* functions perhaps to focus the negative evaluation from the self onto more specific behaviors: to turn scorn to pity and shame to guilt. In effect, remorse tells both others and the self that it is one's behavior, not oneself, that is evil and detestable.

We saw that transgressors who expressed guilt or shame were rated more positively (Stearns and Parrott, 2012). Overt expressions of remorse are often considered in criminal sentencing: such expressions on the part of wrongdoers are typically distrusted as self-serving, but a *lack* of expression of remorse is widely recognized as a sure sign of loathsome depravity. Thus, expressions of remorse have been found to increase the relative positivity of evaluations of drunk drivers (Taylor and Kleinke, 1992) and rapists (Kleinke et al., 1992), and a lack of expressed remorse is associated with psychopathy (Harry, 1992). The experience of remorse may have a less widely recognized function in helping to convince wrongdoers themselves that they are not really despicable persons, but rather that they are sinners who have transgressed, and that it is their behaviors rather than themselves that are execrable.

Evidence supporting the ecological-systems model

The ecological-systems model of social emotions predicts that when secure, persons tend to experience pride in situations where anxious/ambivalent persons experience arrogance; guilt where the others experience shame; envy when the others experience jealousy; and pity when the others experience scorn. Also, detached, avoidant persons tend not to experience any of the social emotions with the frequency or intensity that others do. Again, although direct evidence is lacking, there is considerable evidence in the literature that is consistent with these predictions. This section summarizes such evidence and reports original cross-national research intended to test the ecological-systems model.

Attachment security and social emotions

Attachment security and oxytocin. There is direct evidence that attachment security is related to the functioning of OXY systems which, as we have seen, are heavily involved in prosociality. Buchheim et al. (2009) found that when OXY was administered to insecurely attached men, they experienced an increase in the experience of attachment security. Furthermore, in a study of the effects of OXY on recall of maternal closeness, Bartz et al. (2011) found that OXY in secure men produced recollections that their mothers were more close and caring, while OXY in more anxious attached men produced recollections that their mothers were *less* close and caring.

There is evidence that individual differences in attachment security alter the ability of participants to engage in compassion-focused imagery (CFI), a psychotherapy technique designed to increase self-compassion and openness to compassion from others (Gilbert, 2010). One study found that physiological responses of participants engaging in CFI were associated with calming in securely attached participants, but threat in anxiously attached participants (Rockliff et al., 2008). Another study examined the effects of OXY versus placebo on CFI ability (Rockliff et al., 2011). Female and male adult participants were first tested for attachment security, self-criticism, and social safeness. They then engaged in two CFI sessions, one after being given OXY, the other after placebo, in a counterbalanced and double-blind design. Results revealed that OXY significantly increased abilities to imagine compassion in the group as a whole. However, there were significant individual differences in that the less secure and socially safe, more self-critical participants had a *less* positive experience of CFI under OXY than under placebo. The authors cautioned that the therapeutic use of OXY to activate attachment/affiliative systems may stimulate grief and a yearning for closeness in some persons, and increase their distress.

We considered another double-blind study that found that effects of intranasal OXY on anxiety were moderated by gender and coping style (Cardoso et al., 2012). They found that OXY reduced anxiety only among women with emotion-focused coping styles, which could be interpreted as involving insecure attachment. Moreover, an unexpected result of this study was that both women and men responded to intranasal OXY with significantly higher task-oriented coping scores compared with placebo. The authors suggested that this finding was consistent with the Buchheim et al. (2009) finding that OXY increased reported attachment security: "OXY may promote social affiliation by increasing participants' perceptions of attachment security and solution-oriented coping skills" (Cardoso et al., 2012, p. 89).

Romantic love and attachment. As noted, Hazan and Shaver (1987; Shaver and Hazan, 1993) conceptualized romantic love as an attachment process and found evidence that securely attached persons are, indeed, relatively confident about being loved compared with anxious-ambivalent and avoidant persons. They found that secure participants described their most important love relationships as happy, friendly, and trusting; anxious-ambivalent participants described love as involving more obsession, desire for reciprocation, extreme sexual attraction, and jealousy; and avoidant participants described a fear of intimacy, jealousy, and relatively few positive love experiences. Anxious-ambivalent participants reported experiencing the greatest amount of jealousy and secure participants reported experiencing the least. Only secure participants reported that in some relationships, romantic love never fades. Anxious-ambivalent participants reported that it is easy to fall in love, but both they and avoidant participants reported that it is rare to find true love. Overall, this pattern of results seems consistent with the predictions of ecological-systems theory.

Sex differences in jealousy. Infidelity on the part of the partner is a major source of jealousy for both women and men, but a theory of evolved sex differences predicted that women and men respond differently to different types of infidelity. Women are predicted to experience more jealousy in response to emotional infidelity; while men experience more jealousy in response to sexual infidelity (e.g. Symons, 1979). A meta-analytic review has supported this hypothesized sex difference (Sagarin et al., 2012). This is consistent with the ecological-systems approach to jealousy because this result can be seen to reflect the typical degree of insecurity of women and men regarding emotional and sexual infidelity. All else equal, women are likely to be insecure about paternal investment in her and the young; while men are likely to be insecure about paternity. The differential personal insecurity is reflected in the different patterns of jealousy.

Conclusions. I suggest that social emotions grow naturally out of attachment and dominance relationships demonstrated in many species and are communicated directly via displays which are social affordances. A normally attached human being, or monkey, or dog, or rat experiences feelings within dominance relationships that are presumably associated with neurochemicals including serotonin. These feelings change as the relationship changes: whether the current comparison other is dominant or subordinate to oneself, for example. Also, these feelings change as circumstances change: as the self and comparison other are successful or not in meeting challenges. In human beings, the linguistic identification of such feelings – labeling them as "pride," "shame," "pity" and so on – involve higher-level cognitive processing which takes into account the targets and circumstances in which the feelings occur. One of the implications of this view is that all of the social emotions should be present in all cultures; and that relationships between the social emotions, depression, and serotonin should be the same everywhere. However, cultures may well differ in which social emotions are emphasized by giving them specific labels, considering them to be "basic emotions," and celebrating them in song and story. However, the feelings per se should be universal and primordial.

*The universality of primary social emotions: evidence
from America and Japan*

To test the major propositions of the ecological-systems model, respondents in America and Japan rated emotions experienced in scenarios designed to produce the ecological contingencies (Buck et al., 2005). Hypotheses were that, in both cultures: (1) combinations of ecological contingencies involving relative success and failure in comparison with another person are associated with common emotion labels; and (2) ratings of the ecological contingencies using the common emotion labels will be dynamically interrelated with one another in similar ways.

Methods. University students in America and Japan were asked to pretend that they returned to their high school for a reunion and heard about a CO, described as someone they had known but neither liked nor disliked, but "you were aware of how well or how poorly they did in school – in academics, athletics, extracurricular activities, the dating scene, etc. – in comparison with yourself ... (and) ... they too were aware of your comparative successes and failures." Participants then were asked to imagine the following scenarios:

  I. CO did not go to college, but won a large prize in the lottery and became rich. (Lottery)
 II. CO invented a new computer chip and became rich. (Invention)
III. CO married my prom date, who I am still in love with. (Prom)
 IV. CO was struck by lightning, and is forced to wear a brace. (Lightning)
  V. CO was arrested for selling drugs to children, and went to jail. (Jail)
 VI. CO was dumped by my present lover. (Dump)

The scenarios were designed to be simple, clear, unambiguous, and cross-culturally meaningful, and to evoke ecologically fundamental interpersonal contingencies eliciting the four primary social emotion twins presented in Figure 6.3 by combining instances of success, or positive outcomes; and failure or negative outcomes, with situations that were (1) under O's control, (2) not under O's control, or (3) personally relevant to P.

For each of the scenarios, participants (P) rated how they would feel about O, and how O would feel about them, on the primary social emotions, using equivalent emotion terminology in America and Japan. In fact, the emotion terms did relate to one another as expected: virtually every predicted relationship was found in both America and Japan, and the directions and strengths of these interrelationships were similar in the two nations. Results are presented in Tables 6.1 and 6.2.

Dynamic structure of social emotions. As shown in the right columns of both tables, hypotheses regarding the dynamics of primary social

Table 6.1 Correlations with twinned emotions on the part of the self and other: US sample

	Pride	Arrogance	Guilt	Shame	Envy	Jealousy	Pity	Scorn	Mean r
Twin	0.72		0.71		0.99		-0.31		0.80***
Opposite	-0.68	-0.28	-0.30	-0.68	-0.31	-0.26	-0.78	0.45	-0.40***
Converse	-0.74	-0.58	0.08	-0.04	-0.74	-0.70	-0.10	0.12	-0.39***
Reciprocal	0.16	0.19	0.01	0.60	0.37	0.34	0.41	-0.19	0.25*
Mirror twin	-0.70	-0.40	-0.27	-0.26	-0.93	-0.89	-0.28	0.27	-0.55***
Mirror opposite	0.51	0.07	0.10	0.51	0.43	0.46	0.79	-0.27	0.36***
Mirror converse	0.80	0.78	0.50	0.58	0.84	0.86	0.16	0.53	0.68***
Mirror reciprocal	-0.34	-0.14	-0.01	-0.61	-0.36	-0.34	-0.62	0.30	-0.28**
Mean r	**0.59*****	**0.39*****	**0.16**	**0.49*****	**0.64*****	**0.62*****	**0.50*****	**-0.14**	

N = 12. Within the table, correlation coefficients >0.5 in the predicted direction are significant ($p < 0.05$, one-tailed). Correlation coefficients were transformed to z scores, averaged, evaluated relative to chance with standard error = 1/sqrt (sum [n−3]), and transformed back to rs.

In averaging correlation coefficients for the eight social emotions, correlations with twins were not counted, and signs were reversed when negative relationships were hypothesized.

***$p < 0.001$

**$p < 0.01$

*$p < 0.05$

Table 6.2 Correlations with twinned emotions on the part of the self and other: Japan sample

	誇り hokori (Pride)	傲慢さ goumannsa (Arrog.)	罪悪感 zaiakukann (Guilt)	恥ずかしさ hazukashisa (Shame)	うらや み urayami (Envy)	嫉妬 sitto (Jeal.)	あわれみ awaremi (Pity)	軽蔑 keibetsu (Scorn)	Mean r
Twin	0.83		0.47		0.94		-0.04		0.69***
Opposite	-0.26	0.07	0.16	-0.45	-0.62	-0.46	-0.73	0.01	-0.33**
Converse	-0.41	-0.68	-0.06	-0.53	-0.56	-0.45	-0.23	-0.25	-0.41***
Reciprocal	0.27	0.41	-0.40	0.38	-0.06	0.02	0.31	0.13	0.13
Mirror twin	-0.28	-0.47	-0.24	-0.20	-0.74	-0.59	-0.64	-0.28	-0.46***
Mirror opposite	-0.03	-0.01	-0.22	0.19	0.50	0.50	0.73	-0.09	0.23*
Mirror converse	0.70	0.89	0.42	0.92	0.80	0.75	0.21	0.92	0.77***
Mirror reciprocal	-0.53	-0.41	0.33	-0.74	-0.17	-0.03	-0.61	0.05	-0.31**
Mean r	**0.37****	**0.47*****	**-0.04**	**0.55*****	**0.53*****	**0.44*****	**0.53*****	**0.30****	

N = 12. Within the table, correlation coefficients >0.5 in the predicted direction are significant (p <0.05, one-tailed).
Correlation coefficients were transformed to z scores, averaged, evaluated relative to chance with standard error = 1/sqrt (sum [n–3]), and transformed back to rs.
In averaging correlation coefficients for the eight social emotions, correlations with twins were not counted, and signs were reversed when negative relationships were hypothesized.

Arrog. = Arrogance; Jeal. = Jealousy

***p <0.001

**p <0.01

*p <0.05

emotions were supported in both American and Japanese samples. Specifically, it was expected that, if one experiences a given primary social emotion, it is likely that one would simultaneously experience its twin (average correlation between twins was 0.80 in America/0.69 in Japan); unlikely that one would experience its opposite (−0.40/−0.33), likely that one would experience its reciprocal toward others (0.25/0.13), and unlikely that one would experience its converse toward others (−0.39/−0.41). Similarly, it was expected that if the participant experiences a given primary social emotion, the comparison O is unlikely to simultaneously experience that emotion or its twin (−0.55/−0.46), likely to experience its mirror-opposite (0.36/0.23), unlikely to experience its mirror-reciprocal (−0.28/−0.31), and likely to experience its mirror-converse (0.68/0.77). Thus, the predicted dynamics of the relationships between primary social emotions were supported in both American and Japanese samples, so the dynamics of the primary social emotions predicted and found in an American sample with English emotion terminology are similar to those in a Japanese sample using Japanese emotion terminology.

This result – reflecting ratings from nations with strikingly different histories, cultures, languages, and distinct forms of personal association – is consistent with a key hypothesis in the ecological-systems model, that social emotions are dynamically interrelated in similar ways in distinct cultures. The implication is that this emergence is a universal phenomenon, common to all cultures and to all historical times.

Pity and scorn. Three of the purported twin pairs were highly positively correlated with one another as expected in both American and Japanese samples. Hokori/Pride–Goumannsa/Arrogance correlated +0.72 in America and +0.83 in Japan; Zaiakukann/Guilt–Hazukashisa/ Shame correlated +0.71 in America and +0.47 in Japan; and Urayami/ Envy–Sitto/Jealousy correlated +0.99 in America and +0.94 in Japan. That is, the occurrence of one twin was positively and strongly correlated with the occurrence of the other twin across the scenarios. It was initially expected that Awaremi/Pity and Keibetsu/Scorn would correlate positively as twins, but in fact they were *negatively* correlated with one another in both America (−0.31) and Japan (−0.04). Rather than being twin social emotions, Awaremi/Pity and Keibetsu/Scorn appeared to be alternative ways of responding to failure or negative outcomes of CO.

More generally, these may be alternative ways of responding to the less fortunate. It is noteworthy in this regard that Lakoff (1996) suggested that liberal thought centers around the Nurturing Parent model of the family, as opposed to Strict Father model of morality underlying conservative thought. The liberal model is based upon secure attachment, empathy, fairness, and nurturance: caring about and protecting others and being cared for and protected in return. The conservative model of morality in contrast stresses moral strength through self-discipline and self-denial, versus moral weakness in the forms of a lack of self-control (the lack of self-discipline) and self-indulgence (the failure to engage in self-denial) which are seen as forms of immorality.

This account is consistent with notions that "bleeding heart" liberals tend to pity to the less fortunate, while not-so-compassionate conservatives tend to respond with scorn. This is also consistent with the analysis of Haidt (2003), who although he did not consider "scorn" per se, did consider an analogous "other condemning" family of social/moral emotions: anger, disgust, and contempt. Haidt discussed a conservative "disgust-based moral order" distressing to liberals, which condemns people for what they *are* more than for what they *do*, and tends to ostracize and exclude members of out-groups (based upon ethnicity, religion, social class, sexual orientation, etc.). This suggestion that liberals may tend to pity the less fortunate and conservatives tend to scorn them will be examined in Chapter 7.

Cultural differences in social emotions. At the same time that the primary social emotions were demonstrated to be similar in structure in America and Japan, significant and important national differences were shown for all of the scenarios. Many of these differences were relevant to the differences between American and Japanese culture. American culture has been characterized as giving priority to individual over group values; while in Japan group values have priority (Benedict, 1946; Hall and Hall, 1990; Hofstede, 1980; Najma, 1997; Schwartz, 1994; Triandis, 1995). Markus and Kitayama (1991) characterized this difference in terms of the conception in Asian cultures of individuality based upon *interdependence* of individuals vis-à-vis one another, emphasizing harmony, attention to others, and fitting in; as opposed to the conception in American culture of maintaining *independence* from others and expressing the uniqueness of the individual (Kitayama and Uchida, 2005). This led Kitayama et al. (2006) to suggest that socially disengaging emotions including pride are reinforced in American culture, while it would be more likely that socially engaging emotions including shame are more reinforced in Japan.

In fact, in every one of the scenarios, Americans indicated P would experience greater Hokori/Pride and that CO would experience more admiration of P than did Japanese; while Japanese indicated P would experience more Touwaku/Embarrassment than did Americans. This is consistent with the Kitayama et al. (2006) analysis that American culture promotes socially disengaging emotions while the Japanese encourages socially engaging emotions.

In summary, the pattern of results demonstrates *both* similarity in structure *and* large cultural differences in the occurrence of the social emotions. This constitutes initial evidence that the ecological-systems view of the social emotions has potential as a valid and useful approach to cultural differences as well as uniformities.

Discussion

The ecological-systems view regards the social emotions to be inter-related as a system, and it is a basic principle of cybernetics that systems can be closely coupled or loosely coupled (Rapoport, 1986). The dynamic interrelationships we expect should be apparent *only when the system is closely coupled* – when the social comparisons associated with interpersonal contingencies are clear and unambiguous. In the Buck et al. (2005) study, it was intended that everyone respond similarly to these scenarios, whatever the culture or language. This method was self-correcting, in that if poor choices were made about scenarios or emotion terminology we would not find the results expected because dynamic relationships should be apparent only when the system is closely coupled: when the social comparisons associated with the eco-logical contingencies and emotion labels are clear to participants.

Given that the dynamic interrelationships between social emotions were in fact demonstrated in the data from both America and Japan, it constituted *prima facie* evidence for the pragmatic utility of the labels and scenarios, that is, the emotion labels and scenarios chosen for the studies in fact worked. Only if a closely coupled system was achieved would the primary social emotions interrelate as expected. Choosing inappropriate emotion labels or using inappropriate scen-arios would result in unsystematic error that would undermine expected relationships, causing the rejection of the hypothesis and questioning of the model.

Advantages of the ecological-systems approach

The ecological-systems approach specifies how higher-level social emotions differ from biological emotions (Buck, 1999, 2002a), and it relates social emotions to one another in a systematic and dynamic way. The view of social emotions as interrelated in a self-organizing dynamical system emerging naturally from the ecology of social inter-action is distinct from, yet complementary to, approaches that analyze social emotions separately. The latter approaches emphasize the special characteristics of each emotion and how they differ from one another (Frijda, 1986; Lazarus, 1994; Rosenman, 1984; Scherer, 1984,

1994). In contrast, the ecological-systems view suggests why some social emotions are difficult to distinguish and others are not. The ecological-systems approach also complements the theory that embarrassment, pride, shame, and guilt are "self-conscious emotions" (Tangney and Fischer, 1995; H. B. Lewis, 1971; M. Lewis, 1993), although the assumption of consciousness and elaborate cognitive processing is not shared. Instead, the ecological-systems analysis is more compatible with Haidt's (2001) "social intuitionist" analysis, Kahneman's (2003) "effortless intuition," and research on mirror neurons (Gallese et al., 2004; Nakahara and Miyashita, 2005), suggesting that online social judgments can involve quick affectively laden intuitions: gut feelings which can trigger appraisal and attribution processes. Finally, the ecological-systems approach makes it clear what is "social" about social emotions: that they are born and raised in the give-and-take of social interaction: particularly perhaps in the rough-and-tumble play of the peer affectional system. The importance of social factors is less clear in approaches to self-conscious emotions which emphasize the congruence of behavior with one's identity.

The ecological-systems model goes beyond self-conscious emotion models in several respects. First, it analyzes a wider range of emotions, including emotions such as scorn not considered by most self-conscious emotion approaches. Second, the model suggests a way of differentiating social emotions that does not depend upon how their cognitive attributions differ, or how their action tendencies differ, which have not been entirely successful. Instead, social emotions are differentiated according to the attachment security experienced by the responder at a given time and relative to a given personal relationship, where attachment security is conceived as a state as well as a trait. This allows a flexibility in social emotions which arguably reflects how they actually function: e.g. our success can simultaneously elicit feelings of pride and arrogance depending upon the personal relationship we have in mind: grandma versus high school rival. This is a testable proposition and evidence about how effects of OXY differ according to attachment security is supportive.

Third, the dynamic relationships specified between the social emotions, that are at the heart of the ecological-systems model, have been hinted in other approaches but never presented systematically. They suggest questions that have not previously been asked, and predict and find significant relationships between social emotions that were not conceived by other approaches. For example, other approaches have not hypothesized "reciprocal" relationships between social emotions: that shame for example will be associated with envy/jealousy (+0.60 and +0.38 in America and Japan, respectively). Similarly, other approaches have not considered the "mirror-reciprocal" relationship: that P's guilt and shame would be positively related to O's pity/scorn (+0.50 and +0.42 in America and Japan, respectively for guilt; +0.58 and +0.92 in America and Japan, respectively for shame). Also, P's envy and jealousy are positively related to O's pride/arrogance (+0.84 and +0.80 in America and Japan, respectively for envy; +0.86 and +0.75 in America and Japan, respectively for jealousy). Moreover, other approaches have not considered the "mirror-converse" relationship: that P's shame would be negatively related to O's envy/jealousy (–0.61 and –0.74 in America and Japan, respectively). These questions have *not been asked*, because previous approaches have not recognized the full system of dynamic relationships between multiple social emotions that are at the core of the ecological-systems model.

Fourth, and importantly, in the ecological-systems model, "self-consciousness" itself is not required, which allows a broader conceptualization of social emotions consistent with recent evidence in toddlers (K. C. Barrett, 2005), and with emerging evidence about the complexity of animals' social organization (Morris et al., 2008), mirror neurons (Gallese et al., 2004), and about relationships of sociality to specific neurochemical systems that can operate unconsciously (i.e. that in double-blind studies OXY can increase trusting behavior in human beings (Kosfeld et al., 2005) and alter other prosocial behaviors (Feldman, 2012a)).

In a sense, the ecological-systems approach turns the conventional approach to self-conscious emotions on its head. Many such approaches begin with common emotion labels (pride, guilt, shame), and using a variety of methods seek to differentiate them and specify what is unique to each in terms of its meaning and eliciting circumstances. Such approaches generally deal with one to a few social emotions at a time, and emphasize what is distinctive about each. They also emphasize the cultural uniqueness of social emotions, making cross-cultural comparisons difficult.

In contrast, the ecological-systems model specifies naturally occurring combinations of eliciting circumstances – ecologically fundamental interpersonal contingencies – and suggests that a system of social emotions emerges naturally and effortlessly from these during interaction over the course of development. In this view, social emotions are not invented in the human mind, but rather constitute "natural kinds" that are discovered by the child in the course of interaction. This perspective allows and indeed encourages cross-cultural and comparative research. The ecological contingencies combined with attachment motives specify a dynamic system of primary social emotions that are systematically and similarly interrelated as predicted in America and

Japan; and in addition the findings revealed national differences compatible with the independence/interdependence analysis of these diverse cultures. Thus the ecological-systems perspective of social emotions allowed a systematic approach to the conceptualization, measurement, and understanding of higher-level social emotions. This approach is also relevant to the analysis of higher-level moral emotions across cultures and across historical periods, as we shall see in the next chapter.

Conclusions

Social motives/emotions contribute to a behavior control system that is at once biologically based and outside the individual (Buck, 1988a). Social emotions are based upon innate attachment systems in all human beings and, indeed, in all social animals. Biology confers the immense importance attached to the meeting of social goals that exists in varying degrees in individuals of all cultures, based in part upon their attachment experiences. Furthermore, in all cultures the ravages of early isolation, abuse, and drug addiction can produce detached, avoidant, sociopathic individuals who may become incapable of attachment, who are indifferent to society and its goals, and who therefore are incapable of experiencing pride, guilt, shame, or any of the social emotions. This analysis is at the level of qualities of the individual: qualities of temperament or personality.

Nevertheless, social emotions *function* at the relational level. Individual qualities at a given stage of development naturally confront situational and interpersonal contingencies objectively present in the physical and social environment, and the emergent qualities that materialize from this confrontation have both individual and relational aspects. This is observable in the complex dominant/subordinate relationships that are involved in rough-and-tumble play, as well as the "pecking order" organization of many animal societies (Allee, 1938). Furthermore, social emotions are organized and structured culturally rather than biologically in all human societies. Each society and culture *uses* social emotions in different ways, with different sorts of expectations, different criteria for excellence, and different ways to express and withhold affection and love (Averill, 1994; Schweder, 1994). The result is that the study of the social construction of emotion is a rich and rewarding field for psychologists, sociologists, historians, and anthropologists that has little to do with biology per se.

CHAPTER 7

Moral emotions: the passions of civility

Historically, the study of moral capacities has not typically emphasized the notion of moral emotions. Research has generally focused either upon moral judgment, the ability to tell right from wrong; or moral behavior, the tendency to act in accordance with moral prescriptions when confronted by sometimes-complex situational pressures. However, moral judgments and behaviors rarely occur in an affective vacuum: more often, judgments of right and wrong are accompanied by strong emotions: both positive (moral approbation) and negative (moral indignation). Indeed, moral feelings are some of the strongest and most persistent motivators of human behavior. In introducing a special journal issue on the justice motive in social behavior, Michael J. Lerner asked "why do people care about justice, or act if they care?" (1975, p. 3). Certainly the sense of justice appears to be a powerful motivator: indeed, Lerner also asked "is there anything as powerful in the social dialog as the appeal to justice?" (1975, p. 19).

In Chapters 5 and 6, Tomkins' (1962, 1963) affect theory was applied to higher-level emotions: biologically based curiosity and attachment motives provide the affective "fire" underlying exploratory and social behavior. In addition, both cognitive and social emotions require experience for their competent expression and implementation. Both cognitive and social development and experience are necessary for the mature implementation of moral emotions. Indeed, cognitive and social development, accompanied and motivated by cognitive and social emotions, are not only *necessary* for the development of morality, they are also arguably *sufficient*. Given that a child learns about the workings of the world and cares about others, moral development accompanied by moral emotions is inevitable. Moral teachings from the point of view of a specific religion or ideology are not necessary for the natural acquisition of morality.

Gust/disgust and moral emotions

Gust/disgust: the biological bases of moral emotions?

In moral emotions, curiosity and attachment motives combine with judgments of rightness or wrongness, goodness or badness. This involves two aspects, the more analytic-cognitive knowledge of applicable rules for what is right or wrong, good or bad; and the more syncretic-cognitive *caring* that the right and good prevail. Thus there are two aspects of morality, a rational *morality of justice* and an emotional *morality of caring* that are widely recognized. But, is there a more general motive playing a role in morality that is analogous to the roles played by curiosity and attachment in motivating exploration and affiliation? I noted in Chapter 1 that one general emotion widely associated with moral emotion is disgust, but it seems more relevant to the judgment of wrongness, or what is bad. Is there a general emotion of moral approbation, of judging what is right and good? In 1759 in *The Theory of Moral Sentiments*, Adam Smith posited the notion of general sympathy or fellow feeling (Dawes et al., 2012), implying a general biologically based affective motive of moral approbation. As the opposite of disgust, it might be termed in English *gust*. The notion that it may be useful to posit a general motive of gust is presented here as a speculative hypothesis subject to empirical investigation, rather than an established fact, but as we shall see, at least some suggestive supportive evidence that gust may in fact exist.

Definitions

Moral emotions are associated with learned expectations about what circumstances *should* result in social emotions of pride, guilt, shame, pity, scorn, and so on. These expectations are expressed in notions of distributive and retributive justice, that specify how good and bad outcomes, respectively, *should* be meted out (Homans, 1966). In essence, moral emotions provide the affective motivational force – the "fire" – underlying the sense of justice. As we shall see, the sense of justice can create powerful analogs of social emotions: *triumph/modesty; humiliation/indignation; admiration/resentment;* and *contempt/sympathy*.

In the issue on the justice motive noted earlier, M. J. Lerner (1975) also asked "is there something about people, the way they are built or function which doesn't merely limit the selection of one or another form of justice but actually creates the commitment to justice in its various manifestations?" Lerner rejected the notion of "justice genes" and noted that "any effort to identify universal criteria of justice based on the nature of man will be nothing more than a thinly disguised, more or less conscious manifestation of an ethnocentric bias" (p. 11). Quite true, but if one attempts to identify universal *motivators* of justice in needs to follow/exceed expectations and to be loved, and universal *facilitators* of justice in human tendencies to establish linguistically organized rule systems, the ethnocentric problem is avoided. Different cultures can and do arrive at different principles of justice, but *all do arrive at principles of justice*. Moreover, in all cultures these principles are associated with deep passions.

The development of morality

Moral judgment

Jean Piaget (1971) defined intellectual development as the "spontaneous restructuring of experience," and his theory of moral development suggested that moral judgment emerges from a spontaneous restructuring of social experience. In *The Moral Judgment of the Child* (1932), he applied his methodology and theoretical perspective on cognitive development to the study of moral judgment by asking children about their conceptions of the rules in the game of marbles played on the streets of Geneva. From these observations, he developed hypotheses which he tested by asking children to make moral judgments about stories: for example comparing the guilt of two children, one of whom caused considerable damage accidentally, and the other of whom caused minor damage intentionally. From this evidence, Piaget suggested that younger children tend to use an *authoritarian morality* based upon the one-sided adult-child relationship, while a more *equalitarian morality* requires experience in peer relationships.

Authoritarian morality. According to Piaget (1932), the first stage of moral judgment develops in the preoperational child around the age of 4 and continues to about age 8. It is a morality based upon *moral realism* or the *morality of constraint*: rules are regarded as absolute and unchangeable, and the letter rather than the spirit of the law is emphasized. Good is defined by obedience to authority, and guilt is defined according to the seriousness of the damage caused, without regard to intention. Justice is administered by harsh expiatory punishment: the more serious the consequences, the greater the punishment.

Piaget suggested that moral realism is based jointly upon the child's social experience and level of cognitive development at this age. The relationship naturally established between the child and adults is an authoritarian one in which the adult knows more, has more power, and makes the rules about what is right and wrong. This authoritarian relationship encourages the acceptance of conventional rules and obedience to authority. Piaget argued that the child at this stage of cognitive development is unable fully to appreciate that others have different perspectives, or to judge intention in others. Given this experience with authoritarian social relationships and the child's cognitive limitations, Piaget argued that moral realism represents an adequate equilibration of moral judgment at this stage.

Equalitarian morality. With greater social experience and increasing cognitive skills, disequilibrium increases, and the child is naturally motivated to attain a new level of cognitive organization to encompass these new experiences. The result is *moral relativism* or the *morality of cooperation*, which is characterized by an ethic of mutual respect. Rules are seen as agreed upon by equals in the common interest of all, and they can be changed by mutual consent. Notions of equity and equalitarian distributive justice play a greater role in the child's thinking. Guilt is defined with consideration of extenuating circumstances and the motives and intentions of the actor, and justice is seen as best served by reciprocation or restitution, which seeks to repair the harm. Piaget argued that the morality of cooperation is based upon equalitarian social experience with peers, which develops feelings of mutual respect, solidarity, and trust: the child begins to "feel from within the desire to treat others as he himself would wish to be treated" (Piaget, 1932, p. 196). At the same time, cognitive development makes possible the ability to see the world from other points of view and to judge intention.

The morality of caring

Piaget's theory of moral judgment served as the starting point for studies of moral development by Kohlberg and colleagues, who studied responses to moral dilemmas (for example, judging the morality of a man, Heinz, a poor man who stole expensive medicine to save his sick wife). These studies supported Piaget in most respects (Bronfenbrenner, 1962; Kohlberg, 1963, 1964). However, one aspect of this research stirred considerable controversy: women did not appear to advance as far as did men by Kohlberg's criteria. For example, men tended to judge Heinz's actions in terms of his marital and social obligations, while women tended to emphasize his love of his wife (Bussey and Maughan, 1982). Some suggested that women have a less well-developed sense of moral judgment than men, living up to a stereotyped image of a "good girl" trying to win the affection and approval of others. Gilligan (1977, 1982) argued against this interpretation, contending that women's moral reasoning is *different* from men's, emphasizing attachment and caring in the context of real relationships rather than abstract rights and responsibilities.

In fact, Piaget had explicitly recognized a morality involving caring that exists in parallel to the morality of principle:

> The relations between parent and children are certainly not only those of constraint. There is a spontaneous mutual affection, which from the first prompts the child to acts of generosity and even self-sacrifice ... And here no doubt is the starting point for the *morality of good* which we shall see developing alongside the morality of right or duty, and which in some people completely replaces it.(Piaget, 1932, pp. 193–94; italics added)

Piaget did not investigate the "morality of good" because he recognized that he could not study it using his methods: as he put it, "the affective aspect of cooperation and reciprocity eludes interrogation" (Piaget, 1932, p. 195; cited in Ford and Lowrey, 1986).

There is evidence of the importance of emotional bonds in mediating a variety of behaviors with moral implications: fostering cooperation and altruism and reducing aggression and conflict. Hoffman (1975, 1976) argued that people can seek to benefit others not only to gain indirect self-benefits, but as an end in itself to gain emotional rewards. These emotional rewards may involve increasing feelings of the social affects of pride/arrogance, and decreasing feelings of guilt/shame. Studies of tendencies to give benefits to others have found that in the absence of an emotional attachment, there is more giving if the helper is publicly accountable, but that given attachment to the other person, helping occurs regardless of accountability (Denham, 1986; Shoenrade et al., 1986; Matsumoto et al., 1986).

Moral behavior

From Piaget's and Kohlberg's analyses, one might expect at first glance that once a person has reached a given level of moral judgment and reasoning, he or she would behave accordingly. However, this is not necessarily the case. Actual moral behavior can be influenced by a multitude of situational factors: people will do things in response to situational demands that may violate their own stated moral judgments.

The Character Education Inquiry. An early but large and sophisticated study relating to the effects of situational factors on moral behavior was the *Character Education Inquiry* conducted by Hartshorne and May (1928–30). The ambitious study employed nearly 11,000 5th to 8th grade students in the eastern United States, and measured both moral judgment and behavior. Moral judgment was measured by paper-and-pencil tests of *moral knowledge*, with objectively correct answers (e.g. "Good marks are chiefly a matter of luck"); and *moral opinion* (e.g. "It is one's duty to report another pupil you see cheating").

Moral behavior was studied by giving the children opportunities to lie, cheat, and steal in situations in which they felt safe from discovery but were unobtrusively observed. These opportunities occurred in a variety of settings, including school, home, and in athletics contests and games (Brown, 1965).

An important result of the study was that moral behavior was only moderately correlated across situations, with an average correlation of about +0.34: a child who cheated in one situation was often honest in another. A child might be inconsistent in outwardly similar situations: e.g. cheating on a mathematics test but being honest on a spelling test (Brown, 1965). As Hartshorne and May put it, "A child's conduct in any situation is determined more by the connections that attend the situation than by any mysterious entity residing in the child" (1928–30, vol. 1, p. 610). Moreover, participation in Sunday School and scouting did not guarantee virtue: "... the mere urging of honest behavior by teachers or the discussion of standards and ideals ... has no necessary relation to conduct ... the prevailing ways of inculcating ideals probably do little good and may do some harm" (Hartshorne and May, 1928–30, vol. 1, p. 413). As a consequence, the whole idea of a mysterious entity of "character" residing in the child became questioned in the field, and research on the concept declined (Nucci and Narvaéz, 2008).

Helping behavior. Some of the most dramatic examples of the power of the situation in determining morally relevant behavior have been instances in which people have failed to help someone in critical need of help. One of the best-known of these cases was the murder of Kitty Genovese at Kew Gardens in Queens, New York, in March 1964. She was attacked outside her apartment building by a knife-wielding assailant as she came home from work at 3:00 a.m. Contemporary news reports suggested that thirty-eight of her neighbors watched without calling the police as she was repeatedly attacked for more than half an hour before her death. Another notorious example of the failure to help involved the death of Wang Yue, a 2-year-old Chinese girl who wandered into a busy street in Foshan, Guangdong in October 2011. Surveillance cameras captured her being struck by a van and knocked under the front wheels. The driver paused, but then moved on, at which time his rear wheel drove over the child. As she lay bleeding on the road for more than seven minutes, at least eighteen people walked past her, some pausing to stare. Then a truck ran over Wang's legs with both front and back tires. She was eventually helped by a female rubbish scavenger, Chen Xianmei, and sent to a hospital where she died.

Subsequent investigation revealed that fewer neighbors were aware of Kitty Genovese's plight than contemporary press accounts averred, but the incident and many others prompted John Darley, Bibb Latané, and colleagues to analyze the factors responsible for the failure to help (Darley and Latané, 1968b). They noted that in order to respond to an emergency, people must (a) notice the event; (b) define it as an emergency; and (c) decide that it is their personal responsibility to act. They suggested that, paradoxically, one of the reasons for these events is that there are so many people around, and that the presence of others may make it less likely to notice the event, define it as an emergency, or feel personal responsibility to act. They designed a series of experiments to support these propositions. In one, they showed that men working on a questionnaire were more likely to notice smoke coming into a room when they were alone than when they were with another male; also, solitary men were more likely to define the smoke as an emergency. Apparently when with another person men tended to attend to the questions and did not look around the room, perhaps out of consideration for the privacy of the other male. When the smoke was noticed, both men tended to mask their genuine concern, and looked to the other to compare feelings and reactions, but as the other was also masking, a state of pluralistic ignorance was created in which both were convinced of the other's unconcern. Therefore they were slower both to notice the smoke, and to define it as an emergency (Latané and Darley, 1968). Darley and Latané (1968a) termed the presence of others making it less likely to notice or define an emergency, *direct group inhibition.*

Direct group inhibition may be overcome by factors that ease emotional communication between group members. One such factor is the responsiveness of the other, and Latané and Rodin (1969) tested this with an emergency that could not go unnoticed. Men waited either alone or with a male stranger, who was actually an unresponsive confederate. The female experimenter left the room and then started a tape recording of herself climbing a bookcase to retrieve a stack of papers, then falling with a crash and scream and calling for help: "Oh my God my foot ... I ... I ... can't move it. Oh ... my ankle ... I ... can't get this thing off me!" (Latané and Rodin, 1969, p. 192). Among those who waited alone, 70 percent came out to help; but only 7 percent of those with an unresponsive confederate responded. They were upset and confused, but when they looked at their partner, they apparently decided that the emergency was not serious.

To investigate the effects of acquaintance, Latané and Rodin repeated these procedures with persons who waited either with a stranger who was another real participant, or with a friend. Nearly 70 percent of friend pairs versus 40 percent of stranger pairs responded, and the friend pairs responded more quickly. The authors suggested that the difference was based upon the more accurate emotional communication of the friends: "Strangers ... seemed noticeably confused and concerned ... they often glanced furtively at one another, anxious to discover the other's reaction yet unwilling to meet eyes and betray their own concern. Friends, on the other hand, seemed better able to communicate their concern nonverbally" (Latané and Rodin, 1969, p. 200).

Other evidence of the importance of emotional communication came from a natural experiment in which a passenger staged a collapse on the New York City subway. The number of passengers present had no effect on the speed or amount of helping behavior (Piliavin et al., 1969). Darley et al. (1973) observed that the face-to-face seating arrangement on the subway makes it more likely that people will see the initial spontaneous displays of others to the emergency. They would then know that others are truly concerned and will be less likely to inhibit or mask their own emotional displays. To test this, they repeated the study involving the fall in the next room, but varied the seating arrangement so that some participants faced one another. They found that the participants facing each other responded as quickly and as often as participants waiting alone; whereas participants not facing each other failed to define the event as an emergency. This result demonstrates the importance of spontaneous emotional display and communication in the efficient and prompt response to emergencies.

Another study of helping behavior perhaps supports the relative futility of what Hartshorne and May termed "the mere urging of honest behavior by teachers or the discussion of standards and ideals" (1928–30, vol. 1, p. 413). Darley and Bateson (1973) attempted to replicate the situation presented in the biblical parable of the Good Samaritan, in which a Samaritan helped a man who had been robbed and beaten on the road from Jerusalem to Jericho. Participants were students at the Princeton Theological Seminary, individuals who could perhaps be expected to be both familiar with and concerned about moral standards and ideals. Some read a discussion about future job possibilities for seminarians, while others read the parable of the Good Samaritan. They then were asked to record a short talk on what they had read in a building across campus. One-third were told that they were late for the appointment to record the talk and asked to hurry, one-third were told they were not late but had little time, one-third were told they had plenty of time to make the appointment. On their way to the appointment, the seminarians passed a man slumped coughing and moaning in a doorway. Of the seminarians with plenty of time, 63 percent stopped to help the apparent victim; of those with little time, 43 percent stopped; of those in a hurry, 10 percent stopped. The authors suggested that those under time pressure were less likely to notice the victim or interpret the event as an emergency, while others may have noticed the victim but chosen not to stop because it would conflict with what the experimenter expected and wanted them to do (Darley and Bateson, 1973). Whether they had just read an essay on job opportunities for missionaries, or the parable of the Good Samaritan, made no difference.

The need for social structure

In the last chapter, we considered the power of social influence observed in studies of conformity and obedience, which suggested that people are prevented from violating social expectations or norms by enormous anxiety that is ordinarily unchallenged, and therefore unnoticed. Over time, this social influence comes to function as an online moral compass of sorts, systematically determining attitudes, behaviors, values, sense of right and wrong, and even individual identity. The sociologist Robert K. Merton suggested that the groups that individuals follow and compare themselves to come to embody standards for evaluating themselves and their own behavior. These were termed *reference groups* (Merton, 1996), and their emergence is motivated by a fundamental *need to belong* (Baumeister and Leary, 1995). In this section I consider the process by which a group becomes a reference group, and also what happens when reference groups lose their effectiveness in guiding the individual.

Normal group influence

Personal relationships. Human life is in great part organized in and by personal relationships. The first identification of the individual with the group begins with the infant's attachment to others, which is the prototype for the development of normal social behavior. Group identification is in a sense made up of one's relationships with the specific people that comprise the group, and the specific others with whom a person identifies changes throughout life (Wilmot, 1980). "Much of what human beings spend their time doing concerns such relationships. They think about relationships they are in and those they would like to be in; they gossip about the relationships of others; their moments of greatest joy and sorrow have to do with relationships" (Buck, 1988a, p. 530).

Relationships are structured by the expectations that people have about their own and others' behavior. Expectations develop and change, producing norms and roles specific to a relationship. Importantly, these expectations constitute a source of behavior control that is present when the relationship is salient and absent when it is not, so they are sources of behavior control that are effectively outside the individual. Differences in the salience of relationships are reflected in the strength of the associated expectations, and this is doubtless an important source of situational variability in behavior. The results of many studies of conformity and obedience, and studies of moral behavior and helping, can be considered in this light.

Adaptation to college. The impact of changes in relationships over time is illustrated by a classic study by Theodore Newcomb, which began in 1933. Newcomb was teaching at Bennington College in Vermont, an all-woman college at the time with a strongly liberal political orientation influenced by President Franklin Delano Roosevelt's New Deal. Most of the students who came to Bennington, however, came from upper-middle-class families and social environments which were predominantly politically conservative. Therefore, most students held conservative political attitudes as freshmen. However, most became politically liberal by the time they were seniors. A few, however, remained conservative.

To determine what distinguished the two groups, Newcomb polled members of the 1933 entering class about their political attitudes and values; and polled the same students again in 1937, when they were seniors. He also asked the seniors about their friends and activities, whether they liked the college life at Bennington, whether they had kept up with friends in their home towns, and how often they visited their parents. He found that the women who had adapted and changed their attitudes toward the prevailing liberal view in the college liked the college more and had more friends and activities at the college. In effect, the students accepted the college as their new reference group. Those who had maintained their original conservative attitudes spent more time at home and maintained contact with their families and hometown friends, thus maintaining their original reference groups (Newcomb, 1953).

Long-term effects. Newcomb wondered whether the women who had changed their political attitudes in college would maintain their new liberal attitudes or revert to their original conservative political attitudes after college. The 1960 presidential campaign, in which liberal John Kennedy ran against conservative Richard Nixon, provided an opportunity to explore this question. Newcomb contacted as many of his original participants as possible who were strongly liberal or conservative in 1937. He asked about their political preferences and whether they were active in either campaign. Of the women who were strongly liberal in 1937, 50 percent remained liberal in 1960, 36 percent were intermediate, and 14 percent had reverted to their original conservative positions. Of the conservative women, 62 percent remained conservative, 19 percent were intermediate, and 19 percent had become liberal. Newcomb also asked about the political attitudes of their spouses and friends, and found that he could predict their 1960 political attitudes more readily from the attitudes of the spouses and friends than from their attitudes in 1937. In short, the political attitudes appeared to be determined by the individual's current reference group.

From these studies, Newcomb concluded that a person's political attitudes and values are determined in great part by the people they interact with every day, and tend to be maintained because, all else equal, people tend to choose to interact with people who share them. In effect, attitudes and values tend to be maintained because people tend to choose interpersonal relationships that support their expression. If a non-supportive social environment is chosen for any reason, the reference group tends to change, and the attitudes and values tend to change in conformity to the new social environment.

Stages of group influence. Herbert Kelman (1961) proposed that there are three stages in the process of group influence. The first is *compliance*, where the person disagrees privately with the group but conforms openly. One might think of a freshman in the Newcomb study who did not agree with the liberal political attitudes she was confronted with, but did not object openly. The second stage is termed *identification*, where the person accepts the group opinion as proper and begins to have a satisfying self-defining relationship with that group. An example might be a student who accepted that liberal attitudes are appropriate at Bennington, but continued to maintain her original family and associates as a reference group. The third stage is *internalization*, where the individual actively accepts the group's point of view as her own, and attempts to influence others to follow it. Essentially, the new group has become the reference group.

Group influence in extreme situations

Normally, exposure to group influence is determined by individual choices, so extreme changes in values and attitudes are relatively rare. However, in extreme situations, individuals can involuntarily come under powerful influence from other individuals or groups. Examples include imprisonment, kidnapping, and voluntarily joining a group without realizing its true nature. In such cases, values and attitudes can be profoundly affected, and Kelman's three stages can often be discerned in the process.

Imprisonment. Among the most extreme of situations is imprisonment in a concentration camp. Psychoanalyst Bruno Bettelheim was imprisoned in a Nazi concentration camp in Germany during the

1930s, and kept a secret journal of his observations on hidden scraps of paper (Bettelheim, 1943). One of his most remarkable observations was that a few of the prisoners came to identify with the camp guards. They would walk like the guards, talk like the guards, and alter their prison garb to resemble the guards' uniforms. They persisted even though the guards actually disliked and punished this behavior.

Social psychologist Ivan Steiner (1965, pers. comm.) related Bettelheim's observations to Newcomb's studies and Kelman's model. One of the primary elements in the prisoners' experience as related by Bettelheim (1943) was that they were forced to behave in ways that were both demeaning and highly inconsistent with their own values and attitudes, as well as the values and attitudes of their reference groups. Every day, they were forced to deny and ridicule their own religious or political beliefs, their families, and their heritage, and to support their captors. If they did not comply, they were likely shot. Askenasy (1978) related the experience of a concentration camp victim named Franke who, although cooperative and compliant in other ways, refused to give the Nazi salute to his captors. He was given solitary confinement for a week, then two, and more with increasingly severe beatings until, exhausted, he finally complied.

Bettelheim (1943) noted that the initial reaction of most prisoners was to attempt to bolster and sustain their original values and attitudes. They were eager for news of the outside and attempted to communicate with friends and family not imprisoned. When new prisoners entered the camp they were plied for information. Prisoners would talk with one another about their former lives and activities, and would openly declare that the camp would not change them. In short, they seemed to be highly motivated to protect their values, and to make their previous life and reference group more real. They were utterly opposed to the guards and believed that their brutal actions were entirely unjustified. This pattern resembles Kelman's stage of compliance, where the prisoner conformed openly but disagreed privately. As discussed later in this chapter, this stage is associated with among the most excruciating of emotional states, the moral emotion of *humiliation*, combined with *indignation* and seething *resentment* against the guards.

Many were able to continue in this state of conflict between their values and attitudes, versus how they were compelled to act every day. Some individuals, however, began to act in ways suggesting that to survive they must *adjust to the camp*. This required subtle but real changes in their day-to-day values and attitudes, and their views of the camp, their former lives, and the guards. It implied that actions that were unacceptable on the outside were *acceptable in the camp*. As one captive advised a new arrival:

Don't forget that you're in a concentration camp. Here, every man has to fight for himself and not think of anything else. Even of his father. Here, there are no fathers, no brothers, no friends. Everyone lives and dies for himself alone. (Askenasy, 1978, p. 144)

This pattern resembled Kelman's stage of identification, where the prisoner began to accept the group pressure as legitimate and to comply voluntarily. This reduced somewhat the sense of humiliation, indignation, and resentment, and gave the prisoner at least some sense of personal power over the situation. They began to accept the guards' authority as legitimate, arguing that they were only doing their jobs, and that in any case some of the prisoners deserved the punishment. However, this perspective required changes in the prisoners' orientation to life as it had been prior to imprisonment. Rather than providing support, reminders of their previous lives now provoked conflict and painful feelings of shame and guilt. They knew that they were breaking old rules and acting contrary to their values and attitudes; and that their families and former friends would not approve. So, these prisoners stopped reminiscing about their former lives, and began to actively *resist* news and talk of the outside.

Prisoners who were able to completely block themselves off from their former lives, reference groups, values, and attitudes were able to lessen their guilt and shame, and began to do "easy time" in US prison lingo. A few went further, and actually began to take the guards as their reference group and the camp as their *preferred* home. This is analogous to Kelman's third stage of internalization, where the individual actively accepts the group's values and attitudes, and attempts to influence others to follow them. One of the symptoms of this stage was that the prisoners *no longer cared* about their previous lives and associations. Also, they supported and imitated the guards, and sometimes attempted to get other prisoners to follow insulting and degrading camp rules even in the absence of the guards.

Brainwashing. In Bettelheim's observations, the guards disliked the prisoners' identification with them, but there are other cases in which changes in values and attitudes are actively encouraged. One of the extreme examples of seeking to alter values and attitudes by coercive persuasion is *brainwashing*. The term was originated in a book describing techniques used by Communist cadres under Mao Zedong to change the ideologies of Nationalist Chinese (Hunter, 1951). The concept became popular after the Korean War, when it was found that Chinese and North Korean interrogators were surprisingly able to alter the stated attitudes and values of American prisoners of war (Kinkead, 1959; White, 1957). Analysis of the techniques revealed that the interrogators employed familiar techniques of social influence involving intentional persuasion on the part of the interrogator, who actively attempted to influence the subject; and coercion, where the interrogator controlled outcomes important to the subject (Schein, 1956; Schein et al., 1961).

Similar techniques were employed in programs of "thought reform and ideological remolding" in the People's Republic of China. These often involved techniques of group confrontation and criticism to enforce compliance and conformity. During the Great Leap Forward in the 1950s and the Cultural Revolution of the 1960s, these programs were pursued vigorously and involved considerable abuse. A stated goal of the Cultural Revolution was to actually alter human nature in the service of the social order.

Capture bonding. In other cases of coercive persuasion victims appeared to actually bond with their captors, supporting them, and resisting leaving them. Examples include the kidnappings of Elizabeth Smart in Salt Lake City in 2003 and Jaycee Lee Dugard in California in 1991, and the Stockholm Syndrome of 1973, when a group was held by bank robbers for several days. Among the best-known examples is the kidnapping of Patricia Hearst in 1974. The 19-year-old Hearst family heiress was kidnapped by members of a self-proclaimed group of urban guerrillas, the Symbionese Liberation Army (SLA). The Hearst family complied with their ransom demand that several million dollars' worth of food aid be distributed to the needy, but on the April 4 date scheduled for her release, the young woman announced that she had decided to join the SLA, denounced her parents, and took the pseudonym of "Tanya" after a comrade of Che Guevara. On April 15 she was photographed while robbing a bank in San Francisco, and on May 16 she covered the escape of SLA members William and Emily Harris with automatic weapons fire. When eventually arrested on September 18, 1975, she proclaimed herself to be Tanya, the urban guerilla.

Henson (2006) discussed this seemingly paradoxical phenomenon of hostages becoming emotionally attached to their captors, or *capture bonding*, and suggested that it has evolutionary origins in tribal conflict in the ancestral human environment. Observations of contemporary hunting and gathering tribes has suggested that being captured by nearby tribes must have been relatively common, particularly for women. Henson (2006) reported that, in some tribes including the Yanomamo of South America, as high as one in ten females had been abducted and incorporated into the tribe, and most individuals descended from a captive within the last three generations. As a result, he suggested that a trait of socially reorienting and bonding within a few days was selected. Henson related this to several otherwise puzzling human traits. These included *battered person syndrome*, where abuse and beatings can actually strengthen bonds between abuser and victim; the use of traumatic experiences to produce bonding in *hazing* rituals and military training; and the intense sexual pleasure some derive from bondage, domination, and sadomasochistic (BDSM) practices.

In the case of Patricia Hearst, after her capture and incarceration she experienced long sessions with defense lawyers and psychiatric experts, and regular visits from family and former friends. Tanya began to become confused, then contrite. Friends described her as "coming to her senses" and "becoming her old self again," although cynics suspected that her lawyers were manufacturing a sympathetic pre-trial image. Brainwashing was used for the first time as a formal part of her defense in the bank-robbery trial. Ms. Hearst later stated that her conversion to Tanya reflected the "disgusting vulnerability of the human mind." After almost two years in prison, Ms. Hearst had her sentence commuted by President Jimmy Carter; and in 2001, President Bill Clinton granted her a full presidential pardon.

Emotional group appeals. Capture-bonding may be sustained and magnified by strong emotional appeals to increase the helplessness and confusion of the victim. These can involve expressions of unqualified affection and acceptance: for example, cults have used "love bombing," involving flattery, sharing, and physically caressing. On the other hand, groups have engaged in severe verbal and physical abuse, ranging from verbal confrontation and food and sleep deprivation to extreme torture. Indeed, a combination of these may be particularly powerful: abuse mixed with affection and the opportunity to abuse others. This can be illustrated by the tactics of a California-based group that conducted seminars in "personal development":

> Seminars are usually held in hotel or motel suites, with 18 to 25 students and four or five instructors closeted in marathon sessions. Clients may be deprived of food and sleep, and they are routinely subjected, nude, to hour-long ordeals in "the pit," a cleared area in the center of the seminar room, in which they are badgered, humiliated, and generally tormented by their instructors and their classmates. The object, as one former student describes it, is to make the subject confess his shortcomings and weep. After that, he says, "one of the leaders would holler out, 'he's a man. He divulged everything. He went through hell. We're finding out we're the same. We have to change to become successful.' And he hugged him and told him how great he was." (*Newsweek*, August 27, 1972, p. 68)

This group reportedly tied students to crosses, put them in cages, sealed them in coffins for hours, and forced them to do degrading sexual acts. The students paid $1,000 per man and $640 per woman for the seminar, and most reportedly "emerge rejoicing." The developer of the seminar was described as an ultraconservative businessman who stated, "The total result of it is a helluva great thing," in which a student "reaches a point of honesty with himself ... and [can] live a more creative and constructive life" (*Newsweek*, August 27, 1972, p. 68).

At first glance, it seems paradoxical that people pay to be subjected to such abusive and coercive techniques. Like other phenomena considered in this section, this demonstrates again that in a non-supportive social environment, ties with old reference groups tend to weaken, and attitudes and values tend to come to conform to the new social environment. Beyond this, the evidence from extreme situations reveals that the need for social structure plays on one of the deepest human needs, the need to be accepted by, and play a meaningful role in, a social group. Related to this is the intense reward people can get from painful abuse, due to the close connection between opiates and pain discussed in Chapter 3. On the other hand, there is evidence that rejection from the group is extraordinarily aversive and painful. Certainly, in the ancestral human environment, being rejected, scorned, humiliated, and shunned by the group was a likely death warrant.

Ostracism, exclusion, and rejection

Several research programs have demonstrated the excruciating painfulness of rejection, which may well be a major factor in motivating behavior in studies of conformity and obedience. A classic study by Schachter (1951) demonstrated that, when a person (actually a confederate of the experimenter) disagreed with a group consensus, communication toward the deviate initially increased, then decreased as the group members realized that he could not be changed. Then when given an opportunity, the deviate was voted out of the group. Thus, a certain level of conformity was necessary to maintain meaningful membership in a group.

Direct perception of ostracism: the ball-toss paradigm. The consequences of rejection have been investigated in several experimental paradigms that have shown that even short-term rejection by strangers can have powerfully negative effects on the victim. The *ball-toss* paradigm originated from a personal experience of its developer, Kipling Williams, who reported being briefly included, then excluded, in a game of Frisbee with strangers. He was surprised at the powerful negative emotions and feeling of helplessness that came with exclusion, and decided to use the experience to study ostracism in the laboratory. In this paradigm, three people waiting for an experiment began to toss a ball back and forth, apparently spontaneously. Two of the players were actually confederates of the experimenter, and in the *ostracism* condition, after sharing the ball for a time the two began to throw the ball back and forth to each other, ignoring the real participant. After only a few minutes, this produced a strong negative emotional reaction of painful distress in the participant, with high ratings particularly of sadness and anger. Moreover, ostracized participants showed lower self-reported belonging, control, self-esteem, and meaningful existence (Williams, 2007, 2011).

Williams and colleagues created an online version of the ball toss game termed Cyberball in which participants played an online Internet ball-toss game. This was used to explore the effects of many variables on reactions to ostracism, and it was discovered that the negative effects were surprisingly robust. People reacted badly even though they knew they were playing against a computer instead of people, and even though they were told that the other players were members of out-groups. Ostracism remained painful even when the purported partners were members of a despised out-group – the Ku Klux Klan – and this was emphasized by representing them on the computer screen with small hoods ("The KKK won't let me play!" Gonsalkorale and Williams, 2007). Even when ostracism paid – participants were charged money each time a ball was thrown to them – it still hurt to be ostracized (van Beest and Williams, 2006).

Williams (2007) suggested that ostracism is detected crudely but rapidly: presumably this involves direct perception and the "low road" to cognition. Also, he suggested that the phenomenon recruits the pain mechanism directly: it is felt as pain and it involves much the same neural architecture as physical pain. This was investigated in a study in which participants played Cyberball while fMRI measures were taken (Eisenberger et al., 2003). There was an initial period while the participant watched as two others played the game while the participant was excluded because of extenuating circumstances (equipment problems). This provided a baseline of the participant's brain activity to the task under conditions of implicit social exclusion. This was followed by an inclusion condition where participants played the game without being ostracized, and then by explicit social exclusion as the participant experienced ostracism. Because of the role of pain in social attachment (Panksepp, 1991), brain mechanisms associated with responding to physical pain were examined. As expected, ostracism activated areas of the dorsal anterior cingulate cortex (ACC) linked to the experience of pain in the explicit exclusion condition relative to the inclusion condition. Also, ostracism activated areas of the right ventral prefrontal cortex (RVPFC) implicated in the regulation of pain distress in the explicit exclusion condition relative to the inclusion condition. Moreover, the brain activity was related to self-reports in ways compatible with pain studies. The ACC activation in the explicit exclusion condition was positively and significantly related to self-reported distress, and RVPFC activation in the explicit exclusion condition was negatively related to self-reported distress. The RVPFC distress relationship was mediated by ACC activity, suggesting that the RVPFC regulated ostracism distress by interrupting ACC-mediated distress.

Other manipulations of rejection. Individual personality factors do not appear to play a significant role in the fast, initial response to ostracism as manipulated by ball-tossing or Cyberball, but personality factors do become important in longer-term responses to rejection. Williams (2007, 2011) suggested that two sorts of patterns emerge: one involving ingratiation to improve belonging; the other aggression to get revenge. He suggested moreover that the Cyberball-type paradigm manipulates short-term "minimal" ostracism which is not sensitive to these longer-term responses, but other forms of experimentally manipulating rejection may be. Among those are the *life alone* paradigm, where participants are tested and informed of a prognosis that they will live life alone, without friends or meaningful relationships. Another is the *false feedback* paradigm, where participants converse with others and are then made to think that the others rejected them. These manipulations rely on higher-order cognitive processing and therefore must reflect slower but more differentiated "high-road" cognition. Findings from studies using these paradigms have been inconsistent, reporting both decreases and increases in prosocial behavior following rejection (Twenge et al., 2007; Mead et al., 2011), as well as "emotional blunting," involving reduced sensitivity to pain, emotional insensitivity, a lack of feeling, and a lack of empathy (Baumeister et al., 2007, 2009). It may be that rejection actually sets in motion a wide variety of potential responses which can vary by personality and situational demands. These studies, however, did not examine those emotions arguably most relevant to ostracism and rejection: moral emotions such as humiliation, indignation, admiration, and resentment.

New communication media and social influence

No discussion of contemporary social influence would be complete without consideration of the impact of new communication media upon how social influence is implemented. Both traditional mass media and new communication technologies based on the Internet have altered the very basis of social influence processes, and consequently, social structure; and the emotional and emotional-communication aspects of this transformation are often overlooked.

Spontaneous emotional communication via media. Part of the power of new media technology is that it affords the communication of emotion as never before. We saw in Chapter 4 that social structures emerge naturally from communicative interactions, beginning with nurturing parental care and proceeding as biologically based emotions are played with in communicative social context; and that emotional communication is *necessary and sufficient* for this process to occur. Communication media afford emotional exploration and education because they allow the vicarious exploration, imitation, and modeling of situations that are relatively rare and can be socially dangerous, destructive, or embarrassing.

As communication media change, there is a corresponding change in patterns of emotional communication, and this can have a powerful impact on the transmission of social scripts, roles, and norms. Mirror neuron research has demonstrated the possibility of an "unmediated empathy" via communication media, suggesting the potential for a direct apprehension by the audience of the feelings and desires of senders via video and audio representations of the senders' emotional displays. This has afforded syncretic, holistic, heuristic, and affective KA cognitive processing as opposed to the primarily analytic, linear, sequential, systematic, rational cognitive processing afforded by print media. Indeed, new communication media afford the possibility for immediate, direct spontaneous emotional communication on a global scale (Buck and Powers, 2011).

Social change initiated by communication media. There are a number of examples in which emotional media presentations have effected social changes, indeed transformations. Some years ago, a brief televised news report showing children starving in Ethiopia generated a remarkably compassionate response in viewers which led to assistance on a world-wide scale. The Ethiopian famine was nothing new: it had been going on for two years and had been covered by print media. However, print media lacked the emotional potency of visual media (Chaudhuri and Buck, 1995), and allowed the reader to cognitively manipulate judgments of equity or simply to ignore the material, so that feelings of indignation, guilt, and shame were not generated. But the images of emaciated, anguished children displayed during dinnertime could not be ignored, and they could not be cognitively manipulated.

This can arguably illuminate the situation in the Middle East beginning in the Arab Spring of 2011 and evolving at this writing. This revolution emerged simultaneously in many nations – naturally, organically, and perhaps inevitably – from largely suppressed passions of people in the region combined with the new ecology of emotional communication afforded by social media. The revolution tended to be strongest in societies where repression was the most powerful and effective, and where traditional paths of communication were the most hierarchical and bound by tradition. When suddenly people, and particularly young people, could communicate directly with one another, the release was electric, dramatic, and spectacular. The content of this communication was overwhelmingly emotional: expressing fear, resentment, indignation, hope, and triumph along with such a sense of emotional bonding and solidarity that many people faced knowingly and willingly the prospect of arrest, imprisonment, torture, and violent death.

Another striking example of media-generated social change involves the influence on fertility choices of televised soap operas, or *telenovelas*, in Brazil (La Ferrara et al., 2008). This phenomenon was particularly well-documented because of the way television coverage evolved in Brazil, plus the availability of detailed national population records. Brazil's major broadcaster, Rede Globo, had an effective monopoly on the production of locally produced telenovelas. The Globo telenovelas were high quality programs, with production budgets fifteen times those of Mexican telenovelas, and they emphasized Brazilian identity. They tended to idealize middle- or upper-middle-class consumer-oriented, rich, cosmopolitan, and happy women and men with small families; in contrast with lower-class families which were presented as poor, less happy, and having many children. Globo's major competitor, SBT (Systema Brasiliero de Televisao), relied on imported programming including Mexican and American soap operas. The signals of Globo and SBT entered new markets in Brazil gradually and independently, so that the impact of the entry of the two broadcasters could be compared (La Ferrara et al., 2008).

Investigators examined the penetration of the Globo signal in the Brazilian hinterland from 1965 to 2000, showing a dramatic increase particularly between 1980 and 1990. They then looked at the specific time of introduction of the Globo signal for a given area and calculated fertility statistics before and after the introduction of the signal. The results are presented in Figure 7.1. It illustrates a dramatic decrease in fertility in the year of Globo entry, which was maintained. This period saw a large overall decrease in the total fertility rate in Brazil, which fell from 6.3 children per family in 1960, to 5.8 in 1970, to 4.4 in 1980, to 2.9 in 1991, to 2.3 in 2000 (Lam and Marteleto, 2005). This decline occurred despite resistance in the larger society: abortion is illegal in Brazil, the government enacted no family planning policies over this period, the Catholic church was actively opposed to birth control, and even Globo itself resisted the idea that its programming contributed to the decline in fertility (Downie, 2009).

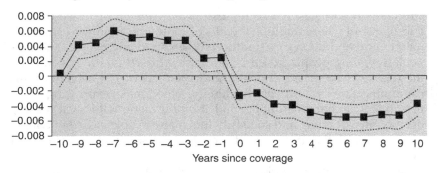

Figure 7.1 Correspondence of fertility decline to the year of
Globo entry in Brazil. See text for details.

The authors considered whether the drop in fertility was specifically
due to the Globo telenovelas. One indication was the fact that expansion of the SBT network had no significant effect on fertility when it was
introduced in new areas. Another was that the probability that the
twenty most popular first names chosen by parents in an area included
the first name of a novela character during the year of the child's birth
was approximately 33 percent if the family had received the Globo
signal and 8.5 percent if it did not (La Ferrara et al., 2008).

There are other international studies of social change seemingly
initiated by communication media, and most involve emotion-laden
issues including divorce rates, body-style preferences, social participation, and trust (Downie, 2009). Communication media have also been
implicated in stirring within-group sentiments and directing hostility
to out-groups, as we shall see later in this chapter.

The neuroscience of morality

In recent years, our understanding of moral judgment, caring, and
behavior has been greatly enriched by the addition of moral emotion
to the mix (Haidt, 2001), and this study of moral emotion was facilitated
by the discovery that dealing with moral situations activated specific
brain mechanisms. A major impetus to this development involved the
study of fMRI responses in morally relevant situations.

Brain responding in moral judgment and behavior

The trolley dilemma and dual-process theory. In one of the first applications
of fMRI measures to moral situations, Greene et al. (2001) investigated
fMRI responses to the consideration of moral dilemmas. The study

involved a family of moral dilemmas puzzling to moral philosophers that typically involve a harmful action that maximizes overall good consequences. For example, in what is known as the *trolley dilemma*, there is a runaway trolley which is headed to hit and kill five people. In the *switch* version of the dilemma, the five would be saved if the participant switched the trolley to another track where one person will be killed instead of five. In the *footbridge* version, the five would be saved if the participant pushed a large stranger off a footbridge over the track, stopping the trolley but killing the stranger. Most people say that they would hit the switch but would not push the stranger off the footbridge, even though the consequences of acting are the same in a utilitarian cost–benefit analysis. Greene et al. suggested that the essential difference between the switch and footbridge versions is that the latter engages the emotions more than the former: "the thought of pushing someone to his death is, we propose, more emotionally salient than the thought of pushing a switch that will cause a trolley to produce similar consequences, and it is this emotional response that accounts for people's tendency to treat these cases differently" (2001, p. 2106).

To test this prediction, Greene et al. (2001) selected a number of moral dilemmas that seemingly engaged emotion more than others, like the footbridge versus the switch versions of the trolley dilemma. They predicted that contemplation of the former, which they termed "moral-personal" dilemmas, would engage brain areas associated with emotion more than contemplation of "moral impersonal" dilemmas. They devised a battery of sixty dilemmas, some moral-personal, some moral-impersonal, and some non-moral (e.g. whether to travel by bus or train). Results supported these predictions: compared to the other two conditions, contemplating the moral-personal dilemmas led to relatively more fMRI activity in brain areas associated in other research with emotion (medial frontal gyrus [BA 9 and 10], posterior cingulate gyrus [BA 31], and angular gyrus [BA 39]); and relatively less activity in areas associated with working memory (right middle frontal gyrus [DLPFC: BA 46] and parietal region [BA 7/40]; see Figure 3.11 for an illustration of Brodmann areas).

To explain this result, Greene proposed a *dual-process* model of moral judgment, involving an implicit, automatic, intuitive, emotional process working with and often competing with a process of explicit, effortful, deliberative, conscious utilitarian judgment in which the welfare of the one is sacrificed for the welfare of the many (Koven, 2011). As Greene put it, "automatic and controlled processes exert distinctive, and in some cases competing, influences on moral judgment" (2011, p. 227). In the dual-process model, "The thought of pushing someone in front of a trolley elicits a prepotent, negative emotional response ... that drives moral disapproval. People also engage in utilitarian moral reasoning (aggregate cost-benefit analysis)" (Greene, 2007, p. 322). Greene suggested that the emotional process is supported particularly by the medial prefrontal cortex (MPFC) and the utilitarian process by the dorsolateral prefrontal cortex (DLPFC). The dual-process model implies that in the realm of morality, reason and emotion function as relatively competitive mechanisms: emotions associated with the MPFC interfere with rational decisions that are based upon a utilitarian cost–benefit analysis that involves the DLPFC (Moll and de Oliveira-Souza, 2007a). The locations of these structures are shown in Figures 3.11 and 3.12.

Brain responses to moral stimuli. At about the same time as the Greene et al. (2001) study, Moll et al. were studying the brain's response to moral stimuli with different methods. One study examined brain activation patterns to an explicit moral reasoning task that was not, however, a moral dilemma. Participants were given statements with explicit moral content (e.g. "we break the law when necessary") and without moral content (e.g. "stones are lighter than water"), and judged each statement simply to be "right" or "wrong" while being scanned in the fMRI (Moll et al., 2001). Results showed activations to moral stimuli in the frontopolar cortex (FPC) and MPFC generally similar to those seen by Greene et al. (2001): activation in the medial frontal gyrus (BA 9 and 10/46) and FPC (BA 10) showed the largest areas of activation to moral judgment; and areas of the right anterior temporal cortex, lenticular nucleus, and cerebellum also were activated during moral judgment. Given their differences in methodology, the agreement between the Moll et al. and Greene et al. results is noteworthy.

A second study by Moll et al. (2002) presented stimuli with moral or non-moral content to participants without requiring an explicit response. Participants were scanned in the fMRI while viewing emotionally charged or neutral pictures. Some presented unpleasant scenes with content implying moral violation, such as scenes of war, physical assault, or poor and abandoned children (Haidt, 2002). Some presented unpleasant pictures without moral content, such as body lesions, body products, and dangerous animals (Rozin et al., 1999). A third type presented pleasant people and landscapes; a fourth, unusual scenes such as surreal images; a fifth, neutral pictures of people and landscapes; a sixth, scrambled images. Participants rated the stimuli for moral content and emotional valence and arousal. Results indicated that both the moral and unpleasant pictures produced significant arousal in brain areas associated with unpleasant emotion: e.g. subcortical, limbic, and cortical regions including the extended amygdala and upper midbrain bilaterally; the periaqueductal gray (PAG); the right thalamus and superior colliculus; the right insula/inferior frontal gyrus (BA 44/45); the right anterior temporal cortex (BA 21/38); posterior temporal/occipital cortices bilaterally (BA 22/27/19); and the right intraparietal sulcus (BA 7). These findings were consistent with other fMRI studies of the neural substrates of unpleasant emotion (Lane et al., 1999; Damasio et al., 2000). In addition, controlling for valence and arousal, the morally relevant scenes produced activation in the right medial OFC (BA 11), the medial frontal gyrus (BA 10), and the right posterior superior temporal sulcus (BA 21/39). Moll et al. suggested that these structures are critical regions in a network which plays a specific role in implicit social behavior, perception, and moral appraisal.

The Ultimatum Game. In a different approach to measuring brain responses in morally relevant situations, Sanfey et al. (2003) used fMRI in the *Ultimatum Game*, which forces participants to consider a proposal that is fair or unfair to themselves personally. In this game, two participants split a sum of money: one player proposes a division that the other must accept or reject. If the recipient accepts the offer, the money is split; if the offer is rejected, neither receives any money. In either case, the game is over. Studies have shown that in industrialized cultures, the modal offer is about 50 percent of the total amount. Low offers (e.g. an 80/20 percent split in favor of the proposer) have about a 50 percent chance of being rejected, even though the recipient loses money. Thus the recipient turns down an often considerable monetary reward if it is seen to be unfair. This rejection is typically accompanied by reports and displays of anger, and Sanfey et al. (2003) suggested that this negative emotion is provoked as an adaptive mechanism to assert and maintain one's social reputation. In the terms of the dual-process model, acceptance of the offer is considered to be rational, and rejection is considered to be emotional.

Sanfey et al. (2003) studied the fMRI responses of receivers to a series of fair and unfair offers, each made supposedly by a different partner. The $10 offers varied from fair ($5 – $5) to progressively unfair ($7 – $3; $8 – $2; $9 – $1). Participants accepted all fair offers, with acceptance declining as offers became less fair. Brain areas that showed greater activation for unfair than fair offers included the DLPFC, the anterior cingulate cortex (ACC), and the anterior insula. The finding of anterior insula activation was of particular interest because of the association of this region with the specific negative emotions of anger and disgust. A higher anterior insula response correlated with a higher proportion of rejections of the offer, which is consistent with the idea that this response is less rational-utilitarian and more emotional. The authors suggested that the high level of DLPFC activation was associated with the rational-utilitarian goal of accumulating money: the more rational-utilitarian accepted offers were associated with relatively less activation of the anterior insula but more activation of the DLPFC; while the more emotional rejected offers showed the opposite pattern. The greater activation of the ACC was also of interest, for as seen in Chapter 3 the ACC is particularly associated with conflict resolution and empathy.

Manipulating the brain: repetitive transcranial magnetic stimulation. Another study investigating the effects of the Ultimatum Game is relevant to the understanding of the DLPFC response (Knoch et al., 2006). This study employed a different method for assessing the brain's involvement in moral reasoning and behavior: it used *repetitive transcranial magnetic stimulation* (rTMS) to transiently disrupt brain activity in the right DLPFC prior to the game. The rTMS procedure involves placing a small device on the skull which carries a coil of wire that can carry electricity to produce a magnetic field. Repeated stimulation by the field can cause the underlying brain tissue to become less active for a period of time. Knoch et al. found that when the right DLPFC was inactivated, participants were much more likely to accept unfair offers, e.g. to behave rationally and selfishly, which was not consistent with a simple dual-process view that the DLPFC is responsible for rational-utilitarian control. Moreover, because of their methodology they could claim that the right DLPFC played a causal role in this, specifically, a "causal role in the implementation of fairness motives when self-interest and fairness are in conflict" (p. 832). Importantly, the right DLPFC inactivation did not affect *judgments* of fairness: participants acknowledged the unfairness of the offers but accepted them anyway. Also interestingly, disruption of the left DLPFC had no effect on the acceptance rate of unfair offers, even though Stanfey et al. (2003) had found that the left as well as right DLPFC is activated by unfair offers. Knoch et al. (2006) noted that these results raise important questions about the interplay of the left and right hemispheres in implementing fairness-related behaviors. These questions remain largely unanswered at this writing.

Tassy et al. (2011) applied the technique of inactivating the right DLPFC using rTMS to the judgment of moral dilemmas. Participants responded to standard dilemmas involving the good of the many at the expense of the few by indicating both an objective moral judgment ("would it be *acceptable* to ...?") and a subjective moral judgment ("would *you* do ...?" e.g. push the person off the footbridge to stop the trolley). In the dual-process model, the DLPFC was seen to underlie rational-utilitarian cost–benefit analysis and to control emotional impulses, so one might assume that disrupting right DLPFC activity should have the effect of decreasing rational-utilitarian judgments (e.g. increasing the effects of emotion). In fact, results indicated that the effects of right DLPFC disruption differed for objective and subjective judgments: objective judgments were actually more rational-utilitarian when the right DLPFC was disrupted; while subjective judgments showed the opposite tendency, particularly for more "high conflict" dilemmas. The authors concluded that, like the Knoch et al. (2006) results, the response to the dilemmas was not compatible with a simple dual-process view of the DLPFC. Moreover, while there was a negative correlation between the emotional intensity of a given dilemma and the probability of a rational-utilitarian response, this correlation was not significant when the right DLPFC was inactivated. Tassy et al. (2011) concluded that the right DLPFC not only participates in a rational-utilitarian control process; it also integrates emotion into the decision process.

Conclusions. The Greene et al. (2001) study was in many respects a game-changer. It demonstrated that emotions that can mediate moral judgment and behavior are associated with remarkably specific neurochemical systems in the brain, and it has been widely cited in the literature on moral emotions. Although the evidence has indicated that the DLPFC plays a critical role in moral judgment and behavior, the notion of an automatic emotional process supported particularly by the MPFC versus a rational-utilitarian process supported by the DLPFC is arguably oversimplified (Frank et al., 2009).

The studies from which the dual-process model emerged employed dilemmas and games in which competition between rational-utilitarian versus emotional systems tended to be enhanced, so that the model perhaps overemphasized the conflict between rational-utilitarian processing and emotion. Moreover, these studies focused primarily upon negative emotions that are generally opposed to rational morality. The dual-process model did not consider the possibility that there may be prosocial emotions that may actually support rational morality in many cases. Moll and de Oliveira-Souza (2007a, 2007b) proposed that prosocial moral sentiments exist, and are associated with the integration, rather than conflict, between rational and emotional mechanisms. In their view, prosocial moral emotions are mediated by the VMPFC and frontopolar cortex (PFC), while the DLPFC supports "self-centered" emotions. This view is consistent with the extensive evidence for the existence of attachment processes and prosocial emotions that we have considered; and also the notion of a fundamental distinction between prosocial and selfish emotions. Also compatible is the contention that these prosocial emotions are ever-present but commonly ignored. As Moll et al. (2002) put it, "humans are endowed with a natural sense of fairness that permeates social perceptions and inter-actions. This moral stance is so ubiquitous that we may not notice ... [this] ... automatic tagging of ordinary social events with moral values" (p. 2730). I return to the topic of the complex and multifaceted nature of moral emotions after considering the effects of frontal lobe brain damage on social and moral functioning.

Brain damage and morality

The celebrated case of Phineas Gage. The recognition of a role for the frontal cortex in moral judgment and decision-making has a long history, dating at least to the widely known case of Phineas Gage, a railroad worker in Vermont in the nineteenth century (Damasio et al., 1994; Macmillan, 2000, 2008). An accidental explosion sent a large iron tamping rod through his cheek and out the top of his head, destroying much of the left frontal lobe. A physician, John Martyn Harlow, vividly described the aftermath of the accident: "The patient bore his sufferings with the most heroic firmness. He recognized me at once, and said he hoped he was not much hurt. He seemed to be perfectly conscious, but was getting exhausted from the hemorrhage ... His person, and the bed on which he was laid, were literally one gore of blood" (Harlow, 1848, pp. 339–42; quoted in Wikipedia: "Phineas Gage").

Although surviving the horrific accident, Gage suffered subsequent personality changes described by Harlow:

> The equilibrium or balance, so to speak, between his intellectual faculties and animal propensities, seems to have been destroyed. He is fitful, irreverent, indulging at times in the grossest profanity (which was not previously his custom), manifesting but little defer-ence for his fellows, impatient of restraint or advice when it conflicts with his desires, at times pertinaciously obstinate, yet capricious and vacillating, devising many plans of future operations, which are no sooner arranged than they are abandoned in turn for others appearing more feasible. A child in his intellectual capacity and manifestations, he has the animal passions of a strong man. Previous to his injury, although untrained in the schools, he possessed a well-balanced mind, and was looked upon by those who knew him as a shrewd, smart businessman, very energetic and persistent in executing all his plans of operation. In this regard his mind was radically changed, so decidedly that his friends and acquaintances said he was "no longer Gage" (Harlow, 1848, pp. 339–42; quoted in Wikipedia: "Phineas Gage")

Some accounts of the Gage case have been distorted and overblown, asserting that he became unable to hold a job and engaged in lying, gambling, brawling, bullying, thievery, drunkenness, abusiveness – even molesting children – but there is no evidence of this (Macmillan,

2000). He apparently held jobs and traveled, appearing for a time as a circus curiosity, and died in 1860 in San Francisco, twelve years after his accident.

The Gage case dramatically illustrated the role of the frontal lobes in decision-making, emotional processing, and social skills that we considered in Chapter 3. Recall that damage to the orbitofrontal cortex (OFC) in humans can lead to disinhibition, antisocial behavior, and impulsiveness (Andersson et al., 1999), and that Damasio's (1994) Somatic Marker Hypothesis stated that appraisal and decision-making involve the ventromedial prefrontal cortex (VMPFC), which includes the OFC. A number of studies have attempted to relate damage to specific parts of the frontal lobes to specific aspects of moral judgment and behavior.

VMPFC damage and moral judgment and behavior. One way of addressing this issue is to test patients with VMPFC damage with moral dilemmas such as the trolley dilemma. This was done by Koenigs et al. (2007) who presented fifty moral-personal, moral-impersonal, and non-moral dilemmas to patients with focal bilateral damage to the VMPFC, brain-damaged comparison patients (BDC) with lesions outside areas of the brain thought to be important for emotion, and normal comparison participants (NC). The VMPFC damaged patients showed a pattern of normal baseline mood and intact intellect, but they had prominent deficits in social emotion, with lower autonomic responding to emotionally loaded pictures and severely low levels of empathy, embarrassment, and guilt. BDC and NC participants had intact emotional processing. Results revealed that the VMPFC damaged patients' responses to non-moral and impersonal moral dilemmas did not differ from those of other groups, but that their responses to personal-moral dilemmas was markedly more rational-utilitarian in that they would more readily choose to inflict harm on one person to save five; e.g. they would say that they would push the person off the footbridge to stop the trolley.

Koenig et al. (2007) divided the personal-moral dilemmas into "low conflict" and "high conflict" dilemmas, based upon the degree of conflict between competing moral principles: e.g. not harming others versus saving multiple lives. For example, pushing a stranger off a footbridge to save five lives is a high conflict dilemma, while pushing your boss off a building to get him out of your life is not and is seen as wrong by virtually everyone. Low conflict personal-moral dilemmas elicited virtually 100 percent agreement from the two comparison groups, such that they unanimously agreed that the action was wrong (e.g. abandoning your baby to avoid the burden of taking care of it). High conflict personal-moral dilemmas did not elicit such agreement (e.g. smothering your baby to save a number of people). The VMPFC damaged patients agreed with the consensus on the low conflict personal-moral scenarios, but they were significantly more likely to endorse the proposed action than either of the comparison groups for all of the high conflict personal-moral scenarios. So, VMPFC damaged patients' moral judgments differed from those of comparison persons only when there was competition between opposing moral principles: an action benefiting the general welfare versus strong emotional aversion to performing that action. The VMPFC damage appeared to blunt the effect of moral emotion.

Using a new set of moral dilemmas, Thomas et al. (2011) found this increased rational-utilitarian response in VMPFC damaged patients even when they would do personal harm to save strangers (e.g. in the high-conflict footbridge dilemma, the one person killed to save five strangers is your daughter). Also, it made no difference whether the pusher was oneself or someone else ("John"): there was a small tendency to behave in a more rational-utilitarian manner when John was doing the pushing, but that was true of both VMPFC and non-brain-damaged groups. Thomas et al. suggested that the VMPFC is involved in joining aversive social-emotional consequences (e.g. feelings of guilt/shame and remorse) to one's actions; so that its damage interferes with the experience of feelings of guilt/shame and remorse.

Koenigs et al. (2007) noted that the apparent lack of emotion on the part of VMPFC damaged patients was not observed in their response to unfair treatment in the Ultimatum Game; in fact their emotional response actually *appeared to be enhanced*. Recall that the Ultimatum Game was designed to elicit frustration by presenting participants with unfair take-it-or-leave-it offers. Employing this game with VMPFC damaged patients, Koenig and Tranel (2007) found, consistent with greater negative emotional responses to injustice, that they "irrationally" rejected unfairly low offers more that did comparison groups. This does not seem consistent with the notion that VMPFC damaged patients are generally emotionally blunted, allowing them to respond in a more rational-utilitarian fashion. Moreover, Koenigs and Tranel (2007) noted that clinical experience with patients with VMPFC damage suggests that they are often short-tempered, angry, irritable, and even abusive, responding aggressively to relatively minor provocations.

Rational and emotional moral involvement

So, on one hand, VMPFC damaged patients appear to demonstrate blunted social emotions such as guilt/shame and remorse, and they behave more "rationally" to scenarios involving strong negative emotional reactions; but on the other hand they behave "irrationally" and with heightened emotion in situations designed to evoke frustration and anger. Moll et al. (2007a) suggested an explanation for this pattern that differs from the dual-process model. The blunted social emotions and increased rational-utilitarian choices on one hand, and increased anger/disgust on the other, are both compatible with a general decrease in prosocial sentiments. That is, the VMPFC damage led to a decrease in prosocial sentiments that on one hand made it easier to sacrifice someone, even your daughter, to save others; and on the other hand heightened frustration and anger when others acted unfairly.

Another way of conceptualizing the duality of emotional versus rational-utilitarian processing is in terms of the distinction between syncretic versus analytic cognitive processing (see Figures 1.3 and 4.1). These forms of processing do not necessarily conflict: in fact they are often positively related to one another. If something is important to us, we generally both think more deeply *and* feel more deeply about it. This principle has been investigated in the context of advertising and marketing (Chaudhuri and Buck, 1995) and can be applied to moral situations. Also, as with consumer products, a wide range of emotions may be involved in moral situations. As the literature on fMRI responses to moral judgment and behavior has been concentrated on moral dilemmas involving highly unpleasant acts like pushing someone off a footbridge, the range of emotions considered has been relatively limited. However, Moll and colleagues pointed out that a variety of prosocial emotions are involved in moral judgment and behavior, and they appear to support as well as oppose rational-utilitarian considerations.

The neuroscience of prosocial moral emotions

The experimental paradigms used to study moral judgment and behavior that we have considered – the moral dilemmas and Ultimatum Game – both involved conflict between rational-utilitarian versus emotional considerations, and both involve negative moral emotions. However, positive moral emotions exist as well: they do not necessarily conflict with rational-utilitarian considerations, and they can be related to specifiable brain mechanisms. Prosocial moral emotions include positively valenced emotions of moral approbation (pride, admiration) as well as negatively valenced emotions (guilt/shame, remorse). Most studies to date have emphasized negatively valenced emotions: there is evidence that specific brain mechanisms associated with moral approbation may include the traditional reward systems combined with systems associated with attachment and empathy.

Brain systems and mindreading. The brain's natural tendency to "mind-read," or to consider the minds of others (ToM) is an analytic-cognitive correlate of prosocial moral emotions. We saw in Chapter 4 that Atzil et al. (2013) found synchrony in the brain activations of mothers and fathers in areas including the MPFC, superior temporal sulcus (STS), inferior frontal gyrus (IFG), and insula which are implicated in empathy, ToM, mirroring, and intuitive understanding. Brain regions most associated with making inferences about the mental states of others include the MPFC (BA 10); temporoparietal junction (TPJ); posterior cingulate cortex (BA 23); retrosplenial area (BA 26, 29, 30); and precuneus (BA 7, 31). The latter three areas are contiguous and together comprise the posteriomedial cortices (PMC). Also, we saw in Chapter 6 that members of scorned groups elicited no MPFC system activation, and that men high in hostile sexism showed less activity in the MPFC, DMPFC, posterior cingulate cortex, and temporal poles when viewing pictures of women in bikinis (Cikara et al., 2010). The scorned persons and sexualized women were, in effect, perceived as objects.

Brain systems associated with prosocial emotions. A number of studies employing a variety of methods and designs have studied brain systems implicated in prosocial emotions. These have included studies involving social scenarios evoking guilt, pity, and embarrassment. For example, we saw that Moll et al. (2002) presented slides with moral content evoking prosocial emotions, versus non-moral content, and found that the prosocial emotion scenes produced activation in the right medial OFC, the medial frontal gyrus, and the right posterior superior temporal sulcus.

Other studies have studied brain responses associated with engaging in altruistic behaviors. For example, Moll et al. (2006) investigated the neural correlates of making charitable donations. They gave participants an initial endowment of US$128, and told them that additional funds were available for anonymous donations to charitable organizations. Participants were told that their decisions in the experiment would determine the final payoff to themselves and the organizations. On each trial, the name of an organization and brief mission statement were presented (e.g. "Death with Dignity: allowing euthanasia for the terminally ill") and the participant was given a choice with a specific payoff type. These were arranged so that the participant could Oppose or Donate to the organization, and that choice could be personally costly or non-costly. For Non-Costly Donation, the organization would receive US$5 and the participant would receive nothing; for Costly Donation, the organization would receive US$5 and the participant would lose US$2; for Costly Opposition, the organization would lose US$5 and the participant would lose US$2; for Non-Costly Opposition, the organization would lose US$5 and the participant would receive nothing; for Pure Reward the organization would get nothing and the participant would gain US$2. Costly Donation and Costly Opposition decisions were defined as altruistic because in both cases the participant would sacrifice for a societal cause: e.g. supporting or opposing a specific charitable organization. At the end of the study, participants indicated their feelings about the organization and its goals, rating both compassion and anger (sympathy and contempt?).

Results indicated that participants did make decisions costly to themselves, losing an average of 40 percent of their original endowment. Also, they rated organizations they donated to as higher in compassion, and those where they opposed donation as higher in anger. The mesolimbic reward system (e.g. the midbrain ventral tegmental area [VTA] medial forebrain bundle [MFB] and the dorsal and ventral striatum) were activated both by Pure Reward and decisions to donate. Moll et al. suggested that the ventral striatum finding is consistent with a hypothesized "joy of giving" or "warm glow" associated with making anonymous donations: the ventral striatum includes the nucleus accumbens (NAcc) "hedonic hotspot," and ventromedial parts of the caudate nucleus and putamen. Furthermore, the ventral striatum and adjoining septal regions were more strongly activated by donation than they were by Pure Reward. The authors concluded that two sorts of reward systems are involved in donating to social causes: the classic subcortical VTA/MFB associated with pure reward; and the paleocortical ventral striatum and septal regions associated with attachment and affiliation. The latter system was "specific for donations and plays key roles in social attachment and affiliative reward systems in humans and other animals" (Moll et al., 2006, p. 15624).

Using a similar methodology, Harbaugh et al. (2007) observed brain responses of female participants to both mandatory giving (analogous to taxation) and voluntary giving to a food bank. In the case of mandatory giving, both increased monetary payment to the participant (pure reward) and increased monetary payment to the food bank produced activation in the ventral striatum (caudate, NAcc, and insula). Consistent with the "warm glow" hypothesis, activity in the caudate and right NAcc and rated satisfaction were higher in the voluntary than the mandatory (taxation) situation. The investigators were able to measure the brain activity associated with conditions in which the reward went only to the food bank or only to the participant herself. Those with relatively more activation to payment to the self than to the charity (termed "egoists") were less likely to give to the charity voluntarily, while the opposite was true for those "altruists" with more striatum activation to payments to the charity than payments to themselves.

Brain systems and prosocial moral emotions during interaction. Prosocial emotions can emerge in interpersonal context in situations involving online cooperation and reciprocal exchange, and procedures have been developed to follow brain responding of two different individuals during such interaction. Kreuger et al. (2007) employed hyperfunctional magnetic resonance imaging (hyperfMRI) to measure the brain responses of two strangers of the same gender as they interacted in a sequential reciprocal trust game. In the game, participant 1 (P1) made an initial move to trust or not trust P2. If P2 was not trusted both P1 and P2 received a small reward ($US.05). If P2 was trusted, P2 could either *reciprocate*, in which case P1 received US$0.10 and P2 received US$0.15; or P2 could *defect*, in which case P1 received nothing and P2 received US$0.25. Participants played thirty-six rounds of non-anonymous games alternating in the roles of P1 and P2, therefore enabling a process of partner building and maintenance, and allowing the potential emergence (or not) of bidirectional trust. The study focused on the decision of P1 to trust, and the mechanisms underlying the emergence of *conditional trust*, which involves both partners developing a strategy assuming that the other is selfish; versus *unconditional trust*, in which both partners assume that the other is trustworthy. The game was divided in two stages: Stage 1 was assumed to involve partner building, and Stage 2, partner maintenance. Pairs were divided into *non-defectors*, in which neither participant defected, and *defectors*, in which some defection was experienced by the pair.

Results indicated that trust was higher in the non-defector group and that it increased over stages, while in the defector group trust decreased across stages. Decisions to trust on the part of P1 were associated with activity in the ACC (BA 9/32) and septal area. Non-defector (i.e. mutually trusting) pairs showed more such ACC activity in Stage 1 and a decrease in ACC activation across stages, while defector pairs showed low initial ACC activity and an increase from Stage 1 to Stage 2. Kreuger et al. (2007) suggested that this early ACC activation was associated with attempting to infer the intentions of the partner, which became less necessary in the non-defector pairs as unconditional trust was established. Also, non-defector pairs showed higher activation in the septal area in Stage 2, and brain-to-brain synchrony in septal area activation increased from Stage 1 to Stage 2 for non-defector pairs but not for defector pairs. Kreuger et al. (2007) suggested that this reflected the emergence of mutual goodwill and social bonding that was also reflected in post-experimental questionnaires in which those in non-defector pairs rated themselves as feeling closer to the partner.

In contrast, defector pairs appeared to adopt a conditional trust strategy whereby their trusting involved evaluating the risks and benefits of cooperation. This led to greater ACC activation and also greater activation of the VTA/MFB reward system in Stage 2 relative to non-defectors. The authors concluded that the ACC was critical in building a trusting relationship by being involved in empathy and inferring the intentions of the partner, and that this interacted with more primitive brain structures in maintaining trust. Conditional trust activated the VTA/MFB reward system associated with evaluating expected and actual reward; and unconditional trust activated the septal area associated with social attachment. The Krueger et al. (2007) study demonstrates how a trusting (or non-trusting) social relationship can emerge over the course of interaction.

Conclusions: doing well versus doing good

Converging evidence from a variety of studies using a variety of methodologies suggests that there are two dissociable albeit overlapping and presumably highly interactive sources of prosocial emotion systems with moral implications. The subcortical VTA/MFB-striatum reward system was considered in Chapter 3 as the Behavioral Activation System (BAS). It is associated with *wanting* in Berridge's analysis, and with the BIS it is involved in evaluating rewarding and punishing circumstances expected in a situation. It appears to involve positive selfish emotions activated with personal success: e.g. doing well.

In comparison, the septal/NAcc areas are subcortical regions that have been considered at several points in this book. MacLean considered the septal division of the limbic system to be associated with emotions concerned with the preservation of the species, e.g. prosocial emotions. The septal/NAcc areas are endorphinergic "hedonic hotspots" associated with Berridge's *liking*. Gorenstein and Newman (1980) noted that septal dysfunctions contribute symptoms similar to disinhibitory psychopathology in humans, including a lack of empathy, guilt, and remorse seen in psychopathy. The septal area both releases and contains receptors for the neuropeptides OXY and AVP, involved in attachment and social bonding. Thus, the septal/NAcc areas may involve "warm glow" prosocial emotions activated by altruistically helping others: e.g. doing good.

These two positive moral emotion systems – the VTA/MFB and septal/NAcc areas – appear to interact with systems of selfish other-critical emotions (anger, frustration, moral disgust) also associated with relatively primitive systems such as the amygdala and anterior insula. We saw in Chapter 3 that the functioning of both of these systems appears to be lateralized. Brain lateralization has not yet been systematically considered in the moral emotion literature, although it is noteworthy that many of the findings we have reviewed have specified right-sided brain structures.

Moll and Schulkin (2009) noted that although systems of social attachment and aversion are based upon evolutionarily ancient subcortical and paleocortical/limbic neurochemical systems, they are tightly integrated with control mechanisms in the frontal cortex, enabling complex prosocial and selfish moral sentiments involving "an intuitive sense of fairness, concern for others, and observance of cultural norms" (Moll et al., 2007b, p. 336). This sense of fairness includes mechanisms of attachment that underlie altruism and empathic concern involving the relatively primitive VTA/MFB and septal/NAcc systems that are tightly integrated with systems in the medial prefrontal cortex including the VMPFC and particularly the FPC. Anger and social disgust involve the amygdala and insula, which are integrated with systems in the lateral prefrontal cortex including lateral sectors of the DLPFC and OFC.

Thus, moral phenomena such as altruism arose, not from conflict between emotion and cognition, but from an integration of moral emotions – syncretic feelings and desires generated by the more primitive systems – and moral judgments – higher-order analytic-cognitive mechanisms involving for example perspective thinking, forecasting outcomes of events and actions, ToM, and the valuation of social choices. "Human altruism has drawn on general mammalian neural systems of reward, social attachment, and aversion. In the context of intertwined social and motivational contingencies, however, altruism tied to abstract moral beliefs relies on the uniquely developed human anterior prefrontal cortex" (Moll et al., 2006, p. 15626). Greater understanding of these systems and their interactions will hopefully help us, in Lieberman's terms (2007, p. 279), to increasingly "carve social processes at their joints."

Doing bad: psychopathy and antisocial personality disorder

The critical role of the subcortical and paleocortical brain systems in mediating moral emotions is of particular interest when considering brain mechanisms associated with psychopathy. Psychopathy is a personality disorder characterized by intact moral reasoning but impaired moral behaviors (Schaich Borg et al., 2011). It is associated with frequent moral transgressions, often involving violence, that are committed without remorse (Harenski and Kiehl, 2011). This emotional detachment differentiates psychopathy from antisocial personality disorder (APD), which involves rule-breaking but not necessarily with a lack of empathy. A well-known example of a sadistic sociopath is Ted Bundy, a charismatic, clean-cut college graduate and law student who confessed to raping and murdering thirty young women. Before his execution in 1989, he stated, "I didn't know what made things tick. I didn't know what made people want to be friends. I didn't know what made people attractive to one another. I didn't know what underlay social interaction" (Wray, 2010). All psychopaths are antisocial, but not all antisocial individuals are psychopaths.

Psychopathy is clinically defined by the Psychopathy Checklist-Revised (PCL-R), which includes items for rating behaviors such as impulsiveness, pathological lying, manipulativeness, and lack of guilt and empathy (Hare, 2003; Anderson and Kiehl, 2012). Understanding of the brain mechanisms involved in psychopathy has been greatly facilitated by research by Kent A. Kiehl and colleagues, who opened a brain research laboratory in a New Mexico prison. This research has implicated disorders in subcortical and paleocortical systems identified by other research on moral emotion: specifically, decreased gray matter has been found in the amygdala, hippocampus, temporal pole, posterior cingulate cortex, and orbitofrontal cortex (Ermer et al., 2012; Ly et.al., 2012; Kiehl, 2006).

Psychopathy relates to a number of issues considered in this book. First, psychopaths are low in inhibition, falling at the extreme right side of Figure 3.5. Their low autonomic responding may enable them to defeat conventional polygraph lie-detector methods. Moreover, they manifest an extreme of the detached style of attachment: recall that Robertson found that a detached style may be a reaction to long isolation from attachment and support (Bretherton, 1992), and indeed, early abuse and neglect are risk factors for psychopathy. As in other examples of brain–behavior relationships we have considered (e.g. gender differences, differences in liberals and conservatives), it is not necessarily the case that the brain abnormalities cause the behavior, and indeed the brain abnormalities may actually reflect experiences in socio-emotional development.

Primary moral emotions

An ecological-systems view of primary moral emotions

We have seen that a variety of words has been used to describe moral emotions. There is considerable overlap with what I have termed social emotions: shame, guilt, embarrassment, remorse, and pity, for example. As noted, the specifically named moral emotions studied this far are

	In oneself		In comparison other	
	Success	Failure	Success	Failure
Social Rules Social Expectations **Fair** (Norms, Roles) **Unfair** Fairness/Equity	Triumph	Humiliation	Admiration	Contempt
	Modesty	Indignation	Resentment	Sympathy

Figure 7.2 The structure of the primary moral emotions. Emotional responses when outcomes to self (P) and comparison other (CO) are judged to be fair or unfair based upon social rules and expectations.

almost uniformly negative. Empathy and altruism are often used to describe positive moral states, but these are not moral emotions per se.

Based upon the ecological systems model, we can offer definitions of *primary moral emotions* that are analogous in general justification to the primary social emotions considered in Chapter 6. Like social emotions, moral emotions are viewed as self-organizing systems naturally emerging from social interaction. Moral emotions are based in ecologically fundamental combinations of interpersonal contingencies experienced by the self (P) versus the comparison other (CO), but instead of involving relative comparisons of positive and negative outcomes of being loved/meeting expectations, the moral emotions involve relative comparisons of positive and negative outcomes that are seen to be fair or unfair. This concept of fairness to self and other is similar to N. T. Feather's (2006) *outcome deservingness* for self and other, and Feather et al. (2011) reported on emotion ratings to scenarios that differed in deservingness and positive and negative outcomes to self and others.

From the viewpoint of the ecological-systems model, if a positive outcome to the self is seen by P as fair, the moral emotion is *triumph*; if it is unfair, the moral emotion is *modesty*. If a negative outcome to the self is seen by P as fair, the moral emotion is *humiliation*; if it is unfair, the moral emotion is *indignation*. If a positive outcome to the CO is seen by P as fair, the moral emotion is *admiration*; if it is unfair, the moral emotion is *resentment*. If a negative outcome to the CO is seen by P as fair, the moral emotion is *contempt*; if it is unfair, the moral emotion is *sympathy* (see Figure 7.2).

The dynamics of primary moral emotions
The ecological-systems analysis implies that, as with the primary social emotions, each primary moral emotion is related to others in specific

respects. Again, this is due to the natural structure of fundamental interpersonal contingencies, combined with the influence of an essential sense of fairness/unfairness. First, each primary social emotion associated with fair outcomes has a twin associated with unfair outcomes: triumph is the twin of modesty, humiliation is the twin of indignation, admiration is the twin of resentment, and contempt is the twin of sympathy.

Second, each primary moral emotion associated with success has an opposite associated with failure. Triumph is the opposite of humiliation, modesty is the opposite of indignation, admiration is the opposite of contempt, and resentment is the opposite of sympathy.

Third, each primary moral emotion has a reciprocal, such that if a person P feels X about him/herself, P would tend to feel its reciprocal toward a comparison other. Triumph is the reciprocal of contempt: that is, triumphant P would tend to have contempt for the CO. Similarly, modesty is the reciprocal of sympathy, humiliation is the reciprocal of admiration, and indignation is the reciprocal of resentment.

Fourth, each primary moral emotion has a converse, which is the opposite of the reciprocal. P would tend *not* to feel the converse about a CO. For example, triumphant P would tend *not* to be admiring of a CO. Similarly, modesty is the converse of resentment, humiliation is the converse of contempt, and indignation is the converse of sympathy.

Again, from the ecological-systems analysis one can make specific hypotheses about the dynamics of primary moral emotions. If one experiences a given primary moral emotion, it is:

1. Likely that one would simultaneously experience its twin (positive correlation).
2. Unlikely that one would experience its opposite (negative correlation).
3. Likely that one would experience its reciprocal toward others (positive correlation).
4. Unlikely that one would experience its converse toward others (negative correlation).

Furthermore, this analysis implies that if P feels a given primary moral emotion about him/herself, a CO would tend to experience a pattern of mirror primary moral emotions in comparison. It is unlikely that a CO will experience the same mirror emotion as P, or its twin. If P is successful in exceeding expectations and feels triumphant, a CO would not tend to feel triumph or modesty. Similarly, humiliation, indignation, admiration, resentment, sympathy, and contempt in P would tend to discourage similar emotions in a CO. Rather, a CO would tend to feel the mirror-opposite of P's emotion: that is, triumph/modesty in

P would tend to encourage feelings of humiliation/indignation in a CO toward P in comparison. On the other hand, P's humiliation/indignation would encourage triumph/modesty in a CO. Moreover, P's admiration/resentment would encourage a CO's contempt/sympathy; and likewise P's contempt/sympathy would encourage a CO's admiration/resentment.

Similarly, a CO would tend *not* to feel the mirror-reciprocal of the moral emotion experienced by P. Triumph/modesty in P would tend to discourage sympathy/contempt in a CO, P's humiliation/indignation would discourage a CO's admiration/resentment. Likewise, sympathy/contempt in P would tend to discourage triumph/modesty in a CO, P's admiration/resentment would discourage a CO's humiliation/indignation. On the other hand, a CO would be likely to feel the mirror-converse of the moral emotion experienced by P. Triumph/modesty in P would tend to encourage admiration/resentment in a CO, and P's humiliation/indignation would encourage a CO's contempt/sympathy. Likewise, admiration/resentment in P would tend to feed triumph/modesty in a CO, and P's sympathy/contempt would encourage a CO's humiliation/indignation.

One can thus specify several additional hypotheses about the dynamics of primary moral emotions. If P experiences a given primary moral emotion, the comparison other is:

5. Unlikely to simultaneously experience that emotion or its twin (negative correlation).
6. Likely to experience its mirror-opposite (positive correlation).
7. Unlikely to experience its mirror-reciprocal (negative correlation).
8. Likely to experience its mirror-converse (positive correlation).

Thus, triumphant/modest P will tend to have sympathy/contempt for the admiring/resentful other, who will feel humiliation/indignation. Figure 7.3 illustrates the case where triumphant P on the left judges outcomes to be fair, and has contempt for the CO on the right. The CO judges the outcomes to be unfair, and responds with indignation and resentment toward P.

Research on primary moral emotions

In contrast with the literature on social emotions, there is relatively little literature concerned with relating and differentiating the moral emotions vis-à-vis one another. However, examination of these terms suggests that such investigation might be fruitful.

Triumph. Triumph can be defined generally as a positive emotional state celebrating a significant victory over a difficult challenge. In

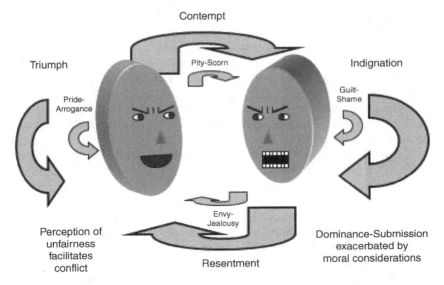

Figure 7.3 Dynamics of moral emotions. Interaction partner P on left perceives unequal outcomes favoring P to be fair and O on right perceives them to be unfair.

triumph, the positive outcome to the self is seen as fair; essentially "I did this and I deserve this!" As such, it is a stronger form of pride, but the typical display of triumph has significant differences from the display of pride, as Matsumoto and Hwang (2012) demonstrated in an analysis of successful Olympic and Paralympic athletes. Specifically, whereas pride typically is associated with a small smile, triumph is associated with a facial grimace or aggressiveness. In pride the head is tilted back, in triumph it is tilted forward. As with pride, the posture shows the torso out and the chest is expanded. Unlike pride, with triumph the arms are raised above the shoulder in a punching motion, and there is a vocal shout or utterance. Matsumoto and Hwang suggested that a possible function of the triumph display was to signal intimidation. Similarly, Aviezer et al. (2012) found body cues, but not facial expressions, discriminated between expressions of triumph and humiliation. Recall that App et al. (2011) found body cues to be more effective than facial and touch cues in displaying dominance status.

As the ecological-systems model regards pride to be a display not only of pride, but of a whole system of social emotions (e.g. of having pity/scorn as well, but *not* being guilty/ashamed or envious/jealous), the same is true of the display of triumph: it is a display of the *system* of moral emotions. It implies feeling contempt/sympathy for the beaten, but *not* feeling humiliation/indignation or admiration/resentment.

Modesty. Modesty is suggested as a "twin" of triumph, in which P succeeds but does not perceive the success to be deserved. Similar terms include "humility" and "simplicity." Expressions of modesty are often expected at times of great success, as the content of innumerable acceptance speeches given at award ceremonies attest. Feather et al. (2011) had a different take on undeserved positive outcome to the self, associating it with guilt and regret.

There is relatively little research devoted to the study of modesty, but its importance in moderating displays of triumph seems evident. In the ecological-systems model, displays of triumph/modesty are likely to be met with their mirror-converse, admiration/resentment, on the part of COs, and one might hypothesize that expressions of modesty might act to reduce resentment and increase admiration. On the other hand, judgments that expressions of modesty are insincere ("false modesty") may be likely to be associated with resentment.

Humiliation. Humiliation involves the judgment that one has failed and that failure is deserved. It is the opposite of triumph and is often displayed as a stronger version of the shame display, with the same submissive posture but with hiding of the face and perhaps weeping. Athletes often display such expressions in the "agony of defeat."

There is interest in the role of humiliation and powerlessness as key factors in the emotional dynamics of oppression (Deutsch, 2006; www.humiliationstudies.org/). Humiliation has been seen as a pervasive and destructive influence which poisons relationships between individuals, groups, and nations; and is a major weapon in the oppression of women, people of color, and other stigmatized groups. Indeed, Lindner (2009) termed humiliation the "nuclear bomb of the emotions." Humiliation has been suggested as a key cause of conflict (Deutsch, 2006), and research has linked humiliation with such diverse but vital issues as adolescent aggression in school (Åslund et al., 2009) and the willingness to act as suicide bombers in the Middle East (Fattah and Fierke, 2009).

Klein (1991) pointed out that what he termed the "humiliation dynamic" demands a victim and a humiliator, as well as a (real or imagined) bystander who witnesses the fact that someone is being rendered helpless. Klein suggested that the very potency of this dynamic is demonstrated by its active denial by the victim. There is a pervasive failure to acknowledge that one is humiliated, particularly among males. The acknowledgement that one is humiliated is, in and of itself, humiliating. As a result, humiliation tends to be not expressed directly, but indirectly in its twin indignation and reciprocal admiration/resentment. This may result in rage and violence, rarely directly toward the oppressor but more typically toward a target at hand that is weak or identified as an out-group member or adversary (Scheff and Retzinger, 1991).

When people are in a position of having little power, there is a risk that they may be intentionally or unintentionally treated in humiliating ways even by individuals and groups (such as social agencies) intended to help them. Because humiliation is rarely acknowledged, this may not be evident. However, emotions opposite to humiliation – triumph, pride, and power – can be measured. In one study, enrollees in a job-training program for at-risk inner-city youth were interviewed about their experiences in the program, including their feelings in terms of how often they had felt specific emotions as part of their involvement with the program. Results revealed that success in the program was not associated with life satisfaction, self-esteem, or most positive or negative emotions. Success was, however, associated with higher ratings of positive power emotions (feeling powerful, strong, and confident), suggesting that the program succeeded if it *worked against* feelings of humiliation and resentment (Singer et al., 2011). In light of indications that humiliation is a key factor in oppression and conflict, this suggests that the role of such emotions in the success of programs intended to help is important and in need of investigation. More generally, this finding suggests that program evaluation should explicitly consider emotional factors – particularly the humiliation dynamic – in assessing program success and effectiveness.

Indignation. The ecological systems approach predicts that Klein's (1991) humiliation dynamic would often involve its twin moral emotion, indignation. Indignation occurs when P regards negative outcomes to the self to be unfair. A common tactic for turning humiliation into indignation is to perceive that CO's victory broke the rules, perhaps by blaming the referee in the case of a closely contested game, or blaming social conditions in the case of oppression. I noted previously the role of new communication technology in the Arab Spring of 2011. The release of suppressed passions that has been widely acknowledged to have motivated this widespread social movement may have been due in great part to the transformation of humiliation to indignation via communication, such that people began simultaneously to define their situation as unfair and to communicate that to their friends.

Admiration. Admiration, involving the judgment that CO's success is deserved, has been considered in several emotion theories. Darwin defined it as "surprise associated with some pleasure and a sense of approval" (1998, p. 269), and Ortony et al. (1998) included it as among the "appreciation emotions" along with appreciation, awe, esteem, and respect. Feather et al. (2011) associated admiration with a deserved positive outcome. Admiration was included as one of the "other-praising" emotions by Haidt (2003), who defined it as the "emotional response to non-moral excellence" (Algoe and Haidt, 2009, p. 107). Algoe and Haidt suggested that admiration is inspirational, stimulating the observer to try to do better. On the other hand, van den Ven et al. (2011) suggested that the response to admiration is more passive, and that envy is more likely to stimulate performance.

It is an interesting implication of the ecological-systems model that admiration is the reciprocal of humiliation, so that we would expect them to be positively related. This seems paradoxical at first glance, but there is evidence that social humiliation may produce tendencies to submit to a strong and charismatic leader. So, the humiliation/indignation dynamic may be associated both with admiration of a strong leader who promises to set things right, and resentment against anyone perceived to be a source of unfairness in one's outcomes. For example, the rise of the Nazi party in 1930s Germany involved the simultaneous resentment of Jews and the terms of the Treaty of Versailles, and admiration of Adolph Hitler; and the Arab Spring may have similarly involved resentment to established authoritarian rulers and simultaneous admiration of emergent charismatic leaders.

Neural correlates of admiration and compassion have been explored by asking participants to view compelling audio/video narratives about real people, 60 to 90 seconds long, designed to evoke admiration or compassion (Immordino-Yang et al., 2009). *Admiration for values* was manipulated by showing people performing highly admirable and virtuous acts; *admiration for skill* was manipulated by showing people performing rare and difficult physical feats; *compassion for social pain* was manipulated by showing people experiencing grief, rejection, or despair; and *compassion for physical pain* was manipulated by showing people experiencing physical injury. Participants were later asked to relive the emotions they felt to the narratives while in the fMRI. Results revealed that, compared to a neutral control narrative, reliving admiration and compassion was associated with activation in subcortical and paleocortical systems including the hypothalamus, mesencephalon, ACC, and anterior insula. Also, both admiration and compassion activated the posteriomedial cortices (PMC) associated with mind-reading. Interestingly, the narratives associated with the psychological state of the other (*admiration for values* and *compassion for social pain*) particularly activated the inferior/posterior portion of the PMC; while those associated with the physical state of the other (*admiration for skill* and *compassion for physical pain*) activated only the superior/anterior portion of the PMC. The authors suggested that these observations provide initial insight into the neural differentiation of higher-level emotions.

Resentment. Feather et al. (2011) associated resentment with a negative outcome to the self or a positive outcome to CO that is undeserved. In the ecological-systems model, the response to an undeserved negative outcome to the self is termed "indignation," and resentment is its reciprocal: indignant P resents the unfair relative success of CO. The model predicts that resentment is a likely output of Klein's (1991) humiliation dynamic, as indignation is the twin of humiliation. Also in the ecological-systems model, resentment is held to be the twin of admiration. This may be controversial because admiration is generally seen to be strongly positive and resentment strongly negative. However, they both do relate to judging CO as relatively successful; it is the fairness of the success that is different, and it is not difficult to imagine admiration tinged with resentment.

Contempt. In the ecological systems model, contempt is P's response to a deserved negative outcome to CO. Contempt was one of the original eight primary affects in Tomkins' theory, paired with disgust as disgust/contempt. The facial expression associated with contempt was asymmetrical, with the corner of the lip tightened and raised on one side of the face more than the other. In a study of the effects of facial expressions during an acquaintance period preceding a Prisoner's Dilemma game, facial expressions of happiness were predictive of cooperation; while expressions of contempt on the part of a sender were related both to defection on the part of the sender and defection on the part of the receiver (Reed et al., 2012). Apparently, the sender's spontaneous display of contempt was accurately detected by the receiver, and more generally, in the acquaintance period participants were able to detect the trustworthiness of their partners via nonverbal communication (Boone and Buck, 2003).

Sympathy. Feather et al. (2011) associated sympathy with a negative outcome to CO that is undeserved, which parallels its definition in the ecological systems model. Feather (2006) reported that participants reported sympathy for a person given a failing grade if the student was deserving of success (e.g. had previously had success based on hard work) and the failure was due to a difficult exam rather than partying before the exam.

A number of studies have analyzed "compassion" as a moral emotion, but as compassion often seems to go beyond considerations of fairness and equity, I suggest "sympathy" as the term in ecological-systems theory. Nevertheless, some studies of compassion arguably apply to sympathy, including the Immordino-Yang et al. (2009) fMRI study summarized previously under admiration. It is noteworthy that Immordino-Yang et al.'s results did not distinguish between the fMRI responses to the attempted manipulation of admiration versus compassion.

From the viewpoint of the ecological-systems model, the communication of sympathy should be important because it expresses that P considered whatever reverse was suffered by CO to be unfair and undeserved. Haidt and Keltner (1999) suggested a facial display of sympathy blending sadness and concerned attention (Eisenberg et al., 1989). However, that is disputed: Widen et al. (2011) could not find evidence for a facial display reliably linked with sympathy/compassion. However, it is possible that compassion is displayed in other ways. App et al. (2011) suggested that compassion is best displayed by touch, as opposed to facial or body expression. That is consistent with the view presented in Chapter 1 that intimate emotions are best displayed and communicated at intimate distances (e.g. Miller, 2012). Several studies have in fact found that sympathy could be accurately communicated, primarily by patting and stroking (Hertenstein et al., 2006a, 2006b, 2009; Thompson and Hampton, 2011).

There is evidence suggesting important gender differences in the experience and expression of sympathy. Hertenstein and Keltner (2011) found that communication of sympathy by touch required at least one female in a dyad. Mercadillo et al. (2011) presented pictures of human suffering known to elicit sympathy/compassion. This study, conducted in Mexico, found no gender difference in self-reported compassion, and both women and men showed activity in the PFC (BA 46, 47), left ACC (BA 24, 32), precuneus (BA 7), and insula (BA 13), which is similar in pattern to other studies of prosocial decision-making. Women showed a greater diversity of activation patterns in the basal ganglia and thalamus, as well as relatively greater activation in prefrontal (BA 46, 47), left ACC (BA 24, 32), and cerebellar regions. Women but not men showed activation in the left superior frontal gyrus (BA 9, 10) and left thalamus. Men but not women showed activation in the parahippocampal cortex (BA 36). The authors concluded that sympathy/compassion in women is accomplished by more elaborate brain processing than in men. Perhaps the morality of caring activates different brain systems than the morality of justice, at least when stimulated by challenging visual images.

Sympathy and contempt are seen to be twins: both responding to negative outcomes to CO. For most twin moral emotions – triumph/modesty, humiliation/indignation, and admiration/resentment – the model predicts that they will tend to be positively correlated across persons and situations. However, we saw this was not found for the purported twin social emotions, pity and scorn. These were negatively related in both American and Japanese participants. This was related to alternative ways of viewing those less fortunate on the part of left- and right-wing political ideologies. Recall Lakoff's (1996) and Haidt's (2003) analyses noted in Chapter 6: liberals tend to blame poverty and other negative social outcomes upon social conditions, while conservatives tend to emphasize individual failings. The same may well be true of the purported twin moral emotions, sympathy and contempt.

Attachment security and moral emotions. We saw in the last chapter that individual differences in attachment security alter the abilities to engage successfully in compassion-focused imagery (CFI: Gilbert, 2010). Engaging in CFI was associated with calming in securely-attached participants, but threat in anxiously-attached participants (Rockliff et al., 2008). And, although OXY significantly increased abilities to imagine compassion in the group as a whole, less secure participants had a more negative experience of CFI under OXY than they did under placebo (Rockliff et al., 2011). Also, Cardoso et al. (2012) found that the effect of intranasal OXY on the mood response to interpersonal stress is moderated by coping style: only women high in emotion-oriented coping (e.g. anxious attachment) showed anxiety decrease following OXY. These results support the proposition that the attachment security of the responder is a critical factor in the differentiation of social emotions.

Other evidence suggests that changes in security versus threat in a society can lead to widespread changes in moral emotions. Social threat can encourage a kind of morality that hearkens back to the authoritarian morality of the child: the morality of subjugation, where the attack, conquest, and even destruction of the enemy become a moral obligation.

The morality of subjugation: authoritarianism and pseudospeciation

We saw in Chapter 4 that attachment is one of the great motivational-emotional systems at the heart of human nature and communication, and there is compelling and converging evidence supporting the *empathy-altruism hypothesis*: that the expression of needs by CO naturally evokes empathic emotions of sympathy and compassion that motivate altruistic responses. Even though the empathy–altruism relationship has been reliably demonstrated, it is all too apparent that human beings do not always help others in need. Batson and Oleson (1991) noted that there are "strong forces working against the arousal of empathy. These include anything and everything that makes it difficult for us to attend to or value another person's welfare" (p. 81). Failing to notice the other's needs, or seeing the other as different from oneself – as "them" rather than "us" – are common. In fact, there is a dark side of the "cuddle hormone" OXY. There is evidence that OXY not only increased trust, empathic concern and interactive synchrony; but also the categorization of others into in-group and out-group (De Dreu, 2012), maternal aggression in defense of the young (Neumann, 2008), and envy or gloating when an opponent was more successful or failed (Shamay-Tsoory et al., 2009).

Schadenfreude: *the dark side of morality*

Exceptions to the empathy–altruism hypothesis go beyond the failure to help the person in need. In some cases people seem to take pleasure in the distress of others: *schadenfreude* (Ben-Ze'ev, 1992). We have seen that a lack of attachment may produce a pattern of psychopathy, where "cold" moral judgment is possible but moral affect is not, but *schadenfreude* is not confined to psychopaths. We noted how televised images of starving Ethiopian children generated world-wide pity, sympathy, compassion, and altruistic action. On the other hand, televised images of a dead American soldier being dragged through the streets of Mogadishu, Somalia, in 1993 generated a very different response in many American viewers: rage, disgust, and deep resentment that might motivate very different responses. Although quite the opposite of altruistic responses, such responses are nonetheless "moral" in the sense that they stem from a sense of injustice. If the persons rejoicing in the death of the American soldier had themselves been suddenly struck down, the response of the American television audience might have involved considerable *schadenfreude*. This is the dark side of morality: the morality that perhaps underlies Lorenz's (1966) *militant enthusiasm* to bond with friend and to subjugate foe. Such dark passions can be stirred by propaganda that presents the world in black and white terms: we are good, they are bad. Such propaganda would be enhanced if it simultaneously stimulated feelings of envy, jealousy, humiliation, and/or resentment toward the enemy.

Some of the darkest and most violent examples of human behavior stem from the morality of subjugation. From earliest human history, entire peoples have been decimated by war, typically for the glory of one god or another. The weak have been subjected to brutal and vicious witch hunts, lynchings, and pogroms, which are not only socially sanctioned but acclaimed. Victims have been made to endure excruciating torture, presumably as a favor to save their souls. The incredible organized horror of the Holocaust was unfortunately not an aberration but an ordinary occurrence in human history in every respect save for its enormous industrial scale and hideous efficiency. Similar events in Bosnia, Cambodia, and Central Africa give grim testimony that socially approved brutality and atrocity toward out-groups are typical of the human species. Such behavior – depraved, iniquitous, despicable but arguably not "immoral" – perhaps reveals the essence of evil.

Equalitarian morality cannot rationalize *schadenfreude*, but the foe is not viewed as a peer worthy of trust, respect, or even mercy. Instead the individual in the grip of militant enthusiasm hearkens back to the authoritarian morality of the child, with its justification of power and expiatory punishment. Friends, the in-group, take on the character of the family, the children of God; while the foe is the incarnation of evil. It is revealing that this return to an authoritarian morality appears to be related to threats to the self-image, often associated with social change and disruption that may challenge attachment security.

The authoritarian personality. The study of authoritarianism began as an attempt to measure the psychological roots of prejudice. T. W. Adorno and colleagues assumed that people are receptive to political ideologies that allow them to express deep-lying personality dispositions (Adorno et al., 1950). They first developed scales to measure ideologies associated with prejudice: anti-Semitism, ethnocentrism, and political-economic conservatism. These were positively correlated with each other in samples of middle-class, white, non-Jewish, native-born Americans. The investigators then studied in clinical interviews persons who differed in ethnocentrism. Themes were found which served as the basis of the development of a new scale which did not directly assess attitudes about minority groups or political issues, but rather a pattern of beliefs that emerged from the clinical data. The result was the *Fascism (F) Scale* (Brown, 1965).

The themes that emerged in the clinical interviews included *conventionalism*, a rigid adherence to middle-class values; *authoritarian submission*, the desire to submit to strong leaders; *authoritarian aggression*, a tendency to condemn and attack unconventional persons; *power and toughness*, the belief that power can solve all problems; *anti-intraception*, opposition to introspection and imagination; *superstition*, an exaggerated belief in mystical forces and the supernatural; *destructiveness and cynicism*, a generalized hostility and low view of human nature; *projectivity*, the attribution of one's own unacceptable impulses to others, and *sex*, a preoccupation with the imagined sexual activities of others. Adorno and colleagues argued that these beliefs are not logically related, but rather are related through dynamic psychological processes. Specifically, they suggested that harsh discipline on the part of parents causes the child to *repress* hostile feelings toward the parents, sexual desires, and personal faults and shortcomings. The repression leads to anti-intraception and to the projection of sexual desires and shortcomings to powerless minorities and outsiders. Also, the repressed hostility toward the parents is *displaced* toward the weak outsiders, and the projection functions to *rationalize* aggressive behaviors.

Prejudiced behavior. Later research suggested that most prejudice is based upon conformity rather than personality (Pettigrew, 1961), and that it may be contemporary threat, rather than threat during childhood, that is responsible for authoritarian tendencies (Rokeach, 1960). Doty et al. distinguished "dispositional authoritarians," who are intrinsically inclined to accept and encourage authoritarian organizations and activities, and "situational authoritarians," who adopt or reject authoritarian behaviors according to the "climate of threat" (1991, p. 639). This view is consistent with the analysis of social movements made by a number of sociologists and political scientists, including Brinton (1938), Hoffer (1951), Kornhauser (1959), and Lipset (1960). These authors claimed that revolutionary social movements are based upon complex problems that threaten security and that a group cannot deal with. The complex problems go unrecognized, and the group in question instead focuses on pseudoproblems that are concrete, simple, and easy to deal with. The discontented group may feel that their irritation is caused by minority groups, particularly when a history of conflict is present, but they may also blame the federal government, the United Nations, socialists, the gold standard, or whatever (Allport, 1954).

Attachment theory and authoritarianism

The description of the authoritarian personality is more in keeping with the descriptions of anxious/ambivalent and avoidant attached individuals than it is securely attached persons. Anxious/ambivalent individuals show a simultaneous longing for warm relationships and intense anger in relationships; avoidant persons manifest suppression and repression of attachment thoughts, affects, and needs; and both manifest a basic insecurity and pessimism and lack a sense of mastery (Mikulincer, 1997; Shaver and Hazan, 1993). Such characteristics could well support many authoritarian characteristics. Thus, all else being equal, one would expect that securely attached persons would not show authoritarian characteristics. On the other hand, contemporary threat may undermine secure attachment, fostering insecurity and pessimism and undermining relationships. It makes sense that anxious-ambivalent and avoidant persons may be more disposed to authoritarian tendencies than securely attached persons. However, a climate of threat may decrease security and encourage authoritarian tendencies in all.

Authoritarian tendencies and social threat. The notion that threat increases authoritarian tendencies has been supported both in experiments (Sales and Friend, 1973) and in studies of archival data on a social level. Sales (1972) found that conversions to authoritarian churches increased during the Great Depression and during an economic upheaval in Seattle, Washington; while conversions to non-authoritarian churches declined. In comparing the threatening 1930s with the less threatening 1920s in the United States, Sales (1973) found increases in a number of indications of authoritarian tendencies. These included power-oriented comic-strip characters such as Superman, cynicism in magazine articles, books and articles on astrology, loyalty oaths for teachers, suppression of erotic materials, less popular interest in psychology and psychiatry, and increased funding for police relative to fire departments (despite reduced crime). This evidence that the authoritarian syndrome increases in times of social threat has been supported in studies of television programming in the United States (Jorgenson, 1975) and Mexico (Robertson, 1976), and of Germany in the years between 1918 and 1940 (Padgett and Jorgenson, 1982). Also, Doty et al. (1991) studied data from the United States where a high threat period (1978–82) was followed by a period of low threat (1983–87).

These archival studies supported Erich Fromm's (1941) thesis in *The Escape from Freedom* that social threat produces self-doubt and feelings of powerlessness and isolation that can lead to the renunciation of personal freedom and submission to a messianic group with powerful leaders. This may be relevant to our current experience of a rise of religious fundamentalism around the world. The universality of this phenomenon suggests the functioning of basic human qualities. The strong emotional need of human beings to conform to what is expected and valued – and thereby to be proud, accepted, and loved – is put under enormous stress by changes in the rules that are not understood and thus cannot be accommodated.

The yearning for a traditional authoritarian morality in response to breakdown of the social order may be species-typical: a feature of human nature. In *Suicide* (1897), sociologist Émile Durkheim described *anomie* as a lack of social norms or shared expectations, resulting in a breakdown of social bonds between individuals and their communities, with a resulting rejection of accepted social standards, values, and practices, and consequent fragmentation of social identity. We have seen that powerful motives to attach and bond constitute a virtual addiction in human beings and other social animals. In human beings this addiction brings about needs to bond, and consequent regulation of behavior by rules, norms, and roles (e.g. expectations structured by language), and these form the basis for self-identity. Thus, the consequences when these rules no longer apply can be devastating. Self-esteem and the ability to act in ways to please others and win affection are founded on knowing and implementing these rules, and when they are questioned it can threaten the very meaning of life. The individual is, in effect, stripped of identity. In response, the individual may cease to trust and respect others and instead fall back upon authoritarian morality: becoming a "true believer," finding a new basis of self-esteem, identity, acceptance, affection, and action in a mass movement headed by a strong, charismatic, and admired leader (Hoffer, 1951).

Humiliation to admiration? I noted previously that one aspect of the ecological-systems model is the reciprocal relationship of humiliation and admiration, which suggests that there might be a tendency of humiliated people to admire others, perhaps particularly if the other is triumphant and expresses sympathy to the humiliated person. Could this be a factor in the tendency of humiliated people to submit to a charismatic leader? We have seen that rejection, exclusion, and ostracism are extremely painful, and that they relate to humiliation, anomie, deindividuation, and a general loss of a social structuring of an individual's life. Would a strong leader with simple answers have a particular appeal to such persons?

Attachment theory and aggression

Pseudospeciation. The identification with a mass movement generally implies the rejection of and hostility toward outsiders. A pattern of cooperation with group members and hostility toward outsiders is a common feature not only of human beings but other social mammals including canids (wild dogs, wolves, coyotes), monkeys, and apes. Intragroup aggression is typically regulated via a dominance hierarchy involving displays of threat and submission, but there is open hostility and conflict between groups. Eibl-Eibesfeldt (1979) suggested that members of other groups are often treated as if they were, in effect, members of other species. This phenomenon is termed *pseudospeciation*, and he argued that it allows human beings to attack humans from other groups with a minimum of inhibition. For example, we saw in Chapter 4 that the pattern of relative cooperation within the group can be combined with deadly hostility toward outsiders (Goodall, 1986).

Deindividuation. Pseudospeciation allows other groups to be attacked with a minimum of inhibition. Such a loss of inhibition is a central feature of *deindividuation*, a concept with roots in LeBon's (1896) analysis of the violent excesses of the street crowds during the French Revolution. LeBon argued that in crowds people lose their individual identities and become part of a homogeneous mass: the *group mind*. A number of studies have confirmed that aggressive behavior increases when people lose self-awareness and see themselves as anonymous (Prentice-Dunn and Rogers, 1980, 1982, 1983; Rogers and Prentice-Dunn, 1981;

Zimbardo, 1969). This is one of the explanations for the abusive behavior observed in a well-known simulated prison experiment conducted at Stanford University in 1971 (Haney et al., 1973). Also, Watson (1973) found that cultures who alter the appearance of warriors prior to battle with masks, face and body painting, and special haircutting, show evidence of more extreme forms of aggression in warfare: killing without quarter, torturing, sacrificing, and mutilating the enemy. Mullen (1986) studied newspaper reports of incidents of lynching, and found that as the number in the lynch mob increased (increasing deindividuation), the degree of atrocity associated with the lynching increased.

We have considered a number of fortunately rare cases in which limbic brain abnormalities trigger aggressive reactions, such as Limbic Psychotic Trigger Reaction (LPTR) and temporal lobe epilepsy (TLE); and psychopathy where long-term deficits in emotional development and socialization are associated with physical traces in the thinning of gray matter in limbic areas. Pseudospeciation and deindividuation, however, occur among "normal" persons, and some of the most destructive and unacceptable manifestations of aggression – lynchings, pogroms, massacres – involve attacks by normal people on the weak and defenseless. Pseudospeciation and deindividuation are related ways in which equalitarian moral constraints can be put aside, at least for the time being, allowing an individual to behave pitilessly without regard to the rules that normally regulate behavior within the group. In pseudospeciation, an outsider is treated as a member of a different species, the usual submissive displays effective within the group are ignored, and sympathy and compassion are denied. In deindividuation, the individual is caught up in the strong spontaneous emotion of the group, and loses awareness of self and the moral affects and linguistically structured rules that normally regulate behavior. In both cases, the moral emotions of a normally socialized person are set aside, and the person becomes functionally a psychopath. But it is important to emphasize that these behaviors while reprehensible are not, in a sense, "immoral." They are, instead, a natural outgrowth of the authoritarian morality of the child, the reversion to which may be a species-typical response of human beings to a fundamental threat to security.

Syndrome E. Itzhak Fried (1997) considered a number of examples where vulnerable members of society have been violently attacked, including the Holocaust in Europe, the Pol Pot massacres in Cambodia in the 1970s, and the Rwandan genocide in the 1990s. He suggested that each case demonstrated a recurring tendency for normal individuals – usually men aged 15–50 – to become transformed into pitiless killers. Due to the uniform nature of this transformation he suggested a common syndrome termed *Syndrome E*. The syndrome is characterized above all by repetitive acts of violence with a compulsion to spare none of the victims, typically in group settings and often involving flat affect or a sense of elation. Some hesitation in the early stages of violence may occur, but desensitization is rapid: conformity increases the apparent uniformity of the group and further increases the power of social influence. Typically this behavior occurs with the approval or encouragement of authority figures. Language, memory, planning, and problem-solving skills remain intact in the perpetrators. Fried suggests that this syndrome is a manifestation "not of a primitive visceral brain released from cortical inhibition, but of a hyperaroused prefrontal cortex disconnected from the regulatory subcortical centres." He concluded: "Thus the prefrontal cortex, the brain region most responsible for the development of human faculties, is also implicated in the most atrocious human behaviour" (Fried, 1998, p. 830).

Liberal vs. conservative morality

Threat versus security. We have encountered differences in motivational-emotional functioning associated with liberal versus conservative attitudes previously, and it dovetails in many respects with the individualist/selfish versus cooperative/prosocial distinction between emotions. These differences also relate to essential concerns with threat as opposed to security. In Chapter 4 we saw that the question of whether human beings are essentially good or evil influenced the conception of the state of nature and the social contract. Thomas Hobbes argued that the state of nature involved a war of all against all, and the social contract was established as a universal peace treaty; while John Locke suggested that people in the state of nature lived together peacefully without leaders according to reason and natural law. Bertrand Russell (1945) argued that these conceptions relate to the basic foundations of modern conservatism and liberalism. Conservatives have historically taken a more pessimistic view of human nature as essentially selfish, requiring constraints by authority and tradition; while liberals tend to have an optimistic view of human perfectibility, preferring the greatest possible freedom of the individual.

In Chapter 3 we reviewed the Kanai et al. (2011) finding of a larger amygdala in persons with a right-wing political orientation, and a larger ACC in those with a left-wing orientation. This is consistent with other evidence that conservatives are often motivated by threat and liberals by sympathy and empathy. For example, Dodd et al. (2012) found that conservatives showed greater physiological responses to threatening images and liberals were more responsive to the positive images. Also, Dawes et al. (2012) found that tendencies toward egalitarian and altruistic behavior correlated with the activation of the left anterior insula associated with empathy and a sense of fairness. Recall that anterior insula activation was found both when a participant rejected unfair offers (Sanfey et al., 2003) and in situations involving admiration and compassion (Immorodino-Yang et al., 2009; Mercadillo et al., 2011). It might be hypothesized that the right and left anterior insula play different roles in this process, with the right more associated with selfish moral disgust and the left with prosocial empathy and altruism.

In Chapter 6 we saw that Buck et al. (2005) found a negative relationship between pity and scorn, suggesting that there are alternative ways of responding to the less fortunate. Based upon the work of Lakoff (1996) and Haidt (2003) it was suggested that liberals may tend to pity the less fortunate and conservatives to scorn them. Moreover, Haidt discussed a conservative moral order which condemns people more for what they *are* rather than what they *do*, and tends to ostracize and exclude members of out-groups.

In the context of the present discussion, if conservatives are indeed particularly responsive to threat, it suggests that all else equal they may be more prone to authoritarian tendencies, including tendencies toward prejudice, ethnocentrism, and pseudospeciation. Moreover, we saw that there is evidence that times of social threat can promote conservative political tendencies (Sales, 1972, 1973). On the other hand, security both on the individual level in the sense of attachment security and low-threat times at the social level should tend to promote liberal tendencies.

Foundations of intuitive ethics. Jonathan Haidt and colleagues have argued that there are five fundamental foundations of intuitive morality, or sources of virtue (Graham et al., 2009). These include concerns for 1. *Fairness*, reciprocity, and justice; 2. *Caring* and nurturing; 3. *Loyalty*, patriotism, and self-sacrifice; 4. *Authority*, obedience, and respect; and 5. *Purity* and sanctity. Graham et al. considered Fairness to correspond to Kohlberg's Morality of Justice, and Caring to Gilligan's Morality of Caring. They referred to Fairness and Caring as *individualizing foundations* because they emphasize the rights and welfare of individuals, and they suggested that these correspond to the "autonomy ethic" of Schweder et al. (1997). In contrast, they suggest that the virtues of Loyalty and Authority correspond to the "community ethic," and Purity to the "divinity ethic." Graham et al. (2009) developed measures of tendencies to use considerations of Fairness, Caring, Loyalty, Authority, and Purity in making morally relevant decisions, e.g. "determining if something is right or wrong." They found that persons identifying themselves as liberal consistently used the Fairness and Caring considerations more than the others; while conservatives endorsed the five foundations of virtue more equally.

Haidt (2007, 2012) argued from this evidence that conservative moral intuition rests upon a broader moral foundation than liberal moral intuition. Liberals emphasize Fairness and Caring more than conservatives, but conservatives are more likely to value loyalty, respect for tradition, and a sense of the sacred. In his discussion, Haidt related the latter values with considerations outside the individual, with an apparent assumption that Fairness and Caring considerations operate at the individual level, as they emphasize the rights and welfare of the individual. For example, in explicating the principle that morality "builds and binds," Haidt stated: "whether people use their mirror neurons to feel another's pain, enjoy a synchronized dance, or bow in unison toward Mecca, it is clear that we are prepared, neurologically, psychologically, and culturally, to link our consciousness, our emotions, and our motor movements with those of other people" (2007, p. 1001). Quite so, and powerfully stated. However, such communicative functions of emotion are not at all foreign to a Morality of Caring, writ rather larger than that analyzed by Haidt.

Like the decision literature considered in Chapter 5, Haidt's analysis rests upon a relatively simplified view of emotion that overlooks its essentially communicative nature. Haidt (2007) defined moral intuition as "fast, automatic, and (usually) affect-laden processes in which an evaluative feeling of good–bad or like–dislike ... appears in consciousness without any awareness of having gone through steps of search, weighing evidence, or inferring a conclusion" (p. 998). This does not acknowledge the complexity of the potential role that emotions – particularly prosocial emotions – may play in contributing to considerations of care and harm. Moral intuition is not necessarily a simple matter of positivity–negativity: it can include a whole range of reptilian, selfish, and prosocial anticipatory emotions, anticipated emotions, and incidental emotions, as well as the feelings and desires experienced at the time of judgment. This is arguably the authentic Morality of Caring of Gilligan (1982), in which factors of emotional expression and communication are paramount and overriding. This reflects the prelinguistic morality that regulates the social organization of nonhuman animals and serves as the developmental foundation of human morality. In essence, the Morality of Caring, implementing the overarching motive of attachment, describes the prelinguistic moral order that naturally exists and has existed in the state of nature, as revealed by the lifestyles of our ancestors in the Garden of Ardi and Lucy. In their linguistically filtered research on the foundations of intuitive ethics, Haidt and colleagues have perhaps analyzed an expanded

Morality of Justice where care and harm in effect are considered to be rational principles coexisting and apparently co-equal with considerations of loyalty, authority, and sanctity.

I suggest that the *sine qua non* of morality is caring, based biologically in attachment. The morality of caring is just that: an affectively based caring that rules are followed. The nature of the rules may differ: they may involve values of justice, nurturing, freedom, loyalty, authority, or purity, and/or a combination of these. But, individuals who do not care are amoral, lacking the capacity for moral emotions. They may thoroughly understand the rules – receive an A+ in an advanced seminar on moral philosophy, for example – but not feel any affective obligation to follow the rules. They do not feel any motivation to treat others as they themselves would wish to be treated. The absence of an affectively based morality of caring – even with an intact ability to reason based upon principles of fairness, caring, loyalty, authority, or purity – is the mark of a psychopath.

Conclusions

In his introduction to the journal issue on the justice motive cited at the beginning of this chapter, M. J. Lerner pointed out that the need for justice is a double-edged sword, on one hand motivating people to right wrongs, but also achieving not justice but justification (Rubin and Peplau, 1975). Due to their social and linguistic-cognitive emotions, human beings are compelled to justify and rationalize the morality of their actions in linguistic accounts, whatever those actions might be. Being the flexible, linguistic creatures that we are, human beings can rationalize virtually any action, even the most abhorrent massacre, even the Holocaust. These accounts are invested with great moral affect, which like social affects may not show unless challenged.

Charles Darwin recognized not only the bloody implications of pseudospeciation in the fostering of human conflict, but also the potential of the human species to extend an equalitarian morality beyond the narrow boundaries of one's own family, nation, racial, and religious group:

> If humanity advances in civilization and smaller tribes are united into bigger communities, the simplest consideration will tell the individual that he must extend his social instincts and sympathies to all the members of the same nation, even if they are personally unknown to him. When that point has once been reached, only an artificial boundary remains that keeps him from extending his sympathies to people of all nations and races. (Darwin, 1859; cited in Eibl-Eibesfeldt, 1979, p. 229)

The GREAT emotions

Phantom moral emotions

When social expectations, roles, and norms are learned, followed, in place, and functional, they are also virtually invisible. Recall that Moll et al. (2002) stated, there is a human "natural sense of fairness ... so ubiquitous that we may not notice ... [the] ... automatic tagging of ordinary social events with moral values" (p. 2730). Social behavior, perception, and moral appraisal are implicit, embedded in natural social behavior. But, this implicit sense of fairness does not reside in one individual. It exists and is functionally expressed and communicated online in face-to-face interaction. This essential sense of fairness actually comprises a number of aspects that are recognized as central to social behavior but are typically considered individually instead of as aspects of a system. These aspects have names in English, which can be conveniently abbreviated into an easily remembered and appropriate acronym – *gratitude, respect, elevation, appreciation,* and *trust* – the GREAT emotions.

Most of the GREAT emotions have received relatively scant attention in the academic literature as emotions per se. The closest analysis is Haidt's notion of the "other praising" of emotions of admiration, gratitude, and elevation (Algoe and Haidt, 2009). Nevertheless, there is reason to believe that: (1) they *are* emotions, and (2) they are at the very heart of social interaction from the earliest interactions of parent and infant. I suggest that they are often overlooked precisely because they are ubiquitous: so omnipresent that they are taken for granted and invisible. The GREAT emotions are considered here as aspects of a single moral emotion system that regulates and lubricates typical online social interaction. They are constantly albeit unconsciously and effortlessly expressed and displayed; and directly, unconsciously, and effortlessly perceived in the course of successful, everyday cooperative interaction. I suggest that a momentary failure to so express these emotions is instantly recognized and associated with an immediate breakdown in the spontaneous flow of interaction. Indeed, I propose that social organization itself is a self-organizing system that emerges naturally from interaction in which partners mutually and simultaneously, albeit unconsciously, are rewarding one another with the GREAT emotions.

The two central features of the GREAT emotions is that (a) they derive biologically from love, bonding, and attachment emotions; and (b) they involve *mutual benefits* in that *all individuals in the relationship accrue rewards and none incur costs.* The GREAT emotions *do not* involve considerations of exchange, equity, reciprocity, or obligation: literally, the more you give these emotions away, the more you receive

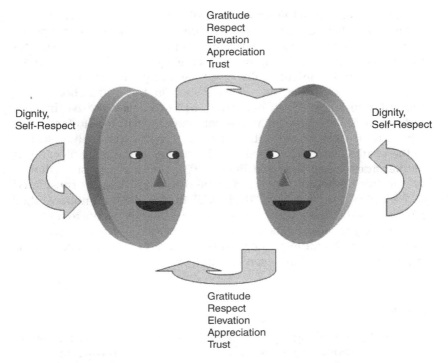

Gratitude
Respect
Elevation
Appreciation
Trust

Dignity,
Self-Respect

Dignity,
Self-Respect

Gratitude
Respect
Elevation
Appreciation
Trust

Figure 7.4 Civility: the dynamics of the GREAT emotions.

in return. Unlike the other social and moral emotions we have considered, the GREAT emotions do not imply differences in status or dominance, and in fact they vitiate against such differences and signal a mutuality that is in important respects an equalitarian relationship. Persons of widely differing social status – for example, a lord and a footman – may have a GREAT relationship if they mutually accept the same social norms and roles and mutually agree that their partner is following them.

The basic social dynamics of the GREAT emotions are illustrated in Figure 7.4. Person P at the left expresses gratitude, respect, elevation, appreciation, and trust for O on the right, which supports CO's self-image and therefore, feelings of dignity and self-respect. O likewise expresses gratitude, respect, elevation, appreciation, and trust for P, supporting P's self-image and therefore, feelings of dignity and self-respect. The more each gives away the GREAT emotions, the more they tend to receive from the partner in return. The displays that signal the GREAT emotions are quite simply the everyday signals of *politeness*.

Some persons have the ability to display the GREAT emotions more successfully than others: this is an important aspect of charisma. In many if not most cases, charisma is in the interest of both partners and is mutually beneficial, but in some cases displays of GREAT emotions can be intentionally used tactically and strategically to manipulate the partner, as we have seen in the last section by. an authoritarian leader. Such deception, however, tends to be difficult, and the exception rather than the rule: normally in face-to-face inter-action the trustworthiness of the partner can be accurately detected, as the results of the Reed et al. (2012) study considered earlier in this chapter attest (see Boone and Buck, 2003). I return to trustworthiness later in this discussion. It must also be recognized that, as considered in the last section, there is a "dark side" to the GREAT emotions: they can be denied to members of out-groups and thereby serve to motivate and justify pseudospeciation, where the rewards of the GREAT emo-tions are reserved for in-group members, and attacking members of the out-group is justified and even encouraged.

Definitions

The emotions making up the GREAT emotions represent different aspects of a spontaneous system of reciprocal social reward that func-tion as a unit. Therefore, each of the GREAT emotions tends to imply all of the others: gratitude implies respect implies elevation implies appreciation implies trust. They occur together. And, they occur together simultaneously in both interactants.

The GREAT emotions are displayed above all by interpersonal synchrony. The discovery of interpersonal synchrony was one of the early triumphs of research in nonverbal communication, or "body language" (Buck, 1984). William Condon defined interpersonal syn-chrony as occurring when the behaviors of a speaker and listener "move in precise synchrony with the articulatory structure of the speaker's speech" (Condon, 1979, p. 161). Ruth Feldman (2012a) defined it more broadly, as the temporal concordance of the biological and social behavior of interactants, and measured it by micro-coding interaction behaviors such as touching, eye contact, emotion display, and soft vocalization.

Condon found evidence of synchrony with spoken language (Chinese and American English) in infants as young as four days old, responding both to live and tape-recorded speech (Condon, 1973a; Condon and Sander, 1974). We saw in Chapter 4 that there is evidence of mutual contingent responsiveness between mother and newborns

(Murray and Trevarthen, 1986); and that given mutual contingent responsiveness, primary intersubjectivity takes place automatically, directly, and naturally; mediated by mirror neuron systems. We also saw that OXY levels in mothers and fathers were synchronized, suggesting that partners shape each other's OXY response through displays of affiliative behavior and attachment (Feldman, 2012a). Also, OXY was associated with the degree of interpersonal synchrony between parents and their 6-month-old children (Feldman et al., 2011). Importantly, we saw that fathers inhaling OXY in a double-blind study showed more frequent touch and longer durations of engagement with the infant, and this was associated with large increases in levels of OXY in the infant, as well as greater readiness for social contact and longer periods of social gaze and toy engagement. There is evidence that the sensory pathways mediating synchrony are "low road" and of old evolutionary origin, and bypass classical sensory pathways to the neocortex (Tamietto et al., 2009).

Such spontaneous social engagement has emotional correlates, generating a pattern of positive feelings associated with basic brain systems of reward and prosociality. These probably include subcortical and paleocortical neurochemical systems involving DA, NE, serotonin, OXY, AVP, and the endorphinergic "hedonic hotspots" discussed in Chapter 4, that are stimulated by the interaction. Studies of moral judgment summarized previously in this chapter suggest the involvement of both VTA/MFB systems underlying individualist "wanting" and septal/NAcc systems underlying prosocial "liking" and the "warm glow." These provide the affective "fire" of the GREAT emotions that, as suggested at the beginning of this book, might be termed *gust*.

The GREAT emotions are not typically noticed as emotions per se: the interactants are seen to be aware of and involved in each other. However, if the pattern of synchrony is broken, the emotional response is palpable, immediate, and negative. In Chapter 4, we saw that Tronick's (1978) "still face" phenomenon – infant distress to a sudden unresponsiveness on the part of a social partner – demonstrates what happens when mutual contingent responsiveness is suddenly interrupted. Also, Trevarthen and Aitken (2001) showed that when either mother or infant communicating over a video link unexpectedly were made to view a playback of the other's behavior, making mutual contingent responsiveness impossible, the communicative flow changed dramatically.

The emotions

Again, the GREAT emotions represent different aspects of a spontaneous system of mutually communicated reciprocal social rewards:

each implies all of the others and all are displayed simultaneously in interpersonal synchrony. Their meaning is detected, grasped, and known by acquaintance, intuitively and directly via mirror neuron systems; even in infants and in nonhuman animals to the extent of their sociality.

Gratitude. Gratitude has been widely studied in the literature, but typically defined in an exchange sense different from that intended here. Gratitude was one of Haidt's (2003) "other praising" emotions, which collectively arise from witnessing exemplary actions of others. Admiration, as noted previously, was defined as a response to non-moral excellence. Haidt defined gratitude in contrast as a "response to generosity, thoughtfulness, or other moral excellence that does benefit to the self" (Algoe and Haidt, 2009, p. 107). This and many other definitions of gratitude have roots in exchange theory, in which a benefactor aids a recipient in some way. This, however, implies a dominance–submission relationship whereby the benefactor is in a higher position relative to the recipient, and this inescapably implies all of the social and moral emotions involved in such relationships, including pride, arrogance, pity, scorn, triumph, modesty, sympathy, and contempt on the part of the benefactor; and guilt, shame, envy, jealousy, humiliation, indignation, admiration, and resentment on the part of the recipient.

Gratitude in this exchange sense is clearly a significant moral emotion that has important implications for behavior (Tangney et al., 2007), but an exclusive emphasis upon gratitude in this sense risks reducing it to mere economics (Emmons, 2004). Rather than this *gratitude of exchange*, gratitude in the GREAT emotion sense is the *gratitude of caring*, that does not involve exchange (Buck, 2004). It is gratitude in Spinoza's (1677) sense of reciprocating love with love (Emmons, 2004). In the GREAT emotion sense, too, gratitude is reciprocated: person P is grateful to CO for following social rules and simultaneously P is grateful to CO for expressing gratitude that P is following the rules.

Respect. Respect is conventionally defined as a positive feeling of esteem for CO. The antonym of respect is contempt. The GREAT emotions involve simultaneous and reciprocal displays of esteem that occur simultaneously with the reciprocal displays of gratitude. P respects CO for following social rules, and displays this respect; CO reciprocates; and simultaneously P respects CO for expressing respect that P is following the rules and expressing respect.

Elevation. Elevation was another of Haidt's "other praising" emotions, defined as a "response to moral excellence that does benefit to the self" (Algoe and Haidt, 2009, p. 107). Haidt (2003) took the term "elevation" from Thomas Jefferson as an emotional response to moral exemplars: when witnessing acts of generosity, charity, gratitude, fidelity of other acts of virtue, "we are deeply impressed with its beauty and feel a strong desire in ourselves of doing charitable and grateful acts also" (Jefferson, cited in Algoe and Haidt, 2009, p. 106). Again, the GREAT emotions involve a mutual, and reciprocal display of elevation that is simultaneous with the mutual and reciprocal displays of gratitude and respect.

Appreciation. Appreciation is defined as the "recognition and enjoyment of the good qualities of someone." The GREAT emotions involve a mutual, and reciprocal display of appreciation that is simultaneous with the mutual and reciprocal displays of gratitude, respect, and elevation.

Trust. Trust is defined as a "reliance on the integrity, ability, or character of a person." Again, the GREAT emotions involve a mutual, and reciprocal display of trust that is simultaneous with the mutual and reciprocal displays of gratitude, respect, elevation, and appreciation.

As we saw in Chapter 4, there is evidence from double-blind studies that trust in human beings can be increased by OXY (Baumgartner et al., 2008; Kosfeld et al., 2005; Kosnik and Tranel, 2011). It seems incredible that higher-level emotions such as trust, which would seem to necessarily involve higher-level cognitive processing including ToM, could be manipulated by a single molecule. In fact, OXY and also AVP are critical neurotransmitters in critical prosocial areas of the brain: the septal area both releases and has receptors for these neuropeptides (Rilling and Insel, 1999). And, we saw that Krueger et al. (2007) followed the emergence of trust within relationships with participants in the fMRI: as relationships came to reflect unconditional trust, the septal area was activated. So, the functioning of the septal area and particularly OXY may actually act to increase the potency of all of the GREAT emotions. The fact that OXY also increases empathic concern and interactive synchrony is consistent with this. I hypothesize that this is the biological essence of "gust."

However, there is also the caution that effects of OXY may vary with attachment security, and that OXY is also associated with the categorizing others into out-groups and other evidence of xenophobia. Did the executors of the Holocaust and other crimes against humanity bask in the warm glow of gust as they perpetrated their appalling crimes? Joseph Mengele, known as the "Angel of Death" responsible for over 200,000 murders at the Auschwitz concentration camp, reportedly experienced "no guilt" (*Miami News*, 1985); Bosnian Serb leader Radovan Karadzic speaking before a war crimes tribunal at The Hague, stated "instead of being accused, I should have been rewarded for all the good things I have done" (*Newsweek*, October 19, 2012, p. 9); and in

1945 Adolf Eichmann reportedly stated: "I will leap into my grave laughing because the feeling that I have five million human beings on my conscience is for me a source of extraordinary satisfaction" (Wikiquote, 2012).

Civility, politeness, and dignity

Civility, politeness, and the GREAT emotions. The GREAT emotions, then – for good or ill – constantly, silently, and imperceptibly lubricate and sustain everyday interpersonal behavior via rituals of politeness, thus lubricating and regulating the course of informal social interaction. The mutual expectancy and acknowledgment that rules are being followed fairly in a relationship, no matter how difficult and contentious that relationship might be in other regards, is arguably among the most fundamental of affectively loaded moral contexts. The (arguably universal) rule is, if I follow the rules fairly and you follow the rules fairly, we can both mutually acknowledge that each of us is acting with *civility*. "Civility" is defined here as acting with justice: following rules and meeting social expectations fairly (Herbst, 2010). Mutual civility, communicated by politeness, results in a kind of mutual admiration one for the other signaled by a mutual display of the GREAT emotions and a relationship of mutual gratitude, respect, elevation, appreciation, and trust. Thus the GREAT emotions depend upon a general expectation that another person will follow rules fairly and act with civility. Note that even someone who is hated and despised can be respected and trusted, albeit perhaps grudgingly. Also, note that the *content of the rules is not specified*. They could involve any of the "big three" moral codes identified by Schweder et al. (1997) – autonomy, community, or divinity – or any of the Graham et al. (2009) five foundations of intuitive ethics: fairness, caring, loyalty, authority, and purity.

The dynamics of social affects in the trusting and respectful relationship were shown in Figure 7.3. Note that, unlike the case in Figures 6.3 and 7.2, both interactants are depicted as happy and satisfied in the context of the relationship. Whereas dominant-submissive relationships tend to be stressful and ultimately unsatisfying to both participants, I hypothesize that relationships characterized by the GREAT emotions serve as bioregulators for both parties, tending to buffer stress and promoting physical health. Again, the parties may dislike one another, as in sworn political enemies. Or, they may differ in dominance status. Nevertheless, if each follows the rules fairly and acts with civility, and each acknowledges the fairness and civility of the other with gratitude, respect, elevation, appreciation, and trust, each can gain a sense of self-affirming satisfaction from the interaction.

As with social and cognitive emotions, the intent here is not to reify terms such as "civility," "respect," "trust," etc. as moral emotions per se. Rather, the intent is to demonstrate an arguably culturally universal confluence of equitable interpersonal contingencies that allows good feelings to be exchanged, as it were, on a basis perceived to be fair, without regard to prior personal relationship, kin-status, or dominance status. One can cooperate even with a hated enemy, as long as civility is maintained, and gain a kind of satisfaction from such cooperation. The English words that seem best to fit this confluence of equitable interpersonal contingencies are words like "civility," "respect," and "trust," but analogs of these words should be found in all languages and historical periods, and they should be broadly applicable to animal as well as human social behavior.

Dignity. The conflict-reducing functions of moral systems are particularly important, as illustrated by the affiliative reconciliation, reassurance, and consolation behavior observed in chimpanzees (de Waal and Roosmalen, 1979). Following rules fairly is an effective way to reduce and avoid conflict. For this reason, I suggest that civil behavior and mutual respect on the part of potentially antagonistic interactants will be valued and rewarded with admiration by third parties, particularly so perhaps if the interactants themselves are bitter enemies. The interactants are seen as trustworthy and worthy of respect by third parties if they act equitably and follow the rules. The particular sort of admiration by third parties associated with perceived civility might be communicated by the English term *dignity*: the potentially antagonistic interactants are seen to be acting with dignity when they follow rules fairly. Again, these terms may well be appropriate for describing the behavior of nonhuman animals as well as human beings. Thus, the mutual acknowledgment of civility sustains the dignity of both interaction partners. This process is so fundamental and so familiar that it becomes invisible: a phantom world of implicit communication that nevertheless is objectively observable, given careful observation, recording, and analysis. It is perhaps most directly visible as interpersonal synchrony.

The GREAT emotions become set in motion during the peer affectional system: to paraphrase a title of a book, all you really need to know you learned in kindergarten. This phantom world is endlessly puzzling and sometimes infuriating to those who did not learn it in kindergarten, such as persons who experienced abuse, neglect, and/or social deprivation, and consequent attachment disorders; and persons with the symptoms of Asperger syndrome or on the autism spectrum, who have difficulty participating in this game where the rules are understood by all but acknowledged by none.

Alternatively, the GREAT emotions can be played coldly, without moral emotion, by a charming psychopath.

Trustworthiness: gateway to the GREAT emotions

Trust is acknowledged to be inherently risky, because it involves relying on another person and the other may fail us (Slovic, 1999). Therefore, the perception and/or judgment that the other is *trustworthy* is a critical prerequisite for the stimulation and implementation of the GREAT emotions in a specific relationship. If a person is not trusted, all of the GREAT emotions fall away and the interaction and relationship are governed by rational economic considerations. As we have seen, this involves wholesale changes in how the relationship and interaction are processed in the brain.

Boone and Buck (2003) suggested that emotional expressivity, or the spontaneous tendency to accurately communicate one's feelings and desires, may act as a marker for trustworthiness and cooperative behavior. They noted that the emotional expressivity of a target person has effects on ratings of liking for that person that are independent of, and as strong as, the physical attractiveness of the target person (Sabatelli and Rubin, 1986; Riggio and Friedman, 1986). There are established evolutionary reasons for the preference for the physically attractive: they have better health outcomes and better fertility outcomes, thus they are marked for success as better potential mates (Langlois et al., 2000). The reasons for the effect of emotional expressivity on interpersonal attractiveness are less clear, but Boone and Buck suggested that one answer may be found in the effect of expressivity on trustworthiness.

Trustworthiness has been investigated in game situations. We saw that participants were able to detect the trustworthiness of their partners via nonverbal communication in an acquaintance period preceding a Prisoner's Dilemma game (Reed et al., 2012). A sender's expressions of contempt were related both to defection on the part of both the sender and the receiver, while expressions of happiness predicted cooperation. The sender's spontaneous display of contempt was accurately detected by the receiver as indicating the sender was not trustworthy, eliciting the anti-GREAT emotion of *suspicion*. On the other hand, the smiling sender was judged to be trustworthy. Krumhuber et al. (2007) similarly demonstrated that brief dynamic representations of smiles in potential partners increased judgments of trustworthiness and cooperative behavior, with the perception of trustworthiness mediating the effect of the facial dynamics on cooperative behavior. On the other hand, Schug et al. (2010) found that, when filmed receiving unfair offers in an Ultimatum Game, cooperators were more expressive facially, and those expressions were not confined to positive expressions. They concluded that general emotional expressivity reliably signals cooperation.

Emotional expressivity, then, signals trustworthiness and thereby opens the gates for the interactants being mutually rewarded by the GREAT emotions, and then in turn the GREAT emotions are displayed and communicated by emotional expressivity in the form of synchronous nonverbal behavior. This is a natural, spontaneous, and automatic process that has its roots in the earliest interactions involving mutual contingent responsiveness of parent and infant, fostering the primary intersubjectivity that is at the heart of empathy. This process is further fostered by new communication media that allow mutual contingent responsiveness over electronic media and the Internet. Of course, the relative ease of establishing apparently GREAT relationships over the Internet has potential downsides, but there is little question that society is being comprehensively transformed by emotional communication via new communication media.

Conclusions: doing well, doing good, destroying the enemy, and avoiding exploitation

Morality involves a sense of what is right and wrong, and while previous analyses have emphasized rational processing, new research has demonstrated the relevance of M. J. Lerner's question: "why do people care about justice, or act if they care?" (1975, p. 3). It appears that there are at least four powerful sorts of motive underlying caring about justice: caring about doing well for oneself, caring about doing good for one's kin and comrade, caring about destroying the enemy, and caring about avoiding being exploited. Each of these motives is associated with strong affective responses identified with subcortical and paleocortical neurochemical systems associated with the VTA/MFB system, the septal system, and the amygdala system, respectively. In human beings these basic motivational/emotional systems, generating gust and disgust, are closely integrated with control mechanisms in the frontal cortex: the VTA/MFB and septal/NAcc systems with systems in the medial prefrontal cortex including the VMPFC and FPC; the amygdala and insula with systems in the lateral prefrontal cortex including lateral sectors of the DLPFC and OFC (Moll and Schulkin, 2009; Moll et al., 2007b). Brain laterality is important to all of this, but remains poorly understood.

The systems controlling moral emotions, judgments, and behaviors offer a specific example of the kind of general mechanism proposed by Tomkins (1962–92, Vol. 2). He saw affect as a separate assembly functioning to amplify other mechanisms of behavior. In the moral emotions, the affect (gust/disgust) is associated with subcortical and paleocortical systems that function to provide the "fire" underlying moral judgment and behavior, themselves mediated by frontal brain mechanisms.

The control of the cognitive and social emotions is analogous: biological systems underlying strong affects associated with curiosity/boredom and attachment/isolation can be viewed as separate assemblies – associated with subcortical and paleocortical brain structures – providing the affective "fire" underlying exploration and social interaction. The "higher-level" nature of cognitive, social, and moral emotions stems from this interaction of more primitive brain systems underlying affect with higher-order processing. So, the understanding of brain mechanisms and how they interact and function can guide and constrain our larger theories of emotion.

The developmental-interactionist theory of emotion views felt affects to be voices of the genes, existing as dissociable but highly interactive modules, and cajoling our behavior with built-in flexibility, enabling the representation of forces of learning and social communication. This allows us to comprehend the hierarchical structure of biologically based primes; and how these function in ecological context via the display and communication of ecologically determined "packages" of these prime states through facial expressions, body postures, gestures, and vocalizations, as well as intimate aromas, touches, and purrs. The voices of the genes are also organized into powerful general motivational/emotional drives involving curiosity, attachment, and a hypothesized general drive of moral approbation termed gust. These interact with ecological contingencies experienced by the individual over the course of development to result in higher-level cognitive, social, and moral emotions. In this biosocial synthesis, emotion is the essential process standing at the conceptual center of the behavioral and social sciences, present from the beginnings of life, and, quietly but constantly and powerfully, whispering directions.

Bibliography

Abelson, J. L., and Nesse, R. M. (1990). Cholecystokinin-4 and panic. *Archives of General Psychiatry*, 47(4): 395.

Acevedo, B. P., Aron, A., Fisher, H. E., and Brown, L. L. (2012). Neural correlates of long-term intense romantic love. *Social Cognitive and Affective Neuroscience*, 7(2): 145–59.

Adams, D. B. (1979). Brain mechanisms for offense, defense, and submission. *Behavioral and Brain Sciences*, 2: 201–43.

Adolphs, R., Tranel, D., Damasio, H., and Damasio, A. (1994). Impaired recognition of emotion in facial expressions following bilateral damage to the human amygdala. *Nature*, 372(6507): 669–72.

Adorno, T. W., Frenkel-Brunswik, E., Levinson, D. J., and Sanford, R. N. (1950). *The Authoritarian Personality*. New York: Harper.

Ainsworth, M. D. S., and Bell, S. M. (1970). Attachment, exploration, and separation: Illustrated by the behavior of one-year-olds in a strange situation. *Child Development*, 41(1): 49–67.

Ainsworth, M. D. S., Blehar, M. C., Waters, E., and Wall, S. (1978). *Patterns of Attachment: A Psychological Study of the Strange Situation*. Hillsdale, NJ: Laurence Erlbaum Associates.

Algoe, S. B., and Haidt, J. (2009). Witnessing excellence in action: The 'other-praising' emotions of elevation, gratitude, and admiration. *Journal of Positive Psychology*, 4(1): 105–27.

Alho, H., Costa, E., Ferrero, P., Fujimoto, M., Cosenza-Murphy, D., and Guidotti, A. (1985). Diazepam-binding inhibitor: A neuropeptide located in selected neuronal populations of rat brain. *Science*, 229(4709): 179–82.

Alkon, D. L. (1989). Memory storage and neural systems. *Scientific American*, 261: 42–51.

Allee, W. C. (1938). *Social Life of Animals*. New York: Norton.

Alley, T. R. (1983). *Social and Applied Aspects of Perceiving Faces*. Hillsdale, NJ: Laurence Erlbaum.

Allport, G. W. (1954). *The Nature of Prejudice*. Cambridge, MA: Addison Wesley.

Amanzio, M., and Benedetti, F. (1999). Neuropharmacological dissection of placebo analgesia: Expectation-activated opioid systems versus conditioning-activated specific subsystems. *Journal of Neuroscience*, 19(1): 484–94.

American Psychiatric Association (1994). *Diagnostic and Statistical Manual of Mental Disorders* (4th edn.). Washington, DC: APA.

Anderson, N. E., and Kiehl, K. A. (2012). The psychopath magnetized: Insights from brain imaging. *Trends in Cognitive Sciences*, 16(1): 52–60.

Anderson, S. W., Bechara, A., Damasio, H., Tranel, D., and Damasio, A. R. (1999). Impairment of social and moral behavior related to early damage in human prefrontal cortex. *Nature Neuroscience*, 2(11): 1032–37.

Andréasson, P., and Dimberg, U. (2008). Emotional empathy and facial feedback. *Journal of Nonverbal Behavior*, 32(4): 215–24.

Andy, O. J., and Stephan, H. (1968). The septum in the human brain. *Journal of Comparative Neurology*, 133(3): 383–409.

Anolli, L., Ciceri, R., and Infantino, M. G. (2002). From "blame by praise" to "praise by blame": Analysis of vocal patterns in ironic communication. *International Journal of Psychology*, 37: 266–77.

App, B., McIntosh, D. N., Reed, C. L., and Hertenstein, M. J. (2011). Nonverbal channel use in communication of emotion: How may depend on why. *Emotion*, 11(3): 603–17.

Ardrey, A. (1966). *The Territorial Imperative*. New York: Delta.

Aristotle (1947). *Poetics*. In R. McKeon (ed.), *Introduction to Aristotle* (pp. 622–67). New York: Modern Library.

Arletti, R., Benelli, A., and Bertolini, A. (1992). Oxytocin involvement in male and female sexual behavior. In C. A. Pedersen, J. D. Caldwell, G. F. Jirikowski, and T. R. Insel (eds.), *Oxytocin in Maternal, Sexual, and Social Behaviors* (pp. 180–93). New York: New York Academy of Sciences.

Arnold, M. B. (1960). *Emotion and personality*, 2 vols. New York: Columbia University Press.

Aron, E. N. (1997). The drama of self-conscious emotions with an antihero called shame. *PsycCRITIQUES*, 42: 589–92.

Aron, A., Fisher, H., Mashek, D. J., Strong, G., Li, H., and Brown, L. L. (2005). Reward, motivation, and emotion systems associated with early-stage intense romantic love. *Journal of Neurophysiology*, 94(1): 327–37.

Asberg, M. (1994). Monoamine transmitters in human aggressiveness and violence: A selected review. *Criminal Behavior and Mental Health*, 4(4): 303–27.

Asch, S. (1952). *Social Psychology*. Englewood Cliffs: Prentice-Hall.

Asher, S. R., and Gottman, J. M. (1981). *The Development of Children's Friendships*. New York: Cambridge University Press.

Ashwin, C., Baron-Cohen, S., Wheelwright, S., O'Riordan, M., and Bullmore, E. T. (2007). Differential activation of the amygdala and the "social brain" during fearful face-processing in Asperger Syndrome. *Neuropsychologia*, 45(1): 2–14.

Asimov, I. (1957). *Only a Trillion*. New York: Abilard-Schuman.

Askenasy, H. (1978). *Are We All Nazis?* Secaucus, NJ: Lyle Stuart.

Åslund, C., Starrin, B., Leppert, J., and Nilsson, K. W. (2009). Social status and shaming experiences related to adolescent overt aggression at school. *Aggressive Behavior*, 35(1): 1–13.

Atzil, S., Hendler, T., and Feldman, R. (2011). Specifying the neurobiological basis of human attachment: Brain, hormones, and behavior in synchronous and intrusive mothers. *Neuropsychopharmacology*, 36(13): 2603–15.

(2013). The brain basis of social synchrony. *Social, Cognitive, and Affective Neuroscience*. September 20. doi:10.1093/scan/nst105 [Epub ahead of print].

Atzil, S., Hendler, T., Zagoory-Sharon, O., Weintbrub, Y., and Feldman, R. (2012). Synchrony and specificity in the maternal and the paternal brain: Relations to oxytocin and vasopressin. *Journal of the American Academy of Child and Adolescent Psychiatry*, 51(8): 798–811.

Averill, J. (1994). It's a small world but a large stage. In P. Ekman and R. Davidson (eds.), *The Nature of Emotion: Fundamental Questions* (pp. 143–45). New York: Oxford University Press.

Aviezer, H., Trope, Y., and Todorov, A. (2012). Body cues, not facial expressions, discriminate between intense positive and negative emotions. *Science*, 338(6111): 1225–29.

Baas, D., Aleman, A., and Kahn, R. S. (2004). Lateralization of amygdala activation: A systematic review of functional neuroimaging studies. *Brain Research Reviews*, 45(2): 96–103.

Bagozzi, R. P., Baumgartner, H., and Pieters, R. (1998). Goal-directed emotions. *Cognition & Emotion*, 12: 1–26.

Baker, K. B., and Kim, J. J. (2004). Amygdalar lateralization in fear conditioning: Evidence for greater involvement of the right amygdala. *Behavioral Neuroscience*, 118(1): 15–23.

Balconi, M., Falbo, L., and Brambilla, E. (2009). BIS/BAS responses to emotional cues: Self report, autonomic measure and alpha band modulation. *Personality and Individual Differences*, 47(8): 858–63.

Bale, T. L., and Dorsa, D. M. (1995). Sex-differences in and effects of estrogen on oxytocin receptor messenger-ribonucleic-acid expression in the ventromedial hypothalamus. *Endocrinology*, 136(1): 27–32.

Balzeau, A., Holloway, R. L., and Grimaud-Hervé, D. (2012). Variations and asymmetries in regional brain surface in the genus Homo. *Journal of Human Evolution*, 62(6): 696–706.

Bandura, A. (1991). Self-regulation of motivation through anticipatory and self-reactive mechanisms. In R. Dienstbier (ed.), *Nebraska Symposium on Motivation 1990: Perspectives on Motivation* (pp. 69–164). Lincoln: University of Nebraska Press.

Bandura, A., and Walters, R. H. (1959). *Adolescent Aggression*. New York: Ronald Press.

(1963). *Social Learning and Personality Development*. New York: Holt, Rinehart & Winston.

Barbas H., and Zikopoulos, B. (2007). The prefrontal cortex and flexible behavior. *The Neuroscientist*, 13(5): 532–55.

Bard, P. (1928). A diencephalic mechanism for the expression of rage with special reference to the sympathetic nervous system. *American Journal of Physiology*, 84: 490–515.

Bargh, J. A., and Ferguson, M. J. (2000). Beyond behaviorism: On the automaticity of higher mental processes. *Psychological Bulletin*, 126(6): 925–45.

Barrett, J., and Fleming, A. S. (2011). Annual research review: All mothers are not created equal – Neural and psychobiological perspectives on mothering and the importance of individual differences. *Journal of Child Psychology and Psychiatry*, 52(4): 368–97.

Barrett, K. C. (2005). The origins of social emotions and self-regulation in toddlerhood: New evidence. *Cognition & Emotion*, 19: 953–79.

Barrett, L. F. (2006). Are emotions natural kinds? *Perspectives on Psychological Science*, 1: 28–58.

Bartal, I. B.-A., Decety, J., and Mason, P. (2011). Empathy and pro-social behavior in rats. *Science*, 334(6061): 1427–30.

Bartels, A., and Zeki, S. (2004). The neural correlates of maternal and romantic love. *NeuroImage*, 21(3): 1155–66.

Bartz, J. A., Zaki, J., Bolger, N., and Ochsner, K. N. (2011). Social effects of oxytocin in humans: Context and person matter. *Trends in Cognitive Sciences*, 15(7): 301–9.

Basbaum, A. I., Clanton, C. H., and Fields, H. L. (1976). Opiate and stimulus-produced analgesia: Functional anatomy of a medullospinal pathway. *Proceedings of the National Academy of Sciences of the United States of America*, 73(12): 4685–88.

Basbaum, A. I., and Fields, H. L. (1978). Endogenous pain control mechanisms: Review and hypothesis. *Annals of Neurology*, 4(5): 451–62.

Basbaum, A. I., Fields, H. L., and Mandel, M. A. (1979). Endogenous pain control mechanisms: Review and hypothesis. *Plastic and Reconstructive Surgery*, 64(3): 431.

Batson, C. D., and Oleson, K. C. (1991). Current status of the empathy–altruism hypothesis. In M. Clark (ed.), *Review of Personality and Social Psychology*, Vol. 12: *Prosocial Behavior* (pp. 62–85). Newbury Park, CA: Sage Publications.

Bauer, H. G. (1954). Endocrine and other clinical manifestations of hypothalamic disease. *Journal of Clinical Endocrinology*, 54: 13–31.

Bauer, R. M. (1984). Autonomic recognition of names and faces in prosopagnosia: A neuropsychological application of the guilty knowledge test. *Neuropsychologia*, 22(4): 457–69.

Baumeister, R. F., Brewer, L. E., Tice, D. M., and Twenge, J. M. (2007). Thwarting the need to belong: Understanding the interpersonal and inner effects of social exclusion. *Social and Personality Psychology Compass*, 1(1): 506–20.

Baumeister, R. F., DeWall, C. N., and Vohs, K. D. (2009). Social rejection, control, numbness, and emotion: How not to be fooled by Gerber and Wheeler (2009). *Perspectives on Psychological Science*, 4(5): 489–93.

Baumeister, R. F., and Leary, M. R. (1995). The need to belong: Desire for interpersonal attachments as a fundamental human motivation. *Psychological Bulletin*, 117(3): 497–529.

Baumeister, R. F., and Tice, D. M. (1990). Anxiety and social exclusion. *Journal of Social and Clinical Psychology*, 9: 165–95.

Baumeister, R. F., Vohs, K. D., DeWall, C. N., and Zhang, L. (2007). How emotion shapes behavior: Feedback, anticipation, and reflection, rather than direct causation. *Personality and Social Psychology Review*, 11(2): 167–203.

Baumgartner, T., Heinrichs, M., Vonlanthen, A., Fischbacher, U., and Fehr, E. (2008). Oxytocin shapes the neural circuitry of trust and trust adaptation in humans. *Neuron*, 58(4): 639–50.

Beasley, Jr., C. M., Tollefson, G. D., and Tran, P. V. (1997). Efficacy of olanapine: An overview of pivotal clinical trials. *Journal of Clinical Psychiatry*, 58(10): 28–36.

Beatty, J. (1995). *Principles of Behavioral Neuroscience*. Madison, WI: Brown & Benchmark.

Beaver, J. D., Lawrence, A. D., van Ditzhuijzen, J., Davis, M. H., Woods, A., and Calder, A. J. (2006). Individual differences in reward drive predict neural responses to images of food. *Journal of Neuroscience*, 26(19): 5160–66.

Bechara, A., and Damasio, A. R. (2005). The somatic marker hypothesis: A neural theory of economic decision. *Games and Economic Behavior*, 52(2): 336–72.

Bechara, A., Dolan, S., and Hindes, A. (2002). Decision-making and addiction (part II): Myopia for the future or hypersensitivity to reward? *Neuropsychologia*, 40(10): 1690–1705.

Behrendt, R.-P. (2011). *Neuroanatomy of Social Behaviour: An Evolutionary and Psychoanalytic Perspective*. London: Karnac Books.

Belzung, C., Pineau, N., Beuzen, A., and Misslin, R. (1994). PD135158, a CCK-B antagonist, reduces "state," but not "trait" anxiety in mice. *Pharmacology, Biochemistry, and Behavior*, 49(2): 433–36.

Benedict, R. (1946). *The Chrysanthemum and the Sword: Patterns of Japanese Culture*. Oxford: Houghton Mifflin.

Benkelfat, C., Bradwejn, J., Meyer, E., Ellenbogen, M., Milot, S., Gjedde, A., and Evans, A. (1995). Functional neuroanatomy of CCK4-induced anxiety in normal healthy volunteers. *American Journal of Psychiatry*, 152(8): 1180–84.

Benson, H. (1975). *The Relaxation Response*. New York: Morrow.

Bentley, D. R., and Hoy, R. R. (1974). The neurobiology of cricket song. *Scientific American*, 231(2): 34–44.

Ben-Ze'ev, A. (1992). Pleasure in others' misfortune. *Iyyun*, 41: 41–61.

Berridge, K. C. (2007). The debate over dopamine's role in reward: The case for incentive salience. *Psychopharmacology*, 191(3): 391–431.

  (2009). "Liking" and "wanting" food rewards: Brain substrates and roles in eating disorders. *Physiology & Behavior*, 97(5): 537–50.

Berridge, K. C., and Kringelbach, M. L. (2008). Affective neuroscience of pleasure: Reward in humans and animals. *Psychopharmacology*, 199(3): 457–80.

Berridge, K. C., and Winkielman, P. (2003). What is an unconscious emotion? The case for unconscious "liking". *Cognition & Emotion*, 17(2): 181–211.

Berry, D. S., and Zebrowitz-McArthur, L. (1988). What's in a face? The impact of facial maturity and defendant intent on the attribution of legal responsibility. *Personality and Social Psychology Bulletin*, 14(1): 23–33.

Bers, S. A., and Rodin, J. (1984). Social-comparison jealousy: A developmental and motivational study. *Journal of Personality and Social Psychology*, 47: 766–79.

Bettelheim, B. (1943). Individual and mass behavior in extreme situations. *Journal of Abnormal and Social Psychology*, 38: 417–52.

Bielsky, I. F., Hu, S. B., and Young, L. J. (2005). Sexual dimorphism in the vasopressin system: Lack of an altered behavioral phenotype in female V1a receptor knockout mice. *Behavioural Brain Research*, 164(1): 132–36.

Birdwhistell, R. L. (1970). *Kinesics and Context*. Philadelphia, PA: University of Pennsylvania Press.

Blanchard, D. C., Sakai, R. R., McEwen, B., Weiss, S. M., and Blanchard, R. J. (1993). Subordination stress: Behavioral, brain, and neuroendocrine correlates. *Behavioral and Brain Research*, 58(1–2): 113–21.

Blass, T. (1991). Understanding behavior in the Milgram obedience experiment: The role of personality, situations, and their interactions. *Journal of Personality and Social Psychology*, 60(3): 398–413.

Block, J. A. (1957). A study of affective responsiveness in a lie-detection situation. *Journal of Abnormal and Social Psychology*, 55(1): 11–15.

Bogen, J. E. (1985). The callosal syndromes. In K. M. Heilman and E. Valenstein (eds.), *Brain Mechanisms Underlying Speech and Language* (pp. 295–338). New York: Grune & Stratton.

Bolles, R. C., and Fanselow, M. S. (1982). Endorphins and behavior. *Annual Review of Psychology*, 33(1): 87–101.

Bongioanni, P. (1991). Platelet MAO activity and personality: An overview. *New Trends in Experimental and Clinical Psychiatry*, 7(1): 17–28.

Boone, R. T., and Buck, R. (2003). Emotional expressivity and trustworthiness: The role of nonverbal behavior in the evolution of cooperation. *Journal of Nonverbal Behavior*, 27(3): 163–82.

Borod, J. (2000). *The Neuropsychology of Emotion*. New York: Oxford University Press.

Borod, J. C., and Koff, E. (1990). Lateralization for facial emotional behavior: A methodological perspective. *International Journal of Psychology*, 25(2): 157–177.

Borod, J., Koff, E., and Buck, R. (1986). The neuropsychology of facial expression: Data from normal and brain-damaged adults. In P. Blanck, R. Buck, and R. Rosenthal (eds.), *Nonverbal Communication in the Clinical Context* (pp. 196–222). University Park, PA: Pennsylvania State University Press.

Borod, J. C., Koff, E., Perlman-Lorch, M., and Nicols, M. (1985). Channels of emotional expression in patients with unilateral brain damage. *Archives of Neurology*, 42(4): 345–48.

Borod, J. C., Koff, E., Yecker, S., Santschi, C., and Schmidt, J. M. (1998). Facial asymmetry during emotional expression: Gender, valence and measurement technique. *Psychophysiology*, 36(11): 1209–15.

Bortolato, M., and Shih, J. C. (2011). Behavioral outcomes of monoamine oxidase deficiency: Preclinical and clinical evidence. *International Review of Neurobiology*, 100: 13–42.

Bos, P. A., Terburga, D., and van Honka, J. (2010). Testosterone decreases trust in socially naïve humans. *Proceedings of the National Academy of Sciences of the United States of America*, 107(22): 9991–95.

Bowers, M. B., Choi, D. C., and Ressler, K. J. (2012). Neuropeptide regulation of fear and anxiety: Implications of cholecystokinin, endogenous opiates, and neuropeptide Y. *Physiology and Behavior*, 107(5): 699–710.

Bowlby, J. (1969–80). *Attachment and Loss*, 3 vols. New York: Basic Books.

(1988). *A Secure Base: Parent–Child Attachment and Healthy Human Development*. London: Routledge.

(1995). *Maternal Care and Mental Health* (2nd edn.). Northvale, NJ: Jason Aronson.

(1999). *Attachment and Loss*, Vol. 1 (2nd edn.). New York: Basic Books.

Bradwejn, J. (1993). Neurobiological investigations into the role of cholecystokinin in panic disorder. *Journal of Psychiatry and Neuroscience*, 18(4): 178–88.

Bradwejn, J., Koszycki, D., Annable, L., Couetoux du Tertre, A., van Megen, H., den Boer, J., and Westenberg, H. (1994). The panicogenic effects of cholecystokinin-tetrapeptide are antagonized by L-365,260, a central cholecystokinin receptor antagonist, in patients with panic disorder. *Archives of General Psychiatry*, 51(6): 486–93.

Bradwejn, J., Koszycki, D., Paradis, M., Reece, P., Hinton, J., and Sedman, A. (1995). Effect of CI-988 on cholecystokinin tetrapeptide-induced panic symptoms in healthy volunteers. *Biological Psychiatry*, 38: 742–46.

Bradwejn, J., Koszycki, D., and Shriqui, C. (1991). Enhanced sensitivity to cholecystokinin tetrapeptide in panic disorder: Clinical and behavioral findings. *Archives of General Psychology*, 48(7): 603–10.

Bradwejn, J., Zhou, Y., Koszycki, D., and Shlik, J. (2000). A double-blind, placebo-controlled study on the effects of gotu kola (*Centella asiatica*) on acoustic startle response in healthy subjects. *Journal of Clinical Psychopharmacology*, 20(6): 680–84.

Breen, C. A., and Atwood, H. L. (1983). Octopamine: A neurohormone with presynaptic activity-dependent effects at crayfish neuromuscular junctions. *Nature*, 303(5919): 716–18.

Brehm, J., and Cohen, A. (1962). *Explorations in Cognitive Dissonance*. New York: John Wiley.

Bremer, F. (1935). Cerveau "isole" et physiologie du sommeil. *Comptes Rendus des Séances de la Société de Biologie et des ses Filiales*, 118: 1235–41.

Bressan, R. A., Erlandsson, K., Jones, H. M., Mulligan, R. S., Ell, P. J., and Pilowsky, L. S. (2002). Optimizing limbic selective D2/D3 receptor occupancy by risperidone: A 123-epidepride SPECT study. *Journal of Clinical Psychopharmacology*, 23(1): 5–14.

Bretherton, I. (1985). Attachment theory: Retrospect and prospect. *Monographs of the Society for Research in Child Development*, 50(1–2): 3–35.

(1992). The origins of attachment theory: John Bowlby and Mary Ainsworth. *Developmental Psychology*, 28(5): 759–75.

Breugelmans, S. M., and Poortinga, Y. H. (2006). Emotion without a word: Shame and guilt among Raramuri Indians and rural Javanese. *Journal of Personality and Social Psychology*, 91: 1111–22.

Brinton, C. (1938). *The Anatomy of Revolution*. New York: Prentice-Hall.

Broca, P. (1861). Remarks on the seat of the faculty of articulated language, following an observation of aphemia (loss of speech). *Bulletin de la Société Anatomique*, 6: 330–57. http://psychclassics.asu.edu/Broca/aphemie-e.html.

Brock, T. C., and Buss, A. H. (1962). Dissonance, aggression, and evaluation of pain. *Journal of Applied Social Psychology*, 65: 403–12.

Bronfenbrenner, U. (1962). The role of age, sex, class, and culture in studies of moral development. *Religious Education Research Supplement*, 57(4): 3–17.

Brown, R. (1965). *Social Psychology*. Glencoe, IL: Free Press.

Brown, S. L., Botsis, A., and van Praag, H. M. (1994). Serotonin and aggression. *Journal of Offender Rehabilitation*, 21: 27–39.

Buchanan, T. W., Tranel, D., and Adolphs, R. (2006). Memories for emotional autobiographical events following unilateral damage to medial temporal lobe. *Brain*, 129(1): 115–27.

Buchheim, A., Heinrichs, M., George, C., Pokorny, D., Koops, E., Henningsen, P., O'Connor, M.-F., and Gündel, H. (2009). Oxytocin enhances the experience of attachment security. *Psychoneuroendocrinology*, 34: 1417–22.

Buchsbaum, R. (1948). *Animals Without Backbones: An Introduction to the Invertebrates*. Chicago: University of Chicago Press.

Buck, R. (1972). Relationships between dissonance-reducing behaviors and tension measures following aggression.Unpublished doctoral dissertation. University of Pittsburgh, Pittsburgh, PA.

(1975). Nonverbal communication of affect in children. *Journal of Personality and Social Psychology*, 31(4): 644–53.

(1976). *Human Motivation and Emotion*. New York: Wiley.

(1977). Nonverbal communication of affect in preschool children: Relationships with personality and skin conductance. *Journal of Personality and Social Psychology*, 35(4): 225–36.

(1979). Individual differences in nonverbal sending accuracy and electrodermal responding: The externalizing-internalizing dimension. In R. Rosenthal (ed.), *Skill in Nonverbal Communication: Individual Differences* (pp. 140–70). Cambridge, MA: Oelgeschlager, Gunn, & Hain.

(1980). Nonverbal behavior and the theory of emotion: The facial feedback hypothesis. *Journal of Personality and Social Psychology*, 38(5): 811–24.

(1983). Emotional development and emotional education. In R. Plutchik and H. Kellerman (eds.), *Emotion in Early Development* (pp. 259–92). New York: Academic Press.

(1984). *The Communication of Emotion*. New York: Guilford Press.

(1985). Prime theory: An integrated view of motivation and emotion. *Psychological Review*, 92(3): 389–413.

(1988a [1976]). *Human Motivation and Emotion* (2nd edn.). New York: John Wiley.

(1988b). Emotional education and mass media: A new view of the global village. In R. P. Hawkins, J. M. Weimann, and S. Pingree (eds.), *Advancing Communication Science: Merging Mass and Interpersonal Perspectives* (pp. 44–76). Beverly Hills, CA: Sage Publications.

(1989a). Emotional communication in personal relationships: A developmental-interactionist view. In C. D. Hendrick (ed.), *Review of Personality and Social Psychology* (Vol. 10, pp. 144–63). Newbury Park, CA: Sage Publications.

(1989b). Subjective, expressive, and peripheral bodily components of emotion. In H. L. Wagner and A. S. R. Manstead (eds.), *Handbook of Psychophysiology: Emotion and Social Behavior* (pp.199–221). Chichester: John Wiley.

(1990). William James, the nature of knowledge, and current issues in emotion, cognition, and communication. *Personality and Social Psychology Bulletin*, 16(4): 612–25.

(1993a). What is this thing called subjective experience? Reflections on the neuropsychology of qualia. *Neuropsychology*, 7(4): 490–99.

(1993b). Spontaneous communication and the foundation of the interpersonal self. In U. Neisser (ed.), *The Perceived Self: Ecological and Interpersonal Sources of Self-Knowledge: Proceedings of the Emory Symposium on Cognition* (Vol. 1, pp. 216–36). Cambridge University Press.

(1993c). Emotional communication, emotional competence, and physical illness: A developmental-interactionist view. In H. Traue and J. W. Pennebaker (eds.), *Emotional Expressiveness, Inhibition, and Health* (pp. 32–56). Seattle, WA: Hogrefe & Huber.

(1993d). The Nebraska Symposium returns to its roots. *PsycCRITIQUES*, 38: 55–57.

(1994a). Social and emotional functions in facial expression and communication: The readout hypothesis. *Biological Psychology*, 38(2–3): 95–115.

(1994b). The neuropsychology of communication: Spontaneous and symbolic aspects. *Journal of Pragmatics*, 22(3–4): 265–78.

(1999). The biological affects: A typology. *Psychological Review*, 106(2): 301–36.

(2002a). The genetics and biology of true love: Prosocial biological affects and the left hemisphere. *Psychological Review*, 109(4): 739–44.

(2002b). "Choice" and "emotion" in altruism: Reflections on the morality of justice versus the morality of caring. *Behavioral and Brain Sciences*, 25(2): 254–55.

(2004). The gratitude of exchange and the gratitude of caring. In R. A. Emmons (ed.), *The Psychology of Gratitude* (pp. 100–22). Oxford University Press.

(2007). The evolutionary bases of social and moral emotions: Dominance, submission, and true love. In J. P. Forgas, M. Haselton, and W. von Hippel (eds.), *The Evolution of the Social Mind: Evolutionary Psychology and Social Cognition* (pp. 89–106). New York: Psychology Press.

(2010a). Emotion is an entity at both biological and ecological levels: The ghost in the machine is language. *Emotion Review*, 2(3): 286–87.

(2010b). Silly love songs: Through love songs we explore strong prosocial feelings. *Psychology Today* Weblog. www.psychologytoday.com/blog/spontaneous-emotion.

(2011). Communicative genes in the evolution of empathy and altruism. *Behavioral Genetics*, 41(6): 876–88.

(2012). Prime elements of subjectively experienced feelings and desires: Imaging the emotional cocktail. *Behavioral and Brain Sciences*, 35(3): 144.

Buck, R., Anderson, E., Chaudhuri, A., and Ray, I. (2004). Emotion and reason in persuasion: Applying the ARI model and the CASC scale. *Journal of Business Research: Marketing Communications and Consumer Behavior*, 57(6): 647–56.

Buck, R., and Boone, R. T. (2009a). Externalizer. In D. Sander and K. Scherer (eds.), *The Oxford Companion to Emotion and the Affective Sciences* (p. 169). New York: Oxford University Press.

(2009b). Internalizer. In D. Sander and K. Scherer (eds.), *The Oxford Companion to Emotion and the Affective Sciences* (p. 375). New York: Oxford University Press.

Buck, R., and Chaudhuri, A. (1994). Affect, reason, and involvement in persuasion: The ARI model. In Forschungsgruppe Konsum und Verhalten (Hrsg.), *Konsumenten Forschung [Consumer Research]* (pp.107–17). Munich: Verlag Franz Vahlen.

Buck, R., and Davis, W. A. (2010). Marketing risk: Emotional appeals can promote the mindless acceptance of risk. In S. Roeser (ed.), *Emotions and Risky Technologies* (Vol. 5, pp. 61–80). New York: Springer.

Buck, R., and Duffy, R. (1980). Nonverbal communication of affect in brain damaged patients. *Cortex*, 16(3): 351–62.

Buck, R., Easton, C. J., and Goldman, C. K. (1995). A developmental-interactionist theory of motivation, emotion, and cognition: Implications for understanding psychopathology. *The Japanese Journal of Research on Emotions*, 3(1): 1–16.

Buck, R., and Ferrer, R. (2012). Emotion, warnings, and the ethics of risk communication. In S. Roeser, R. Hillerbrand, P. Sandin, and M. Peterson (eds.), *Handbook of Risk Theory* (pp. 694–723). New York: Springer.

Buck, R., and Ginsburg, B. (1991). Emotional communication and altruism: The communicative gene hypothesis. In E. M. Clark (ed.), *Review of Personality and Social Psychology* (Vol. 12, pp. 149–75). Newbury Park, CA: Sage Publications.

(1997a). Communicative genes and the evolution of empathy. In W. Ickes (ed.), *Empathetic Accuracy* (pp. 17–43). New York: Guilford Press.

(1997b). Selfish and social emotions as voices of selfish and social genes. In C. S. Carter, I. I. Lederhendler, and B. Kirkpatrick (eds.), *The Integrative Neurobiology of Affiliation*, Annals of the New York Academy of Sciences (Vol. 807, pp. 481–83). New York: New York Academy of Sciences.

Buck, R., Goldman, C. K., Easton, C. J., and Smith, N. N. (1998). Social learning and emotional education: Emotional expression and communication in behaviorally-disordered children and schizophrenic patients. In W. F. Flack and J. D. Laird (eds.), *Emotions in Psychopathology* (pp. 298–314). New York: Oxford University Press.

Buck, R., Kenny, D. A., Powers, S. R., Boone, R. T., Triantis, G., Ferrer, R., and Iwamitsu, Y. (2007). Individual and dyad-level factors in emotional communication. Symposium on The Communication of Emotion in Close Relationships. Chair: Joan K. Monin. Presented at the meeting of the Society of Personality and Social Psychology, Memphis, TN, USA January 2007.

Buck, R. W., Miller, R. E., and Caul, W. F. (1974). Sex, personality, and physiological variables in the communication of emotion via facial expression. *Journal of Personality and Social Psychology*, 30(4): 587–96.

Buck, R., Nakamura, M., Vieira, E. T., Jr., and Polonsky M. (2005). A developmental-interactionist theory of biological and higher level emotions: A cross-national comparison of America and Japan. Plenary presentation at the Symposium on New Perspectives in Affective Science. Kyoto University, Kyoto, Japan. January 2005. Paper submitted for publication.

Buck, R., and Powers, S. R. (2006). The biological foundations of social organization: The dynamic emergence of social structure through nonverbal communication. In V. Manusov and M. Patterson (eds.), *The Sage Handbook of Nonverbal Communication* (pp. 119–38). Thousand Oaks, CA: Sage Publications.

(2010). Mirror neurons, primary intersubjectivity, and the affective and rational aspects of empathy: A developmental-interactionist view. Invited presentation at the Symposium on the Neuroscience of Empathy. Emotion Preconference. Society of Personality and Social Psychology Annual Meeting, Las Vegas, NV, January 14.

(2011). Emotion, media, and the global village. In K. Doveling, C. von Scheve, and E. A. Konijn (eds.), *The Routledge Handbook of Emotions and Mass Media* (pp. 181–94). New York: Routledge.

(2013). Encoding and display: A developmental-interactionist model of nonverbal sending accuracy. In J. Hall and M. Knapp (eds.), *Nonverbal Communication: Handbook of Communication Sciences* (pp. 403–40). Berlin and Boston: Mouton de Gruyter.

Buck, R., Powers, S. R., and Kapp, W. (2011). Developing the communication of affect receiving ability test-spontaneous-posed-regulated. Presented at the International Communication Association Convention, Boston, May.

Buck, R. W., Savin, V. J., Miller, R. E., and Caul, W. F. (1972). Nonverbal communication of affect in humans. *Journal of Personality and Social Psychology*, 23: 362–71.

Buck, R., and Van Lear, C. A. (2002). Verbal and nonverbal communication: Distinguishing symbolic, spontaneous, and pseudo-spontaneous nonverbal behavior. *Journal of Communication*, 52(3): 522–41.

Burgdorf, J., and Panksepp, J. (2001). Tickling induces reward in adolescent rats. *Physiology & Behavior*, 72(1–2): 167–73.

Burgoon, J., Stern, L. A., and Dillman, L. (1995). *Interpersonal Adaptation: Dyadic Interaction Patterns*. Cambridge University Press.

Burt, D. M., and Perrett, D. I. (1995). Perception of age in adult Caucasian male faces: Computer graphic manipulation of shape and colour information. *Proceedings of the Royal Society of London B*, 259(1355): 137–43.

(1997). Perceptual asymmetries in judgments of facial attractiveness, age, gender, speech, and expression. *Neuropsychologia*, 35(5): 685–93.

Buss, A. H., and Brock, T. C. (1963). Repression and guilt in relation to aggression. *Journal of Applied Social Psychology*, 66: 345–50.

Bussey, K., and Maughan, B. (1982). Gender differences in moral reasoning. *Journal of Personality and Social Psychology*, 42: 701–6.

Butler, E. A., Wilhelm, F. H., and Gross, J. J. (2006). Respiratory sinus arrhythmia, emotion, and emotion regulation during social interaction. *Psychophysiology*, 43(6): 612–22.

Butler, R. (1994). Teacher communications and student interpretations: Effects of teacher responses to failing students on attributional inferences in two age groups. *British Journal of Educational Psychology*, 64(2): 277–94.

Cacioppo, J. T., and Berntson, G. G. (1992). Social psychological contributions to the decade of the brain: Doctrine of multilevel analysis. *American Psychologist*, 47(8): 1019–28.

Cahill, L. (2005). His brain, her brain. *Scientific American*, 292(5): 40–47.

Cahill, L., Uncapher, M., Kilpatrick, L., Alkire, M. T., and Turner, J. (2004). Sex-related hemispheric lateralization of amygdala function in emotionally influenced memory: An fMRI investigation. *Learning and Memory*, 11(3): 261–66.

Calder, A. J. (2003). Disgust discussed. *Annals of Neurology*, 53(4): 427–28.

Calder, A. J., Beaver, J. D., Davis, M. H., van Ditzhuijzen, J., Keane, J., and Lawrence, A. D. (2007). Disgust sensitivity predicts the insula and pallidal response to pictures of disgusting foods. *European Journal of Neuroscience*, 25(11): 3422–28.

Calder, A. J., Keane, J., Manes, F., Antoun, N., and Young, A. W. (2000). Impaired recognition and experience of disgust following brain injury. *Nature Neuroscience*, 3(11): 1077–78.

Caldwell, H. K., Dike, O. E., Stevenson, E. L., Storck, K., and Young, W. S. III (2010). Social dominance in male vasopressin 1b receptor knockout mice. *Hormones and Behavior*, 58(2): 257–63.

Caldwell, J. D. (1992). Central oxytocin and female sexual behavior. In C. A. Pedersen, J. D. Caldwell, G. F. Jirikowski, and T. R. Insel (eds.), *Oxytocin in Maternal, Sexual, and Social Behaviors* (pp. 166–79). New York: New York Academy of Sciences.

Campbell, C. B. G. (1992). The triune brain in the evolution [Review of P. D. MacLean, *The Triune Brain in Evolution: Role in Paleocerebral Functions*]. *American Scientist*, 80: 497–98.

Campbell, W. K., Foster, J. D., and Brunell, A. B. (2004). Running from shame or reveling in pride? Narcissism and the regulation of self-conscious emotions. *Psychological Inquiry*, 15(2): 150–53.

Campos, J. J., Walle, E. A., and Dahl, A. (2010). What is missing in the study of the development of jealousy? In S. L. Hart, and M. Legerstee (eds.), *Handbook of Jealousy: Theory, Research, and Multidisciplinary Approaches* (pp. 312–28). New York: Wiley-Blackwell.

Cannon, W. B. (1927). The James–Lange theory of emotions: A critical examination and an alternative theory. *American Journal of Psychology*, 39(1): 106–24.

(1932). *The Wisdom of the Body*. New York: W. W. Norton.

Cardoso, C., Linnen, A., Joober, R., and Ellenbogen, M. A. (2012). Coping style moderates the effect of intranasal oxytocin on the mood response to interpersonal stress. *Experimental and Clinical Psychopharmacology*, 20(2): 84–91.

Carter, C. S. (1992). Oxytocin and sexual behavior. *Neuroscience and Biobehavioral Reviews*, 16(2): 131–44.

(1998). Neuroendocrine perspectives on social attachment and love. *Psychoneuroendocrinology*, 23(8): 779–818.

Carter, C. S., Boone, E. M., Pournajafi-Nazarloo, H., and Bales, K. L. (2009). Consequences of early experiences and exposure to oxytocin and vasopressin are sexually dimorphic. *Developmental Neuroscience*, 31(4): 332–41.

Carter, C. S., and DeVries, A. C. (1999). Stress and soothing: An endocrine perspective. In M. Lewis and R. Douglas (eds.), *Soothing and Stress* (pp. 3–18). Mahwah, NJ: Lawrence Erlbaum Associates.

Carter, C. S., Grippo, A. J., Pournajafi-Nazarloo, H., Ruscio, M. G., Porges, S. W., Inga, D. N., and Rainer, L. (2008). Oxytocin, vasopressin and sociality. *Progress in Brain Research*, 170: 331–36.

Carter, C. S., Lederhendler, I. I., and Kirkpatrick, B. (eds.) (1997). *The Integrative Neurobiology of Affiliation*, Annals of the New York Academy of Sciences, Vol. 807. New York: New York Academy of Sciences.

Carver, C. S., and Miller, C. J. (2006). Relations of serotonin function to personality: Current views and a key methodological issue. *Psychiatry Research*, 144(1): 1–15.

Castrogiovanni, P., Maremmani, I., Bongioanni, P., and Marazziti, D. (1990). Platelet monoaminooxidase activity and behavioural characteristics in humans. *Neuropsychobiology*, 23: 173–76.

Cattaert, D., Delbecque, J.-P., Edwards, D. H., and Issa, F. A. (2010). Social interactions determine postural network sensitivity to 5-HT. *Journal of Neuroscience*, 30(16): 5603–16.

Chaiken, S. (1980). Heuristic versus systematic information processing and the use of source versus message cues in persuasion. *Journal of Personality and Social Psychology*, 39(5): 752–66.

(1987). The heuristic model of persuasion. In M. P. Zanna, J. M. Olson, and C. P. Herman (eds.), *Social Influence: The Ontario Symposium* (Vol. 5, pp. 3–39). Hillsdale, NJ: Lawrence Erlbaum Associates.

Chaiken, S., and Eagley, A. H. (1983). Communication modality as a determinant of persuasion: The role of communicator salience. *Journal of Personality and Social Psychology*, 45(2): 241–56.

Chattwood, A., and Thompson, C. R. (2011). Non-genetic heterogeneity and cell fate choice in Dictyostelium discoideum. *Development, Growth, and Differentiation*, 53(4): 558–66.

Chaudhuri, A., and Buck, R. (1995). Media differences in rational and emotional responses to advertising. *Journal of Broadcasting & Electronic Media*, 39(1): 109–25.

Chhatwal, J. P., Gutman, A. R., Maguschak, K. A., Bowser, M. E., Yang, Y., Davis, M., and Ressler, K. J. (2009). Functional interactions between endocannabinoid and CCK neurotransmitter systems may be critical for extinction learning. *Neuropsychopharmacology*, 34(2): 509–21.

Chomsky, N. (1972). *Language and Mind*. New York: Harcourt Brace Jovanovich.

(1980). *Rules and Representations*. New York: Columbia University Press.

Churchland, P. S., and Winkielman, P. (2012). Modulating social behavior with oxytocin: How does it work? What does it mean? *Hormones and Behavior*, 61(3): 392–99.

Chwalisz, K., Diener, E., and Gallagher, D. (1988). Autonomic arousal feedback and emotional experience: Evidence from the spinal cord injured. *Journal of Personality and Social Psychology*, 54(5): 820–28.

Cikara, M., Eberhardt, J. L., and Fiske, S. T. (2010). From agents to objects: Sexist attitudes and neural responses to sexualized targets. *Journal of Cognitive Neuroscience*, 23(3): 540–51.

Clynes, M. (1977). *Sentics: The Touch of Emotions*. New York: Doubleday/Anchor.

(1980). The communication of emotion: Theory of sentics. In R. Plutchik and H. Kellerman (eds.), *Emotion: Theory, Research and Experience*, Vol. 1: *Theories of Emotion* (pp. 271–300). New York: Academic Press.

(1988). Generalised emotion, its production, and sentic cycle therapy. In M. Clynes and J. Panksepp (eds.), *Emotions and Psychopathology* (pp. 107–70). New York: Plenum.

Coccaro, E. F. (1992). Impulsive aggression and central serotonergic system function in humans: An example of a dimensional brain-behavior relationship. *International Clinical Psychopharmacology*, 7(1): 3–12.

Coccaro, E. F., Kavoussi, R. J., Hauger, R. L., Cooper, T. B., and Ferris, C. F. (1998). Cerebrospinal fluid vasopressin levels: Correlates with aggression and serotonin function in personality-disordered subjects. *Archives of General Psychiatry*, 55(8): 708–14.

Cohen, J. D., Braver, T. S., and Brown, J. W. (2002). Computational perspectives on dopamine function in prefrontal cortex. *Current Opinion in Neurobiology*, 12(2): 223–29.

Cohen, T. R., Wolff, S. T., Panter, A. T., and Insko, C. A. (2011). Introducing the GASP scale: A new measure of guilt and shame proneness. *Journal of Personality and Social Psychology*, 100(5): 947–66.

Coleman-Mesches, K., and McGaugh, J. L. (1995a). Differential involvement of the right and left amygdalae in expression of memory for aversively motivated training. *Brain Research*, 670(1): 75–81.

(1995b). Muscimol injected into the right or left amygdaloid complex differentially affects retention performance following aversively motivated training. *Brain Research*, 676(1): 183–88.

(1995c). Muscimol injected into the right or left amygdaloid complex differentially affects retention performance following aversively motivated training. *Brain Research*, 676: 183–88.

Coleman-Mesches, K., Salinas, J. A., and McGaugh, J. L. (1996). Unilateral amygdala inactivation after training attenuates memory for reduced reward. *Behavioral Brain Research*, 77: 175–80.

Common Sense Media (2012). www.commonsensemedia.org/.

Condon, W. S. (1973a). An analysis of behavioral organization. In S. Weitz (ed.), *Nonverbal Communication* (2nd edn., pp. 149–67). New York: Oxford University Press.

(1973b). Communication and order: The micro-rhythm hierarchy of speaker behavior. Paper presented at the Convention of School Psychologists, New York.

(1979). Neonatal entrainment and enculturation. In M. Bullowa (ed.), *Before Speech: The Beginning of Interpersonal Communication* (pp. 131–68). Cambridge University Press.

(1982). Cultural microrhythms. In M. Davis (ed.), *Interaction Rhythms: Periodicity in Communicative Behavior* (pp. 53–76). New York: Human Sciences.

Condon, W. S., and Ogston, W. D. (1966). Sound film analysis of normal and pathological behavior. *Journal of Neurological and Mental Diseases*, 143 (4): 338–47.

Condon, W. S., and Sander, L. W. (1974). Neonate movement is synchronized with adult speech: Interactional participation and language acquisition. *Science*, 183: 99–101.

Cornelius, R. R. (1996). *The Science of Emotion: Research and Tradition in Psychology and Emotion*. Upper Saddle River, NJ: Prentice Hall.

Cory, G. A. (2002). Reappraising MacLean's triune brain concept. In G. A. Cory and R. Gardner (eds.), *The Evolutionary Neuroethology of Paul D. MacLean: Convergences and Frontiers* (pp. 9–27). Westport, CT: Praeger.

Cory, G. A., and Gardner, R. (eds.) (2002). *The Evolutionary Neuroethology of Paul D. MacLean: Convergences and Frontiers*. Westport, CT: Praeger.

Costa, E., and Guidotti, A. (1991). Diazepam binding inhibitor (DBI): A peptide with multiple biological actions. *Life Sciences*, 49(5): 325–44.

Coursey, R. D., Buchsbaum, M. S., and Murphy, D. L. (1979). Platelet MAO activity and evoked potentials in the identification of subjects biologically at risk for psychiatric disorders. *British Journal of Psychiatry*, 134: 372–81.

Craig, I. W. (2005). The role of monoamine oxidase A, MAOA, in the aetiology of antisocial behaviour: The importance of gene-environment interactions. In G. Bock and J. Goode (eds.), *Molecular Mechanisms Influencing Aggressive Behaviours: The Novartis Foundation Symposium 268* (pp. 227–37). Chichester: John Wiley.

Creighton, M. R. (1990). Revisiting shame and guilt cultures: A forty-year pilgrimage. *Ethos*, 18(3): 279–307.

Cruciani, F., Trombetta, B., Massaia, A., Destro-Bisol, G., Sellitto, D., and Scozzari, R. (2011). A revised root for the human Y chromosomal phylogenetic tree: The origin of patrilineal diversity in Africa. *American Journal of Human Genetics*, 88(6): 814–18.

Damasio, A. (1994). *Decartes' Error: Emotion, Reason, and the Human Brain*. New York: Gosset/Putnam.

Damasio, A. R., Grabowski, T. J., Bechara, A., Damasio, H., Ponto, L. L. B., Parvizi, J., and Hichwa, R. D. (2000). Subcortical and cortical brain activity during the feeling of self-generated emotions. *Nature Neuroscience*, 3: 1049–56.

Damasio, H., Grabowski, T., Frank, R., Galaburda, A. M., and Damasio, A. R. (1994). The return of Phineas Gage: Clues about the brain from the skull of a famous patient. *Science*, 264(5162): 1102–5.

Darley, J. M., and Batson, C. D. (1973). "From Jerusalem to Jericho": A study of situational and dispositional variables in helping behavior. *Journal of Personality and Social Psychology*, 27(1): 107–8.

Darley, J. M., and Latané, B. (1968a). Bystander intervention in emergencies: Diffusion of responsibility. *Journal of Personality and Social Psychology*, 8: 377–83.

(1968b). When will people help in a crisis? *Psychology Today*, 2: 54–71.

Darley, J. M., Teger, A. I., and Lewis, L. D. (1973). Do groups always inhibit individuals' responses to potential emergencies? *Journal of Personality and Social Psychology*, 26: 395–99.

Darwin, C. (1998 [1872]). *The expression of the emotions in man and animals* (3rd edn.), ed. C. Ekman. London: Oxford University Press.

Davidson, L., and Schaffner, B. (1977). Contrasts and similarities in the handling of emotions in two different cultures. *Hiroshima Forum for Psychology*, 4: 59–67.

Davidson, R. J., and Fox, N. A. (1982). Asymmetrical brain activity discriminates between positive and negative affective stimuli in human infants. *Science*, 218(4578): 1235–37.

Davidson, R. J., and Irwin, W. (1999). The functional neuroanatomy of emotion and affective style. *Trends in Cognitive Sciences*, 3(1): 11–21.

Dawes, C. T., Loewen, P. J., Schreiber, D., Simmons, A. N., Flagan, T., McElreath, R., Bokemper, S. E., Fowler, J. H., and Paulus, M. P. (2012). Neural basis of egalitarian behavior. *Proceedings of the National Academy of Sciences of the United States of America*, 109(17): 6479–83.

Deacon, T. W. (1988). Evolution of human language circuits. In H. Jerison, and I. Jerison (eds.), *Intelligence and Evolutionary Biology*. New York: Springer Verlag.

(1989). The neural circuitry underlying primate calls and human language. *Human Evolution*, 4(5): 367–401.

de Beun, R., Geerts, N. E., Jansen, E., Slangen, J. L., and van de Poll, N. E. (1991). Luteinizing hormone releasing hormone-induced conditioned place-preference in male rats. *Pharmacology Biochemistry and Behavior*, 39(1): 143–47.

Decety, J., and Jackson, P. L. (2004). The functional architecture of human empathy. *Behavioral and Cognitive Neuroscience Reviews*, 3(2): 71–100.

de Charms, R. (1968). *Personal Causation*. New York: Academic Press.

Deci, E. L. and Ryan, R. M. (1991). A motivational approach to self: Integration in personality. In R. Dienstbier (ed.), *Nebraska Symposium on Motivation 1990: Perspectives on Motivation* (pp. 237–88). Lincoln: University of Nebraska Press.

Deckel, A. W. (1995). Laterality of aggressive responses in Anolis. *Journal of Experimental Zoology*, 272(3): 194–200.

De Dreu, C. K. W. (2012). Oxytocin modulates cooperation within and competition between groups: An integrative review and research agenda. *Hormones and Behavior*, 61(3): 419–28.

Delgado, J. M. R. (1969). *Physical Control of the Mind*. New York: Harper & Row.

Delgado, J. M. R., Roberts, W. W., and Miller, N. E. (1954). Learning motivated by electrical stimulation of the brain. *American Journal of Physiology*, 179(3): 587–93.

Delis, D. C., Robertson, L. C., and Efron, R. (1986). Hemispheric specialization of memory for visual hierarchical stimuli. *Neuropsychologia*, 24(2): 205–14.

de Montigny, C. (1989). Cholecystokinin tetrapeptide induces panic-like attacks in healthy volunteers. *Archives of General Psychology*, 46(6): 511–17.

Denenberg, V. H. (1981). Hemispheric laterality in animals and the effects of early experience. *Behavioral and Brain Sciences*, 4(1): 1–21.

(1984). Behavioral asymmetry. In N. Geschwind and A. M. Galaburda (eds.), *Cerebral Dominance: The Biological Foundations* (pp. 114–33). Cambridge, MA: Harvard University Press.

Denenberg, V. H., and Yutzey, D. (1985). Hemispheric specialization of memory for visual hierarchical stimuli. *Neuropsychologia*, 24: 205–14.

Denham, S. A. (1986). Social cognition, prosocial behavior, and emotion in preschoolers: Contextual validation. *Child Development*, 57(1): 194–201.

DePaulo, B., Rosenthal, R., Eisenstat, R., Rogers, P., and Finkelstein, S. (1978). Decoding discrepant nonverbal cues. *Journal of Personality and Social Psychology*, 36: 313–23.

de Rivera, Joseph (1989). Comparing experiences across cultures: Shame and guilt in American and Japanese. *Hiroshima Forum for Psychology*, 14: 13–20.

Des Roches, A. D. B., Richard-Yris, M. A., Henry, S., Ezzaouïa, M., and Hausberger, M. (2008). Laterality and emotions: Visual laterality in the domestic horse (*Equus caballus*) differs with objects' emotional value. *Physiology & Behavior*, 94(3): 487–90.

Deutsch, J. A. (1972). Brain reward: ESB and ecstasy. *Psychology Today*, 6: 45–48.

Deutsch, M. (2006). A framework for thinking about oppression and its change. *Social Justice Research*, 19(1): 7–41.

De Vries, G. J. (1996). Brain sexual dimorphism and parental behavior. Presentation at the New York Academy of Sciences Conference on the Integrative Neurobiology of Affiliation, Georgetown University, Washington, DC, March 14–17.

De Vries, G. J., Buijs, R. M., van Leeuwen, F. W., Caffé, A. R., and Swaab, D. F. (1985). The vasopressinergic innervation of the brain in normal and castrated rats. *Journal of Comparative Neurology*, 233(2): 236–54.

De Vries, G. J. and Villalba, C. (1997). Brain sexual dimorphism and parental and other social behaviors. In C. S. Carter, I. I. Lederhendler, and B. Kirkpatrick (eds.), *The Integrative Neurobiology of Affiliation*, Annals of the New York Academy of Sciences (Vol. 807, pp. 273–86). New York: New York Academy of Sciences.

De Vries, G. J., Wang, Z., Bullock, N. A., and Numan, S. (1994). Sex differences in the effects of testosterone and its metabolites on vasopressin messenger RNA levels in the bed nucleus of the stria terminalis of rats. *Journal of Neuroscience*, 14(3): 1789–94.

de Waal, F. B. M. (2002). Evolutionary psychology: The wheat and the chaff. *Current Directions in Psychological Science*, 11: 187–91.

(2008). Putting the altruism back into altruism: The evolution of empathy. *Annual Review of Psychology*, 59: 279–300.

de Waal, F. B. M., and Aureli, F. (1997). Conflict resolution and distress alleviation in monkeys and apes. In C. S. Carter, I. I. Lederhendler, and B. Kirkpatrick (eds.), *The Integrative Neurobiology of Affiliation*, Annals of the New York Academy of Sciences (Vol. 807, pp. 317–28). New York: New York Academy of Sciences.

de Waal, F. B. M., and Roosmalen, A. (1979). Reconciliation and consolation among chimpanzees. *Behavioral Ecology and Sociobiology*, 5(1): 55–66.

DeWied, D., and Gispen, W. H. (1977). Behavioral effects of peptides. In H. Gainer (ed.), *Peptides in Neurobiology* (pp. 397–448). New York: Plenum.

Dijker, A. J. (2001). The influence of perceived suffering and vulnerability on the experience of pity. *European Journal of Social Psychology*, 31(6): 659–77.

Dijker, A. J., and Koomen, W. (2003). Extending Weiner's attribution–emotion model of stigmatization of ill persons. *Basic & Applied Social Psychology*, 25: 51–69.

Dimberg, U., Thunberg, M., and Elmehed, K. (2000). Unconscious facial reactions to emotional facial expressions. *Psychological Science*, 11(1): 86–89.

Di Pellegrino, G., Fadiga, L., Fogassi, L., Gallese, V., and Rizzolatti, G. (1992). Understanding motor events: A neurophysiological study. *Experimental Brain Research*, 91(1): 176–80.

Dixon, D., Jenkens, I., Moody, R. T. J., and Zhuravlev, A. Y. (2001). *Atlas of Life on Earth*. New York: Barnes & Noble.

Dixon, T. (2012). "Emotion": The history of a keyword in crisis. *Emotion Review*, 4: 338–44.

Dodd, M. D., Balzer, A., Jacobs, C., Gruszczynski, M., Smith, K. B., and Hibbing, J. R. (2012). The political left rolls with the good, the political right confronts the bad: Physiology and cognition in politics. *Philosophical Transactions of the Royal Society B*, 367(1589): 640–49.

Domes, G., Heinrichs, M., Gläscher, J., Büchel, C., Braus, D. F., and Herpertz, S. C. (2007a). Oxytocin attenuates amygdala responses to emotional faces regardless of valence. *Biological Psychiatry*, 62(10): 1187–90.

Domes, G., Heinrichs, M., Michel, A., Berger, C., and Herpertz, S. C. (2007b). Oxytocin improves "mind-reading" in humans. *Biological Psychiatry*, 61(6): 731–33.

Donaldson, Z. R., and Young, L. J. (2008). Oxytocin, vasopressin, and the neurogenetics of sociality. *Science*, 322(5903): 900–4.

Donegan, N. H., Sanislow, C. A., Blumberg, H. P., Fulbright, R. K., Lacadie, C., Skudlarski, P., Gore, J. C., Olson, I. R., McGlashan, T. H., and Wexler, B. E. (2003). Amygdala hyperreactivity in borderline personality disorder: Implications for emotional dysregulation. *Biological Psychiatry*, 54(11): 1284–93.

Doty, R. M., Peterson, B. E., and Winter, D. G. (1991). Threat and authoritarianism in the United States, 1978–1987. *Journal of Personality and Social Psychology*, 61(4): 614–28.

Downie, A. (2009). Brazil's popular soap operas have done more than just entertain people. *The Telegraph*, April 4. www.telegraph.co.uk/news/world news/southamerica/brazil/5106647/Brazils-racy-telenovelas-inspire-drop-in-birth-rate-rise-in-divorce.html.

Duffy, R. J., and Buck, R. (1979). A study of the relationship between propositional (pantomime) and subpropositional (facial expression) extraverbal behavior in aphasics. *Folia Phoniatrica*, 31: 129–36.

Duffy, R. J., and Duffy, J. R. (1981). Three studies of deficits in pantomimic expression and pantomimic recognition in aphasia. *Journal of Speech and Hearing Research*, 24(1): 70–84.

Duffy, R. J., Duffy, J. R., and Pearson, K. (1975). Pantomime recognition in aphasics. *Journal of Speech and Hearing Disorders*, 44: 156–168.

Dunn, J., Slomkowski, C., and Beardsall, L. (1994). Sibling relationships from the preschool period through middle childhood and early adolescence. *Developmental Psychology*, 30: 315–24.

Durkheim, E. (1897). *Le suicide*. Paris: Alcan.

Dziobek, I., Bahnemann, M., Convit, A., and Heekeren, H. R. (2010). The role of the fusiform-amygdala system in the pathophysiology of autism. *Archives of General Psychiatry*, 67(4): 397–405.

Eagly, A. H. (1976). Sex differences in influenceability. *Psychological Bulletin*, 85: 86–116.

(1983). Gender and social influence: A social psychological analysis. *American Psychologist*, 38(9): 971–81.

Easterbrook, J. A. (1969). The effect of emotion of cue utilization and the organization of behavior. *Psychological Review*, 66: 183–201.

Easton, C. J. (1994). Expression and communication of emotion in schizophrenic patients. *Dissertation Abstracts International*, 55(9): 147.

Eberhard, A., Burlingame, A. L., Eberhard, C., Kenyon, G. L., Nealson, K. H., and Oppenheimer, N. J. (1981). Structural identification of autoinducer of Photobacterium fischeri luciferase. *Biochemistry*, 20(9): 2444–49.

Eccles, J. (1965). The synapse: From electrical to chemical transmission. *Scientific American*, 212: 56–66.

Eibl-Eibesfeldt, I. (1970). *Ethology: The Biology of Behavior*, trans. Erich Klinghammer. New York: Holt, Rinehart, & Winston.

(1979). *The Biology of Peace and War*. New York: Viking.

Eisenberg, N., Fabes, R. A., Miller, P. A., Fultz, J., Shell, R., Mathy, R. M., and Reno, R. R. (1989). Relation of sympathy and personal distress to prosocial behavior: A multimethod study. *Journal of Personality and Social Psychology*, 57(1): 55–66.

Eisenberger, N. I., Lieberman, M. D., and Williams, K. D. (2003). Does rejection hurt? An fMRI study of social exclusion. *Science*, 302(5643): 290–92.

Ekman, P. (1994). All emotions are basic. In P. Ekman and R. Davidson (eds.), *The Nature of Emotion: Fundamental Questions* (pp. 15–19). New York: Oxford University Press.

Ekman, P., and Davidson, R. (eds.) (1994). *The Nature of Emotion: Fundamental Questions*. New York: Oxford University Press.

Ekman, P., and Friesen, W. V. (1969a). Nonverbal leakage and cues to deception. *Psychiatry*, 32(1): 88–105.

(1969b). The repertoire of nonverbal behavior: Categories, origins, usage, and coding. *Semiotica*, 1: 49–98.

(1971). Constants across cultures in the face and emotion. *Journal of Personality and Social Psychology*, 17(2): 124–29.

(1975). *Unmasking the Face*. Englewood Cliffs, NJ: Prentice-Hall.

Ekman, P., Friesen, W. V., and Ellsworth, P. (1972). *Emotion in the Human Face*. New York: Pergamon.

Ekman, P., Sorenson, E. R., and Friesen, W. V. (1969). Pan-cultural elements in facial displays of emotion. *Science*, 164(3875): 86–88.

Emmons, R. A. (2004). The psychology of gratitude: An introduction. In R. A. Emmons (ed.), *The Psychology of Gratitude*. Oxford University Press.

Engebrecht, J., Nealson, K., and Silverman, M. (1983). Bacterial bioluminescence: Isolation and genetic analysis of functions from Vibrio fischeri. *Cell*, 32(3): 773–81.

Epstein, S., Pacini, R., Denes-Raj, V., and Heier, H. (1996). Individual differences in intuitive–experiential and analytical–rational thinking styles. *Journal of Personality and Social Psychology*, 71(2): 390–405.

Ermer, E., Cope, L. M., Nyalakanti, P. K., Calhoun, V. D., and Kiehl, K. A. (2012). Aberrant paralimbic gray matter in criminal psychopathy. *Journal of Abnormal Psychology*, 121(3): 649–58.

Esch, T., and Stefano, G. (2004). The neurobiology of pleasure, reward processes, addiction and their health implications. *Neuroendocrine Letters*, 25(4): 235–51.

Eysenck, H. J. (1967). *The Biological Basis of Personality*. Springfield, IL: Charles C. Thomas.

Farook, J. M., Zhu, Y. Z., Wang, H., Moochhala, S., Lee, L., and Wong, P. T. (2001). Strain differences in freezing behavior of PVG hooded and Sprague-Dawley rats: Differential cortical expression of cholecystokinin-sub-2 receptors. *Neuroreport: For Rapid Communication of Neuroscience Research*, 12(12): 2717–20.

Fattah, K., and Fierke, K. M. (2009). A clash of emotions: The politics of violence in the Middle East. *European Journal of International Relations*, 15(1): 67–93.

Feather, N. T. (2006). Deservingness and emotions: Applying the structural model of deservingness to the analysis of affective reactions to outcomes. *European Review of Social Psychology*, 17: 38–73.

Feather, N. T., McKee, I. R., and Bekker, N. (2011). Deservingness and emotions: Testing a structural model that relates to the perceived deservingness of positive or negative outcomes. *Motivation and Emotion*, 35(1): 1–13.

Feldman, R. (2012a). Oxytocin and social affiliation in humans. *Hormones and Behavior*, 61(3): 380–91.

(2012b). Parent–infant synchrony: A bio-behavioral model of mutual influences in the formation of affiliative bonds. *Monographs of the Society for Research in Child Development*, 77(2): 42–51.

Feldman, R., and Bamberger, E. (submitted for publication). Father–child reciprocity from infancy to adolescence shapes children's social and dialogical skills.

Feldman, R., Gordon, I., and Zagoory-Sharon, O. (2010). The cross-generation transmission of oxytocin in humans. *Hormones and Behavior*, 58(4): 669–76.

(2011). Maternal and paternal plasma, salivary, and urinary oxytocin and parent-infant synchrony: Considering stress and affiliation components of human bonding. *Developmental Science*, 14(4): 752–61.

Feldman, R., Weller, A., Zagoory-Sharon, O., and Levine, A. (2007). Evidence for a neuroendocrinological foundation of human affiliation: Plasma oxytocin levels across pregnancy and the postpartum period predict mother-infant bonding. *Psychological Science*, 18(11): 965–70.

Feldman, R., Zagoory-Sharon, O., Weisman, O., Schneiderman, I., Gordon, I., Maoz, R., Shalev, I., and Ebstein, R. P. (2012). Sensitive parenting is associated with plasma oxytocin and polymorphisms in the OXTR and CD38 genes. *Biological Psychiatry*, 72(3): 175–81.

Fendt, M., Koch, M., Kungel, M., and Schnitzler, H. U. (1995). Cholecystokinin enhances the acoustic startle response in rats. *Neuroreport: An International Journal for the Rapid Communication of Research in Neuroscience*, 6(15): 2081–84.

Fergusson, D. M., Boden, J. M., Horwood, L. J., Miller, A. L., and Kennedy, M. A. (2011). MAOA, abuse exposure and antisocial behaviour: 30-year longitudinal study, *British Journal of Psychiatry*, 198(6): 457–63.

Ferrarese, C., Appollonio, I., Bianchi, G., Frigo, M., Marzorati, C., Pecora, N., Perego, M., Pierpaoli, C., and Frattola, L. (1993). Benzodiazepine receptors and diazepam binding inhibitor: A possible link between stress, anxiety, and the immune system. *Psychoneuroendocrinology*, 18(1): 3–22.

Ferrer, R. A. (2007). The role of emotion in relation to information, motivation, and behavioral skills in obesity-related behaviors. Unpublished master's thesis. University of Connecticut, Storrs, CT.

(2009). Addressing the role of emotion in HIV risk behavior. Unpublished doctoral dissertation. University of Connecticut, Storrs, CT.

Ferrer, R. A., Fisher, J. D., Buck, R., and Amico, K. R. (2011). Pilot test of an emotional education intervention component for sexual risk reduction. *Health Psychology*, 30(5): 656–60.

Ferris, C. F., Stolberg, T., Kulkarni, P., Murugavel, M., Blanchard, R., Blanchard, D. C., Febo, M., Brevard, M., and Simon, N. G. (2008). Imaging the neural circuitry and chemical control of aggressive motivation. *BMC Neuroscience*, 9: 111.

Festinger, L. (1950). Informal social communication. *Psychological Review*, 57: 271–82

(1954). A theory of social comparison processes. *Human Relations*, 7: 117–40.

(1957). *A Theory of Cognitive Dissonance*. Stanford University Press.

Fichetti, M. (2011). Your brain in love: Cupid's arrows, laced with neurotransmitters, find their marks. *Scientific American*, January 18, 304: 92.

Fields, H. L., and Basbaum, A. I. (1984). Endogenous pain control mechanisms. In P. D. Wall and R. Melzack (eds.), *Textbook of Pain* (pp. 142–52). Edinburgh: Churchill Livingstone.

Fine, C., Lumsden, J., and Blair, R. J. (2001). Dissociation between "theory of mind" and executive functions in a patient with early left amygdala damage. *Brain*, 124(Pt. 2): 287–98.

Fischer, P., Greitemeyer, T., Kastenmuller, A., Vongrincic, C., and Saur, A. (2011). The effects of risk-glorifying media exposure on risk-positive cognitions, emotions, and behaviors: A meta-analytic review. *Psychological Bulletin*, 137(3): 367–90.

Fischman, M. W. (1984). The behavioral pharmacology of cocaine in humans. In J. Grabowski (ed.), *Cocaine: Pharmacology, Effects and Treatment of Abuse* (pp. 73–92). Washington, DC: US Government Printing Office.

Fisher, H. E., Brown, L. L., Aron, A., Strong, G., and Mashek, D. (2010). Reward, addiction, and emotion regulation systems associated with rejection in love. *Journal of Neurophysiology*, 104(1): 51–60.

Fiske, S. T. (2010a). Envy up, scorn down: How comparison divides us. *American Psychologist*, 65(8): 698–706.

(2010b). Interpersonal stratification: Status, power, and subordination. In S. T. Fiske, D. T. Gilbert, and G. Lindzey (eds.), *Handbook of Social Psychology* (5th edn., pp. 941–82). New York: John Wiley.

Flavell, J. (1968). *The Development of Role-Taking and Communication Skills in Children*. New York: John Wiley.

Fontaine, J. R. J., Luyten, P., De Boeck, P., Corveleyn, P., Fernandez, J., Herrera, M., Ittzés, A., and Tomcsányi, T. (2006). Untying the Gordian knot of guilt and shame: The structure of guilt and shame reactions based on situation and person variation in Belgium, Hungary, and Peru. *Journal of Cross-Cultural Psychology*, 37(3): 273–92.

Ford, M. R., and Lowrey, C. R. (1986). Gender differences in moral reasoning: A comparison of the use of justice and care orientations. *Journal of Personality and Social Psychology*, 50: 777–83.

Forgas, J. P. (1995). Mood and judgment: The affect infusion model (AIM). *Journal of Personality and Social Psychology*, 117(1): 39–66.

Frank, M. J., Cohen, M. X., and Sanfey, A. G. (2009). Multiple systems in decision making: A neurocomputational perspective. *Current Directions in Psychological Science*, 18(2): 73–77.

Frankland, P. W., Josselyn, S. A., Bradwejn, J., Vaccarino, F. J. and Yeomans, J. S. (1996). Intracerebroventricular infusion of the CCK-sub(B) receptor agonist pentagastrin potentiates acoustic startle. *Brain Research*, 733(1): 129–32.

Frattaroli, J. (2005). Experimental disclosure and its moderators: A meta-analysis. Dissertation Abstracts International: Section B: The Sciences and Engineering, Vol. 66(6-B).

Fredrickson, B. L. (2001). The role of positive emotions in positive psychology: The broaden-and-build theory of positive emotions. *American Psychologist*, 56(3): 218–26.

Fried, I. (1997). Syndrome E. *The Lancet*, 350: 1845–47.

(1998). Author's reply. *The Lancet*, 351, March 14, p. 830.

Frijda, N. (1986). *The Emotions*. New York: Cambridge University Press.

(1994). Emotions require cognitions, even if simple ones. In P. Ekman and R. J. Davidson (eds.), *The Nature of Emotion: Fundamental Questions* (pp. 197–202). New York: Oxford University Press.

(2009). Emotions, individual differences and time course: Reflections. *Cognition & Emotion*, Special issue: *Individual Differences in Emotion*, 23: 1444–61.

Frodi, A. M., Lamb, M. E., Leavitt, L. A., and Donovan, W. L. (1978). Fathers' and mothers' responses to infant smiles and cries. *Infant Behavior and Development*, 1: 187–98.

Fromm, E. (1941). *Escape from Freedom*. New York: Holt, Rinehart & Winston.

Fuentes, A. (2000). Hylobatid communities: Changing views on pair bonding and social organization in hominoids. *Yearbook of Physical Anthropology*, 43: 33–60.

Fusar-Poli, P., Placentino, A., Carletti, F., Landi, P., Allen, P., Surguladze, S., ... and Politi, P. (2009). Functional atlas of emotional faces processing: A voxel-based meta-analysis of 105 functional magnetic resonance imaging studies. *Journal of Psychiatry and Neuroscience*, 34(6): 418–32.

Gable, S. L., and Haidt, J. (2005) What (and why) is positive psychology? *Review of General Psychology*, 9: 103–10.

Gainotti, G. (2000). Neuropsychological theories of emotion. In J. Borod (ed.), *The Neuropsychology of Emotion* (pp. 214–36). New York: Oxford University Press.

Galaburda, A. M., and Pandya, D. N. (1982). Role of architectonics and connections in the study of primate brain evolution. In E. Armstrong and D. Falk (eds.), *Primate Brain Evolution* (pp. 203–16). New York: Plenum.

Gallese, V. (2001). The "shared manifold" hypothesis: From mirror neurons to empathy. *Journal of Consciousness Studies*, 8(5–7): 33–50.

Gallese, V., Fadiga, L., Fogassi, L., and Rizzolatti, G. (1996). Action recognition in the premotor cortex. *Brain*, 119(2): 593–609.

Gallese, V., and Goldman, A. I. (1998). Mirror neurons and the simulation theory of mind-reading. *Trends in Cognitive Sciences*, 2(12): 493–501.

Gallese, V., Keysers, C., and Rizzolatti, G. (2004). A unifying view of the basis of social cognition. *Trends in Cognitive Sciences*, 8(9): 396–403.

Gallese, V., and Rizzolatti, G. (2002). Hearing sounds, understanding actions: Action representation in mirror neurons. *Science*, 297(5582): 846–48.

Gallio, M., Sturgill, G., Rather, P., and Kylsten, P. (2002). A conserved mechanism for extracellular signalling in eukaryotes and prokaryotes. *Proceedings of the National Academy of Sciences of the United States of America*, 99(19): 12208–13.

Gamer, M., Zurowskia, B., and Büchel, C. (2011). Different amygdala subregions mediate valence related and attentional effects of oxytocin in humans. *Proceedings of the National Academy of Sciences of the United States of America*, 107(20): 9400–5.

Gangestead, S. W., Garver-Apgar, C. E., Simpson, J. A., and Cousins, A. J. (2007). Changes in women's mate preferences across the ovulatory cycle. *Journal of Personality and Social Psychology*, 92(1): 151–63.

Gangestead, S. W., and Simpson, J. A. (2000). The evolution of human mating: Trade-offs and strategic pluralism. *Behavioral and Brain Sciences*, 23(4): 573–644.

Gangestead, S. W., Simpson, J. A., Cousins, A. J., Garver-Apgar, C. E., and Christensen P. N. (2004). Women's preferences for male behavioral displays changes across the menstrual cycle. *Psychological Science*, 15(3): 203–7.

Gangestead, S. W., Thornbill, R., and Garver-Apgar, C. E. (2005). Adaptations to ovulation. In D. M. Buss (ed.), *The Handbook of Evolutionary Psychology* (pp. 68–95). Hoboken, NJ: John Wiley.

Gantt, S. P., and Agazarian, Y. M. (2011). The group mind, systems-centred functional sub-grouping, and interpersonal neurobiology. In E. Hopper and H. Weinberg (eds.), *The Social Unconscious in Persons, Groups, and Societies* (Vol. 1, pp. 99–123). London: Karnac Books.

Gat, A. (2009). So why do people fight? Evolutionary theory and the causes of war. *European Journal of International Relations*, 15(4): 571–99.

Gazzola, V., Rizzolatti, G., Wicker, B., and Keysers, C. (2007). The anthropomorphic brain: The mirror neuron system responds to human and robotic actions. *NeuroImage*, 35(4): 1674–84.

George, D. T., Umhau, J. C., Phillips, M. J., Emmela, D., Ragan, P. W., Shoaf, S. E., and Rawlings, R. R. (2001). Serotonin, testosterone and alcohol in the etiology of domestic violence. *Psychiatry Research*, 104(1): 27–37.

Gerdes, K. E. (2011). Empathy, sympathy, and pity: 21st-century definitions and implications for practice and research. *Journal of Social Science Research*, 37(3): 230–41.

Geschwind, N. (1979). Specializations of the human brain. *Scientific American*, 241: 180–99.

Ghiglieri, M. P. (1985). The social ecology of chimpanzees. *Scientific American*, 252: 102–13.

Gibbons, A. (1993). Pleistocene population explosions. *Science*, 262: 27–28.

Gibson, J. J. (1966). *The Senses Considered as Perceptual Systems*. Boston: Houghton Mifflin.

(1977). The theory of affordances. In R. E. Shaw and J. Bransford (eds.), *Perceiving, Acting and Knowing: Toward an Ecological Psychology* (pp. 67–82). Hillsdale, NJ: Lawrence Erlbaum Associates.

(1979). *The Ecological Approach to Visual Perception*. Boston: Houghton Mifflin.

Gilbert, P. (2010). Compassion focused therapy: A special section. *International Journal of Cognitive Therapy*, 3: 95–96.

Gilligan, C. (1977). In a different voice: Women's conceptions of self and of morality. *Harvard Educational Review*, 47: 481–517.

(1982). *In a Different Voice*. Cambridge, MA: Harvard University Press.

Gingrich, B. S., Huot, R. L., Wang, Z., and Insel, T. R. (1997). Differential fos expression following microinjection of oxytocin or vasopressin in the prairie vole brain. In C. S. Carter, I. I. Lederhendler, and B. Kirkpatrick (eds.), *The Integrative Neurobiology of Affiliation*, Annals of the New York Academy of Sciences (Vol. 807, pp. 504–5). New York: New York Academy of Sciences.

Ginsburg, B. E. (1991). Origins and dynamics of social organization in primates and in wolves: Cooperation, aggression, and hierarchy. In A. Somit and R. Wildenmann (eds.), *Hierarchy and Democracy* (pp. 45–62). Baden Baden: Nomos.

Glickman, S. E., and Schiff, B. B. (1967). A biological theory of reinforcement. *Psychological Review*, 74: 81–109.

Goffman, E. (1956). Embarrassment and social organization. *American Journal of Sociology*, 62: 264–71.

(1967). *Interaction Ritual: Essays on Face-to-Face Behavior.* Garden City, NY: Anchor.

Goldman, C. (1994). The relationship of emotional communication to social competence: The role of communication accuracy in behaviorally disordered children's social functioning. Unpublished doctoral dissertation. University of Connecticut, Storrs, CT.

Gomes, C. M., and Boesch, C. (2009). Wild chimpanzees exchange meat for sex on a long-term pasis. *PLoS One,* 4: 1–5.

Gonsalkorale, K., and Williams, K. D. (2007). The KKK won't let me play: Ostracism even by a despised outgroup hurts. *European Journal of Social Psychology,* 37(6): 1176–86.

Goodall, J. (1986). *The Chimpanzees of Gombe: Patterns of 'Behavior.* Cambridge, MA: Belknap Press.

Gordon, I., Zagoory-Sharon, O., Leckman, J. F., and Feldman, R. (2010a). Oxytocin and the development of parenting in humans. *Biological Psychiatry,* 68(4): 377–82.

(2010b). Prolactin, oxytocin, and the development of paternal behavior across the first six months of fatherhood. *Hormones and Behavior,* 58(3): 513–18.

Gordon, I., Zagoory-Sharon, O., Schneiderman, I., Leckman, J. F., Weller, A., and Feldman, R. (2008). Oxytocin and cortisol in romantically unattached young adults: Associations with bonding and psychological distress. *Psychophysiology,* 45(3): 349–52.

Gore, R. (2003). The rise of mammals. *National Geographic,* 203(4): 2–37.

Goren-Inbar, N., Alperson, N., Kislev, M. E., Simchoni, O., Melamed, Y., Ben-Nun, A., and Werker, E. (2004). Evidence of hominin control of fire at Gesher Benot Ya'aqov, Israel. *Science,* 304(5671): 725–27.

Gorenstein, E. E., and Newman, J. P. (1980). Disinhibitory psychopathology: A new perspective and a model for research. *Psychological Review,* 87(3): 301–15.

Gottlieb, G. (1984). Evolutionary trends and evolutionary origins: Relevance to theory in comparative psychology. *Psychological Review,* 91(4): 448–56.

Gottman, J. M. (1979). *Marital Interaction: Experimental Investigations.* New York: Academic Press.

Graham, J., Haidt, J., and Nosek, B. (2009). Liberals and conservatives rely on different sets of moral foundations. *Journal of Personality and Social Psychology,* 96(5): 1029–46.

Graham, S., Doubleday, C., and Guarino, P. A. (1984). The development of relations between perceived controllability and the emotions of pity, anger, and guilt. *Child Development,* 55: 561–65.

Graham, S., and Weiner, B. (1986). From an attributional theory of emotion to developmental psychology: A round-trip ticket? *Social Cognition,* 4: 152–79.

(1991). Testing judgments about attribution–emotion–action linkages: A lifespan approach. *Social Cognition,* 9: 254–76.

Gray, J. (1993). *Men are from Mars, Women are from Venus: A Practical Guide for Improving Communication and Getting What You Want in Your Relationships.* New York: HarperCollins.

Gray, J. A. (1971). *The Psychology of Fear and Stress.* New York: McGraw-Hill.

(1977). Drug effects on fear and frustration: Possible limbic site of action of minor tranquilizers. In L. L. Iversen, S. D. Iversen, and S. H. Snyder (eds.), *Handbook of Psychopharmacology,* Vol. 8: *Drugs, Neurotransmitters, and Behavior* (pp. 433–529). New York: Plenum.

(1982a). *The Neuropsychological Theory of Anxiety: An Investigation of the Septal-Hippocampal System*. Cambridge University Press.

(1982b). *The Neuropsychology of Anxiety: An Enquiry into the Functions of the Septo-Hippocampal System*. New York: Oxford University Press.

(1987). *The Psychology of Fear and Stress*. New York: McGraw-Hill.

Gray, J. A., and McNaughton, N. (2000). *The Neuropsychology of Anxiety: An Enquiry into the Functions of the Septo-Hippocampal System*. New York: Oxford University Press.

Greene, J. D. (2007). Why are VMPFC patients more utilitarian? A dual-process theory of moral judgment explains. *Trends in Cognitive Sciences*, 11(8): 322–23.

(2011). Emotion and morality: A tasting menu. *Emotion Review*, 3: 227–29.

Greene, J. D., Sommerville, R. B., Nystrom, L. E., Darley, J. M., and Cohen, J. D. (2001). An fMRI investigation of emotional engagement in moral judgment. *Science*, 293(5537): 2105–8.

Gross, J. J., and Levenson, R. W. (1997). Hiding feelings: The acute effects of inhibiting negative and positive emotion. *Journal of Abnormal Psychology*, 106(1): 95–103.

Gross, K. (1901). *The Play of Man*. New York: Appleton.

Grossman, S. (1967). *Essentials of Physiological Psychology*. New York: John Wiley.

Grunberg, N. E., and Straub, R. O. (1992). The role of gender and taste class in the effects of stress on eating. *Health Psychology*, 11: 97–100.

Guarneri, P., Guidotti, A., and Costa, E. (1990). On the processing of diazepam-binding inhibitor (DBI) in human brain. In G. Biggio and E. Costa (eds.), *Advances in Biochemical Pharmacology*, Vol. 46: *GABA and Benzodiazepine Receptor Subtypes: Molecular Biology, Pharmacology, and Clinical Aspects* (pp. 201–11). New York: Raven Press.

Guastella, A. J., and MacLeod, C. (2012). A critical review of the influence of oxytocin nasal spray on social cognition in humans: Evidence and future directions. *Hormones and Behavior*, 61(3): 410–18.

Guastella, A. J., Mitchell, P. B., and Mathews, F. (2008). Oxytocin enhances the encoding of positive social memories in humans. *Biological Psychiatry*, 64(3): 256–58.

Guerrero, L. K., Trost, M. R., and Yoshimura, S. M. (2005). Romantic jealousy: Emotions and communicative responses. *Personal Relationships*, 12(2): 233–52.

Gur, R. C., Mozley, L. H., Mozley, P. D., Resnick, S. M., Karp, J. S., Alavi, A., Arnold, S. E., and Gur, R. E. (1995). Sex differences in regional cerebral glucose metabolism during a resting state. *Science*, 267(5197): 528–31.

Haenisch, B., Bilkei-Gorzo, A., Caron, M. G., and Bönisch, H. (2009). Knockout of the norepinephrine transporter and pharmacologically diverse antidepressants prevent behavioral and brain neurotrophin alterations in two chronic stress models of depression. *Journal of Neurochemistry*, 111(2): 403–16.

Hahn, T., Dresler, T., Ehlis, A., Plichta, M. M., Heinzel, S., Polak, T., Lesch, K. P., Breuer, F., Jakob, P. M., and Fallgatter, A. J. (2009). Neural response to reward anticipation is modulated by gray's impulsivity. *NeuroImage*, 46(4): 1148–53.

Haidt, J. (2001). The emotional dog and its rational tail: A social intuitionist approach to moral judgment. *Psychological Review*, 108(4): 814–34.

(2002). Dialogue between my head and my heart: Affective influences on moral judgment. *Psychological Inquiry*, 13: 54–56.

(2003). The moral emotions. In R. J. Davidson, K. R. Scherer, and H. H. Goldsmith (eds.), *Handbook of Affective Sciences* (pp. 852–70). Oxford University Press.

(2007). The new synthesis in moral psychology. *Science*, 316(5827): 998–1002.

(2012). *The Righteous Mind: Why Good People are Divided on Politics and Religion*. New York: Pantheon.

Haidt, J., and Keltner, D. (1999). Culture and facial expression: Open-ended methods find more faces and a gradient of recognition. *Cognition & Emotion*, 13: 225–26.

Hall, C. S., and Lindzey, G. (1970). *Theories of Personality*. New York: Wiley.

Hall, E. T. (1966). *The Hidden Dimension*. Garden City, NY: Doubleday.

(1973). The hidden dimension. *Leonardo*, 6(1): 94.

Hall, E. T., and Hall, M. R. (1990). *Understanding Cultural Differences*. Yarmouth, ME: Intercultural Press.

Han, S., Lerner, J. S., and Keltner, D. (2007). Feelings and consumer decision making: The appraisal-tendency framework. *Journal of Consumer Psychology*, 17(3): 158–68.

Haney, C., Banks, W. C., and Zimbardo, P. G. (1973). Study of prisoners and guards in a simulated prison. *Naval Research Reviews*, 9: 1–17.

Hansen, C. H., and Hansen, R. D. (1988). Finding the face in the crowd: An anger superiority effect. *Journal of Personality and Social Psychology*, 54(6): 917–24.

Harari, H., Shamay-Tsoory, S. G., Ravid, M., and Levkovitz, Y. (2010). Double dissociation between cognitive and affective empathy in borderline personality disorder. *Psychiatry Research*, 175(3): 277–79.

Harbaugh, W. T., Mayr, U., and Burghart, D. R. (2007). Neural responses to taxation and voluntary giving reveal motives for charitable donations. *Science*, 316(5831): 1622–25.

Hardee, J. E., Thompson, J. C., and Puce, A. (2008). The left amygdala knows fear: Laterality in the amygdala response to fearful eyes. *Social Cognitive & Affective Neuroscience*, 3(1): 47–54.

Harder, B. (2002). Was the humble sponge Earth's first animal? *National Geographic News*, April 1. http://news.nationalgeographic.com/news/2002/04/0401_0401_shapeoflife1_2.html.

Harenski, C. L., and Kiehl, K. A. (2011). Emotion and morality in psychopathy and paraphilias. *Emotion Review*, 3(3): 299–301.

Harlé, K. M., and Sanfey, A. G. (2007). Incidental sadness biases social economic decisions in the ultimatum game. *Emotion*, 7(4): 876–81.

Harlow, H. F. (1971). *Learning to Love*. San Francisco: Albion.

Harlow, H. F., and Mears, C. E. (1983). Emotional sequences and consequences. In R. Plutchik and A. Kellerman (eds.), *Emotion: Theory, Research, and Experience*, Vol. 2: *Emotions in Early Development* (pp. 171–97). New York: Academic Press.

Harlow, J. M. (1999). Passage of an iron rod through the head. *Journal of Neuropsychiatry and Clinical Neuroscience*, 11(2): 281–83.

Harro, J., Vasar, E., and Bradwejn, J. (1993). CCK in animal and human research on anxiety. *Trends in Pharmacological Sciences*, 14(6): 244–49.

Harry, B. (1992). Criminals' explanations of their criminal behavior. II: A possible role for psychopathy. *Journal of Forensic Sciences*, 37(5): 1334–40.

Hart, S. L. (2010). The ontogenesis of jealousy in the first year of life: A theory of jealousy as a biologically-based dimension of temperament. In S. L. Hart and M. Legerstee (eds.), *Handbook of Jealousy: Theory, Research, and Multidisciplinary Approaches* (pp. 57–82). Malden, MA: Wiley-Blackwell.

Hartshorne, H., and May, M. (1928–30). *Studies in the Nature of Character*, 3 vols. New York: Macmillan.

Hatfield, E., and Sprecher, S. (1986). Measuring passionate love in intimate relationships. *Journal of Adolescence*, 9(4): 383–410.

Haviland, W. A., Prins, H. E. L., Walrath, D., and McBride, B. (2009). *The Essence of Anthropolgy*. Belmont, CA: Wadsworth.

Hazan, C., and Shaver, P. R. (1987). Romantic love conceptualized as an attachment process. *Journal of Personality and Social Psychology*, 52(3): 511–24.

(1990). Love and work: An attachment-theoretical perspective. *Journal of Personality and Social Psychology*, 59(2): 270–80.

(1994). Attachment as an organizational framework for research on close relationships. *Psychological Inquiry*, 5(1): 1–22.

Heath, R. G. (ed.) (1964). *The Role of Pleasure in Behavior*. New York: Harper & Row.

Hebb, A. L., Zacharko, R. M., Dominguez, H., Trudel, F., Laforest, S., and Drolet, G. (2002). Odor-induced variation on anxiety-like behavior in mice is associated with discrete and differential effects on mesocorticolimbic cholecystokinin mRNA expression. *Neuropsychopharmacology*, 27(5): 744–55.

Hebb, D. O. (1949). *The Organization of Behavior*. New York: John Wiley.

Heider, F. (1944). Social perception and phenomenal causality. *Psychological Review*, 51: 358–74.

(1946). Attitudes and cognitive organization. *Journal of Psychology*, 21: 107–12.

(1958). *The Psychology of Interpersonal Relations*. New York: John Wiley.

Heilman, K. M., Blonder, L. X., Bowers, D., and Crucian, G. P. (2000). Neurological disorders and emotional dysfunction. In J. Borod (ed.), *The Neuropsychology of Emotion* (pp. 367–412). New York: Oxford University Press.

Henson, H. K. (2006). Evolutionary psychology, memes and the origin of war. *Mankind Quarterly*, 46(4): 443–59.

Herbst, S. (2010). *Rude Democracy: Civility and Incivility in American Politics*. Philadelphia, PA: Temple University Press.

Hertenstein, M. J., Holmes, R., McCullough, M., and Keltner, D. (2009). The communication of emotion via touch. *Emotion*, 9(4): 566–73.

Hertenstein, M. J., and Keltner, D. (2011). Gender and the communication of emotion via touch. *Sex Roles*, 64(1–2): 70–80.

Hertenstein, M. J., Keltner, D., App, B., Bulleit, B. A., and Jaskolka, A. R. (2006). Touch communicates distinct emotions. *Emotion*, 6(3): 528–33.

Hertenstein, M. J., Verkamp, J. M., Kerestes, A. M., and Holmes, R. M. (2006). The communicative functions of touch in humans, nonhuman primates, and rats: A review and synthesis of the empirical research. *Genetic, Social, and General Psychology Monographs*, 132(1): 5–94.

Hess, W. R. (1928). Stammganglien-reizversuche [Brainstem stimulation attempts]. *Berliner Gesellschaft fur Physiologie*, 42: 554.

Hess, W. R., and Brugger, M. (1943). Das subkortikale zentrum der afektiven abwehrreaktion. *Helvetica Physiological et Pharacological Acta*, 1: 33–52.

Hetherington, R., and Reid, R. G. B. (2010). *The Climate Connection: Climate Change and Modern Human Evolution*. New York: Cambridge University Press.

Hoffer, E. (1951). *The True Believer*. New York: Harper.

Hoffman, M. L. (1975). Developmental synthesis of affect and cognition and its implications for altruistic motivation. *Developmental Psychology*, 11: 607–22.

(1976). Empathy, role-taking, guilt, and development of altruistic motives. In T. Lickona (ed.), *Moral Development and Behavior: Theory, Research, and Social Issues* (pp. 124–43). New York: Holt, Rinehart & Winston.

Hofstadter, R. (1959). *Social Darwinism in American Thought*. New York: George Braziller.

Hofstede, G. H. (1980). *Culture's Consequences: International Differences in Work-Related Values*. Beverly Hills, CA: Sage Publications.

Hohmann, G. W. (1966). Some effects of spinal cord lesions on experienced emotional feelings. *Psychophysiology*, 3(2): 143–56.

Holland, N. H. (2009). Your brain on movies. *PSYART: A Hyperlink Journal for the Psychological Study of the Arts*. December 15. www.psyartjournal.com/ article/show/n_holland-your_brain_on_movies.

Holst, E., and von Saint Paul, U. (1962). Electrically-controlled behavior. *Scientific American*, 203: 50–59.

Holstege, G., Georgiadis, J. R., Paans, A. M. J., Meiners, L. C., Ferdinand, H. C. E., van der Graaf, F. H. C. E., and Reinders, A. A. T. S. (2003). Brain activation during human male ejaculation. *Journal of Neuroscience*, 23(27): 9185–93.

Homans, G. C. (1966). *Social Behavior: Its Elementary Forms*. New York: Harcourt, Brace & World.

Hughes, J., Smith, T., Morgan, B., and Fothergill, L. (1975). Purification and properties of enkephalin: The possible endogenous ligand for the morphine receptor. *Life Sciences*, 16(12): 1753–58.

Hunter, E. (1951). *Brainwashing in Red China*. New York: Vanguard.

Hupka, R. B., Lenton, A. P., and Hutchison, K. A. (1999). Universal development of emotion categories in natural language. *Journal of Personality and Social Psychology*, 77(2): 247–78.

Ichikawa, J., Li, Z., Dai, J., and Meltzer, H. Y. (2002). Atypical antipsychotic drugs, quetiapine, iloperidone, and melperone, preferentially increase dopamine and acetylcholine release in rat medial prefrontal cortex: Role of 5-HT-1A receptor agonism. *Brain Research*, 956(2): 349–57.

Immordino-Yang, M. H., McColl, A., Damasio, H., and Damasio, A. (2009). Neural correlates of admiration and compassion. *Proceedings of the National Academy of Sciences of the United States of America*, 106(19): 8021–26.

Immordino-Yang, M. H., and Sylvan, L. (2010). Admiration for virtue: Neuroscientific perspectives on a motivating emotion. *Contemporary Educational Psychology*, 35(2): 110–15.

Insel, T. R. (1992). Oxytocin: A neuropeptide for affiliation: Evidence from behavioral, receptor autoradiographic, and comparative studies. *Psychoneuroendocrinology*, 17(1): 3–35.

(2000). Toward a neurobiology of attachment. *Review of General Psychology*, 4(2): 176–85.

(2002). Implications for the neurobiology of love. In S. G. Post and L. G. Underwood (eds.), *Altruism and Altruistic Love: Science, Philosophy, and Religion in Dialogue* (pp. 254–63). Oxford University Press.

Insel, T. R., and Young, L. J. (2001). Opinion: The neurobiology of attachment. *Nature Reviews Neuroscience*, 2(2): 129–36.

Insel, T. R., Young, L., and Wang, Z. (1997). Molecular aspects of monogamy. In C. S. Carter, I. I. Lederhendler, and B. Kirkpatrick (eds.), *The Integrative Neurobiology of Affiliation*, Annals of the New York Academy of Sciences (Vol. 807, pp. 302–16). New York: New York Academy of Sciences.

Iversen, L. (1979). The chemistry of the brain. *Scientific American*, 241(3): 134–49.

Iwamitsu, Y., and Buck, R. (2008). Toward psychological intervention for cancer: Emotional suppression, psychological distress, and coping with cancer. In L. K. Jacobs (ed.), *Coping with Cancer* (pp. 77–93). Hauppauge, NY: Nova Science Publishers.

Iwamitsu, Y., Shimoda, K., Abe, H., Tani, T., Okawa, M., and Buck, R. (2005a). Anxiety, emotional suppression, and psychological distress before and after breast cancer diagnosis. *Psychosomatics*, 46(1): 1–6.

(2005b). The relationship between negative emotional suppression and emotional distress in breast cancer patients. *Health Communication*, 18(3): 201–15.

Izard, C. E. (1971). *The Face of Emotion*. New York: Appleton Century Crofts.

(1977). *Human Emotions*. New York: Plenum.

(1978). On the ontogenesis of emotions and emotion-cognition relationships in infancy. In M. Lewis and L. A. Rosenbloom (eds.), *The Development of Affect* (pp. 389–413). New York: Plenum.

(ed.) (1979). *Emotions in Personality and Psychopathology*. Oxford: Plenum.

Jackson, P. L., Brunet, E., Meltzoff, A. N., and Decety, J. (2006). Empathy examined through the neural mechanisms involved in imagining how I feel versus how you feel pain: An event-related fMRI study. *Neuropsychologia*, 44(5): 752–61.

Jaffe, J. H. (1985). Drug addiction and drug abuse. In A. G. Gilman, L. S. Goodman, T. W. Rail, and F. Murad (eds.), *Goodman and Gilman's The Pharmacologic Basis of Therapeutics* (7th edn., pp. 532–81). New York: Macmillan.

James, W. (1884/1968). What is an emotion? *Mind*, 9: 188–205. Reprinted in M. Arnold (ed.), *The Nature of Emotion* (pp. 188–205). Baltimore, MD: Penguin.

(1890). *The Principles of Psychology*, Vol. 1. New York: Henry Holt.

Janata, P. (2009). The neural architecture of music-evoked autobiographical memories. *Cerebral Cortex*, 19(11): 2579–94.

Jankowiak, W. R., and Fischer, E. F. (1992). A cross-cultural perspective on romantic love. *Ethnology*, 31(2): 149–55.

Janssen, S. A., and Arntz, A. (2001). Real-life stress and opioid-mediated analgesia in novice parachute jumpers. *Journal of Psychophysiology*, 15(2): 106–13.

Janszky, J., Szücs, A., Halász, P., Borbély, C., Holló, A., Barsi, P., and Mirnics, Z. (2002). Orgasmic aura originates from the right hemisphere. *Neurology*, 58 (2): 302–4.

Javanmard, M., Shlik, J., Kennedy, S. H., Vaccarino, F. J., Houle, S., and Bradwejn, J. (1999). Neuroanatomic correlates of CCK-4-induced panic attacks in healthy humans: A comparison of two time points. *Biological Psychiatry*, 45(7): 872–82.

Jenkins, J., Jimenez-Pabon, E., Shaw, R., and Sefer, J. (1975). *Schuell's Aphasia in Adults*. New York: Harper & Row.

Jerabek, I., Boulenger, J. P., Lavallee, Y. J., and Jolicoeur, F. B. (1998). Psychological predictors of CCK-sub-4-induced panic-like symptoms. *Human Psychopharmacology Clinical and Experimental*, 13(1): 35–42.

John, O. P., and Robins, R. W. (1993). Determinants of interjudge agreement on personality traits: The Big Five domains, observability, evaluativeness, and the unique perspective of the self. *Journal of Personality*, 61(4): 521–51.

Johnson, R. G. (1972). *Aggression in Man and Animals*. Philadelphia: W. B. Saunders.

Johnson, R. T., and Breedlove, S. M. (2012). Human trust: Testosterone raises suspicion. *Proceedings of the National Academy of Sciences of the United States of America*, 107(25): 11149–50.

Jones, H. E. (1960). The longitudinal method in the study of personality. In I. Iscoe and H. W. Stevenson (eds.), *Personality Development in Children* (pp. 3–27). University of Chicago Press.

Jorgenson, D. O. (1975). Economic threat and authoritarianism in television programs: 1950–1974. *Psychological Reports*, 37: 1153–54.

Josselyn, S. A., Frankland, P. W., Petrisano, S., Bush, D. E., Yeomans, J. S., and Vaccarino, F. J. (1995). The CCK-sub(b) antagonist, L-365,260, attenuates fear-potentiated startle. *Peptides*, 16(7): 1313–15.

Jung, C. G. (1977). *Collective Psychiatric Studies*. Princeton University Press.

Jürgens, U. (1979). Neural control of vocalization in nonhuman primates. In H. L. Steklis and M. J. Raleigh (eds.), *Neurobiology of Social Communication in Primates* (pp. 11–14). New York: Academic Press.

Jürgens, U., and Ploog, D. (1981). On the neural control of mammalian vocalization. *Trends in Neurosciences*, 4: 135–37.

Kagan, J. (2007). *What is Emotion? History, Measures, and Meanings*. New Haven, CT: Yale University Press.

Kagan, J., Reznick, J. S., Clarke, C., Snidman, N., and Garcia-Coll, C. (1984). Behavioral inhibition to the unfamiliar. *Child Development*, 55(6): 2212–25.

Kagan, J., Snidman, N., Kahn, V., Towsley, S., Steinberg, S., and Fox, N. A. (2007). The preservation of two infant temperaments into adolescence. *Monographs of the Society for Research in Child Development*, 72(2): 1–95.

Kahneman, D. (2003). Maps of bounded rationality: Psychology for behavioral economics. *American Economic Review*, 93(5): 1449–75.

Kanai, R., Feilden, T., Firth, C., Rees, G. (2011). Political orientations are correlated with brain structure in young adults. *Current Biology*, 21(8): 677–80.

Kandell, S., Schwarts, J. and Jessell, T. (eds.) (2000). *Principles of Neural Science* (4th edn.). New York: McGraw-Hill.

Katsura, M., Mohri, Y., Shuto, K., Tsujimura, A., Ukai, M., and Ohkuma, S. (2002). Psychological stress, but not physical stress, causes increase in diazepam binding inhibitor (DBI) mRNA expression in mouse brains. *Molecular Brain Research*, 104(1): 103–9.

Katz, M. M., and Maas, J. W. (1994). Psychopharmacology and the etiology of psychopathologic states: Are we looking in the right way? *Neuropsychopharmacology*, 10(2): 139–44.

Kavaliers, M., and Hirst, M. (1986). An octadecaneuropeptide (ODN) derived from diazepam binding inhibitor increases aggressive interactions in mice. *Brain Research*, 383(1–2): 343–49.

Kelley, H. H. (1967). Attribution theory in social psychology. In D. Levine (ed.), *Nebraska Symposium on Motivation* (Vol. 15, pp. 192–238). Lincoln: University of Nebraska Press.

Kelly, G. A. (1955). *The Psychology of Personal Constructs*. New York: W. W. Norton.

Kelman, H. C. (1961). *Social Influence and Personal Belief*. New York: John Wiley.

Keltner, D. (1995). The signs of appeasement: Evidence for the distinct displays of embarrassment, amusement, and shame. *Journal of Personality and Social Psychology*, 68: 441–54.

(1997). Signs of appeasement: Evidence for the distinct displays of embarrassment, amusement, and shame. In P. Ekman and E. Rosenberg (eds.), *What the Face Reveals: Basic and Applied Studies of Spontaneous Expression Using the Facial Action Coding System (FACS)* (pp. 133–60). New York: Oxford University Press.

Keltner, D., and Buswell, B. W. (1996). Evidence for the distinctness of embarrassment, shame, and guilt: A study of recalled antecedents and facial expressions of emotion. *Cognition & Emotion*, 10(2): 155–71.

(1997). Embarrassment: Its distinct form and appeasement functions. *Psychological Bulletin*, 122(3): 250–70.

Keltner, D., and Harker, L. (1998). The forms and functions of the nonverbal signal of shame. In P. Gilbert and B. Andrews (eds.), *Shame: Interpersonal Behavior, Psychopathology, and Culture* (pp. 78–98). New York: Oxford University Press.

Keltner, D., Young, R. C., Heerey, E. A., Oemig, C., and Monarch, N. D. (1998). Teasing in hierarchical and intimate relations. *Journal of Personality and Social Psychology*, 75(5): 1231–37.

Kendon, A. (1970). Movement coordination in social interaction: Some examples described. *Acta Psychologica*, 32: 100–25.

Kennedy, J. L., Bradwejn, J., Koszycki, D., King, N., Crowe, R., Vincent, J., and Fourie, O. (1999). Investigation of cholecystokinin system genes in panic disorder. *Molecular Psychiatry*, 4(3): 284–85.

Keysers, C. (2011). *The Empathic Brain*. Social Brain Press.

Keysers, C., Kaas, J. H., and Gazzola, V. (2010). Somatosensation in social perception. *Nature Reviews Neuroscience*, 11(6): 417–28.

Keysers, C., Kohler, E., Umiltà, M. A., Nanetti, L., Fogassi, L., and Gallese, V. (2003). Audiovisual mirror neurons and action recognition. *Experimental Brain Research*, 153(4): 628–36.

Kiecolt-Glaser, J. K., Bane, C., Glaser, R., and Malarkey, W. B. (2003). Love, marriage, and divorce: Newlyweds' stress hormones foreshadow relationship changes. *Journal of Consulting and Clinical Psychology*, 71(1): 176–88.

Kiehl, K. A. (2006). A cognitive neuroscience perspective on psychopathy: Evidence for paralimbic system dysfunction. *Psychiatry Research*, 142(2–3): 107–28.

Killgore, W. D. S., Oki, M., and Yurgelun-Todd, D. A. (2001). Sex-specific developmental changes in amygdala responses to affective faces. *Neuroreport*, 12(2): 427–33.

Killgore, W. D. S., and Yurgelun-Todd, D. A. (2001). Sex differences in amygdala activation during the perception of facial affect. *Neuroreport*, 12(11): 2543–47.

Kim, P., Feldman, R., Mayes, L. C., Eicher, V., Thompson, N., Leckman, J. F., and Swain, J. E. (2011). Breastfeeding, brain activation to own infant cry, and maternal sensitivity. *Journal of Child Psychology and Psychiatry*, 52(8): 907–15.

King, H. E. (1961). Psychological effects of excitation in the limbic system. In D. E. Sheer (ed.), *Electrical Stimulation of the Brain* (pp. 477–86). Austin: University of Texas Press.

Kinkead, E. (1959). *In Every War But One*. New York: W. W. Norton.

Kinsbourne, M. (2002). The role of imitation in body ownership and mental growth. In A. Meltzoff and W. Prinz (eds.), *The Imitative Mind* (pp. 311–30). Cambridge University Press.

Kircanski, K., Lieberman, M. D., and Craske, M. G. (2012). Feelings into words: Contributions of language to exposure therapy. *Psychological Science*, 23 (10): 1086–91.

Kitayama, S., Mesquita, B., and Karasawa, M. (2006). Cultural affordances and emotional experience: Socially engaging and disengaging emotions in Japan and the United States. *Journal of Personality and Social Psychology*, 91 (5): 890–903.

Kitayama, S., and Uchida, Y. (2005). Interdependent agency: An alternative system for action. In R. M. Sorrentino, D. Cohen, J. M. Olson, and M. P. Zanna (eds.), *Cultural and Social Behavior: The Ontario Symposium* (Vol. 10, pp. 137–64). Mahwah, NJ: Lawrence Erlbaum Associates.

Klein, D. C. (1991). The humiliation dynamic: An overview. *Journal of Primary Prevention*, 12(2): 93–121.

Kleinginna, P. R., and Kleinginna, A. M. (1981a). A categorized list of motivation definitions, with a suggestion for a consensual definition. *Motivation and Emotion*, 5(3): 263–91.

(1981b). A categorized list of emotion definitions, with suggestions for a consensual definition. *Motivation and Emotion*, 5(4): 348–79.

Kleinhans, N. M., Richards, T., Sterling, L., Stegbauer, K. C., Mahurin, R., Johnson, L. C., Greenson, J., Dawson, G., and Aylward, E. (2008). Abnormal functional connectivity in autism spectrum disorders during face processing. *Brain*, 131(4): 1000–12.

Kleinke, C. L., Wallis, R., and Stalder, K. (1992). Evaluation of a rapist as a function of expressed intent and remorse. *Journal of Social Psychology*, 132: 525–37.

Klinnert, M., Campos, J. J., Sorce, J. F., Emde, R. N., and Svedja, M. (1983). Social referencing: Emotional expressions as behavior regulators in emotion. *Theory, Research, and Experience*, 2: 57–86.

Klüver, H., and Bucy, P. C. (1937). "Psychic blindness" and other symptoms following bilateral temporal lobectomy in Rhesus monkeys. *American Journal of Physiology*, 119: 352–53.

(1938). An analysis of certain effects of bilateral temporal lobectomy in the rhesus monkey, with special reference to "psychic blindness." *Journal of Psychology*, 5(1): 33–54.

(1939). Preliminary analysis of functions of the temporal lobe in monkeys. *Archives of Neurology and Psychiatry*, 42(6): 979–1000.

Knoch, D., Pascual-Leone, A., Meyer, K., Treyer, V., and Fehr, E. (2006). Diminishing reciprocal fairness by disrupting the right prefrontal cortex. *Science*, 314(5800): 829–32.

Kober, H., Barrett, L. F., Joseph, J., Bliss-Moreau, E., Lindquist, K. and Wager, T. D. (2008). Functional grouping and cortical–subcortical interactions in emotion: A meta-analysis of neuroimaging studies. *NeuroImage*, 42(2): 998–1031.

Koenigs, M., and Tranel, D. (2007). Irrational economic decision-making after ventromedial prefrontal damage: Evidence from the Ultimatum Game. *Journal of Neuroscience*, 27(4): 951–56.

Koenigs, M., Young, L., Adolphs, R., Tranel, D., Cushman, F. A., Hauser, M. D., and Damasio, A. (2007). Damage to the prefrontal cortex increases utilitarian moral judgments. *Nature*, 446(7138): 908–11.

Koenigsberg, H. W., Siever, L. J., Lee, H., Pizzarello, S., New, A. S., Goodman, M., Cheng, H., Flory, J, and Prohovnik, I. (2009). Neural correlates of emotion processing in borderline personality disorder. *Psychiatry Research: Neuroimaging*, 172(3): 192–99.

Kohlberg, L. (1963). Moral development and identification. In H. W. Stevenson (ed.), *Child Psychology* (pp. 277–332). University of Chicago Press.

(1964). Development of moral character and moral ideology. In M. L. Hoffman and L. W. Hoffman (eds.), *Review of Child Development Research* (Vol. 1, pp. 383–431). New York: Sage Publications.

Kohler, E., Keysers, C., Umiltà, M. A., Fogassi, L., Gallese, V., and Rizzolatti, G. (2002). Hearing sounds, understanding actions: Action representation in mirror neurons. *Science*, 297(5582): 846–48.

Kolak, A. M., and Volling, B. L. (2011). Sibling jealousy in early childhood: Longitudinal links to sibling relationship quality. *Infant and Child Development*, 20(2): 213–26.

Kolber, B. J., Boyle, M. P., Wieczorek, L., Kelley, C. L., Onwuzurike, C. C., Nettles, S. A., Vogt, S. K., and Muglia, L. J. (2010). Transient early-life forebrain corticotropin-releasing hormone elevation causes long-lasting anxiogenic and despair-like changes in mice. *Journal of Neuroscience*, 30(7): 2571–81.

Kolmer, M., Roos, C., Tirronen, M., Myöhänen, S., and Alto, H. (1994). Tissue-specific expressions of the diazepam-binding inhibitor in Drosophila melanogaster: Cloning, structure, and localization of the genes. *Molecular Cell Biology*, 14(10): 6983–95.

Koolhaas, J. M., van den Brink, T. H. C., Roozendaal, B., and Boorsma, F. (1990). Medial amygdala and aggressive behavior: Interaction between testosterone and vasopressin. *Aggressive Behavior*, 16(3): 223–29.

Kornhauser, W. (1959). *The Politics of Mass Society*. Glencoe, IL: Free Press.

Koscik, T. R., and Tranel, D. (2011). The human amygdala is necessary for developing and expressing normal interpersonal trust. *Neuropsychologia*, 49(4): 602–11.

Kosfeld, M., Heinrichs, M., Zak, P. J., Fischbacher, U., and Fehr, E. (2005). Oxytocin increases trust in humans. *Nature*, 435(7042): 673–76.

Koszycki, D., Cox, B. J., and Bradwejn, J. (1993). Anxiety sensitivity and response to cholecystokinin tetrapeptide in healthy volunteers. *American Journal of Psychiatry*, 150(12): 1881–83.

Koven, N. S. (2011). Specificity of meta-emotion effects on moral decision-making. *Emotion*, 11(5): 1255–61.

Kowal, C. J. (2012). Sell to me: looking at the effects of facial expressions on persuasion. Unpublished doctoral dissertation. University of Connecticut, Storrs, CT.

Kravitz, E. A. (1988). Hormonal control of behavior: Amines and the biasing of behavioral output in lobsters. *Science*, 241(4874): 1775–81.

Krøll, J. B., Nøhr, J., Gregersen, N., Kristiansen, K., and Mandrup, S. (1996). Structure of the rat gene encoding the multifunctional acyl-CoA-binding protein: Conservation of intron 1 sequences in rodents and man. *Gene*, 173 (2): 239–40.

Krueger, F., McCabe, K., Moll, J., Kriegeskorte, N., Zahn, R. Strenziok, M., Heinecke, A., and Grafman, J. (2007). Neural correlates of trust. *Proceedings of the National Academy of Sciences of the United States of America*, 104(50): 20084–89.

Krumhuber, E., Manstead, A. S. R., Cosker, D., Marshall, D., Rosin, P. D., and Kappas, A. (2007). Facial dynamics as indicators of trustworthiness and cooperative behavior. *Emotion*, 7(4): 730–35.

Lackie, J. M. (1986). *Cell Movement and Cell Behaviour*. London: Allen & Unwin.

La Ferrara, E., Chong, A., and Duryea, S. (2008). *Soap Operas and Fertility: Evidence from Brazil*. Research report for the Inter-American Development Bank. Washington, DC. www.iadb.org/document.cfm?id=1856122.

Laird, J. D. (1996). Emotional feelings are knowledge, by acquaintance. *International Journal of Psychology*, 31: 222.

Lakoff, G. (1996). *Moral Politics: What Conservatives Know That Liberals Don't*. University of Chicago Press.

Lam, D. and Marteleto, L. (2005). Small families and large cohorts: The impact of the demographic transition on schooling in Brazil. In C. Lloyd, J. Behrman, N. Stromquist, and B. Cohen (eds.), *The Changing Transitions to Adulthood in Developing Countries: Selected Studies* (pp. 56–83). Washington, DC: National Academy of Sciences.

Landis, C. (1924). Studies of emotional reactions: General behavior and facial expression. *Journal of Comparative Psychology*, 4(5): 447–510.

(1929). The interpretation of facial expression in emotion. *Journal of General Psychology*, 2(1): 59–72.

(1932). An attempt to measure emotional traits in juvenile delinquency. In K. S. Lashley (ed.), *Studies in the Dynamics of Behavior* (pp. 265–326). University of Chicago Press.

Lane, R. D., Chua, P. M., and Dolan, R. J. (1999). Common effects of emotional valence, arousal and attention on neural activation during visual processing of pictures. *Neuropsychologia*, 37(9): 989– 97.

Langer, E., Blank, A., and Chanowitz, B. (1978). The mindlessness of ostensibly thoughtful action: The role of placebic information in interpersonal interaction. *Journal of Personality and Social Psychology*, 36(6): 635–42.

Langlois, J. H., Kalakanis, L., Rubenstein, A. J., Larson, A., Hallam, M., and Smoot, M. (2000). Maxims or myths of beauty? A meta-analytic and theoretical review. *Psychological Bulletin*, 126(3): 390–423.

Larsen, K. S., Coleman, D., Forbes, J., and Johnson, R. (1972). Is the subject's personality of the experimental situation a better predictor of a subject's willingness to administer shock to a victim? *Journal of Personality and Social Psychology*, 22: 287–95.

Latané, B., and Darley, J. M. (1968). Group inhibition of bystander intervention in emergencies. *Journal of Personality and Social Psychology*, 10(3): 215–21.

Latané, B., and Rodin, J. (1969). A lady in distress: Inhibiting effects of friends and strangers on bystander interventions. *Journal of Experimental Social Psychology*, 5(2): 189–202.

Lawrence, E. J., Shaw, P., Giampietro, V. P., Surguladze, S., Brammer, M. J., and David, A. S. (2006). The role of "shared representations" in social perception and empathy: An fMRI study. *NeuroImage*, 29(4): 1173–84.

Lazarus, R. S. (1966). *Psychological Stress and the Coping Process*. New York: McGraw-Hill.

(1984). On the primacy of cognition. *American Psychologist*, 39(2): 124–29.

(1991a). Cognition and motivation in emotion. *American Psychologist*, 46(4): 352–67.

(1991b). *Emotion and Adaptation*. New York: Oxford University Press.

(1994). Universal antecedents of emotion. In P. Ekman and R. J. Davidson (eds.), *The Nature of Emotion: Fundamental Questions* (pp. 163–71). New York: Oxford University Press.

Lazarus, R. S., and Alfert, E. (1964). Short-circuiting of threat by experimentally altering cognitive appraisal. *Journal of Abnormal and Social Psychology*, 69(2): 195–205.

Leakey, R. E., and Lewin, R. (1992). *Origins Reconsidered: In Search of What Makes Us Human*. New York: Doubleday.

Le Bon, G. (1896). *The Crowd*. London: Ernest Benn.

Leckman, J. F. (2011). Variations in maternal behavior: Oxytocin and reward pathways – Peripheral measures matter?! *Neuropsychopharmacology*, 36(13), 2587–88.

LeDoux, J. E. (1982). Neuroevolutionary mechanisms of cerebral asymmetry in man. *Brain, Behavior and Evolution*, 30: 197–213.

(1986). A neurobiological view of the psychology of emotion. In J. LeDoux and W. Hirst (eds.), *Mind and Brain: Dialogues between Cognitive Psychology and Neuroscience* (pp. 355–58). New York: Cambridge University Press.

(1993). Emotional networks in the brain. In M. Lewis and J. Haviland (eds.), *Handbook of Emotions* (pp. 109–18). New York: Guilford Press.

(1996). *The Emotional Brain: The Mysterious Underpinnings of Emotional Life*. New York: Simon & Schuster.

LeDoux, J. E., Romanski, L. M., and Xagoraris, A. (1989). Indelibility of subcortical emotional memories. *Journal of Cognitive Neuroscience*, 1(3): 238–43.

LeDoux, J. E., Sakaguchi, A., and Reis, D. J. (1984). Subcortical efferent projections of the medial geniculate nucleus mediate emotional responses conditioned to acoustic stimuli. *Journal of Neuroscience*, 4(3): 683–98.

LePage, J. F., and Théoret, H. (2007). The mirror neuron system: Grasping others' actions from birth? *Developmental Science*, 10(5): 513–23.

Le Poire, B., Shepard, C., and Duggan, A. (1999). Nonverbal involvement, expressiveness, and pleasantness as predicted by parental and partner attachment style. *Communication Monographs*, 66(4): 293–311.

Lerner, J. S., and Keltner, D. (2000). Beyond valence: Toward a model of emotion-specific influences on judgment and choice. *Cognition & Emotion*, 14(4): 473–93.

(2001). Fear, anger, and risk. *Journal of Personality & Social Psychology*, 81: 146–59.

Lerner, J. S., Small, D. A., and Loewenstein, G. F. (2004). Heart strings and purse strings: Carry-over effects of emotions on economic transactions. *Psychological Science*, 15: 337–41.

Lerner, M. J. (1975). The justice motive in social behavior: Introduction. *Journal of Social Issues*, 31: 1–20.

LeRoith, D., Liotta, A. S., Roth, J., Shiloach, J., Lewis, M. E., Pert, C. B., and Krieger, D. T. (1982). Corticotropin and β-endorphin-like materials are native to unicellular organisms. *Proceedings of the National Academy of Sciences of the United States of America*, 79(6): 2086–90.

LeRoith, D., Shiloach, J., Roth, J., and Lesniak, M. A. (1980). Evolutionary origins of vertebrate hormones: Substances similar to mammalian insulin are native to unicellular eukaryotes. *Proceedings of the National Academy of Sciences of the United States of America*, 77(10): 6184–88.

Leventhal, H., and Scherer, K. (1987). The relationship of emotion to cognition: A functional approach to a semantic controversy. *Cognition & Emotion*, 1(1): 3–28.

Levine, J. D., Gordon, N. C., Jones, R. T., and Fields, H. L. (1978). The narcotic antagonist naloxone enhances clinical pain. *Nature*, 272: 826–27.

Lévi-Strauss, C. (1969). *The Elementary Structures of Kinship*, ed. Rodney Needham, trans. J. H. Bell, J. R. von Sturmer, and Rodney Needham (*Les Structures élémentaires de la parenté*, 1949). London: Eyre & Spottiswoode.

Lewejohann, L., Kloke, V., Heiming, R. S., Jansen, F., Kaiser, S., Schmitt, A., Lesch, K. P., and Sachser, N. (2010). Social status and day-to-day behaviour of male serotonin transporter knockout mice. *Behavioural Brain Research*, 211(2): 220–28.

Lewin, K. (1951). *Field Theory in Social Science: Selected Theoretical Papers*. New York: Harper.

Lewis, H. B. (1971). *Shame and Guilt in Neurosis*. New York: International Universities Press.

Lewis, M. (1993). Self-conscious emotions: Embarrassment, pride, shame, and guilt. In M. Lewis and J. M. Haviland (eds.), *Handbook of Emotions* (pp. 563–573). New York: Guilford Press.

Ley, R. G., and Bryden, M. P. (1979). Hemispheric difference in processing emotions and faces. *Brain and Language*, 7(1): 127–38.

Lhermitte, J., Chain, F., Escourolle, R., Ducarne, B., and Pillon, B. (1972). Etude anatamo-clinique d'un cas de prosopagnosie. *Revue Neurologique*, 126: 329–46.

Lieberman, M. D. (2007). Social cognitive neuroscience: A review of core processes. *Annual Review of Psychology*, 58: 259–89.

Lieberman, M. D., Eisenberger, N. I., Crockett, M. J., Tom, S. M., Pfeifer, J. H., and Way, B. M. (2007). Putting feelings into words: Affect labeling disrupts amygdala activity in response to affective stimuli. *Psychological Science*, 18 (5): 421–28.

Lindner, E. (2009). Why there can be no conflict resolution as long as people are being humiliated. *International Review of Education*, 55: 157–81.

Lindquist, K. A., Wager, T. D., Bliss-Moreau, E., Kober, H., and Feldman-Barrett, B. L. (2012a). What are emotions and how are they created in the brain? *Behavioral and Brain Sciences*, 35(3): 172–202.

Lindquist, K. A., Wager, T. D., Kober, H., Bliss-Moreau, E., and Feldman-Barrett, L. (2012b). The brain basis of emotion: A meta-analytic review. *Behavioral and Brain Sciences*, 35(3): 121–43.

Lindsley, D. B. (1951). Emotion. In S. S. Stevens (ed.), *Handbook of Experimental Psychology* (pp. 473–516). New York: John Wiley.

(1957). Psychophysiology and motivation. In M. R. Jones (ed.), *Nebraska Symposium on Motivation* (pp. 44–105). Lincoln: University of Nebraska Press.

Lipset, J. M. (1960). *Political Man: The Social Bases of Politics*. New York: Doubleday.

Livingstone, M. S., Harris-Warrick, R. M., and Kravitz, E. A. (1980). Serotonin and octopamine produce opposite postures in lobsters. *Science*, 208(4439): 76–79.

Loewenstein, G. F. (1996). Out of control: Visceral influences on behavior. *Organizational Behavior and Human Decision Processes*, 65(3): 272–92.

Loewenstein, G. F., and Lerner, J. S. (2003). The role of affect in decision making. In R. Davidson, K. Scherer, and H. Goldsmith (eds.), *Handbook of Affective Science* (pp. 619–42). New York: Oxford University Press.

Loewenstein, G. F., Rick, S., and Cohen, J. D. (2008). Neuroeconomics. *Annual Review of Psychology*, 59: 647–72.

Loewenstein, G. F., Weber, E. U., Hsee, C. K., and Welch, N. (2001). Risk as feelings. *Psychological Bulletin*, 127(2): 267–86.

Lorenz, K. (1966). *On Aggression*. New York: Harcourt, Brace & World.

Loumaye, E., Thorner, J., and Catt, K. J. (1982). Yeast mating pheromone activates mammalian gonadotropins: Evolutionary conservation of a reproductive hormone? *Science*, 218(4579): 1323–25.

Lovejoy, C. O. (2009). Reexamining human origins in light of *Ardipithecus ramidus*. *Science*, 326(2): 74.

Lowe, J., and Carroll, D. (1985). The effects of spinal injury on the intensity of emotional experience. *British Journal of Clinical Psychology*, 64: 135–36.

Lutz, C. (1988). Ethnographic perspectives on the emotion lexicon. In V. Hamilton, G. H. Bower, and N. H. Frijda (eds.), *Cognitive Perspectives on Emotion and Motivation* (pp. 399–419). New York: Kluwer Academic/Plenum.

Ly, M., Motzkin, J. C., Philippi, C. L., Kirk, G. R., Newman, J. P., Kiehl, K. A., and Koenigs, M. (2012). Cortical thinning in psychopathy. *American Journal of Psychiatry*, 169(7): 743–49.

Lynch, T. R., Rosenthal, M. Z., Kosson, D. S., Cheavens, J. S., Lejuez, C. W., and Blair, R. J. R. (2006). Heightened sensitivity to facial expressions of emotion in borderline personality disorder. *Emotion*, 6(4): 647–55.

Ma, P. M., and Weiger, W.A. (1993). Serotonin-containing neurons in lobsters: The actions of γ-aminobutyric acid, octopamine, serotonin, and proctolin on activity of a pair of identified neurons in the first abdominal ganglion. *Journal of Neurophysiology*, 69: 2015–29.

Maas, J. W., Katz, M. M., Frazer, A., and Bowden, C. L. (2001). Current evidence regarding biological hypotheses of depression and accompanying pathophysiological processes: A critique and synthesis of results using clinical and basic research results. *Integrative Psychiatry*, 7(3–4): 155–69.

Macbeth, A. H., Stepp, J. E., Lee, H.-J., Young, W. S. III, and Caldwell, H. K. (2010). Normal maternal behavior, but increased pup mortality, in conditional oxytocin receptor knockout females. *Behavioral Neuroscience*, 124(5): 677–85.

MacDonald, K. (1993). Parent–child play: An evolutionary perspective. In K. MacDonald (ed.), *Parent–Child Play: Descriptions and Implications* (pp. 113–43). Albany, NY: State University of New York Press.

MacDonald, K., and MacDonald, T. M. (2010). The peptide that binds: A systematic review of oxytocin and its prosocial effects in humans. *Harvard Review of Psychiatry*, 18(1): 1–21.

MacLean, P. D. (1952). Some psychiatric implications of physiological studies on frontotemporal portion of limbic system (visceral brain). *Electroencephalography and Clinical Neurophysiology*, 4(4): 407–18.

(1958). Contrasting functions of limbic and neocortical systems of the brain and their relevance to psychophysiological aspects of medicine. *American Journal of Medicine*, 25(4): 611–26.

(1969). The hypothalamus and emotional behavior. In W. Haymaker, E. Anderson, and W. J. H. Nauta (eds.), *The Hypothalamus*. Springfield, IL: Charles C. Thomas.

(1973). *A Triune Concept of the Brain and Behaviour*. University of Toronto Press.

(1990). *The Triune Brain in Evolution: Role in Paleocerebral Functions*. New York: Plenum.

(1993). Cerebral evolution of emotion. In M. Lewis and J. Haviland (eds.), *Handbook of Emotions* (pp. 67–83). New York: Guilford Press.

(2001). Ongoing discussion of book reviews of Jaak Panksepp (1998), Affective Neuroscience (Vol. 2, No. 2), commentary by Paul D. MacLean. *Neuropsychoanalysis*, 3(1): 81–85.

MacLean, P. D., and Ploog, D. W. (1962). Cerebral representation of penile erection. *Journal of Neurophysiology*, 25(1): 29–55.

Macmillan, M. (2000). Restoring Phineas Gage: A 150th retrospective. *Journal of the History of the Neurosciences*, 9(1): 46–66.

(2001). An odd kind of fame: Stories of Phineas Gage. *Canadian Bulletin of Medical History*, 20(1): 195.

(2008). Phineas Gage: Unraveling the myth. *The Psychologist*, 21(9): 828–31.

(2009a). Phineas Gage: Unanswered questions, July 30. www.deakin.edu.au/hmnbs/psychology/gagepage/PgQuestn.php.

(2009b). The Phineas Gage Information Page. www.deakin.edu.au/health/psychology/gagepage/.

Mar, R. A., Kelley, W. M., Heatherton, T. F., and Macrae, C. N. (2007). Detecting agency from the biological motion of veridical versus animated agents. *Social, Cognitive, and Affective Neuroscience*, 2(3): 199–205.

Margulis, L., and Sagan, D. (1995). *What is Life?* New York: Simon & Schuster.

Mark, V., and Ervin, F. V. (1970). *Violence and the Brain*. New York: Harper & Row.

Markova, G., Stieben, J., and Legerstee, M. (2010). Neural structures of jealousy: Infant's experience of social exclusion with caregivers and peers. In S. L. Hart and M. Legerstee (eds.), *Handbook of Jealousy: Theory, Research, and Multidisciplinary Approaches* (pp. 83–100). New York: Wiley-Blackwell.

Markowitsch, H. J. (1998). Differential contribution of right and left amygdala to affective information processing. *Behavioural Neurology*, 11(4): 233–44.

Markus, H. M., von Dawans, B., and Domes, G. (2009). Oxytocin, vasopressin, and human social behavior. *Frontiers in Neuroendocrinology*, 30(4): 548–57.

Markus, H. R., and Kitayama, S. (1991). Culture and the self: Implications for cognition, emotion, and motivation. *Psychological Review*, 98: 224–53.

Marsh, R. C. (1956). *Bertrand Russell: Logic and Language*. London: Allen & Unwin.

Marsicano, G., Wotjak, C. T., Azad, S. C., Bisogno, T., Rammes, G., Cascio, M. G., ... and Lutz, B. (2002). The endogenous cannabinoid system controls extinction of aversive memories. *Nature*, 418(6897): 530–34.

Martínez, I., Rosa, M., Arsuaga, J. L., Jarabo, P., Quam, R., Lorenzo, C., Gracia, A., Carretero, J. M., Bermúdez de Castro, J., and Carbonell, E. (2004). Auditory capacities in Middle Pleistocene humans from the Sierra de Atapuerca in Spain. *Proceedings of the National Academy of Sciences of the United States of America*, 101(27): 9976–81.

Marx, J. L. (1985). "Anxiety peptide" found in brain. *Science*, 227(4689): 934.

Maslow, A. H. (1954). *Motivation and Personality*. New York: Harper.

Masters, R. D. (2002). MacLean's evolutionary neuroethology: Environmental pollution, brain chemistry, and violent crime. In G. A. Cory, and R. Gardner (eds.), *The Evolutionary Neuroethology of Paul MacLean: Convergences and Frontiers* (pp. 275–97). Westport, CT: Praeger.

Masters, W. H., and Johnson, V. E. (1966). *Human Sexual Response*. Toronto and New York: Bantam Books.

Matsumoto, D., Haan, N., Yabrove, G., Theodorou, P., and Carney, C. C. (1986). Preschoolers' moral actions and emotions in Prisoner's Dilemma. *Developmental Psychology*, 22(5): 663–70.

Matsumoto, D., and Hwang, H. S. (2012). Evidence for a nonverbal expression of triumph. *Evolution and Human Behavior*, 33(5): 520–29.

Matthews, G. G. (1949). *Neurobiology: Molecules, Cells, and Systems*. Oxford: Blackwell Science.

    (1998). *Neurobiology: Molecules, Cells, and Systems* (2nd edn.). Oxford: Blackwell Science.

Mayer, D. J., Price, D. D., and Rafii, A. (1977). Antagonism of acupuncture analgesia in man by the narcotic antagonist naloxone. *Brain Research*, 121 (2): 368–72.

McArthur, L. Z., and Baron, R. (1983). Toward an ecological theory of social perception. *Psychological Review*, 90(3): 215–38.

McCarthy, M. M. (1990). Oxytocin inhibits infanticide in female house mice (*Mus domesticus*). *Hormones and Behavior*, 24(3): 365–75.

McGuire, M. T., Raleigh, M. J., and Brammer, G. L. (1984). Adaptation, selection, and benefit–cost balances: Implications of behavioral-physiological studies of social dominance in male vervet monkeys. *Ethology and Sociobiology*, 5: 269–77.

McPherron, S. P., Alemseged, Z., Marean, C. W., Wynn, J. G., Reed, D., Geraads, D., ... and Bearat, H. A. (2010). Evidence for stone-tool-assisted consumption of animal tissues before 3.39 million years ago at Dikika, Ethiopia. *Nature*, 466: 857–60.

Mead, N. L., Baumeister, R. F., Stillman, T. F., Rawn, C. D., and Vohs, K. D. (2011). Social exclusion causes people to spend and consume strategically in the service of affiliation. *Journal of Consumer Research*, 37(5): 902–19.

Meltzer, H. Y. (2001). Serotonin as a target for antipsychotic drug action. In A. Breier, P. V. Tran, J. M. Herrera, G. D. Tollefson, and F. P. Bymaster (eds.), *Current Issues in the Psychopharmacology of Schizophrenia* (pp. 289–303). Philadelphia, PA: Lippincott Williams & Wilkins.

Meltzoff, A. N. (1990). Towards a developmental cognitive science: The implications of cross-modal matching and imitation for the development of representation and memory in infancy. *Annals of the New York Academy of Sciences*, 608(1): 1–31.

Meltzoff, A. N., and Decety, J. (2003). What imitation tells us about social cognition: A rapprochement between developmental psychology and cognitive neuroscience. *Philosophical Transactions of the Royal Society London B, Biological Sciences*, 358(1431): 491–500.

Meltzoff, A. N., and Moore, M. K. (1977). Imitation of facial and manual gestures by human neonates. *Science*, 198(4312): 75–78.

    (1983). Newborn infants imitate adult facial gestures. *Child Development*, 54(3): 702–9.

    (1997). Explaining facial imitation: A theoretical model. *Early Development and Parenting*, 6(3–4): 179–92.

Melzack, R., and Wall, P. D. (1965). Pain mechanisms: A new theory. *Science*, 150(3699): 971–79.

Mendoza, S., and Mason, W. A. (1997). Attachment relationships in New World primates. In C. S. Carter, I. I. Lederhendler, and B. Kirkpatrick (eds.), *The Integrative Neurobiology of Affiliation*, Annals of the New York Academy of Sciences (Vol. 807, pp. 203–9). New York: New York Academy of Sciences.

Mercadillo, R. E., Diaz, J. L., Pasaye, E. H., and Barrios, F. A. (2011). Perception of suffering and compassion experience: Brain gender disparities. *Brain and Cognition*, 76(1): 5–14.

Meredith, M., and Fernandez-Fewell, G. (1994). Vomeronasal system, LHRH, and sex behaviour. *Psychoneuroendocrinology*, 19(5–7): 657–72.

Meredith, M., and Fewell, G. (2001). Vomeronasal organ: Electrical stimulation activates fos in mating pathways and in GnRH neurons. *Brain Research*, 922(1): 87–94.

Merton, R. K. (1938). Social structure and anomie. *American Sociological Review*, 3(5): 672–82.

(1968). *Social Theory and Social Structure*. New York: Free Press.

(1996). *On Social Structure and Science*, ed. P. Sztompka. University of Chicago Press.

Meyer-Lindenberg, A., Domes, G., Kirsch, P., and Heinrichs, M. (2011). Oxytocin and vasopressin in the human brain: Social neuropeptides for translational medicine. *Nature Reviews Neuroscience*, 12(9): 524–38.

Miami News (1985). Mengele son: Dad felt "no guilt." June 18. http://news. google.com/newspapers?nid=2206&dat=19850618&id=lqAmAAAAIBAJ& sjid=nQEGAAAAIBAJ&pg=2306,358981.

Michotte, A. E. (1963). *The Perception of Causality*. New York: Basic Books.

Mikulincer, M. (1997). Adult attachment style and information processing: Individual differences in curiosity and cognitive closure. *Journal of Personality and Social Psychology*, 72(5): 1217–30.

(1998a). Attachment working models and the sense of trust: An exploration of interaction goals and affect regulation. *Journal of Personality and Social Psychology*, 74(5): 1209–24.

(1998b). Adult attachment style and affect regulation: Strategic variables in self-appraisals. *Journal of Personality and Social Psychology*, 75(2): 420–35.

Mikulincer, M., and Florian, V. (2008). The complex and multifaceted nature of the fear of personal death: The multidimensional model of Victor Florian. In A. Tomer, G. T. Eliason, and P. T. P. Wong (eds.), *Existential and Spiritual Issues in Death Attitudes* (pp. 39–64). Mahwah, NJ: Lawrence Erlbaum Associates.

Mikulincer, M., and Shaver, P. (2003). The attachment behavioral system in adulthood: Activation, psychodynamics, and interpersonal processes. In M. P. Zanna (ed.), *Advances in Experimental Social Psychology* (Vol. 35, pp. 53–152). San Diego, CA: Academic Press.

(2005). Mental representation of attachment security: Theoretical foundation for a positive social psychology. In M. W. Baldwin (ed.), *Interpersonal Cognition* (pp. 233–66). New York: Guilford Press.

Milgram, S. (1963). Behavioral study of obedience. *Journal of Abnormal and Social Psychology*, 67: 371–78.

(1965). Some conditions of obedience and disobedience to authority. In I. D. Steiner and M. Fishbein (eds.), *Current Studies in Social Psychology* (pp. 243–62). New York: Holt, Rinehart, & Winston.

Miller, E. (1974). Review of "A triune concept of the brain and behaviour." *Canadian Psychologist/Psychologie Canadienne*, 15(4), 394–96.

Miller, G., Tybur, J. M., and Jordan, B. D. (2007). Ovulatory cycle effects on tip earnings by lap dancers: Economic evidence for human estrus? *Evolution and Human Behavior*, 28(6): 375–81.

Miller, M. (2012). Emotion communication using physical touch: Intentions, symbol systems, and individual predispositions. Unpublished doctoral dissertation, University of Connecticut.

Miller, R. E., Caul, W. F., and Mirsky, I. A. (1967). Communication of affects between feral and socially isolated monkeys. *Journal of Personality and Social Psychology*, 7(3): 231–39.

Miller, R. S. (1995a). Embarrassment and social behavior. In J. P. Tangney and K. W. Fischer (eds.), *Self-Conscious Emotions. The Psychology of Shame, Guilt, Embarrassment, and Pride* (pp. 322–39). New York: Guilford Press.

(1995b). On the nature of embarrassability: Shyness, social evaluation, and social skill. *Journal of Personality*, 63(2): 315–39.

(1996). *Embarrassment: Poise and Peril in Everyday Life*. New York: Guilford Press.

Miller, W. L., Baxter, J. D., and Eberhardt, N. L. (1983). Peptide hormone genes: Structure and evolution. In D. T. Krieger and J. B. Martin (eds.), *Brain Peptides* (pp. 15–78). New York: John Wiley.

Mitani, J. C. (1984). The behavioral regulation of monogamy in gibbons (*Hylobates muelleri*). *Behavioral Ecology and Sociobiology*, 15(3): 225–29.

Mize, K. D., and Jones, N. A. (2012). Infant physiological and behavioral responses to loss of maternal attention to a social-rival. *International Journal of Psychophysiology*, 83: 16–23.

Moll, J., and de Oliveira-Souza, R. (2007a). Moral judgments, emotions and the utilitarian brain. *Trends in Cognitive Sciences*, 11(8): 319–21.

(2007b). Response to Greene: Moral sentiments and reason – Friends or foes? *Trends in Cognitive Sciences*, 11(8): 323–24.

Moll, J., de Oliveira-Souza, R., Eslinger, P. J., Bramati, I. E., Mourao-Miranda, J., Andreiulo, P. A., and Pessoa, L. (2002). The neural correlates of moral sensitivity: A functional magnetic resonance imaging investigation of basic and moral emotions. *Journal of Neuroscience*, 22(7): 2730–36.

Moll, J., de Oliveira-Souza, R., Garrido, G. J., Bramati, I. E., Caparelli-Daquer, E. M., Paiva, M. L., Zahn, R., and Grafman, J. (2007). The self as a moral agent: linking the neural bases of social agency and moral sensitivity. *Social Neuroscience*, 2(3–4): 336–52.

Moll, J., de Oliveira-Souza, R., and Zahn, R. (2008). The neural basis of moral cognition: Sentiments, concepts, and values. *Annals of the New York Academy of Sciences*, 1124: 161–80.

Moll, J., de Oliveira-Souza, R., Zahn, R., and Grafman, J. (2007). The cognitive neuroscience of moral emotions. In W. Sinnott-Armstrong (ed.), *Moral Psychology* (Vol. 3, pp. 1–17). Cambridge, MA: MIT Press.

Moll, J., Eslinger, P. J., and de Oliveira-Souza, R. (2001). Frontopolar and anterior temporal cortex activation in a moral judgment task. *Arquivos de Neuro-Psiquiatria*, 59(3-B): 657–64.

Moll, J., Krueger, F., Zahn, R., Pardini, M., de Oliveira-Souza, R., and Grafman, J. (2006). Human fronto-mesolimbic networks guide decisions about charitable donation. *Proceedings of the National Academy of Sciences of the United States of America*, 103(42): 15623–28.

Moll, J., and Schulkin, J. (2009). Social attachment and aversion in human moral cognition. *Neuroscience and Biobehavioral Reviews*, 33(3): 456–65.

Moll, J., Zahn, R, de Oliveira-Souza, R., Bramati, I. E., Krueger, F., Tura, B., Cavanagh, A. L., and Grafman, J. (2011). Impairment of prosocial sentiments is associated with frontopolar and septal damage in frontotemporal dementia. *NeuroImage*, 54(2): 1735–42.

Moll, J., Zahn, R., de Oliveira-Souza, R., Krueger, F., and Grafman, J. (2005). The neural basis of human moral cognition. *Nature Reviews Neuroscience*, 6: 799–809.

Molnar-Szakacs, I., Iacoboni, M., Koski, L., and Mazziotta, J. (2005). Functional segregation within pars opercularis of the inferior frontal gyrus: Evidence from fMRI studies of imitation and action observation. *Cerebral Cortex*, 15 (7): 986–94.

Moon-Fanelli, A. (2011). The ontogeny of expression of communicative genes in coyote–beagle hybrids. *Behavior Genetics*, 41: 858–75.

Moore, F. L. (1987). Behavioral actions of neurohypophysial peptides. In D. Crews (ed.), *Psychobiology of Reproductive Behavior: An Evolutionary Perspective* (pp. 61–87). Englewood Cliffs, NJ: Prentice-Hall.

Moors, A., and De Houwer, J. (2005). Automatic processing of dominance and submissiveness. *Experimental Psychology*, 52(4): 296–302.

Morris, D. (1967). *The Naked Ape*. London: Constable.

Morris, J. S., Ohman, A., and Dolan, R. J. (1998). Conscious and unconscious emotional learning in the amygdala. *Nature*, 393(6684): 467–70.

Morris, P. H., Doe, C., and Godsell, E. (2008). Secondary emotions in non-primate species? Behavioral reports and subjective claims by animal owners. *Cognition & Emotion*, 22(1): 3–20.

Moruzzi, G., and Magoun, H. W. (1949). Brain stem reticular formation and activation of the EEG. *Electroencephalography and Clinical Neurophysiology*, 1 (4): 455–73.

Moskowitz, D. S., Pinard, G., Zuroff, D. C., Annable, L., and Young, S. N. (2001). The effect of tryptophan on social interaction in everyday life: A placebo-controlled study. *Neuropsychopharmacology*, 25: 277–89.

Moyer, K. E. (1968). Kinds of aggression and their physiological bases. *Communications in Behavior and Biology*, 2(2): 65–87.

Mukamel, R., Ekstrom, A. D., Kaplan, J., Iacoboni, M., and Fried, I. (2010). Single-neuron responses in humans during execution and observation of actions. *Current Biology*, 20(8): 750–56.

Mullen, B. (1986). Atrocity as a function of lynch mob composition: A self-attention perspective. *Personality and Social Psychology Bulletin*, 12(2): 187–94.

Murphy, D. L. (1973). Technical strategies for the study of catecholamines in man. In E. Usdin and S. Snyder (eds.), *Frontiers in Catecholamine Research* (pp. 1077–82). Oxford: Pergamon.

Murphy, M. R., MacLean, P. D., and Hamilton, S. C. (1981). Species-typical behavior of hamsters deprived from birth of the neocortex. *Science*, 213 (4506): 459–61.

Murray, L., and Trevarthen, C. (1986). The infant's role in mother–infant communications. *Journal of Child Language*, 13: 15–29.

Najma, J. (1977). Shame and guilt in Japan. *Hiroshima Forum for Psychology*, 4: 69–71.

Nakahara, K., and Miyashita, Y. (2005). Understanding intentions: Through the looking glass. *Science*, 308(5722): 644–45.

Napier, J. (1960). Fossil hand bones from Olduvai Gorge. *Nature*, 196: 409–11.

Neumann, I. D. (2008). Brain oxytocin: A key regulator of emotional and social behaviours in both females and males. *Journal of Neuroendocrinology*, 20(6): 858–65.

New, A. S., Hazlett, E. A., Buchsbaum, M. S., Goodman, M., Reynolds, D., Mitropoulou, V., Sprung, L., Shaw, R. B., Koenigsberg, H., Platholi, J., Silverman, J., and Siever, L. J. (2002). Blunted prefrontal cortical[18] fluorodeoxyglucose positron emission tomography response to meta-chlorophenylpiperazine in impulsive aggression. *Archives of General Psychiatry*, 59(7): 621–29.

Newcomb, T. (1953). An approach to the study of communicative acts. *Psychological Review*, 60: 93–404.

Newell, P. C. (1995). Signal transduction and motility of Dictyostelium. *Bioscience Reports*, 15: 445–62.

Niall, H. D. (1982). The evolution of peptide hormones. *Annual Review of Physiology*, 44(1): 615–24.

Niedenthal, P. M., and Brauer, M. (2012). Social functionality of human emotion. *Annual Review of Psychology*, 63: 259–85.

Nucci, L. P., and Narvaéz, D. (2008). *Handbook of Moral and Character Education*. New York: Taylor & Francis.

Oades, R. D. (1985). The role of noradrenaline in tuning and dopamine in switching between signals in the CNS. *Neuroscience & Biobehavioral Reviews*, 9(2): 261–82.

Ochsner, K. N., Bunge, S. A., Gross, J. J., and Gabrieli, J. D. (2002). Rethinking feelings: An fMRI study of the cognitive regulation of emotion. *Journal of Cognitive Neuroscience*, 14(8): 1215–29.

Ochsner, K. N., Ray, R. D., Cooper, J. C., Robertson, E. R., Chopra, S., Gabrieli, J. D., and Gross, J. J. (2004). For better or for worse: Neural systems supporting the cognitive down- and up-regulation of negative emotion. *NeuroImage*, 23(2): 483–99.

Oda, R., Naganawa, T., Yamauchi, S., Yamagata, N., and Matsumoto-Oda, A. (2009). Altruists are trusted based on non-verbal cues. *Biology Letters*, 5(6): 752–54.

Öhman, A., and Dimberg, U. (1978). Facial expressions as conditioned stimuli for electrodermal responses: A case of "preparedness"? *Journal of Personality and Social Psychology*, 36(11): 1251–58.

Olds, J. (1956). Pleasure centers in the brain. *Scientific American*, 195, 105–16.

(1958). Self-stimulation of the brain. *Science*, 127(3294): 315–24.

Olds, J., and Milner, P. (1954). Positive reinforcement produced by electrical stimulation of septal area and other regions of rat brain. *Journal of Comparative and Physiological Psychology*, 47(6): 419–27.

Olds, M. E., and Olds, J. (1963). Approach-avoidance analysis of rat diencephalon. *Journal of Comparative Neurology*, 120(2): 259–95.

Olson, S. (1989). *Shaping the Future: Biology and Human Values*. Washington, DC: National Academy Press.

Ophir, A. G., Gessel, A., Zheng, D. J., and Phelps, S. M. (2012). Oxytocin receptor density is associated with male mating tactics and social monogamy. *Hormones and Behavior*, 61(3): 445–53.

Ortony, A., Clore, G. L., and Collins, A. (1988). *The Cognitive Structure of Emotions*. Cambridge University Press.

Owens, G. P., Sinha, A. K., Sikela, J. M., and Hahn, W. E. (1989). Sequence and expression of the murine diazepam binding inhibitor. *Molecular Brain Research*, 6: 101–8.

Padgett, V. R., and Jorgenson, D. O. (1982). Superstition and economic threat. *Personality and Social Psychology Bulletin*, 8(4): 736–41.

Panksepp, J. (1981). Hypothalamic integration of behavior. In P. Morgane and J. Panksepp (eds.), *Handbook of the Hypothalamus*, Vol. 3: *Behavioral Studies of the Hypothalamus* (pp. 289–437). New York: Marcel Bekker.

(1982). Toward a general psychobiological theory of emotions. *Behavioral and Brain Sciences*, 5(3): 407–67.

(1986). The neurochemistry of behavior. *Annual Review of Psychology*, 37(1): 77–107.

(1991). Brain opioids: A neurochemical substrate for narcotic and social dependence. In S. Cooper (ed.), *Theory in Psychopharmacology* (pp. 149–75). London: Academic Press.

(1992). Oxytocin effects on emotional processes: Separation distress, social bonding, and relationship to psychiatric disorders. *Annals of the New York Academy of Sciences*, 652: 243–52.

(1993). Neurochemical control of moods and emotions: Amino acids to neuropeptides. In M. Lewis and J. Haviland (eds.), *Handbook of Emotions* (pp. 87–107). New York: Guilford Press.

(1996). The roles of brain opioids, oxytocin and prolactin in social affect and social bonding. Presentation at the New York Academy of Sciences Conference on the Integrative Neurobiology of Affiliation, Georgetown University, Washington, DC.

(1998). *Affective Neuroscience: The Foundations of Human and Animal Emotions.* New York: Oxford University Press.

(2002). Foreword: The MacLean legacy and some modern trends in emotion research. In G. A. Cory and R. Gardner (eds.), *The Evolutionary Neuroethology of Paul MacLean: Convergences and Frontiers* (pp. ix–xxxvi). Westport, CT: Praeger.

(2003). Feeling the pain of social loss. *Science*, 302(5643): 237–39.

Panksepp, J., and Burgdorf, J. (1999). Laughing rats? Playful tickling arouses high frequency ultrasonic chirping in young rodents. In S. Hameroff, C. Chalmers, and C. Kazniak (eds.), *Toward a Science of Consciousness*, Vol. 3: *The Third Tucson Discussions and Debates* (pp. 231–44). Cambridge, MA: MIT Press.

(2000). 50-kHz chirping (laughter?) in response to conditioned and unconditioned tickle-induced reward in rats: Effects of social housing and genetic variables. *Behavioural Brain Research*, 115(1): 25–38.

Panksepp, J., Nelson, E., and Bekkedal, M. (1997). Brain systems for the mediation of social separation-distress and social-reward: Evolutionary antecedents and neuropeptide intermediaries. In C. S. Carter, I. I. Lederhendler, and B. Kirkpatrick (eds.), *The Integrative Neurobiology of Affiliation*, Annals of the New York Academy of Sciences (Vol. 807, pp. 78–100). New York: New York Academy of Sciences.

Papathanassoglou, E. D., Giannakopoulou, M., Mpouzika, M., Bozas, E., and Karabinis, A. (2010). Potential effects of stress in critical illness through the role of stress neuropeptides. *Nursing in Critical Care*, 15(4): 204–16.

Papez, J. W. (1937). A proposed mechanism of emotion. *Archives of Neurology and Psychiatry*, 38(4): 725–43.

Pappu, S., Gunnell, Y., Akhilesh, K., Braucher, R., Taieb, M., Demory, F., and Thouveny, N. (2001). Early Pleistocene presence of Acheulian hominins in south India. *Science*, 331(6024): 1596–99.

Parkinson, B. (1997). Untangling the appraisal–emotion connection. *Personality and Social Psychology Review*, 1(1): 62–79.

Parrott, W. G. (1991). The emotional experience of envy and jealousy. In P. Salovey (ed.), *The Psychology of Jealousy and Envy* (pp. 3–30). New York: Guilford Press.

Parrott, W. G., and Smith, R. H. (1983). Distinguishing the experiences of envy and jealousy. *Journal of Personality and Social Psychology*, 64: 906–20.

     (1991). Embarrassment: Actual vs. typical cases, classical vs. prototypical representations. *Cognition & Emotion*, 5: 467–88.

Patton, P. (2008). One world, many minds. *Scientific American Mind*, 19: 72–79.

Pavlov, I. P. (1927). *Conditioned Reflexes: An Investigation of the Physiological Activity of the Cerebral Cortex*, trans. G. V. Anrep. Oxford: Clarendon Press.

Pederson, C. A. (1997). Oxytocin control of maternal behavior: Regulation by sex steroids and offspring stimuli. In C. S. Carter, I. I. Lederhendler, and B. Kirkpatrick (eds.), *The Integrative Neurobiology of Affiliation*, Annals of the New York Academy of Sciences (Vol. 807, pp. 126–45). New York: New York Academy of Sciences.

Pederson, C. A., Caldwell, J. D., and Brooks, P. J. (1990). Neuropeptide control of parental and reproductive behavior. In D. Ganten and D. Pfaff (eds.), *Current Topics in Neuroendocrinology: Behavioral Aspects of Neuroendocrinology* (Vol. 10, pp. 81–113). Berlin: Springer-Verlag.

Peery, J. C. (1978). Magnification of affect using frame-by-frame film analysis. *Environmental Psychology and Nonverbal Behavior*, 3(1): 58–61.

Pelphrey, K. A., Mitchell, T. V., McKeown, M. J., Goldstein, J., Allison, T., and McCarthy, G. (2003). Brain activity evoked by the perception of human walking: Controlling for meaningful coherent motion. *Journal of Neuroscience*, 23(17): 6819–25.

Pelphrey, K. A., Morris, J. P., and McCarthy, G. (2004). Grasping the intentions of others: The perceived intentionality of an action influences activity in the superior temporal sulcus during social perception. *Journal of Cognitive Neuroscience*, 16(10): 1706–16.

Pennebaker, J. W. (1997). Writing about emotional experiences as a therapeutic process. *Psychological Science*, 8(3): 164–66.

Pennebaker, J. W., and Chung, C. K. (2007). Expressive writing, emotional upheavals, and health. In H. S. Friedman and R. C. Silver (eds.), *Foundations of Health Psychology* (pp. 263–84). New York: Oxford University Press.

Pennisi, E. (2006). Was Lucy's a fighting family? Look at her legs. *Science*, 311 (5759): 330–31.

Pert, C. (1985). Neuropeptides and their receptors: Substrates for the biochemistry of emotion. Keynote address at the inaugural meeting of the International Society for Research on Emotions. Harvard University, Cambridge, MA.

     (1997). *Molecules of Emotion: Why You Feel The Way You Feel*. New York: Scribner.

Pert, C. B., and Snyder, S. H. (1973). Opiate receptor: Demonstration in nervous tissue. *Science*, 179(4077): 1011–14.

Pettigrew, T. F. (1961). Social psychology and desegregation research. *American Psychologist*, 16: 105–12.

Petty, R. E., and Cacioppo, J. T. (1986). *Communication and Persuasion: Central and Peripheral Routes to Attitude Change*. New York: Springer Verlag.

Piaget, J. (1932). *The Moral Judgment of the Child*. Glencoe, IL: Free Press.

(1971). Piaget's theory. In P. Mussen (ed.), *Handbook of Child Development*, Vol. 1: *Theoretical Models of Human Development* (pp. 703–32). New York: John Wiley.

Piliavin, I. M., Rodin, J., and Piliavin, J. A. (1969). Good samaritanism: An underground phenomenon? *Journal of Personality and Social Psychology*, 13(4): 298–99.

Pincus, J. H. (2001). *Base Instincts: What Makes Killers Kill?* New York: MetroBooks.

Pinel, J. P. J. (1993). *Biopsychology* (2nd edn.). Needham Heights, MA: Allyn & Bacon.

Pinker, S. (1994). *The Language Instinct: How the Mind Creates Language*. New York: Morrow.

Pitkow, L. J., Sharer, C. A., Ren, X., Insel, T. R., Terwilliger, E. F., and Young, L. J. (2001). Facilitation of affiliation and pair-bond formation by vasopressin receptor gene transfer into the ventral forebrain of a monogamous vole. *Journal of Neuroscience*, 21(18): 7392–96.

Ploog, D. (1981). Neurobiology of primate audio-vocal behavior. *Brain Research Reviews*, 3(1): 35–61.

(1988). Neurobiology and pathology of subhuman vocal communication and human speech. In D. Todt, P. Symmes, and D. Goedeking (eds.), *Primate Vocal Communication* (pp. 195–212). Berlin: Springer Verlag.

(1992). Neuroethological foundations of biological psychiatry. In H. M. Engert and M. Weigand (eds.), *Integrative Biological Psychiatry* (pp. 3–35). Berlin: Springer Verlag.

Polonsky, M., and Buck, R. (2003). Gender and relationship effects on social and moral emotions. Paper presented at the meeting of the National Communication Association, Miami, FL, November 2003.

Pontius, A. A. (1997). Homicide linked to moderate repetitive stresses kindling limbic seizures in 14 cases of limbic psychotic trigger reaction. *Aggression and Violent Behavior*, 2(2): 125–41.

(2002). Neuroethology, exemplified by limbic seizures with motiveless homicide in "limbic psychotic trigger reaction." In G. A. Cory and R. Gardner (eds.), *The Evolutionary Neuroethology of Paul MacLean: Convergences and Frontiers* (pp. 167–92). Westport, CT: Praeger.

Porges, S. W. (1995). Cardiac vagal tone: A physiological index of stress. *Neuroscience & Biobehavioral Reviews*, 19(2): 225–33.

Potegal, M., and Ferris, C. F. (1989). Intraspecific aggression in male hamsters is inhibited by intrahypothalamic vasopressin-receptor antagonist. *Aggressive Behavior*, 15(4): 311–20.

Powers, S. R. (2009). Toward using more ecologically valid emotion displays in brain research: a functional neuroimaging study of the communication of affect receiving ability test. Unpublished doctoral dissertation. University of Connecticut, Storrs, CT.

Powers, S. R., Buck, R., Kiehl, K., and Schaich-Borg, J. (2007). An fMRI study of neural responses to spontaneous emotional expressions: Evidence for a communicative theory of empathy. Paper presented at the 93rd Annual Convention of the National Communication Association, Chicago, IL.

Powers, S. R., Rauh, C., Buck, R., Henning, R., and West, T. V. (2011). The effect of video feedback delay on frustration and emotion communication accuracy. *Computers in Human Behavior*, 27(5): 1651–57.

Prentice-Dunn, S., and Rogers, R. W. (1980). Effects of deindividuating situational cues and aggressive models on subjective deindividuation and aggression. *Journal of Personality and Social Psychology*, 39: 104–13.

(1982). Effects of public and private self-awareness on deindividuation and aggression. *Journal of Personality and Social Psychology*, 43: 503–13.

(1983). Deindividuation in aggression. In R. G. Green and E. I. Donnerstein (eds.), *Aggression: Theoretical and Empirical Reviews*, Vol. 2: *Issues in Research* (pp. 155–71). New York: Academic Press.

Preston, S. D., and de Waal, F. B. M. (2002). Empathy: Its ultimate and proximate bases. *Behavioral and Brain Sciences*, 25(1): 1–72.

Prideaux, E. (1920). The psychogalvanic reflex: A review. *Brain*, 43(1): 50–73.

Prodan, C. I., Orbelo, D. M., Testa, J. A., and Ross, E. D. (2001). Hemispheric differences in recognizing upper and lower facial displays of emotion. *Neuropsychiatry, Neuropsychology, & Behavioral Neurology*, 14(4): 206–12.

Prohovnik, I., Skudlarski, P., Fulbright, R. K., Gore, J. C., and Wexler, B. E. (2004). Functional MRI changes before and after onset of reported emotions. *Psychiatry Research: Neuroimaging*, 132(3): 239–50.

Pulaski, M. (1999). Sex, power and rock 'n roll: An investigation of information processing and emotional views of liking for music videos. Thesis C66 1999. Doctoral dissertation, University of Connecticut, Storrs. Dissertation Abstracts International.

Purves, D., Augenstine, G. J., Fitzpatrick, D., Katz, L. C., LaMantia, A.-S., and McNamara, J. O. (1997). *Neuroscience*. Sunderland, MA: Sinauer.

Raleigh, M. J., McGuire, M. T., Brammer, G. L., Pollack, D. B., and Yuwiler, A. (1991). Serotonergic mechanisms promote dominance acquisition in adult male vervet monkeys. *Brain Research*, 559(2): 181–90

Ramnani, N., and Miall, C. R. (2004). A system in the human brain for predicting the actions of others. *Nature Neuroscience*, 7(1): 85–90.

Rampello, L., Alvano, A., Chiechio, S., Raffaele, R., Vecchio, I., and Malaguarnera, M. (2005). An evaluation of efficacy and safety of reboxetine in elderly patients affected by "retarded" post-stroke depression: A random, placebo-controlled study. *Archives of Gerontology and Geriatrics*, 40(3): 275–85.

Raphael, D. D. (1960). *The Paradox of Tragedy*. Bloomington, IN: Indiana University Press.

Rapoport, A. (1986). *General Systems Theory: Essential Concepts and Applications*. New York: Routledge.

Reardon, K. K., and Buck, R. (1989). Emotion, reason, and communication in coping with cancer. *Health Communication*, 1: 41–54.

Redmond, Jr., D. E., and Murphy, D. L. (1975). Behavioral correlates of platelet monoamine oxidase (MAO) activity in rhesus monkeys. *Psychosomatic Medicine*, 37: 80.

Redmond, Jr., D. E., Murphy, D. L., and Baulu, J. (1979). Platelet monoamine oxidase activity correlates with social affiliative and agonistic behaviors in normal rhesus monkeys. *Psychosomatic Medicine*, 41: 87–100.

Reed, L. I., Zeglen, K. N., and Schmidt, K. L. (2012). Facial expressions as honest signals of cooperative intent in a one-shot anonymous Prisoner's Dilemma game. *Evolution and Human Behavior*, 33(3): 200–9.

Reiman, E. M., Fusselman, M. J., Fox, P. T., and Raichle, M. E. (1989). Neuroanatomical correlates of anticipatory anxiety. *Science*, 243(4894): 1071–74.

Reiner, A. (1990). An explanation of behavior [Review of P. D. MacLean, *The Triune Brain in Evolution*]. *Science*, 250(4978): 303–5.

Reti, I. M., Xu, J. Z., Yanofski, J., McKibben, J., Uhart, M., Cheng, Y. J., Zandi, P., ... and Nestadt, G. (2011). Monoamine oxidase A regulates antisocial personality in whites with no history of physical abuse. *Comprehensive Psychiatry*, 52(2): 188–94.

Retzinger, S. M. (1991). *Violent Emotions: Shame and Rage in Marital Quarrels*. Newbury Park, CA: Sage Publications.

(1995). Shame and anger in personal relationships. In S. Duck, and J. T. Wood (eds.), *Confronting Relationship Challenges* (pp. 22–42). Thousand Oaks, CA: Sage Publications.

Reynolds, D. V. (1971). Neural mechanisms of laughter. Paper presented at the Midwestern Psychological Association Convention, April, Detroit, MI.

Richard, P., Moos, F., and Freund-Mercier, M. J. (1991). Central effects of oxytocin. *Physiological Reviews*, 71(2): 331–70.

Ridley, M. (1998). *The Origins of Virtue*. New York: Penguin.

Riedel, K., and Ebert, L. (2002). Communication in bacterial biofilms. *Biomedical Progress*, 15: 69–74.

Riedl, R., and Javor, A. (2012). The biology of trust: Integrating evidence from genetics, endocrinology, and functional brain imaging. *Journal of Neuroscience, Psychology, and Economics*, 5(2): 63–91.

Riem, M. M., Bakermans-Kranenburg, M. J., Pieper, S., Tops, M., Boksem, M. A., Vermeiren, R. R., van IJzendoorn, M. H., and Rombouts, S. A. (2011). Oxytocin modulates amygdala, insula, and inferior frontal gyrus responses to infant crying: A randomized controlled trial. *Biological Psychiatry*, 70(3): 291–97.

Riem, M. M., van IJzendoorn, M. H., Tops, M., Boksem, M. A., Rombouts, S. A., and Bakermans-Kranenburg, M. J. (2011). No laughing matter: Intranasal oxytocin administration changes functional brain connectivity during exposure to infant laughter. *Neuropsychopharmacology*, 37(5): 1257–66.

Riggio, R. E., and Friedman, H. S. (1986). Impression formation: The role of expressive behavior. *Journal of Personality and Social Psychology*, 50(2): 421–27.

Rightmire, G. P. (1998). Human evolution in the Middle Pleistocene: The role of *Homo heidelbergensis*. *Evolutionary Anthropology*, 6: 218–27.

Rilling, J. K., and Insel, T. R. (1999). The primate neocortex in comparative perspective using magnetic resonance imaging. *Journal of Human Evolution*, 37(2): 191–223.

Rimmele, U., Hediger, K., Heinrichs, M., and Klaver, P. (2009). Oxytocin makes a face in memory familiar. *Journal of Neuroscience*, 29(1): 38–42.

Risch, S. C. (ed.) (1991). *Central Nervous System Peptide Mechanisms in Stress and Depression*. Washington, DC: American Psychiatric Press.

Rizzolatti, G., and Fabbri-Destro, M. (2010). Mirror neurons: From discovery to autism. *Experimental Brain Research*, 200(3–4): 223–37.

Roberts, W. W., and Kiess, H. O. (1964). Motivational properties of hypothalamic aggression in cats. *Journal of Comparative and Physiological Psychology*, 58(2): 187–93.

Robertson, M. (1976). Economic threat and authoritarianism in Mexico: 1950 to 1974. Paper presented at the meeting of the California Psychological Association, Los Angeles, CA.

Rockliff, H., Gilbert, P., McEwan, K., Lightman, S., and Glover, D. (2008). A pilot exploration of heart rate variability and salivary cortisol responses to compassion-focused imagery. *Journal of Clinical Neuropsychiatry*, 5(3): 132–139.

Rockliff, H., Karl, A., McEwan, K., Gilbert, J., Matos, M., and Gilbert, P. (2011). Effect of oxytocin on compassion-focused imagery. *Emotion*, 11: 1388–96.

Rodriguez de Fonesca, F., Carrera, M., Rocio, A., Navarro, M., Koob, G. F., and Weiss, F. (1997). Activation of corticotropin-release factor in the limbic system during cannabinoid withdrawal. *Science*, 276(5321): 2050–54.

Rogers, C. (1951). *Client-Centered Therapy*. Boston: Houghton-Mifflin.

Rogers, R. W., and Prentice-Dunn, S. (1981). Deindividuation and anger-mediated interracial aggression: Unmasking regressive racism. *Journal of Personality and Social Psychology*, 41: 63–73.

Rokeach, M. (1960). *The Open and Closed Mind*. New York: Basic Books.

Rolls, E. T. (1999). *The Brain and Emotion*. New York: Oxford University Press.

Rosenman, I. (1984). Cognitive determinants of emotion: A structural theory. In P. Shaver (ed.), *Review of Personality and Social Psychology*, Vol. 5: *Emotions, Relationships, and Health* (pp. 11–36). Beverly Hills, CA: Sage Publications.

Rosenthal, R., Hall, J. A., DiMatteo, M. R., Rogers, P. L., and Archer, D. (1979). *Sensitivity to Nonverbal Communication: The PONS Test*. Baltimore: Johns Hopkins University Press.

Ross, E. D. (1981). The aprosodias: Functional-anatomic organization of the affective components of language in the right hemisphere. *Archives of Neurology*, 38(9): 561–69.

(1992). Lateralization of affective prosody in the brain. *Neurology*, 42(Suppl. 3): 411.

Ross, E. D., Homan, R. W., and Buck, R. (1994). Differential hemispheric lateralization of primary and social emotions. *Neuropsychiatry, Neuropsychology, and Behavioral Neurology*, 7(1): 1–19.

Roth, B. L. (1994). Multiple serotonin receptors: Clinical and experimental aspects. *Annals of Clinical Psychiatry*, 6: 67–78.

Rothbart, M. K. (2012). Advances in temperament: History, concepts, and measures. In M. Zentner and R. L. Shiner (eds.), *Handbook of Temperament* (pp. 3–20). New York: Guilford Press.

Rotter, J. (1966). Generalized expectancies for internal versus external control of reinforcement. *Psychological Monographs: General and Applied*, 80(1): 1–28.

Roy, A. (1991). Cerebrospinal fluid diazepam binding inhibitor in depressed patients and normal controls. *Neuropharmacology*, 30(12B): 1441–44.

Roy, A., Pickar, D., Gold, P., Barbaccia, M., Guidotti, A., Costa, E., and Linnoila, M. (1989). Diazepam-binding inhibitor and corticotropin-releasing hormone in cerebrospinal fluid. *Acta Psychiatrica Scandinavica*, 80(3): 287–91.

Rozin, P. (1999). The process of moralization. *Psychological Science*, 10(3): 218–21.

Rozin, P., and Fallon, A. E. (1987). A perspective on disgust. *Psychological Review*, 94(1): 23–41.

Rozin, P., Fallon, A., and Augustoni-Ziskind, M. (1985). The child's conception of food: The development of contamination sensitivity to "disgusting" substances. *Developmental Psychology*, 21: 1075–79.

Rozin, P., Haidt, J., and McCauley, C. R. (1993). Disgust. In M. Lewis and J. Haviland (eds.), *Handbook of Emotions* (pp. 575–94). New York: Guilford Press.

Rozin, P., Lowery, L., and Ebert, R. (1994). Varieties of disgust faces and the structure of disgust. *Journal of Personality and Social Psychology*, 66(5): 870–81.

Rozin, P., Lowery, L., Imada, S., and Haidt, J. (1999). The CAD triad hypothesis: A mapping between three moral emotions (contempt, anger, disgust) and three moral codes (community, autonomy, divinity). *Journal of Personality and Social Psychology*, 76(4): 574–86.

Rozin, P., Millman, L., and Nemeroff, C. (1986). Operation of the laws of sympathetic magic in disgust and other domains. *Journal of Personality and Social Psychology*, 50: 703–12.

Rubin, Z., and Peplau, L. A. (1975). Who believes in a just world? *Journal of Social Issues*, 31(3): 65–89.

Ruby, E. G., and McFall-Ngai, M. J. (1999). Oxygen-utilizing reactions and symbiotic colonization of the squid light organ by Vibrio fischeri. *Trends in Microbiology*, 7(10): 414–20.

Russell, B. (1912). *Problems of Philosophy*. New York: Simon & Schuster.

(1945). *A History of Western Philosophy*. New York: Simon & Schuster.

Ryle, G. (1949). *The Concept of Mind*. New York: Barnes & Noble.

Sabatelli, R. M., Buck, R., and Kenny, D. A. (1986). A social relations analysis of nonverbal communication accuracy in married couples. *Journal of Personality*, 54(3): 513–27.

Sabatelli, R. M. and Rubin, M. (1986). Nonverbal expressiveness and physical attractiveness as mediators of interpersonal perceptions. *Journal of Nonverbal Behavior*, 10(2): 120–33.

Safer, M. A., and Leventhal, H. (1977). Ear differences in evaluating emotional tones of voice and verbal content. *Journal of Experimental Psychology: Human Perception and Performance*, 3(1): 75–82.

Sagarin, B. J., Martin, A. L., Coutinho, S. A., Edlund, J. E., Patel, L., Skowronski, J. J., and Zengel, B. (2012). Sex differences in jealousy: A meta-analytic examination. *Evolution and Human Behavior*, 33(6): 595–614.

Sales, S. (1972). Need for stimulation as a factor in preferences for different stimuli. *Journal of Personality Assessment*, 36: 55–61.

(1973). Threat as a factor in authoritarianism: An analysis of archival data. *Journal of Personality and Social Psychology*, 36: 988–99.

Sales, S., and Friend, K. E. (1973). Success and failure as determinants of level of authoritarianism. *Behavioral Science*, 18: 163–72.

Salovey, P., and Rodin, J. (1984). Some antecedents and consequences of social-comparison jealousy. *Journal of Personality and Social Psychology*, 47: 780–92.

(1986). The differentiation of social-comparison jealousy and romantic jealousy. *Journal of Personality and Social Psychology*, 50: 1100–12.

Sanfey, A. G. (2007a). Social decision-making: Insights from game theory and neuroscience. *Science*, 318(5850): 598–602.

(2007b). Decision neuroscience: New directions in studies of judgment and decision making. *Current Directions in Psychological Science*, 16(3): 151–55.

Sanfey, A. G., Rilling, J. K., Aronson, J. A., Nystrom, L. E., and Cohen, J. D. (2003). The neural basis of economic decision-making in the ultimatum game. *Science*, 300(5626): 1755–58.

Savaskan, E., Ehrhardt, R., Schulz, A., Walter, M., and Schachinger, H. (2008). Post-learning intranasal oxytocin modulates human memory for facial identity. *Psychoneuroendocrinology*, 33(3): 368–74.

Sawada, M. (2010). Developmental features of envy. *Japanese Psychological Review*, 53: 110–23.

Schachter, S. (1951). Deviation, rejection, and communication. *Journal of Abnormal and Social Psychology*, 46(2): 190–207.

Schachter, S., and Singer, J. (1962). Cognitive, social, and physiological determinants of emotional state. *Psychological Review*, 69: 379–99.

Schaich Borg, J., Sinnott-Armstrong, W., Calhoun, V. D., and Kiehl, K. A. (2011). Neural basis of moral verdict and moral deliberation. *Social Neuroscience*, 6 (4): 398–413.

Schally, A. V., Coy, D. H., Arimura, A., Redding, T. W., Kastin, A. J., Meyers, C., ... and Millar, R. (1978). Hypothalamic peptide hormones and their analogues. In B. Cox, I. D. Morris, and A. H. Weston (eds.), *Pharmacology of the Hypothalamus* (pp. 161–201). Baltimore: University Park Press.

Scheff, T. J. (1988). Shame and conformity: The deference-emotion system. *American Sociological Review*, 53(3): 395–406.

(1995). Self-defense against verbal assault: Shame, anger, and the social bond. *Family Process*, 34: 271–86.

(1997). Shame in social theory. In M. R. Lansky and A. P. Morrison (eds.), *The Widening Scope of Shame* (pp. 205–30). Mahwah, NJ: Analytic Press.

Scheff, T. J., and Retzinger, S. M. (1991). *Emotions and Violence: Shame and Rage in Destructive Conflicts*. Lexington, MA: D. C. Heath.

Schein, E. H. (1956). The Chinese indoctrination program for prisoners of war. *Psychiatry: Journal for the Study of Interpersonal Processes*, 19: 149–72.

Schein, E. H., Schneider, I., and Barker, C. H. (1961). *Coercive Persuasion*. New York: W. W. Norton.

Scherer, K. R. (1984). On the nature and function of emotion: A component-process approach. In K. Scherer and P. Ekman (eds.), *Approaches to Emotion* (pp. 293–318). Hillsdale, NJ: Lawrence Erlbaum Associates.

(1993). Studying the emotion-antecedent appraisal process: An expert system approach. *Cognition & Emotion*, 7(3–4): 325–55.

(1994). An emotion's occurrence depends on the relevance of an event to the organism's goal/need hierarchy. In P. Ekman and R. Davidson (eds.), *The Nature of Emotion: Fundamental Questions* (pp. 227–31). New York: Oxford University Press.

Schneider, D. J., Hastorf, F. A. H., and Ellsworth, P. C. (1979). *Person Perception*. Reading, MA: Addison-Wesley.

Schneiderman, I., Zagoory-Sharon, O., Leckman, J. F., and Feldman, R. (2012). Oxytocin during the initial stages of romantic attachment: Relations to couples' interactive reciprocity. *Psychoneuroendocrinology*, 37(8): 1277–85.

Schoenrade, P. A., Batson, C. D., Brandt, J. R., and Loud, R. E. (1986). Attachment, accountability, and motivation to benefit another not in distress. *Journal of Personality and Social Psychology*, 51: 557–63.

Schug, J., Matsumoto, D., Horita, Y., Yamagishi, T., and Bonnet, K. (2010). Emotional expressivity as a signal of cooperation. *Evolution and Human Behavior*, 31(2): 87–94.

Schultz, R. T, Grelotti, D. J., Klin, A., Kleinman, J., Van der Gaag, C., Marois, R., and Skudlarski, P. (2003). The role of the fusiform face area in social cognition: Implications for the pathobiology of autism. *Philosophical Transactions of the Royal Society of London B, Biological Sciences*, 358(1430): 415–27.

Schwartz, C. E., Wright, C. I., Shin, L. M., Kagan, J., Whalen, P. J., McMullin, K. G., and Rauch, S. L. (2003). Differential amygdalar response to novel versus newly familiar neutral faces: A functional MRI probe developed for studying inhibited temperament. *Biological Psychiatry*, 53(10): 854–62.

Schwartz, S. (1975). The justice of need and the activation of humanitarian norms. *Journal of Social Issues*, 31(3): 111–36.

(1994). Beyond individualism/collectivism: New cultural dimensions of values. In U. Kim, H. C. Triandis, and G. Yoon (eds.), *Individualism and Collectivism* (pp. 85–117). London: Sage Publications.

Schweder, R. A. (1994). "You're not sick, you're just in love": Emotion as an interpretive system. In P. Ekman and R. Davidson (eds.), *The Nature of Emotion: Fundamental Questions* (pp. 32–44). New York: Oxford University Press.

Schweder, R. A., Much, N. C., Mahapatra, M., and Park, L. (1997). The "big three" of morality (autonomy, community, and divinity), and the "big three" explanations of suffering. In A. Brandt and P. Rozin (eds.), *Morality and Health* (pp. 119–69). New York: Routledge.

Scott, J. P. (1974). Effects of psychotropic drugs on separation distress in dogs. *Exerpta Medica, International Congress Series*, 359: 735–45.

Seligman, M. E. P. (2002). Positive psychology, positive prevention, and positive therapy. In C. R. Snyder and S. J. Lopez (eds.), *Handbook of Positive Psychology* (pp. 3–9). New York: Oxford University Press.

(2011). *Flourish: A Visionary New Understanding of Happiness and Well-Being*. New York: Free Press.

Selye, H. (1950). *The Physiology and Pathology of Exposure to Stress*. Amsterdam: North Holland Publishing Company.

(1956). *The Stress of Life*. New York: McGraw-Hill.

Sem-Jacobson, C. W. (1968). *Depth-Electroencephalographic Stimulation of the Human Brain and Behavior*. Springfield, IL: Charles C. Thomas.

Semrud-Clikeman, M., Fine, J. G., and Zhu, D. C. (2011). The role of the right hemisphere for processing of social interactions in normal adults using functional magnetic resonance imaging. *Neuropsychobiology*, 64(1): 47–51.

Shahrokh, D. K., Zhang, T. Y., Diorio, J., Gratton, A., and Meaney, M. J. (2010). Oxytocin-dopamine interactions mediate variations in maternal behavior in the rat. *Endocrinology*, 151(5): 2276–86.

Shamay-Tsoory, S. G., Fischer, M., Dvash, J., Harari, H., Perach-Bloom, N., and Levkovitz, Y. (2009). Intranasal administration of oxytocin increases envy and schadenfreude (gloating). *Biological Psychiatry*, 66(9): 864–70.

Shamay-Tsoory, S. G., Lavidor, M., and Aharon-Peretz, J. (2008). Social learning modulates the lateralization of emotional valence. *Brain and Cognition*, 67 (3): 280–91.

Shaver, P., and Hazan, C. (1993). Adult romantic attachment: Theory and evidence. In D. Perlman and W. Jones (eds.), *Advances in Personal Relationships* (Vol. 4, pp. 29–70). London: Kingsley.

Sher, K. J., Bylund, D. B., Walitzer, K. S., Hartmann, J., and Ray-Prenger, C. (1994). Platelet monoamine oxidase (MAO) activity: Personality, substance use, and the stress-response-dampening effect of alcohol. *Experimental and Clinical Psychopharmacology*, 2(1): 53–81.

Sheridan, C. L., and King, R. G. (1972). Obedience to authority with an authentic victim. *Proceedings of the 80th Annual Convention of the American Psychological Association*, 7: 165–66.

Sherif, M. (1936). *The Psychology of Social Norms*. New York: Harper.

(1965). Formation of social norms. In H. Proshansky and B. Seidenberg (eds.), *Basic Studies in Social Psychology* (pp. 461–71). New York: Holt, Rinehart & Winston.

Siever, L., and Trestman, R. L. (1993). The serotonin system and aggressive personality disorder. *International Clinical Psychopharmacology*, 8(2): 33–39.

Simpson, J. A., and Lapaglia, J. (2007). An evolutionary account of strategic pluralism in human mating. In J. P. Forgas, M. Haselton, and W. von Hippel (eds.), *The Evolution of the Social Mind: Evolutionary Psychology and Social Cognition* (pp. 161–77). New York: Psychology Press.

Singer, M., Britner, P., Milan, S., and Buck, R. (2011). *Youth Work and Learn at Our Piece of the Pie (OPP): Preliminary Findings of a Pilot Policy Review of Connecticut's Youth Development Model.* Report prepared by the Center for Health, Intervention and Prevention, University of Connecticut; for the Department of Children and Families, the Court Support Services Division (Judicial Branch), and the Office for Workforce Competitiveness.

Singer, T. (2006). The neuronal basis and ontogeny of empathy and mind reading: Review of literature and implications for future research. *Neuroscience & Biobehavioral Reviews*, 30(6): 855–63.

Singer, T., Seymour, B., O'Doherty, J., Kaube, H., Dolan, R. J., and Frith, C. D. (2004). Empathy for pain involves the affective but not sensory components of pain. *Science*, 303(5661): 1157–62.

Skinner, B. F. (1945). The operational analysis of psychological terms. *Psychological Review*, 52(5): 270–77.

(1953). *Science and Human Behavior*. New York: Macmillan.

Slater, M., Antley, A., Davison, A., Swapp, D., Guger, C., Barker, C., Pistrang, N., and Sanchez-Vives, M. V. (2006). A virtual reprise of the Stanley Milgram obedience experiments. *PLoS ONE* 1(1): e39.

Slotnik, B. M. (1967). Disturbances of maternal behavior in the rat following lesions of the cingulate cortex. *Behaviour*, 29(2): 204–36.

Slovic, P. (1999). Trust, emotion, sex, politics, and science: Surveying the risk-assessment battlefield. *Risk Analysis*, 19(4): 689–701.

Smith, C. A., and Ellsworth, P. C. (1985). Patterns of cognitive appraisal in emotion. *Journal of Personality and Social Psychology*, 48(4): 813–38.

Smith, K. S., Tindell, A. J., Aldridge, J. W., and Berridge, K. C. (2009). Ventral pallidum roles in reward and motivation. *Behavioral Brain Research*, 196(2): 155–67.

Smith, R. H., Kim, S.-H., and Parrott, W. G. (1988). Envy and jealousy: Semantic problems and experiential distinctions. *Personality and Social Psychology Bulletin*, 14(2): 401–9.

Smith, R. H., Turner, T. J., Garonzik, R., Leach, C. W., Urch-Druskat, V., and Weston, C. M. (1996). Envy and Schadenfreude. *Personality and Social Psychology Bulletin*, 22: 158–68.

Smith, S. D., Abou-Khalil, B., and Zald, D. H. (2008). Post-traumatic stress disorder in a patient with no left amygdala. *Journal of Abnormal Psychology*, 117(2): 479–84.

Smuts, B. (1987). What are friends for? *Natural History*, 96: 36–45.

Soares, P., Ermini, L., Thomson, N., Mormina, M., Rito, T., Röhl, A., . . . and Richards, M. B. (2009). Correcting for purifying selection: an improved human mitochondrial molecular clock. *American Journal of Human Genetics*, 84(6): 740–59.

Sokoloff, P., Giros, B., Martres, M. P., Bouthenet, M. L., and Schwartz, J. C. (1990). Molecular cloning and characterization of a novel dopamine receptor (D_3) as a target for neuroleptics. *Nature*, 347(6289): 146–51.

Sperry, R. W., Zaidel, E., and Zaidel, D. (1979). Self recognition and social awareness in the deconnected minor hemisphere. *Neuropsychologia*, 17(2): 153–66.

Spinoza, B. (1677). *Ethica Ordine Geometrico Demonstrata [The Ethics]*. www. gutenberg.org/ebooks/3800.

Spitz, R. A. (1945). Hospitalism: An inquiry into the genesis of psychiatric conditions in early childhood. *Psychoanalytic Study of the Child*, 1: 53–74.

Stamm, J. S. (1955). The function of the median cerebral cortex in maternal behavior of rats. *Journal of Comparative and Physiological Psychology*, 48(4): 347–56.

Stayton, D. J., Hogan, R., and Ainsworth, M. D. (1971). Infant obedience and maternal behavior: The origins of socialization reconsidered. *Child Development*, 42(4): 1057–69.

Stearns, D. C., and Parrott, W. G. (2012). When feeling bad makes you look good: Guilt, shame, and person perception. *Cognition & Emotion*, 26: 407–30.

Stein, L. (1964). Reciprocal action of reward and punishment mechanisms. In R. G. Heath (ed.), *The Role of Pleasure in Behavior* (pp. 113–39). New York: Hoeber.

(1978). Reward neurotransmitters: Catecholamines and opioid peptides. In M. A. Lipton, A. DiMascio, and K. F. Killam (eds.), *Psychopharmacology: A Generation of Progress* (pp. 569–581). New York: Raven Press.

Steiner, J. E. (1979). Human facial expressions in response to taste and smell stimulation. *Advances in Child Development and Behavior*, 13: 257–95.

Stephan, H. (1983). Evolutionary trends in limbic structures. *Neuroscience & Biobehavioral Reviews*, 7(3): 367–74.

Steriade, M. (1996). Arousal: Revisiting the reticular activating system. *Science*, 272(5259): 225–26.

Stifano, S. C. (2008). Movies, meaning, and social influence: A developmental-interactionist theory of film communication. Unpublished MA thesis, University of Connecticut.

(2009). Movies, meaning, and social influence: A developmental-interactionist theory of film communication. Unpublished paper, University of Connecticut. www.stephenstifano.com/docs/ditheory.pdf.

(2010a). Examining the empathy dimension in film communication. Paper presented at the meeting of the Eastern Communication Association, Baltimore, MD, April 22.

(2010b). Cinematic marketing: A developmental-interactionist approach to television advertising. Paper presented at the meeting of the Eastern Communication Association, Baltimore, MD, April 23.

(2011). Make belief: Examining the interaction of reason and emotion in film communication. Unpublished doctoral dissertation, University of Connecticut. Paper AAI3485421. http://digitalcommons.uconn.edu/dissertations/AAI3485421.

Stipek, D., Weiner, B., and Li, K. (1989). Testing some attribution–emotion relations in the People's Republic of China. *Journal of Personality and Social Psychology*, 56: 109–16.

Stouffer, S. A., Lumsdane, A. A., Lumsdane, M. H., Williams, R. M., Jr., Smith, M. B., Janis, I. L., Star, S. A., and Cottrell, Jr., L. S., (1949). *The American Soldier: Combat and its Aftermath*, Vol. 2. New York: Wiley.

Strack, F. (1996). Feeling and knowing: Multiple representations of human experience. *International Journal of Psychology*, 31: 222.

Strathearn, L., Fonagy, P., Amico, J., and Montague, P. R. (2009). Adult attachment predicts maternal brain and oxytocin response to infant cues. *Neuropsychopharmacology*, 34(13): 2655–66.

Straube, T., Dietrich, C., Mothes-Lasch, M., Mentzel, H-J., and Miltner, W. H. R. (2010). The volatility of the amygdala response to masked fearful eyes. *Human Brain Mapping*, 31, 1601–8.

Strauss, E. (1986). Cerebral representation of emotion. In P. Blanck, R. Buck, and R. Rosenthal (eds.), *Nonverbal Communication in the Clinical Context* (pp. 176–96). University Park, PA: Pennsylvania State University Press.

Strizhakova, Y., Kang, Y., and Buck, R. (2007). Assessment of emotional gratifications: Development of the EGRATS Scale. Unpublished paper, Suffolk University, Boston, MA.

Suberi, M., and McKeever, W. F. (1977). Differential right hemispheric memory of emotional and non-emotional faces. *Neuropsychologie*, 15: 757–68.

Suda, M., Takei, Y., Aoyama, Y., Narita, K., Sakurai, N., Fukuda, M., and Mikuni, M. (2011). Autistic traits and brain activation during face-to-face conversations in typically developed adults. *PLoS ONE*, 6(5): 1–8.

Summers, C. H., and Greenberg, N. (1995). Activation of central biogenic amines following aggressive interaction in male lizards, *Anolis carolinensis*. *Brain, Behavior and Evolution*, 45: 339–49.

Suttie, J. (2011). A course correction for positive psychology [Review of M. Seligman, *Flourish: A Visonary New Understanding of Happiness and Well-Being*]. *Greater Good Magazine*, August 11.

Swain, J. E., Lorberbaum, J. P., Kose, S., and Strathearn, L. (2007). Brain basis of early parent–infant interactions: Psychology, physiology, and in vivo functional neuroimaging studies. *Journal of Child Psychology and Psychiatry*, 48(3–4): 262–87.

Symons, D. (1979). *The Evolution of Human Sexuality*. New York: Oxford University Press.

(1980). Precis of "The Evolution of Human Sexuality". *Behavioral and Brain Sciences*, 3: 171–214.

Szabo, C. A., Xiong, J., Lancaster, J. L., Rainey, L., and Fox, P. (2001). Amygdalar and hippocampal volumetry in control participants. *American Journal of Neuroradiology*, 22(7): 1342–45.

Tamietto, M., Castelli, L., Vighetti, S., Perozzo, P., Geminiani, G., Weiskrantz, L., and de Gelder, B. (2009). Unseen facial and bodily expressions trigger fast emotional reactions. *Proceedings of the National Academy of Sciences of the United States of America*, 106(42): 17662–66.

Tangney, J. P. (1992). Situational determinants of shame and guilt in young adulthood. *Personality and Social Psychology Bulletin*, 18: 199–206.

(1995a). Shame and guilt in interpersonal relationships. In J. P. Tangney and K. W. Fischer (eds.), *Self-Conscious Emotions: The Psychology of Shame, Guilt, Embarrassment, and Pride* (pp. 114–39). New York: Guilford Press.

(1995b). Recent advances in the empirical study of shame and guilt. *American Behavioral Scientist*, 38: 1132–45.

(1999). The self-conscious emotions: Shame, guilt, embarrassment, and pride. In T. Dalgleish, and M. Power (eds.), *Handbook of Cognition and Emotion* (pp. 541–68). New York: John Wiley.

Tangney, J. P., and Fischer, K. W. (eds.) (1995). *Self-Conscious Emotions: The Psychology of Shame, Guilt, Embarrassment, and Pride.* New York: Guilford Press.

Tangney, J. P., Miller, R. S., Flicker, L., and Barlow, D. H. (1996). Are shame, guilt, and embarrassment distinct emotions? *Journal of Personality and Social Psychology,* 70(6): 1256–69.

Tangney, J. P., Stuewig, J., and Hafez, L. (2011). Shame, guilt, and remorse: Implications for offender populations. *Journal of Forensic Psychiatry and Psychology,* 22(5): 706–23.

Tangney, J. P., Stuewig, J., and Mashek, D. J. (2007). Moral emotions and moral behavior. *Annual Review of Psychology,* 58: 345–72.

Tarazi, F. I., Zhang, Z., and Baldessarini, R. J. (2001). Long-term effects of olanzapine, risperidone, and quetiapine on dopamine receptor types in regions of rat brain: Implications for antipsychotic drug treatment. *Journal of Pharmacology and Experimental Therapeutics,* 297(2): 711–17.

(2002). Long-term effects of olanzapine, risperidone, and quetiapine on serotonin 1A, 2A, and 3C receptors in rat forebrain regions. *Psychopharmacology,* 161(3): 263–70.

Tassy, S., Oullier, O., Duclos, Y., Coulon, O., Mancini, J., Deruelle, C., Attarian, S., Felician, O., and Wicker, B. (2011). Disrupting the right prefrontal cortex alters moral judgement. *Social, Cognitive, and Affective Neuroscience,* 7(3): 282–88.

Tatara, M. (1989). Deeper understanding of personality functioning in different cultures: Comments on Dr. de Rivera's paper. *Hiroshima Forum for Psychology,* 14: 21–22.

Tauscher, J., Küfferle, B., Asenbaum, S., Tauscher-Wisniewski, S., and Kaspar, S. (2002). Striatal dopamine-2 receptor occupancy as measured with 123I iodobenzamide and SPECT predicted the occurrence of EPS in patients treated with atypical antipsychotics and haloperidol. *Psychopharmacology,* 162(1): 42–49.

Tavris, C. (1974). A conversation with Stanley Milgram. *Psychology Today,* 8: 71–80.

Taylor, C., and Kleinke, C. L. (1992). Effects of severity of accident, history of drunk driving, intent, and remorse on judgments of a drunk driver. *Journal of Applied Social Psychology,* 22(21): 1641–55.

Taylor, S. E., Klein, L. C., Lewis, B. P., Gruenewald, T. L., Gurung, R. A. R., and Updegraff, J. A. (2000). Biobehavioral responses to stress in females: Tend-and-befriend, not fight-or-flight. *Psychological Review,* 107 (3): 411–29.

Tenaza, R. R. (1975). Territory and monogamy among Kloss' gibbons (*Hylobates klossii*) in Siberut Island, Indonesia. *Folia-Primatologica,* 24(1): 60–80.

Tennov, D. (1979). *Love and Limerance: The Experience of Being in Love in New York.* New York: Stein & Day.

ter Riet, G., de Craen, A. J. M., de Boer, A., and Kessels, A. G. H. (1998). Is placebo analgesia mediated by endogenous opioids? *Pain: A Systematic Review,* 76(3): 273–75.

Terzian, H., and Ore, D. G. (1955). Symptoms of Klüver and Bucy reproduced in man by bilateral removal of the temporal lobes. *Neurology,* 5: 373–80.

Tesser, A., and Collins, J. E. (1988). Emotion in social reflection and comparison situations: Intuitive, systematic, and exploratory approaches. *Journal of Personality and Social Psychology,* 55: 695–709.

Thomas, A., Chess, S., and Burch, H. G. (1970). The origin of personality. *Scientific American*, 223: 102–9.

Thomas, B. C., Croft, K. E., and Tranel, D. (2011). Harming kin to save strangers: Further evidence for abnormally utilitarian moral judgments after ventro-medial prefrontal damage. *Journal of Cognitive Neuroscience*, 23(9): 2186–96.

Thompson, E. H., and Hampton, J. A. (2011). The effect of relationship status on communicating emotions through touch. *Cognition & Emotion*, 25(2): 295–306.

Thompson, R. A. (1987). Development of children's inferences of the emotions of others. *Developmental Psychology*, 23(1): 124–31.

Thompson, R. R., George, K., Walton, J. C., Orr, S. P., and Benson, J. (2006). Sex-specific influences of vasopressin on human social communication. *Proceedings of the National Academy of Sciences of the United States of America*, 103(20): 7889–94.

Tomkins, S. S. (1962–92). *Affect, Imagery, Consciousness*, 4 vols. New York: Springer.

(1982). Affect theory. In P. Ekman (ed.), *Emotion in the Human Face* (2nd edn. pp. 353–95). Cambridge University Press.

Tomkins. S. S., and McCarter, R. (1964). What and where are the primary affects? Some evidence for a theory. *Perceptual and Motor Skills*, 18: 119–58.

Tracy, J. L., and Matsumoto, D. (2008). The spontaneous display of pride and shame: Evidence for biologically innate nonverbal displays. *Proceedings of the National Academy of Sciences of the United States of America*, 105(16): 11655–60.

Tracy, J. L., and Prehn, C. (2012). Arrogant or self-confident? The use of contextual knowledge to differentiate hubristic and authentic pride from a single nonverbal expression. *Cognition & Emotion*, 26(1): 14–24.

Tracy, J. L., and Robins, R. W. (2004a). Keeping the self in self-conscious emotions: Further arguments for a theoretical model. *Psychological Inquiry*, 15(2): 171–77.

(2004b). Putting the self into self-conscious emotions: A theoretical model. *Psychological Inquiry*, 15(2): 103–25.

(2004c). Show your pride: Evidence for a discrete emotion expression. *Psychological Science*, 15(3): 194–97.

(2006). Appraisal antecedents of shame and guilt: Support for a theoretical model. *Personality and Social Psychology Bulletin*, 32(10): 1339–51.

(2008). The nonverbal expression of pride: Evidence for cross-cultural recognition. *Journal of Personality and Social Psychology*, 94(3): 516–30.

Tranel, D., and Damasio, A. R. (1985). Knowledge without awareness: An autonomic index of facial recognition by prosopagnosics. *Science*, 228 (4706): 1453–54.

Tremblay, R. E. (2010). Developmental origins of disruptive behaviour problems: The "original sin" hypothesis, epigenetics and their consequences for prevention. *Journal of Child Psychology and Psychiatry*, 51(4): 341–67.

Trevarthan, C. (1979). Communication and cooperation in early infancy: A description of primary intersubjectivity. In M. Bullowa (ed.), *Before Speech: The Beginning of Human Communication* (pp. 321–47). Cambridge University Press.

Trevarthan, C., and Aitken, K. J. (2001). Infant intersubjectivity: Research, theory, and clinical applications. *Journal of Child Psychology and Psychiatry*, 42(1): 3–48.

Triandis, H. (1995). *Individualism and Collectivism*. Boulder, CO: Westview Press.

Tronick, E. (1978). The infant's response to entrapment between contradictory messages in a face-to-face interaction. *Journal of the American Academy of Child Psychiatry*, 17: 1–13.

Tse, W. S., and Bond, A. J. (2002a). Difference in serotonergic and noradrenergic regulation of human social behaviours. *Psychopharmacology*, 159(2): 216–21.

(2002b). Serotonergic intervention affects both social dominance and affiliative behaviour. *Psychopharmacology*, 161(3): 324–30.

Tsutsumi, T., Akiyoshi, J., Hikichi, T., Kiyota, A., Kohno, Y., Katsuragi, S., . . . and Nagayama, H. (2001). Suppression of conditioned fear by administration of CCKB receptor antisense oligodeoxynucleotide into the lateral ventricle. *Pharmacopsychiatry*, 34(6): 232–37.

Tucker, D. M. (1981). Lateral brain function, emotion, and conceptualization. *Psychological Bulletin*, 89(1): 19–46.

Tuinier, S., Verhoeven, W. M., and van Praag, H. M. (1995). Cerebrospinal fluid 5-hydroxyindolacetic acid and aggression: A critical reappraisal of the clinical data. *International Clinical Psychopharmacology*, 10(3): 147–56.

Twenge, J. M., Zhang, L., Catanese, K. R., Dolan-Pascoe, B., Lyche, L. R., and Baumeister, R. F. (2007). Replenishing connectedness: Reminders of social activity reduce aggression after social exclusion. *British Journal of Social Psychology*, 46: 205–24.

Uzefovsky, F., Shalev, I., Israel, S., Knafo, A., and Ebstein, R. P. (2012). Vasopressin selectively impairs emotion recognition in men. *Psychoneuroendocrinology*, 37(4): 576–80.

Vaish, A., Missana, M., and Tomasello, M. (2011). Three-year-old children intervene in third-party moral transgressions. *British Journal of Developmental Psychology*, 29(1): 124–30.

Van Beest, I., and Williams, K. D. (2006). When inclusion costs and ostracism pays, ostracism still hurts. *Journal of Personality and Social Psychology*, 91(5): 918–28.

Van Daal, J. H. H. M., De Kok, Y. J. M., Jenks, B. G., Wendelaar Bonga, S. E., and Van Abeelen, J. H. F. (1987). A genotype-dependent hippocampal dynorphinergic mechanism controls mouse exploration. *Pharmacology, Biochemistry and Behavior*, 28(4): 465–68.

van de Ven, N., Zeelenberg, M., and Pieters, R. (2011). Why envy outperforms admiration. *Personality and Social Psychology Bulletin*, 37(6): 784–95.

Van IJzendoorn, M. H., and Bakermans-Kranenburg, M. J. (2012). A sniff of trust: Meta-analysis of the effects of intranasal oxytocin administration on face recognition, trust to in-group, and trust to out-group. *Psychoneuroendocrinology*, 37(3): 438–43.

Vecchio, R. (2005). Explorations in employee envy: Feeling envious and feeling envied. *Cognition & Emotion*, 19(1): 69–81.

von Rohr, C. R., Koski, S. E., Burkart, J. M., Caws, C., Fraser, O. N., Ziltener, A., and van Schaik, C. P. (2012). Impartial third-party interventions in captive chimpanzees: A reflection of community concern. *PLoS ONE*, 7 (3): e32494.

Vytal, K., and Hamann, S. (2010). Neuroimaging support for discrete neural correlates of basic emotions: A voxel-based meta-analysis. *Journal of Cognitive Neuroscience*, 22(12): 2864–85.

Wager, T. D., Barrett, L. F., Bliss-Moreau, E., Lindquist, K. A., Duncan, S., Kober, H., . . . and Mize, J. (2008). The neuroimaging of emotion. In

M. Lewis, J. M. Haviland-Jones, and L. F. Barrett (eds.), *Handbook of Emotions* (3rd edn., pp. 249–71). New York: Guilford Press.

Wagner, A. W., and Linehan, M. M. (1999). Facial expression recognition ability among women with borderline personality disorder: implications for emotion regulation? *Journal of Personality Disorders*, 13(4): 329–44.

Walker, R. J., Brooks, H. L., and Holden-Dye, L. (1996). Evolution and overview of classical transmitter molecules and their receptors. *Parasitology*, 113: 3–33.

Walker, W. F. (1987). *Functional Anatomy of the Vertebrates: An Evolutionary Perspective*. Philadelphia: Saunders.

Walter, H. (2012). Social cognitive neuroscience of empathy: Concepts, circuits, and genes. *Emotion Review*, 4(1): 9–17.

Wang, Z., Yu, G., Cascio, C., Liu, Y., Gingrich, B., and Insel, T. R. (1999). Dopamine D2 receptor-mediated regulation of partner preferences in female prairie voles (*microtus ochrogaster*): A mechanism for pair bonding? *Behavioral Neuroscience*, 113(3): 602–11.

Watson, J. B. (1919). *Psychology from the Standpoint of a Behaviorist*. Philadelphia: Lippincott.

Watson, R. I. (1973). Investigation into deindividuation using a cross-cultural survey technique. *Journal of Personality and Social Psychology*, 25: 242–45.

Weiger, W. A., and Ma, P. M. (1993). Serotonin-containing neurons in lobsters: Origins and characterization of inhibitory postsynaptic potentials. *Journal of Neurophysiology*, 69: 2003–14.

Weiner, B. (1986). *An Attributional Theory of Motivation and Emotion*. New York: Springer Verlag.

(1987). The social psychology of emotion: Applications of a naive psychology. *Journal of Social and Clinical Psychology*, 5: 405–19.

Weiner, B., Graham, S., and Chandler, C. (1982). Pity, anger, and guilt: An attributional analysis. *Personality and Social Psychology Bulletin*, 8(2): 226–32.

Welten, S. C. M., Zeelenberg, M., and Breugelmans, S. M. (2012). Vicarious shame. *Cognition & Emotion*, 26(5): 836–46.

Wernicke, C. (1874). *Der Aphasiche Symptomen-complex*. Breslau: Cohen & Weigert.

Wernicke, K. (1875/1995). The aphasia symptom-complex: A psychological study on an anatomical basis. In P. Eling (ed.), *Reader in the History of Aphasia: From Franz Gall to Norman Geschwind* (pp. 69–89). Amsterdam: John Benjamins.

Whalen, P. J. (1998). Fear, vigilance, and ambiguity: Initial neuroimaging studies of the human amygdala. *Current Directions in Psychological Science*, 7(6): 177–88.

Wheeler, W. (1928). *The Social Insects: Their Origin and Evolution*. New York: Harcourt, Brace & Company.

White, J. C. (1940). Autonomic discharge from stimulation of the hypothalamus in man. *Research Publications of the Association for Research in Nervous and Mental Disease*, 20: 854–63.

White, R. W. (1959). Motivation reconsidered: The concept of competence. *Psychological Review*, 66: 297–333.

White, W. L. (1957). *The Captives of Korea*. New York: Scribner's.

Wicker, B., Keysers, C., Plailly, J., Royet, J., Gallese, V., and Rizzolatti, G. (2003). Both of us disgusted in my insula: The common neural basis of seeing and feeling disgust. *Neuron*, 40(3): 655–64.

Widen, C., Christy, A. M., Hewett, K., Russell, J. A. (2011). Do proposed facial expressions of contempt, shame, embarrassment, and compassion communicate the predicted emotion? *Cognition & Emotion*, 25(5): 898–906.

Wikiquote. http://en.wikiquote.org/wiki/Adolf_Eichmann, accessed October 2012.

Williams, J. R., Insel, T. R., Harbaugh, C. R., and Carter, C. S. (1994). Oxytocin administered centrally facilitates formation of a partner preference in prairie voles (*Microtus ochrogaster*). *Journal of Neuroendocrinology*, 6(3): 247–50.

Williams, K. D. (2007). Ostracism. *Annual Review of Psychology*, 58: 425–52.

——— (2011). Ostracism. Presentation at the meeting of the Society of Experimental Social Psychology. Washington, DC.

Williams, L. A., and DeSteno, D. (2010). Pride in parsimony. *Emotion Review*, 2 (2): 180–81.

Wilmot, W. W. (1980). *Dyadic Communication* (2nd edn.). Reading, MA: Addison-Wesley.

Wilson, E. O. (1975). *Sociobiology: The New Synthesis*. Cambridge, MA: Belknap Press.

Windslow, J. T., Hastings, N., Carter, C. S., Harbaugh, C. R., and Insel, T. R. (1993). A role for central vasopressin in pair bonding in the monogamous prairie vole. *Nature*, 365(6446): 545–48.

Winkielman, P., and Berridge, K. (2003). Irrational wanting and subrational liking: How rudimentary motivational and affective processes shape preferences and choices. *Political Psychology*, 24(4): 657–80.

Wise, R. A., and Bozarth, M. A. (1987). A psychomotor stimulant theory of addiction. *Psychological Review*, 94(4): 469–92.

Wittgenstein, L. (1965). *The Blue and Brown Books*. New York: Philosophical Library.

Wohlschläger, A., and Bekkering, H. (2002). Is human imitation based on a mirror-neuron system? Some behavioural evidence. *Experimental Brain Research*, 143: 335–41.

Wray, H. (2010). The sick logic of a psychopath. *Huffington Post*, November 6. www.huffingtonpost.com/wray-herbert.the-sick-logic-of-a-psych_b_778969. html.

Yanase, H., Shimizu, H., Yamada, K., and Iwanaga, T. (2002). Cellular location of the diazepam binding inhibitor in glial cells with special reference to its coexistence with brain-type fatty acid binding protein. *Archives of Histology and Cytology*, 65(1): 27–36.

Young, K. A., Gobrogge, K. L., Liu, Y., and Wang, Z. (2011). The neurobiology of pair bonding: Lessons from a socially monogamous rodent. *Frontiers in Neuroendocrinology*, 32(1): 53–69.

Young, L. J. (2001). Social deficits in oxytocin knockout mice. Presentation at the National Institution of Child Health and Human Development/ACC 2001 Conference: Potential Cellular and Molecular Mechanisms in Autism and Related Disorders. Bethesda, MD.

——— (2002). The neurobiology of social recognition, approach, and avoidance. *Biological Psychiatry*, 51(1): 18–26.

Young, L. J., Lim, M. M., Gingrich, B., and Insel, T. R. (2001). Cellular mechanisms of social attachment. *Hormones and Behavior*, 40(2): 133–38.

Young, P. T. (1961). *Motivation and Emotion*. New York: John Wiley.

Zajonc, R. B. (1980). Feeling and thinking: Preferences need no inferences. *American Psychologist*, 35(2): 151–75.

(1984). On the primacy of affect. *American Psychologist*, 39(2): 117–23.

Zhu, X., Wang, X., Parkinson, C., Cai, C., Gao, S., and Hu, P. (2010). Brain activation evoked by erotic films varies with different menstrual phases: An fMRI study. *Behavioural Brain Research*, 206(2): 279–85.

Zhuo, M. (2008). Cortical plasticity and chronic pain. *Trends in Neuroscience*, 31: 199–207.

Zikopoulos, B., and Barbas, H. (2012). Pathways for emotions and attention converge on the thalamic reticular nucleus in primates. *Journal of Neuroscience*, 32(15): 5338–50.

Zimbardo, P. G. (1969). The human choice: Individuation, reason, and order versus deindividuation, impulse, and chaos. In W. J. Arnold and D. Levine (eds.), *Nebraska Symposium on Motivation*. Lincoln: University of Nebraska Press.

(2007). When good people do evil. *Yale Alumni Magazine*, 1–7. www.yalealumnimagazine.com/issues/2007_01/milgram.html.

Zuckerman, M. (1993). P-impulsive sensation seeking and its behavioral, psychophysiological, biochemical correlates. *Neuropsychobiology*, 28(1–2): 30–36.

Zuckerman, M., Buchsbaum, M. S., and Murphy, D. L. (1980). Sensation seeking and its biological correlates. *Psychological Bulletin*, 88(1): 187–214.

Index

abandonment, *132*
abuse, 175, 208, 257, 295, 309–10, **331**, **359**
ACC, 116, 328, **340**
  in emergence of trusting relationship, **329**
  left-wing political orientation and, 116
  prosocial emotions and, 116
accessibility, 21
  definition, 12
accommodation, 236
  definition, 212
accurate emotional communication
  OXY and, 190
Acetylcholine (ACh)
  definition, 42
acetylcholine esterase (AChE)
  definition, 43
Acheulean industry, 165
ACTH, 37, 48, 53, 67
activation, xvi, 5, 7–9, 25, 38, 53–54, 57–58, 64,
    67, 72–73, 89–91, 103, 105, 107, 116,
    128, 131–33, 136–38, 155, 187–90,
    192, 194, 196, 205, 209, 252, 257–58,
    277, 280, 313, 318–19, 326, 338,
    364–65, 389, 392, 395, 402–3, 413,
    416, 422
activation systems
  reticular formation and, 25
actor–viewer empathy (film)
  definition, 235
acupuncture
  opiates and, 51
adaptation, 67, 69, 147, 230
addiction, 116
  definition, 43, 51
addiction to love, 87, 256
admiration, 278, 325, **352**
  definition, **337**
    as primary moral emotion, **332**
  humiliation and
    authoritarian leadership, **338**
  research on, **338**
admiration/resentment, **340**
  as primary moral emotions, 297

adrenal-cortico-tropic hormone (ACTH)
  stress and, 39, 67
adrenocorticotropic hormone (ACTH)
  Beta-lopotropin and
    in microbes, 48
adult attachment, 270
  definition, 177
advertising, 179
affect
  definition, 20, 39, 113, 205
affect (noun)
  definition, 8, 11
affect dimensions, 8
affect infusion model (AIM)
  definition, 237
affect labeling
  definition, 242
affection, 263
affectional stages
  definition, 181
affective attunement, 195
affective communication, 260
affective curiosity
  definition, 21
affective empathy, *132*
affective environment, 96
affective microscope, 199
affective neuroscience, 10
affective *qualia*
  definition, 33
  peptides and, 49
affects, 219
  definition, 8
affects, higher-level, 8
affects, primary, 8
affordances, 217, 261
  bodily
    Emotion III and, 17
  definition, 16
    Gibsonian theory, 261
  social, 16
  terrestrial, 16
aggression, *134*
aggressive behavior, 86, 125

423

Studies in Emotion and Social Interaction